CORRECTNESS

P9-DVG-182

A Canadian Writer's Reference

FIFTH EDITION

A Canadian Writer's Reference

Diana Hacker

Nancy Sommers
Harvard University

Contributing ESL Specialist
Marcy Carbajal Van Horn
St. Edward's University

BEDFORD / ST. MARTIN'S   BOSTON ◆ NEW YORK

Editorial advisory board for the Fifth Edition

Brian Diemert, Brescia University College
Jeannie M. Martin, Vancouver Island University
Jonathan Finn, Wilfrid Laurier University
Robert G. May, Queen's University, Kingston
Joseph Khoury, St. Francis Xavier University
Melanie Sexton, University of Ottawa

For Bedford/St. Martin's

Executive Editor: Michelle M. Clark
Senior Development Editor: Barbara G. Flanagan
Development Editor: Mara Weible
Associate Editor: Alicia Young
Senior Production Editor: Rosemary R. Jaffe
Assistant Production Editor: Lindsay DiGianvittorio
Assistant Production Manager: Joe Ford
Marketing Manager: Marjorie Adler
Editorial Assistant: Kylie Paul
Copy Editors: Linda McLatchie, Dawn Hunter
Indexer: Ellen Kuhl Repetto
Permissions Manager: Kalina Ingham Hintz
Senior Art Director: Anna Palchik
Text Design: Claire Seng-Niemoeller
Cover Design: Donna Lee Dennison
Composition: Nesbitt Graphics, Inc.
Printing and Binding: RR Donnelley and Sons

President: Joan E. Feinberg
Editorial Director: Denise B. Wydra
Editor in Chief: Karen S. Henry
Director of Marketing: Karen R. Soeltz
Director of Production: Susan W. Brown
Associate Director, Editorial Production: Elise S. Kaiser
Managing Editor: Elizabeth M. Schaaf

Library of Congress Control Number: 2011921711

Manufactured in the United States of America.

6   5   4   3
g   f   e

For information, write: Bedford/St. Martin's, 75 Arlington Street, Boston, MA 02116   (617-399-4000)

ISBN: 978-0-312-56617-3 (Student Edition)
ISBN: 978-1-4576-0245-0 (Instructor's Edition)

ACKNOWLEDGMENTS

Acknowledgments and copyrights can be found at the back of the book on pages 593–96, which constitute an extension of the copyright page. It is a violation of the law to reproduce these selections by any means whatsoever without the written permission of the copyright holder.

A Canadian Writer's Reference

How to use this book and its companion Web site

A Canadian Writer's Reference is designed to save you time and will answer most of the questions you are likely to ask as you plan, draft, revise, and edit a piece of writing: How do I choose and narrow a topic? How do I know when to begin a new paragraph? Should I write *each was* or *each were*? When should I place a comma before *and*? What is counterargument? How do I cite a source from the Web?

The book's companion Web site extends the book beyond its covers. See pages x–xi for details.

How to find information with an instructor's help

When you are revising an essay that your instructor has marked, tracking down information is simple. If your instructor uses a code such as S1-a or MLA-2b to indicate a problem, you can turn directly to the appropriate section of the handbook. Just flip through the tabs at the tops of the pages until you find the code in question.

If your instructor uses an abbreviation such as *w* or *dm*, consult the list of abbreviations and revision symbols on the next-to-last page of the book. There you will find the name of the problem (*wordy*; *dangling modifier*) and the number of the section to consult.

If your instructor provides advice without codes or abbreviations, use the index at the back of the book to look up specific terms. (See pp. ix and xii for more about the index.)

Lund 3

the other snowmobiles" (Johnson 7). Whether such noise adversely affects the park's wildlife remains a debated question, but the possibility exists. **Smart use of counterargument**
Some who favor keeping the park open to snowmobiles argue that newer, four-stroke machines cause less air and noise pollution than older models. While this is true, the new machines still pollute more than cars, and their decibel level is reduced only slightly ("Snowmobile" B25). Also, because the newer snowmobiles cost at least $3,000 more than the older ones, it is unlikely that individuals would choose to buy them or that rental companies could afford to upgrade. At present there are no strict guarantees that only the newer models would be allowed into the park.
Like most federal agencies, budget constraints face the *dm* National Park Service. Funds that should be used to preserve Yellowstone National Park and its wildlife have been diverted to deal with the snowmobile issue. A single environmental impact study of the problem cost taxpayers nearly $250,000 in early 2002 (Greater Yellowstone Coalition), and the park service estimates that implementing the new plan

Revision Symbols
Letter-number codes refer to sections of

abbr	
adj	
add	
adv	
agr	
appr	
art	
awk	
cap	
case	
cliché	
coh	coherence C4-d
coord	faulty coordination S6-c
cs	comma splice G6
dev	inadequate development C4-b
dm	dangling modifier S3-e
-ed	error in -ed ending G2-d
emph	emphasis S6
ESL	ESL grammar M1, M2, M3, M4, M5

S3-e Repair dangling modifiers.

A dangling modifier fails to refer logically to any word in the Dangling modifiers are easy to repair, but they can be hard especially in your own writing.

Recognizing dangling modifiers

Dangling modifiers are usually word groups (such as verb that suggest but do not name an actor. When a sentence

ix

How to find information on your own

This handbook is designed to allow you to find information quickly without an instructor's help—usually by consulting the main menu inside the front cover. At times, you may also consult the detailed menu inside the back cover, the index, the glossary of usage, the list of revision symbols, or one of the directories to documentation models. The tutorials on pages xii–xv give you opportunities to practise finding information in different ways.

THE MAIN MENU   The main menu inside the front cover displays the handbook's contents briefly and simply. Each of the twelve sections in the main menu leads you to a colour-coded tabbed divider (such as C/Composing and Revising), where you can find a more detailed menu.

Let's say that you want to find out how to make your sentences parallel. Your first step is to scan the main menu for the appropriate topic—in this case, S1, "Parallelism." Then you can browse the section numbers at the tops of the pages to find section S1.

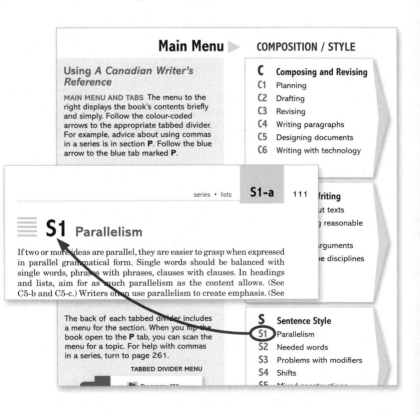

Main Menu ▶ COMPOSITION / STYLE

Using *A Canadian Writer's Reference*

MAIN MENU AND TABS The menu to the right displays the book's contents briefly and simply. Follow the colour-coded arrows to the appropriate tabbed divider. For example, advice about using commas in a series is in section **P**. Follow the blue arrow to the blue tab marked **P**.

C Composing and Revising
C1 Planning
C2 Drafting
C3 Revising
C4 Writing paragraphs
C5 Designing documents
C6 Writing with technology

series • lists   **S1-a**   111   Iriting

ut texts

≡ **S1** Parallelism

reasonable

If two or more ideas are parallel, they are easier to grasp when expressed in parallel grammatical form. Single words should be balanced with single words, phrases with phrases, clauses with clauses. In headings and lists, aim for as much parallelism as the content allows. (See C5-b and C5-c.) Writers often use parallelism to create emphasis. (See

rguments

e disciplines

The back of each tabbed divider includes a menu for the section. When you flip the book open to the **P** tab, you can scan the menu for a topic. For help with commas in a series, turn to page 261.

TABBED DIVIDER MENU

S Sentence Style
S1 Parallelism
S2 Needed words
S3 Problems with modifiers
S4 Shifts

THE DETAILED MENU The detailed menu appears inside the back cover. When the section you're looking for is broken up into quite a few subsections, try consulting this menu. For instance, if you have a question about the proper use of commas after introductory elements, this menu will quickly lead you from P/Punctuation to P1, "The comma" to P1-b, "Introductory elements."

Once you find the right subsection in the book, you will see three kinds of advice to help you edit your writing—a rule, an explanation, and one or more examples that show editing.

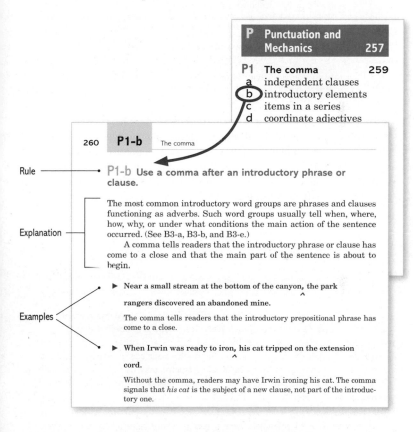

THE INDEX If you aren't sure which topic to choose from one of the menus, consult the index at the back of the book. For example, you may not realize that the question of whether to use *have* or *has* is a matter of subject-verb agreement (section G1). In that case, simply look up "*has* vs. *have*" in the index. You will be directed to specific pages covering subject-verb agreement.

MAKING THE MOST OF YOUR HANDBOOK   You will find your way to helpful advice by using the index, the menus, or the tabbed dividers. Once you get to the page with the advice you are looking for, you may also find a "Making the most of your handbook" box that pulls together additional related advice and models for your assignment.

> drilling, for example, imagine a jury that represents those who have a stake in the matter: environmentalists, policymakers, oil company executives, and consumers.
>
> At times, you can deliberately narrow your audience. If you are working within a word limit, for example, you might not have the space in which to address all the concerns surrounding the offshore drilling debate. Or you might be primarily interested in reaching one segment of a general

> **Making the most of your handbook**
>
> You may need to consider a specific audience for your argument.
> ► Writing in a particular discipline, such as business or psychology: A4

THE GLOSSARY OF USAGE   When in doubt about the correct use of a particular word (such as *affect* and *effect*), consult the glossary of usage, section W1. This glossary explains the difference between commonly confused words; it also includes words that are inappropriate in formal written English.

MORE ONLINE

Using the book's companion Web site: hackerhandbooks.com/writersref

Throughout *A Canadian Writer's Reference,* Fifth Edition, you will see references to more advice and help on the book's Web site. These are labelled PRACTICE (for interactive exercises), MODELS (for model papers and other documents), and THE WRITING CENTRE (for tips on getting help with your assignments). Here is a complete list of resources on the site. Your instructor may use some of this material in class; each area of the site, however, has been developed for you to use on your own whenever you need it.

> \> Practice exercises
> More than 1800 interactive writing, grammar, and research/documentation exercise items, all with immediate feedback. Research exercises include topics such as integrating quotations and documenting sources in MLA, APA, and CMS (*Chicago*) styles.
> \> Model papers
> Annotated sample papers, organized by style (MLA, APA, CMS [*Chicago*], CSE) and by genre (research paper, argument paper, review of the literature, and so on)
> \> *Research and Documentation Online*
> Advice on finding sources in a variety of academic disciplines and up-to-date guidelines for documenting print and online sources in MLA, APA, CMS (*Chicago*), and CSE styles

DIRECTORIES TO DOCUMENTATION MODELS   When you are documenting sources in a research paper with MLA, APA, or CMS (*Chicago*) style, you can find documentation models by consulting the appropriate colour-coded directories.

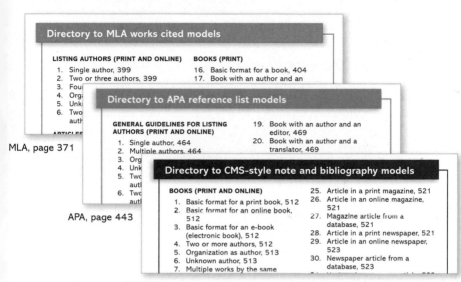

MLA, page 371

APA, page 443

CMS (*Chicago*), page 498

> **Multilingual/ESL**
> Resources, strategies, model papers, and exercises to help multilingual students improve their academic writing skills
> **Revision**
> Papers in progress and models of global and sentence-level revisions
> **Writing centre resources**
> Revision checklists and helpsheets for common writing problems
> **Language Debates**
> Mini-essays exploring controversial issues of grammar and usage
> **Exercise PDFs, diagnostics, and test prep**
> Print-format practice exercises, interactive diagnostic tests, and links to additional online resources for every part of the book
> **Nancy Sommers videos**
> From the book's coauthor, advice on revising, reading and responding to texts, working with teacher comments, and developing an argument
> **Re:Writing**
> A free collection of resources for composition and other university and college classes: help with preparing presentation slides, avoiding plagiarism, evaluating online sources, and more
> **E-book**
> An online version of *A Writer's Reference*, with interactive exercises, audio commentary on model papers, and short movies that teach essential academic skills such as integrating sources in a research paper and revising with peer comments (This area of the Web site requires an activation code.)

Tutorials

The following tutorials will give you practice using the book's menus, index, glossary of usage, and MLA directory. Answers to the tutorials begin on page xvi.

TUTORIAL 1: Using the menus

Each of the following "rules" violates the principle it expresses. Using the main menu inside the front cover or the detailed menu inside the back cover, find the section in *A Canadian Writer's Reference* that explains the principle. Then fix the problem. Example:

> *Tutors in*
> ▶ ~~In~~ the writing centre/~~they~~ say that vague pronoun reference is
>   ^
>   unacceptable. *G3-b*

1. A verb have to agree with its subject.
2. About sentence fragments. You should avoid them.
3. Its important to use apostrophe's correctly.
4. If your sentence begins with a long introductory word group use a comma to separate the word group from the rest of the sentence.

TUTORIAL 2: Using the index

Assume that you have written the following sentences and want to know the answers to the questions in brackets. Use the index at the back of the book to locate the information you need, and edit the sentences if necessary.

1. Each of the candidates have decided to participate in tonight's debate. [Should the verb be *has* or *have* to agree with *Each*?]
2. We had intended to go surfing but spent most of our vacation lying on the beach. [Should I use *lying* or *laying*?]
3. In some cultures, it is considered ill mannered for you to accept a gift. [Is it OK to use *you* to mean "anyone in general"?]
4. In Quebec, Joanne picked up several bottles of maple syrup for her sister and me. [Should I write *for her sister and I*?]

TUTORIAL 3: Using the menus or the index

Imagine that you are in the following situations. Using either the menus or the index, find the information you need.

1. You are a student studying health administration, and you're editing a report you've just written on the benefits of community-based urgent

care clinics. You recall learning to put a comma between all items in a series except the last two. But you have noticed that most writers use a comma between all items. You're curious about the rule. Which section of *A Canadian Writer's Reference* will you consult?

2. You are tutoring in your university's writing centre. A composition student comes to you for help with her first essay. She is revising a draft and struggling with her use of articles (*a*, *an*, and *the*). You know how to use articles, but you aren't able to explain the complicated rules on their correct use. Which section in *A Canadian Writer's Reference* will you and the student, a multilingual writer, consult?

3. You have been assigned to write a response to an essay you read for your composition class. Your instructor has asked that you use at least three quotations from the text in your response, which must be written in MLA style. You aren't quite sure how to integrate words from another source in your own writing. Which section in this handbook will help?

4. You supervise interns at a housing agency. Two of your interns have trouble with the *-s* endings on verbs. One tends to drop *-s* endings; the other tends to add them where they don't belong. You suspect that both problems stem from dialects spoken at home. The interns are in danger of losing their jobs because your boss thinks that anyone who writes "the tenant refuse . . ." or "the landlords insists . . ." is beyond hope. You disagree. Where can you direct your interns for help in *A Canadian Writer's Reference*?

TUTORIAL 4: Using the glossary of usage

Consult the glossary of usage to see if the italicized words are used correctly. Then edit any sentences containing incorrect usage. Example:

> ▶ The pediatrician gave my daughter *a̸* injection for her allergy.

(insertion: *an*)

1. Changing attitudes toward alcohol have *effected* the beer industry.
2. It is *mankind's* nature to think wisely and act foolishly.
3. Our goal this year is to *grow* our profits by 9 percent.
4. Most sleds are pulled by no *less* than two dogs and no more than ten.

TUTORIAL 5: Using the directory to MLA works cited models

Let's say that you have written a short research essay on the origins of hip-hop music. You have cited the following four sources in your essay, using MLA style, and you are ready to type your list of works cited. Turn to pages 371–72 and use the MLA directory to locate the appropriate models. Then write a correct entry for each source and arrange the entries in a properly formatted list of works cited.

A book by Jeff Chang titled *Can't Stop, Won't Stop: A History of the Hip-Hop Generation*. The book was published in New York by St. Martin's Press in 2005.

An online article by Kay Randall called "Studying a Hip Hop Nation." The article appeared on the University of Texas at Austin Web site. The title of the site is *University of Texas at Austin*. You accessed the site on April 13, 2010; the last update was October 9, 2008.

A sound recording entitled "Rapper's Delight" performed by the Sugarhill Gang on the CD *Sugarhill Gang*. The CD was released in 2008 by DBK Works.

A magazine article accessed online through the database *Expanded Academic ASAP*. The article, "The Roots Redefine Hip-Hop's Past," was written by Kimberly Davis and published in *Ebony* magazine in June 2003. The article appears on pages 162–64. You found this article on April 13, 2010.

Answers to the Tutorials

TUTORIAL 1

1. A verb has to agree with its subject. (G1-a)
2. Avoid sentence fragments. (G5)
3. It's important to use apostrophes correctly. (P4)
4. If your sentence begins with a long introductory word group, use a comma to separate the word group from the rest of the sentence. (P1-b)

TUTORIAL 2

1. The index entry *"each"* mentions that the word is singular, so you might not need to look further to realize that the verb should be *has*, not *have*. The first page reference takes you to the entry for *each* in the glossary of usage (W1), which directs you to G1-e and G3-a for details about why *has* is correct. The index entry *"has* vs. *have"* leads you to the chart in G1.
2. The index entry *"lying* vs. *laying"* takes you to section G2-b, where you will learn that *lying* (meaning "reclining or resting on a surface") is correct.
3. Looking up *"you*, inappropriate use of"* leads you to the glossary of usage (W1) and section G3-b, which explain that *you* should not be used to mean "anyone in general." You can revise the sentence by using *a person* or *one* instead of *you*, or you can restructure the sentence completely: *In some cultures, accepting a gift is considered ill mannered.*
4. The index entries *"I* vs. *me"* and *"me* vs. *I"* take you to section G3-c, which explains why *for her sister and me* is correct.

TUTORIAL 3

1. Section P1-c states that, although usage varies, most experts advise using a comma between all items in a series—to prevent possible misreadings or ambiguities. To find this section, you would probably use the menu system.
2. You and the student would consult section M2, on articles. This section is easy to locate in the menu system.

3. In the menu system, you will find "MLA papers" and then section MLA-3, "Integrating sources."
4. You can send your interns to sections G1 and G2-c, which you can find in the menu system if you know to look under "Subject-verb agreement" or "Verb forms, tenses, and moods." If you aren't sure about the grammatical terminology, you can look in the index under "-*s*, as verb ending" or "Verbs, -*s* form of."

TUTORIAL 4

1. Changing attitudes toward alcohol have *affected* the beer industry.
2. It is *human* nature to think wisely and act foolishly.
3. Our goal this year is to *increase* our profits by 9 percent.
4. Most sleds are pulled by no *fewer* than two dogs and no more than ten.

TUTORIAL 5

Chang, Jeff. *Can't Stop, Won't Stop: A History of the Hip-Hop Generation.* New York: St. Martin's, 2005. Print.

Davis, Kimberly. "The Roots Redefine Hip-Hop's Past." *Ebony* June 2003: 162-64. *Expanded Academic ASAP.* Web. 13 Apr. 2010.

Randall, Kay. "Studying a Hip Hop Nation." *University of Texas at Austin.* U of Texas at Austin, 9 Oct. 2008. Web. 13 Apr. 2010.

Sugarhill Gang. "Rapper's Delight." *Sugarhill Gang.* DBK Works, 2008. CD.

Preface for instructors

Everywhere I travel, instructors tell me that they love *A Writer's Reference*—from which *A Canadian Writer's Reference* is adapted—for its clear, concise explanations and respectful tone and for its ease of use inside and outside the classroom. I understand why *A Writer's Reference* inspires such affection; it is the book I too have always loved, the book my students trust and keep, and the one that teaches one patient lesson at a time. Millions of students and instructors have turned to *A Writer's Reference* for the straightforward, reliable, and comprehensive support that Diana Hacker always offered. It has been one of the great pleasures of my own teaching career to build on that foundation as the coauthor of *A Writer's Reference*.

Many people have asked, *How do you revise the most successful handbook in the country—the handbook that everyone loves?* To prepare for the current edition, I traveled to more than forty-five colleges and universities to learn how students use their handbooks and how instructors teach from them. I listened, everywhere, for clues about how to make the handbook an even more helpful companion for students throughout their academic careers and an even stronger resource for the teachers guiding their development as writers. Throughout my travels, I heard students puzzle out the unfamiliar elements of academic writing, particularly those related to working with sources. I watched creative instructors show their students how to build arguments, synthesize sources, and strengthen their ideas through revision. I observed writing centre tutors responding to students' questions about thesis statements and counterargument. And I listened to librarians expertly explain how to approach research assignments and evaluate sources. I wanted this edition to capture the vibrant energy and creativity that surround conversations about student writing, wherever they take place.

As you look through the book, you'll discover many innovations inspired by these conversations. One of the new features I'm most excited about is "Revising with Comments." During my travels, I asked students about the comments they receive most frequently and asked instructors to show me the comments they write most frequently on their students' drafts. The answers to these questions, combined with my own research on responding to student writers, shaped this feature, which helps students and instructors make the most of reviewing and commenting. In keeping with the Hacker tradition, this new feature teaches one lesson at a time—how to revise an unclear thesis or how to consider opposing viewpoints, for instance—and directs students to specific sections of the handbook to guide their revision strategies.

In *A Writer's Reference*, Diana Hacker created the most innovative and practical reference—the one that responds most directly to student writers' questions and challenges. This edition carries on that tradition. You'll find that the book you've always loved now includes a new argument paper, a stepped-out approach to writing and revising thesis statements, new coverage of synthesizing sources, expanded attention to writing assignments across the disciplines, and many more practical innovations. As a classroom teacher, I know how much a trusted and reliable handbook can help students make the most of their writing experiences in college or university and beyond. And

now as the coauthor of this new edition, I am eager to share this book with you, knowing that you'll find everything you and your students love and trust about *A Writer's Reference*.

Nancy Sommers

Features of the fifth edition of *A Canadian Writer's Reference*

What's new

TARGETED CONTENT FOR TODAY'S STUDENTS: ACADEMIC WRITING AND RESEARCH

- *Synthesis.* Many of today's academic writing assignments require that students synthesize—analyze sources and work them into a conversation that helps develop an argument.

New coverage of synthesis, with annotated examples in MLA and APA styles, helps students work with sources to meet the demands of academic writing. (See MLA-3c and APA-3c.)

- *A new sample argument paper* shows students how to state and support an argumentative thesis, address counterarguments, integrate visuals, and document sources. (See pp. 87–91.)

- *A new annotated advertisement* illustrates how one student analyzes key elements of a visual to begin building an interpretation. (See p. 70.)

- *A new case study* follows one student's research and writing process, providing an illustrated model for strategizing about a research assignment, using search tools and techniques, evaluating sources, taking notes, thinking critically about how best to use sources in a paper, and integrating a source responsibly. This section (MLA-5b) directs students to more detailed information throughout the book. (See pp. 432–35.)

- *A new section on writing about literature.* A new tabbed section, L, includes advice on interpreting and writing about works of literature with two annotated student essays.

- *New advice for distinguishing scholarly and popular sources.* (See pp. 350–51.)

- *Integrating evidence in analytical papers.* Section A1-d shows—at the sentence level—how to introduce, include, and interpret a passage in an analytical paper. (See p. 74.)

- *More help with writing assignments in other disciplines and in various genres.* For students who work with evidence in disciplines other than English, we have included annotated assignments and excerpts from model papers in psychology, business, biology, and nursing. (See pp. 105–08.)

- *New documentation models, many annotated.* Eighty-six new models across the three styles (MLA, APA, CMS [*Chicago*]) include sources students are using today—podcasts, online videos, blogs, and DVD features. Annotations for many models help students see at a glance how to gather information about sources and format citations. (See p. 419 for an example.)

- *New chart on avoiding plagiarism.* (See pp. 364–65.)

CONCRETE STRATEGIES FOR REVISING

- *New coverage of portfolio keeping.* For students who are asked to maintain and submit a writing portfolio, a new section, C3-e, "Prepare a portfolio; reflect on your writing," covers types of portfolios, offers tips for writing a reflective cover document, and provides a sample reflective essay. (See pp. 28–31.)

- *Revising with comments.* Based on research with sixty-five students at colleges and universities, this new feature helps students understand common instructor comments such as "unclear thesis," "develop more," or "cite your source" and gives students revision strategies they can apply to their own work. (See pp. 23–27.)

- *Specific strategies for revising thesis statements.* We know that writers often need help reworking thesis statements, in whatever discipline they are writing. A new stepped-out approach helps students identify a problem in a draft thesis, ask relevant questions, and use their own responses to revise. (See pp. 16–18.)

NEW EXAMPLES, RELEVANT GRAMMAR COVERAGE

- *Academic examples that reflect the types of sentences students are expected to write in university and college.* A new type of hand-edited example ("Writing with sources") shows typical errors students make—and how they can correct them—when they integrate sources in MLA, APA, and CMS (*Chicago*) papers. (See p. 270 for an example.)

- *More ESL coverage.* Part M, Multilingual Writers and ESL Challenges, offers more accessible advice and more support for multilingual writers across the disciplines.

- *Basic grammar content that is more straightforward than ever.* Tabbed section B, Basic Grammar, the handbook's reference within a reference, now teaches with everyday example sentences.

NAVIGATION HELP THAT MAKES SENSE TO STUDENTS

- *Making the most of your handbook.* These new boxes, running throughout the book, help students pull together the advice they need to complete writing assignments in any class. The boxes teach students to use their handbook as a reference by prompting them to consult related advice and examples from different parts of the book as they write and revise. (See p. 347 for an example.)

- *Plain-language navigation for quick and easy reference.* In the upper right-hand corner of every page, terms like *main idea*, *flow*, and *presenting the other side* will help students see at a glance the exact page they need.

A NEW COLLECTION OF RESOURCES THAT HELPS INSTRUCTORS MAKE THE MOST OF THEIR HANDBOOK

- *Teaching with Hacker Handbooks*, by Marcy Carbajal Van Horn, offers practical advice on common topics such as designing a composition course, crafting writing assignments, and teaching multilingual writers. Ten lesson plans, each including strategies and materials that are ready to use or customize, support common course goals, like teaching argument, teaching paragraphs, and teaching with peer review. The collection also includes a wealth of handouts, syllabi, and other resources for integrating a Hacker handbook into your course. Available in print and online (hackerhandbooks.com/teaching).

What's the same

The features that have made *A Canadian Writer's Reference* work so well for so many students and instructors are still here.

Colour-coded main menu and tabbed dividers. The main menu directs students to yellow, blue, and green tabbed dividers; the colour coding makes it easy for students to identify and flip to the section they need. The documentation sections are further colour-coded: orange for MLA, dark green for APA, and purple for CMS (*Chicago*).

User-friendly index. Even students who are unsure of grammar terminology will find help fast by consulting the user-friendly index. When facing a choice between *I* and *me*, for example, students may not know to look for "Case" or "Pronoun case." They are more likely to look up "*I*" or "*me*," so the index includes entries for "*I* vs. *me*" and "*me* vs. *I*." Similar entries appear throughout the index.

Citation at a glance. Annotated visuals show students where to find the publication information they need to cite common types of sources in MLA, APA, and CMS (*Chicago*) styles. (See p. 416 for an example.)

Quick-access charts and an uncluttered design. This edition has what instructors and students have come to expect of a Hacker handbook: a clear and navigable presentation of information, with charts that summarize key content.

What's on the companion Web site?
hackerhandbooks.com/writersref

See page xxi for a list of resources available on the handbook's companion Web site.

Grammar, writing, and research exercises with feedback for every item. More than 1800 items offer students plenty of extra practice, and our new scorecard gives instructors flexibility in viewing students' results.

Annotated model papers in MLA, APA, CMS (*Chicago*), and CSE styles. Student writers can see formatting conventions and effective writing in traditional academic essays and in other common genres: annotated bibliographies, literature reviews, lab reports, business proposals, and clinical documents.

Research and Documentation Online. Written by a college librarian, this award-winning resource gives students a jump start with research in thirty academic disciplines. In addition to coverage of MLA, APA, and CMS (*Chicago*) styles of documentation, the site includes complete documentation advice for writing in the sciences (CSE style).

Resources for writers and tutors. Checklists, hints, tips, and helpsheets are available in downloadable format.

Resources for multilingual writers and ESL. Writers will find advice and strategies for understanding postsecondary expectations and completing writing assignments. Also included are charts, exercises, activities, and an annotated essay in draft and final form.

Language Debates. Twenty-two brief essays provide opportunities for critical thinking about grammar and usage issues.

Access to premium content. New copies of the print handbook can be packaged with a free activation code for premium content: the e-book, a series of online video tutorials, and a collection of games, activities, readings, guides, and more.

Supplements for instructors

PRACTICAL

Teaching with Hacker Handbooks (in print and online at hackerhandbooks.com/teaching)

A Writer's Reference instructor resources (on the companion Web site at hackerhandbooks.com/writersref)

PROFESSIONAL

Teaching Composition: Background Readings

The Bedford Guide for Writing Tutors, Fifth Edition

The Bedford Bibliography for Teachers of Writing, Sixth Edition

Supplements for students

PRINT

Exercises for A Canadian Writer's Reference

Developmental Exercises for A Writer's Reference

Working with Sources: Exercises for A Writer's Reference

Research and Documentation in the Electronic Age

Resources for Multilingual Writers and ESL

Writing in the Disciplines: Advice and Models

Strategies for Online Learners

ONLINE

A Writer's Reference e-Book

CompClass for A Writer's Reference

Acknowledgments

I am grateful for the expertise, enthusiasm, and classroom wisdom that so many individuals brought to this edition.

Reviewers

For their participation in a focus group on *A Writer's Reference* at the 2010 Conference on College Composition and Communication, I would like to thank Jennifer Cellio, Northern Kentucky University; Robert Cummings, University of Mississippi; Karen Gardiner, University of Alabama; Letizia Guglielmo, Kennesaw State College; Liz Kleinfeld, Metropolitan State College of Denver; and Melinda Knight, Montclair State University.

I thank those professors whose meticulous feedback helped shape *Strategies for Online Learners*: Jill Dahlman, University of Hawaii; Dana Del George, Santa Monica College; Larry Giddings, Pikes Peak Community College; David Hennessy, Broward College; Neil Plakcy, Broward College; and Rolando Regino, Riverside Community College.

I am indebted to the members of our Librarian Advisory Board: Barbara Fister, Gustavus Adolphus College; Susan Gilroy, Harvard University; John Kupersmith, University of California, Berkeley; and Monica Wong, El Paso Community College.

For their invaluable input, I would like to thank an insightful group of reviewers who answered detailed questionnaires about the previous edition: Susan Achziger, Community College of Aurora; Michelle Adkerson, Nashville State Community College; Chanon Adsanatham, Community College of Aurora; Martha Ambrose, Edison Community College; Kimberley Aslett, Lake Superior State University; Laurel Barlow, Weber State University; Cynthia Bates, University of California, Davis; Fiona C. Brantley, Kennesaw State University; Max Brzezinski, Wake Forest University; Ken A. Bugajski, University of Saint Francis; Jeff Calkins, Tacoma Community College; Erin E. Campbell, Abraham Baldwin Agricultural College; Elizabeth Canfield, Virginia Commonwealth University; Eric Cash, Abraham Baldwin College; Michael Chamberlain, Azusa Pacific University; Deborah Chedister, SUNY Orange County Community College; Rong Chen, SUNY at Stony Brook; Michele J. Cheung, University of Southern Maine; Denise-Marie Coulter, Atlantic Cape Community College; Meriah Crawford, Virginia Commonwealth University; Tony Cruz, SUNY Orange County Community College; Janet Dean, Bryant College; Jeffrey L. Decker, University of California, Los Angeles; Sarah Doetschman, University of Alaska, Fairbanks; Elizabeth Evans, Wake Forest University; Martin Fertig, Montgomery County Community College; Christina D. French, Diablo Valley College; Marilyn Gilbert, The Art Institute of Seattle; William Gorski, West Los Angeles College; Ann H. Gray, Scott Community College; Jeanette Gregory, Cloud County Community College; Wendy Harrison, Abraham Baldwin Agricultural College; Catherine Hutcheson, Troy University; Melissa Jenkins, Wake Forest University; Elizabeth C. Jones, Wor-Wic Community College; Kristen Katzin-Nystrom, SUNY Orange County Community College; Lolann A. King, Trinity Valley Community College; Jamison Klagmann, University of Alaska, Fairbanks; Cheryl Laz, University of Southern Maine; Mark Leidner, Abraham Baldwin Agricultural College; Lindsay Lewan, Arapahoe Community College; Keming Liu, Medgar Evers College; Jeanette Lonia, Delaware Technical & Community College; Stefanie Low, Brooklyn College; Angie Macri, Pulaski Technical College; Edward W. Maine, California State University, Fullerton; Diane McDonald, Montgomery County Community College; Vickie Melograno, Atlantic Cape Community College; Priya Menon, Troy University; Gayla Mills, Randolph-Macon College; Frank Nigro, Shasta College; Diana Palmer, Montgomery County Community College; Peter J. Pellegrin, Cloud County Community College; Brenton Phillips, Cloud County Community College; J. Andrew Prall, University of Saint Francis; Mary Jean Preston, Carthage College; Molly Pulda, Brooklyn College; Tiffany A. Rayl, Montgomery County Community College; Jessica Richard, Wake Forest University; S. Randall Rightmire, University of California, Santa Barbara; Charles Riley, Baruch College/CUNY;

Rekha Rosha, Wake Forest University; Mitchell Rowat, University of Western Ontario; Kirsti Sandy, Keene State College; Robert M. Sanford, University of Southern Maine; Su Senapati, Abraham Baldwin Agricultural College; Shant Shahoian, Glendale Community College; Michele Singletary, Nashville State Community College; Michel Small, Shasta College; Matt Smith, University of Saint Francis; Marcia A. Sol, Cloud Community College; Stephen E. Sullivan, University of Saint Francis; Judith K. Taylor, Northern Kentucky University; Matt Theado, Gardner-Webb University; Jennifer Thomas, Azusa Pacific University; Matthew A. Thomas, Azusa Pacific University; Katherine E. Tirabassi, Keene State College; Cliff Toliver, Missouri Southern State University; Elaine Torda, SUNY Orange County Community College; Monica Trent, Montgomery College, Rockville; Ellen Vance, Art Institute of Seattle; Travis Wagner, University of Southern Maine; Karen Woods Weierman, Worcester State College; and Kelli Wood, El Paso Community College. We would also like to thank our anonymous reviewers from Brooklyn College, the University of Colorado at Denver, Glendale Community College, Ithaca College, Northern Kentucky University, Pulaski Technical College, and Wake Forest University.

Contributors

I am grateful to the following individuals, fellow teachers of writing, for their smart revisions of two key supplements: Joe Bizup, Boston University, updated *Writing about Literature* with fresh selections and relevant advice; and Jon Cullick, Northern Kentucky University, and Terry Myers Zawacki, George Mason University, tackled *Writing in the Disciplines*, expanding the advice to cover nine disciplines with the addition of music, engineering, and criminology. I am enormously grateful to Marcy Carbajal Van Horn, ESL specialist, experienced composition instructor, and former online writing lab director, who lent her expertise on several projects: She served as lead author for two brand-new resources, *Teaching with Hacker Handbooks* and *Strategies for Online Learners*, and she improved our coverage for multilingual writers both in the handbook and on the companion Web site.

Six instructors from Canadian colleges and universities lent their expertise to "Teaching with *A Canadian Writer's Reference*" in the instructor's edition. Thanks for tips, assignments, and teaching activities to Brian Diemert, Brescia University College; Jonathan Finn, Wilfrid Laurier University; Joseph Khoury, St. Francis Xavier University; Jeannie M. Martin, Vancouver Island University; Robert G. May, Queen's University at Kingston; and Melanie Sexton, University of Ottawa.

Student contributors

A number of bright and willing students helped identify which instructor comments provide the best guidance for revision. From Green River Community College: Kyle Baskin, Josué Cardona, Emily Dore, Anthony Hines, Stephanie Humphries, Joshua Kin, Jessica Llapitan, James Mitchell, Derek Pegram, Charlie Piehler, Lindsay Allison Rae Richards, Kristen Saladis, Jacob Simpson, Christina Starkey, Ariana Stone, and Joseph Vreeburg. From Northern Kentucky University: Sarah Freidhoff, Marisa Hempel, Sarah Laughlin, Sean Moran, Laren Reis, and Carissa Spencer. From Palm Beach Community College: Alexis Day, Shawn Gibbons, Zachary Jennison, Jean Lacz, Neshia Neal, Sarah Reich, Jude Rene, and Sam Smith. And from the University of Maine at Farmington: Nicole Carr, Hannah Courtright, Timothy Doyle, Janelle Gallant, Amy Hobson, Shawn Menard, Jada Molton, Jordan Nicholas, Nicole Phillips, Tessa Rockwood, Emily Rose, Nicholas Tranten, and Ashley Wyman. I also thank the students who have let us use and adapt their papers as models in the handbook and on its companion Web site: Ned Bishop, Lucy Bonilla, Jamal Hammond, Sam Jacobs, Albert Lee, Luisa Mirano, Anna Orlov, Emilia Sanchez, and Matt Watson.

Bedford/St. Martin's

A handbook is truly a collaborative writing project, and it is a pleasure to acknowledge and thank the enormously talented Bedford/ St. Martin's editorial team, whose deep commitment to students informs each new feature of *A Writer's Reference*. Joan Feinberg, Bedford's president and Diana Hacker's first editor, offers her superb judgment on every aspect of the book. Joan's graceful and generous leadership, both within Bedford and in the national composition community, is a never-ending source of inspiration for those who work closely with her. Michelle Clark, executive editor; Mara Weible, lead development editor; and Barbara Flanagan, senior editor, are treasured friends and colleagues, the kind of editors every author dreams of having. Michelle, an endless source of creativity and joy, combines wisdom with patience, imagination with practicality, and hard work with good cheer. Mara's brilliant, close, and careful attention to each detail of the handbook comes from her teacher's sensibility and editor's unerring eye. And Barbara, who has worked on Diana Hacker's handbooks for more than twenty-five years, brings to this edition her unrelenting insistence on both clarity and precision as well as her editorial patience and perseverance. Thanks to Alicia Young, associate editor, for expertly managing the review process, preparing documents, and editing several ancillaries. Thanks also to Kylie Paul, editorial assistant and newest member of the handbook team, for managing many small details related to both our Web and print projects.

The passionate commitment to *A Writer's Reference* of many Bedford colleagues — Denise Wydra, editorial director; Karen Henry, editor in chief; Marjorie Adler, marketing manager; and John Swanson, senior executive marketing manager — ensures that this edition remains the most innovative and practical handbook on the market. Special thanks go to Jimmy Fleming, senior English specialist, for his abundant contributions, always wise and judicious, and for his enthusiasm and support as we traveled to colleges near and far. Many thanks to Rosemary Jaffe, senior production editor, who kept us on schedule and efficiently and gracefully turned a manuscript into a handbook. And thanks to Linda McLatchie, copyeditor, for her thoroughness and attention to detail; to Claire Seng-Niemoeller, text designer, who always has clarity and ease of use in mind as she designs *A Writer's Reference*; to Donna Dennison, art director, who has given the book a strikingly beautiful cover; and to Sarah Ferguson, new media editor, who developed the book's companion Web site and e-book. Canadian editor Dawn Hunter has thoroughly updated this edition of *A Canadian Writer's Reference*, adding examples based on Canadian culture and literature throughout the text, substituting numerous Canadian sources for the documentation models, and ensuring that the text conforms to Canadian conventions.

Most important, I want to thank Diana Hacker. To create the best writing help for her students at Prince George's Community College, she studied their practices and puzzled out their challenges. What she learned inspired her to create the best reference for all students of academic writing. I'm honoured to acknowledge her work, her legacy, and her innovative spirit — and pleased to continue in the tradition of this brilliant teacher and writer.

And last, but never least, I offer thanks to Maxine Rodburg, Laura Saltz, and Kerry Walk, friends and colleagues, for sustaining conversations about teaching writing; to Joshua Alper, an attentive reader of life and literature, for his steadfastness across the drafts; to Sam and Kate for lively conversations about writing; and to Rachel and Alexandra, whose good-natured and humorous observations about their real lives as college writers are a constant source of instruction and inspiration.

Nancy Sommers

Composing
and Revising

C Composing and Revising

Writing is a process of figuring out what you think, not a matter of recording already developed thoughts. Since it's not possible to think about everything all at once, most experienced writers handle a piece of writing in stages. You will generally move from planning to drafting to revising, but be prepared to return to earlier stages as your ideas develop.

C1 Planning

C1-a Assess the writing situation.

Begin by taking a look at your writing situation. Consider your subject, your purpose, your audience, available sources of information, and any assignment requirements such as length, document design, and deadlines (see the checklist on p. 6). It is likely that you will make final decisions about all of these matters later in the writing process—after a first draft, for example—but you can save yourself time by thinking about as many of them as possible in advance.

In many writing situations, part of your challenge will be determining your purpose, or your reason, for writing. The wording of an assignment may suggest its purpose. If no guidelines are given, you may need to ask yourself, "Why am I communicating with my readers?" or "What do I want to accomplish?" University and college writers most often write for the following purposes:

to inform	to analyze
to explain	to synthesize
to summarize	to propose
to recommend	to call readers to action
to evaluate	to change attitudes
to persuade	to express feelings

Audience analysis can often help you determine how to accomplish your purpose—how much detail or explanation to provide, what kind of tone and language to use, and what potential objections to address. You may need to consider multiple audiences. The audience for a business report, for example, might include readers who want details and those who prefer a quick overview. For a service learning course, the audience for a proposal might include both your instructor and the supervisor at the organization at which you volunteered. The checklist on page 6 includes questions that will help you analyze your audience and develop an effective strategy for reaching your readers.

Academic English What counts as good writing varies from culture to culture and even among groups within cultures. In some situations, you will need to become familiar with the writing styles—such as direct or indirect, personal or impersonal, plain or embellished—that are valued by the culture or discipline for which you are writing.

C1-b Experiment with ways to explore your subject.

Instead of just plunging into a first draft, experiment with one or more techniques for exploring your subject: talking and listening, reading and annotating texts, listing, clustering, freewriting, asking questions, keeping a journal, blogging. Whatever technique you turn to, the goal is the same: to generate ideas that will lead you to a question, a problem, or a topic that you want to explore. At this early stage of the writing process, don't censor yourself. Sometimes an idea that initially seems trivial or far-fetched will turn out to be worthwhile.

Talking and listening

Because writing is a process of figuring out what you think about a subject, it can be useful to try out your ideas on other people. Conversation can deepen and refine your ideas before you even begin to set them down on paper. By talking and listening to others, you can also discover what they find interesting, what they are curious about, and where they disagree with you. If you are planning to advance an argument, you can try it out on listeners with other points of view.

Many writers begin a writing project by brainstorming ideas in a group, debating a point with friends, or chatting with an instructor. Others prefer to record themselves talking through their own thoughts. Some writers exchange ideas by sending e-mails or instant messages or by posting to discussion boards or blogs. You may be encouraged to share ideas with your classmates and instructor in an online workshop, where you can begin to refine your thoughts before starting a draft.

THE WRITING CENTRE   hackerhandbooks.com/writersref
> Resources for writers and tutors > Tips from writing tutors:
Invention strategies

Understanding an assignment

Determining the purpose of the assignment

Usually the wording of an assignment will suggest its purpose. You might be expected to do one of the following in an academic writing assignment:

- summarize information from books, lectures, or research (See A1-c.)
- analyze ideas and concepts (See A1-d.)
- take a position and defend it with evidence (See A2.)
- synthesize (combine ideas from) several sources and create an original argument (See MLA-3.)

Understanding how to answer an assignment's questions

Many assignments will ask you to answer a *how* or *why* question. Such questions cannot be answered using only facts; instead, you will need to take a position. For example, the question "*What* are the survival rates for people with leukemia?" can be answered by reporting facts. The question "*Why* are the survival rates for people with leukemia in one province lower than they are in a neighbouring province?" must be answered with both facts and interpretation.

If a list of prompts appears in the assignment, be careful—instructors rarely expect you to answer all of the questions in order. Look instead for topics, themes, or ideas that will help you ask your own questions.

Recognizing implied questions

When you are asked to *discuss, analyze, argue,* or *consider,* your instructor will often expect you to answer a *how* or *why* question.

Discuss the effects of the Copyright Modernization Act on the protection of intellectual property.	= How has the Copyright Modernization Act affected the protection of intellectual property?
Consider the recent rise in the number of autism diagnoses.	= Why is the number of autism diagnoses rising?

Recognizing disciplinary expectations

When you are asked to write in a specific discipline, pay attention to the expectations and features of the writing in that discipline. Look closely at the key terms and specialized vocabulary of the assignment and the kinds of evidence and citation style your instructor expects. (See A4.)

Checklist for assessing the writing situation

Subject

- Has the subject (or a range of possible subjects) been given to you, or are you free to choose your own?
- What interests you about your subject? What questions would you like to explore?
- Why is your subject worth writing about? How might readers benefit from reading about it?
- Do you need to narrow your subject to a more specific topic (because of length restrictions, for instance)?

Purpose and audience

- Why are you writing: To inform readers? To persuade them? To entertain them? To call them to action? Some combination of these?
- Who are your readers? How well informed are they about the subject? What do you want them to learn?
- How interested and attentive are they likely to be? Will they resist any of your ideas?
- What is your relationship to your readers: Student to instructor? Employee to supervisor? Citizen to citizen? Expert to novice?

Sources of information

- Where will your information come from: Reading? Personal experience? Research? Direct observation? Interviews? Questionnaires?
- What kinds of evidence will best serve your subject, purpose, and audience?
- What sort of documentation style is required: MLA? APA? CMS?

Length and document design

- Do you have any length specifications? If not, what length seems appropriate, given your subject, purpose, and audience?
- Does the assignment call for a particular kind of paper: A report? A proposal? An essay? An analysis of data? A reflection?
- Is a particular format required? If so, do you have guidelines to follow or examples to consult?
- How might visuals — charts, graphs, tables, images — help you convey information?

Reviewers and deadlines

- Who will be reviewing your draft in progress: Your instructor? A writing centre tutor? Your classmates?
- What are your deadlines? How much time will you need for each stage, including proofreading and printing the final draft?

Reading and annotating texts

Reading is an important way to deepen your understanding of a topic and expand your perspective. Annotating a text, written or visual, encourages you to read actively—to highlight key concepts, to note possible contradictions in an argument, or to raise questions for further research and investigation. Here, for example, is a paragraph from an essay on medical ethics as one student annotated it:

M:
o

Read c.
notes before yc

▶ Guidelines for active reading: page 68
▶ Taking notes: R3-c
▶ Analyzing texts: A1-d

What breakthroughs? Do all breakthroughs have the same consequences?

tem cell esearch

        Breakthroughs in genetics present us with a promise and a predicament. The promise is that we may soon be able to treat and prevent a host of debilitating diseases. The predicament is that our newfound genetic knowledge may also enable us to manipulate our own nature—to enhance our muscles, memories, and moods; to choose the sex, height, and other genetic traits of our children; to make ourselves "better than well." When science moves faster than moral understanding, as it does today, men and women struggle to articulate their unease. In liberal societies they reach first for the language of autonomy, fairness, and individual rights. But this part of our moral vocabulary is ill equipped to address the hardest questions posed by genetic engineering. The genomic revolution has induced a kind of moral vertigo.

Sandel's key dilemma

What does he mean by "moral understanding"?

s everyone eally uneasy? s something a reakthrough if creates a redicament?

Which questions? He doesn't seem to be taking sides.

                          —Michael Sandel, "The Case against Perfection"

Listing

Listing ideas—a technique sometimes known as *brainstorming*—is a good way to figure out what you know and what questions you have.

        Here is a list one student jotted down for an essay about community service requirements for high school students in Ontario:

- Volunteered throughout high school.
- Teaching adults to read motivated me to study education.
- "The best way to find yourself is to lose yourself in the service of others."   —Gandhi

unteering helps students find interests and career paths.
Volunteering as requirement? Contradiction?
- Some students need to work to save for university tuition.
- Enough time to study, work, and volunteer?
- Can't students volunteer for their own reasons?
- What schools have community service requirements?
- What do students say about community service requirements?

Listing questions and ideas helped the writer narrow her subject and identify her position. In other words, she treated her early list as a record of her thoughts and a springboard to new ideas, not as an outline.

Clustering

Unlike listing, clustering highlights relationships among ideas. To cluster ideas, write your subject in the centre of a sheet of paper, draw a circle around it, and surround the circle with related ideas connected to it with lines. If some of the satellite ideas lead to more specific clusters, write them down as well. The writer of the following cluster diagram was exploring ideas for an essay on obesity in children.

CLUSTER DIAGRAM

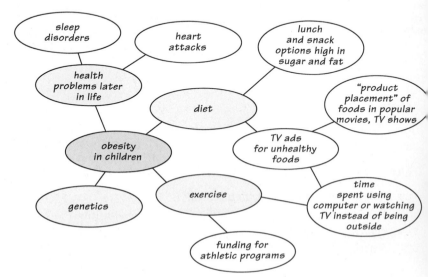

Freewriting

In its purest form, freewriting is simply nonstop w
ten minutes or so and write whatever comes to m
to think about word choice, spelling, or even meanin
you can write about being stuck, but you should keep your i
ing. If nothing much happens, you have lost only ten minutes. It's i
likely, though, that something interesting will emerge—perhaps an
eloquent sentence, a genuine expression of curiosity, or an idea worth
further investigation.

To explore ideas on a particular topic, consider using a technique
called *focused freewriting*. Again, you write quickly and freely, but this
time you focus on a subject and pay attention to the connections among
your ideas.

Asking questions

When gathering material for a story, journalists routinely ask them
selves Who? What? When? Where? Why? and How? In addition to
helping journalists get started, these questions ensure that they will
not overlook an important fact.

Whenever you are writing about events, whether current or historical, asking the journalist's questions is one way to get started.
One student, whose topic was the negative reaction in 1915 to D. W.
Griffith's silent film *The Birth of a Nation*, began exploring her topic
with this set of questions:

Who objected to the film?

What were the objections?

When were the protests first voiced?

Where were protests most strongly expressed?

Why did protesters object to the film?

How did protesters make their views known?

In the academic world, scholars often
generate ideas by posing questions related
to a specific discipline: one set of questions
for analyzing short stories, another for evaluating experiments in social psychology,
still another for reporting field experiences
in criminal justice.

> **Making the most
> of your handbook**
>
> Effective writers begin by
> asking questions.
>
> ▶ Asking questions in
>   academic disciplines:
>   A4-b

If you are writing in a particular disci-
pline, you might begin your writing process by finding out which questions scholars in that discipline typically explore.

eeping a journal

A journal is a collection of informal, exploratory, sometimes experimental writing. In a journal, often meant for your eyes only, you can take risks. You might freewrite, pose questions, comment on an interesting idea from one of your classes, or keep a list of questions that occur to you while reading and researching. You might imagine a conversation between yourself and your readers or stage a debate to understand opposing positions. A journal can also serve as a sourcebook of ideas to draw on in future essays.

Blogging

Although a blog (Weblog) is a type of journal, it is a public writing space rather than a private one. In a blog, you might express opinions, make observations, recap events, have fun with language, or interpret an image. Since most blogs have a commenting feature, you can create a conversation by inviting readers to give you feedback—ask questions, pose counterarguments, or suggest other readings on a topic.

C1-c Draft a working thesis.

As you explore your topic and identify questions to investigate, you will begin to see possible ways to focus your material. At this point, try to settle on a tentative central idea. The more complex your topic, the more your focus will change as your drafts evolve. For many types of writing, you will be able to assert your central idea in a sentence or two. Such a statement, which ordinarily appears in the opening paragraph of your finished essay, is called a *thesis statement* (see also C2-a).

A thesis is often one or more of the following:

- the answer to a question you have posed
- the solution for a problem you have identified
- a statement that takes a position on a debatable topic

A tentative or working thesis will help you organize your draft. Don't worry about the exact wording because your main point may change as you refine and focus your ideas. Here, for example, are one student's efforts to pose a question and draft a thesis statement for an essay in his film course.

QUESTION
In *Rebel without a Cause,* how does the filmmaker show that the main character becomes alienated from his family and friends?

Testing a working thesis

Once you have come up with a working thesis, you can use the following questions to evaluate it.

- Does your thesis answer a question, propose a solution to a problem, or take a position in a debate?
- Does the thesis require an essay's worth of development? Or will you run out of points too quickly?
- Is the thesis too obvious? If you cannot come up with interpretations that oppose your own, consider revising your thesis.
- Can you support your thesis with the evidence available?
- Can you explain why readers will want to read an essay with this thesis? Can you respond when a reader asks "So what?"

WORKING THESIS

In *Rebel without a Cause*, Jim Stark, the main character, is often seen literally on the edge of physical danger, suggesting that he is becoming more and more agitated by family and society.

The working thesis will need to be revised as the student thinks through and revises his paper, but it provides a useful place to start writing.

Here another student identifies a problem to focus an argument paper.

PROBLEM

Canadians who earn average incomes cannot run effective national political campaigns.

WORKING THESIS

Parliament should pass legislation that would make it possible for Canadians who are not wealthy to be viable candidates in national political campaigns.

The student has roughed out language for how to solve the problem — enacting federal legislation. As she learns more about her topic, she will be able to refine her thesis and suggest a more specific solution, such as federal restriction of campaign spending.

Keep in mind as you draft your working thesis that an effective thesis is a promise to a reader; it points both the writer and the reader in a definite direction. For a more detailed discussion of thesis, see C2-a.

C1-d Sketch a plan.

Once you have drafted a working thesis, listing and organizing your supporting ideas is a good next step. Creating outlines, whether formal or informal, can help you make sure your writing is credible and logical.

When to use an informal outline

You might want to sketch an informal outline to see how you will support your thesis and to figure out a tentative structure for your ideas. Informal outlines can take many forms. Perhaps the most common is simply the thesis followed by a list of major ideas.

> Working thesis: Television advertising should be regulated nationally to help prevent childhood obesity.

- Children watch more television than ever.
- Snacks marketed to children are often unhealthy and fattening.
- Childhood obesity can cause sleeping disorders and other health problems.
- Addressing these health problems costs taxpayers billions of dollars.
- Therefore, these ads are actually costing the public money.
- In Quebec, all advertising to children under thirteen is prohibited. Can this model be used nationally?
- We regulate alcohol and cigarette ads on television, so why not advertisements for pop and junk food?

If you began by jotting down a list of ideas (see pp. 7–8), you can turn that list into a rough outline by crossing out some ideas, adding others, and putting the ideas in a logical order.

When to use a formal outline

Early in the writing process, rough outlines have certain advantages: They can be produced quickly, they are obviously tentative, and they can be revised easily. However, a formal outline may be useful later in the writing process, after you have written a rough draft, especially if your topic is complex. It can help you see whether the parts of your essay work together and whether your essay's structure is logical.

The following formal outline brought order to the research paper that appears in MLA-5c, on Internet surveillance in the workplace. The student's thesis is an important part of the outline. Everything else in the outline supports it, directly or indirectly.

FORMAL OUTLINE

Thesis: Although companies often have legitimate concerns that lead them to monitor employees' Internet usage—from expensive security breaches to reduced productivity—the benefits of electronic surveillance are outweighed by its costs to employees' privacy and autonomy.

I. Although employers have always monitored employees, electronic surveillance is more efficient.

   A. Employers can gather data in large quantities.

   B. Electronic surveillance can be continuous.

   C. Electronic surveillance can be conducted secretly, with keystroke logging programs.

II. Some experts argue that employers have legitimate reasons to monitor employees' Internet usage.

   A. Unmonitored employees could accidentally breach security.

   B. Companies are legally accountable for the online actions of employees.

III. Despite valid concerns, employers should value employee morale and autonomy and avoid creating an atmosphere of distrust.

   A. Setting the boundaries for employee autonomy is difficult in the wired workplace.

   1. Using the Internet is the most popular way of wasting time at work.

   2. Employers can't tell easily if employees are working or surfing the Web.

   B. Surveillance can create resentment among employees.

   1. Web surfing can relieve stress, and restricting it can generate tension between managers and workers.

   2. Enforcing Internet usage can seem arbitrary.

IV. Surveillance may not increase employee productivity, and trust may benefit productivity.

   A. A company shouldn't care how many hours salaried employees work as long as they get the job done.

   B. Casual Internet use can actually benefit companies.

   1. The Internet may spark business ideas.

   2. The Internet may suggest ideas about how to operate more efficiently.

V. Employees' rights to privacy are not well defined by the law.

   A. Few federal guidelines on electronic surveillance exist.

   B. Employers and employees are negotiating the boundaries without legal guidance.

   C. As technological capabilities increase, the need to define boundaries will also increase.

Guidelines for constructing an outline

1. Put the thesis at the top.
2. Make items at the same level parallel grammatically (see S1).
3. Use sentences unless phrases are clear.
4. Use the conventional system of numbers, letters, and indents:

I.
   A.
   B.
      1.
      2.
         a.
         b.
II.
   A.
   B.
      1.
      2.
         a.
         b.

5. Always include at least two items at each level.
6. Limit the number of major sections in the outline; if the list of roman numerals (at the first level) gets too long, try clustering the items into fewer major categories with more subcategories.

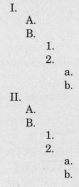

C2 Drafting

Generally, the introduction to a piece of writing announces the main point; the body develops it, usually in several paragraphs; the conclusion drives it home. You can begin drafting, however, at any point. If you find it difficult to introduce a paper that you have not yet written, try drafting the body first and saving the introduction for later.

C2-a For most types of writing, draft an introduction that includes a thesis.

Drafting an introduction

Your introduction will usually be a paragraph of 50 to 150 words (in a longer paper, it may be more than one paragraph). Perhaps the most common strategy is to open the paragraph with a few sentences that engage the reader and establish your purpose for writing and then state your main point. The statement of your main point is called the *thesis*. (See also C1-c.)

In the following introductions, the thesis is highlighted.

> Credit card companies love to extend credit to college students, especially those just out of high school. Ads for credit cards line campus bulletin boards, flash across commercial Web sites for students, and get stuffed into shopping bags at college bookstores. Why do the companies market their product so vigorously to a population that lacks a substantial credit history and often has no steady source of income? The answer is that significant profits can be earned through high interest rates and assorted penalties and fees. By granting college students liberal lending arrangements, credit card companies often hook them on a cycle of spending that can ultimately lead to financial ruin.   —Matt Watson, student

> As the United States industrialized in the nineteenth century, using immigrant labor, social concerns took a backseat to the task of building a prosperous nation. The government did not regulate industries and did not provide an effective safety net for the poor or for those who became sick or injured on the job. Immigrants and the poor did have a few advocates, however. Settlement houses such as Hull-House in Chicago provided information, services, and a place for reform-minded individuals to gather and work to improve the conditions of the urban poor. Alice Hamilton was one of these reformers. Hamilton's efforts helped to improve the lives of immigrants and drew attention and respect to the problems and people that until then had been ignored.   —Laurie McDonough, student

Ideally, the introductory sentences leading to the thesis should hook the reader, perhaps with one of the following:

- a startling statistic or an unusual fact
- a vivid example
- a description or an image
- a paradoxical statement
- a quotation or a bit of dialogue
- a question
- an analogy
- an anecdote

Whether you are writing for a scholarly audience, a professional audience, or a general audience, you cannot assume your readers' interest in the topic. The hook should spark curiosity and offer readers a reason to continue.

Although the thesis frequently appears at the end of the introduction, it can also appear at the beginning. Much work-related writing, for example, requires a straightforward approach and commonly begins with the thesis.

> Flextime scheduling, which has proved effective at the Library of Congress, should be introduced on a trial basis at the main branch of the Montgomery County Public Library. By offering flexible work hours, the library can boost employee morale, cut down on absenteeism, and expand its hours of operation.   —David Warren, student

For some types of writing, it may be difficult or impossible to express the central idea in a thesis statement; or it may be unwise or unnecessary to include a thesis statement in the essay. A personal narrative, for example, may have a focus that is too subtle to be distilled in a single statement. Strictly informative writing, like that found in many business memos, may be difficult to summarize in a thesis. In such instances, do not try to force the central idea into a thesis sentence. Instead, think in terms of an overriding purpose, which may or may not be stated directly.

> **Making the most of your handbook**
>
> The thesis statement is central to many types of writing.
>
> ▶ Writing about texts: A1
>
> ▶ Constructing reasonable arguments: A2
>
> ▶ Writing research papers: MLA-1, APA-1, CMS-1

Academic English If you come from a culture that prefers an indirect approach in writing, you may feel that asserting a thesis early in an essay sounds unrefined or even rude. In Canada, however, readers appreciate a direct approach; when you state your point as directly as possible, you show that you understand your topic and value your readers' time.

Writing effective thesis statements

An effective thesis statement is a central idea that requires supporting evidence; its scope is appropriate for the required length of the essay; and it is sharply focused. It should answer a question you have posed, resolve a problem you have identified, or take a position in a debate.

When constructing a thesis statement, ask yourself whether you can successfully develop it with the sources available to you and for the purposes you've identified. Also ask if you can explain why readers should be interested in reading an essay that explores this thesis.

A thesis must require proof or further development through facts and details; it cannot itself be a fact or a description.

DRAFT
THESIS
The first polygraph was developed by Dr. John A. Larson in 1921.

PROBLEM The thesis is *too factual.* A reader could not disagree with it or debate it; no further development of this idea is required.

STRATEGY *Enter a debate* by posing a question about your topic that has more than one possible answer. For example: Should the polygraph be used by private employers? Your thesis should be your answer to the question.

REVISED
THESIS
Because the polygraph has not been proven reliable, even under controlled conditions, its use by employers should be banned.

A thesis should be an answer to a question, not a question itself.

DRAFT
THESIS
Did Prime Minister John Diefenbaker make the decision to halt production of the Avro Arrow?

PROBLEM The thesis is a *question*, not an answer to a question.

STRATEGY *Take a position* on your topic by answering the question you have posed. Your thesis should be your answer to the question.

REVISED
THESIS
Although Prime Minister John Diefenbaker made the announcement that production of the Avro Arrow would be halted, an analysis of the evidence suggests that the decision was not his alone.

A thesis should be of sufficient scope for your assignment; it should not be too broad.

DRAFT
THESIS
Mapping the human genome has many implications for health and science.

PROBLEM The thesis is *too broad.* Even in a very long research paper, you would not be able to discuss all the implications of mapping the human genome.

STRATEGY *Consider subtopics of your original topic.* Once you have chosen a subtopic, take a position in an ongoing debate and pose a question that has more than one answer. For example: Should people be tested for genetic diseases? Your thesis should be your answer to the question.

REVISED
THESIS
Although scientists can now detect genetic predisposition for specific diseases, policymakers should establish guidelines about whom to test and under what circumstances.

A thesis also should not be too narrow.

DRAFT
THESIS
A person who carries a genetic mutation linked to a particular disease might or might not develop that disease.

PROBLEM The thesis is *too narrow.* It does not suggest any argument or debate about the topic.

STRATEGY *Identify challenging questions* that readers might have about your topic. Then pose a question that has more than one answer. For example: Do the risks of genetic testing outweigh its usefulness? Your thesis should be your answer to this question.

REVISED
THESIS
Though positive results in a genetic test do not guarantee that the disease will develop, such results can cause psychological trauma; genetic testing should therefore be avoided in most cases.

A thesis should be sharply focused, not too vague. Avoid fuzzy, hard-to-define words such as *interesting, good,* or *disgusting.*

DRAFT
THESIS
Memorial Hall in the Canadian War Museum is an interesting place.

PROBLEM This thesis is *too fuzzy and unfocused.* It's difficult to define *interesting,* and the sentence doesn't give the reader any cues about where the essay is going.

STRATEGY *Focus your thesis with concrete language and a clear plan.* Pose a question about the topic that has more than one answer. For example: How does the physical structure of Memorial Hall shape the experience of visitors? Your thesis—your answer to the question—should use specific language that engages readers to follow your argument.

REVISED
THESIS
The design of Memorial Hall in the Canadian War Museum encourages an interactive experience—almost forcing visitors, with its "spotlight" effect, to reflect on the sacrifices of Canada's soldiers.

C2-b Draft the body.

The body of your essay develops support for your thesis, so it's important to have at least a working thesis before you start writing. What does your thesis promise readers? Try to keep your response to that question in mind as you draft the body.

You may already have written an introduction that includes your working thesis. If not, as long as you have a draft thesis, you can begin developing the body and return later to the introduction. If your thesis suggests a plan or if you have sketched a preliminary outline, try to block out your paragraphs accordingly. Draft the body of your essay by writing at least a paragraph about each supporting point you listed in the planning stage. If you do not have a plan, pause for a few moments and sketch one (see C1-d).

Keep in mind that often you might not know what you want to say until you have written a draft. It is possible to begin without a plan—assuming you are prepared to treat your first attempt as a "discovery draft" that will be radically rewritten once you discover what you really want to say. Whether or not you have a plan when you begin drafting, you can often figure out a workable order for your ideas by stopping each time you start a new paragraph, to think about what your readers will need to know to follow your train of thought.

For more detailed advice about paragraphs in the body of an essay, see C4. For specific help with drafting paragraphs, see C4-b.

TIP: As you draft, keep careful notes and records of any sources you read and consult. (See R3.) If you quote, paraphrase, or summarize a source, include a citation, even in your draft. You will save time and avoid plagiarism if you follow the rules of citation and documentation while drafting.

C2-c Draft a conclusion.

A conclusion should remind readers of the essay's main idea without repeating it. Often the concluding paragraph can be relatively short. By the end of the essay, readers should already understand your main point; your conclusion drives it home and, perhaps, gives readers something larger to consider.

In addition to echoing your main idea, a conclusion might

- briefly summarize your essay's key points
- propose a course of action
- offer a recommendation
- discuss the topic's wider significance or implications
- pose a question for future study

To conclude an essay analyzing the shifting roles of women in the military services, one student discusses her topic's implications for society as a whole:

As the military continues to train women in jobs formerly reserved for men, our understanding of women's roles in society will no doubt continue to change. As news reports of women training for and taking part in combat operations become commonplace, reports of women becoming CEOs, police chiefs, and even president of the United States will cease to surprise us. Or perhaps we have already reached this point.
—Rosa Broderick, student

To make the conclusion memorable, you might include a detail, an example, or an image from the introduction to bring readers full circle; a quotation or a bit of dialogue; an anecdote; or a witty or ironic comment.

Whatever concluding strategy you choose, keep in mind that an effective conclusion is decisive and unapologetic. Avoid introducing wholly new ideas at the end of an essay. And because the conclusion is so closely tied to the rest of the essay in both content and tone, be prepared to rework it (or even replace it) as you revise your draft.

C3 Revising

Revising is rarely a one-step process. Global matters—focus, purpose, organization, content, and overall strategy—generally receive attention first. Improvements in sentence structure, word choice, grammar, punctuation, and mechanics come later.

C3-a Make global revisions.

Many of us resist global revisions because we find it difficult to view our work from our audience's perspective. To distance yourself from a draft, put it aside for a while, preferably overnight or even longer. When you return to it, try to play the role of your audience as you read. If possible, enlist friends or family to be the audience for your draft. Or visit your school's writing centre to go over your draft with a writing tutor. Ask your reviewers to focus on the larger issues of writing, such as purpose and organization, not on word- or sentence-level issues. The checklist for global revision on the next page may help you and your reviewers get started.

> **Making the most of your handbook**
>
> Seeking and using feedback are critical steps in revising a paper.
>
> ▶ Guidelines for peer reviewers: page 22
> ▶ Revising with comments: C3-c

PRACTICE AND MODELS hackerhandbooks.com/writersref
  > Composing and revising > C3–1 and C3–2
  > Revising > Sample global revision
        > Sample sentence-level revision

Checklist for global revision

Purpose and audience

- Does the draft address a question, a problem, or an issue that readers care about?
- Is the draft appropriate for its audience? Does it account for the audience's knowledge of and possible attitudes toward the subject?

Focus

- Is the thesis clear? Is it prominently placed?
- If there is no thesis, is there a good reason for omitting one?
- Are any ideas obviously off the point?

Organization and paragraphing

- Are there enough organizational cues for readers (such as topic sentences or headings)?
- Are ideas presented in a logical order?
- Are any paragraphs too long or too short for easy reading?

Content

- Is the supporting material relevant and persuasive?
- Which ideas need further development?
- Are the parts proportioned sensibly? Do major ideas receive enough attention?
- Where might material be deleted?

Point of view

- Is the dominant point of view—first person (*I* or *we*), second person (*you*), or third person (*he, she, it, one,* or *they*)—appropriate for your purpose and audience? (See S4-a.)

C3-b Revise and edit sentences.

Much of this book offers advice on revising sentences for clarity and on editing them for grammar, punctuation, and mechanics. Some writers handle sentence-level revisions directly at the computer, experimenting with a variety of possible improvements. Other writers prefer to print out a hard copy of the draft and mark it up before

> ### Guidelines for peer reviewers
>
> - View yourself as a coach, not a judge. Work with the writer to identify the draft's strengths and areas for improvement.
> - Restate the writer's main ideas to check that they are clearly expressed.
> - Where possible, give specific compliments. Let the writer know which of his or her strategies are successful.
> - Ask to hear more about passages you find confusing or interesting.
> - Express interest in reading the next draft.

making changes in the file. Here is a rough-draft paragraph as one student edited it on-screen for a variety of sentence-level problems.

Although some cities have found creative ways to improve access to public transportation for passengers with physical disabilities, ~~and to fund other programs, there have been problems in~~ our city has struggled with ~~due to the need to address~~ budget constraints and competing ~~needs~~ priorities. ~~This~~ The budget crunch has led citizens to question how funds are distributed.~~?~~ For example, last year ~~when~~ city officials voted to use available funds to support ~~had to choose between allocating funds for accessible transportation or allocating funds to~~ after-school programs rather than transportation upgrades. ~~, they voted for the after-school programs.~~ It is not clear to some citizens why ~~these~~ after-school programs are more important.

The original paragraph was flawed by wordiness, a problem that can be addressed through any number of revisions. The following revision would also be acceptable:

> Some cities have funded improved access to public transportation for passengers with physical disabilities. Because of budget constraints, our city chose to fund after-school programs rather than transportation programs. As a result, citizens have begun to question how funds are distributed and why certain programs are more important than others.

Some of the paragraph's improvements do not involve choice and must be fixed in any revision. The hyphen in *after-school programs* is necessary; a noun must be substituted for the pronoun *these* in the last sentence; and the question mark in the second sentence must be changed to a period.

C3-c Revising with comments

To revise is to "re-see," and the comments you receive from your instructors, peers, and writing centre tutors will help you re-see your draft from your readers' point of view. Sometimes these comments are written as shorthand commands—"Be specific!"—and sometimes as questions—"What is your main point?" Such comments don't immediately show you *how* to revise, but they do identify places where global and sentence-level revisions can improve your draft.

When instructors, peers, and writing tutors comment on your work, you won't be able to incorporate everyone's advice. Sort through the comments you receive with your purpose and audience in mind.

You may also want to keep a revision and editing log, a list of the global and sentence-level concerns that come up repeatedly in your reviewers' comments. When you apply lessons from one assignment to another, comments can help you become a more effective writer.

Remember not to take criticism personally. Your readers are responding to your essay, not to you. It may be frustrating to hear that you still have more work to do, but taking feedback seriously— and revising accordingly—will make your essay stronger. This section addresses common types of comments an instructor or peer might make in response to your writing.

THE COMMENT: **Unclear thesis**

SIMILAR COMMENTS: **Vague thesis · State your position · What is your main point?**

UNDERSTANDING THE COMMENT   When readers point out that your thesis is unclear, the comment often signals that they have a hard time identifying your essay's main point.

the mother or other relatives.

drives to dance lessons,

eball team, hosts birthday

omework help. Do more **Unclear thesis**

r hinder the development of

STRATEGIES FOR REVISING

- *Ask questions.* What is the thesis, position, or main point of the draft? Can you support it with the available evidence? (See C1-c, A2-c, and A2-d.)
- *Reread your entire draft.* Because ideas develop as you write, you may find that your conclusion contains a clearer statement of your main point than does your working thesis. Or you may find your thesis elsewhere in your draft. (See C-2a.)
- *Try framing your thesis* as an answer to a question you pose, the resolution of a problem you identify, or a position you take in a

debate. And put your thesis to the "So what?" test: Why would a reader be interested in this thesis? (See C1-c and p. 11.)

THE COMMENT: **Narrow your introduction**

SIMILAR COMMENTS: **Unfocused intro · Too broad**

UNDERSTANDING THE COMMENT When readers point out that your introduction needs to be "narrowed," the comment often signals that the beginning sentences of your essay are not specific or focused.

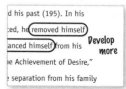

even believe that rituals
actions influence the outcome
e fans go beyond cheering, and **Narrow**
ssment, and chanted slurs **your**
orts. **introduction**

STRATEGIES FOR REVISING

- *Reread your introduction and ask questions.* Are the sentences leading to your thesis specific enough to engage readers and communicate your purpose? Do these sentences lead logically to your thesis? Do they spark your readers' curiosity and offer them a reason to continue reading? (See C-2a.)

- *Try engaging readers with a "hook" in your introduction*—a question, a quotation, a paradoxical statement, a vivid example, or an image. (See p. 15.)

THE COMMENT: **Develop more**

SIMILAR COMMENTS: **Undeveloped · Give examples · Explain**

UNDERSTANDING THE COMMENT When readers suggest that you "develop more," the comment often signals that you stopped short of providing a full and detailed discussion of your idea.

d his past (195). In his
ed, he removed himself
anced himself from his **Develop**
more
e Achievement of Desire,"
e separation from his family

STRATEGIES FOR REVISING

- *Read your paragraph to a peer or a tutor* and ask specific questions. What's missing? Do readers need more background information or examples to understand your point? Do they need more evidence to be convinced? Is it clear what point you're making with your details? (See A2-d.)

- *Keep your purpose in mind.* Your assignment probably asks you to do more than summarize sources or list examples and evidence. Make sure you discuss the examples and illustrations you provide and analyze your evidence. (See A2-e.)

- *Think about why your main point matters to your readers.* Take another look at your points and support and answer the question "So what?" (See p. 11.)

THE COMMENT: **Be specific**

SIMILAR COMMENTS: **Need examples · Evidence?**

UNDERSTANDING THE COMMENT When readers say that you need to "be specific," the comment often signals that you could strengthen your writing with additional details.

cultural differences between the
Italy. Italian citizens do not share
Be specific
attitudes or values as Canadian
rences make it hard for some
feel comfortable coming to the

STRATEGIES FOR REVISING

- *Reread your topic sentence* to understand the focus of the paragraph. (See C4-a.)

- *Ask questions.* Does the paragraph contain claims that need support? Have you provided evidence—specific examples, vivid details and illustrations, statistics and facts—to help readers understand your ideas and find them persuasive? (See A2-e.)

- *Interpret your evidence.* Remember that details and examples don't speak for themselves. You'll need to show readers how evidence supports your claims. (See A1-d and A2-e.)

THE COMMENT: **Consider opposing viewpoints**

SIMILAR COMMENTS: **What about the other side? · Counterargument?**

UNDERSTANDING THE COMMENT When readers suggest that you "consider opposing viewpoints," the comment often signals that you need to recognize and respond to possible objections to your argument.

stile work environment
chers Shepard and Clifton
es using drug-testing **Consider**
ave lower productivity **opposing**
viewpoints
ve not adopted such

STRATEGIES FOR REVISING

- *Read more* to learn about the debates surrounding the topic. (See p. 7.)

- *Ask questions:* Are there other sides to the issue? Would a reasonable person offer an alternative explanation for the evidence or provide counterevidence? (See p. 85.)

- *Be open-minded.* Although it might seem illogical to introduce opposing arguments, you'll show your knowledge of the topic by recognizing that not everyone draws the same conclusion. (See A2-f, A2-g, and p. 376.)

- *Introduce and counter objections* with phrases like these: "Some readers might point out that . . ." or "Critics of this view argue that. . . ." (See p. 85.)
- *Revise your thesis*, if necessary, to account for other points of view.

THE COMMENT: **Summarize less, analyze more**

SIMILAR COMMENTS: **Too much summary · Show, don't tell · Go deeper**

UNDERSTANDING THE COMMENT When readers point out that you need to include more analysis and less summary, the comment often signals that they are looking for your interpretation of the text.

> ...ages she speaks with
> For example, she speaks
> ...uébécois French with her   **Summarize**   **less,**
> ...s English at school (327).   **analyze**
> ...r experience with speaking   **more**

STRATEGIES FOR REVISING

- *Reread your paragraph and highlight the sentences that summarize.* Then, in a different colour, highlight the sentences that contain your analysis. (Summary describes what the text says; analysis offers a judgment or interpretation of the text.) (See A1-c and A1-d.)
- *Reread the text* (or passages of the text) that you are analyzing. Pay attention to how the language and structure of the text contribute to its meaning. (See A1-a.)
- *Ask questions.* What strategies does the author use and how do those strategies help convey the author's message? What insights about the text can you share with your readers? How can you deepen your reader's understanding of the author's main points? (See A3 and A1-d.)

THE COMMENT: **More than one point in this paragraph**

SIMILAR COMMENTS: **Unfocused · Lacks unity · Hard to follow**

UNDERSTANDING THE COMMENT When readers tell you that you have "more than one point in this paragraph," the comment often signals that not all sentences in your paragraph support the topic sentence.

> ...he believes the social
> ...omic benefits. Many
> ...Most important, casino   **More than**
> ...reas of the province   **one point**
> ...ecent years.   **in this**
>   **paragraph**

STRATEGIES FOR REVISING

- *Reread your paragraph and ask questions.* What is the main point of the paragraph? Is there a topic sentence that signals to readers what to expect in the rest of the paragraph? Have you included sentences that perhaps belong elsewhere in your draft? (See C4-a.)

- *Revisit your topic sentence.* It should serve as an important signpost for readers. Make sure the wording of your topic sentence is precise and that you have enough evidence to support it in the paragraph. (See C4-b.)

THE COMMENT: **Your words?**

SIMILAR COMMENTS: **Source?** • **Who's talking here?**

UNDERSTANDING THE COMMENT   When readers ask "Your words?" the comment often signals that it is unclear whether you are using only your own words or are mixing in some words of your sources.

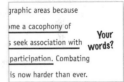

> graphic areas because
>
> me a cacophony of
>
> seek association with **Your words?**
>
> participation. Combating
>
> is now harder than ever.

STRATEGIES FOR REVISING

- *Check that you have clearly marked the boundaries* between your source material and your own words. Have you borrowed words from sources without properly acknowledging them? (See MLA-2, APA-2, and CMS-2.)

- *Use a signal phrase* to introduce each source and provide context. Doing so prepares readers for a source's words. (See MLA-3b, APA-3b, and CMS-3b.)

- *Use quotation marks* to enclose language that you borrow word-for-word from a source and follow each quotation with a parenthetical citation. (See MLA-2b, APA-2b, and CMS-2b.)

- *Put summaries and paraphrases in your own words* and always cite your sources. (See MLA-2c, APA-2c, and CMS-2c.)

As you revise your paper, you might request feedback or clarification from instructors or peers by e-mail. Because e-mail communication can be quick and convenient, it's natural to think of it as informal, but be sure to keep your audience in mind. You should usually use a formal greeting for an instructor (*Dear Professor Brink*) instead of a casual one (*Hey!*) and use standard formatting and language (avoiding emoticons, abbreviations like *LOL,* and unconventional capitalization). You can often be more flexible with peers, but use a more formal style at the beginning of the semester, until you get to know them. And make sure you have a clear purpose in mind: Are you trying to share an observation? Asking for another perspective on your topic? Requesting feedback on a particular paragraph? For more on using e-mail in business and academic contexts, see C5-f.

C3-d Proofread the final manuscript.

After revising and editing, you are ready to prepare the final manuscript. (See C5-e for guidelines.) Make sure to allow yourself enough time for proofreading—the final and most important step in manuscript preparation.

Proofreading is a special kind of reading: a slow and methodical search for misspellings, typographical mistakes, and omitted words or word endings. Such errors can be difficult to spot in your own work because you may read what you intended to write, not what is actually on the page. To fight this tendency, try proofreading out loud, articulating each word as it is actually written. You might also try proofreading your sentences in reverse order, a strategy that takes your attention away from the meanings you intended and forces you to focus on one word at a time.

Although proofreading may be slow, it is crucial. Errors strewn throughout an essay are distracting and annoying. If the writer doesn't care about this piece of writing, the reader might wonder, why should I? A carefully proofread essay, however, sends a positive message that you value your writing and respect your readers.

C3-e Prepare a portfolio; reflect on your writing.

At the end of the semester, your instructor may ask you to submit a portfolio, or collection, of your writing. A writing portfolio often consists of drafts, revisions, and reflections that demonstrate a writer's thinking and learning processes or showcase the writer's best work. Your instructor may give you the choice of submitting a paper portfolio or an e-portfolio.

Reflection—the process of stepping back periodically to examine your decisions, preferences, strengths, and challenges as a writer—is the backbone of portfolio keeping. Your instructor may ask you to submit a reflective document in which you introduce or comment on the pieces in your portfolio and discuss your development as a writer throughout the course. This reflection may take the form of an essay, a cover letter, or some other kind of statement—often, but not always, placed as an introductory piece. You might try one or more of the following strategies:

- Discuss, in depth, your best entry. Explain why it is your best and how it represents what you learned in the course.

- Describe in detail the revisions you've made to one key piece and the improvements and changes you want readers to notice. Include specific passages from the piece.

- Demonstrate what this portfolio illustrates about you as a writer, student, researcher, or critical thinker.

- Reflect on what you've learned about writing and reading throughout the course.

- Reflect on how you plan to use the skills and experiences from your writing course in other courses where writing will be assigned.

SAMPLE REFLECTIVE LETTER FOR A PORTFOLIO

December 11, 2010

Professor Todd Andersen

Humanities Department

Johnson State College

Dear Professor Andersen,

    This semester has been more challenging than I had anticipated. I have always been a good writer, but I discovered this semester that I had to stretch myself in ways that weren't always comfortable. I learned that if I wanted to reach my readers, I needed to understand that not everyone sees the world the way I do. I needed to work with my peers and write multiple drafts to understand that a first draft is just a place to start. I have chosen three pieces of writing for my portfolio: "Negi and the Other Girl: Nicknames and Identity," "School Choice Is a Bad Choice," and "Flat-footed Advertising." Each shows my growth as a writer in different ways, and the final piece was my favorite assignment of the semester.

    The peer review sessions that our class held in October helped me with my analytical response paper. My group and I chose to write about

Reflective writing can take various forms. Bonilla wrote her reflection as a letter.

Reflective writing often calls for first person ("I").

Bonilla lists the pieces included in her portfolio by title.

"Jíbara," by Esmeralda Santiago, for the Identity unit. My first and second drafts were unfocused. I spent my first draft basically retelling the events of the essay. I think I got stuck doing that because the details of Santiago's essay are so interesting—the biting termites, the burning metal, and the *jíbara* songs on the radio—and because I didn't understand the differences between summary and analysis. My real progress came when I decided to focus the essay on one image—the mirror hanging in Santiago's small house, a mirror that was hung too high for her to look into. Finding a focus helped me move from listing the events of the essay to interpreting those events. I thought my peers would love my first draft, but they found it confusing. Some of their comments were hard to take, but their feedback (and all the peer feedback I received this semester) helped me see my words through a reader's eyes.

Bonilla comments on a specific area of growth.

While my Identity paper shows my struggle with focus, my next paper shows my struggle with argument. For my argument essay, I wrote about charter schools. My position is that the existence of charter schools weakens the quality of public schools. In my first draft, my lines of argument were not in the best order. When I revised, I ended the paper with my most powerful argument: Because they refuse to adopt open enrollment policies and are unwilling to admit students with severe learning or behavior problems, charter schools are elitist. While revising, I also introduced a counterargument in my final draft because our class discussion showed me that many of my peers disagree with me. To persuade them, I needed to address their arguments in favor of charter schools. My essay is stronger because I acknowledged that both the proponents and opponents of abandoning charters want improved education for America's children. It took me a while to understand that including counterarguments would actually make my argument more convincing, especially to readers who don't already agree with me. Understanding the importance of counterargument helped me with other writing I did in this course, and it will help me in the writing I do for my major, political science.

Even in the reflective document, Bonilla includes elements of good writing, such as using transitions.

Bonilla reflects on how skills from her writing course will carry over to other courses.

Another stretch for me this semester was seeing visuals as texts that are worth more than a five-second response. The final assignment was my favorite because it involved a number of surprises. I wasn't so much surprised by the idea that ads make arguments because I understand that they are designed to persuade. What was surprising was being able to see all the elements of a visual and write about how they work together to convey a clear message. For my essay "Flat-footed Advertising," I chose the EAS Performance Nutrition ad "The New Theory of Evolution for Women." In my summary of the ad, I noted that the woman who follows the EAS program for twelve weeks and "evolves" is compared to modern humans and our evolution from apes as shown in the classic 1966 *March of Progress* illustration (Howell 41). It was these familiar poses of "Nicolle," the woman in the image, that drew me to study this ad. In my first draft, I made all of the obvious points, looking only literally at the comparison and almost congratulating the company on such a clever use of a classic scientific drawing. Your comments on my draft were a little unsettling because you asked me "So what?"—why would my ideas matter to a reader? You pushed me to consider the ad's assumptions and to question the meaning of the word *evolve*. In my revised essay, I argue that even though Nicolle is portrayed as powerful, satisfied, and "fully evolved," the ad campaign rests on the assumption that performance is best measured by physical milestones. In the end, an ad that is meant to pay homage to woman's strength is in fact demeaning. My essay evolved from draft to draft because I allowed my thinking to change and develop as I revised. I've never revised as much as I did with this final assignment. I cared about this paper and wanted to show my readers why my argument mattered.

> Bonilla mentions how comments on her draft helped her revise.

The expectations for college writing are different from those for high school writing. I believe that my portfolio pieces show that I finished this course as a stronger writer. I have learned to take risks in my writing and to use the feedback from you and my peers, and now I know how to acknowledge the points of view of my audience to be more persuasive. I'm glad to have had the chance to write a reflection at the end of the course. I hope you enjoy reading this portfolio and seeing the evolution of my work this semester.

> In her conclusion, Bonilla summarizes her growth in the course.

Sincerely,

Lucy Bonilla

Lucy Bonilla

C4 Writing paragraphs

Except for special-purpose paragraphs, such as introductions and conclusions (see C2-a and C2-c), paragraphs are clusters of information supporting an essay's main point (or advancing a story's action). Aim for paragraphs that are clearly focused, well developed, organized, coherent, and neither too long nor too short for easy reading.

C4-a Focus on a main point.

A paragraph should be unified around a main point. The main point should be clear to readers, and every sentence in the paragraph should relate to it.

Stating the main point in a topic sentence

As a rule, you should state the main point of a paragraph in a topic sentence—a one-sentence summary that tells readers what to expect as they read on. Usually the topic sentence (highlighted in the following example) comes first in the paragraph.

> All living creatures manage some form of communication. The dance patterns of bees in their hive help to point the way to distant flower fields or announce successful foraging. Male stickleback fish regularly swim upside-down to indicate outrage in a courtship contest. Male deer and lemurs mark territorial ownership by rubbing their own body secretions on boundary stones or trees. Everyone has seen a frightened dog put his tail between his legs and run in panic. We, too, use gestures, expressions, postures, and movement to give our words point.   —Olivia Vlahos, *Human Beginnings*

In academic writing, topic sentences are often necessary to advance or clarify the lines of an argument or to report the research in a field. In business writing, topic sentences (along with headings) are essential because readers often scan for information and summary statements. Sometimes the topic sentence is introduced by a transitional sentence linking the paragraph to earlier material, and occasionally the topic sentence is withheld until the end of the paragraph.

> **Making the most of your handbook**
>
> Topic sentences let your reader know how a body paragraph relates to your essay's thesis.
>
> ▶ Effective thesis statements: **page 16**

Sticking to the point

Sentences that do not support the topic sentence destroy the unity of a paragraph. If the paragraph is otherwise focused, such sentences can simply be deleted or perhaps moved elsewhere. In the following paragraph describing the inadequate facilities in a high school, the information about the chemistry instructor (highlighted) is clearly off the point.

> As the result of tax cuts, the educational facilities of Fort Richmond Collegiate have reached an all-time low. Some of the books date back to 1990 and have long since shed their covers. The few computers in working order must share one printer. The lack of lab equipment makes it necessary for four or five students to work at one table, with most watching rather than performing experiments. Also, the chemistry instructor left to have a baby at the beginning of the semester, and most of the students don't like the substitute. As for the furniture, many of the upright chairs have become recliners, and the desk legs are so unbalanced that they play seesaw on the floor.

Sometimes the solution for a disunified paragraph is not as simple as deleting or moving material. Writers often wander into uncharted territory because they cannot think of enough evidence to support a topic sentence. Feeling that it is too soon to break into a new paragraph, they move on to new ideas for which they have not prepared the reader. When this happens, the writer is faced with a choice: Either find more evidence to support the topic sentence or adjust the topic sentence to mesh with the evidence that is available.

C4-b Develop the main point.

Though an occasional short paragraph is fine, particularly if it functions as a transition or emphasizes a point, a series of brief paragraphs suggests inadequate development. How much development is enough? That varies, depending on the writer's purpose and audience.

For example, when health columnist Jane Brody wrote a paragraph attempting to convince readers that it is impossible to lose fat quickly, she knew that she would have to present a great deal of evidence because many dieters want to believe the opposite. She did *not* write only the following:

> When you think about it, it's impossible to lose—as many diets suggest—10 pounds of *fat* in ten days, even on a total fast. Even a moderately active person cannot lose so much weight so fast. A less active person hasn't a prayer.

This three-sentence paragraph is too skimpy to be convincing. But the paragraph that Brody did write contains enough evidence to convince even skeptical readers.

> When you think about it, it's impossible to lose—as many . . . diets suggest—10 pounds of *fat* in ten days, even on a total fast. A pound of body fat represents 3,500 calories. To lose 1 pound of fat, you must expend 3,500 more calories than you consume. Let's say you weigh 170 pounds and, as a moderately active person, you burn 2,500 calories a day. If your diet contains only 1,500 calories, you'd have an energy deficit of 1,000 calories a day. In a week's time that would add up to a 7,000-calorie deficit, or 2 pounds of real fat. In ten days, the accumulated deficit would represent nearly 3 pounds of lost body fat. Even if you ate nothing at all for ten days and maintained your usual level of activity, your caloric deficit would add up to 25,000 calories. . . . At 3,500 calories per pound of fat, that's still only 7 pounds of lost fat.
>
> —Jane Brody, *Jane Brody's Nutrition Book*

C4-c Choose a suitable pattern of organization.

Although paragraphs (and indeed whole essays) may be patterned in any number of ways, certain patterns of organization occur frequently, either alone or in combination:

- examples and illustrations (p. 34)
- narration (p. 35)
- description (p. 36)
- process (p. 36)
- comparison and contrast (p. 36)
- analogy (p. 37)
- cause and effect (p. 38)
- classification and division (p. 38)
- definition (p. 39)

These patterns (sometimes called *methods of development*) have different uses, depending on the writer's subject and purpose.

Examples and illustrations

Providing examples, perhaps the most common method of development, is appropriate whenever the reader might be tempted to ask, "For example?"

Normally my parents abided scrupulously by "The Budget," but
several times a year Dad would dip into his battered black strongbox
and splurge on some irrational, totally satisfying luxury. Once he
bought over a hundred comic books at a flea market, doled out to us
thereafter at the tantalizing rate of two a week. He always got a
whole flat of pansies, Mom's favorite flower, for us to give her on
Mother's Day. One day a boy stopped at our house selling fifty-cent
raffle tickets on a sailboat, and Dad bought every ticket the boy had
left—three books' worth.   —Connie Hailey, student

Illustrations are extended examples, frequently presented in story
form. When well selected, they can be a vivid and effective means of
developing a point.

Part of [Harriet Tubman's] strategy of conducting was,
as in all battle-field operations, the knowledge of how and when
to retreat. Numerous allusions have been made to her moves
when she suspected that she was in danger. When she feared the
party was closely pursued, she would take it for a time on a train
southward bound. No one seeing Negroes going in this direction
would for an instant suppose them to be fugitives. Once on her
return she was at a railroad station. She saw some men reading
a poster and she heard one of them reading it aloud. It was a
description of her, offering a reward for her capture. She took
a southbound train to avert suspicion. At another time when
Harriet heard men talking about her, she pretended to read
a book which she carried. One man remarked, "This can't be the
woman. The one we want can't read or write." Harriet devoutly
hoped the book was right side up.

                    —Earl Conrad, *Harriet Tubman*

Narration

A paragraph of narration tells a story or part of a story. The following
paragraph recounts one of the author's experiences in the African wild.

One evening when I was wading in the shallows of the lake to
pass a rocky outcrop, I suddenly stopped dead as I saw the sinuous
black body of a snake in the water. It was all of six feet long, and
from the slight hood and the dark stripes at the back of the neck I
knew it to be a Storm's water cobra—a deadly reptile for the bite of
which there was, at that time, no serum. As I stared at it an
incoming wave gently deposited part of its body on one of my feet. I
remained motionless, not even breathing, until the wave rolled back
into the lake, drawing the snake with it. Then I leaped out of the
water as fast as I could, my heart hammering.

                    —Jane Goodall, *In the Shadow of Man*

Description

A descriptive paragraph sketches a portrait of a person, place, or thing by using concrete and specific details that appeal to one or more of the senses—sight, sound, smell, taste, and touch. Consider, for example, the following description of the grasshopper invasions that devastated the midwestern United States in the late 1860s.

They came like dive bombers out of the west. They came by the millions with the rustle of their wings roaring overhead. They came in waves, like the rolls of the sea, descending with a terrifying speed, breaking now and again like a mighty surf. They came with the force of a williwaw and they formed a huge, ominous, dark brown cloud that eclipsed the sun. They dipped and touched earth, hitting objects and people like hailstones. But they were not hail. These were *live* demons. They popped, snapped, crackled, and roared. They were dark brown, an inch or longer in length, plump in the middle and tapered at the ends. They had transparent wings, slender legs, and two black eyes that flashed with a fierce intelligence.

—Eugene Boe, "Pioneers to Eternity"

Process

A process paragraph is structured in chronological order. A writer may choose this pattern either to describe how something is made or done or to explain to readers, step by step, how to do something. The following paragraph explains how to perform a "roll cast," a popular fly-fishing technique.

Begin by taking up a suitable stance, with one foot slightly in front of the other and the rod pointing down the line. Then begin a smooth, steady draw, raising your rod hand to just above shoulder height and lifting the rod to the 10:30 or 11:00 position. This steady draw allows a loop of line to form between the rod top and the water. While the line is still moving, raise the rod slightly, then punch it rapidly forward and down. The rod is now flexed and under maximum compression, and the line follows its path, bellying out slightly behind you and coming off the water close to your feet. As you power the rod down through the 3:00 position, the belly of line will roll forward. Follow through smoothly so that the line unfolds and straightens above the water.

—*The Dorling Kindersley Encyclopedia of Fishing*

Comparison and contrast

To compare two subjects is to draw attention to their similarities, although the word *compare* also has a broader meaning that includes a consideration of differences. To contrast is to focus only on differences.

Whether a paragraph stresses similarities or differences, it may be patterned in one of two ways. The two subjects may be presented one at a time, as in the following paragraph of contrast.

> So Grant and Lee were in complete contrast, representing two diametrically opposed elements in American life. Grant was the modern man emerging; beyond him, ready to come on the stage, was the great age of steel and machinery, of crowded cities and a restless, burgeoning vitality. Lee might have ridden down from the old age of chivalry, lance in hand, silken banner fluttering over his head. Each man was the perfect champion of his cause, drawing both his strengths and his weaknesses from the people he led.
>
> —Bruce Catton, "Grant and Lee: A Study in Contrasts"

Or a paragraph may proceed point by point, treating the two subjects together, one aspect at a time. The following paragraph uses the point-by-point method to contrast speeches given by Abraham Lincoln in 1860 and Barack Obama in 2008.

> Two men, two speeches. The men, both lawyers, both from Illinois, were seeking the presidency, despite what seemed their crippling connection with extremists. Each was young by modern standards for a president. Abraham Lincoln had turned fifty-one just five days before delivering his speech. Barack Obama was forty-six when he gave his. Their political experience was mainly provincial, in the Illinois legislature for both of them, and they had received little exposure at the national level—two years in the House of Representatives for Lincoln, four years in the Senate for Obama. Yet each was seeking his party's nomination against a New York senator of longer standing and greater prior reputation—Lincoln against Senator William Seward, Obama against Senator Hillary Clinton. They were both known for having opposed an initially popular war—Lincoln against President Polk's Mexican War, raised on the basis of a fictitious provocation; Obama against President Bush's Iraq War, launched on false claims that Saddam Hussein possessed WMDs [weapons of mass destruction] and had made an alliance with Osama bin Laden.
>
> —Garry Wills, "Two Speeches on Race"

Analogy

Analogies draw comparisons between items that appear to have little in common. Writers can use analogies to make something abstract or unfamiliar easier to grasp or to provoke fresh thoughts about a common subject. In the following paragraph, physician Lewis Thomas draws an analogy between the behaviour of ants and that of humans.

Ants are so much like human beings as to be an embarrassment. They farm fungi, raise aphids as livestock, launch armies into wars, use chemical sprays to alarm and confuse enemies, capture slaves. The families of weaver ants engage in child labor, holding their larvae like shuttles to spin out the thread that sews the leaves together for their fungus gardens. They exchange information ceaselessly. They do everything but watch television.

—Lewis Thomas, "On Societies as Organisms"

Cause and effect

A paragraph may move from cause to effects or from an effect to its causes. The topic sentence in the following paragraph mentions an effect; the rest of the paragraph lists several causes.

The fantastic water clarity of the Mount Gambier sinkholes results from several factors. The holes are fed from aquifers holding rainwater that fell decades—even centuries—ago, and that has been filtered through miles of limestone. The high level of calcium that limestone adds causes the silty detritus from dead plants and animals to cling together and settle quickly to the bottom. Abundant bottom vegetation in the shallow sinkholes also helps bind the silt. And the rapid turnover of water prohibits stagnation.

— Hillary Hauser, "Exploring a Sunken Realm in Australia"

Classification and division

Classification is the grouping of items into categories according to some consistent principle. The following paragraph classifies species of electric fish.

Scientists sort electric fishes into three categories. The first comprises the strongly electric species like the marine electric rays or the freshwater African electric catfish and South American electric eel. Known since the dawn of history, these deliver a punch strong enough to stun a human. In recent years, biologists have focused on a second category: weakly electric fish in the South American and African rivers that use tiny voltages for communication and navigation. The third group contains sharks, nonelectric rays, and catfish, which do not emit a field but possess sensors that enable them to detect the minute amounts of electricity that leak out of other organisms.

—Anne and Jack Rudloe, "Electric Warfare:
The Fish That Kill with Thunderbolts"

Division takes one item and divides it into parts. As with classification, division should be made according to some consistent principle.

The following paragraph describes the components that make up a baseball.

> Like the game itself, a baseball is composed of many layers. One of the delicious joys of childhood is to take apart a baseball and examine the wonders within. You begin by removing the red cotton thread and peeling off the leather cover—which comes from the hide of a Holstein cow and has been tanned, cut, printed, and punched with holes. Beneath the cover is a thin layer of cotton string, followed by several hundred yards of woolen yarn, which makes up the bulk of the ball. Finally, in the middle is a rubber ball, or "pill," which is a little smaller than a golf ball. Slice into the rubber and you'll find the ball's heart—a cork core. The cork is from Portugal, the rubber from southeast Asia, the covers are American, and the balls are assembled in Costa Rica.
>
> —Dan Gutman, *The Way Baseball Works*

Definition

A definition puts a word or concept into a general class and then provides enough details to distinguish it from other members in the same class. In the following paragraph, the writer defines *envy* as a special kind of desire.

> Envy is so integral and so painful a part of what animates behavior in market societies that many people have forgotten the full meaning of the word, simplifying it into one of the synonyms of desire. It is that, which may be why it flourishes in market societies: democracies of desire, they might be called, with money for ballots, stuffing permitted. But envy is more or less than desire. It begins with an almost frantic sense of emptiness inside oneself, as if the pump of one's heart were sucking on air. One has to be blind to perceive the emptiness, of course, but that's just what envy is, a selective blindness. *Invidia*, Latin for envy, translates as "non-sight," and Dante has the envious plodding along under cloaks of lead, their eyes sewn shut with leaden wire. What they are blind to is what they have, God-given and humanly nurtured, in themselves.
>
> —Nelson W. Aldrich Jr., *Old Money*

C4-d Make paragraphs coherent.

When sentences and paragraphs flow from one to another without discernible bumps, gaps, or shifts, they are said to be coherent. Coherence can be improved by strengthening the ties between old information and new. A number of techniques for strengthening those ties are detailed in this section.

Linking ideas clearly

Readers expect to learn a paragraph's main point in a topic sentence early in the paragraph. Then, as they move into the body of the paragraph, they expect to encounter specific details, facts, or examples that support the topic sentence—either directly or indirectly. In the following paragraph, all of the sentences following the topic sentence directly support it.

> A passenger list of the early years [of the Orient Express] would read like a *Who's Who of the World*, from art to politics. Sarah Bernhardt and her Italian counterpart Eleonora Duse used the train to thrill the stages of Europe. For musicians there were Toscanini and Mahler. Dancers Nijinsky and Pavlova were there, while lesser performers like Harry Houdini and the girls of the Ziegfeld Follies also rode the rails. Violinists were allowed to practice on the train, and occasionally one might see trapeze artists hanging like bats from the baggage racks.   —Barnaby Conrad III, "Train of Kings"

If a sentence does not support the topic sentence directly, readers expect it to support another sentence in the paragraph and therefore to support the topic sentence indirectly. The following paragraph begins with a topic sentence. The highlighted sentences are direct supports, and the rest of the sentences are indirect supports.

> Though the open-space classroom works for many children, it is not practical for my son, David. First, David is hyperactive. When he was placed in an open-space classroom, he became distracted and confused. He was tempted to watch the movement going on around him instead of concentrating on his own work. Second, David has a tendency to transpose letters and numbers, a tendency that can be overcome only by individual attention from the instructor. In the open classroom, he was moved from teacher to teacher, with each one responsible for a different subject. No single teacher worked with David long enough to diagnose the problem, let alone help him with it. Finally, David is not a highly motivated learner. In the open classroom, he was graded "at his own level," not by criteria for a certain grade. He could receive a B in reading and still be a grade level behind, because he was doing satisfactory work "at his own level."
> —Margaret Smith, student

Repeating key words

Repetition of key words is an important technique for gaining coherence. To prevent repetitions from becoming dull, you can use variations of the key word (*hike, hiker, hiking*), pronouns referring to the word (*gamblers . . . they*), and synonyms (*run, spring, race, dash*). In the following paragraph describing plots among indentured servants in the seventeenth century, historian Richard Hofstadter binds sentences together by repeating the key word *plots* and echoing it with a variety of synonyms (which are highlighted).

> Plots hatched by several servants to run away together occurred mostly in the plantation colonies, and the few recorded servant uprisings were entirely limited to those colonies. Virginia had been forced from its very earliest years to take stringent steps against mutinous plots, and severe punishments for such behavior were recorded. Most servant plots occurred in the seventeenth century: a contemplated uprising was nipped in the bud in York County in 1661; apparently led by some left-wing offshoots of the Great Rebellion, servants plotted an insurrection in Gloucester County in 1663, and four leaders were condemned and executed; some discontented servants apparently joined Bacon's Rebellion in the 1670's. In the 1680's the planters became newly apprehensive of discontent among the servants "owing to their great necessities and want of clothes," and it was feared they would rise up and plunder the storehouses and ships; in 1682 there were plant-cutting riots in which servants and laborers, as well as some planters, took part.
>
> —Richard Hofstadter, *America at 1750*

Using parallel structures

Parallel structures are frequently used within sentences to underscore the similarity of ideas (see S1). They may also be used to bind together a series of sentences expressing similar information. In the following passage describing folk beliefs, anthropologist Margaret Mead presents similar information in parallel grammatical form.

> Actually, almost every day, even in the most sophisticated home, something is likely to happen that evokes the memory of some old folk belief. The salt spills. A knife falls to the floor. Your nose tickles. Then perhaps, with a slightly embarrassed smile, the person who spilled the salt tosses a pinch over his left shoulder. Or someone recites the old rhyme, "Knife falls, gentleman calls." Or as you rub your nose you think, That means a letter. I wonder who's writing?
>
> —Margaret Mead, "New Superstitions for Old"

Maintaining consistency

Coherence suffers whenever a draft shifts confusingly from one point of view to another or from one verb tense to another. In addition, coherence can suffer when new information is introduced with the subject of each sentence. For advice on avoiding shifts, see S4.

Providing transitions

Transitions are bridges between what has been read and what is about to be read. Transitions help readers move from sentence to sentence; they also alert readers to more global connections of ideas— those between paragraphs or even larger blocks of text.

Academic English   Choose transitions carefully and vary them appropriately. Each transition has a different meaning; if you use a transition with an inappropriate meaning, you might confuse your reader.

▶ Although taking eight o'clock classes may seem

unappealing, coming to school early has its advan-
         For example,
tages. ~~Moreover~~, students who arrive early typically
         ^

avoid the worst traffic and find the best parking spaces.

SENTENCE-LEVEL TRANSITIONS   Certain words and phrases signal connections between (or within) sentences. Frequently used transitions are included in the chart on page 43.

Skilled writers use transitional expressions with care, making sure, for example, not to use *consequently* when *also* would be more precise. They are also careful to select transitions with an appropriate tone, perhaps preferring *so* to *thus* in an informal piece, *in summary* to *in short* for a scholarly essay.

In the following paragraph, an excerpt from an argument that dinosaurs had the "'right-sized' brains for reptiles of their body size," biologist Stephen Jay Gould uses transitions (highlighted) to guide readers from one idea to the next.

> I don't wish to deny that the flattened, minuscule head of large bodied Stegosaurus houses little brain from our subjective, top-heavy perspective, but I do wish to assert that we should not expect more of the beast. First of all, large animals have relatively smaller brains than related, small animals. The correlation of brain size with body size among kindred animals (all reptiles, all mammals, for example) is remarkably regular. As we move from small to large

Common transitions

TO SHOW ADDITION	and, also, besides, further, furthermore, in addition, moreover, next, too, first, second
TO GIVE EXAMPLES	for example, for instance, to illustrate, in fact, specifically
TO COMPARE	also, similarly, likewise
TO CONTRAST	but, however, on the other hand, in contrast, nevertheless, still, even though, on the contrary, yet, although
TO SUMMARIZE OR CONCLUDE	in other words, in short, in conclusion, to sum up, therefore
TO SHOW TIME	after, as, before, next, during, later, finally, meanwhile, since, then, when, while, immediately
TO SHOW PLACE OR DIRECTION	above, below, beyond, farther on, nearby, opposite, close, to the left
TO INDICATE LOGICAL RELATIONSHIP	if, so, therefore, consequently, thus, as a result, for this reason, because, since

animals, from mice to elephants or small lizards to Komodo dragons, brain size increases, but not so fast as body size. In other words, bodies grow faster than brains, and large animals have low ratios of brain weight to body weight. In fact, brains grow only about two-thirds as fast as bodies. Since we have no reason to believe that large animals are consistently stupider than their smaller relatives, we must conclude that large animals require relatively less brain to do as well as smaller animals. If we do not recognize this relationship, we are likely to underestimate the mental power of very large animals, dinosaurs in particular.

—Stephen Jay Gould, "Were Dinosaurs Dumb?"

PARAGRAPH-LEVEL TRANSITIONS   Paragraph-level transitions usually link the *first* sentence of a new paragraph with the *first* sentence of the previous paragraph. In other words, the topic sentences signal global connections.

Look for opportunities to allude to the subject of a previous paragraph (as summed up in its topic sentence) in the topic sentence of the next one. In his essay "Little Green Lies," Jonathan H. Alder uses this strategy in the topic sentences of the following paragraphs, which appear in a passage describing the benefits of plastic packaging.

Consider aseptic packaging, the (synthetic packaging) for the "juice boxes" so many children bring to school with their lunch. One criticism of aseptic packaging is that it is nearly impossible to recycle, yet on almost every other count, aseptic packaging is environmentally preferable to the packaging alternatives. Not only do aseptic containers not require refrigeration to keep their contents from spoiling, but their manufacture requires less than one-10th the energy of making glass bottles.

What is true for juice boxes is also true for other forms of (synthetic packaging.) The use of polystyrene, which is commonly (and mistakenly) referred to as "Styrofoam," can reduce food waste dramatically due to its insulating properties. (Thanks to these properties, polystyrene cups are much preferred over paper for that morning cup of coffee.) Polystyrene also requires significantly fewer resources to produce than its paper counterpart.

TRANSITIONS BETWEEN BLOCKS OF TEXT   In long essays, you will need to alert readers to connections between blocks of text that are more than one paragraph long. You can do this by inserting transitional sentences or short paragraphs at key points in the essay. Here, for example, is a transitional paragraph from a student research paper. It announces that the first part of the paper has come to a close and the second part is about to begin.

> Although the great apes have demonstrated significant language skills, one central question remains: Can they be taught to use that uniquely human language tool we call grammar, to learn the difference, for instance, between "ape bite human" and "human bite ape"? In other words, can an ape create a sentence?

C4-e If necessary, adjust paragraph length.

Most readers feel comfortable reading paragraphs that range between one hundred and two hundred words. Shorter paragraphs can require too much starting and stopping, and longer ones can strain the reader's attention span. There are exceptions to this guideline, however. Paragraphs longer than two hundred words frequently appear in scholarly writing, where writers explore complex ideas. Paragraphs shorter than one hundred words occur in business writing and on Web sites, where readers routinely skim for main ideas; in newspapers because of narrow columns; and in informal essays to quicken the pace.

In an essay, the first and last paragraphs will ordinarily be the introduction and the conclusion. These special-purpose paragraphs are likely to be shorter than those in the body of the essay. Typically, the body paragraphs will follow the essay's outline: one paragraph per point in short essays, several per point in longer ones. Some ideas require more development than others, however, so it is best to be flexible. If an idea stretches to a length unreasonable for a paragraph, you should divide the paragraph, even if you have presented comparable points in the essay in single paragraphs.

Paragraph breaks are not always made for strictly logical reasons. Writers use them for all of the following reasons.

REASONS FOR BEGINNING A NEW PARAGRAPH

- to mark off the introduction and the conclusion
- to signal a shift to a new idea
- to indicate an important shift in time or place
- to emphasize a point (by placing it at the beginning or the end, not in the middle, of a paragraph)
- to highlight a contrast
- to signal a change of speakers (in dialogue)
- to provide readers with a needed pause
- to break up text that looks too dense

Beware of using too many short, choppy paragraphs, however. Readers want to see how your ideas connect, and they become irritated when you break their momentum by forcing them to pause every few sentences. Here are some reasons you might have for combining some of the paragraphs in a rough draft.

REASONS FOR COMBINING PARAGRAPHS

- to clarify the essay's organization
- to connect closely related ideas
- to bind together text that looks too choppy

C5 Designing documents

The term *document* is broad enough to describe anything you might write in a university or college class, in the business world, or in everyday life. How you design a document (format it for the printed page or for a computer screen) will affect how readers respond to it.

Good document design promotes readability, but what *readability* means depends on your purpose and audience and perhaps on other elements of your writing situation, such as your subject and any length restrictions. All of your design choices—formatting options, headings, and lists—should be made with your writing situation in mind. Likewise, visuals—tables, charts, and images—can support your writing if they are used appropriately.

C5-a Determine layout and format to suit your purpose and audience.

Similar documents share common design features. Together, these features—layout, margins and line spacing, alignment, fonts, and font styles—can help guide readers through a document.

Layout

Most readers have set ideas about how different kinds of documents should look. Advertisements, for example, have a distinctive appearance, as do newsletters and brochures. Instructors have expectations about how a university or college paper should look (see C5-e). Employers, too, expect documents such as letters, résumés, memos, and e-mail messages to be presented in standard ways (see C5-f).

Unless you have a compelling reason to stray from convention, it's best to choose a document layout that conforms to your readers' expectations. If you're not sure what readers expect, look at examples of the kind of document you are producing.

Margins and line spacing

Margins help control the look of a page. For most academic and business documents, leave a margin of 1 to 1.5 inches (2.5 to 3.5 cm) on all sides. These margins create a visual frame for the text and provide room for annotations, such as an instructor's comments or a peer's suggestions. Tight margins generally make a page crowded and difficult to read.

Most manuscripts in progress are double-spaced to allow room for editing. Final copy is often double-spaced as well, since single-spaced text is less inviting to read. If you are unsure about margin and spacing requirements for your document, check with your instructor or consult documents similar to the one you are writing. At times, the advantages of wide margins and double-spaced lines are offset by other considerations. For example, most business and technical documents are single-spaced, with double-spacing between paragraphs, to save paper and to promote quick scanning. Keep your purpose and audience in mind as you determine appropriate margins and line spacing for your document.

Planning a document: Design checklist for purpose and audience

- What is the purpose of your document? How can your document design help you achieve this purpose?
- Who are your readers? What are their expectations?
- What format is required? What format options—layout, margins, line spacing, and font styles—will readers expect?
- How can you use visuals—charts, graphs, tables, images—to help you convey information and achieve your purpose?

Fonts

If you have a choice, select a font that fits your writing situation in an easy-to-read size (usually 10–12 points). Although offbeat fonts may seem attractive, they slow readers down and can distract them from your ideas. For example, using Comic Sans, a font with a handwritten, childish feel, can make an essay seem too informal or unpolished, regardless of how well it's written. Fonts that are easy to read and appropriate for academic and workplace documents include the following: Arial, Courier, Georgia, Times New Roman, and Verdana. Check with your instructor; he or she may expect or prefer a particular font.

Font styles

Font styles—such as **boldface**, *italics*, and <u>underlining</u>—can be useful for calling attention to parts of a document. On the whole, it is best to use restraint when selecting styles. Applying too many different styles within a document can result in busy-looking pages and can confuse readers.

TIP: Never write an academic document in all capital or all lowercase letters. Although some readers have become accustomed to instant messages and e-mails that omit capital letters entirely, their absence makes a piece of writing too informal and difficult to read.

C5-b Use headings when appropriate.

In short essays, you will have little need for headings, especially if you use paragraphing and clear topic sentences to guide readers. In more complex documents, however, such as longer essays, research papers, business reports, and Web sites, headings can be a useful visual cue for readers.

Headings help readers see at a glance the organization of a document. If more than one level of heading is used, the headings also indicate the hierarchy of ideas—as they do throughout this book.

Headings serve a number of functions for your readers, depending on the needs of different readers. When readers are looking for specific information and don't want to read the entire document, headings can guide them to the right place quickly. When readers are scanning, hoping to pick up a document's meaning or message, headings can provide an overview. Even when readers are committed enough to read every word, headings can help them preview a document before they begin reading or easily revisit a specific section after they've read through the document once.

> **Making the most of your handbook**
>
> Headings can help writers plan and readers understand a document.
>
> ▶ Papers organized with headings: pages 485 and 530

TIP: While headings can be useful, they cannot substitute for transitions between paragraphs (see p. 43).

Phrasing headings

Headings should be as brief and as informative as possible. Certain styles of headings—the most common being *-ing* phrases, noun phrases, questions, and imperative sentences—work better for some purposes, audiences, and subjects than for others.

Whatever style you choose, use it consistently. Headings on the same level of organization should be written in parallel structure (see S1), as in the following examples from a report, a history textbook, a financial brochure, and a nursing manual, respectively.

-ING PHRASES AS HEADINGS

Safeguarding Earth's atmosphere

Charting the path to sustainable energy

Conserving global forests

NOUN PHRASES AS HEADINGS

The civil rights movement

The antiwar movement

The feminist movement

QUESTIONS AS HEADINGS

How do I buy shares?

How do I redeem shares?

How has the fund performed in the past three years?

IMPERATIVE SENTENCES AS HEADINGS

Ask the patient to describe current symptoms.

Take a detailed medical history.

Record the patient's vital signs.

Placing and formatting headings

Headings on the same level of organization should be placed and formatted in a consistent way. If you have more than one level of heading, you might centre your first-level headings and make them boldface; then you might make the second-level headings left-aligned and italicized, like this:

First-level heading

Second-level heading

A university or college paper with headings typically has only one level, and the headings are often centred, as in the sample paper on pages 488–96. In a report or a brochure, important headings can be highlighted by using white space above and below them. Less important headings can be downplayed by using less white space or by running them into the text.

C5-c Use lists to guide readers.

Lists are easy to read or scan when they are displayed, item by item, rather than run into your text. You might choose to display the following kinds of lists:

- steps in a process
- advice or recommendations
- items to be discussed
- criteria for evaluation (as in checklists)
- parts of an object

Lists are usually introduced with an independent clause followed by a colon (*All mammals share the following five characteristics:*).

Periods are not used after items in a list unless the items are complete sentences. Lists should be in parallel grammatical form (see S1).

Use bullets (circles or squares) or dashes to draw readers' eyes to a list and to emphasize individual items. If you are describing a sequence or a set of steps, number your list with Arabic numerals (1, 2, 3) followed by periods.

Although lists can be useful visual cues, don't overdo them. Too many will clutter a document.

C5-d Add visuals to support your purpose.

Visuals can convey information concisely and powerfully. Charts, graphs, and tables, for example, can simplify complex numerical information. Images—including photographs and diagrams—often express an idea more vividly than words can. With access to the Internet, digital photography, and word processing or desktop publishing software, you can download or create your own visuals to enhance your document. Keep in mind that if you download a visual—or use published information to create your own visual—you must credit your source (see R3).

Choosing appropriate visuals

Use visuals to supplement your writing, not to substitute for it. Always consider how a visual supports your purpose and how your audience might respond to it. A student writing about online news used two screen shots to illustrate a point about hyperlinked text (see A2-h). Another student, writing about treatments for childhood obesity, created a table to display data she had found in two different sources and discussed in her paper (see APA-5b).

In many cases, the same information can be presented visually in different formats. When deciding whether to display data in a table or a graph, for example, think about the message you want to convey and the information your readers need. (See the examples on p. 51.) If your discussion refers to specific numbers, a table will be more useful to readers. If, however, you want readers to grasp at a glance that the value of petroleum exports increased from 2001 to 2008, a line graph will be more effective (see p. 51).

As you draft and revise a document, carefully choose the visuals that support your main point, and avoid overloading your text with too many images. The chart on pages 52–53 describes eight types of visuals and their purposes.

INFORMATION DISPLAYED IN TWO TYPES OF VISUALS   These visuals present the same information in two different ways. The table provides exact numbers for comparison. The line graph allows readers to see the trend in the value of exports.

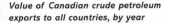

Value of Canadian crude petroleum exports to all countries, by year

Year	Crude exported (millions of dollars)
2001	16 083
2002	18 015
2003	20 514
2004	25 174
2005	29 994
2006	37 942
2007	41 830
2008	67 439

Source: Statistics Canada (2010).

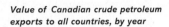

Value of Canadian crude petroleum exports to all countries, by year

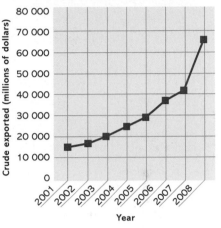
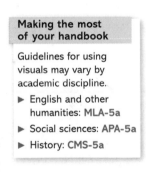

Placing and labelling visuals

A visual may be placed in the text of a document, near a discussion to which it relates, or it can be put in an appendix, labelled, and referred to in the text. Placing visuals in the text of a document can be tricky. Usually you will want a visual to appear close to the sentences that relate to it, but page breaks won't always allow this placement. At times, you may need to insert the visual at a later point and tell readers where it can be found; sometimes you can make the text flow, or wrap, around the visual. No matter where you place a visual, refer to it in your text. Don't expect visuals to speak for themselves.

Making the most of your handbook

Guidelines for using visuals may vary by academic discipline.

▶ English and other humanities: MLA-5a

▶ Social sciences: APA-5a

▶ History: CMS-5a

Most of the visuals you include in a document will require some sort of label. A label, which is typically placed above or below the visual, should be brief but descriptive. Most commonly, a visual is labelled with the word "Figure" or the abbreviation "Fig.," followed by a number: *Fig. 4.* Sometimes a title might be included to explain how the visual relates to the text: *Fig. 4. Voter turnout by age.*

Choosing visuals to suit your purpose

Pie chart

Pie charts compare a part or parts to the whole. Segments of the pie represent percentages of the whole (and always total 100 percent).

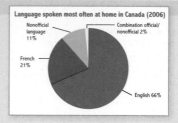

Language spoken most often at home in Canada (2006)

Nonofficial language 11%
Combination official/nonofficial 2%
French 21%
English 66%

Line graph

Line graphs highlight trends over a period of time or compare numerical data.

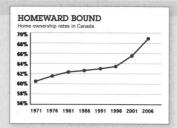

HOMEWARD BOUND
Home ownership rates in Canada

1971 1976 1981 1986 1991 1996 2001 2006

Bar graph

Bar graphs, like line graphs, show trends or comparisons at a glance. This bar graph displays the same data as in the line graph above.

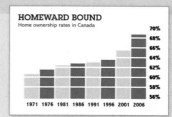

HOMEWARD BOUND
Home ownership rates in Canada

1971 1976 1981 1986 1991 1996 2001 2006

Table

Tables display numbers and words in columns and rows. They can be used to organize complicated numerical information into an easily understood format.

Sources [top to bottom]: Statistics Canada; Statistics Canada; Statistics Canada; UNAIDS.

Prices of daily doses of AIDS drugs ($US)

Drug	Brazil	Uganda	Côte d'Ivoire	US
3TC (Lamuvidine)	1.66	3.28	2.95	8.70
ddC (Zalcitabine)	0.24	4.17	3.75	8.80
Didanosine	2.04	5.26	3.48	7.25
Efavirenz	8.96	n/a	6.41	13.13
Indinavir	10.32	12.79	9.07	14.93
Nelfinavir	4.14	4.45	4.39	6.47
Nevirapine	5.04	n/a	n/a	8.46
Saquinavir	6.24	7.37	5.52	6.50
Stavudine	0.56	6.19	4.10	9.07
ZDV/3TC	1.44	7.34	n/a	18.78
Zidovudine	1.08	4.34	2.43	10.12

Source: UNAIDS, 2000

Photograph

Photographs can be used to vividly depict people, scenes, or objects discussed in a text.

Diagram

Diagrams, useful in scientific and technical writing, concisely illustrate processes, structures, or interactions.

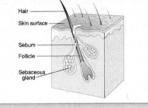

Flowchart

Flowcharts show structures (the hierarchy of employees at a company, for example) or steps in a process and their relation to one another. (For another example, see p. 122.)

Map

Maps illustrate distances, historical information, or demographics and often use symbols for geographic features and points of interest.

Sources [top to bottom]: Fred Zwicky; NIAMS; Arizona Board of Regents; Lynn Hunt et al.

Using visuals responsibly

Most word processing and spreadsheet software will allow you to produce your own visuals. If you create a chart, a table, or a graph using information from your research, you must cite the source of the information even though the visual is your own. The visual at the right credits the source of its data.

If you download a photograph from the Web or scan an image from a magazine or book, you must credit the person or organization that created it, just as you would cite any other source you use in a paper (see R3). Make sure any cropping or other changes you make to the visual do not distort the meaning of the original. If your document is written for publication outside the classroom, you will need to request permission to use any visual you borrow.

VISUAL WITH A SOURCE CREDITED

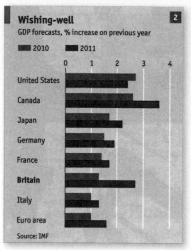

Source: International Monetary Fund (2010).

C5-e Use standard academic formatting.

Instructors have certain expectations about how an academic paper should look. If your instructor provides guidelines for formatting an essay, a report, a research paper, or another document, you should follow them. Otherwise, use the manuscript format that is recommended for your academic discipline.

In most English and other humanities classes, you will be asked to use MLA (Modern Language Association) format (see pp. 55–56 and MLA-5). In most social science classes, such as psychology and sociology, and in most education, business, and health-related classes, you will be asked to use APA (American Psychological Association) format (see APA-5). In history and some other humanities classes, you will be asked to use CMS (*Chicago*) format (see CMS-5).

MLA PAPER FORMAT

1″ (2.5 cm)

¹/₂″ (1.5 cm)

Orlov 1

Anna Orlov

Professor Willis

1″ (2.5 cm) English 101

17 March 2009

Online Monitoring:

Title is centred.

A Threat to Employee Privacy in the Wired Workplace

As the Internet has become an integral tool of businesses, company policies on Internet usage have become as common as policies regarding vacation days or sexual harassment. A 2005 study by the American Management Association and ePolicy Institute found that 76% of companies monitor employees' use of the Web, and the number of companies that block employees' access to certain Web sites has increased 27% since 2001 (1). Unlike other company rules, however, Internet usage policies often include language authorizing companies to secretly monitor their employees, a practice that raises questions about rights in the workplace. Although companies often have legitimate concerns that lead them to monitor employees' Internet usage—from expensive security breaches to reduced productivity—the benefits of electronic surveillance are outweighed by its costs to employees' privacy and autonomy.

1″ (2.5 cm)

Double-spacing is used throughout.

¹/₂″ (1.5 cm) While surveillance of employees is not a new phenomenon, electronic surveillance allows employers to monitor workers with unprecedented efficiency. In his book *The Naked Employee,* Frederick Lane describes offline ways in which employers have been permitted to intrude on employees' privacy for decades, such as drug testing, background checks, psychological exams, lie detector tests, and in-store video surveillance. The difference, Lane argues, between these old methods of data gathering and electronic surveillance involves quantity:

First line of each paragraph is indented.

1″ (2.5 cm) Technology makes it possible for employers to gather enormous amounts of data about employees, often far beyond what is necessary to satisfy safety or productivity concerns. And the trends that drive technology—faster, smaller, cheaper—make it possible for larger and larger numbers of employers to gather ever-greater amounts of personal data. (3-4)

Long quotation is indented in MLA style.

In an age when employers can collect data whenever employees use their

1″ (2.5 cm)

Marginal annotations indicate MLA-style formatting.

MLA PAPER FORMAT (continued)

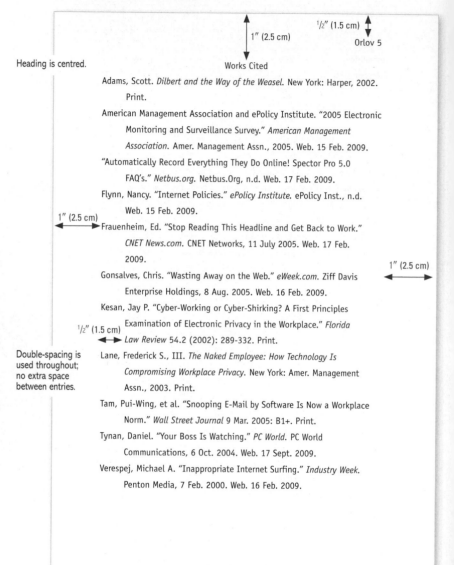

1″ (2.5 cm)

½″ (1.5 cm)

Orlov 5

Heading is centred.

Works Cited

Adams, Scott. *Dilbert and the Way of the Weasel*. New York: Harper, 2002.
Print.

American Management Association and ePolicy Institute. "2005 Electronic
Monitoring and Surveillance Survey." *American Management
Association*. Amer. Management Assn., 2005. Web. 15 Feb. 2009.

"Automatically Record Everything They Do Online! Spector Pro 5.0
FAQ's." *Netbus.org*. Netbus.Org, n.d. Web. 17 Feb. 2009.

Flynn, Nancy. "Internet Policies." *ePolicy Institute*. ePolicy Inst., n.d.
Web. 15 Feb. 2009.

1″ (2.5 cm)

Frauenheim, Ed. "Stop Reading This Headline and Get Back to Work."
CNET News.com. CNET Networks, 11 July 2005. Web. 17 Feb.
2009.

1″ (2.5 cm)

Gonsalves, Chris. "Wasting Away on the Web." *eWeek.com*. Ziff Davis
Enterprise Holdings, 8 Aug. 2005. Web. 16 Feb. 2009.

Kesan, Jay P. "Cyber-Working or Cyber-Shirking? A First Principles
Examination of Electronic Privacy in the Workplace." *Florida
Law Review* 54.2 (2002): 289-332. Print.

½″ (1.5 cm)

Double-spacing is
used throughout;
no extra space
between entries.

Lane, Frederick S., III. *The Naked Employee: How Technology Is
Compromising Workplace Privacy*. New York: Amer. Management
Assn., 2003. Print.

Tam, Pui-Wing, et al. "Snooping E-Mail by Software Is Now a Workplace
Norm." *Wall Street Journal* 9 Mar. 2005: B1+. Print.

Tynan, Daniel. "Your Boss Is Watching." *PC World*. PC World
Communications, 6 Oct. 2004. Web. 17 Sept. 2009.

Verespej, Michael A. "Inappropriate Internet Surfing." *Industry Week*.
Penton Media, 7 Feb. 2000. Web. 16 Feb. 2009.

C5-f Use standard business formatting.

This section provides guidelines for preparing business letters, résumés, and memos.

BUSINESS LETTER IN FULL BLOCK STYLE

FrancophoneVoice

March 16, 2010 ──┐├─────── Date

Jonathan Ross ──┐
Managing Editor
Francophone World Today ────────── Inside address
2023 Meadow Place
Victoria, BC V8R 1R2 ──┘

Dear Mr. Ross: ──┐├─────── Salutation

Thank you very much for taking the time yesterday to speak to the University of Victoria's Francophone Club. A number of students have told me that they enjoyed your presentation and found your job search suggestions to be extremely helpful.

As I mentioned to you when we first scheduled your appearance, the club publishes a monthly newsletter, *Francophone Voice*. Our purpose is to share up-to-date information and expert advice with members of the university's Francophone population. Considering how much students benefited from your talk, I would like to publish excerpts from it in our newsletter.

Body ──

I have taken the liberty of transcribing parts of your presentation and organizing them into a question-and-answer format for our readers. When you have a moment, would you mind looking through the enclosed article and letting me know if I may have your permission to print it? I would be happy, of course, to make any changes or corrections that you request. I'm hoping to include this article in our next newsletter, so I would need your response by April 4.

Once again, Mr. Ross, thank you for sharing your experiences with us. You gave an informative and entertaining speech, and I would love to be able to share it with the students who couldn't hear it in person.

Sincerely, ─────── Close

Jeffrey Richardson ──────── Signature

Jeffrey Richardson
Associate Editor

Enc.

210 Student Centre University of Victoria Victoria BC V8W 2Y2

Business letters

In writing a business letter, be direct, clear, and courteous. State your purpose or request at the beginning of the letter and include only relevant information in the body. By being as direct and concise as possible, you show that you value your reader's time. For the format of the letter, use established business conventions. A sample business letter in full block style appears on page 57.

Résumés and cover letters

An effective résumé gives relevant information in a clear, concise form. You may be asked to produce a traditional résumé, a scannable résumé, or a Web résumé. The cover letter gives a prospective employer a reason to look at your résumé. The goal is to present yourself in a favourable light without including unnecessary details.

COVER LETTERS   Always include a cover letter to introduce yourself, state the position you seek, and tell where you learned about it. The letter should also highlight past experiences that qualify you for the position and emphasize what you can do for the employer (not what the job will do for you). End the letter with a suggestion for a meeting, and tell your prospective employer when you will be available.

TRADITIONAL RÉSUMÉS   Traditional résumés are produced on paper, and they are screened by people, not by computers. Because screeners often face stacks of applications, they may spend very little time looking at each résumé. Therefore, you need to make your résumé as reader-friendly as possible. Here are a few guidelines:

- Limit your résumé to one page if possible, two pages at most.
- Organize your information into clear categories—Education, Experience, and so on.
- Present the information in each category in reverse chronological order to highlight your most recent accomplishments.
- Use bulleted lists or some other simple, clear visual device to organize information.
- Use strong, active verbs to emphasize your accomplishments. For current activities, use present-tense verbs, such as *manage*; for past activities, use past-tense verbs, such as *managed*.

TRADITIONAL RÉSUMÉ

Jeffrey Richardson
608 Harbinger Avenue
Victoria, BC V8V 4J1
205-555-2651
jrichardson@example.net

OBJECTIVE	To obtain an editorial internship with a magazine
EDUCATION Fall 2007– present	University of Victoria • BA expected in June 2011 • Double major: English and journalism • GPA: 3.7 (on a 4-point scale)
EXPERIENCE Fall 2009– present	Associate editor, *Francophone Voice*, newsletter of Francophone Club • Assign and edit feature articles • Coordinate community outreach
Fall 2008– present	Photo editor, *The Martlet*, student paper • Shoot and organize photos for print and online publication • Oversee photo staff assignments; evaluate photos
Summer 2009	Intern, *The Globe*, Nanaimo, British Columbia • Wrote stories about local issues and personalities • Interviewed political condidates • Edited and proofread copy • Coedited "The Landscapes of Northern Canada: A Photoessay"
Summers 2008, 2009	Tutor, Nanaimo ESL Program • Tutored English language learners • Trained new tutors
ACTIVITIES	Photographers' Workshop, Francophone Club
PORTFOLIO	Available at http://jrichardson.example.net/jrportfolio.htm
REFERENCES	Available upon request

SCANNABLE RÉSUMÉS   Scannable résumés can be submitted on paper, by e-mail, or through an online employment service. The résumés are scanned and searched electronically, and a database matches keywords in the employer's job description with keywords in the résumés. A human screener then looks through the résumés selected by the database.

A scannable résumé must be formatted simply so that the scanner can accurately pick up its content. In general, follow these guidelines when preparing a scannable résumé:

- Include a Keywords section that lists words likely to be searched by a scanner. Use nouns, such as *manager*, not verbs, such as *manage*.

- Use standard résumé headings (for example, Education, Experience, References).

- Avoid special characters, graphics, or font styles.

- Avoid formatting such as tabs, indents, columns, or tables.

WEB RÉSUMÉS   Posting your résumé on a Web site is an easy way to provide recent information about your employment goals and accomplishments. Most guidelines for traditional résumés apply to Web résumés. You may want to include a downloadable version of your résumé and link to an electronic portfolio. Always list the date that you last updated your résumé.

Memos

Usually brief and to the point, a memo reports information, makes a request, or recommends an action. The format of a memo, which varies from company to company, is designed for easy distribution, quick reading, and efficient filing.

Most memos display the date, the name of the recipient, the name of the sender, and the subject on separate lines at the top of the page. Many companies have preprinted forms for memos, and most word processing programs have memo templates.

The subject line of a memo should describe the topic as clearly and concisely as possible, and the introductory paragraph should get right to the point. In addition, the body of the memo should be well organized and easy to skim. To promote skimming, use headings where possible and set off any items that deserve special attention (in a list, for example, or in boldface).

E-mail

In business and academic contexts, you will want to show readers that you value their time. Your e-mail message may be just one of many that your readers have to wade through. Here are some strategies for writing effective e-mails:

- Use a meaningful, concise subject line to help readers sort through messages and set priorities.

BUSINESS MEMO

Commonwealth Press

MEMORANDUM

February 25, 2010

To:	Editorial assistants, Advertising Department
cc:	Stephen Chapman
From:	Helen Brown
Subject:	New database software

The new database software will be installed on your computers next week. I have scheduled a training program to help you become familiar with the software and with our new procedures for data entry and retrieval.

Training program
A member of our IT staff will teach in-house workshops on how to use the new software. If you try the software before the workshop, please be prepared to discuss any problems you encounter.

We will keep the training groups small to encourage hands-on participation and to provide individual attention. The workshops will take place in the training room on the third floor from 10:00 a.m. to 2:00 p.m.

Lunch will be provided in the cafeteria.

Sign-up
Please sign up by March 1 for one of the following dates by adding your name in the department's online calendar:

- Wednesday, March 3
- Friday, March 5
- Monday, March 8

If you will not be in the office on any of those dates, please let me know by March 1.

- Put the most important part of your message at the beginning so that your reader sees it without scrolling.
- For long, detailed messages, provide a summary at the beginning.
- Write concisely, and keep paragraphs fairly short.
- Avoid writing in all capital letters or all lowercase letters.
- Be sparing with boldface, italics, and special characters; not all e-mail systems handle such elements consistently.
- Proofread for typos and obvious errors that are likely to slow down readers.

You will also want to use e-mail responsibly by following conventions of good etiquette and not violating standards of academic integrity. Here are some strategies for writing responsible e-mails:

- Remember that your messages can easily be forwarded to others and reproduced. Do not write anything that you would not want attributed to you. And do not forward another person's message without asking his or her consent.
- If you write an e-mail message that includes someone else's words — opinions, statistics, song lyrics, and so forth — it's best to let your reader know where any borrowed material begins and ends and the source for that material.
- Remember to choose your words carefully and judiciously because e-mail messages can easily be misread. Without your voice, facial gestures, or body language, a message can be misunderstood. Pay careful attention to tone and avoid writing anything that you wouldn't be comfortable saying directly to a reader.

C6 Writing with technology

C6-a Use software tools wisely.

Grammar checkers, spell checkers, and autoformatting are software tools designed to help you avoid errors and save time. These tools can alert you to possible errors in words, sentence structures, or formatting. But they're not always right. If a program suggests or makes a change, be sure the change is one you really want to make. Familiarizing yourself with your software's settings can help you use these tools effectively.

Grammar checkers

Grammar checkers can help with some of the sentence-level problems in a typical draft. But they will often misdiagnose errors, especially because they cannot account for your intended meaning. When the grammar checker makes a suggestion for revision, you must decide whether the change is more effective than your original.

It's just as important to be aware of what your grammar checker isn't picking up on. If you count on your grammar checker to identify trouble spots, you might overlook problems with coordination and subordination (see S6), sentence variety (see S7), sexist language (see W4-e), and passive verbs (see W3-a), for example.

Spell checkers

Spell checkers flag words not found in their dictionaries; they will suggest a replacement for any word they don't recognize. They can help you spot many errors, but don't let them be your only proof-reader. If you're writing about the health benefits of a Mediterranean diet, for example, don't let your software change *briam* (a vegetable dish) to *Brian*. Even if your spell checker identifies a real misspelling, the replacement word it suggests might carry a different connotation or even be nonsensical. After misspelling *probably*, you might end up with *portly*. Consider changes carefully before accepting them. If you're not sure what word or spelling you need, consult a dictionary, such as *Merriam-Webster's Collegiate Dictionary*. (See also W6-a.)

Because spell checkers flag only unrecognized words, they won't catch misused words, such as *accept* when you mean *except*. For help with commonly confused or misused words and with avoiding informal speech and jargon, consult the glossary of usage (W1).

Autoformatting

As you write, your software may attempt to save you effort with auto-formatting. It might recognize that you've typed a URL and turn it into a link. Or if you're building a list, it might add numbering for you. Be aware of such changes and make sure they are appropriate for your paper and applied to the right text.

C6-b Manage your files.

Your instructor may ask you to complete assignments in stages, including notes, outlines, annotated bibliographies, rough drafts, and a final draft. Keeping track of all of these documents can be challenging. Be sure to give your files distinct names that reflect the appropriate stage of your writing process, and store them in a logical place.

> **My English 101 Portfolio**
>
> Address C:\My English 101 Portfolio
>
> Name ▲
> Essay 1 - Literacy narrative
> Essay 2 - Argument paper
> Essay 3 - Ad analysis
> Essay 4 - Research paper Navajo art
> Portfolio cover letter 12.3.09
>
> Address C:\My English 101 Portfolio\Essay 3 - Ad analysis
>
> Name ▲
> Ad analysis draft 10.13.09
> Ad analysis FINAL 10.28.09
> Ad analysis peer response 10.18.09
> Ad analysis revised 10.20.09

Writing online or in a word processing program can make writing and revising easier. You can undo changes or return to an earlier draft if a revision misfires. Applying the following steps can help you explore revision possibilities with little risk.

- Create folders and subfolders for each assignment. Save notes, outlines, and drafts together.

- Label revised drafts with different file names and dates.

- Print hard copies, make backup copies, and press the Save button early and often. Save work every five to ten minutes.

- Always record complete bibliographic information about sources, including images.

- Use a comment function to make notes to yourself or to respond to the drafts of peers.

Academic
Writing

A Academic Writing

When you write in university or college, you pose questions, explore ideas, and engage in scholarly debates and conversations. To join in those conversations, you will analyze and respond to texts, evaluate other people's arguments, and put forth your own ideas.

≡ **A1** Writing about texts

The word *texts* can refer to a variety of works, including essays, articles, government reports, books, Web sites, advertisements, and photographs. Most assignments that ask you to respond to a text call for a summary or an analysis or both.

> **Making the most of your handbook**
>
> Knowing the expectations for a writing assignment is a key first step in drafting.
>
> ▶ Understanding writing assignments: A4-f

A summary is neutral in tone and demonstrates that you have understood the author's key ideas. Assignments calling for an analysis of a text vary widely, but they usually ask you to look at how the text's parts contribute to its central argument or purpose, often with the aim of judging its evidence or overall effect.

When you write about a text, you will need to read it—or, in the case of a visual text, view it—several times to discover meaning. Two techniques will help you move beyond a superficial first reading: (1) annotating the text with your observations and questions and (2) outlining the text's key points. These techniques will help you analyze both written and visual texts.

A1-a Read actively: Annotate the text.

Read actively by jotting down your questions and thoughts in a notebook or in the margins of the text or visual. Use a pencil instead of a highlighter; with a pencil you can underline key concepts, mark points, or circle elements that intrigue you. If you change your mind, you can erase your early annotations and replace them with new ones. To annotate an electronic document, take notes in a separate file or use software features to highlight, underline, or insert comments.

Guidelines for active reading

Familiarize yourself with the basic features and structure of a text.

- What kind of text are you reading: An essay? An editorial? A scholarly article? An advertisement? A photograph? A Web site?
- What is the author's purpose: To inform? To persuade? To call to action?
- Who is the audience? How does the author appeal to the audience?
- What is the author's thesis? What question does the text attempt to answer?
- What evidence does the author provide to support the thesis?
- What key terms does the author define?

Note details that surprise, puzzle, or intrigue you.

- Has the author revealed a fact or made a point that counters your assumptions? Is anything surprising?
- Has the author made a generalization you disagree with? Can you think of evidence that would challenge the generalization?
- Do you see any contradictions or inconsistencies in the text?
- Does the text contain words, statements, or phrases that you don't understand? If so, what reference materials do you need to consult?

Read and reread to discover meaning.

- What do you notice on a second or third reading that you didn't notice earlier?
- Does the text raise questions that it does not resolve?
- If you could address the author directly, what questions would you pose? Where do you agree and disagree with the author? Why?

Apply additional critical thinking strategies to visual texts.

- What first strikes you about the visual text? What elements do you notice immediately?
- Who or what is the main subject of the visual text?
- What colours and textures dominate?
- What is in the background? In the foreground?
- What role, if any, do words or numbers play in the text?
- When was the visual created or the information collected?

On this page and on page 70 are an article from *CQ Researcher*, a newsletter about social and political issues, and an advertisement, both annotated by students. The students, Emilia Sanchez and Ren Yoshida, were assigned to analyze these texts. They began by reading actively.

ANNOTATED ARTICLE

Big Box Stores Are Bad for Main Street
BETSY TAYLOR

There is plenty of reason to be concerned about the proliferation of Wal-Marts and other so-called "big box" stores. The question, however, is not whether or not these types of stores create jobs (although several studies claim they produce a net job loss in local communities) or whether they ultimately save consumers money. The real concern about having a 25-acre slab of concrete with a 100,000 square foot box of stuff land on a town is whether it's good for a community's soul.

Opening strategy— the problem is not x, it's y.

Sentimental— what is a community's soul?

The worst thing about "big boxes" is that they have a tendency to produce Ross Perot's famous "big sucking sound"—sucking the life out of cities and small towns across the country. On the other hand, small businesses are great for a community. They offer more personal service; they won't threaten to pack up and leave town if they don't get tax breaks, free roads and other blandishments; and small-business owners are much more responsive to a customer's needs. (Ever try to complain about bad service or poor quality products to the president of Home Depot?)

Lumps all big boxes together.

Assumes all small businesses are attentive.

Logic problem? Why couldn't customer complain to store manager?

Yet, if big boxes are so bad, why are they so successful? One glaring reason is that we've become a nation of hyper-consumers, and the big-box boys know this. Downtown shopping districts comprised of small businesses take some of the efficiency out of overconsumption. There's all that hassle of having to travel from store to store, and having to pull out your credit card so many times. Occasionally, we even find ourselves chatting with the shopkeeper, wandering into a coffee shop to visit with a friend or otherwise wasting precious time that could be spent on acquiring more stuff.

True?

Taylor wishes for a time that is long gone or never was.

But let's face it—bustling, thriving city centers are fun. They breathe life into a community. They allow cities and towns to stand out from each other. They provide an atmosphere for people to interact with each other that just cannot be found at Target, or Wal-Mart or Home Depot.

Community vs. economy. What about prices?

Is it anti-American to be against having a retail giant set up shop in one's community? Some people would say so. On the other hand, if you board up Main Street, what's left of America?

Ends with emotional appeal.

ANNOTATED ADVERTISEMENT

empowering
FARMERS

When you choose Equal Exchange fairly traded coffee, tea or chocolate, you join a network that empowers farmers in Latin America, Africa, and Asia to:

- Stay on their land
- Care for the environment
- Farm organically
- Support their family
- Plan for the future

www.equalexchange.coop

Photo: Jesus Choqueheranca de Quevero,
Coffee farmer & CEPICAFE Cooperative member, Peru

Source: Equal Exchange.

What is being exchanged?

"Empowering" — why in an elegant font? Who is empowering farmers?

"Farmers" in all capital letters — shows strength?

Straightforward design and not much text.

Outstretched hands. Is she giving a gift? Inviting a partnership?

Raw coffee is red: earthy, natural, warm.

Positive verbs: consumers choose, join, empower; farmers stay, care, farm, support, plan.

A1-b Sketch a brief outline of the text.

After reading, rereading, and annotating a text, try to outline it. Seeing how the author has constructed a text can help you understand it. As you sketch an outline, pay special attention to the text's thesis (central idea) and its topic sentences. The thesis of a written text usually appears in the introduction, often in the first or second paragraph. Topic sentences can be found at the beginnings of most body paragraphs, where they announce a shift to a new topic. (See C2-a and C4-a.)

In your outline, put the author's thesis and key points in your own words. Here, for example, is the outline that Emilia Sanchez developed as she prepared to write her summary and analysis of the text on page 69. Notice that Sanchez's informal outline does not trace the author's ideas paragraph by paragraph; instead, it sums up the article's central points.

OUTLINE OF "BIG BOX STORES ARE BAD FOR MAIN STREET"

Thesis: Whether or not they take jobs away from a community or offer low prices to consumers, we should be worried about "big-box" stores like Wal-Mart, Target, and Home Depot because they harm communities by taking the life out of downtown shopping districts.

I.   Small businesses are better for cities and towns than big-box stores are.
  A.   Small businesses offer personal service, but big-box stores do not.
  B.   Small businesses don't make demands on community resources as big-box stores do.
  C.   Small businesses respond to customer concerns, but big-box stores do not.
II. Big-box stores are successful because they cater to consumption at the expense of benefits to the community.
  A.   Buying everything in one place is convenient.
  B.   Shopping at small businesses may be inefficient, but it provides opportunities for socializing.
  C.   Downtown shopping districts give each city or town a special identity.

Conclusion: Although some people say that it's anti-American to oppose big-box stores, actually these stores threaten the communities that make up America by encouraging buying at the expense of the traditional interactions of Main Street.

A visual often doesn't state an explicit thesis or an explicit line of reasoning. Instead, you must sometimes infer the meaning beneath the image's surface and interpret its central point and supporting ideas from the elements of its design. One way to outline a visual text is to try to define its purpose and sketch a list of its key elements. Here, for example, are the key features that Ren Yoshida identified for the advertisement printed on page 70.

OUTLINE OF EQUAL EXCHANGE ADVERTISEMENT

Purpose: To persuade readers that they can improve the lives of organic farmers and their families by purchasing Equal Exchange coffee.

Key features:

- The farmer's heart-shaped hands are outstretched, offering the viewer partnership and the product of her hard work.
- The coffee beans are surprisingly red, fruitlike, and fresh—natural and healthy looking.
- Words above and below the photograph describe the equal exchange between farmers and consumers.
- Consumer support leads to a higher quality of life for the farmers and for all people, since these farmers care for the environment and plan for the future.
- The simplicity of the design echoes the simplicity of the exchange. The consumer only has to buy a cup of coffee to make a difference.
- Equal Exchange is selling more than a product—coffee. It is selling the idea that together farmers and consumers hold the future of land, environment, farms, and family in their hands.

A1-c Summarize to demonstrate your understanding.

Your goal in summarizing a text is to state the work's main ideas and key points simply, briefly, and accurately in your own words. Writing a summary does not require you to judge the author's ideas. If you have sketched a brief outline of the text (see A1-b), refer to it as you draft your summary.

To summarize a written text, first find the author's central idea—the thesis. Then divide the whole piece into a few major and perhaps minor ideas. Since a summary

Making the most of your handbook

Summarizing is a key research skill.

▶ Summarizing without plagiarizing: R3-c

▶ Putting summaries and paraphrases in your own words: MLA-2c, APA-2c, CMS-2c

Guidelines for writing a summary

- In the first sentence, mention the title of the text, the name of the author, and the author's thesis or the visual's central point.
- Maintain a neutral tone; be objective.
- Use the third-person point of view and the present tense: *Taylor argues.* . . .
- Keep your focus on the text. Don't state the author's ideas as if they were your own.
- Put all or most of your summary in your own words; if you borrow a phrase or a sentence from the text, put it in quotation marks and give the page number in parentheses.
- Limit yourself to presenting the text's key points.
- Be concise; make every word count.

must be fairly short, you must make judgments about what is most important.

To summarize a visual text, begin with essential information such as who created the visual, who the intended audience is, where the visual appeared, and when it was created. Briefly explain the visual's main point or purpose and identify its key features (see p. 72).

Following is Emilia Sanchez's summary of the article that is printed on page 69.

> In her essay "Big Box Stores Are Bad for Main Street," Betsy Taylor argues that chain stores harm communities by taking the life out of downtown shopping districts. Explaining that a community's "soul" is more important than low prices or consumer convenience, she argues that small businesses are better than stores like Home Depot and Target because they emphasize personal interactions and don't place demands on a community's resources. Taylor asserts that big-box stores are successful because "we've become a nation of hyper-consumers" (1011), although the convenience of shopping in these stores comes at the expense of benefits to the community. She concludes by suggesting that it's not "anti-American" to oppose big-box stores because the damage they inflict on downtown shopping districts extends to America itself.
>
> — Emilia Sanchez, student

A1-d Analyze to demonstrate your critical thinking.

Whereas a summary most often answers the question of *what* a text says, an analysis looks at *how* a text makes its point.

Typically, an analysis takes the form of an essay that makes its own argument about a text. Include an introduction that briefly summarizes the text, a thesis that states your own judgment about the text, and body paragraphs that support your thesis with evidence. If you are analyzing a visual, examine it as a whole and then reflect on how the individual elements contribute to its overall meaning. If you have written a summary of the text or visual, you may find it useful to refer to the main points of the summary as you write your analysis.

> **Making the most of your handbook**
>
> When you analyze a text, you weave words and ideas from the source into your own writing.
>
> ▶ Guidelines for using quotation marks: **R3-c**
>
> ▶ Quoting or paraphrasing: **MLA-2, APA-2, CMS-2**
>
> ▶ Using signal phrases: **MLA-3b, APA-3b, CMS-3b**

Using interpretation in an analysis

Student writer Emilia Sanchez begins her essay about Betsy Taylor's article (see p. 69) by summarizing Taylor's argument. She then states her own thesis, or claim, which offers her judgment of Taylor's article, and begins her analysis. In her first body paragraph, Sanchez interprets Taylor's use of language.

> Topic sentence includes Sanchez's claim.

> Quoted material shows Taylor's language and is placed in quotation marks.

> Transition to Sanchez's next point.

Taylor's use of colorful language reveals that she has a sentimental view of American society and does not understand economic realities. In her first paragraph, Taylor refers to a big-box store as a "25-acre slab of concrete with a 100,000 square foot box of stuff" that "land[s] on a town," evoking images of a powerful monster crushing the American way of life (1011). But she oversimplifies a complex issue. Taylor does not consider. . . .

> Signal phrase introduces a quotation from the text.

> Quotation is followed by Sanchez's interpretation of Taylor's language.

A1-e Sample student essay: Analysis of an article

Beginning on the next page is Emilia Sanchez's analysis of the article by Betsy Taylor (see p. 69). Sanchez used Modern Language Association (MLA) style to format her paper and cite the source.

MODELS　**hackerhandbooks.com/bedhandbook**
> Model papers > MLA analysis papers: Sanchez; Lee; Lopez

Sanchez 1

Emilia Sanchez

Professor Goodwin

English 10

23 October 2009

Rethinking Big-Box Stores

In her essay "Big Box Stores Are Bad for Main Street," Betsy Taylor focuses not on the economic effects of large chain stores but on the effects these stores have on the "soul" of America. She argues that stores like Home Depot, Target, and Wal-Mart are bad for America because they draw people out of downtown shopping districts and cause them to focus on consumption. In contrast, she believes that small businesses are good for America because they provide personal attention, encourage community interaction, and make each city and town unique. But Taylor's argument is unconvincing because it is based on sentimentality—on idealized images of a quaint Main Street—rather than on the roles that businesses play in consumers' lives and communities. By ignoring the complex economic relationship between large chain stores and their communities, Taylor incorrectly assumes that simply getting rid of big-box stores would have a positive effect on America's communities.

Taylor's use of colorful language reveals that she has a sentimental view of American society and does not understand economic realities. In her first paragraph, Taylor refers to a big-box store as a "25-acre slab of concrete with a 100,000 square foot box of stuff" that "land[s] on a town," evoking images of a powerful monster crushing the American way of life (1011). But she oversimplifies a complex issue. Taylor does not consider that many downtown business districts failed long before chain stores moved in, when factories and mills closed and workers lost their jobs. In cities with struggling economies, big-box stores can actually provide much-needed jobs. Similarly, while Taylor blames big-box stores for harming local economies by asking for tax breaks, free roads, and other perks, she doesn't acknowledge that these stores also enter into economic partnerships with the surrounding communities by offering financial benefits to schools and hospitals.

Opening briefly summarizes the article's purpose and thesis.

Sanchez begins to analyze Taylor's argument.

Thesis expresses Sanchez's judgment of Taylor's article.

Signal phrase introduces quotations from the source; Sanchez uses an MLA in-text citation.

Sanchez begins to identify and challenge Taylor's assumptions.

Transition to another point in Sanchez's analysis.

Marginal annotations indicate MLA-style formatting and effective writing.

Clear topic sentence announces a shift to a new topic.

    Taylor's assumption that shopping in small businesses is always better for the customer also seems driven by nostalgia for an old-fashioned Main Street rather than by the facts. While she may be right that many small businesses offer personal service and are responsive to customer complaints, she does not consider that many customers appreciate the

Sanchez refutes Taylor's claim.

service at big-box stores. Just as customer service is better at some small businesses than at others, it is impossible to generalize about service at all big-box stores. For example, customers depend on the lenient return policies and the wide variety of products at stores like Target and Home Depot.

    Taylor blames big-box stores for encouraging American "hyper-consumerism," but she oversimplifies by equating big-box stores with bad values and small businesses with good values. Like her other points, this claim ignores the economic and social realities of American society today. Big-box stores do not force Americans to buy more. By offering lower prices in a convenient setting, however, they allow consumers to save time and purchase goods they might not be able to afford from small businesses. The existence of more small businesses would not change what most Americans can afford, nor would it reduce their desire to buy affordable merchandise.

Sanchez treats the author fairly.

Conclusion returns to the thesis and shows the wider significance of Sanchez's analysis.

    Taylor may be right that some big-box stores have a negative impact on communities and that small businesses offer certain advantages. But she ignores the economic conditions that support big-box stores as well as the fact that Main Street was in decline before the big-box store arrived. Getting rid of big-box stores will not bring back a simpler America populated by thriving, unique Main Streets; in reality, Main Street will not survive if consumers cannot afford to shop there.

Work Cited

Work cited page is in MLA style.

Taylor, Betsy. "Big Box Stores Are Bad for Main Street." *CQ Researcher*
        9.44 (1999): 1011. Print.

Guidelines for analyzing a text

Written texts

Instructors who ask you to analyze an essay or an article often expect you to address some of the following questions.

- What is the author's thesis or central idea? Who is the audience?
- What questions (stated or unstated) does the author address?
- How does the author structure the text? What are the key parts, and how do they relate to one another and to the thesis?
- What strategies has the author used to generate interest in the argument and to persuade readers of its merit?
- What evidence does the author use to support the thesis? How persuasive is the evidence? (See A2-d and A2-e.)
- Does the author anticipate objections and counter opposing views? (See A2-f.)
- Does the author use any faulty reasoning? (See A3-a.)

Visual texts

If you are analyzing a visual text, the following additional questions will help you evaluate an image's purpose and meaning.

- What confuses, surprises, or intrigues you about the image?
- What is the source of the visual, and who created it? What is its purpose?
- What clues suggest the visual text's intended audience? How does the image appeal to its audience?
- If the text is an advertisement, what product is it selling? Does it attempt to sell an idea or a message as well?
- If the visual text includes words, how do the words contribute to the meaning?
- How do design elements—colours, shapes, perspective, background, foreground—help convey the visual text's meaning or serve its purpose?

A2 Constructing reasonable arguments

In writing an argument, you take a stand on a debatable issue. The question being debated might be a matter of public policy:

> Should religious groups be allowed to meet on public school property?
>
> What is the least dangerous way to dispose of hazardous waste?
>
> Should motorists be banned from texting while driving?
>
> Should a province limit the number of charter schools?

On such questions, reasonable people may disagree.

Reasonable men and women also disagree about many scholarly issues. Psychologists debate the role of genes and environment in determining behaviour; historians interpret the causes of the War of 1812 quite differently; biologists challenge one another's predictions about the effects of global warming.

When you construct a *reasonable* argument, your goal is not simply to win or to have the last word. Your aim is to explain your understanding of the truth about a subject or to propose the best solution to

---

Academic English   Some cultures value writers who argue with force; other cultures value writers who argue subtly or indirectly. Academic audiences in Canada will expect your writing to be assertive and confident—neither aggressive nor passive. You can create an assertive tone by acknowledging different positions and supporting your ideas with specific evidence.

TOO AGGRESSIVE	Of course only registered organ donors should be eligible for organ transplants. It's selfish and shortsighted to think otherwise.
TOO PASSIVE	I might be wrong, but I think that maybe people should have to register as organ donors if they want to be considered for a transplant.
ASSERTIVE	If only registered organ donors are eligible for transplants, more people will register as donors.

If you are uncertain about the tone of your work, ask for help at your school's writing centre.

a problem—without being needlessly combative. In constructing your argument, you join a conversation with other writers and readers. Your aim is to convince readers to reconsider their positions by offering new reasons to question existing viewpoints.

A2-a Examine your issue's social and intellectual contexts.

Arguments appear in social and intellectual contexts. Public policy debates arise in social contexts and are conducted among groups with competing values and interests. For example, the debate over offshore oil drilling has been renewed in Canada in light of skyrocketing energy costs—with environmentalists, policymakers, oil company executives, and consumers all weighing in on the argument. Most public policy debates also have intellectual dimensions that address scientific or theoretical questions. In the case of the drilling issue, geologists, oceanographers, and economists all contribute their expertise.

Scholarly debates play out in intellectual contexts, but they have a social dimension as well. For example, scholars respond to the contributions of other specialists in the field, often building on others' views and refining them, but at times challenging them.

Because many of your readers will be aware of the social and intellectual contexts in which your issue is grounded, you will be at a disadvantage if you are not informed. That's why it is a good idea to conduct some research before preparing your argument; consulting even a few sources can deepen your understanding of the debates surrounding your topic. For example, the student whose paper appears on pages 87–91 became more knowledgeable about his issue—the shift from print to online news—after reading and annotating a few sources.

> **Making the most of your handbook**
>
> Supporting your claims with evidence from sources can strengthen your argument.
>
> ▶ Conducting research: R1

A2-b View your audience as a panel of jurors.

Do not assume that your audience already agrees with you; instead, envision skeptical readers who, like a panel of jurors, will make up their minds after listening to all sides of the argument. If you are arguing a public policy issue, aim your paper at readers who represent a variety of positions. In the case of the debate over offshore drilling, for example, imagine a jury that represents those who have a stake in the matter: environmentalists, policymakers, oil company executives, and consumers.

At times, you can deliberately narrow your audience. If you are working within a word limit, for example, you might not have the space in which to address all the concerns surrounding the offshore drilling debate. Or you might be primarily interested in reaching one segment of a general audience, such as consumers. In such instances, you can still view your audience as a panel of jurors; the jury will simply be a less diverse group.

> **Making the most of your handbook**
>
> You may need to consider a specific audience for your argument.
> ▶ Writing in a particular discipline, such as business or psychology: A4

In the case of scholarly debates, you will be addressing readers who share your interest in a discipline, such as literature or psychology. Such readers belong to a group with an agreed-upon way of investigating and talking about issues. Though they generally agree about disciplinary methods of asking questions and share specialized vocabulary, scholars in an academic discipline often disagree about particular issues. Once you see how they disagree about your issue, you should be able to imagine a jury that reflects the variety of positions they hold.

A2-c In your introduction, establish credibility and state your position.

When you are constructing an argument, make sure your introduction contains a thesis that states your position on the issue you have chosen to debate (see also C2-a). In the sentences leading up to the thesis, establish your credibility with readers by showing that you are knowledgeable and fair-minded. If possible, build common ground with readers who may not at first agree with your views and show them why they should consider your thesis.

> **Making the most of your handbook**
>
> When you write an argument, you state your position in a thesis.
> ▶ Writing effective thesis statements: C1-c, C2-a

In the following introduction, student Kevin Smith presents himself as someone worth listening to. Because Smith introduces both sides of the debate, readers are likely to approach his essay with an open mind.

Smith shows that he is familiar with the legal issues surrounding school prayer.

Although the Supreme Court has ruled against prayer in public schools on First Amendment grounds, many people still feel that prayer should be allowed. Such people value prayer as a practice central to their faith and believe that prayer is a way for schools to reinforce moral principles. They also compellingly point out a paradox in the First Amendment itself: at what point does the separation of church and state restrict the freedom of those who wish to practice their religion? What proponents of school prayer fail to realize, however, is that the Supreme Court's decision, although it was made on legal grounds, makes sense on religious grounds as well. Prayer is too important to be trusted to our public schools.

Smith is fair-minded, presenting the views of both sides.

Smith's thesis builds common ground.

—Kevin Smith, student

TIP: A good way to test a thesis while drafting and revising is to imagine a counterargument to your argument (see A2-f). If you can't think of an opposing point of view, rethink your thesis and ask a classmate or writing centre tutor to respond to your argument.

A2-d Back up your thesis with persuasive lines of argument.

Arguments of any complexity contain lines of argument that, when taken together, might reasonably persuade readers that the thesis has merit. The following, for example, are the main lines of argument that Sam Jacobs used in his paper about the shift from print to online news (see pp. 87–91).

CENTRAL CLAIM	Thesis: The shift from print to online news provides unprecedented opportunities for readers to become more engaged with the news, to hold journalists accountable, and to participate as producers, not simply as consumers.
SUPPORTING CLAIMS	• Print news has traditionally had a one-sided relationship with its readers, delivering information for passive consumption.

(continued)

THE WRITING CENTRE **hackerhandbooks.com/writersref**
> Resources for writers and tutors > Tips from writing tutors:
Writing assignments;
Writing essays in English

SUPPORTING
CLAIMS
(continued)

- Online news invites readers to participate in a collaborative process—to question and even contribute to the content.
- Links within news stories provide transparency, allowing readers to move easily from the main story to original sources, related articles, or background materials.
- Technology has made it possible for readers to become news producers—posting text, audio, images, and video of news events.
- Citizen journalists can provide valuable information, sometimes more quickly than traditional journalists can.

If you sum up your main lines of argument, as Jacobs did, you will have a rough outline of your essay. In your paper, you will provide evidence for each of your claims.

A2-e Support your claims with specific evidence.

You will need to support your central claim and any subordinate claims with evidence: facts, statistics, examples and illustrations, visuals, expert opinion, and so on. Most debatable topics require that you consult some written sources. As you read through the sources, you will learn more about the arguments and counterarguments at the centre of your debate.

Remember that you must document your sources. Documentation gives credit to the authors and shows readers how to locate a source in case they want to assess its credibility or explore the issues further.

Making the most of your handbook

Sources, when used responsibly, can provide evidence to support an argument.

▶ Paraphrasing, summarizing, and quoting sources: R3-c

▶ Punctuating direct quotations: P5-a

▶ Citing sources: MLA-2, APA-2, CMS-2

Using facts and statistics

A fact is something that is known with certainty because it has been objectively verified: The capital of Nunavut is Iqaluit. Carbon has an atomic weight of 12. Pierre Laporte was murdered by the FLQ on October 17, 1970. Statistics are collections of numerical facts: Alcohol use by drivers is a factor in about 30 percent of traffic fatalities. Almost one million women in Canada are self-employed.

Most arguments are supported at least to some extent by facts and statistics. For example, in the following passage the writer uses statistics to show that postsecondary students in the United States are granted unreasonably high credit limits.

> A 2009 study by Sallie Mae revealed that undergraduates are carrying record-high credit card balances and are relying on credit cards more than ever, especially in the economic downturn. The average credit card debt per college undergraduate is $3,173, and 82 percent of undergraduates carry balances and incur finance charges each month (Sallie Mae).

Writers often use statistics in selective ways to bolster their own positions. If you suspect that a writer's handling of statistics is not quite fair, track down the original sources for those statistics or read authors with opposing views, who may give you a fuller understanding of the numbers.

Using examples and illustrations

Examples and illustrations (extended examples, often in story form) rarely prove a point by themselves, but when used in combination with other forms of evidence they flesh out an argument with details and specific instances and bring it to life. Because examples are often concrete and sometimes vivid, they can reach readers in ways that statistics and abstract ideas cannot.

In a paper arguing that online news provides opportunities for readers that print news does not, Sam Jacobs describes how regular citizens armed with only cell phones and laptops helped save lives during Hurricane Katrina by relaying critical news updates.

Using visuals

Visuals—charts, graphs, diagrams, photographs—can support your argument by providing vivid and detailed evidence and by capturing your readers' attention. Bar or line graphs, for instance, describe and organize complex statistical data; photographs can immediately and evocatively convey abstract ideas. Writers in almost every academic field use visual evidence to support their arguments or to counter opposing arguments. For example, to explain a conflict among Southeast Asian countries, a historian might choose a map to illustrate the geographic situation and highlight particular issues. Or to refute another scholar's hypothesis about the dangers of a vegetarian diet, a nutritionist might support her claims by using a table to organize and highlight detailed numerical information. (See C5-d.)

As you consider using visual evidence, ask yourself the following questions:

- Is the visual accurate, credible, and relevant?

- How will the visual appeal to readers? Logically? Ethically? Emotionally?

- How will the visual evidence function? Will it provide background information? Present complex numerical information or an abstract idea? Lend authority? Anticipate or refute counter-arguments?

> **Making the most of your handbook**
>
> Integrating visuals can strengthen your writing.
> - ▶ Choosing appropriate visuals: **page 50**
> - ▶ Placing and labelling visuals: **page 51**
> - ▶ Using visuals responsibly: **page 54**

Like all forms of evidence, visuals don't speak for themselves; you'll need to analyze and interpret the evidence to show readers how the visuals inform and support your argument.

Citing expert opinion

Although they are no substitute for careful reasoning of your own, the views of an expert can contribute to the force of your argument. For example, to help him make the case that print journalism has a one-sided relationship with its readers, Sam Jacobs integrates an expert's key description:

> With the rise of the Internet, however, this one-sided relationship has been criticized by journalists such as Dan Gillmor, founder of the Center for Citizen Media, who argues that traditional print journalism treats "news as a lecture," whereas online news is "more of a conversation" (xxiv).

When you rely on expert opinion, make sure that your source is an expert in the field you are writing about. In some cases, you may need to provide credentials showing why your source is worth listening to. When including expert testimony in your paper, you can summarize or paraphrase the expert's opinion or you can quote the expert's exact words. You will of course need to document the source, as Jacobs did in the example just given.

Anticipating and countering opposing arguments

To anticipate a possible objection to your argument, consider the following questions:

- Could a reasonable person draw a different conclusion from your facts or examples?
- Might a reader question any of your assumptions?
- Could a reader offer an alternative explanation of this issue?
- Is there any evidence that might weaken your position?

The following questions may help you respond to a reader's potential objection:

- Can you concede the point to the opposition but challenge the point's importance or usefulness?
- Can you explain why readers should consider a new perspective or question a piece of evidence?
- Should you explain how your position responds to contradictory evidence?
- Can you suggest a different interpretation of the evidence?

When you write, use phrasing to signal to readers that you're about to present an objection. Often the signal phrase can go in the lead sentence of a paragraph:

> Critics of this view argue that. . . .
>
> Some readers might point out that. . . .
>
> Researchers challenge these claims by. . . .

A2-f Anticipate objections; counter opposing arguments.

Readers who already agree with you need no convincing, but indifferent or skeptical readers may resist your arguments. To be willing to give up a position that seems reasonable, a reader has to see that there is an even more reasonable one. In addition to presenting your own case, therefore, you should consider the opposing arguments and attempt to counter them.

It might seem at first that drawing attention to an opposing point of view or contradictory evidence would weaken your argument. But by anticipating and countering objections, you show yourself as a reasonable and well-informed writer. You also establish your purpose, demonstrate the significance of the issue you are debating, and ultimately strengthen your argument.

There is no best place in an essay to deal with opposing views. Often it is useful to summarize the opposing position early in your essay. After stating your thesis but before developing your own arguments, you might have a paragraph that addresses the most important counterargument. Or you can anticipate objections paragraph by paragraph as you develop your case. Wherever you decide to address opposing arguments, you will enhance your credibility if you explain the arguments of others accurately and fairly.

A2-g Build common ground.

As you counter opposing arguments, try to seek out one or two assumptions you might share with readers who do not initially agree with your views. If you can show that you share their concerns, your readers may be more likely to acknowledge the validity of your argument. For example, to persuade people opposed to controlling the deer population with a regulated hunting season, a provincial wildlife department would have to show that it too cares about preserving deer and does not want them to die needlessly. Having established these values in common, the department might be able to persuade critics that reducing the total number of deer prevents starvation caused by overpopulation.

People believe that intelligence and decency support their side of an argument. To be persuaded, they must see these qualities in your argument. Otherwise they will persist in their opposition.

A2-h Sample argument paper

In the paper that begins on the next page, student Sam Jacobs argues that the shift from print to online news benefits readers by providing them with opportunities to become more engaged with the news, to hold journalists accountable, and to participate as producers, not simply as consumers. Notice that he is careful to present opposing views fairly before providing his counterarguments.

In writing the paper, Jacobs consulted both print and online sources. When he quotes or uses information from a source, he cites the source with an MLA (Modern Language Association) in-text citation. Citations in the paper refer readers to the list of works cited at the end of the paper. (For more details about citing sources, see MLA-4.)

MODELS   hackerhandbooks.com/writersref
> Model papers > MLA argument papers: Jacobs; Hammond; Lund; Sanghvi
> MLA papers: Orlov; Daly; Levi

Sam Jacobs

Professor Alperini

English 101

March 19, 2010

From Lecture to Conversation: Redefining What's "Fit to Print"

"All the news that's fit to print," the motto of the *New York Times*
since 1896, plays with the word *fit*, asserting that a news story must be
newsworthy and must not exceed the limits of the printed page. The
increase in online news consumption, however, challenges both meanings
of the word *fit*, allowing producers and consumers alike to rethink who
decides which topics are worth covering and how extensive that coverage
should be. Any cultural shift usually means that something is lost, but in
this case there are clear gains. The shift from print to online news provides
unprecedented opportunities for readers to become more engaged with the
news, to hold journalists accountable, and to participate as producers, not
simply as consumers.

Guided by journalism's code of ethics—accuracy, objectivity, and
fairness—print news reporters have gathered and delivered stories according
to what editors decide is fit for their readers. Except for op-ed pages and
letters to the editor, print news has traditionally had a one-sided relationship
with its readers. The print news media's reputation for objective reporting
has been held up as "a stop sign" for readers, sending a clear message that
no further inquiry is necessary (Weinberger). With the rise of the Internet,
however, this model has been criticized by journalists such as Dan Gillmor,
founder of the Center for Citizen Media, who argues that traditional print
journalism treats "news as a lecture," whereas online news is "more of a
conversation" (xxiv). Print news arrives on the doorstep every morning as a
fully formed lecture, a product created without participation from its
readership. By contrast, online news invites readers to participate in a
collaborative process—to question and even help produce the content.

One of the most important advantages online news offers over print
news is the presence of built-in hyperlinks, which carry readers from one
electronic document to another. If readers are curious about the definition
of a term, the roots of a story, or other perspectives on a topic, links
provide a path. Links help readers become more critical consumers of

Marginal annotations:

Jacobs provides
background in
opening sentences
for his thesis.

Thesis states the
main point.

Jacobs does not
need a citation for
common knowledge.

Transition moves
from Jacobs's main
argument to specific
examples.

Marginal annotations indicate MLA-style formatting and effective writing.

information by engaging them in a totally new way. For instance, the link embedded in the story "Window into Fed Debate over a Crucial Program" (Healy) allows readers to find out more about the trends in consumer spending and to check the journalist's handling of an original source (see Fig. 1). This kind of link gives readers the opportunity to conduct their own evaluation of the evidence and verify the journalist's claims.

But economists greeted the news with a small cheer because sales excluding automobiles actually grew in September, suggesting that consumer spending was stabilizing.

Over all, retail sales fell 1.5 percent in September from a month earlier, the Commerce Department reported, better than an anticipated decline of 2.1 percent.

Retail sales excluding automobiles and parts grew 0.5 percent, largely because of higher sales at gas stations and grocery stores.

Auto dealers bore the brunt of the month's declines.

Consumers swamped dealerships in late July and August to take advantage of the government's $3 billion cash-for-clunkers program, which offered rebates of up to $4,500 to entice people to swap their older cars for more fuel-efficient models.

Sales at auto dealers surged in August, but fell 11 percent in September.

Sign in to Recommend

A version of this article appeared in print on October 15, 2009, on page B3 of the New York edition.   More Articles in Business »

INSIDE NYTIMES.COM

Timothy Winters / Ian Thomas   CB09-154
Service Sector Statistics Division
(301) 763-2713

U.S. Census Bureau News
U.S. Department of Commerce · Washington, D.C. 20233

FOR IMMEDIATE RELEASE

WEDNESDAY, OCTOBER 14, 2009 AT 8:30 A.M. EDT

**ADVANCE MONTHLY SALES FOR RETAIL TRADE
AND FOOD SERVICES
SEPTEMBER 2009**

The U.S. Census Bureau announced today that advance estimates of U.S. retail and food services sales for September, adjusted for seasonal variation and holiday and trading-day differences, but not for price changes, were $344.7 billion, a decrease of 1.5 percent (±0.5%) from the previous month and 5.7 percent (±0.7%) below September 2008. Total sales for the July through September 2009 period were down 6.6 percent (±0.3%) from the same period a year ago. The July to

Fig. 1. Links embedded in online news articles allow readers to move from the main story to original sources, related articles, or background materials. The link in this online article (Healy) points to a government report, the original source of the author's data on consumer spending.

Jacobs 3

Links provide a kind of transparency impossible in print because they allow readers to see through online news to the "sources, disagreements, and the personal assumptions and values" that may have influenced a news story (Weinberger). The International Center for Media and the Public Agenda underscores the importance of news organizations letting "customers in on the often tightly held little secrets of journalism." To do so, they suggest, will lead to "accountability and accountability leads to credibility" ("Openness"). These tools alone don't guarantee that news producers will be responsible and trustworthy, but they encourage an open and transparent environment that benefits news consumers.

Not only has technology allowed readers to become more critical news consumers, but it also has helped some to become news producers. The Web gives ordinary people the power to report on the day's events. Anyone with an Internet connection can publish on blogs and Web sites, engage in online discussion forums, and contribute video and audio recordings. Citizen journalists with laptops, cell phones, and digital camcorders have become news producers alongside large news organizations.

Not everyone embraces the spread of unregulated news reporting online. Critics point out that citizen journalists are not necessarily trained to be fair or ethical, for example, nor are they subject to editorial oversight. Acknowledging that citizen reporting is more immediate and experimental, critics also question its accuracy and accountability: "While it has its place . . . it really isn't journalism at all, and it opens up information flow to the strong probability of fraud and abuse. . . . Information without journalistic standards is called gossip," writes David Hazinski in the *Atlanta Journal-Constitution* (23A). In his book *Losing the News*, media specialist Alex S. Jones argues that what passes for news today is in fact "pseudo news" and is "far less reliable" than traditional print news (27). Even a supporter like Gillmor is willing to agree that citizen journalists are "nonexperts," but he argues that they are "using technology to make a profound contribution, and a real difference" (140).

Citizen reporting made a difference in the wake of Hurricane Katrina in 2005. Armed with cell phones and laptops, regular citizens relayed critical news updates in a rapidly developing crisis, often before traditional journalists were even on the scene. In 2006, the enormous contributions of

---

Jacobs clarifies key terms (*transparency* and *accountability*).

Source is cited in MLA style.

Jacobs develops the thesis.

Opposing views are presented fairly.

Jacobs counters opposing arguments.

A vivid example helps Jacobs make his point.

Jacobs 4

citizen journalists were recognized when the New Orleans *Times-Picayune* received the Pulitzer Prize in public service for its online coverage—largely citizen-generated—of Hurricane Katrina. In recognizing the paper's "meritorious public service," the Pulitzer Prize board credited the newspaper's blog for "heroic, multi-faceted coverage of [the storm] and its aftermath" ("2006 Pulitzer"). Writing for the *Online Journalism Review*, Mark Glaser emphasizes the role that blog updates played in saving storm victims' lives. Further, he calls the *Times-Picayune*'s partnership with citizen journalists a "watershed for online journalism."

The Internet has enabled consumers to participate in a new way in reading, questioning, interpreting, and reporting the news. Decisions about appropriate content and coverage are no longer exclusively in the hands of news editors. Ordinary citizens now have a meaningful voice in the conversation—a hand in deciding what's "fit to print." Some skeptics worry about the apparent free-for-all and loss of tradition. But the expanding definition of news provides opportunities for consumers to be more engaged with events in their communities, their nations, and the world.

Jacobs uses specific evidence for support.

Conclusion echoes the thesis without dully repeating it.

Jacobs 5

Works Cited

Gillmor, Dan. *We the Media: Grassroots Journalism by the People, for the People*. Sebastopol: O'Reilly, 2006. Print.

Glaser, Mark. "NOLA.com Blogs and Forums Help Save Lives after Katrina." *OJR: The Online Journalism Review*. Knight Digital Media Center, 13 Sept. 2005. Web. 2 Mar. 2010.

Hazinski, David. "Unfettered 'Citizen Journalism' Too Risky." *Atlanta Journal-Constitution* 13 Dec. 2007: 23A. *General OneFile*. Web. 2 Mar. 2010.

Healy, Jack. "Window into Fed Debate over a Crucial Program." *New York Times*. New York Times, 14 Oct. 2009. Web. 4 Mar. 2010.

Jones, Alex S. *Losing the News: The Future of the News That Feeds Democracy*. New York: Oxford UP, 2009. Print.

"Openness and Accountability: A Study of Transparency in Global Media Outlets." *ICMPA: International Center for Media and the Public Agenda*. Intl. Center for Media and the Public Agenda, 2006. Web. 26 Feb. 2010.

"The 2006 Pulitzer Prize Winners: Public Service." *The Pulitzer Prizes*. Columbia U, n.d. Web. 2 Mar. 2010.

Weinberger, David. "Transparency Is the New Objectivity." *Joho the Blog*. David Weinberger, 19 July 2009. Web. 26 Feb. 2010.

Works cited page uses MLA style.

List is alphabetized by authors' last names (or by title when a work has no author).

Abbreviation "n.d." indicates that the online source has no update date.

A3 Evaluating arguments

In your reading and in your own writing, evaluate all arguments for logic and fairness. Many arguments can stand up to critical scrutiny. Sometimes, however, a line of argument that at first seems reasonable turns out to be illogical, unfair, or both.

A3-a Distinguish between reasonable and fallacious argumentative tactics.

A number of unreasonable argumentative tactics are known as *logical fallacies*. Most of the fallacies—such as hasty generalizations and false analogies—are misguided or dishonest uses of legitimate argumentative strategies. The examples in this section suggest when such strategies are reasonable and when they are not.

Generalizing (inductive reasoning)

Writers and thinkers generalize all the time. We look at a sample of data and conclude that data we have not observed will most likely conform to what we have seen. From a spoonful of soup, we conclude just how salty the whole bowl will be. After numerous unpleasant experiences with an airline, we decide to book future flights with a competitor.

When we draw a conclusion from an array of facts, we are engaged in inductive reasoning. Such reasoning deals in probability, not certainty. For a conclusion to be highly probable, it must be based on evidence that is sufficient, representative, and relevant. (See the chart on p. 94.)

The fallacy known as *hasty generalization* is a conclusion based on insufficient or unrepresentative evidence.

HASTY GENERALIZATION

In a single year, scores on standardized tests in Alberta's public schools rose by ten points. Therefore, more children than ever are succeeding in Canada's public school systems.

Data from one province do not justify a conclusion about the whole of Canada.

A *stereotype* is a hasty generalization about a group. Here are a few examples.

STEREOTYPES

Women are bad bosses.

All politicians are corrupt.

Athletes are never strong students.

Stereotyping is common because of our tendency to perceive selectively. We tend to see what we want to see; we notice evidence confirming our already formed opinions and fail to notice evidence to the contrary. For example, if you have concluded that all politicians are corrupt, this stereotype will be confirmed by news reports of legislators being indicted—even though every day the media describe conscientious officials serving the public honestly and well.

Academic English   Many hasty generalizations contain words such as *all*, *ever*, *always*, and *never*, when qualifiers such as *most*, *many*, *usually*, and *seldom* would be more accurate.

Drawing analogies

An analogy points out a similarity between two things that are otherwise different. Analogies can be an effective means of arguing a point. Our system of judicial decision making, or case law, which relies heavily on previous decisions, makes extensive use of reasoning by analogy. One lawyer may point out, for example, that specific facts or circumstances resemble those from a previous case and will thus argue for a similar result or decision. In response, the opposing lawyer may maintain that such facts or circumstances bear only a superficial resemblance to those in the previous case and that in legally relevant respects they are quite different and thus require a different result or decision.

It is not always easy to draw the line between a reasonable and an unreasonable analogy. At times, however, an analogy is clearly off base, in which case it is called a *false analogy*.

FALSE ANALOGY

If we can send a spacecraft to Pluto, we should be able to find a cure for the common cold.

The writer has falsely assumed that because two things are alike in one respect, they must be alike in others. Exploring the outer reaches of the solar system and finding a cure for the common cold are both scientific challenges, but the problems confronting medical researchers are quite different from those solved by space scientists.

Testing inductive reasoning

Though inductive reasoning leads to probable and not absolute truth, you can assess a conclusion's likely probability by asking three questions. This chart shows how to apply those questions to a sample conclusion based on a survey.

CONCLUSION The majority of students on our campus would volunteer at least five hours a week in a community organization if the school provided a placement service for volunteers.

EVIDENCE In a recent survey, 723 of 1215 students questioned said they would volunteer at least five hours a week in a community organization if the school provided a placement service for volunteers.

1. Is the evidence sufficient?

   That depends. On a small campus (say, 3000 students), the pool of students surveyed would be sufficient for market research, but on a large campus (say, 30 000), 1215 students are only 4 percent of the population. If that 4 percent were known to be truly representative of the other 96 percent, however, even such a small sample would be sufficient (see question 2).

2. Is the evidence representative?

   The evidence is representative if those responding to the survey reflect the characteristics of the entire student population: age, sex, race, field of study, overall number of extracurricular commitments, and so on. If most of those surveyed are majors in a field like social work, however, the researchers would be wise to question the survey's conclusion.

3. Is the evidence relevant?

   Yes. The results of the survey are directly linked to the conclusion. Evidence based on a survey about the number of hours students work for pay, by contrast, would not be relevant because it would not be about *choosing to volunteer*.

Tracing causes and effects

Demonstrating a connection between causes and effects is rarely simple. For example, to explain why a chemistry course has a high failure rate, you would begin by listing possible causes: inadequate preparation of students, poor teaching, lack of qualified tutors, and so on. Next you would investigate each possible cause. Only after investigating the possible causes would you be able to weigh the relative impact of each cause and suggest appropriate remedies.

Because cause-and-effect reasoning is so complex, it is not surprising that writers frequently oversimplify it. In particular, writers sometimes assume that because one event follows another, the first is the cause of the second. This common fallacy is known as *post hoc*, from the Latin *post hoc, ergo propter hoc*, meaning "after this, therefore because of this."

POST HOC FALLACY

Since Premier Cho took office, unemployment of minorities in the province has decreased by 7 percent. Premier Cho should be applauded for reducing unemployment among minorities.

The writer must show that Premier Cho's policies are responsible for the decrease in unemployment; it is not enough to show that the decrease followed the premier's taking office.

Weighing options

Especially when reasoning about problems and solutions, writers must weigh options. To be fair, a writer should mention the full range of options, showing why one is superior to the others or might work well in combination with others.

It is unfair to suggest that there are only two alternatives when in fact there are more. When writers set up a false choice between their preferred option and one that is clearly unsatisfactory, they create an *either . . . or* fallacy.

EITHER . . . OR FALLACY

Our current war against drugs has not worked. Either we should legalize drugs or we should turn the drug war over to our armed forces and let them fight it.

Clearly there are other options, such as increased funding for drug abuse prevention and treatment.

Making assumptions

An assumption is a claim that is taken to be true—without the need of proof. Most arguments are based to some extent on assumptions, since writers rarely have the time and space to prove all the conceivable claims on which an argument is based. For example, someone arguing about the best means of limiting population growth in developing countries might well assume that the goal of limiting population growth is worthwhile. For most audiences, there would be no need to articulate this assumption or to defend it.

There is a danger, however, in failing to spell out and prove a claim that is clearly controversial. Consider the following short argument, in which a key claim is missing.

ARGUMENT WITH MISSING CLAIM

Violent crime is increasing. Therefore, we should vigorously enforce the death penalty.

The writer seems to be assuming that the death penalty deters violent criminals—and that most audiences will agree. The writer also assumes that the death penalty is a fair punishment for violent crimes. These are not safe assumptions; the writer will need to state and support both claims.

When a missing claim is an assertion that few would agree with, we say that a writer is guilty of a *non sequitur* (Latin for "it does not follow").

NON SEQUITUR

Leah loves good food; therefore, she will be an excellent chef.

Few people would agree with the missing claim—that lovers of good food always make excellent chefs.

Deducing conclusions (deductive reasoning)

When we deduce a conclusion, we—like Sherlock Holmes—put things together. We establish that a general principle is true, that a specific case is an example of that principle, and that therefore a particular conclusion about that case is a certainty. In real life, such absolute reasoning rarely happens. Approximations of it, however, sometimes occur.

Deductive reasoning can often be structured in a three-step argument called a *syllogism*. The three steps are the major premise, the minor premise, and the conclusion.

1. Anything that increases radiation in the environment is dangerous to public health. (Major premise)
2. Nuclear reactors increase radiation in the environment. (Minor premise)
3. Therefore, nuclear reactors are dangerous to public health. (Conclusion)

The major premise is a generalization. The minor premise is a specific case. The conclusion follows from applying the generalization to the specific case.

Deductive arguments break down if one of the premises is not true or if the conclusion does not logically follow from the premises. In the following argument, the major premise is very likely untrue.

UNTRUE PREMISE

The police do not give speeding tickets to people driving less than eight kilometres per hour over the limit. Dominic is driving ninety-five kilometres per hour in a ninety-kilometre-per-hour zone. Therefore, the police will not give Dominic a speeding ticket.

The conclusion is true only if the premises are true. If the police sometimes give speeding tickets for driving less than eight kilometres per hour over the limit, Dominic cannot safely conclude that he will avoid a ticket.

In the following argument, both premises might be true, but the conclusion does not follow logically from them.

CONCLUSION DOES NOT FOLLOW

All members of our club ran in this year's Manitoba Marathon. Jay ran in this year's Manitoba Marathon. Therefore, Jay is a member of our club.

The fact that Jay ran the marathon is no guarantee that he is a member of the club. Presumably, many marathon runners are nonmembers.

Assuming that both premises are true, the following argument holds up.

CONCLUSION FOLLOWS

All members of our club ran in this year's Manitoba Marathon. Jay is a member of our club. Therefore, Jay ran in this year's Manitoba Marathon.

A3-b Distinguish between legitimate and unfair emotional appeals.

There is nothing wrong with appealing to readers' emotions. After all, many issues worth arguing about have an emotional as well as a logical dimension. Even the Greek logician Aristotle lists *pathos* (emotion) as a legitimate argumentative tactic. For example, in an essay criticizing big-box stores, writer Betsy Taylor has a good reason for tugging at readers' emotions: Her subject is the decline of city and town life. In her conclusion, Taylor appeals to readers' emotions by invoking their national pride.

LEGITIMATE EMOTIONAL APPEAL

Is it anti-American to be against having a retail giant set up shop in one's community? Some people would say so. On the other hand, if you board up Main Street, what's left of America?

As we all know, however, emotional appeals are frequently misused. Many of the arguments we see in the media, for instance, strive to win our sympathy rather than our intelligent agreement. A TV commercial suggesting that you will be thin and sexy if you drink a certain diet beverage is making a pitch to emotions. So is a political speech that recommends electing a candidate because he is a devoted husband and father who serves as a volunteer firefighter.

The following passage illustrates several types of unfair emotional appeals.

UNFAIR EMOTIONAL APPEALS

This progressive proposal to build a ski resort has been carefully researched by RBC, the largest bank in the province; furthermore, it is favoured by a majority of the local merchants. The only opposition comes from narrow-minded, hippie environmentalists who care more about trees than they do about people; one of their leaders was actually arrested for disturbing the peace several years ago.

Words with strong positive or negative connotations, such as *progressive* and *hippie*, are examples of *biased language*. Attacking the people who hold a belief (environmentalists) rather than refuting their argument is called *ad hominem*, a Latin term meaning "to the man." Associating a prestigious name (RBC) with the writer's side is called *transfer*. Claiming that an idea should be accepted because a large number of people (the majority of merchants) are in favour is called the *bandwagon appeal*. Bringing in irrelevant issues (the arrest) is a *red herring*, named after a trick used in fox hunts to mislead the dogs by dragging a smelly fish across the trail.

A3-c Judge how fairly a writer handles opposing views.

The way in which a writer deals with opposing views is revealing. Some writers address the arguments of the opposition fairly, conceding points when necessary and countering others, all in a civil spirit. Other writers will do almost anything to win an argument: either ignoring opposing views altogether or misrepresenting such views and attacking their proponents.

In your own writing, you build credibility by addressing opposing arguments fairly. (See also A2-f.) In your reading, you can assess the credibility of your sources by looking at how they deal with views not in agreement with their own.

Describing the views of others

Writers and politicians often deliberately misrepresent the views of others. One way they do this is by setting up a "straw man," a character so weak that he is easily knocked down. The *straw man* fallacy consists of an oversimplification or outright distortion of opposing views. For example, in a British Columbia debate over attempts to control the cougar population, pro-cougar groups characterized their opponents as trophy hunters bent on shooting harmless cougars and sticking them on the walls of their dens. In truth, such hunters were only one faction of those who saw a need to control the cougar population.

During the District of Columbia's struggle for voting representation, some politicians set up a straw man, as shown in the following example.

STRAW MAN FALLACY

Washington, DC, residents are lobbying for statehood. Giving a city such as the District of Columbia the status of a state would be unfair.

The straw man wanted statehood. In fact, most District citizens lobbied for voting representation in any form, not necessarily through statehood.

Quoting opposing views

Writers often quote the words of writers who hold opposing views. In general, this is a good idea, for it ensures some level of fairness and accuracy. At times, though, both the fairness and the accuracy are an illusion.

A source may be misrepresented when it is quoted out of context. All quotations are to some extent taken out of context, but a fair writer will explain the context to readers. To select a provocative sentence from a source and to ignore the more moderate sentences surrounding it is both unfair and misleading. Sometimes a writer deliberately distorts a source through the device of ellipsis dots. Ellipsis dots tell readers that words have been omitted from the original source. When those words are crucial to an author's meaning, omitting them is obviously unfair. (See P6-c.)

ORIGINAL SOURCE

Johnson's *History of the American West* is riddled with inaccuracies and astonishing in its blatantly racist description of the Indian wars. —B. R., reviewer

MISLEADING QUOTATION

According to B. R., Johnson's *History of the American West* is "astonishing in its . . . description of the Indian wars."

A4 Writing in the disciplines

University and college courses expose you to the thinking of scholars in many disciplines, such as the humanities (literature, music, art), the social sciences (psychology, anthropology, sociology), the sciences (biology, physics, chemistry), and the professions and applied sciences (nursing, education, forestry). Writing in any discipline provides opportunities to practise the methods used by scholars in these fields and to enter into their debates. Each field has its own questions, evidence, language, and conventions, but all disciplines share certain expectations for good writing.

A4-a Find commonalities across disciplines.

A good paper in any field needs to communicate a writer's purpose to an audience and to explore an engaging question about a subject. Effective writers make an argument and support their claims with evidence. Writers in most fields need to show the thesis they're developing (or, in the sciences, the hypothesis they're testing) and counter opposition from other writers. All disciplines require writers to document where they found their evidence and from whom they borrowed ideas.

A4-b Recognize the questions writers in a discipline ask.

Disciplines are characterized by the kinds of questions their scholars attempt to answer. Historians, for example, often ask questions about the causes and effects of events and about the connections between current and past events. One way to understand how disciplines ask different questions is to look at assignments on the same subject in

Writing advice for all your courses

When writing for any course in any discipline, keeping the following steps in mind can help you write a strong academic paper. Consult sections of this handbook that are appropriate to your assignment.

- Understand the writing assignment: C1-b, A4-f
- Determine and communicate a purpose: C1-a, C1-b
- Consider your audience: C1-a, C1-b
- Ask questions appropriate to the field: A4-b
- Formulate a thesis: C2-a, MLA-1a, APA-1a, CMS-1a
- Determine what types of evidence to gather: A4-c, C5-d
- Conduct research: R1
- Support your claim: A2-d, A2-e, MLA-1c, APA-1c, CMS-1c
- Counter opposing arguments or objections: A2-f
- Identify the appropriate documentation style: A4-e, R4
- Integrate sources: MLA-3, APA-3, CMS-3
- Document your sources: MLA-4, APA-4, CMS-4
- Design and format your document: C5, MLA-5a, APA-5a, CMS-5a

various fields. In many disciplines, for example, writers might discuss disasters. The following are some questions that writers in different fields might ask about this subject.

EDUCATION	Should the elementary school curriculum teach students how to cope in disasters?
FILM	How has the disaster film genre changed since the advent of computer-generated imagery (CGI) in the early 1970s?
HISTORY	How did the formation of the Canadian Red Cross reshape disaster relief in Canada?
ENGINEERING	What recent innovations in levee design are most promising?
PSYCHOLOGY	What are the most effective ways to identify and treat post-traumatic stress disorder (PTSD) in disaster survivors?

The questions you ask in any discipline will form the basis of the thesis for your paper. The questions themselves don't communicate a central idea, but they may lead you to one. For an education paper, for example, you might begin with the question "Should the elementary school curriculum teach students how to cope in disasters?" After considering the issues involved, you might draft the following working thesis.

School systems should adopt age-appropriate curriculum units that introduce children to the risks of natural and human-made disasters and that allow children to practise coping strategies.

Whenever you write for a university or college course, try to determine the kinds of questions scholars in the field might ask about a topic. You can find clues in assigned readings, lecture or discussion topics, e-mail discussion groups, and the paper assignment itself.

A4-c Understand the kinds of evidence writers in a discipline use.

Regardless of the discipline in which you're writing, you must support any claims you make with evidence—facts, statistics, examples and illustrations, visuals, expert opinion, and so on.

The kinds of evidence used in different disciplines commonly overlap. Students of geography, media studies, and political science, for example, might use census data to explore different topics. The evidence that one discipline values, however, might not be sufficient to support an interpretation or a conclusion in another field. You might use anecdotes or interviews in an anthropology paper, for example, but such evidence would be irrelevant in a biology lab report. The chart on page 103 lists the kinds of evidence typically used in various disciplines.

A4-d Become familiar with a discipline's language conventions.

Every discipline has a specialized vocabulary. As you read the articles and books in a field, you'll notice certain words and phrases that come up repeatedly. Sociologists, for example, use terms such as *independent variables*, *political opportunity resources*, and *dyads* to describe social phenomena; computer scientists might refer to *algorithm design* and *loop invariants* to describe programming methods. Practitioners in health fields such as nursing use terms like *treatment plan* and *systemic assessment* to describe patient care. Use discipline-specific terms only when you are certain that you and your readers fully understand their meaning.

In addition to vocabulary, many fields of study have developed specialized conventions for point of view and verb tense. See the chart on page 104.

Evidence typically used in various disciplines

Humanities: Literature, art, film, music, philosophy

- Passages of text or lines of a poem
- Details from an image, a film, or a work of art
- Passages of a musical composition
- Critical essays that analyze original works

Humanities: History

- Primary sources such as photographs, letters, maps, and government documents
- Scholarly books and articles that interpret evidence

Social sciences: Psychology, sociology, political science, anthropology

- Data from original experiments
- Results of field research such as interviews, observations, or surveys
- Statistics from government agencies
- Scholarly books and articles that interpret data from original experiments and from other researchers' studies

Sciences: Biology, chemistry, physics

- Data from original experiments
- Scholarly articles that report findings from experiments

A4-e Use a discipline's preferred citation style.

In any discipline, you must give credit to those whose ideas or words you have borrowed. Avoid plagiarism by citing sources honestly and accurately (see R3).

While all disciplines emphasize careful documentation, each follows a particular system of citation that its members have agreed on. Writers in the humanities usually use the system established by the Modern Language Association (MLA). Scholars in some social sciences, such as psychology and anthropology, follow the style guidelines of the American Psychological Association (APA); scholars in history and some humanities typically follow *The Chicago Manual of Style*. For guidance on using the MLA, APA, or *Chicago* (CMS) format, see MLA-4, APA-4, or CMS-4, respectively. (For CSE [Council of Science Editors] style, see hackerhandbooks.com/resdoc.)

Point of view and verb tense in academic writing

Point of view

- Writers of analytical or research essays in the humanities usually use the third-person point of view: *Austen presents . . .* or *Castel describes the battle as. . . .*

- Scientists and most social scientists, who depend on quantitative research to present findings, tend to use the third-person point of view: *The results indicated. . . .*

- Writers in the humanities and in some social sciences occasionally use the first person in discussing their own experience or in writing a personal narrative: *After spending two years interviewing families affected by the war, I began to understand that . . .* or *Every July as we approached the Bay of Fundy, we could sense. . . .*

Present or past tense

- Literature scholars use the present tense to discuss a text: *Hughes effectively dramatizes different views of minority assertiveness.* (See MLA-3.)

- Science and social science writers use the past tense to describe experiments and the present tense to discuss the findings: *In 2003, Berkowitz released the first double-blind placebo study. . . . These results paint a murky picture.* (See APA-3.)

- Writers in history use the present tense or the present perfect tense to discuss a text: *Shelby Foote describes the scene like this . . .* or *Shelby Foote has described the scene like this. . . .* (See CMS-3.)

A4-f Understand writing assignments in the disciplines.

When you are asked to write in a specific discipline, become familiar with the distinctive features of the writing in that discipline. Then read the assignment carefully and identify the purpose of the assignment and the types of evidence you are expected to use.

On the following pages are examples of assignments in four disciplines—psychology, business, biology, and nursing—along with excerpts from student papers that were written in response to the assignments.

MODELS   hackerhandbooks.com/writersref
> Model papers > APA literature review: Charat
> APA business proposal: Ratajczak
> CSE laboratory report: Johnson and Arnold
> APA nursing practice paper: Riss

Psychology

ASSIGNMENT: LITERATURE REVIEW

```
      ┌───── 1 ─────┐              ┌─ 2 ─┐
Write a literature review in which you report on and
┌─ 2 ─┐     ┌──────── 3 ────────┐     ┌──────── 1 ────────┐
evaluate the published research on a behavioural disorder.
```

1 Key terms
2 Purpose: to report on and evaluate a body of evidence
3 Evidence: research of other psychologists

ADHD IN BOYS VS. GIRLS   3

Always Out of Their Seats (and Fighting):

Why Are Boys Diagnosed with ADHD More Often Than Girls?

Attention deficit hyperactivity disorder (ADHD) is a commonly

diagnosed disorder in children that affects social, academic, or occupational

functioning. As the name suggests, its hallmark characteristics are

hyperactivity and lack of attention as well as impulsive behavior. For

decades, studies have focused on the causes, expression, prevalence, and

outcome of the disorder, but until recently very little research investigated

gender differences. In fact, until the early 1990s most research focused

exclusively on boys (Brown, Madan-Swain, & Baldwin, 1991), perhaps

because many more boys than girls are diagnosed with ADHD. Researchers

have speculated on the possible explanations for the disparity, citing

reasons such as true sex differences in the manifestation of the disorder's

symptoms, gender biases in those who refer children to clinicians, and

possibly even the diagnostic procedures themselves (Gaub & Carlson, 1997).

But the most persuasive reason is that ADHD is often a comorbid

condition—that is, it coexists with other behavior disorders that are not

diagnosed properly and that do exhibit gender differences.

It has been suggested that in the United States children are often

misdiagnosed as having ADHD when they actually suffer from a behavior

disorder such as conduct disorder (CD) or a combination of ADHD and

another behavior disorder (Disney, Elkins, McGue, & Iancono, 1999;

Lilienfeld & Waldman, 1990). Conduct disorder is characterized by negative

and criminal behavior in children and is highly correlated with adult

diagnoses of antisocial personality disorder (ASPD). This paper first

considers research that has dealt only with gender difference in the

Marginal annotations:

Background and explanation of writer's purpose.

Evidence from research the writer has reviewed.

APA citations and specialized language (*ADHD, comorbid*).

Thesis: writer's argument.

Two sources in one parenthetical citation are separated by a semicolon.

Marginal annotations indicate appropriate formatting and effective writing.

Business

ASSIGNMENT: PROPOSAL

Write a proposal, as a memo, for improving or adding a service at a company where you have worked. Address the pros and cons of your proposal; draw on relevant studies, research, and your knowledge of the company.

1 Key terms
2 Purpose: to analyze certain evidence and make a proposal based on that analysis
3 Appropriate evidence: relevant studies, research, personal experience

---

MEMORANDUM

To: Jay Crosson, Senior Vice President, Human Resources

From: Kelly Ratajczak, Intern, Purchasing Department

Subject: Proposal to Add a Wellness Program

Date: April 24, 2009

Writer's main idea.

Health care costs are rising. In the long run, implementing a wellness program in our corporate culture will decrease the company's health care costs.

Data from recent study as support for claim.

APA citation style, typical in business.

Business terms familiar to readers (costs, productivity, absenteeism).

Research indicates that nearly 70% of health care costs are from common illnesses related to high blood pressure, overweight, lack of exercise, high cholesterol, stress, poor nutrition, and other preventable health issues (Hall, 2006). Health care costs are a major expense for most businesses, and they do not reflect costs due to the loss of productivity or absenteeism. A wellness program would address most, if not all, of these health care issues and related costs.

Headings define sections of proposal.

Benefits of Healthier Employees

Not only would a wellness program substantially reduce costs associated with employee health care, but our company would prosper through many other benefits. Businesses that have wellness programs show a lower cost in production, fewer sick days, and healthier employees ("Workplace Health," 2006). Our healthier employees will help to cut not only our production and absenteeism costs but also potential costs such as higher

Biology

ASSIGNMENT: LABORATORY REPORT

Write a report on an experiment you conduct on the distribution pattern of a plant species indigenous to the Northeast. Describe your methods for collecting data and interpret your experiment's results.

1 Key terms
2 Purpose: to describe and interpret the results of an experiment
3 Evidence: data collected during the experiment

Distribution Pattern of Dandelion 1

	CSE style, typical in sciences.

Distribution Pattern of Dandelion (*Taraxacum officinale*)

on an Abandoned Golf Course

ABSTRACT

This paper reports our study of the distribution pattern of the common dandelion (*Taraxacum officinale*) on an abandoned golf course in Hilton, NY, on 10 July 2005. An area of 6 ha was sampled with 111 randomly placed 1×1 m^2 quadrats. The dandelion count from each quadrat was used to test observed frequencies against expected frequencies based on a hypothesized random distribution. [Abstract continues.]

Abstract: an overview of hypothesis, experiment, and results.

Specialized language (aggregated, random, uniformly distributed).

INTRODUCTION

Theoretically, plants of a particular species may be aggregated, random, or uniformly distributed in space [1]. The distribution type may be determined by many factors, such as availability of nutrients, competition, distance of seed dispersal, and mode of reproduction [2].

The purpose of this study was to determine if the distribution pattern of the common dandelion (*Taraxacum officinale*) on an abandoned golf course was aggregated, random, or uniform.

Introduction: context and purpose of experiment. Instead of a thesis in the introduction, a lab report interprets the data in a later Discussion section.

METHODS

The study site was an abandoned golf course in Hilton, NY. The vegetation was predominantly grasses, along with dandelions, broad-leaf plantain (*Plantago major*), and bird's-eye speedwell (*Veronica chamaedrys*). We sampled an area of approximately 6 ha on 10 July 2005, approximately two weeks after the golf course had been mowed.

Scientific names for plant species.

Nursing

ASSIGNMENT: NURSING PRACTICE PAPER

Write a client history, a nursing diagnosis, recommendations

for care, your rationales, and expected and actual outcomes.

Use interview notes, the client's health records, and relevant

research findings.

1 Key terms
2 Purpose: to provide client history, diagnosis, recommendations, and outcomes
3 Evidence: interviews, health records, and research findings

---

ALL AND HTN IN ONE CLIENT   1

Acute Lymphoblastic Leukemia and Hypertension in One Client:
A Nursing Practice Paper

Physical History

> Evidence from client's medical chart for overall assessment.

E.B. is a 16-year-old white male 5'10" tall weighing 190 lb. He was
admitted to the hospital on April 14, 2006, due to decreased platelets and
a need for a PRBC transfusion. He was diagnosed in October 2005 with
T-cell acute lymphoblastic leukemia (ALL), after a 2-week period of
decreased energy, decreased oral intake, easy bruising, and petechia. The
client had experienced a 20-lb weight loss in the previous 6 months. At the
time of diagnosis, his CBC showed a WBC count of 32, an H & H of 13/38,
and a platelet count of 34,000. His initial chest X-ray showed an anterior

> Specialized nursing language (*echo-cardiogram, chemo-therapy*, and so on).

mediastinal mass. Echocardiogram showed a structurally normal heart. He
began induction chemotherapy on October 12, 2005, receiving
vincristine, 6-mercaptopurine, doxorubicin, intrathecal methotrexate, and
then high-dose methotrexate per protocol. During his hospital stay, he

> Instead of a thesis, or main claim, the writer gives a diagnosis, recommendations for care, and expected outcomes, all supported by evidence from observations and client records.

required packed red cells and platelets on two different occasions. He
was diagnosed with hypertension (HTN) due to systolic blood pressure
readings consistently ranging between 130s and 150s and was started on
nifedipine. E.B. has a history of mild ADHD, migraines, and deep vein
thrombosis (DVT). He has tolerated the induction and consolidation
phases of chemotherapy well and is now in the maintenance phase, in
which he receives a daily dose of mercaptopurine, weekly doses of
methotrexate, and intermittent doses of steroids.

Sentence Style

S Sentence Style

☰ **S1** Parallelism

If two or more ideas are parallel, they are easier to grasp when expressed in parallel grammatical form. Single words should be balanced with single words, phrases with phrases, clauses with clauses. In headings and lists, aim for as much parallelism as the content allows. (See C5-b and C5-c.) Writers often use parallelism to create emphasis. (See p. 134.)

A kiss can be a comma, a question mark, or an exclamation point.
— Mistinguett

This novel is not to be tossed lightly aside, but to be hurled with great force.
— Dorothy Parker

Politics is about compromise; business is about doing.
— Paul Martin

S1-a Balance parallel ideas in a series.

Readers expect items in a series to appear in parallel grammatical form. When one or more of the items violate readers' expectations, a sentence will be needlessly awkward.

▶ Children who study music also learn confidence, discipline, and
creativity.
~~they are creative.~~
 ^
The revision presents all the items in the series as nouns: *confidence*, *discipline*, and *creativity*.

▶ Impressionist painters believed in focusing on ordinary subjects,
using
capturing the effects of light on those subjects, and ~~to use~~ short
 ^
brushstrokes.

The revision uses *-ing* forms for all the items in the series: *focusing*, *capturing*, and *using*.

PRACTICE   hackerhandbooks.com/writersref
> Sentence style > S1–2 to S1–5

▶ Racing to get to work on time, Sam drove down the middle of the
                                  ignored
road, ran one red light, and two stop signs.
                                ^

The revision adds a verb to make the three items parallel: *drove*, *ran*, and *ignored*.

S1-b Balance parallel ideas presented as pairs.

When pairing ideas, underscore their connection by expressing them in similar grammatical form. Paired ideas are usually connected in one of these ways:

- with a coordinating conjunction such as *and*, *but*, or *or*
- with a pair of correlative conjunctions such as *either . . . or* or *not only . . . but also*
- with a word introducing a comparison, usually *than* or *as*

Parallel ideas linked with coordinating conjunctions

Coordinating conjunctions (*and*, *but*, *or*, *nor*, *for*, *so*, and *yet*) link ideas of equal importance. When those ideas are closely parallel in content, they should be expressed in parallel grammatical form.

▶ Emily Dickinson's poetry features the use of dashes and
    the capitalization of
   ~~capitalizing~~ common words.
  ^

The revision balances the nouns *use* and *capitalization*.

▶ Many cities are reducing property taxes for home owners
     extending
and ~~extend~~ financial aid in the form of tax credits to renters.
  ^

The revision balances the verb *reducing* with the verb *extending*.

Parallel ideas linked with correlative conjunctions

Correlative conjunctions come in pairs: *either . . . or, neither . . . nor, not only . . . but also, both . . . and, whether . . . or*. Make sure that the grammatical structure following the second half of the pair is the same as that following the first half.

▶ Thomas Edison was not only a prolific inventor but also ~~was~~

a successful entrepreneur.

The words *a prolific inventor* immediately follow *not only*, so *a successful entrepreneur* should follow *but also*. Repeating *was* after *also* creates an unbalanced effect.

$\overset{to}{}$
▶ The clerk told me either to change my flight or $\overset{\wedge}{\text{take}}$ the train.

To change, which follows *either*, should be balanced with *to take*, which follows *or*.

Comparisons linked with *than* or *as*

In comparisons linked with *than* or *as*, the elements being compared should be expressed in parallel grammatical structure.

$\overset{to\ ground}{}$
▶ It is easier to speak in abstractions than ~~grounding~~ $\overset{\wedge}{}$ one's

thoughts in reality.

To speak is balanced with *to ground*.

$\overset{writing}{}$
▶ In Pueblo culture, according to Silko, ~~to write~~ $\overset{\wedge}{}$ down the

stories of a tribe is not the same as "keeping track of all the

stories" (290).

> Writing
> with
> sources
> MLA-style
> citation

When you are quoting from a source, parallel grammatical structure—such as *writing . . . keeping*—helps create continuity between your sentence and the words from the source.

Comparisons should also be logical and grammatically complete. (See S2-c.)

S1-c Repeat function words to clarify parallels.

Function words such as prepositions (*by, to*) and subordinating conjunctions (*that, because*) signal the grammatical nature of the word groups to follow. Although you can sometimes omit such function words, be sure to include them whenever they signal parallel structures that readers might otherwise miss.

▶ Our study revealed that left-handed students were more likely
that
to have trouble with classroom desks and rearranging desks
^
for exam periods was useful.

A second subordinating conjunction helps readers sort out the two parallel ideas: *that* left-handed students have trouble with classroom desks and *that* rearranging desks was useful.

S2 Needed words

Sometimes writers leave out words intentionally, and the meaning of the sentence is not affected. But leaving out words can occasionally cause confusion for readers or make the sentence ungrammatical. Readers need to see at a glance how the parts of a sentence are connected.

ESL Languages sometimes differ in the need for certain words. In particular, be alert for missing articles, verbs, subjects, or expletives. See M2, M3-a, and M3-b.

S2-a Add words needed to complete compound structures.

In compound structures, words are often left out for economy: *Tom is a man who means what he says and [who] says what he means.* Such omissions are acceptable as long as the omitted words are common to both parts of the compound structure.

If a sentence defies grammar or idiom because an omitted word is not common to both parts of the compound structure, the simplest solution is to put the word back in.

▶ Successful advertisers target customers whom they identify through
who
demographic research or have purchased their product in the past.
^
The word *who* must be included because *whom . . . have purchased* is not grammatically correct.

accepted
▶ Mayor Davis never has and never will accept a bribe.
^
Has . . . accept is not grammatically correct.

> *in*
> ▶ Many South Pacific islanders still believe and live by ancient laws.
> ⌃

Believe . . . by is not idiomatic in English. (For a list of common idioms, see W5-d.)

NOTE: Even when the omitted word is common to both parts of the compound structure, occasionally it must be repeated to avoid ambiguity.

My favourite *professor* and *mentor* influenced my career choice. [Professor and mentor are the same person.]

My favourite *professor* and *my mentor* influenced my career choice. [Professor and mentor are two different people; *my* must be repeated.]

S2-b Add the word *that* if there is any danger of misreading without it.

If there is no danger of misreading, the word *that* may be omitted when it introduces a subordinate clause. *The value of a principle is the number of things [that] it will explain.* Occasionally, however, a sentence might be misread without *that*.

> ▶ In his famous obedience experiments, psychologist Stanley
> *that*
> Milgram discovered ordinary people were willing to inflict
> ⌃
> physical pain on strangers.

Milgram didn't discover ordinary people; he discovered that ordinary people were willing to inflict pain on strangers. The word *that* tells readers to expect a clause, not just *ordinary people*, as the direct object of *discovered*.

S2-c Add words needed to make comparisons logical and complete.

Comparisons should be made between items that are alike. To compare unlike items is illogical and distracting.

> ▶ The forests of North America are much more extensive than
> *those of*
> Europe.
> ⌃

Forests must be compared with forests, not with all of Europe.

▶ ~~The death rate of~~ <u>I</u>nfantry soldiers ~~is~~ generally much higher than <u>die at a</u> <u>rate</u>

other combat troops.

The death rate cannot logically be compared with troops. The writer could revise the sentence by inserting *that of* after *than*, but the revision shown here is more concise.

▶ Some say that Ella Fitzgerald's renditions of Cole Porter's songs
are better than any other ~~singer.~~ *singer's.*

Ella Fitzgerald's renditions cannot logically be compared with a singer. The revision uses the possessive form *singer's*, with the word *renditions* being implied.

Sometimes the word *other* must be inserted to make a comparison logical.

▶ Jupiter is larger than any *other* planet in our solar system.

Jupiter is a planet, and it cannot be larger than itself.

Sometimes the word *as* must be inserted to make a comparison grammatically complete.

▶ The city of Lowell is as old, *as* if not older than, the neighbouring city

of Lawrence.

The construction *as old* is not complete without a second *as*: *as old as . . . the neighbouring city of Lawrence.*

Comparisons should be complete enough to ensure clarity. The reader should understand what is being compared.

INCOMPLETE   Brand X is less salty.

COMPLETE   Brand X is less salty than Brand Y.

Finally, comparisons should leave no ambiguity for readers. If more than one interpretation is possible, revise the sentence to state clearly which interpretation you intend. In the following ambiguous sentence, two interpretations are possible.

AMBIGUOUS   Ken helped me more than my roommate.

CLEAR   Ken helped me more than *he helped* my roommate.

CLEAR   Ken helped me more than my roommate *did*.

S2-d Add the articles *a*, *an*, and *the* where necessary for grammatical completeness.

It is not always necessary to repeat articles with paired items: *We bought a computer and printer.* However, if one of the items requires *a* and the other requires *an*, both articles must be included.

▶ We bought a computer and ^an^ antivirus program.

Articles are sometimes omitted in recipes and other instructions that are meant to be followed while they are being read. In nearly all other forms of writing, whether formal or informal, such omissions are inappropriate.

> **ESL**   Choosing and using articles can be challenging for multi-lingual writers. See M2.

S3 Problems with modifiers

Modifiers, whether they are single words, phrases, or clauses, should point clearly to the words they modify. As a rule, related words should be kept together.

S3-a Put limiting modifiers in front of the words they modify.

Limiting modifiers such as *only*, *even*, *almost*, *nearly*, and *just* should appear in front of a verb only if they modify the verb: *At first, I couldn't even touch my toes, much less grasp them.* If modifiers limit the meaning of some other word in the sentence, they should be placed in front of that word.

▶ St. Vitus Cathedral, commissioned by Charles IV in the
mid-fourteenth century, ~~almost~~ ^almost^ took six centuries to complete.

Almost limits the meaning of *six centuries*, not *took*.

PRACTICE   hackerhandbooks.com/writersref
> Sentence style > S3–3 to S3–5

▶ If you ~~just~~ interview *just* chemistry majors, your picture of the

student body's response to the new grading policies will be

incomplete.

The adverb *just* limits the meaning of *chemistry majors*, not *interview*.

When the limiting modifier *not* is misplaced, the sentence usually suggests a meaning the writer did not intend.

▶ ~~All~~ *Not all* of Canada's coal ~~does not come~~ *comes* from Alberta.

The original sentence says that no coal comes from Alberta. The revision makes the writer's real meaning clear: Some (but not all) of Canada's coal comes from Alberta.

S3-b Place phrases and clauses so that readers can see at a glance what they modify.

Although phrases and clauses can appear at some distance from the words they modify, make sure your meaning is clear. When phrases or clauses are oddly placed, absurd misreadings can result.

MISPLACED	The soccer player returned to the clinic where he had undergone emergency surgery in 2009 in a limousine sent by Adidas.
REVISED	Travelling in a limousine sent by Adidas, the soccer player returned to the clinic where he had undergone emergency surgery in 2009.

The revision corrects the false impression that the soccer player underwent emergency surgery in a limousine.

▶ ~~There~~ *On the walls* are many pictures of comedians who have performed at

Gavin's. ~~on the walls.~~

The comedians weren't performing on the walls; the pictures were on the walls.

▶ The robber was described as ~~a~~ *an eighty-kilogram* man with a heavy mustache.

~~weighing eighty kilograms.~~

The robber, not the mustache, weighed eighty kilograms.

Occasionally the placement of a modifier leads to an ambiguity—a squinting modifier. In such a case, two revisions will be possible, depending on the writer's intended meaning.

AMBIGUOUS   The exchange students we met for coffee occasionally questioned us about our latest slang.

CLEAR   The exchange students we occasionally met for coffee questioned us about our latest slang.

CLEAR   The exchange students we met for coffee questioned us occasionally about our latest slang.

In the original version, it was not clear whether the meeting or the questioning happened occasionally. Both revisions eliminate the ambiguity.

S3-c Move awkwardly placed modifiers.

As a rule, a sentence should flow from subject to verb to object, without lengthy detours along the way. When a long adverbial word group separates a subject from its verb, a verb from its object, or a helping verb from its main verb, the result is often awkward.

▶ ~~Hong Kong,~~ *A*fter more than 150 years of British rule, *Hong Kong* was

transferred back to Chinese control in 1997.

There is no reason to separate the subject, *Hong Kong*, from the verb, *was transferred*, with a long phrase.

▶ ~~Donez Xiques discusses,~~ *I*n her biography of Margaret Laurence,
Donez Xiques discusses
the writer's frequent theme of "the significance of freedom and

responsibility" (149).

Writing with sources
MLA-style citation

When you quote from a source, the phrase or clause that you use to introduce the source should be as straightforward as possible. There is no reason to separate the verb, *discusses*, from its object, *theme*, with two prepositional phrases.

> **ESL**   English does not allow an adverb to appear between a verb and its object. See M3-f.
>
> *easily*
> ▶ Yolanda lifted ~~easily~~ the twenty-five-kilogram weight.

S3-d Avoid split infinitives when they are awkward.

An infinitive consists of *to* plus the base form of a verb: *to think*, *to run*, *to dance*. When a modifier appears between *to* and the verb, an infinitive is said to be "split": *to carefully balance, to completely understand*.

When a long word or a phrase appears between the parts of the infinitive, the result is usually awkward.

▶ The patient should try to ~~if possible~~ avoid putting weight on
   If possible, the
his foot.

Attempts to avoid split infinitives can result in equally awkward sentences. When alternative phrasing sounds unnatural, most experts allow—and even encourage—splitting the infinitive.

AWKWARD   We decided actually to enforce the law.

BETTER   We decided to actually enforce the law.

At times, neither the split infinitive nor its alternative sounds particularly awkward. In such situations, it is usually better to unsplit the infinitive, especially in formal writing.

▶ Nursing students learn to ~~accurately~~ record a patient's vital
               accurately.
signs/

S3-e Repair dangling modifiers.

A dangling modifier fails to refer logically to any word in the sentence. Dangling modifiers are easy to repair, but they can be hard to recognize, especially in your own writing.

Recognizing dangling modifiers

Dangling modifiers are usually word groups (such as verbal phrases) that suggest but do not name an actor. When a sentence opens with such a modifier, readers expect the subject of the next clause to name the actor. If it doesn't, the modifier dangles.

▶ Understanding the need to create checks and balances on power,
   the framers of
the Constitution divided the government into three branches.

PRACTICE hackerhandbooks.com/writersref
> Sentence style > S3–6 to S3–8

The framers of the Constitution (not the document itself) understood the need for checks and balances.

> women have often been denied
> ► After completing seminary training, ~~women's~~ access to the
>   ^
> priesthood. ~~has often been denied.~~
>   ^
> Women (not their access to the priesthood) complete the training.

The following sentences illustrate four common kinds of dangling modifiers.

DANGLING *Deciding to join the navy*, the recruiter enthusiastically pumped Joe's hand. [Participial phrase]

DANGLING *Upon entering the doctor's office*, a skeleton caught my attention. [Preposition followed by a gerund phrase]

DANGLING *To satisfy her mother*, the piano had to be practised every day. [Infinitive phrase]

DANGLING *Though not eligible for the clinical trial*, the doctor was willing to prescribe the drug for Ethan on compassionate grounds. [Elliptical clause with an understood subject and verb]

These dangling modifiers falsely suggest that the recruiter decided to join the navy, that the skeleton entered the doctor's office, that the piano intended to satisfy the mother, and that the doctor was not eligible for the clinical trial.

Although most readers will understand the writer's intended meaning in such sentences, the inadvertent humour can be distracting.

Repairing dangling modifiers

To repair a dangling modifier, you can revise the sentence in one of two ways:

- Name the actor in the subject of the sentence.
- Name the actor in the modifier.

Depending on your sentence, one of these revision strategies may be more appropriate than the other.

Checking for dangling modifiers

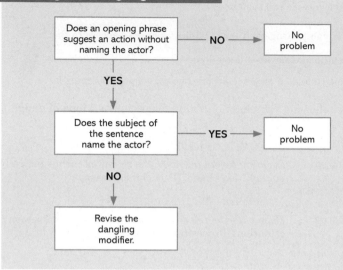

ACTOR NAMED IN SUBJECT

I noticed
▶ Upon entering the doctor's office, a skeleton. ~~caught my attention.~~
              ^   ^
Jing-mei had to practise
▶ To satisfy her mother, the piano ~~had to be practised~~ every day.
                 ^

ACTOR NAMED IN MODIFIER

When Joe decided
▶ ~~Deciding~~ to join the navy, the recruiter enthusiastically pumped
  ^
his
~~Joe's~~ hand.
 ^
Ethan was
▶ Though not eligible for the clinical trial, the doctor was willing to
  ^   *him*
prescribe the drug for ~~Ethan~~ on compassionate grounds.
                       ^

NOTE: You cannot repair a dangling modifier just by moving it. Consider, for example, the sentence about the skeleton. If you put the modifier at the end of the sentence (*A skeleton caught my attention upon entering the doctor's office*), you are still suggesting—absurdly, of course—that the skeleton entered the office. The only way to avoid the problem is to put the word *I* in the sentence, either as the subject or in the modifier.

I noticed
▶ Upon entering the doctor's office, a skeleton. ~~caught my attention.~~
                    ^   ^

As I entered
▶ ~~Upon entering~~ the doctor's office, a skeleton caught my attention.
   ^

▤ S4 Shifts

The following sections can help you avoid unnecessary shifts that might distract or confuse your readers: shifts in point of view, in verb tense, in mood or voice, or from indirect to direct questions or quotations.

S4-a Make the point of view consistent in person and number.

The point of view of a piece of writing is the perspective from which it is written: first person (*I* or *we*), second person (*you*), or third person (*he, she, it, one, they,* or any noun).

The *I* (or *we*) point of view, which emphasizes the writer, is a good choice for informal letters and writing based primarily on personal experience. The *you* point of view, which emphasizes the reader, works well for giving advice or explaining how to do something. The third-person point of view, which emphasizes the subject, is appropriate in formal academic and professional writing.

Writers who are having difficulty settling on an appropriate point of view sometimes shift confusingly from one to another. The solution is to choose a suitable perspective and then stay with it.

▶ Our class practised rescuing a victim trapped in a wrecked car.
                                                              We
  We learned to dismantle the car with the essential tools. ~~You~~ were
              our   *our*   ^
  graded on ~~your~~ speed and ~~your~~ skill in freeing the victim.
            ^   ^

The writer should have stayed with the *we* point of view. *You* is inappropriate because the writer is not addressing readers directly. *You* should not be used in a vague sense meaning "anyone." (See G3-b.)

You need
▶ ~~One needs~~ a password and a credit card number to access the
  ^
  database. You will be billed at an hourly rate.

You is appropriate because the writer is giving advice directly to readers.

▶ According to the US National Institute of Mental Health (2007),
children
~~a child~~ with attention deficit hyperactivity disorder may have trouble
   ^

sitting still and may gradually stop paying attention to their teachers

(Symptoms section, para. 2).

In describing reports or results of studies, writers are often tempted to generalize with singular nouns, such as *child*, and then later in the passage find
themselves shifting from singular to plural. Here the writer might have
changed *their* to the singular *his or her* to agree with *child*, but the revision
making both terms plural is more concise. (See also W4-e and G3-a.)

S4-b Maintain consistent verb tenses.

Consistent verb tenses clearly establish the time of the actions being described. When a passage begins in one tense and shifts without warning
and for no reason to another, readers are distracted and confused.

▶ There was no way I could fight the current and win. Just as I was
                            jumped   *swam*
losing hope, a stranger ~~jumps~~ off a passing boat and ~~swims~~
                          ^   ^

toward me.

The writer thought that the present tense (*jumps, swims*) would convey
immediacy and drama. But having begun in the past tense (*could fight, was
losing*), the writer should follow through in the past tense.

Writers often encounter difficulty with verb tenses when writing
about literature. Because fictional events occur outside the time frames
of real life, the past tense and the present tense may seem equally
appropriate. The literary convention, however, is to describe fictional
events consistently in the present tense. (See p. 192.)

▶ The scarlet letter is a punishment sternly placed on Hester's
                                      is
breast by the community, and yet it ~~was~~ a fanciful and
                                      ^

imaginative product of Hester's own needlework.

S4-c Make verbs consistent in mood and voice.

Unnecessary shifts in the mood of a verb can be distracting and confusing
to readers. There are three moods in English: the *indicative*, used for facts,
opinions, and questions; the *imperative*, used for orders or advice; and the

subjunctive, used in certain contexts to express wishes or conditions contrary to fact (see G2-g).

The following passage shifts confusingly from the indicative to the imperative mood.

▶ The counsellor advised us to spread out our core requirements over
two or three semesters. ~~Also,~~ *She also suggested that we* pay attention to prerequisites for
elective courses.

The writer began by reporting the counsellor's advice in the indicative mood (*counsellor advised*) and switched to the imperative mood (*pay attention*); the revision puts both sentences in the indicative.

A verb may be in either the active voice (with the subject doing the action) or the passive voice (with the subject receiving the action). (See W3-a.) If a writer shifts without warning from one to the other, readers may be left wondering why.

▶ Each student completes a self-assessment, *gives it* ~~The self-assessment~~
~~is then given~~ *exchanges* to the teacher, and a copy ~~is exchanged~~ with a
classmate.

Because the passage began in the active voice (*student completes*) and then switched to the passive (*self-assessment is given, copy is exchanged*), readers are left wondering who gives the self-assessment to the teacher and the classmate. The active voice, which is clearer and more direct, leaves no ambiguity.

S4-d Avoid sudden shifts from indirect to direct questions or quotations.

An indirect question reports a question without asking it: *We asked whether we could visit Miriam.* A direct question asks directly: *Can we visit Miriam?* Sudden shifts from indirect to direct questions are awkward. In addition, sentences containing such shifts are impossible to punctuate because indirect questions must end with a period and direct questions must end with a question mark. (See P6-a.)

▶ I wonder whether Karla knew of the theft and, if so, ~~did she report~~ *whether she reported* it
to the police.

The revision poses both questions indirectly. The writer could also ask both questions directly: *Did Karla know of the theft, and, if so, did she report it to the police?*

An indirect quotation reports someone's words without quoting word-for-word: *Annabelle said that she is a Virgo.* A direct quotation presents the exact words of a speaker or writer, set off with quotation marks: *Annabelle said, "I am a Virgo."* Unannounced shifts from indirect to direct quotations are distracting and confusing, especially when the writer fails to insert the necessary quotation marks, as in the following example.

▶ The patient said she had been experiencing heart palpitations and
asked me to   *was*
~~please~~ run as many tests as possible to find out what̶'̶s̶ wrong.
^   ^
The revision reports the patient's words indirectly. The writer also could quote the words directly: *The patient said, "I have been experiencing heart palpitations. Please run as many tests as possible to find out what's wrong."*

S5 Mixed constructions

A mixed construction contains sentence parts that do not sensibly fit together. The mismatch may be a matter of grammar or of logic.

S5-a Untangle the grammatical structure.

Once you begin a sentence, your choices are limited by the range of grammatical patterns in English. (See B2 and B3.) You cannot begin with one grammatical plan and switch without warning to another. Often you must rethink the purpose of the sentence and revise.

MIXED   For most drivers who have a blood alcohol level of
0.05 percent double their risk of causing an accident.

The writer begins the sentence with a long prepositional phrase and makes it the subject of the verb *double*. But a prepositional phrase can serve only as a modifier; it cannot be the subject of a sentence.

REVISED   For most drivers who have a blood alcohol level of
0.05 percent, the risk of causing an accident is doubled.

REVISED   Most drivers who have a blood alcohol level of
0.05 percent double their risk of causing an accident.

PRACTICE   hackerhandbooks.com/writersref
> Sentence style > S5–2 to S5–4

In the first revision, the writer begins with the prepositional phrase and finishes the sentence with a proper subject and verb (*risk . . . is doubled*). In the second revision, the writer stays with the original verb (*double*) and heads into the sentence another way, making *drivers* the subject of *double*.

▶ ~~When the country elects~~ *Electing* a governing party is the most important
    ^

responsibility in a democracy.

The adverb clause *When the country elects a governing party* cannot serve as the subject of the verb *is*. The revision replaces the adverb clause with a gerund phrase, a word group that can function as a subject. (See B3-e and B3-b.)

▶ Although Canada is one of the wealthiest nations in the world,

~~but~~ more than one million of our children live in poverty.

The coordinating conjunction *but* cannot link a subordinate clause (*Although Canada . . .*) with an independent clause (*more than one million of our children live in poverty*).

Occasionally a mixed construction is so tangled that it defies grammatical analysis. When this happens, back away from the sentence, rethink what you want to say, and then rewrite the sentence.

MIXED   In the whole-word method, children learn to recognize entire words rather than by the phonics method in which they learn to sound out letters and groups of letters.

REVISED   The whole-word method teaches children to recognize entire words; the phonics method teaches them to sound out letters and groups of letters.

ESL English does not allow double subjects, nor does it allow an object or an adverb to be repeated in an adjective clause. Unlike some other languages, English does not allow a noun and a pronoun to be repeated in a sentence if they have the same grammatical function. See M3-c and M3-d.

▶ My father ~~he~~ moved to Peru before he met my mother.

▶ ~~The final exam~~ I should really study for ~~it~~ *the final exam* to pass the course.
                                                ^

S5-b Straighten out the logical connections.

The subject and the predicate (the verb and its modifiers) should make sense together; when they don't, the error is known as *faulty predication.*

>   *Tiffany*
> ▶ We decided that ~~Tiffany's welfare~~ would not be safe living
>   ^
> with her mother.

Tiffany, not her welfare, would not be safe.

>   *the double personal exemption for*
> ▶ Under the revised plan, seniors/~~who now receive a double~~
>   ^
> ~~personal exemption,~~ will be abolished.

The exemption, not seniors, will be abolished.

An appositive is a noun that renames a nearby noun. When an appositive and the noun it renames are not logically equivalent, the error is known as *faulty apposition.* (See B3-c.)

>   *Tax accounting,*
> ▶ ~~The tax accountant,~~ a very lucrative profession, requires intelligence,
>   ^
> patience, and attention to mathematical detail.

The tax accountant is a person, not a profession.

S5-c Avoid *is when, is where,* and *reason . . . is because* constructions.

In formal English, readers sometimes object to *is when, is where,* and *reason . . . is because* constructions on grammatical or logical grounds.

> ▶ The ~~reason the~~ experiment failed ~~is~~ because conditions in the lab
> were not sterile.

Grammatically, the verb *is* should not be followed by an adverb clause beginning with *because.* (See B2-b and B3-e.) The writer might have changed *because* to *that* (*The reason the experiment failed is that conditions in the lab were not sterile*), but the preceding revision is more concise.

>   *a disorder suffered by people who*
> ▶ Anorexia nervosa is ~~where people~~ think they are too fat and diet
>   ^
> to the point of starvation.

Where refers to places. Anorexia nervosa is a disorder, not a place.

S6 Sentence emphasis

Within each sentence, emphasize your point by expressing it in the subject and verb of an independent clause, the words that receive the most attention from readers (see S6-a to S6-e).

Within longer stretches of prose, you can draw attention to ideas that deserve special emphasis by using a variety of techniques, often involving an unusual twist or some element of surprise (see S6-f).

S6-a Coordinate equal ideas; subordinate minor ideas.

When combining two or more ideas in one sentence, you have two choices: coordination or subordination. Choose coordination to indicate that the ideas are equal or nearly equal in importance. Choose subordination to indicate that one idea is less important than another.

Coordination

Coordination draws attention equally to two or more ideas. To coordinate single words or phrases, join them with a coordinating conjunction or with a pair of correlative conjunctions: bananas *and* strawberries; *not only* a lackluster plot *but also* inferior acting (see B1-g).

To coordinate independent clauses—word groups that express a complete thought and that can stand alone as a sentence—join them with a comma and a coordinating conjunction (*and, but, or, nor, for, so, yet*) or with a semicolon. The semicolon is often accompanied by a conjunctive adverb such as *moreover, furthermore, therefore,* or *however* or by a transitional phrase such as *for example, in other words,* or *as a matter of fact*. (For longer lists, see P3-a.)

> Social networking Web sites offer ways for people to connect in the virtual world, but they do not replace face-to-face social interaction.

> Social networking Web sites offer ways for people to connect in the virtual world; however, they do not replace face-to-face social interaction.

Subordination

To give unequal emphasis to two or more ideas, express the major idea in an independent clause and place any minor ideas in subordinate clauses or phrases. (See B3.) Subordinate clauses, which cannot stand alone, typically begin with one of the following subordinating conjunctions or relative pronouns.

after	since	whether
although	so that	which
as	that	while
as if	though	who
because	unless	whom
before	until	whose
even though	when	
if	where	

Let your intended meaning determine which idea you emphasize. Consider the two ideas about social networking Web sites.

Social networking Web sites offer ways for people to connect in the virtual world. They do not replace face-to-face social interaction.

If your purpose is to stress the ways that people can connect in the virtual world rather than the limitations of these connections, subordinate the idea about the limitations.

Although they do not replace face-to-face social interaction, social networking Web sites offer ways for people to connect in the virtual world.

To focus on the limitations of the virtual world, subordinate the idea about the Web sites.

Although social networking Web sites offer ways for people to connect in the virtual world, they do not replace face-to-face social interaction.

S6-b Combine choppy sentences.

Short sentences demand attention, so you should use them primarily for emphasis. Too many short sentences, one after the other, make for a choppy style.

If an idea is not important enough to deserve its own sentence, try combining it with a sentence close by. Put any minor ideas in subordinate structures such as phrases or subordinate clauses. (See B3.)

▶ The Parks Department keeps the use of insecticides to a minimum/
  because the
  ~~The~~ city is concerned about the environment.
  ^

The writer wanted to emphasize that the Parks Department minimizes its use of chemicals, so she put the reason in a subordinate clause beginning with *because*.

▶ The Great Lakes St. Lawrence Seaway, ~~is~~ a 3700-kilometre
 ^
waterway that opened in 1959. ~~It~~ is a major source of
 ^
transportation for goods in North America.

A minor idea is now expressed in an appositive phrase (*a 3700-kilometre waterway that opened in 1959*).

 E
▶ ~~Sister Consilio was~~ ἐnveloped in a black robe with only her face and
 ^
 Sister Consilio
hands visible. ~~She~~ was an imposing figure.
 ^

Because Sister Consilio's overall impression was more important to the writer's purpose, the writer put the description of the clothing in a participial phrase beginning with *Enveloped*.

Although subordination is ordinarily the most effective technique for combining short, choppy sentences, coordination is appropriate when the ideas are equal in importance.

 and
▶ At 3:30 p.m., Forrest displayed a flag of truce. ~~Forrest~~ sent in a
 ^
demand for unconditional surrender.

Combining two short sentences by joining their predicates (*displayed . . . sent*) is an effective coordination technique.

ESL Unlike some other languages, English does not repeat objects or adverbs in adjective clauses. The relative pronoun (*that, which, whom*) or relative adverb (*where*) in the adjective clause represents the object or adverb. See M3-d.

▶ The apartment that we rented ~~it~~ needed repairs.

The pronoun *it* cannot repeat the relative pronoun *that*.

▶ The small town where my grandfather was born ~~there~~ is now

a big city.

The adverb *there* cannot repeat the relative adverb *where*.

S6-c Avoid ineffective or excessive coordination.

Coordinate structures are appropriate only when you intend to draw readers' attention equally to two or more ideas: *Professor Sakellarios praises loudly, and she criticizes softly.* If one idea is more important than another—or if a coordinating conjunction does not clearly signal the relationship between the ideas—you should subordinate the less important idea.

| INEFFECTIVE COORDINATION | Closets were taxed as rooms, and most colonists stored their clothes in chests or clothespresses. |
| IMPROVED WITH SUBORDINATION | Because closets were taxed as rooms, most colonists stored their clothes in chests or clothespresses. |

Because it is so easy to string ideas together with *and*, writers often rely too heavily on coordination in their rough drafts. Revising for excessive coordination is important: Look for opportunities to tuck minor ideas into subordinate clauses or phrases.

> *After four hours,*
> ▶ ~~Four hours went by, and~~ a rescue truck finally arrived, but by that
>   ^
> time we had been evacuated in a helicopter.

Three independent clauses were excessive. The least important idea has become a prepositional phrase.

S6-d Do not subordinate major ideas.

If a sentence buries its major idea in a subordinate construction, readers may not give the idea enough attention. Make sure to express your major idea in an independent clause and to subordinate any minor ideas.

> *defeated Louis St-Laurent,*
> ▶ John Diefenbaker, who was the unexpected winner of the 1957
>   ^
> federal election /. ~~defeated Louis St-Laurent.~~
>   ^

The writer wanted to focus on Diefenbaker's unexpected victory, but the original sentence buried this information in an adjective clause. The revision puts the more important idea in an independent clause and tucks the less important idea into an adjective clause (*who defeated Louis St-Laurent*).

> *As*
> ▶ I was driving home from my new job, heading down Hougue
>   ^
> Road, ~~when~~ my car suddenly overheated.

The writer wanted to emphasize that the car overheated, not the fact of driving home. The revision expresses the major idea in an independent clause and places the less important idea in an adverb clause (*As I was driving home from my new job*).

S6-e Do not subordinate excessively.

In attempting to avoid short, choppy sentences, writers sometimes go to the opposite extreme, putting more subordinate ideas into a sentence than its structure can bear. Sentences that become too complicated can sometimes be restructured. More often, however, such sentences must be divided.

▶ In *Animal Liberation*, Peter Singer argues that animals possess
nervous systems and can feel pain. ~~and that~~ H̶e therefore believes
that "the ethical principle on which human equality rests requires
us to extend equal consideration to animals" (1).

Writing with sources

MLA-style citation

Excessive subordination makes it difficult for the reader to focus on the quoted passage. By splitting the original sentence into two separate sentences, the writer draws attention to Peter Singer's main claim, that animals should be given "equal consideration" to humans.

S6-f Experiment with techniques for gaining special emphasis.

By experimenting with certain techniques, usually involving some element of surprise, you can draw attention to ideas that deserve special emphasis. Use such techniques sparingly, however, or they will lose their punch. The writer who tries to emphasize everything ends up emphasizing nothing.

Using sentence endings for emphasis

You can highlight an idea simply by withholding it until the end of a sentence. The technique works something like a punch line. In the following example, the sentence's meaning is not revealed until its very last word.

> The only completely consistent people are the dead.
>
> — Aldous Huxley

Using parallel structure for emphasis

Parallel grammatical structure draws special attention to paired ideas or to items in a series. (See S1.) When parallel ideas are paired, the emphasis falls on words that underscore comparisons or contrasts, especially when they occur at the end of a phrase or clause.

> *Americans* are *benevolently ignorant* about Canada, while *Canadians* are *malevolently well informed* about the United States.
>
> — J. Bartlet Brebner

In a parallel series, the emphasis falls at the end, so it is generally best to end with the most dramatic or climactic item in the series.

> Sister Charity enjoyed passing out writing punishments: translate the Ten Commandments into Latin, type a thousand-word essay on good manners, copy the New Testament with a quill pen.
>
> —Marie Visosky, student

Using an occasional short sentence for emphasis

Too many short sentences in a row will fast become monotonous (see S6-b), but an occasional short sentence, when played off against longer sentences in the same passage, will draw attention to an idea.

> The women who have achieved success in the various fields of labour have won the victory for us, but unless we all follow up and press onward the advantage will be lost. Yesterday's successes will not do for today!   —Nellie McClung

▤ **S7** Sentence variety

When a rough draft is filled with too many sentences that begin the same way or have the same structure, try injecting some variety—as long as you can do so without sacrificing clarity or ease of reading.

S7-a Use a variety of sentence structures.

A writer should not rely too heavily on simple sentences and compound sentences, for the effect tends to be both monotonous and choppy. (See S6-b and S6-c.) Too many complex or compound-complex sentences, however, can be equally monotonous. If your style tends to one or the other extreme, try to achieve a better mix of sentence types.

For a discussion of sentence types, see B4-a.

S7-b Vary your sentence openings.

Most sentences in English begin with the subject, move to the verb, and continue to the object, with modifiers tucked in along the way or put at the end. For the most part, such sentences are fine. Put too many of them in a row, however, and they become monotonous.

Adverbial modifiers are easily movable when they modify verbs; they can often be inserted ahead of the subject. Such modifiers might be single words, phrases, or clauses.

▶ *Eventually a*
  A few drops of sap ~~eventually~~ began to trickle into the bucket.

Like most adverbs, *eventually* does not need to appear close to the verb it modifies (*began*).

▶ *Just as the sun was coming up, a*
  A pair of black ducks flew over the pond. ~~just as the sun was~~

~~coming up.~~

The adverb clause, which modifies the verb *flew*, is as clear at the beginning of the sentence as it is at the end.

Adjectives and participial phrases can frequently be moved to the beginning of a sentence without loss of clarity.

▶ *Dejected and withdrawn,*
  Edward/~~dejected and withdrawn,~~ nearly gave up his search

for a job.

▶   *A*   *John and I*
  ~~John and I,~~ Anticipating a peaceful evening, sat down at the

campfire to brew a cup of coffee.

TIP: When beginning a sentence with an adjective or a participial phrase, make sure that the subject of the sentence names the person or thing described in the introductory phrase. If it doesn't, the phrase will dangle. (See S3-e.)

S7-c Try inverting sentences occasionally.

A sentence is inverted if it does not follow the normal subject-verb-object pattern. Many inversions sound artificial and should be avoided except in the most formal contexts. But if an inversion sounds natural, it can provide a welcome touch of variety.

> *Opposite the produce section is a*
> Ⱥ refrigerated case of cheeses. ~~is opposite the produce section.~~
>   ^   ^

The revision inverts the normal subject-verb order by moving the verb, *is*, ahead of its subject, *case*.

> *Placed at the top two corners of the stage were huge*
> ~~Huge~~ lavender hearts outlined in bright white lights. ~~were~~
>   ^   ^
> ~~at the top two corners of the stage.~~

In the revision, the subject, *hearts*, appears after the verb, *were placed*. The two parts of the verb are also inverted—and separated from each other (*Placed . . . were*)—without any awkwardness or loss of meaning.

Inverted sentences are used for emphasis as well as for variety (see S6-f).

W

Word Choice

W Word Choice

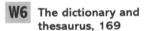

W1 Glossary of usage

This glossary includes words commonly confused (such as *accept* and *except*), words commonly misused (such as *aggravate*), and words that are nonstandard (such as *hisself*). It also lists colloquialisms and jargon. Colloquialisms are casual expressions that may be appropriate in informal speech but are inappropriate in formal writing. Jargon is needlessly technical or pretentious language that is inappropriate in most contexts. If an item is not listed here, consult the index. For irregular verbs (such as *sing, sang, sung*), see G2-a. For idiomatic use of prepositions, see W5-d.

a, an Use *an* before a vowel sound, *a* before a consonant sound: *an apple*, *a peach*. Problems sometimes arise with words beginning with *h* or *u*. If the *h* is silent, the word begins with a vowel sound, so use *an*: *an hour*, *an honourable deed*. If the *h* is pronounced, the word begins with a consonant sound, so use *a*: *a hospital*, *a historian*, *a hotel*. Words such as *university* and *union* begin with a consonant sound (a *y* sound), so use *a*: *a union*. Words such as *uncle* and *umbrella* begin with a vowel sound, so use *an*: *an underground well*. When an abbreviation or an acronym begins with a vowel sound, use *an*: *an EKG*, *an MRI*, *an AIDS prevention program*.

accept, except *Accept* is a verb meaning "to receive." *Except* is usually a preposition meaning "excluding." *I will accept all the packages except that one. Except* is also a verb meaning "to exclude." *Please except that item from the list.*

adapt, adopt *Adapt* means "to adjust or become accustomed"; it is usually followed by *to. Adopt* means "to take as one's own." *Our family adopted a Vietnamese child, who quickly adapted to his new life.*

adverse, averse *Adverse* means "unfavourable." *Averse* means "opposed" or "reluctant"; it is usually followed by *to. I am averse to your proposal because it could have an adverse impact on the economy.*

advice, advise *Advice* is a noun, *advise* a verb. *We advise you to follow John's advice.*

affect, effect *Affect* is usually a verb meaning "to influence." *Effect* is usually a noun meaning "result." *The drug did not affect the disease, and it had adverse side effects. Effect* can also be a verb meaning "to bring about." *Only the president can effect such a dramatic change.*

aggravate *Aggravate* means "to make worse or more troublesome." *Overgrazing aggravated the soil erosion.* In formal writing, avoid the use of *aggravate* meaning "to annoy or irritate." *Her babbling annoyed* (not *aggravated*) *me.*

agree to, agree with *Agree to* means "to give consent to." *Agree with* means "to be in accord with" or "to come to an understanding with." *He agrees with me about the need for change, but he won't agree to my plan.*

ain't *Ain't* is nonstandard. Use *am not, are not (aren't)*, or *is not (isn't)*. *I am not* (not *ain't*) *going home for spring break.*

all ready, already *All ready* means "completely prepared." *Already* means "previously." *Susan was all ready for the concert, but her friends had already left.*

all right *All right* is written as two words. *Alright* is nonstandard.

all together, altogether *All together* means "everyone or everything in one place." *Altogether* means "entirely." *We were not altogether certain that we could bring the family all together for the reunion.*

allude To *allude* to something is to make an indirect reference to it. Do not use *allude* to mean "to refer directly." *In his lecture, the professor referred* (not *alluded*) *to several pre-Socratic philosophers.*

allusion, illusion An *allusion* is an indirect reference. An *illusion* is a misconception or false impression. *Did you catch my allusion to Shakespeare? Mirrors give the room an illusion of depth.*

a lot *A lot* is two words. Do not write *alot*. *Sam lost a lot of weight.* See also *lots, lots of*.

among, between See *between, among*.

amongst In Canadian English, *among* is preferred.

amoral, immoral *Amoral* means "neither moral nor immoral"; it also means "not caring about moral judgments." *Immoral* means "morally wrong." *Until recently, most business courses were taught from an amoral perspective. Murder is immoral.*

amount, number Use *amount* with quantities that cannot be counted; use *number* with those that can. *This recipe calls for a large amount of sugar. We have a large number of toads in our garden.*

an See *a, an*.

and etc. *Et cetera (etc.)* means "and so forth"; *and etc.* is redundant. See also *etc.*

and/or Avoid the awkward construction *and/or* except in technical or legal documents.

angry at, angry with Use *angry with*, not *angry at*, when referring to a person. *The coach was angry with the referee.*

ante-, anti- The prefix *ante-* means "earlier" or "in front of"; the prefix *anti-* means "against" or "opposed to." *The people running the antismoking* *campaign put up signs in the antechamber. Anti-* should be used with a hyphen when it is followed by a capital letter or a word beginning with *i*.

anxious *Anxious* means "worried" or "apprehensive." In formal writing, avoid using *anxious* to mean "eager." *We are eager* (not *anxious*) *to see your new house.*

anybody, anyone *Anybody* and *anyone* are singular. (See G1-e and G3-a.)

anymore Use the adverb *anymore* in a negative context to mean "any longer" or "now." *The factory isn't producing shoes anymore.* Using *anymore* in a positive context is colloquial; in formal writing, use *now* instead. *We order all our food online now* (not *anymore*).

anyone See *anybody, anyone.*

anyone, any one *Anyone*, an indefinite pronoun, means "any person at all." *Any one*, the pronoun *one* preceded by the adjective *any*, refers to a particular person or thing in a group. *Anyone from the winning team may choose any one of the games on display.*

anyplace In formal writing, use *anywhere*.

anyways, anywheres *Anyways* and *anywheres* are nonstandard. Use *anyway* and *anywhere*.

as Do not use *as* to mean "because" if there is any chance of ambiguity. *We cancelled the picnic because* (not *as*) *it began raining. As* here could mean either "because" or "when."

as, like See *like, as.*

as to *As to* is jargon for *about. He inquired about* (not *as to*) *the job.*

averse See *adverse, averse.*

awful The adjective *awful* and the adverb *awfully* are not appropriate in formal writing.

awhile, a while *Awhile* is an adverb; it can modify a verb, but it cannot be the object of a preposition such as *for*. The two-word form *a while* is a noun preceded by an article and therefore can be the object of a preposition. *Stay awhile. Stay for a while.*

back up, backup *Back up* is a verb phrase. *Back up the car carefully. Be sure to back up your hard drive. Backup* is a noun meaning "a copy of electronically stored data." *Keep your backup in a safe place. Backup* can also be used as an adjective. *I regularly create backup disks.*

bad, badly *Bad* is an adjective, *badly* an adverb. *They felt bad about ruining the surprise. Her arm hurt badly after she slid into second base.* (See G4-a and G4-b.)

being as, being that *Being as* and *being that* are nonstandard expressions. Write *because* instead. *Because* (not *Being as*) *I slept late, I had to skip breakfast.*

USAGE hackerhandbooks.com/writersref
> Language Debates > Pronoun-antecedent agreement
> *bad* versus *badly*

beside, besides *Beside* is a preposition meaning "at the side of" or "next to." *She kept a stack of books beside her bed. Besides* is a preposition meaning "except" or "in addition to." *No one besides Terrie can have that ice cream. Besides* is also an adverb meaning "in addition." *I'm not hungry; besides, I don't like ice cream.*

between, among Ordinarily, use *among* with three or more entities, *between* with two. *The prize was divided among several contestants. You have a choice between carrots and beans.*

bring, take Use *bring* when an object is being transported toward you, *take* when it is being moved away. *Please bring me a glass of water. Please take these forms to Mr. Scott.*

burst, bursted; bust, busted *Burst* is an irregular verb meaning "to come open or fly apart suddenly or violently." Its past tense is *burst*. The past-tense form *bursted* is nonstandard. The verbs *bust* and *busted* are slang for *burst* and, along with *bursted*, should not be used in formal writing.

can, may The distinction between *can* and *may* is fading, but some writers still observe it in formal writing. *Can* is traditionally reserved for ability, *may* for permission. *Can you fix the broken printer? May I help you?*

censor, censure *Censor* means "to remove or suppress material considered objectionable." *Censure* means "to criticize severely." *The administration's policy of censoring books has been censured by the media.*

cite, site *Cite* means "to quote as an authority or example." *Site* is usually a noun meaning "a particular place." *He cited the zoning law in his argument against the proposed site of the gas station.* Locations on the Internet are usually referred to as *sites. The library's Web site improves every week.*

climactic, climatic *Climactic* is derived from *climax*, the point of greatest intensity in a series or progression of events. *Climatic* is derived from *climate* and refers to meteorological conditions. *The climactic period in the dinosaurs' reign was reached just before severe climatic conditions brought on an ice age.*

coarse, course *Coarse* means "crude" or "rough in texture." *The coarse weave of the wall hanging gave it a three-dimensional quality. Course* usually refers to a path, a playing field, or a unit of study; the expression *of course* means "certainly." *I plan to take a course in car repair this summer. Of course, you are welcome to join me.*

compare to, compare with *Compare to* means "to represent as similar." *She compared him to a wild stallion. Compare with* means "to examine similarities and differences." *The study compared the language ability of apes with that of dolphins.*

complement, compliment *Complement* is a verb meaning "to go with or complete" or a noun meaning "something that completes." As a verb, *compliment* means "to flatter"; as a noun, it means "flattering remark." *Her* *skill at rushing the net complements his skill at volleying. Martha's flower arrangements receive many compliments.*

conscience, conscious *Conscience* is a noun meaning "moral principles." *Conscious* is an adjective meaning "aware or alert." *Let your conscience be your guide. Were you conscious of his love for you?*

continual, continuous *Continual* means "repeated regularly and frequently." *She grew weary of the continual telephone calls. Continuous* means "extended or prolonged without interruption." *The broken siren made a continuous wail.*

could care less *Could care less* is nonstandard. Write *couldn't care less* instead. *He couldn't* (not *could*) *care less about his psychology final.*

could of *Could of* is nonstandard for *could have*. *We could have* (not *could of*) *taken the train.*

council, counsel A *council* is a deliberative body, and a *councillor* is a member of such a body. *Counsel* usually means "advice" and can also mean "lawyer"; a *counsellor* is one who gives advice or guidance. *The councillors met to draft the council's position paper. The pastor offered wise counsel to the troubled teenager.*

criteria *Criteria* is the plural of *criterion*, which means "a standard or rule or test on which a judgment or decision can be based." *The only criterion for the scholarship is ability.*

data *Data* is a plural noun technically meaning "facts or results." But *data* is increasingly being accepted as a singular noun. *The new data suggest* (or *suggests*) *that our theory is correct.* (The singular *datum* is rarely used.)

different from, different than Ordinarily, write *different from. Your sense of style is different from Jim's.* However, *different than* is acceptable to avoid an awkward construction. *Please let me know if your plans are different than* (to avoid *from what*) *they were six weeks ago.*

differ from, differ with *Differ from* means "to be unlike"; *differ with* means "to disagree with." *My approach to the problem differed from hers. She differed with me about the wording of the agreement.*

disinterested, uninterested *Disinterested* means "impartial, objective"; *uninterested* means "not interested." *We sought the advice of a disinterested counsellor to help us solve our problem. Mark was uninterested in anyone's opinion but his own.*

don't *Don't* is the contraction for *do not. I don't want any. Don't* should not be used as the contraction for *does not*, which is *doesn't. He doesn't* (not *don't*) *want any.*

due to *Due to* is an adjective phrase and should not be used as a preposition meaning "because of." *The trip was cancelled because of* (not *due to*) *lack of interest. Due to* is acceptable as a subject complement and usually follows a form of the verb *be. His success was due to hard work.*

each *Each* is singular. (See G1-e and G3-a.)

effect See *affect, effect*.

e.g. In formal writing, replace the Latin abbreviation *e.g.* with its English equivalent: *for example* or *for instance*.

either *Either* is singular. (See G1-e and G3-a.) For *either . . . or* constructions, see G1-d and G-3a.

elicit, illicit *Elicit* is a verb meaning "to bring out" or "to evoke." *Illicit* is an adjective meaning "unlawful." *The reporter was unable to elicit any information from the police about illicit drug traffic.*

emigrate from, immigrate to *Emigrate* means "to leave one country or region to settle in another." *In 1903, my great-grandfather emigrated from Russia to escape the religious pogroms. Immigrate means "to enter another country and reside there." In 2006, half of the people who immigrated to Canada settled in Ontario.*

eminent, imminent *Eminent* means "outstanding" or "distinguished." *We met an eminent professor of Greek history. Imminent means "about to happen." The snowstorm is imminent.*

enthused Many people object to the use of *enthused* as an adjective. Use *enthusiastic* instead. *The children were enthusiastic* (not *enthused*) *about going to the circus.*

etc. Avoid ending a list with *etc.* It is more emphatic to end with an example, and in most contexts readers will understand that the list is not exhaustive. When you don't want to end with an example, *and so on* is more graceful than *etc.* (See also *and etc.*)

eventually, ultimately Often used interchangeably, *eventually* is the better choice to mean "at an unspecified time in the future," and *ultimately* is better to mean "the furthest possible extent or greatest extreme." *He knew that eventually he would complete his degree. The existentialists considered suicide the ultimately rational act.*

everybody, everyone *Everybody* and *everyone* are singular. (See G1-e and G3-a.)

everyone, every one *Everyone* is an indefinite pronoun. *Every one*, the pronoun *one* preceded by the adjective *every*, means "each individual or thing in a particular group." *Every one* is usually followed by *of. Everyone wanted to go. Every one of the missing books was found.*

except See *accept, except*.

expect Avoid the informal use of *expect* meaning "to believe, think, or suppose." *I think* (not *expect*) *it will rain tonight.*

explicit, implicit *Explicit* means "expressed directly" or "clearly defined"; *implicit* means "implied, unstated." *I gave him explicit instructions not to go swimming. My mother's silence indicated her implicit approval.*

farther, further   *Farther* usually describes distances. *Further* usually suggests quantity or degree. *Saskatoon is farther from Kenora than I thought. I would be grateful for further suggestions.*

fewer, less   Use *fewer* for items that can be counted; use *less* for items that cannot be counted. *Fewer people are living in the city. Please put less sugar in my tea.*

finalize   *Finalize* is jargon meaning "to make final or complete." Use ordinary English instead. *The architect prepared final drawings* (not *finalized the drawings*).

firstly   *Firstly* sounds pretentious, and it leads to the ungainly series *firstly, secondly, thirdly,* and so on. Write *first, second, third* instead.

further   See *farther, further*.

get   *Get* has many colloquial uses. In writing, avoid using *get* to mean the following: "to evoke an emotional response" (*That music always gets to me*); "to annoy" (*After a while his sulking got to me*); "to take revenge on" (*I got back at her by leaving the room*); "to become" (*He got sick*); "to start or begin" (*Let's get going*). Avoid using *have got to* in place of *must. I must* (not *have got to*) *finish this paper tonight.*

good, well   *Good* is an adjective, *well* an adverb. (See G4-a and G4-b.) *He hasn't felt good about his game since he sprained his wrist last season. She performed well on the uneven parallel bars.*

graduate   Both of the following uses of *graduate* are standard: *My sister was graduated from UBC last year. My sister graduated from UBC last year.* It is nonstandard, however, to drop the word *from: My sister graduated UBC last year.* Though this usage is common in informal English, many readers object to it.

grow   Phrases such as *to grow the economy* and *to grow a business* are jargon. Usually the verb *grow* is intransitive (it does not take a direct object). *Our business has grown very quickly.* Use *grow* in a transitive sense, with a direct object, to mean "to cultivate" or "to allow to grow." *We plan to grow tomatoes this year. John is growing a beard.*

hanged, hung   *Hanged* is the past-tense and past-participle form of the verb *hang* meaning "to execute." *The prisoner was hanged at dawn. Hung* is the past-tense and past-participle form of the verb *hang* meaning "to fasten or suspend." *The expensive paintings were hung in the gallery.*

hardly   Avoid expressions such as *can't hardly* and *not hardly*, which are considered double negatives. *I can* (not *can't*) *hardly describe my surprise at getting the job.* (See G4-d.)

has got, have got   *Got* is unnecessary and awkward in such constructions. It should be dropped. *We have* (not *have got*) *three days to prepare for the opening.*

he At one time *he* was commonly used to mean "he or she." Today such usage is inappropriate. (See W4-e and G3-a.)

he/she, his/her In formal writing, use *he or she* or *his or her*. For alternatives to these wordy constructions, see W4-e and G3-a.

hisself *Hisself* is nonstandard. Use *himself*.

hopefully *Hopefully* means "in a hopeful manner." *We looked hopefully to the future.* Some usage experts object to the use of *hopefully* as a sentence adverb, apparently on grounds of clarity. To be safe, avoid using *hopefully* in sentences such as the following: *Hopefully, your son will recover soon.* Instead, indicate who is doing the hoping: *I hope that your son will recover soon.*

however In the past, some writers objected to the conjunctive adverb *however* at the beginning of a sentence, but current experts allow placing the word according to the intended meaning and emphasis. All of the following sentences are correct. *Pam decided, however, to attend the lecture. However, Pam decided to attend the lecture.* (She had been considering other activities.) *Pam, however, decided to attend the lecture.* (Unlike someone else, Pam chose to attend the lecture.) (See P1-f.)

hung See *hanged, hung*.

i.e. In formal writing, replace the Latin abbreviation *i.e.* with its English equivalent: *that is.*

if, whether Use *if* to express a condition and *whether* to express alternatives. *If you go on a trip, whether to Nebraska or Italy, remember to bring traveller's cheques.*

illusion See *allusion, illusion*.

immigrate See *emigrate from, immigrate to*.

imminent See *eminent, imminent*.

immoral See *amoral, immoral*.

implement *Implement* is a pretentious way of saying "do," "carry out," or "accomplish." Use ordinary language instead. *We carried out* (not *implemented*) *the director's orders.*

imply, infer *Imply* means "to suggest or state indirectly"; *infer* means "to draw a conclusion." *John implied that he knew all about computers, but the interviewer inferred that John was inexperienced.*

in, into *In* indicates location or condition; *into* indicates movement or a change in condition. *They found the lost letters in a box after moving into the house.*

in regards to *In regards to* confuses two different phrases: *in regard to* and *as regards.* Use one or the other. *In regard to* (or *As regards*) *the contract, ignore the first clause.*

USAGE hackerhandbooks.com/writersref
> Language Debates > Sexist language
> *however* at the beginning of a sentence

irregardless   *Irregardless* is nonstandard. Use *regardless*.

is when, is where   These mixed constructions are often incorrectly used in definitions. *A run-off election is a second election held to break a tie* (not *is when a second election is held to break a tie*). (See S5-c.)

its, it's   *Its* is a possessive pronoun; *it's* is a contraction for *it is*. (See P4-a and P4-b.) *It's always fun to watch a dog chase its tail*.

kind(s)   *Kind* is singular and should be treated as such. Don't write *These kind of chairs are rare*. Write instead *This kind of chair is rare*. *Kinds* is plural and should be used only when you mean more than one kind. *These kinds of chairs are rare*.

kind of, sort of   Avoid using *kind of* or *sort of* to mean "somewhat." *The movie was somewhat* (not *sort of*) *boring*. Do not put *a* after either phrase. *That kind of* (not *kind of a*) *salesclerk annoys me*.

lay, lie   See *lie, lay*.

lead, led   *Lead* is a metallic element; it is a noun. *Led* is the past tense of the verb *lead*. *He led me to the treasure*.

learn, teach   *Learn* means "to gain knowledge"; *teach* means "to impart knowledge." *I must teach* (not *learn*) *my sister to read*.

leave, let   *Leave* means "to exit." Avoid using it with the nonstandard meaning "to permit." *Let* (not *Leave*) *me help you with the dishes*.

less   See *fewer, less*.

let, leave   See *leave, let*.

liable   *Liable* means "obligated" or "responsible." Do not use it to mean "likely." *You're likely* (not *liable*) *to trip if you don't tie your shoelaces*.

lie, lay   *Lie* is an intransitive verb meaning "to recline or rest on a surface." Its forms are *lie, lay, lain*. *Lay* is a transitive verb meaning "to put or place." Its forms are *lay, laid, laid*. (See G2-b.)

like, as   *Like* is a preposition, not a subordinating conjunction. It can be followed only by a noun or a noun phrase. *As* is a subordinating conjunction that introduces a subordinate clause. In casual speech, you may say *She looks like she hasn't slept* or *You don't know her like I do*. But in formal writing, use *as*. *She looks as if she hasn't slept. You don't know her as I do*. (See also B1-f and B1-g.)

loose, lose   *Loose* is an adjective meaning "not securely fastened." *Lose* is a verb meaning "to misplace" or "to not win." *Did you lose your only loose pair of work pants?*

lots, lots of   *Lots* and *lots of* are informal substitutes for *many*, *much*, or *a lot*. Avoid using them in formal writing.

mankind   Avoid *mankind* whenever possible. It offends many readers because it excludes women. Use *humanity, humans, the human race,* or *humankind* instead. (See W4-e.)

may   See *can, may.*

maybe, may be   *Maybe* is an adverb meaning "possibly." *Maybe the sun will shine tomorrow. May be* is a verb phrase. *Tomorrow may be brighter.*

may of, might of   *May of* and *might of* are nonstandard for *may have* and *might have.* We *might have* (not *might of*) *had too many cookies.*

media, medium   *Media* is the plural of *medium. Of all the media that cover the Olympics, television is the medium that best captures the spectacle of the events.*

most   *Most* is informal when used to mean "almost" and should be avoided. *Almost* (not *Most*) *everyone went to the parade.*

must of   See *may of.*

myself   *Myself* is a reflexive or intensive pronoun. Reflexive: *I cut myself.* Intensive: *I will drive you myself.* Do not use *myself* in place of *I* or *me. He gave the flowers to Melinda and me* (not *myself*). (See also G3-c.)

neither   *Neither* is singular. (See G1-e and G3-a.) For *neither . . . nor* constructions, see G1-d and G3-a.

none   *None* may be singular or plural. (See G1-e.)

nowheres   *Nowheres* is nonstandard. Use *nowhere* instead.

number   See *amount, number.*

of   Use the verb *have,* not the preposition *of,* after the verbs *could, should, would, may, might,* and *must. They must have* (not *must of*) *left early.*

off of   *Off* is sufficient. Omit *of. The ball rolled off* (not *off of*) *the table.*

OK, O.K., okay   All three spellings are acceptable, but avoid these expressions in formal speech and writing.

parameters   *Parameter* is a mathematical term that has become jargon for "fixed limit," "boundary," or "guideline." Use ordinary English instead. *The task force worked within certain guidelines* (not *parameters*).

passed, past   *Passed* is the past tense of the verb *pass. Ann passed me another slice of cake. Past* usually means "belonging to a former time" or "beyond a time or place." *Our past president spoke until past midnight. The hotel is just past the next intersection.*

percent, per cent, percentage   *Percent* (also spelled *per cent*) is always used with a specific number. *Percentage* is used with a descriptive term such as *large* or *small,* not with a specific number. *The candidate won*

80 percent of the primary vote. A large percentage of registered voters turned out for the election.

phenomena *Phenomena* is the plural of *phenomenon*, which means "an observable occurrence or fact." *Strange phenomena occur at all hours of the night in that house, but last night's phenomenon was the strangest of all.*

plus *Plus* should not be used to join independent clauses. *This raincoat is dirty; moreover* (not *plus*), *it has a hole in it.*

practice, practise *Practice* is a noun, *practise* a verb. *You should practise the flute at home every day, even if you have band practice at school.*

precede, proceed *Precede* means "to come before." *Proceed* means "to go forward." *As we proceeded up the mountain path, we noticed fresh tracks in the mud, evidence that a group of hikers had preceded us.*

principal, principle *Principal* is a noun meaning "the head of a school or an organization" or "a sum of money." It is also an adjective meaning "most important." *Principle* is a noun meaning "a basic truth or law." *The principal expelled her for three principal reasons. We believe in the principle of equal justice for all.*

proceed, precede See *precede, proceed.*

quote, quotation *Quote* is a verb; *quotation* is a noun. Avoid using *quote* as a shortened form of *quotation. Her quotations* (not *quotes*) *from current movies intrigued us.*

raise, rise *Raise* is a transitive verb meaning "to move or cause to move upward." It takes a direct object. *I raised the shades. Rise* is an intransitive verb meaning "to go up." *Heat rises.*

real, really *Real* is an adjective; *really* is an adverb. *Real* is sometimes used informally as an adverb, but avoid this use in formal writing. *She was really* (not *real*) *angry.* (See G4-b.)

reason . . . is because Use *that* instead of *because. The reason she's cranky is that* (not *because*) *she didn't sleep last night.* (See S5-c.)

reason why The expression *reason why* is redundant. *The reason* (not *The reason why*) *Jones lost the election is clear.*

relation, relationship *Relation* describes a connection between things. *Relationship* describes a connection between people. *There is a relation between poverty and infant mortality. Our business relationship has cooled over the years.*

respectfully, respectively *Respectfully* means "showing or marked by respect." *Respectively* means "each in the order given." *He respectfully submitted his opinion to the judge. John, Tom, and Larry were a butcher, a baker, and a lawyer, respectively.*

sensual, sensuous *Sensual* means "gratifying the physical senses," especially those associated with sexual pleasure. *Sensuous* means "pleasing to the senses," especially those involved in the experience of art, music, and nature. *The sensuous music and balmy air led the dancers to more sensual movements.*

set, sit *Set* is a transitive verb meaning "to put" or "to place." Its past tense is *set*. *Sit* is an intransitive verb meaning "to be seated." Its past tense is *sat*. *She set the dough in a warm corner of the kitchen. The cat sat in the doorway.*

shall, will *Shall* was once used in place of the helping verb *will* with *I* or *we*: *I shall, we shall*. Today, however, *will* is generally accepted even when the subject is *I* or *we*. The word *shall* occurs primarily in polite questions (*Shall I find you a pillow?*) and in legalistic sentences suggesting duty or obligation (*The applicant shall file form A by December 31*).

should of *Should of* is nonstandard for *should have*. *They should have* (not *should of*) *been home an hour ago.*

since Do not use *since* to mean "because" if there is any chance of ambiguity. *Because* (not *Since*) *we won the game, we have been celebrating with a pitcher of root beer. Since* here could mean "because" or "from the time that."

sit See *set, sit.*

site See *cite, site.*

somebody, someone *Somebody* and *someone* are singular. (See G1-e and G3-a.)

something *Something* is singular. (See G1-e.)

sometime, some time, sometimes *Sometime* is an adverb meaning "at an indefinite or unstated time." *Some time* is the adjective *some* modifying the noun *time* and means "a period of time." *Sometimes* is an adverb meaning "at times, now and then." *I'll see you sometime soon. I haven't lived there for some time. Sometimes I see him at the library.*

suppose to Write *supposed to.*

sure and Write *sure to. We were all taught to be sure to* (not *sure and*) *look both ways before crossing a street.*

take See *bring, take.*

than, then *Than* is a conjunction used in comparisons; *then* is an adverb denoting time. *That pizza is more than I can eat. Tom laughed, and then we recognized him.*

that See *who, which, that.*

that, which Many writers reserve *that* for restrictive clauses, *which* for nonrestrictive clauses. (See P1-e.)

theirselves *Theirselves* is nonstandard for *themselves*. *The crash victims pushed the car out of the way themselves* (not *theirselves*).

them The use of *them* in place of *those* is nonstandard. *Please take those* (not *them*) *flowers to the patient in room 220.*

then, than See *than, then*.

there, their, they're *There* is an adverb specifying place; it is also an expletive (placeholder). Adverb: *Sylvia is lying there unconscious.* Expletive: *There are two plums left. Their* is a possessive pronoun. *Fred and Jane finally washed their car. They're* is a contraction of *they are. They're later than usual today.*

they The use of *they* to indicate possession is nonstandard. Use *their* instead. *Cindy and Sam decided to sell their* (not *they*) *1975 Corvette.*

they, their The use of the plural pronouns *they* and *their* to refer to singular nouns or pronouns is nonstandard. *No one handed in his or her* (not *their*) *draft on time.* (See G3-a.)

this kind See *kind(s)*.

to, too, two *To* is a preposition; *too* is an adverb; *two* is a number. *Too many of your shots slice to the left, but the last two were just right.*

toward, towards *Toward* and *towards* are generally interchangeable.

try and *Try and* is nonstandard for *try to*. *The teacher asked us all to try to* (not *try and*) *write an original haiku.*

ultimately, eventually See *eventually, ultimately*.

unique Avoid expressions such as *most unique, more straight, less perfect, very round*. Either something is unique or it isn't. It is illogical to suggest degrees of uniqueness. (See G4-c.)

usage The noun *usage* should not be substituted for *use* when the meaning is "employment of." *The use* (not *usage*) *of insulated shades has cut fuel costs dramatically.*

use to Write *used to*.

utilize *Utilize* means "to make use of." It often sounds pretentious; in most cases, *use* is sufficient. *I used* (not *utilized*) *the laser printer.*

wait for, wait on *Wait for* means "to be in readiness for" or "to await." *Wait on* means "to serve." *We're only waiting for* (not *waiting on*) *Ruth to take us to the museum.*

ways *Ways* is colloquial when used to mean "distance." *The city is a long way* (not *ways*) *from here.*

weather, whether The noun *weather* refers to the state of the atmosphere. *Whether* is a conjunction referring to a choice between alternatives. *We wondered whether the weather would clear.*

---

well, good   See *good, well*.

where   Do not use *where* in place of *that*. *I heard that* (not *where*) *the crime rate is increasing.*

which   See *that, which* and *who, which, that*.

while   Avoid using *while* to mean "although" or "whereas" if there is any chance of ambiguity. *Although* (not *While*) *Gloria lost money in the slot machine, Tom won it at roulette.* Here *While* could mean either "although" or "at the same time that."

who, which, that   Do not use *which* to refer to persons. Use *who* instead. *That*, though generally used to refer to things, may be used to refer to a group or class of people. *The player who* (not *that* or *which*) *made the basket at the buzzer was named MVP. The team that scores the most points in this game will win the tournament.*

who, whom   *Who* is used for subjects and subject complements; *whom* is used for objects. (See G3-d.)

who's, whose   *Who's* is a contraction of *who is*; *whose* is a possessive pronoun. *Who's ready for more popcorn? Whose coat is this?* (See P4-b and P4-a.)

will   See *shall, will*.

would of   *Would of* is nonstandard for *would have*. *She would have* (not *would of*) *had a chance to play if she had arrived on time.*

you   In formal writing, avoid *you* in an indefinite sense meaning "anyone." (See G3-b.) *Any spectator* (not *You*) *could tell by the way John caught the ball that his throw would be too late.*

your, you're   *Your* is a possessive pronoun; *you're* is a contraction of *you are. Is that your new bike? You're in the finals.* (See P4-a and P4-b.)

USAGE   hackerhandbooks.com/writersref
　　> Language Debates > *who* versus *which* or *that*
　　　　　　　　　　　> *who* versus *whom*
　　　　　　　　　　　> *you*

W2 Wordy sentences

Long sentences are not necessarily wordy, nor are short sentences always concise. A sentence is wordy if it can be tightened without loss of meaning.

W2-a Eliminate redundancies.

Writers often repeat themselves unnecessarily, thinking that expressions such as *cooperate together*, *yellow in colour*, or *basic essentials* add emphasis to their writing. In reality, such redundancies do just the opposite. There is no need to say the same thing twice.

▶ Daniel ~~is now employed~~ at a private rehabilitation centre
   ^ works
   ~~working~~ as a registered physical therapist.

Though modifiers ordinarily add meaning to the words they modify, occasionally they are redundant.

▶ Sylvia ~~very hurriedly~~ scribbled her name, address, and phone

number on a greasy napkin.

The word *scribbled* already suggests that Sylvia wrote very hurriedly.

▶ Gabriele Muccino's film *The Pursuit of Happyness* tells the story

of a single father determined ~~in his mind~~ to pull himself and his

son out of homelessness.

The word *determined* contains the idea that his resolution formed in his mind.

W2-b Avoid unnecessary repetition of words.

Though words may be repeated deliberately, for effect, repetitions will seem awkward if they are clearly unnecessary. When a more concise version is possible, choose it.

PRACTICE   hackerhandbooks.com/writersref
   > Word choice > W2–3 to W2–6

▶ Our fifth patient, in room six, is a~~~~ very difficult. ~~patient.~~

Writing
with
sources

APA-style
citation

▶ A study by the Henry J. Kaiser Family Foundation (2004)
  measured
  ~~studied~~ the effects of diet and exercise on childhood
  obesity.

The repetition of *study . . . studied* is awkward and redundant. By using the descriptive verb *measured* instead, the writer conveys more precisely the purpose of the study and suggests its function in the paper.

W2-c Cut empty or inflated phrases.

An empty phrase can be cut with little or no loss of meaning. Common examples are introductory word groups that weaken the writer's authority by apologizing or hedging: *in my opinion, I think that, it seems that, one must admit that,* and so on.

O
▶ ~~In my opinion,~~ Our current immigration policy is misguided.

Inflated phrases can be reduced to a word or two without loss of meaning.

INFLATED	CONCISE
along the lines of	like
as a matter of fact	in fact
at all times	always
at the present time	now, currently
at this point in time	now, currently
because of the fact that	because
by means of	by
by virtue of the fact that	because
due to the fact that	because
for the purpose of	for
for the reason that	because
have the ability to	be able to, can
in light of the fact that	because
in order to	to
in spite of the fact that	although, though
in the event that	if
in the final analysis	finally
in the nature of	like
in the neighbourhood of	about
until such time as	until

> *now.*
> ▶ We are unable to provide funding ~~at this point in time.~~
>   ^

W2-d Simplify the structure.

If the structure of a sentence is needlessly indirect, try simplifying it. Look for opportunities to strengthen the verb.

> ▶ The financial analyst claimed that because of volatile market
>
>   conditions she could not ~~make an~~ estimate ~~of~~ the company's
>
>   future profits.

> The verb *estimate* is more vigorous and concise than *make an estimate of*.

The colourless verbs *is, are, was*, and *were* frequently generate excess words. (See also W3-b.)

> *examined*
> ▶ Investigators ~~were involved in examining~~ the effect of classical
>   ^
>   music on unborn babies.

> The revision is more direct and concise. The action (*examining*), originally appearing in a subordinate structure, has become a strong verb, *examined*.

The expletive constructions *there is* and *there are* (or *there was* and *there were*) can also generate excess words. The same is true of expletive constructions beginning with *it*.

> *A*
> ▶ ~~There is~~ another module ~~that~~ tells the story of Charles Darwin
>   ^
>   and introduces the theory of evolution.

> *A* *must*
> ▶ ~~It is imperative that~~ all night managers follow strict procedures
>   ^ ^
>   when locking the safe.

Finally, verbs in the passive voice may be needlessly indirect. When the active voice expresses your meaning as effectively, use it. (See also W3-a.)

> *our coaches have recruited*
> ▶ All too often, athletes with marginal academic skills. ~~have~~
>   ^ ^
>   ~~been recruited by our coaches.~~

W2-e Reduce clauses to phrases, phrases to single words.

Word groups functioning as modifiers can often be made more compact. Look for any opportunities to reduce clauses to phrases or phrases to single words.

▶ We took a side trip to Gravenhurst, ~~which was~~ the birthplace of

Dr. Norman Bethune.

▶ In ~~the~~ essay*this*, ~~that follows,~~ I argue against Immanuel Kant's
problematic
claim that we should not lie under any circumstances*/*. ~~which~~

~~is a problematic assertion.~~

W3 Active verbs

As a rule, choose an active verb and pair it with a subject that names the person or thing doing the action. Active verbs express meaning more emphatically and vigorously than their weaker counterparts—forms of the verb *be* or verbs in the passive voice.

PASSIVE	The pumps *were destroyed* by a surge of power.
***BE* VERB**	A surge of power *was* responsible for the destruction of the pumps.
ACTIVE	A surge of power *destroyed* the pumps.

Verbs in the passive voice lack strength because their subjects receive the action instead of doing it. Forms of the verb *be* (*be, am, is, are, was, were, being, been*) lack vigour because they convey no action.

Although passive verbs and the forms of *be* have legitimate uses, choose an active verb if it can carry your meaning. Even among active verbs, some convey action more vigorously than others. Carefully selected verbs can energize a piece of writing.

▶ The goalie crouched low, ~~reached~~*swept* out his stick, and ~~sent~~*hooked* the

rebound away from the mouth of the net.

Academic English   Although you may be tempted to avoid the passive voice completely, keep in mind that some writing situations call for it, especially scientific writing. For appropriate uses of the passive voice, see pages 157 and 158; for advice about forming the passive voice, see M1-b and B2-b.

W3-a Use the active voice unless you have a good reason for choosing the passive.

In the active voice, the subject of the sentence does the action; in the passive voice, the subject receives the action. Although both voices are grammatically correct, the active voice is usually more effective because it is clearer and more direct.

ACTIVE   Hernando *caught* the fly ball.

PASSIVE   The fly ball *was caught* by Hernando.

Passive sentences often identify the actor in a phrase beginning with *by*, as in the preceding example. Sometimes, however, that phrase is omitted, and who or what is responsible for the action becomes unclear: *The fly ball was caught.*

Most of the time, you will want to emphasize the actor, so you should use the active voice. To replace a passive verb with an active one, make the actor the subject of the sentence.

▶ The settlers stripped the land of timber before realizing
  ~~The land was stripped of timber before the settlers realized~~
  ^
the consequences of their actions.

The revision emphasizes the actors (*settlers*) by naming them in the subject.

▶ The contractor removed the
  ~~The~~ debris ~~was removed~~ from the construction site.
  ^

Sometimes the actor does not appear in a passive-voice sentence. To turn such a sentence into the active voice, the writer must determine an appropriate subject, in this case *contractor*.

The passive voice is appropriate if you want to emphasize the receiver of the action or to minimize the importance of the actor.

APPROPRIATE PASSIVE	Many farmers *were forced* to leave their homes after the flooding.
APPROPRIATE PASSIVE	As the time for harvest approaches, the tobacco plants *are sprayed* with a chemical to retard the growth of suckers.

The writer of the first sentence wanted to emphasize the receiver of the action, *farmers*. The writer of the second sentence wanted to focus on the tobacco plants, not on the people spraying them.

In much scientific writing, the passive voice properly emphasizes the experiment or process being described, not the researcher. Check with your instructor for the preference in your discipline.

APPROPRIATE PASSIVE	The solution *was heated* to the boiling point, and then it was reduced in volume by 50%.

W3-b Replace *be* verbs that result in dull or wordy sentences.

Not every *be* verb needs replacing. The forms of *be* (*be, am, is, are, was, were, being, been*) work well when you want to link a subject to a noun that clearly renames it or to an adjective that describes it: *Orchard House was the home of Louisa May Alcott. The harvest will be bountiful after the summer rains.* And *be* verbs are essential as helping verbs before present participles (*is flying, are disappearing*) to express ongoing action: *Derrick was fighting the fire when his wife went into labour.* (See G2-f.)

If using a *be* verb makes a sentence needlessly dull and wordy, however, consider replacing it. Often a phrase following the verb will contain a noun or an adjective (such as *violation, resistant*) that suggests a more vigorous, active verb (*violate, resist*).

▶ Burying nuclear waste in Antarctica would ~~be in violation of~~ an
violate
^
international treaty.

Violate is less wordy and more vigorous than *be in violation of*.

▶ When Rosa Parks ~~was resistant to~~ giving up her seat on the bus,
resisted
^
she became a civil rights hero.

Resisted is stronger than *was resistant to*.

≣ **W4** Appropriate language

Language is appropriate when it suits your subject, engages your audience, and blends naturally with your own voice.

W4-a Stay away from jargon.

Jargon is specialized language used among members of a trade, profession, or group. Use jargon only when readers will be familiar with it; even then, use it only when plain English will not do as well.

> **JARGON** We outsourced the work to a firm in Alberta because we didn't have the bandwidth to tackle it in-house.

> **REVISED** We hired a company in Alberta because we had too few employees to do the work.

Broadly defined, jargon includes puffed-up language designed more to impress readers than to inform them. The following are common examples from business, government, higher education, and the military, with plain English alternatives in parentheses.

ameliorate (improve)	indicator (sign)
commence (begin)	optimal (best, most favourable)
components (parts)	parameters (boundaries, limits)
endeavour (try)	peruse (read, look over)
facilitate (help)	prior to (before)
impact (v.) (affect)	utilize (use)

Sentences filled with jargon are hard to read and often wordy.

▶ All ~~employees functioning in the capacity of~~ work-study students
  must prove that they are currently enrolled.
  ~~are required to give evidence of current enrollment.~~
  ^

▶ The CEO should ~~dialogue~~ *talk* with investors about ~~partnering~~ *working* with
  ^   ^ *poor neighbourhoods.* ^
  clients to buy land in ~~economically deprived zones.~~
  ^

W4-b Avoid pretentious language, most euphemisms, and "doublespeak."

Hoping to sound profound or poetic, some writers embroider their thoughts with large words and flowery phrases. Such pretentious language is so ornate and wordy that it obscures the writer's meaning.

PRACTICE hackerhandbooks.com/writersref
> Word choice > W4–5

▶ Taylor's ~~employment of multihued means of expression draws~~ *use of colorful language reveals that she has a* ~~back the curtains and lets slip the~~ sentimental ~~vantage point from~~ *view of* ~~which she observes~~ American society ~~as well as her lack of~~ *and does not understand* ~~comprehension of~~ economic realities.

Euphemisms — nice-sounding words or phrases substituted for words thought to sound harsh or ugly — are sometimes appropriate. Many cultures, for example, accept euphemisms when speaking or writing about excretion (*I have to go to the bathroom*), sexual intercourse (*They did not sleep together*), and the like.

Most euphemisms, however, are needlessly evasive or even deceitful. Like pretentious language, they obscure the intended meaning.

EUPHEMISM	PLAIN ENGLISH
adult entertainment	pornography
preowned automobile	used car
economically deprived	poor
strategic withdrawal	retreat or defeat
revenue enhancers	taxes
chemical dependency	drug addiction
downsize	lay off, fire
correctional facility	prison

The term *doublespeak* applies to any deliberately evasive or deceptive language, including euphemisms. Doublespeak is especially common in politics and business. A military retreat is described as *tactical redeployment*, *enhanced interrogation* is a euphemism for "torture," and *downsizing* really means "firing employees."

W4-c In most contexts, avoid slang, regional expressions, and nonstandard English.

Slang is an informal and sometimes private vocabulary that expresses the solidarity of a group such as teenagers, rock musicians, or football fans; it is subject to more rapid change than standard English. For example, the slang teenagers use to express approval changes every few years; *cool, groovy, neat, awesome, phat*, and *sick* have replaced one another within the last four decades. Sometimes slang becomes so widespread that it is accepted as standard vocabulary. *Jazz*, for example, started out as slang but is now a standard term for a style of music.

Although slang has a certain vitality, it is a code that not everyone understands, and it is very informal. Therefore, it is inappropriate in most written work.

▶ When the server crashed unexpectedly, three hours of unsaved _we lost_

data. ~~went down the tubes.~~
   ^

▶ The government's "filth" guidelines for food will ~~gross you out.~~ _disgust you._
   ^

Regional expressions are common to a group in a geographic
area. _He's from away_ (for _He wasn't born here_) is an expression in
Prince Edward Island, for example. Regional expressions have the
same limitations as slang and are therefore inappropriate in most
writing.

▶ John was four blocks from the house before he remembered to
   turn on
   ~~cut~~ the headlights. ~~on.~~
   ^   ^

▶ Seamus wasn't ~~for~~ sure, but he thought the whales might be

   migrating during his visit to British Columbia.

Standard English is the language used in all academic, business,
and professional fields. Nonstandard English is spoken by people with
a common regional or social heritage. Although nonstandard English
may be appropriate when spoken within a close group, it is out of place
in most formal and informal writing.

▶ The premier said he ~~don't~~ know if he will approve the budget _doesn't_
   ^

   without the clean air provision.

If you speak a nonstandard dialect, try to identify the ways in which
your dialect differs from standard English. Look especially for the following features of nonstandard English, which commonly cause problems in writing.

Misusing verb forms such as _began_ and _begun_ (See G2-a.)

Leaving _-s_ endings off verbs (See G2-c.)

Leaving _-ed_ endings off verbs (See G2-d.)

Leaving out necessary verbs (See G2-e.)

Using double negatives (See G4-d.)

W4-d Choose an appropriate level of formality.

In deciding on a level of formality, consider both your subject and your audience. Does the subject demand a dignified treatment, or is a relaxed tone more suitable? Will readers be put off if you assume too close a relationship with them, or might you alienate them by seeming too distant?

For most academic and professional writing, some degree of formality is appropriate. In a job application letter, for example, it is a mistake to sound too breezy and informal.

> **TOO INFORMAL**   I'd like to get that sales job you've got in the paper.
>
> **MORE FORMAL**   I would like to apply for the position of sales associate advertised in the *Brandon Sun*.

Informal writing is appropriate for private letters, personal e-mail and text messages, and business correspondence between close associates. In choosing a level of formality, above all be consistent. When a writer's voice shifts from one level of formality to another, readers receive mixed messages.

▶ Once a pitcher for the Blue Jays, Jorge shared with me the secrets
of his trade. His lesson ~~commenced~~ *began* with his famous curveball,
~~implemented~~ *thrown* by tucking the little finger behind the ball. Next
he ~~elucidated~~ *revealed* the mysteries of the sucker pitch, a slow ball
coming behind a fast windup.

Commenced and *elucidated* are inappropriate for the subject, and they clash with informal terms such as *sucker pitch* and *fast windup*.

W4-e Avoid sexist language.

Sexist language is language that stereotypes, excludes, or demeans women or men. Using nonsexist language is a matter of courtesy—of respect for and sensitivity to the feelings of others.

Recognizing sexist language

Some sexist language is easy to recognize because it reflects genuine contempt for women: referring to a woman as a "chick," for example, or calling a lawyer a "lady lawyer."

Other forms of sexist language are less blatant. The following practices, while they may not result from conscious sexism, reflect stereotypical thinking: referring to members of one profession as exclusively male or exclusively female (teachers as women or computer engineers as men, for instance) or using different conventions when naming or identifying women and men.

STEREOTYPICAL LANGUAGE

After a nursing student graduates, *she* must face a difficult licensing examination. [Not all nursing students are women.]

Running for city council are Boris Stotsky, a lawyer, and *Mrs.* Cynthia Jones, a professor of English and *mother of three*. [The title *Mrs.* and the description *mother of three* are irrelevant.]

Still other forms of sexist language result from outdated traditions. The pronouns *he*, *him*, and *his*, for instance, were traditionally used to refer generically to persons of either sex. Some writers now use *she*, *her*, and *hers* generically or substitute the female pronouns alternately with the male pronouns.

GENERIC PRONOUNS

A journalist is motivated by *his* deadline.

A good interior designer treats *her* clients' ideas respectfully.

But both forms are sexist — for excluding one sex entirely and for making assumptions about the members of particular professions.

Similarly, the nouns *man* and *men* were once used to refer generically to persons of either sex. Current usage demands gender-neutral terms for references to both men and women.

INAPPROPRIATE	APPROPRIATE
chairman	chairperson, moderator, chair, head
fireman	firefighter
foreman	supervisor
mailman	mail carrier, postal worker, letter carrier
to man	to operate, to staff
mankind	people, humans
manpower	personnel, staff
policeman	police officer
weatherman	forecaster, meteorologist
workman	worker

Revising sexist language

When revising sexist language, you may be tempted to substitute *he or she* and *his or her*. These terms are inclusive but wordy; fine in small doses, they can become awkward when repeated throughout an essay. A better revision strategy is to write in the plural; yet another strategy is to recast the sentence so that the problem does not arise.

SEXIST

A journalist is motivated by *his* deadline.

A good interior designer treats *her* clients' ideas respectfully.

ACCEPTABLE BUT WORDY

A journalist is motivated by *his or her* deadline.

A good interior designer treats *his or her* clients' ideas respectfully.

BETTER: USING THE PLURAL

Journalists are motivated by *their* deadlines.

Good interior designers treat *their* clients' ideas respectfully.

BETTER: RECASTING THE SENTENCE

A journalist is motivated by *a* deadline.

A good interior designer treats clients' ideas respectfully.

For more examples of these revision strategies, see G3-a.

W4-f Revise language that may offend groups of people.

Obviously it is impolite to use offensive terms such as *Polack* and *redneck*, but biased language can take more subtle forms. Because language evolves over time, names once thought acceptable may become offensive. When describing groups of people, choose names that the groups currently use to describe themselves.

▶ Nunavut takes its name from the ~~Eskimo~~ Inuit word meaning "our land."

▶ Many ~~Oriental~~ Asian immigrants have recently settled in our town.

Negative stereotypes (such as "drives like a teenager" or "sour as a spinster") are of course offensive. But you should avoid stereotyping a person or a group even if you believe your generalization to be positive.

▶ It was no surprise that Greer, ~~a Chinese Canadian,~~ an excellent math and science student, was selected for the honours chemistry program.

☰ **W5** Exact language

Two reference works will help you find words to express your meaning: a good dictionary, such as the *Canadian Oxford Dictionary*, which is also available online, or the *Nelson Canadian Dictionary of the English Language*, and a thesaurus, such as *Roget's International Thesaurus*. (See W6.)

TIP: Do not turn to a thesaurus in search of flowery or impressive language. Look instead for words that exactly express your meaning.

W5-a Select words with appropriate connotations.

In addition to their strict dictionary meanings (or *denotations*), words have *connotations*, emotional colourings that affect how readers respond to them. The word *steel* denotes "commercial iron that contains carbon," but it also calls up a cluster of images associated with steel. These associations give the word its connotations—cold, hard, smooth, unbending.

If the connotation of a word does not seem appropriate for your purpose, your audience, or your subject matter, you should change the word. When a more appropriate synonym does not come quickly to mind, consult a dictionary or a thesaurus. (See W6.)

▶ When Canadian soldiers returned home after World War II, many
       left
  women a̶b̶a̶n̶d̶o̶n̶e̶d̶ their jobs in favour of marriage.
   ^

The word *abandoned* is too negative for the context.

W5-b Prefer specific, concrete nouns.

Unlike general nouns, which refer to broad classes of things, specific nouns point to particular items. *Film*, for example, names a general class, *fantasy film* names a narrower class, and *The Golden Compass* is more specific still.

Unlike abstract nouns, which refer to qualities and ideas (*justice, beauty, realism, dignity*), concrete nouns point to immediate, often sensory experience and to physical objects (*steeple, asphalt, lilac, stone, garlic*).

Specific, concrete nouns express meaning more vividly than general or abstract ones. Although general and abstract language is sometimes necessary to convey your meaning, use specific, concrete words whenever possible.

▶ The senator spoke about the challenges of our country's future: *pollution, dwindling natural resources, and overcrowded prisons.* ~~the environment and crime.~~
   ^

Nouns such as *thing, area, aspect, factor,* and *individual* are especially dull and imprecise.

▶   *motherhood, and memory.*
   Toni Morrison's *Beloved* is about slavery, ~~among other things.~~
      ^

▶   *experienced technician.*
   Try pairing a new employee with an ~~individual with technical~~
      ^
   ~~experience.~~

W5-c Do not misuse words.

If a word is not in your active vocabulary, you may find yourself misusing it, sometimes with embarrassing consequences. When in doubt, check the dictionary.

▶   *climbing*
   Fans who arrived late were ~~migrating~~ up the bleachers in search of
      ^
   seats.

Writing
with
sources

MLA-style
citation
▶   *argues*
   Marie Winn ~~quarrels~~ that television viewing is bad for families
      ^
   because it "serves to anesthetize parents into accepting their

   family's diminished state" (357).

   When you are introducing a quotation with a signal phrase, be sure to choose a verb that clearly reflects the source's intention. *Quarrel* suggests a heated or angry dispute; *argue* is a more neutral word. (See also MLA-3b on using signal phrases.)

Be especially alert for misused word forms—using a noun such as *absence, significance,* or *persistence,* for example, when your meaning requires the adjective *absent, significant,* or *persistent.*

▶   *persistent*
   Most dieters are not ~~persistence~~ enough to make a permanent change
      ^
   in their eating habits.

W5-d Use standard idioms.

Idioms are speech forms that follow no easily specified rules. Native speakers of a language seldom have problems with idioms, but prepositions (such as *with*, *to*, *at*, and *of*) sometimes cause trouble, especially when they follow certain verbs and adjectives. When in doubt, consult a dictionary.

UNIDIOMATIC	IDIOMATIC
abide with (a decision)	abide by (a decision)
according with	according to
agree to (an idea)	agree with (an idea)
angry at (a person)	angry with (a person)
capable to	capable of
comply to	comply with
desirous to	desirous of
different than (a person or thing)	different from (a person or thing)
intend on doing	intend to do
off of	off
plan on doing	plan to do
preferable than	preferable to
prior than	prior to
similar than	similar to
superior than	superior to
sure and	sure to
think on	think of, about
try and	try to
type of a	type of

ESL Because idioms follow no particular rules, you must learn them individually. You may find it helpful to keep a list of idioms that you frequently encounter in conversation and in reading. See M5.

W5-e Do not rely heavily on clichés.

The pioneer who first announced that he had "slept like a log" no doubt amused his companions with a fresh, unlikely comparison. Today, however, that comparison is a cliché, a saying that can no longer add emphasis or surprise.

PRACTICE **hackerhandbooks.com/writersref**
> Word choice > W5–7

To see just how dully predictable clichés are, put your hand over the right-hand column in the following list and then finish the phrases on the left.

cool as a	cucumber
beat around	the bush
blind as a	bat
busy as a	bee, beaver
crystal	clear
out of the frying pan and	into the fire
light as a	feather
like a bull	in a china shop
playing with	fire
nutty as a	fruitcake
selling like	hotcakes
starting out at the bottom	of the ladder
water under the	bridge
white as a	sheet, ghost
avoid clichés like the	plague

The solution for clichés is simple: Just delete them or rewrite them.

> When I received a full scholarship from my second-choice school,
> *felt squeezed to settle for second best.*
> I ~~found myself between a rock and a hard place.~~
>   ^

Sometimes you can write around a cliché by adding an element of surprise. One student, for example, who had written that she had butterflies in her stomach, revised her cliché like this:

If all of the action in my stomach is caused by butterflies, there must be a horde of them, with horseshoes on.

The image of butterflies wearing horseshoes is fresh and unlikely, not predictable like the original cliché.

W5-f Use figures of speech with care.

A figure of speech is an expression that uses words imaginatively (rather than literally) to make abstract ideas concrete. Most often, figures of speech compare two seemingly unlike things to reveal surprising similarities.

In a *simile*, the writer makes the comparison explicitly, usually by introducing it with *like* or *as*: *By the time cotton had to be picked, Grandfather's neck was as red as the clay he plowed.* In a *metaphor*, the *like* or *as* is omitted, and the comparison is implied. For example, in Shakespeare's *As You Like It*, a young man compares life to a play: *All the world's a stage, and all the men and women merely players.*

Although figures of speech are useful devices, writers sometimes use them without thinking through the images they evoke. The result is sometimes a *mixed metaphor*, the combination of two or more images that don't make sense together.

▶ Our manager decided to put all controversial issues ~~in a holding pattern~~ on a back burner until after the annual meeting.

Here the writer is mixing airplanes (*holding pattern*) and stoves (*back burner*). Simply deleting one of the images corrects the problem.

W6 The dictionary and thesaurus

W6-a The dictionary

A good dictionary, whether print or online—such as the *Canadian Oxford Dictionary* or the *Nelson Canadian Dictionary of the English Language* or, for US spelling and word use, *The American Heritage Dictionary of the English Language* or *Merriam-Webster's Collegiate Dictionary*—is an indispensable writer's aid.

A sample print dictionary entry, taken from *The American Heritage Dictionary*, appears on page 170. Labels show where various kinds of information about a word can be found in that dictionary.

A sample online dictionary entry, taken from *Merriam-Webster Online Dictionary*, appears on page 171.

Spelling, word division, and pronunciation

The main entry (*re•gard* in the sample entries) shows the correct spelling of the word. When there are two correct spellings of a word (as in *collectible, collectable*, for example), both are given, with the preferred spelling usually appearing first.

The main entry also shows how the word is divided into syllables. The dot between *re* and *gard* separates the two syllables and indicates where the word should be divided if it can't fit at the end of a line of type (see P7-h). When a word is compound, the main entry shows how to write it: as one word (*crossroad*), as a hyphenated word (*cross-stitch*), or as two words (*cross section*).

The word's pronunciation is given just after the main entry. The accents indicate which syllables are stressed; the other marks are explained in the dictionary's pronunciation key. In print dictionaries, this key usually appears at the bottom of every page or every other page. Many online entries include an audio link to a person's voice pronouncing the word. And most online dictionaries have an audio pronunciation guide.

Word endings and grammatical labels

When a word takes endings to indicate grammatical functions (called *inflections*), the endings are listed in boldface, as with *-garded, -garding,* and *-gards* in the following sample print entry.

PRINT DICTIONARY ENTRY

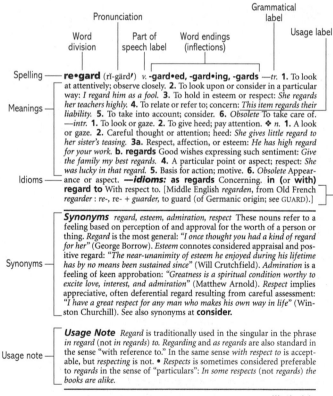

Labels for the parts of speech and for other grammatical terms are sometimes abbreviated, as they are in the print entry. The most commonly used abbreviations are these:

n.	noun	adj.	adjective
pl.	plural	adv.	adverb
sing.	singular	pron.	pronoun
v.	verb	prep.	preposition
tr.	transitive verb	conj.	conjunction
intr.	intransitive verb	interj.	interjection

ONLINE DICTIONARY ENTRY

AN ENCYCLOPÆDIA BRITANNICA COMPANY

Merriam-Webster

m-w.com

Dictionary | Thesaurus | Spanish-English | Medical

regard

regard — Part of speech label

3 ENTRIES FOUND:

1) **regard** (noun) •

Alternative entries — 2) **regard** (verb) — Audio pronunciation link
self-regard (noun) — Pronunciation

¹**re·gard** ◀)) *noun* \ri-ˈgärd\

Definition of REGARD

Usage label — •1 *archaic* **:** APPEARANCE

2 **a :** ATTENTION, CONSIDERATION <due *regard* should be given to all facets of the question>

Meanings (synonyms shown as hyperlinks) —
b : a protective interest **:** CARE <has no *regard* for her health>

3 **:** LOOK, GAZE

4 **a :** the worth or estimation in which something or someone is held <a man of small *regard*>

b (1) **:** a feeling of respect and affection **:** ESTEEM <she soon won the *regard* of her colleagues> (2) *plural* **:** friendly greetings implying such feeling <give him my *regards*>

. . .

Idioms —
— **in regard to**
 : with respect to **:** CONCERNING
— **with regard to**
 : in regard to

Link for multilingual writers — 🖉 See regard defined for English-language learners »

. . .

Word origin (etymology) —
Origin of REGARD
Middle English, from Anglo-French, from *regarder*
First Known Use: 14th century

Source: Merriam-Webster, www.Merriam-Webster.com (2010).

Meanings, word origin, synonyms, and antonyms

Each meaning for the word is given a number. Occasionally a word's use is illustrated in a quoted sentence. Sometimes a word can be used as more than one part of speech (*regard*, for instance, can be used as either a verb or a noun). In such a case, all the meanings for one part of speech are given before all the meanings for another, as in the sample entries. The entries also give idiomatic uses of the word.

The origin of the word, called its *etymology*, appears after all the meanings in the print and online versions.

Synonyms, words similar in meaning to the main entry, are frequently listed. In the sample print entry (p. 170), the dictionary draws distinctions in meaning among the various synonyms. In the online entry (p. 171), synonyms appear as hyperlinks. Antonyms, which do not appear in the sample entries, are words having a meaning opposite from that of the main entry.

Usage

Usage labels indicate when, where, or under what conditions a particular meaning for a word is appropriately used. Common labels are *informal* (or *colloquial*), *slang*, *archaic*, *poetic*, *nonstandard*, *dialect*, *obsolete*, and *British*. In the sample print entry (p. 170), two meanings of *regard* are labelled *obsolete* because they are no longer in use. The sample online entry (p. 171) has one meaning labelled *archaic*.

Dictionaries sometimes include usage notes as well. In the sample print entry, the dictionary offers advice on several uses of *regard* not specifically covered by the meanings. Such advice is based on the opinions of many experts and on actual usage in current magazines, newspapers, and books.

W6-b The thesaurus

When you are looking for just the right word, you may want to consult a collection of synonyms and antonyms such as *Roget's International Thesaurus*. Look up the adjective *still*, for example, and you will find synonyms such as *tranquil*, *quiet*, *quiescent*, *reposeful*, *calm*, *pacific*, *halcyon*, *placid*, and *unruffled*. The list will likely contain words you've never heard of or with which you are only vaguely familiar. Whenever you are tempted to use one of these words, first look it up in the dictionary to avoid misusing it.

Do not turn to a thesaurus in search of exotic, fancy words to embellish your essays. Look instead for words that express your meaning exactly and that are familiar to both you and your readers.

G

Grammatical Sentences

G Grammatical Sentences

G 173 – 222

G1 Subject-verb agreement

In the present tense, verbs agree with their subjects in number (singular or plural) and in person (first, second, or third): *I sing, you sing, he sings, she sings, we sing, they sing.* Even if your ear recognizes the standard subject-verb combinations presented in G1-a, you will no doubt encounter tricky situations such as those described in G1-b to G1-k.

G1-a Consult this section for standard subject-verb combinations.

This section describes the basic guidelines for making present-tense verbs agree with their subjects. The present-tense ending *-s* (or *-es*) is used on a verb if its subject is third-person singular (*he*, *she*, *it*, and singular nouns); otherwise the verb takes no ending. Consider, for example, the present-tense forms of the verbs *love* and *try*, given at the beginning of the chart on the following page.

The verb *be* varies from this pattern; unlike any other verb, it has special forms in *both* the present and the past tense. These forms appear at the end of the chart on page 176.

If you aren't confident that you know the standard forms, use the charts on pages 176 and 177 as you proofread for subject-verb agreement. You may also want to look at G2-c on *-s* endings of regular and irregular verbs.

G1-b Make the verb agree with its subject, not with a word that comes between.

Word groups often come between the subject and the verb. Such word groups, usually modifying the subject, may contain a noun that at first appears to be the subject. By mentally stripping away such modifiers, you can isolate the noun that is in fact the subject.

The *samples* on the tray in the lab *need* testing.

▶ High levels of air pollution causes damage to the respiratory

tract.

The subject is *levels*, not *pollution*. Strip away the phrase *of air pollution* to hear the correct verb: *levels cause*.

PRACTICE   hackerhandbooks.com/writersref
  > Grammatical sentences > G1–3 to G1–5

Subject-verb agreement at a glance

Present-tense forms of *love* and *try* (typical verbs)

	SINGULAR		PLURAL	
FIRST PERSON	I	love	we	love
SECOND PERSON	you	love	you	love
THIRD PERSON	he/she/it*	loves	they**	love

	SINGULAR		PLURAL	
FIRST PERSON	I	try	we	try
SECOND PERSON	you	try	you	try
THIRD PERSON	he/she/it*	tries	they**	try

Present-tense forms of *have*

	SINGULAR		PLURAL	
FIRST PERSON	I	have	we	have
SECOND PERSON	you	have	you	have
THIRD PERSON	he/she/it*	has	they**	have

Present-tense forms of *do* (including negative forms)

	SINGULAR		PLURAL	
FIRST PERSON	I	do/don't	we	do/don't
SECOND PERSON	you	do/don't	you	do/don't
THIRD PERSON	he/she/it*	does/doesn't	they**	do/don't

Present-tense and past-tense forms of *be*

	SINGULAR		PLURAL	
FIRST PERSON	I	am/was	we	are/were
SECOND PERSON	you	are/were	you	are/were
THIRD PERSON	he/she/it*	is/was	they**	are/were

*And singular nouns (*child, Roger*)
**And plural nouns (*children, the Mannings*)

▶ The slaughter of pandas for their pelts ~~have~~ *has* caused the
panda population to decline drastically.

The subject is *slaughter*, not *pandas* or *pelts*.

NOTE: Phrases beginning with the prepositions *as well as, in addition to, accompanied by, together with,* and *along with* do not make a singular subject plural.

When to use the -s (or -es) form of a present-tense verb

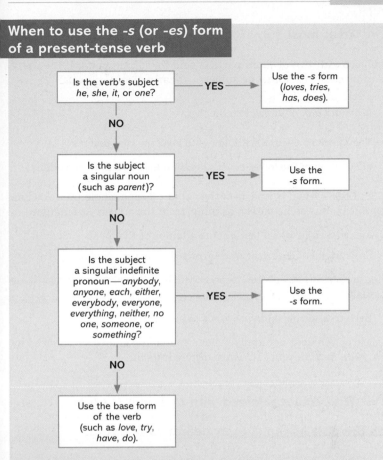

Is the verb's subject *he, she, it,* or *one?* — **YES** → Use the -s form (*loves, tries, has, does*).

NO ↓

Is the subject a singular noun (such as *parent*)? — **YES** → Use the -s form.

NO ↓

Is the subject a singular indefinite pronoun—*anybody, anyone, each, either, everybody, everyone, everything, neither, no one, someone,* or *something?* — **YES** → Use the -s form.

NO ↓

Use the base form of the verb (such as *love, try, have, do*).

EXCEPTION: Choosing the correct present-tense form of *be* (*am, is,* or *are*) is not always so simple. See the chart on the previous page for both present- and past-tense forms of *be*.

ESL TIP: Do not use the -s form of a verb if it follows a modal verb such as *can, must,* or *should* or another helping verb. (See M1-c.)

> ▶ The premier as well as his press secretary ~~were~~ *was* on
>   the plane.

To emphasize that two people were on the plane, the writer could use *and* instead: *The premier and his press secretary were on the plane.*

G1-c Treat most subjects joined with *and* as plural.

A subject with two or more parts is said to be compound. If the parts are connected with *and*, the subject is nearly always plural.

Leon and Jan often *jog* together.

▶ The Supreme Court's willingness to hear the case and its
    have
    affirmation of the lower court's decision ~~has~~ set a new precedent.

EXCEPTIONS: When the parts of the subject form a single unit or when they refer to the same person or thing, treat the subject as singular.

Fish and chips was a last-minute addition to the menu.

Sue's friend and adviser was surprised by her decision.

When a compound subject is preceded by *each* or *every*, treat it as singular.

Each tree, shrub, and vine needs to be sprayed.

This exception does not apply when a compound subject is followed by *each*: *Alan and Marcia each have different ideas.*

G1-d With subjects joined with *or* or *nor* (or with *either . . . or* or *neither . . . nor*), make the verb agree with the part of the subject nearer to the verb.

A driver's *licence* or credit *card is* required.

A driver's *licence* or two credit *cards are* required.

is
▶ If an infant or a child ~~are~~ having difficulty breathing, seek

    medical attention immediately.

▶ Neither the chief financial officer nor the marketing
    were
    managers ~~was~~ able to convince the client to reconsider.

The verb must be matched with the part of the subject closer to it: *child is* in the first sentence, *managers were* in the second.

NOTE: If one part of the subject is singular and the other is plural, put the plural one last to avoid awkwardness.

subjects with *and* • subjects with *or, not, either . . . or* •
pronouns like *anyone, each* • nouns like *family, audience*

G1-f

179

G1-e Treat most indefinite pronouns as singular.

Indefinite pronouns are pronouns that do not refer to specific persons or things. The following commonly used indefinite pronouns are singular.

anybody	each	everyone	nobody	somebody
anyone	either	everything	no one	someone
anything	everybody	neither	nothing	something

Many of these words appear to have plural meanings, and they are often treated as plural in casual speech. In formal written English, however, they are nearly always treated as singular.

Everyone on the team *supports* the coach.

▶ Each of the furrows ~~have~~ has been seeded.

▶ Nobody who participated in the clinical trials ~~were~~ was given a placebo.

The subjects of these sentences are *Each* and *Nobody*. These indefinite pronouns are third-person singular, so the verbs must be *has* and *was*.

A few indefinite pronouns (*all, any, none, some*) may be singular or plural depending on the noun or pronoun they refer to.

SINGULAR   *Some* of our *luggage was* lost.

None of his *advice makes* sense.

PLURAL   *Some* of the *rocks are* slippery.

None of the *eggs were* broken.

NOTE: When the meaning of *none* is emphatically "not one," *none* may be treated as singular: *None* [meaning "Not one"] *of the eggs was broken.* Using *not one* instead is sometimes clearer: *Not one of the eggs was broken.*

G1-f Treat collective nouns as singular unless the meaning is clearly plural.

Collective nouns such as *jury, committee, audience, crowd, troop, family,* and *couple* name a class or a group. In Canadian English, collective nouns are nearly always treated as singular: They emphasize the group as a unit. Occasionally, when there is some reason to draw attention to the individual members of the group, a collective noun may be treated as plural. (See also p. 198.)

SINGULAR   The *class respects* the teacher.

PLURAL   The *class are* debating among themselves.

To emphasize the notion of individuality in the second sentence, many writers would add a clearly plural noun.

PLURAL   The class *members are* debating among themselves.

> *meets*
> The board of trustees ~~meet~~ in Denver twice a year.

The board as a whole meets; there is no reason to draw attention to its individual members.

> *were*
> A young couple ~~was~~ arguing about politics while holding hands.

The meaning is clearly plural. Only separate individuals can argue and hold hands.

NOTE: The phrase *the number* is treated as singular, *a number* as plural.

SINGULAR   *The number* of school-age children *is* declining.

PLURAL   *A number* of children *are* attending the wedding.

NOTE: In general, when fractions or units of measurement are used with a singular noun, treat them as singular; when they are used with a plural noun, treat them as plural.

SINGULAR   *Three-fourths* of the salad *has* been eaten.

Fifty *centimetres* of wallboard *was* covered with mud.

PLURAL   *One-fourth* of the drivers *were* texting.

Two *kilograms* of blueberries *were* used in the jam.

G1-g Make the verb agree with its subject even when the subject follows the verb.

Verbs ordinarily follow subjects. When the normal order is reversed, it is easy to be confused. Sentences beginning with *there is* or *there are* (or *there was, there were*) are inverted; the subject follows the verb.

There *are* surprisingly few *honeybees* left in southern China.

▶ There ~~was~~ *were* a social worker and a neighbour at the scene of the crash.

The subject, *worker and neighbour*, is plural, so the verb must be *were*.

Occasionally you may invert a sentence for variety or effect. If you do, check to make sure that your subject and verb agree.

▶ Of particular concern ~~is~~ *are* penicillin and tetracycline, antibiotics

used to make animals more resistant to disease.

The subject, *penicillin and tetracycline*, is plural, so the verb must be *are*.

G1-h Make the verb agree with its subject, not with a subject complement.

One basic sentence pattern in English consists of a subject, a linking verb, and a subject complement: *Jack is a lawyer.* Because the subject complement (*lawyer*) names or describes the subject (*Jack*), it is sometimes mistaken for the subject. (See B2-b on subject complements.)

▶ A major force in today's economy ~~are~~ *is* children — as consumers,

decision makers, and trend spotters.

Force is the subject, not *children*. If the corrected version seems too awkward, make *children* the subject: *Children are a major force in today's economy — as consumers, decision makers, and trend spotters.*

▶ A tent and a sleeping bag ~~is~~ *are* the required equipment for all campers.

Tent and bag is the subject, not *equipment*.

G1-i *Who, which,* and *that* take verbs that agree with their antecedents.

Like most pronouns, the relative pronouns *who, which,* and *that* have antecedents, nouns or pronouns to which they refer. Relative pronouns used as subjects of subordinate clauses take verbs that agree with their antecedents.

Take a *course that prepares* you for classroom management.

One of the

Constructions such as *one of the students who* [or *one of the things that*] may cause problems for writers. Do not assume that the antecedent must be *one*. Instead, consider the logic of the sentence.

▶ Our ability to use language is one of the things that set/s us

apart from animals.

The antecedent of *that* is *things*, not *one*. Several things set us apart from animals.

Only one of the

When the word *only* comes before *one*, you are safe in assuming that *one* is the antecedent of the relative pronoun.

▶ Veronica was the only one of the first-year French students who
was
~~were~~ fluent enough to apply for the exchange program.
^
The antecedent of *who* is *one*, not *students*. Only one student was fluent enough.

G1-j Words such as *athletics*, *economics*, *mathematics*, *physics*, *politics*, *statistics*, *measles*, and *news* are usually singular, despite their plural form.

is
▶ Politics ~~are~~ among my mother's favourite pastimes.
^

EXCEPTION: Occasionally some of these words, especially *economics*, *mathematics*, *politics*, and *statistics*, have plural meanings:

Office politics often sway decisions about hiring and promotion.

The economics of the building plan are prohibitive.

G1-k Titles of works, company names, words mentioned as words, and gerund phrases are singular.

describes
▶ *Lost Cities* ~~describe~~ the discoveries of fifty ancient civilizations.
^
specializes
▶ Delmonico Brothers ~~specialize~~ in organic produce and
^
additive-free meats.

is
▶ *Controlled substances* ~~are~~ a euphemism for illegal drugs.
  ^

A gerund phrase consists of an *-ing* verb form followed by any objects, complements, or modifiers (see B3-b). Treat gerund phrases as singular.

makes
▶ Encountering long hold times ~~make~~ customers impatient with
  ^

telephone tech support.

☰ G2 Verb forms, tenses, and moods

Section G-1 deals with subject-verb agreement, and section W3 offers advice on active and passive verbs. This section describes other potential challenges with verbs:

a. irregular verb forms (such as *drive, drove, driven*)
b. *lie* and *lay*
c. *-s* (or *-es*) endings on verbs
d. *-ed* endings on verbs
e. omitted verbs
f. tense
g. subjunctive mood

> **ESL** If English is not your first language, see also M1 for more help with verbs.

G2-a Choose standard English forms of irregular verbs.

Except for the verb *be*, all verbs in English have five forms. The following list shows the five forms and provides a sample sentence in which each might appear.

BASE FORM	Usually I (*walk, ride*).
PAST TENSE	Yesterday I (*walked, rode*).
PAST PARTICIPLE	I have (*walked, ridden*) many times before.
PRESENT PARTICIPLE	I am (*walking, riding*) right now.
-S FORM	He/she/it (*walks, rides*) regularly.

The verb *be* has eight forms instead of the usual five: *be, am, is, are, was, were, being, been.*

For all regular verbs, the past-tense and past-participle forms are the same (ending in *-ed* or *-d*), so there is no danger of confusion. This is not true, however, for irregular verbs, such as the following.

BASE FORM	PAST TENSE	PAST PARTICIPLE
go	went	gone
break	broke	broken
fly	flew	flown
sing	sang	sung

The past-tense form always occurs alone, without a helping verb. It expresses action that occurred entirely in the past: *I rode to work yesterday. I walked to work last Tuesday.* The past participle is used with a helping verb. It forms the perfect tenses with *has, have,* or *had;* it forms the passive voice with *be, am, is, are, was, were, being,* or *been.* (See B1-c for a complete list of helping verbs and G2-f for a survey of tenses.)

PAST TENSE	Last July, we *went* to Paris.
HELPING VERB + PAST PARTICIPLE	We *have gone* to Paris twice.

The list of common irregular verbs beginning at the bottom of this page will help you distinguish between the past tense and the past participle. Choose the past-participle form if the verb in your sentence requires a helping verb; choose the past-tense form if the verb does not require a helping verb. (See verb tenses in G2-f.)

▶ Yesterday we ~~seen~~ *saw* a documentary about Isabel Allende.

The past-tense *saw* is required because there is no helping verb.

▶ The truck was apparently ~~stole~~ *stolen* while the driver ate lunch.

▶ By Friday, the stock market had ~~fell~~ *fallen* two hundred points.

Because of the helping verbs *was* and *had,* the past-participle forms are required: *was stolen, had fallen.*

Common irregular verbs

BASE FORM	PAST TENSE	PAST PARTICIPLE
arise	arose	arisen
awake	awoke, awaked	awaked, awoke, awoken
be	was, were	been

BASE FORM	PAST TENSE	PAST PARTICIPLE
beat	beat	beaten, beat
become	became	become
begin	began	begun
bend	bent	bent
bite	bit	bitten, bit
blow	blew	blown
break	broke	broken
bring	brought	brought
build	built	built
burst	burst	burst
buy	bought	bought
catch	caught	caught
choose	chose	chosen
cling	clung	clung
come	came	come
cost	cost	cost
deal	dealt	dealt
dig	dug	dug
dive	dived, dove	dived
do	did	done
drag	dragged	dragged
draw	drew	drawn
dream	dreamed, dreamt	dreamed, dreamt
drink	drank	drunk
drive	drove	driven
eat	ate	eaten
fall	fell	fallen
fight	fought	fought
find	found	found
fly	flew	flown
forget	forgot	forgotten, forgot
freeze	froze	frozen
get	got	gotten, got
give	gave	given
go	went	gone
grow	grew	grown
hang (execute)	hanged	hanged
hang (suspend)	hung	hung
have	had	had
hear	heard	heard
hide	hid	hidden
hurt	hurt	hurt
keep	kept	kept
know	knew	known
lay (put)	laid	laid
lead	led	led
lend	lent	lent
let (allow)	let	let

BASE FORM	PAST TENSE	PAST PARTICIPLE
lie (recline)	lay	lain
lose	lost	lost
make	made	made
prove	proved	proven, proved
read	read	read
ride	rode	ridden
ring	rang	rung
rise (get up)	rose	risen
run	ran	run
say	said	said
see	saw	seen
send	sent	sent
set (place)	set	set
shake	shook	shaken
shoot	shot	shot
shrink	shrank	shrunk
sing	sang	sung
sink	sank	sunk
sit (be seated)	sat	sat
slay	slew	slain
sleep	slept	slept
speak	spoke	spoken
spin	spun	spun
spring	sprang	sprung
stand	stood	stood
steal	stole	stolen
sting	stung	stung
strike	struck	struck
swear	swore	sworn
swim	swam	swum
swing	swung	swung
take	took	taken
teach	taught	taught
throw	threw	thrown
wake	woke, waked	waked, woken
wear	wore	worn
wring	wrung	wrung
write	wrote	written

G2-b Distinguish among the forms of *lie* and *lay*.

Writers and speakers frequently confuse the various forms of *lie* (meaning "to recline or rest on a surface") and *lay* (meaning "to put or place something"). *Lie* is an intransitive verb; it does not take a direct object: *The tax forms lie on the table.* The verb *lay* is transitive; it takes a direct object: *Please lay the tax forms on the table.* (See B2-b.)

In addition to confusing the meaning of *lie* and *lay*, writers and speakers are often unfamiliar with the standard English forms of these verbs.

BASE FORM	PAST TENSE	PAST PARTICIPLE	PRESENT PARTICIPLE
lie ("recline")	lay	lain	lying
lay ("put")	laid	laid	laying

▶ Sue was so exhausted that she ~~laid~~ *lay* down for a nap.

The past-tense form of *lie* ("to recline") is *lay*.

▶ The patient had ~~laid~~ *lain* in an uncomfortable position all night.

The past-participle form of *lie* ("to recline") is *lain*. If the correct English seems too stilted, recast the sentence: *The patient had been lying in an uncomfortable position all night.*

▶ The prosecutor ~~lay~~ *laid* the pistol on a table close to the jurors.

The past-tense form of *lay* ("to place") is *laid*.

▶ Letters dating from World War I were ~~laying~~ *lying* in the corner of the

chest.

The present participle of *lie* ("to rest on a surface") is *lying*.

G2-c Use *-s* (or *-es*) endings on present-tense verbs that have third-person singular subjects.

All singular nouns (*child*, *tree*) and the pronouns *he*, *she*, and *it* are third-person singular; indefinite pronouns such as *everyone* and *neither* are also third-person singular. When the subject of a sentence is third-person singular, its verb takes an *-s* or *-es* ending in the present tense. (See also G1.)

	SINGULAR		PLURAL	
FIRST PERSON	I	know	we	know
SECOND PERSON	you	know	you	know
THIRD PERSON	he/she/it	knows	they	know
	child	knows	parents	know
	everyone	knows		

>   *drives*
> My neighbour ~~drive~~ to North Bay every weekend.
>   ^

>   *turns*   *dissolves*   *eats*
> Sulphur dioxide ~~turn~~ leaves yellow, ~~dissolve~~ marble, and ~~eat~~ away
>   ^   ^   ^
>
> iron and steel.

The subjects *neighbour* and *sulphur dioxide* are third-person singular, so the verbs must end in *-s*.

TIP: Do not add the *-s* ending to the verb if the subject is not third-person singular. The writers of the following sentences, knowing they sometimes dropped *-s* endings from verbs, overcorrected by adding the endings where they don't belong.

> I prepares program specifications and logic diagrams.

The writer mistakenly concluded that the *-s* ending belongs on present-tense verbs used with *all* singular subjects, not just *third-person* singular subjects. The pronoun *I* is first-person singular, so its verb does not require the *-s*.

> The dirt floors requires continual sweeping.

The writer mistakenly thought that the verb needed an *-s* ending because of the plural subject. But the *-s* ending is used only on present-tense verbs with third-person *singular* subjects.

In nonstandard speech, the *-s* verb form *has*, *does*, or *doesn't* is sometimes replaced with *have*, *do*, or *don't*. In standard English, use *has*, *does*, or *doesn't* with a third-person singular subject. (See also G1-a.)

>   *has*
> This respected musician always ~~have~~ a message in his work.
>   ^
>
> *Does*
> ~~Do~~ she know the correct procedure for the experiment?
> ^
>
>   *doesn't*
> My uncle ~~don't~~ want to change jobs right now.
>   ^

G2-d Do not omit *-ed* endings on verbs.

Speakers who do not fully pronounce *-ed* endings sometimes omit them unintentionally in writing. Leaving off *-ed* endings is common in many dialects and in informal speech even in standard English. In the following frequently used words and phrases, for example, the *-ed* ending is not always fully pronounced.

advised	developed	prejudiced	supposed to
asked	fixed	pronounced	used to
concerned	frightened	stereotyped	

When a verb is regular, both the past tense and the past participle are formed by adding *-ed* (or *-d*) to the base form of the verb.

Past tense

Use the ending *-ed* or *-d* to express the past tense of regular verbs. The past tense is used when the action occurred entirely in the past.

▶ Over the weekend, Ed ~~fix~~ *fixed* his brother's skateboard and tuned up
  ^
  his mother's 1991 Fiat.

▶ Last summer, my counsellor ~~advise~~ *advised* me to ask my chemistry
  ^
  instructor for help.

Past participles

Past participles are used in three ways: (1) following *have, has,* or *had* to form one of the perfect tenses; (2) following *be, am, is, are, was, were, being,* or *been* to form the passive voice; and (3) as adjectives modifying nouns or pronouns. The perfect tenses are listed on page 191, and the passive voice is discussed in W3. For a discussion of participles as adjectives, see B3-b.

▶ Robin has ~~ask~~ *asked* for more housing staff for next year.
  ^
  Has asked is present perfect tense (*have* or *has* followed by a past participle).

▶ Though it is not a new phenomenon, domestic violence is now
  ~~publicize~~ *publicized* more than ever.
  ^
  Is publicized is a verb in the passive voice (a form of *be* followed by a past participle).

▶ All kickboxing classes end in a cool-down period to stretch
  ~~tighten~~ *tightened* muscles.
  ^
  The past participle *tightened* functions as an adjective modifying the noun *muscles.*

G2-e Do not omit needed verbs.

Although standard English allows some linking verbs and helping verbs to be contracted in informal contexts, it does not allow them to be omitted.

Linking verbs, used to link subjects to subject complements, are frequently a form of *be: be, am, is, are, was, were, being, been.* (See B2-b.) Some of these forms may be contracted (*I'm, she's, we're, you're, they're*), but they should not be omitted altogether.

>   *are*
> When we quiet in the evening, we can hear crickets in the woods.
>   ^

Helping verbs, used with main verbs, include forms of *be, do,* and *have* and the modal verbs *can, will, shall, could, would, should, may, might,* and *must.* (See B1-c.) Some helping verbs may be contracted (*he's leaving, we'll celebrate, they've been told*), but they should not be omitted altogether.

>   *have*
> We been in Moncton since last Thursday.
> ^

ESL   Some languages do not require a linking verb between a subject and its complement. English, however, requires a verb in every sentence. See M3-a.

>   *am*
> Every night, I read a short book to my daughter. When I
>   ^
> too busy, my husband reads to her.

G2-f Choose the appropriate verb tense.

Tenses indicate the time of an action in relation to the time of the speaking or writing about that action.

The most common problem with tenses — shifting confusingly from one tense to another — is discussed in section S4. Other problems with tenses are detailed in this section, after the following survey of tenses.

Survey of tenses

Tenses are classified as present, past, and future, with simple, perfect, and progressive forms for each.

missing verbs • linking verbs (*is, were*) • tenses •
simple (*walk*) • perfect (*had walked*) • progressive (*am walking*)

G2-f 191

SIMPLE TENSES The simple tenses indicate relatively simple time relations. The *simple present* tense is used primarily for actions occurring at the same time they are being discussed or for actions occurring regularly. The *simple past* tense is used for actions completed in the past. The *simple future* tense is used for actions that will occur in the future. In the following table, the simple tenses are given for the regular verb *walk*, the irregular verb *ride*, and the highly irregular verb *be*.

SIMPLE PRESENT

SINGULAR		PLURAL	
I	walk, ride, am	we	walk, ride, are
you	walk, ride, are	you	walk, ride, are
he/she/it	walks, rides, is	they	walk, ride, are

SIMPLE PAST

SINGULAR		PLURAL	
I	walked, rode, was	we	walked, rode, were
you	walked, rode, were	you	walked, rode, were
he/she/it	walked, rode, was	they	walked, rode, were

SIMPLE FUTURE

I, you, he/she/it, we, they	will walk, ride, be

PERFECT TENSES More complex time relations are indicated by the perfect tenses. A verb in one of the perfect tenses (a form of *have* plus the past participle) expresses an action that was or will be completed at the time of another action.

PRESENT PERFECT

I, you, we, they	have walked, ridden, been
he/she/it	has walked, ridden, been

PAST PERFECT

I, you, he/she/it, we, they	had walked, ridden, been

FUTURE PERFECT

I, you, he/she/it, we, they	will have walked, ridden, been

PROGRESSIVE FORMS The simple and perfect tenses have progressive forms that describe actions in progress. A progressive verb consists of a form of *be* followed by a present participle. The progressive forms are not normally used with certain verbs, such as *believe, know, hear, seem,* and *think*.

PRESENT PROGRESSIVE

I	am walking, riding, being
he/she/it	is walking, riding, being
you, we, they	are walking, riding, being

PAST PROGRESSIVE

| I, he/she/it | was walking, riding, being |
| you, we, they | were walking, riding, being |

FUTURE PROGRESSIVE

| I, you, he/she/it, we, they | will be walking, riding, being |

PRESENT PERFECT PROGRESSIVE

| I, you, we, they | have been walking, riding, being |
| he/she/it | has been walking, riding, being |

PAST PERFECT PROGRESSIVE

| I, you, he/she/it, we, they | had been walking, riding, being |

FUTURE PERFECT PROGRESSIVE

| I, you, he/she/it, we, they | will have been walking, riding, being |

ESL   See M1-a for more specific examples of verb tenses that can be challenging for multilingual writers.

Special uses of the present tense

Use the present tense when expressing general truths, when writing about literature, and when quoting, summarizing, or paraphrasing an author's views.

General truths or scientific principles should appear in the present tense unless such principles have been disproved.

> *revolves*
> ▶ Galileo taught that the earth ~~revolved~~ around the sun.
> ⌃

Because Galileo's teaching has not been discredited, the verb should be in the present tense. The following sentence, however, is acceptable: *Ptolemy taught that the sun revolved around the earth.*

When writing about a work of literature, you may be tempted to use the past tense. The convention, however, is to describe fictional events in the present tense.

> *reaches*
> ▶ In Masuji Ibuse's *Black Rain*, a child ~~reached~~ for a pomegranate
>   ^
>   *is*
> in his mother's garden, and a moment later he ~~was~~ dead, killed
>   ^
> by the blast of the atomic bomb.

When you are quoting, summarizing, or paraphrasing the author of a nonliterary work, use present-tense verbs such as *writes, reports, asserts*, and so on to introduce the source. This convention is usually followed even when the author is dead (unless a date or the context specifies the time of writing).

> *argues*
> ▶ Dr. Jerome Groopman ~~argued~~ that doctors are "susceptible
>   ^
> to the subtle and not so subtle efforts of the pharmaceutical
>
> industry to sculpt our thinking" (9).

Writing
with
sources
MLA-style
citation

In MLA style, signal phrases are written in the present tense, not the past tense. (See also MLA-3b.)

APA NOTE: When you are documenting a paper with the APA (American Psychological Association) style of in-text citations, use past tense verbs such as *reported* or *demonstrated* or present perfect verbs such as *has reported* or *has demonstrated* to introduce the source.

> E. Wilson (1994) reported that positive reinforcement alone was a less effective teaching technique than a mixture of positive reinforcement and constructive criticism.

The past perfect tense

The past perfect tense consists of a past participle preceded by *had* (*had worked, had forgotten*). This tense is used for an action already completed by the time of another past action or for an action already completed at some specific past time.

> Everyone *had spoken* by the time I arrived.
>
> I pleaded my case, but Paula *had made up* her mind.

Writers sometimes use the simple past tense when they should use the past perfect.

> ▶ We built our cabin high on a pine knoll, fifteen metres above an
>   *had been*
> abandoned quarry that ~~was~~ flooded in 1920 to create a lake.
>   ^

The building of the cabin and the flooding of the quarry both occurred in the past, but the flooding was completed before the time of building.

had
▶ By the time dinner was served, the guest of honour left.
                                                        ^

The past perfect tense is needed because the action of leaving was already completed at a specific past time (when dinner was served).

Some writers tend to overuse the past perfect tense. Do not use the past perfect if two past actions occurred at the same time.

wrote
▶ When Ernest Hemingway lived in Cuba, he ~~had written~~ *For Whom*
                                             ^
the Bell Tolls.

Sequence of tenses with infinitives and participles

An infinitive is the base form of a verb preceded by *to*. (See B3-b.) Use the present infinitive to show action occurring at the same time as or later than the action of the verb in the sentence.

raise
▶ The club had hoped to ~~have raised~~ fifteen thousand dollars by
                          ^
April 1.

The action expressed in the infinitive (*to raise*) occurred later than the action of the sentence's verb (*had hoped*).

Use the perfect form of an infinitive (*to have* followed by the past participle) for an action occurring earlier than that of the verb in the sentence.

have joined
▶ Dan would like to ~~join~~ the navy, but he did not pass the physical.
                     ^
The liking occurs in the present; the joining would have occurred in the past.

Like the tense of an infinitive, the tense of a participle is governed by the tense of the sentence's verb. Use the present participle (ending in *-ing*) for an action occurring at the same time as that of the sentence's verb.

Hiking the Crowsnest Pass in early spring, we spotted many wildflowers.

Use the past participle (such as *given* or *helped*) or the present perfect participle (*having* plus the past participle) for an action occurring before that of the verb.

tenses with infinitives (*to see*), participles (*given*) • verbs with *if, when* •
conditional • subjunctive • contrary-to-fact • wishes

G2-g 195

Discovered off the coast of Nova Scotia, the barque yielded many treasures.

Having skied all day, Lee collapsed in front of the fire.

G2-g Use the subjunctive mood in the few contexts that require it.

There are three moods in English: the *indicative*, used for facts, opinions, and questions; the *imperative*, used for orders or advice; and the *subjunctive*, used in certain contexts to express wishes, requests, or conditions contrary to fact. For many writers, the subjunctive causes the most problems.

Forms of the subjunctive

In the subjunctive mood, present-tense verbs do not change form to indicate the number and person of the subject (see G1-a). Instead, the subjunctive uses the base form of the verb (*be, drive, employ*) with all subjects.

It is important that you *be* [not *are*] prepared for the interview.

We asked that she *drive* [not *drives*] more slowly.

Also, in the subjunctive mood, there is only one past-tense form of *be*: *were* (never *was*).

If I *were* [not *was*] you, I'd try a new strategy.

Uses of the subjunctive

The subjunctive mood appears in only a few contexts: in contrary-to-fact clauses beginning with *if* or expressing a wish; in *that* clauses following verbs such as *ask, insist, recommend, request,* and *suggest*; and in certain set expressions.

IN CONTRARY-TO-FACT CLAUSES BEGINNING WITH *IF* When a subordinate clause beginning with *if* expresses a condition contrary to fact, use the subjunctive *were* in place of *was*.

▶ The astronomers would be able to see the moons of Jupiter

were
tonight if the weather ~~was~~ clearer.
^

The verb in the subordinate clause expresses a condition that does not exist: The weather is not clear.

were
▶ If I ~~was~~ a member of the Senate, I would vote for that bill.
        ^

The writer is not a member of the Senate, so the verb in the *if* clause must be *were*.

Do not use the subjunctive mood in *if* clauses expressing conditions that exist or may exist.

If Dana *wins* the contest, she will leave for Barcelona in June.

IN CONTRARY-TO-FACT CLAUSES EXPRESSING A WISH   In formal English, use the subjunctive *were* in clauses expressing a wish or desire. While use of the indicative is common in informal speech, it is not appropriate in academic writing.

> **INFORMAL**   I wish that Dr. Vaughn *was* my professor.
>
> **FORMAL**   I wish that Dr. Vaughn *were* my professor.

IN *THAT* CLAUSES FOLLOWING VERBS SUCH AS *ASK*, *INSIST*, *REQUEST*, AND *SUGGEST*   Because requests have not yet become reality, they are expressed in the subjunctive mood.

                                               be
▶ Professor Moore insists that her students ~~are~~ on time.
                                                ^
                                file
▶ We recommend that Lambert ~~files~~ form NR73 soon.
                                 ^

IN CERTAIN SET EXPRESSIONS   The subjunctive mood appears in certain expressions: *be that as it may*, *as it were*, *far be it from me*, and so on.

G3 Pronouns

Pronouns are words that substitute for nouns (see B1-b). Pronoun errors are typically related to the four topics discussed in this section:

    a.   pronoun-antecedent agreement (singular vs. plural)
    b.   pronoun reference (clarity)
    c.   pronoun case (personal pronouns such as *I* vs. *me*, *she* vs. *her*)
    d.   pronoun case (*who* vs. *whom*)

For more help with pronouns, consult the glossary of usage (W1).

G3-a Make pronouns and antecedents agree.

Many pronouns have antecedents, nouns or pronouns to which they refer. A pronoun and its antecedent agree when they are both singular or both plural.

SINGULAR   *Dr. Ava Berto* finished *her* rounds.

PLURAL   The hospital *interns* finished *their* rounds.

> **ESL**   The pronouns *he*, *his*, *she*, *her*, *it*, and *its* must agree in gender (masculine, feminine, or neuter) with their antecedents, not with the words they modify.
>
>   *Steve* visited *his* [not *her*] sister in Gander.

Indefinite pronouns

Indefinite pronouns refer to nonspecific persons or things. Even though some of the following indefinite pronouns may seem to have plural meanings, treat them as singular in formal English.

anybody	each	everyone	nobody	somebody
anyone	either	everything	no one	someone
anything	everybody	neither	nothing	something

Everyone performs at *his or her* [not *their*] own fitness level.

When a plural pronoun refers mistakenly to a singular indefinite pronoun, you can usually choose one of three options for revision:

1. Replace the plural pronoun with *he or she* (or *his or her*).
2. Make the antecedent plural.
3. Rewrite the sentence so that no agreement problem exists.

▶ When someone travels outside Canada for the first time,
   he or she needs
   ~~they need~~ to apply for a passport.
     ^

▶ When ~~someone travels~~ outside Canada for the first time,
   people travel
     ^
   they need to apply for a passport.

Anyone who
▶ ~~When someone~~ travels outside Canada for the first time./
  ^
  needs
  ~~they need~~ to apply for a passport.
  ^

Because the *he or she* construction is wordy, often the second or third revision strategy is more effective. Using *he* (or *his*) to refer to persons of either sex, while less wordy, is considered sexist, as is using *she* (or *her*) for all persons. See W4-e for strategies that avoid sexist usage.

NOTE: If you change a pronoun from singular to plural (or vice versa), check to be sure that the verb agrees with the new pronoun (see G1-e).

Generic nouns

A generic noun represents a typical member of a group, such as a typical student, or any member of a group, such as any lawyer. Although generic nouns may seem to have plural meanings, they are singular.

Every *runner* must train rigorously if *he or she wants* [not *they want*] to excel.

When a plural pronoun refers mistakenly to a generic noun, you will usually have the same revision options as on page 197.

                              he or she wants
▶ A medical student must study hard if ~~they want~~ to succeed.
                                          ^
  Medical students
▶ ~~A medical student~~ must study hard if they want to succeed.
  ^

▶ A medical student must study hard ~~if they want~~ to succeed.

Collective nouns

Collective nouns such as *jury, committee, audience, crowd, class, troop, family, team,* and *couple* name a group. Ordinarily the group functions as a unit, so the noun should be treated as singular; if the members of the group function as individuals, however, the noun should be treated as plural. (See also G1-f.)

AS A UNIT   The *committee* granted *its* permission to build.

AS INDIVIDUALS   The *committee* put *their* signatures on the letter.

When treating a collective noun as plural, many writers prefer to add a clearly plural antecedent such as *members* to the sentence: *The members of the committee put their signatures on the letter.*

▶ Defence lawyer Charles Fitzpatrick urged the jury to find his client

Louis Riel not guilty by reason of insanity. The jury disagreed,
                        its
returning ~~their~~ verdict of guilty but recommending mercy.
          ^

There is no reason to draw attention to the individual members of the jury, so *jury* should be treated as singular.

Compound antecedents

Treat most compound antecedents joined with *and* as plural.

In 1988, *Reagan and Mulroney* held a summit where *they* signed the Canada-US Free Trade Agreement.

With compound antecedents joined with *or* or *nor* (or with *either . . . or* or *neither . . . nor*), make the pronoun agree with the nearer antecedent.

Either *Bruce* or *Tom* should receive first prize for *his* poem.

Neither the *mouse* nor the *rats* could find *their* way through the maze.

NOTE: If one of the antecedents is singular and the other plural, as in the second example, put the plural one last to avoid awkwardness.

EXCEPTION: If one antecedent is male and the other female, do not follow the traditional rule. The sentence *Either Bruce or Elizabeth should receive first prize for her short story* makes no sense. A better solution is to recast the sentence: *The prize for best short story should go to either Bruce or Elizabeth.*

G3-b Make pronoun references clear.

In a sentence like *After Andrew intercepted the ball, he kicked it as hard as he could*, the pronouns *he* and *it* substitute for the nouns *Andrew* and *ball*. The word a pronoun refers to is called its *antecedent*.

Ambiguous reference

Ambiguous pronoun reference occurs when a pronoun could refer to two possible antecedents.

PRACTICE   hackerhandbooks.com/writersref
  > Grammatical sentences > G3–11 to G3–13

> ▶ ~~When Gloria set the pitcher~~ on the glass-topped table~~. it broke.~~
>   ^   ^
>   *The pitcher broke when Gloria set it*
>
> ▶ Tom told James~~, that he had~~ won the lottery."
>   ^   ^
>   *"You have*

What broke—the pitcher or the table? Who won the lottery—Tom or James? The revisions eliminate the ambiguity.

Implied reference

A pronoun should refer to a specific antecedent, not to a word that is implied but not present in the sentence.

> ▶ After braiding Ann's hair, Sue decorated ~~them~~ with colourful
>   ^
>   *the braids*
>
>   silk ribbons.

The pronoun *them* referred to Ann's braids (implied by the term *braiding*), but the word *braids* did not appear in the sentence.

Modifiers, such as possessives, cannot serve as antecedents. A modifier may strongly imply the noun that a pronoun might logically refer to, but it is not itself that noun.

Writing
with
sources
MLA-style
citation

> ▶ In ~~Jamaica Kincaid's~~ "Girl," ~~she~~ describes the advice a mother
>   ^
>   *Jamaica Kincaid*
>
>   gives her daughter, including the mysterious warning not to be
>
>   "the kind of woman who the baker won't let near the bread" (454).

Using the possessive form of an author's name to introduce a source leads to a problem later in this sentence: The pronoun *she* cannot refer logically to a possessive modifier (*Jamaica Kincaid's*). The revision substitutes the noun *Jamaica Kincaid* for the pronoun *she*, thereby eliminating the problem.

Broad reference of *this, that, which, and* it

For clarity, the pronouns *this, that, which,* and *it* should ordinarily refer to specific antecedents rather than to whole ideas or sentences. When a pronoun's reference is needlessly broad, either replace the pronoun with a noun or supply an antecedent to which the pronoun clearly refers.

> ▶ By pooling their money, members of an investment club gain
>   purchasing power. ~~This~~ allows/ for more diversification, which
>   ^
>   *The larger sums*
>
>   lowers the risks.

For clarity, the writer substituted the noun *sums* for the pronoun *This*, which referred broadly to the idea expressed in the preceding sentence.

▶ Romeo and Juliet were both too young to have acquired much
      a fact
wisdom, ~~and~~ that accounts for their rash actions.
   ^

The writer added an antecedent (*fact*) that the pronoun *that* clearly refers to.

Indefinite use of *they, it,* and *you*

Do not use the pronoun *they* to refer indefinitely to persons who have not been specifically mentioned. *They* should always refer to a specific antecedent.

     the board
▶ In June, ~~they~~ announced that parents would have to pay a fee
   ^

   for their children to participate in sports and music programs

   starting in September.

The word *it* should not be used indefinitely in constructions such as *It is said on television . . .* or *In the article, it says that. . . .*

  The
▶ ~~In the~~ encyclopedia ~~it~~ states that male moths can smell female
  ^

  moths from several kilometres away.

The pronoun *you* is appropriate only when the writer is addressing the reader directly: *Once you have kneaded the dough, let it rise in a warm place.* Except in informal contexts, however, *you* should not be used to mean "anyone in general." Use a noun instead.

             a guest
▶ Ms. Pickersgill's *Guide to Etiquette* stipulates that ~~you~~
                ^

  should not arrive at a party too early or leave too late.

G3-c Distinguish between pronouns such as *I* and *me*.

The personal pronouns in the following chart change what is known as *case form* according to their grammatical function in a sentence. Pronouns functioning as subjects or subject complements appear in the *subjective* case; those functioning as objects appear in the *objective* case; and those showing ownership appear in the *possessive* case.

PRACTICE   **hackerhandbooks.com/writersref**
    > Grammatical sentences > G3-14 and G3-15
                   > G3-17 and G3-18 (pronoun review)

	SUBJECTIVE CASE	OBJECTIVE CASE	POSSESSIVE CASE
SINGULAR	I	me	my
	you	you	your
	he/she/it	him/her/it	his/her/its
PLURAL	we	us	our
	you	you	your
	they	them	their

Pronouns in the subjective and objective cases are frequently confused. Most of the rules in this section specify when to use one or the other of these cases (*I* or *me*, *he* or *him*, and so on). See page 205 for a special use of pronouns and nouns in the possessive case.

Subjective case (I, you, he, she, it, we, they)

When a pronoun functions as a subject or a subject complement, it must be in the subjective case.

SUBJECT	Sylvia and *he* shared the award.
SUBJECT COMPLEMENT	Greg announced that the winners were Sylvia and *he*.

Subject complements—words following linking verbs that complete the meaning of the subject—frequently cause problems for writers, since we rarely hear the correct form in casual speech. (See B2-b.)

▶ During the trial, David Milgaard repeatedly denied that the

　　　　　he.
killer was ~~him.~~
　　　　　^

If *killer was he* seems too stilted, rewrite the sentence: *During the trial, David Milgaard repeatedly denied that he was the killer.*

Objective case (me, you, him, her, it, us, them)

When a personal pronoun is used as a direct object, an indirect object, or the object of a preposition, it must be in the objective case.

DIRECT OBJECT	Bruce found Tony and brought *him* home.
INDIRECT OBJECT	Alice gave *me* a surprise party.
OBJECT OF A PREPOSITION	Jessica wondered if the call was for *her*.

I, you, he/she/it, we, they • subject pronouns • *me, you, him/her/it, us, them* • object pronouns • words that rename nouns • appositives

G3-c   203

Compound word groups

When a subject or an object appears as part of a compound structure, you may occasionally become confused. To test for the correct pronoun, mentally strip away all of the compound word group except the pronoun in question.

▶ Joel ran away from home because his stepfather and ~~him~~ had
    he

quarrelled.

His stepfather and he is the subject of the verb *had quarrelled.* If we strip away the words *his stepfather and,* the correct pronoun becomes clear: *he had quarrelled* (not *him had quarrelled*).

▶ The most traumatic experience for her father and ~~I~~ occurred long
    me

after her operation.

Her father and me is the compound object of the preposition *for.* Strip away the words *her father and* to test for the correct pronoun: *for me* (not *for I*).

When in doubt about the correct pronoun, some writers try to avoid making the choice by using a reflexive pronoun such as *myself.* Using a reflexive pronoun in such situations is nonstandard.

▶ The Indian cab driver gave my cousin and ~~myself~~ some good tips
    me

on travelling in New Delhi.

My cousin and me is the indirect object of the verb *gave.* For correct uses of *myself,* see the glossary of usage (W1).

Appositives

Appositives are noun phrases that rename nouns or pronouns. A pronoun used as an appositive has the same function (usually subject or object) as the word(s) it renames.

▶ The chief strategists, Dr. Bell and ~~me,~~ could not agree on a plan.
    I,

The appositive *Dr. Bell and I* renames the subject, *strategists.* Test: *I could not agree* (not *me could not agree*).

▶ The newspaper reporter interviewed only two witnesses, the bicyclist
and ~~I.~~
    me.

The appositive *the bicyclist and me* renames the direct object, *witnesses*. Test: *interviewed me* (not *interviewed I*).

We or us *before a noun*

When deciding whether *we* or *us* should precede a noun, choose the pronoun that would be appropriate if the noun were omitted.

▶ <u>Us</u> tenants would rather fight than move.
  We

▶ Management is shortchanging <s>we</s> tenants.
  us

No one would say *Us would rather fight than move* or *Management is shortchanging we*.

Comparisons with *than or as*

When a comparison begins with *than* or *as*, your choice of a pronoun will depend on your meaning. To test for the correct pronoun, mentally complete the sentence: *My roommate likes football more than I [do]*.

▶ In our position paper supporting nationalized health care in the

  United States, we argued that Canadians are much better off
  than <s>us</s>.
  we.

We is the subject of the verb *are*, which is understood: *Canadians are much better off than we [are]*. If the correct English seems too formal, you can always add the verb.

▶ We respected no other candidate for the city council as much
  as <s>she</s>.
  her.

This sentence means that we respected no other candidate as much as *we respected her*. *Her* is the direct object of the understood verb *respected*.

Subjects and objects of infinitives

An infinitive is the word *to* followed by the base form of a verb. (See B3-b.) Subjects of infinitives are an exception to the rule that subjects must be in the subjective case. Whenever an infinitive has a subject, it must be in the objective case. Objects of infinitives also are in the objective case.

▶ Ms. Wilson asked John and <s>I</s> to drive the senator and <s>she</s> to the
  me   *her*

  airport.

we or us with noun • with than or as • me, you, him, etc.
with infinitive (to see) • my, your, their, etc. with -ing form

G3-d 205

John and me is the subject of the infinitive *to drive*; *senator and her* is the direct object of the infinitive.

Possessive case to modify a gerund

A pronoun that modifies a gerund or a gerund phrase should be in the possessive case (*my, your, his, her, its, our, their*). A gerund is a verb form ending in *-ing* that functions as a noun. Gerunds frequently appear in phrases; when they do, the whole gerund phrase functions as a noun. (See B3-b.)

> *your*
> ▶ The chances of ~~you~~ being hit by lightning are about two million
>   ^
> to one.

Your modifies the gerund phrase *being hit by lightning*.

Nouns as well as pronouns may modify gerunds. To form the possessive case of a noun, use an apostrophe and an *-s* (*victim's*) or just an apostrophe (*victims'*). (See P4-a.)

> *aristocracy's*
> ▶ The old order in France paid a high price for the ~~aristocracy~~
>   ^
> exploiting the lower classes.

The possessive noun *aristocracy's* modifies the gerund phrase *exploiting the lower classes*.

G3-d Distinguish between *who* and *whom*.

The choice between *who* and *whom* (or *whoever* and *whomever*) occurs primarily in subordinate clauses and in questions. *Who* and *whoever*, subjective-case pronouns, are used for subjects and subject complements. *Whom* and *whomever*, objective-case pronouns, are used for objects.

An exception to this general rule occurs when the pronoun functions as the subject of an infinitive (see p. 207).

In subordinate clauses

When *who* and *whom* (or *whoever* and *whomever*) introduce subordinate clauses, their case is determined by their function within the clause they introduce.

PRACTICE   hackerhandbooks.com/writersref
> Grammatical sentences > G3–16
                        > G3–17 and G3–18 (pronoun review)

In the following two examples, the pronouns *who* and *whoever* function as the subjects of the clauses they introduce.

▶ First prize goes to the runner ~~whom~~ earns the most points.
         who

The subordinate clause is *who earns the most points*. The verb of the clause is *earns*, and its subject is *who*.

▶ Maya Angelou's *I Know Why the Caged Bird Sings* should be read
 by ~~whomever~~ is interested in the effects of racial prejudice on
   whoever
children.

The writer selected the pronoun *whomever*, thinking that it was the object of the preposition *by*. However, the object of the preposition is the entire subordinate clause *whoever is interested in the effects of racial prejudice on children*. The verb of the clause is *is*, and the subject of the verb is *whoever*.

When functioning as an object in a subordinate clause, *whom* (or *whomever*) appears out of order, before the subject and verb. To choose the correct pronoun, you can mentally restructure the clause.

▶ You will work with our senior traders, ~~who~~ you will meet after
           whom

your orientation.

The subordinate clause is *whom you will meet after your orientation*. The subject of the clause is *you*, and the verb is *will meet*. *Whom* is the direct object of the verb. The correct choice becomes clear if you mentally restructure the clause: *you will meet whom*.

When functioning as the object of a preposition in a subordinate clause, *whom* is often separated from its preposition.

▶ The tutor ~~who~~ I was assigned to was very supportive.
  whom

Whom is the object of the preposition *to*. In this sentence, the writer might choose to drop *whom*: *The tutor I was assigned to was very supportive*.

NOTE: Inserted expressions such as *they know, I think,* and *she says* should be ignored in determining whether to use *who* or *whom*.

▶ The speech pathologist reported a particularly difficult session
 with a stroke patient ~~whom~~ she knew was suffering from aphasia.
        who

Who is the subject of *was suffering*, not the object of *knew*.

In questions

The case of an interrogative pronoun is determined by its function within the question.

> *Who*
> ▶ ~~Whom~~ was responsible for creating that computer virus?
>   ^
>   *Who* is the subject of the verb *was*.

When *whom* functions as the object in a question, it appears out of normal order. To choose the correct pronoun, you can mentally restructure the question.

> *Whom*
> ▶ ~~Who~~ did the New Democratic Party nominate in 2004?
>   ^
>   *Whom* is the direct object of the verb *did nominate*. This becomes clear if you restructure the question: *The New Democratic Party did nominate whom in 2004?*

For subjects or objects of infinitives

An infinitive is the word *to* followed by the base form of a verb. (See B3-b.) Subjects of infinitives are an exception to the rule that subjects must be in the subjective case. The subject of an infinitive must be in the objective case. Objects of infinitives also are in the objective case. (See also p. 204.)

> *whom*
> ▶ When it comes to money, I know ~~who~~ to believe.
>   ^
>   The infinitive phrase *whom to believe* is the direct object of the verb *know*, and *whom* is the subject of the infinitive *to believe*.

G4 Adjectives and adverbs

Adjectives modify nouns or pronouns. They usually come before the word they modify; occasionally they function as complements following the word they modify. Adverbs modify verbs, adjectives, or other adverbs. (See B1-d and B1-e.)

Many adverbs are formed by adding *-ly* to adjectives (*normal, normally; smooth, smoothly*). But don't assume that all words ending in *-ly* are adverbs or that all adverbs end in *-ly*. Some adjectives end in *-ly* (*lovely, friendly*), and some adverbs don't (*always, here, there*). When in doubt, consult a dictionary.

PRACTICE   hackerhandbooks.com/writersref
  > Grammatical sentences > G4–3 and G4–4

> **ESL**   Placement of adjectives and adverbs can be a tricky matter for multilingual writers. See M3-f and M4-b.

G4-a Use adjectives to modify nouns.

Adjectives ordinarily precede the nouns they modify. But they can also function as subject complements or object complements, following the nouns they modify.

> **ESL**   In English, adjectives are not pluralized to agree with the words they modify: *The red* [not *reds*] *roses were a surprise.*

Subject complements

A subject complement follows a linking verb and completes the meaning of the subject. (See B2-b.) When an adjective functions as a subject complement, it describes the subject.

Justice is *blind.*

Problems can arise with verbs such as *smell, taste, look,* and *feel,* which sometimes, but not always, function as linking verbs. If the word following one of these verbs describes the subject, use an adjective; if the word following the verb modifies the verb, use an adverb.

ADJECTIVE   The detective looked *cautious.*

ADVERB   The detective looked *cautiously* for fingerprints.

The adjective *cautious* describes the detective; the adverb *cautiously* modifies the verb *looked.*

Linking verbs suggest states of being, not actions. Notice, for example, the different meanings of *looked* in the preceding examples. To look cautious suggests the state of being cautious; to look cautiously is to perform an action in a cautious way.

▶ The lilacs in our backyard smell especially ~~sweetly~~ ^sweet^ this year.

The verb *smell* suggests a state of being, not an action. Therefore, it should be followed by an adjective, not an adverb.

▶ The drawings looked ~~well~~ ^good^ after the architect made a few changes.

The verb *looked* is a linking verb suggesting a state of being, not an action. The adjective *good* is appropriate following the linking verb to describe *drawings*. (See also the note on p. 210.)

When the verb *feel* refers to the state of a person's health or emotions, it is a linking verb and should be followed by an adjective (such as *bad*) instead of an adverb (such as *badly*).

▶ We felt ~~badly~~ when we heard of your grandmother's death.
       bad

Object complements

An object complement follows a direct object and completes its meaning. (See B2-b.) When an adjective functions as an object complement, it describes the direct object.

Sorrow makes *us wise*.

Object complements occur with verbs such as *call, consider, create, find, keep,* and *make.* When a modifier follows the direct object of one of these verbs, use an adjective to describe the direct object; use an adverb to modify the verb.

ADJECTIVE   The referee called the plays *perfect*.

ADVERB   The referee called the plays *perfectly*.

The first sentence means that the referee considered the plays to be perfect; the second means that the referee did an excellent job of calling the plays.

G4-b Use adverbs to modify verbs, adjectives, and other adverbs.

When adverbs modify verbs (or verbals), they nearly always answer the question When? Where? How? Why? Under what conditions? How often? or To what degree? When adverbs modify adjectives or other adverbs, they usually qualify or intensify the meaning of the word they modify. (See B1-e.)

Adjectives are often used incorrectly in place of adverbs in casual or nonstandard speech.

▶ The transportation arrangement worked out ~~perfect~~ for everyone.
                                perfectly

▶ The manager must see that the office runs ~~smooth~~ and ~~efficient~~.
                                      smoothly   efficiently.

The adverb *perfectly* modifies the verb *worked out*; the adverbs *smoothly* and *efficiently* modify the verb *runs*.

▶ The chance of recovering any property lost in the fire looks
really
~~real~~ slim.
^

Only adverbs can modify adjectives or other adverbs. *Really* intensifies the meaning of the adjective *slim*.

NOTE: The incorrect use of the adjective *good* in place of the adverb *well* to modify a verb is especially common in casual and nonstandard speech. Use *well*, not *good*, to modify a verb in your writing.

well
▶ We were glad that Sanya had done ~~good~~ on the CFA exam.
^

The adverb *well* should be used to modify the verb *had done*.

The word *well* is an adjective, however, when it means "healthy," "satisfactory," or "fortunate": *I feel very well today. All is well. It is just as well.*

For more help with *well* and *good*, consult the glossary of usage (W1).

ESL The placement of adverbs varies from language to language. Unlike some languages, such as French and Spanish, English does not allow an adverb between a verb (*poured*) and its direct object (*the liquid*). See M3-f.

slowly
▶ In the last stage of our experiment, we poured ~~slowly~~ the
^

liquid into the container.

G4-c Use comparatives and superlatives with care.

Most adjectives and adverbs have three forms: the positive, the comparative, and the superlative.

POSITIVE	COMPARATIVE	SUPERLATIVE
soft	softer	softest
fast	faster	fastest
careful	more careful	most careful
bad	worse	worst
good	better	best

Comparative versus superlative

Use the comparative to compare two things, the superlative to compare three or more.

▶ Which of these two low-carb drinks is ~~best?~~ *better?*

▶ Though Shaw and Jackson are impressive, Hobbs is the ~~more~~ *most*

qualified of the three candidates running for mayor.

Forming comparatives and superlatives

To form comparatives and superlatives of one-syllable adjectives, use the endings *-er* and *-est*: *smooth, smoother, smoothest; dark, darker, darkest*. For adjectives with three or more syllables, use *more* and *most* (or *less* and *least* for downward comparisons): *exciting, more exciting, most exciting; interesting, less interesting, least interesting*. Two-syllable adjectives form comparatives and superlatives in both ways: *lovely, lovelier, loveliest; helpful, more helpful, most helpful*.

Some one-syllable adverbs take the endings *-er* and *-est* (*fast, faster, fastest*), but longer adverbs and all of those ending in *-ly* form the comparative and superlative with *more* and *most* (or *less* and *least*).

The comparative and superlative forms of some adjectives and adverbs are irregular: *good, better, best; well, better, best; bad, worse, worst; badly, worse, worst*.

▶ The Kirov is the ~~talentedest~~ *most talented* ballet company we have seen.

▶ According to our projections, sales at local businesses will be ~~worser~~ *worse* than those at the chain stores this winter.

Double comparatives or superlatives

Do not use double comparatives or superlatives. When you have added *-er* or *-est* to an adjective or adverb, do not also use *more* or *most* (or *less* or *least*).

▶ Of all her family, Julia is the ~~most~~ happiest about the move.

▶ All the polls indicated that Harper was more ~~likelier~~ *likely* to win than Martin.

Absolute concepts

Avoid expressions such as *more straight, less perfect, very round,* and *most unique.* Either something is unique or it isn't. It is illogical to suggest that absolute concepts come in degrees.

> ► That is the most ~~unique~~ ^{unusual} wedding gown I have ever seen.

> ► The painting would have been even more ~~priceless~~ ^{valuable} had it been
>
> signed.

G4-d Avoid double negatives.

Standard English allows two negatives only if a positive meaning is intended: *The orchestra was not unhappy with its performance* (meaning that the orchestra was happy). Using a double negative to emphasize a negative meaning is nonstandard.

Negative modifiers such as *never, no,* and *not* should not be paired with other negative modifiers or with negative words such as *neither, none, no one, nobody,* and *nothing.*

> ► Management is not doing ~~nothing~~ ^{anything} to see that the trash is picked up.
>
> The double negative *not . . . nothing* is nonstandard.

The modifiers *hardly, barely,* and *scarcely* are considered negatives in standard English, so they should not be used with negatives such as *not, no one,* or *never.*

> ► Maxine is so weak that she ~~can't~~ ^{can} hardly climb stairs.

G5 Sentence fragments

A sentence fragment is a word group that pretends to be a sentence. Sentence fragments are easy to recognize when they appear out of context, like these:

When the cat leaped onto the table.

Running for the bus.

And immediately popped their flares and life vests.

PRACTICE   hackerhandbooks.com/writersref
> Grammatical sentences > G5–3 to G5–6

Test for fragments

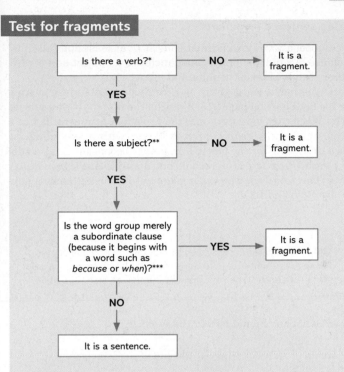

*Do not mistake verbals for verbs. A verbal is a verb form (such as *walking, to act*) that does not function as a verb of a clause. (See B3-b.)
**The subject of a sentence may be *you*, understood. (See B2-b.)
***A sentence may open with a subordinate clause, but the sentence must also include an independent clause. (See G5-a and B4-a.)

If you find any fragments, try one of these methods of revision (see G5-a to G5-c):

1. Attach the fragment to a nearby sentence.

2. Rewrite the fragment as a complete sentence.

When fragments appear next to related sentences, however, they are harder to spot.

> We had just sat down to dinner. When the cat leaped onto the table.
>
> I tripped and twisted my ankle. Running for the bus.
>
> The pilots ejected from the burning plane, landing in the water not far from the ship. And immediately popped their flares and life vests.

Recognizing sentence fragments

To be a sentence, a word group must consist of at least one full independent clause. An independent clause includes a subject and a verb, and it either stands alone or could stand alone.

To test whether a word group is a complete sentence or a fragment, use the flowchart on page 213. By using the flowchart, you can see exactly why *When the cat leaped onto the table* is a fragment: It has a subject (*cat*) and a verb (*leaped*), but it begins with a subordinating word (*When*). *Running for the bus* is a fragment because it lacks a subject and a verb (*Running* is a verbal, not a verb). *And immediately popped their flares and life vests* is a fragment because it lacks a subject. (See also B3-b and B3-e.)

> **ESL**   Unlike some other languages, English requires a subject and a verb in every sentence (except in commands, where the subject *you* is understood but not present: *Sit down*). See M3-a and M3-b.
>
>   *It is*
> ▶ ~~Is~~ often hot and humid during the summer.
>   ^
>
>   *are*
> ▶ Students usually very busy at the end of the semester.
>   ^

Repairing sentence fragments

You can repair most fragments in one of two ways:

1. Pull the fragment into a nearby sentence.
2. Rewrite the fragment as a complete sentence.

                            when
▶ We had just sat down to dinner/~~When~~ the cat leaped onto the
                            ^
table.

   Running for the bus,
▶ I tripped and twisted my ankle. ~~Running for the bus.~~
^

▶ The pilots ejected from the burning plane, landing in the water
               They
not far from the ship. ~~And~~ immediately popped their flares and
          ^
life vests.

G5-a Attach fragmented subordinate clauses or turn them into sentences.

A subordinate clause is patterned like a sentence, with both a subject and a verb, but it begins with a word that marks it as subordinate. The following words commonly introduce subordinate clauses.

after	before	so that	until	while
although	even though	than	when	who
as	how	that	where	whom
as if	if	though	whether	whose
because	since	unless	which	why

Subordinate clauses function within sentences as adjectives, as adverbs, or as nouns. They cannot stand alone. (See B3-e.)

Most fragmented clauses beg to be pulled into a sentence nearby.

▶ Canadians have come to fear the West Nile virus/ ~~Because~~
  because
  it is transmitted by the common mosquito.

> *Because* introduces a subordinate clause, so it cannot stand alone. (For punctuation of subordinate clauses at the end of a sentence, see P2-f.)

If a fragmented clause cannot be attached to a nearby sentence or if you feel that attaching it would be awkward, try turning the clause into a sentence. The simplest way to do this is to delete the opening word or words that mark it as subordinate.

▶ Population increases and uncontrolled development are taking
  a deadly toll on the environment. ~~So that across~~ the globe, fragile
  Across
  ecosystems are collapsing.

G5-b Attach fragmented phrases or turn them into sentences.

Like subordinate clauses, phrases function within sentences as adjectives, as adverbs, or as nouns. They cannot stand alone. Fragmented phrases are often prepositional or verbal phrases; sometimes they are appositives, words or word groups that rename nouns or pronouns. (See B3-a, B3-b, and B3-c.)

Often a fragmented phrase may simply be pulled into a nearby sentence.

> *examining*
> ► The archaeologists worked slowly/, ~~Examining~~ and labelling
>   ^
> every pottery shard they uncovered.

The word group beginning with *Examining* is a verbal phrase.

> *a*
> ► The patient displayed symptoms of ALS/, ~~A~~ neurodegenerative
>   ^
> disease.

A neurodegenerative disease is an appositive renaming the noun *ALS*. (For punctuation of appositives, see P1-e.)

If a fragmented phrase cannot be pulled into a nearby sentence effectively, turn the phrase into a sentence. You may need to add a subject, a verb, or both.

> *She also taught us*
> ► Jamie explained how to access our new database. ~~Also~~ how to
>   ^
> submit expense reports and request vendor payments.

The revision turns the fragmented phrase into a sentence by adding a subject and a verb.

G5-c Attach other fragmented word groups or turn them into sentences.

Other word groups that are commonly fragmented include parts of compound predicates, lists, and examples introduced by *for example*, *in addition*, or similar expressions.

Parts of compound predicates

A predicate consists of a verb and its objects, complements, and modifiers (see B2-b). A compound predicate includes two or more predicates joined with a coordinating conjunction such as *and*, *but*, or *or*. Because the parts of a compound predicate have the same subject, they should appear in the same sentence.

> ► The woodpecker finch of the Galápagos Islands carefully selects a
> *and*
> twig of a certain size and shape/ ~~And~~ then uses this tool to pry out
>   ^
> grubs from trees.

The subject is *finch*, and the compound predicate is *selects . . . and . . . uses*. (For punctuation of compound predicates, see P2-a.)

Lists

To correct a fragmented list, often you can attach it to a nearby sentence with a colon or a dash. (See P3-d and P6-b.)

▶ The smallest bones in the human body are in the middle ear~~/~~: the ~~The~~ incus, the malleus, and the stapes.

Sometimes terms like *especially*, *like*, and *such as* introduce fragmented lists. Such fragments can usually be attached to the preceding sentence.

▶ In the twentieth century, Canada produced some great writers~~/~~, such ~~Such~~ as Margaret Atwood, Robertson Davies, Michael Ondaatje, Alice Munro, and June Callwood.

Examples introduced by for example, in addition, or similar expressions

Expressions that introduce examples or explanations can lead to fragments. Although a sentence may begin with a word or phrase like the following, the rest of the sentence must include a subject and a verb.

also	for example	mainly
and	for instance	or
but	in addition	that is

Often the easiest solution is to turn the fragment into a sentence.

▶ A streaming gauge is useful for measuring a river's height and flow. In addition, ~~providing~~ *it provides* residents with early flood warnings.

The writer corrected this fragment by adding a subject—*it*—and substituting the verb *provides* for the verbal *providing*.

▶ Tannen claims that men and women have different ideas about communication. For example, *she explains* that a woman "expects her husband to be a new and improved version of her best friend" (441).

A quotation must be part of a complete sentence. *That a woman "expects her husband to be a new and improved version of her best friend"* is a fragment—a subordinate clause. Adding a signal phrase that includes a subject and a verb (*she explains*) corrects the fragment.

G5-d Exception: A fragment may be used for effect.

Writers occasionally use sentence fragments for special purposes.

FOR EMPHASIS	Following the dramatic Americanization of their children, even my parents grew more publicly confident. *Especially my mother.* —Richard Rodriguez
TO ANSWER A QUESTION	Are these new drug tests 100 percent reliable? *Not in the opinion of most experts.*
TRANSITIONS	*And now the opposing arguments.*
EXCLAMATIONS	*Not again!*
IN ADVERTISING	*Fewer carbs. Improved taste.*

Although fragments are sometimes effective, writers and readers do not always agree on when they are appropriate. That's why you will find it safer to write in complete sentences.

G6 Run-on sentences

Run-on sentences are independent clauses that have not been joined correctly. An independent clause is a word group that can stand alone as a sentence. (See B4-a.) When two independent clauses appear in one sentence, they must be joined in one of these ways:

- with a comma and a coordinating conjunction (*and, but, or, nor, for, so, yet*)
- with a semicolon (or occasionally with a colon or a dash)

Recognizing run-on sentences

There are two types of run-on sentences. When a writer puts no mark of punctuation and no coordinating conjunction between independent clauses, the result is called a *fused sentence.*

FUSED   ┌——— INDEPENDENT CLAUSE ———┐ ┌———
Air pollution poses risks to all humans it can be

┌—— INDEPENDENT CLAUSE ——┐
deadly for people with asthma.

A far more common type of run-on sentence is the *comma splice*—two or more independent clauses joined with a comma but without a coordinating conjunction. In some comma splices, the comma appears alone.

COMMA   Air pollution poses risks to all humans, it can be
SPLICE   deadly for people with asthma.

In other comma splices, the comma is accompanied by a joining word that is *not* a coordinating conjunction (*and, but, or, nor, for, so,* and *yet*).

COMMA   Air pollution poses risks to all humans, however, it can
SPLICE   be deadly for people with asthma.

However is a transitional expression and cannot be used with only a comma to join two independent clauses (see G6-b).

Revising run-on sentences

To revise a run-on sentence, you have four choices.

1. Use a comma and a coordinating conjunction (*and, but, or, nor, for, so, yet*).

▶ Air pollution poses risks to all humans, *but* it can be deadly for

people with asthma.

2. Use a semicolon (or, if appropriate, a colon or a dash). A semicolon may be used alone or with a transitional expression.

▶ Air pollution poses risks to all humans*;* it can be deadly for

people with asthma.

▶ Air pollution poses risks to all humans*; however,* it can be deadly for

people with asthma.

3. Make the clauses into separate sentences.

▶ Air pollution poses risks to all humans*. It* ~~it~~ can be deadly for

people with asthma.

4. Restructure the sentence, perhaps by subordinating one of the clauses.

▶ *Although air* ~~Air~~ pollution poses risks to all humans, it can be deadly for

people with asthma.

One of these revision techniques usually works better than the others for a particular sentence. The fourth technique, the one requiring the most extensive revision, is often the most effective.

G6-a Consider separating the clauses with a comma and a coordinating conjunction.

There are seven coordinating conjunctions in English: *and, but, or, nor, for, so,* and *yet.* When a coordinating conjunction joins independent clauses, it is usually preceded by a comma. (See P1-a.)

> ▶ Some lesson plans include exercises, ~~completing~~ them should not
>   *but*
>
>   be the focus of all class periods.

G6-b Consider separating the clauses with a semicolon (or, if appropriate, with a colon or a dash).

When the independent clauses are closely related and their relation is clear without a coordinating conjunction, a semicolon is an acceptable method of revision. (See P3-a.)

> ▶ Tragedy depicts the individual confronted with the fact of death/;
>
>   comedy depicts the adaptability of human society.

A semicolon is required between independent clauses that have been linked with a transitional expression (such as *however, therefore, moreover, in fact,* or *for example*). For a longer list, see P3-a.

> ▶ In his film adaptation of the short story "Killings," Todd
>
>   Field changed key details of the plot/; as a matter of fact,
>
>   he added whole scenes that do not appear in the story.

A colon or a dash may be more appropriate if the first independent clause introduces the second or if the second clause summarizes or explains the first. (See P3-d and P6-b.) In formal writing, the colon is usually preferred to the dash.

>   *This*
> ▶ Nuclear waste is hazardous: ~~this~~ is an indisputable fact.
>
> ▶ The female black widow spider is often a widow of her own
>
>   making/ she has been known to eat her partner after mating.

Recognizing run-on sentences

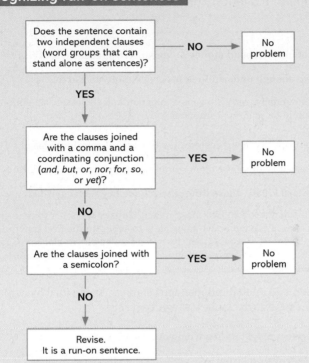

Does the sentence contain two independent clauses (word groups that can stand alone as sentences)? — **NO** → No problem

YES

Are the clauses joined with a comma and a coordinating conjunction (*and*, *but*, *or*, *nor*, *for*, *so*, or *yet*)? — **YES** → No problem

NO

Are the clauses joined with a semicolon? — **YES** → No problem

NO

Revise. It is a run-on sentence.

If you find an error, choose an effective method of revision. See G6-a to G6-d for revision strategies.

A colon is an appropriate method of revision if the first independent clause introduces a quoted sentence.

▶ Saul Bellow, winner of the Nobel Prize in Literature, had this

to say about characters/: "We all know what it is to be
  ∧

tired of 'characters.' Human types have become false and

boring."

G6-c Consider making the clauses into separate sentences.

▶ Why should we spend money on expensive space exploration/?
 We
 ~~we~~ have enough underfunded programs here on Earth.
 ^

Since one independent clause is a question and the other is a statement, they should be separate sentences.

Writing
with
sources

APA-style
citation

▶ Some studies have suggested that the sexual relationships of
                                                          A
 bonobos set them apart from common chimpanzees/. Åccording
                                                        ^
 to Stanford (1998), these differences have been exaggerated.

Using a comma to join two independent clauses creates a comma splice. In this example, an effective revision is to separate the first independent clause (*Some studies . . .*) from the second independent clause (*these differences . . .*) and to keep the signal phrase with the second clause. (See also APA-3.)

NOTE: When two quoted independent clauses are divided by explanatory words, make each clause its own sentence.

▶ "It's always smart to learn from your mistakes," quipped my
        "It's
 boss/. ~~"it's~~ even smarter to learn from the mistakes of others."
      ^

G6-d Consider restructuring the sentence, perhaps by subordinating one of the clauses.

If one of the independent clauses is less important than the other, turn it into a subordinate clause or a phrase. (For more about subordination, see S6, especially the list on p. 130.)

▶ One of the most famous advertising slogans is Wheaties
                                          which
 cereal's "Breakfast of Champions," ~~it~~ was penned in 1933.
                                     ^

▶ Alfred Fitzpatrick, ~~was~~ a reverend and a pioneer in education,
                    ^
 ~~he~~ founded Frontier College in 1899.

Multilingual
Writers and
ESL Challenges

M Multilingual Writers and ESL Challenges

This section of *A Canadian Writer's Reference* is primarily for multilingual writers. You may find this section helpful if you learned English as a second language (ESL) or if you speak a language other than English with your friends and family.

≡ **M1** Verbs

Both native speakers of English and English language learners encounter challenges with verbs. Section M1 focuses on specific challenges that multilingual writers sometimes face. You can find more help with verbs in other sections in the book:

> making subjects and verbs agree (G1)
>
> using irregular verb forms (G2-a, G2-b)
>
> leaving off verb endings (G2-c, G2-d)
>
> choosing the correct verb tense (G2-f)
>
> avoiding inappropriate uses of the passive voice (W3-a)

M1-a Use the appropriate verb form and tense.

This section offers a brief review of English verb forms and tenses. For additional help, see G2-f and B1-c.

Basic verb forms

Every main verb in English has five forms, which are used to create all of the verb tenses in standard English. The chart on page 226 shows these forms for the regular verb *help* and the irregular verbs *give* and *be*. See G2-a for the forms of other common irregular verbs.

Verb tenses

Section G2-f describes all the verb tenses in English, showing the forms of a regular verb, an irregular verb, and the verb *be* in each tense. The chart on pages 227–28 provides more details about the tenses commonly used in the active voice in writing; the chart on page 229 gives details about tenses commonly used in the passive voice.

PRACTICE AND MODELS   hackerhandbooks.com/writersref
> Multilingual/ESL > Charts and study help
> Sample student paper (draft and final)
> Exercises
> Links to online resources

Basic verb forms

	REGULAR VERB *HELP*	IRREGULAR VERB *GIVE*	IRREGULAR VERB *BE**
BASE FORM	help	give	be
PAST TENSE	helped	gave	was, were
PAST PARTICIPLE	helped	given	been
PRESENT PARTICIPLE	helping	giving	being
-*S* FORM	helps	gives	is

*Be also has the forms *am* and *are*, which are used in the present tense.

M1-b To write a verb in the passive voice, use a form of *be* with the past participle.

When a sentence is written in the passive voice, the subject receives the action instead of doing it. (See B2-b.)

> The solution *was measured* by the lab assistant.

> Melissa *was taken* to the hospital.

To form the passive voice, use a form of *be*—*am*, *is*, *are*, *was*, *were*, *being*, *be*, or *been*—followed by the past participle of the main verb: *was chosen*, *are remembered*. (Sometimes a form of *be* follows another helping verb: *will be stopped*, *could have been broken*.)

For details on forming the passive in various tenses, consult the chart on page 229. (For appropriate uses of the passive voice, see W3-a.)

> written
> ▶ The novel *Before Green Gables* was ~~writing~~ by Budge Wilson.
> ^

In the passive voice, the past participle *written*, not the present participle *writing*, must follow *was* (the past tense of *be*).

> be
> ▶ Senator Dixon will defeated.
> ^

The passive voice requires a form of *be* before the past participle.

> teased.
> ▶ The child was being ~~tease.~~
> ^

The past participle *teased*, not the base form *tease*, must be used with *was being* to form the passive voice.

Verb tenses commonly used in the active voice

For descriptions and examples of all verb tenses, see G2-f. For verb tenses commonly used in the passive voice, see the chart on page 229.

Simple tenses
For general facts, states of being, habitual actions

Simple present — **Base form or -s form**

- general facts — Busy students often *study* late at night.
- states of being — Water *becomes* steam at 100 °C.
- habitual, repetitive actions — We *donate* to a different charity each year.
- scheduled future events — The train *arrives* tomorrow at 6:30 p.m.

NOTE: For advice about using the present tense in writing about literature, see page 192.

Simple past — **Base form + -ed or -d or irregular form**

- completed actions at a specific time in the past — The storm *destroyed* their property. She *drove* to Montreal three years ago.
- facts or states of being in the past — When I *was* young, I usually *walked* to school with my sister.

Simple future — ***will* + base form**

- future actions, promises, or predictions — I *will exercise* tomorrow. The snowfall *will begin* around midnight.

Simple progressive forms
For continuing actions

Present progressive — ***am, is, are* + present participle**

- actions in progress at the present time, not continuing indefinitely — The students *are taking* an exam in Room 105. Jonathan *is parking* the car.
- future actions (with *go, leave, come, move,* etc.) — I *am leaving* tomorrow morning.

Past progressive — ***was, were* + present participle**

- actions in progress at a specific time in the past — They *were swimming* when the storm struck.
- *was going to, were going to* for past plans that did not happen — We *were going to* drive to Banff for spring break, but the car broke down.

→

Verb tenses commonly used in the active voice (continued)

NOTE: Some verbs are not normally used in the progressive: *appear, believe, belong, contain, have, hear, know, like, need, see, seem, taste, understand*, and *want*.

    want
▶ I ~~am wanting~~ to see Norm Foster's *Bedtime Stories*.
    ^

Perfect tenses
For actions that happened or will happen before another time

Present perfect   *has, have* + past participle

- repetitive or constant actions that began in the past and continue to the present

    I *have loved* cats since I was a child. Alicia *has worked* in Kenya for ten years.

- actions that happened at an unknown or unspecific time in the past

    Stephen *has visited* Wales three times.

Past perfect   *had* + past participle

- actions that began or occurred before another time in the past

    She *had* just *crossed* the street when the runaway car crashed into the building.

NOTE: For more discussion of uses of the past perfect tense, see G2-f. For advice about using the past perfect in conditional sentences, see M1-e.

Perfect progressive forms
For continuous past actions before another time

Present perfect progressive   *has, have* + *been* + present participle

- continuous actions that began in the past and continue to the present

    Yolanda *has been trying* to get a job in Winnipeg for five years.

Past perfect progressive   *had* + *been* + present participle

- actions that began and continued in the past until some other past action

    By the time I moved to Halifax, I *had been supporting* myself for five years.

tenses • active voice (*study, will perform*) •
passive voice (*are served, is being shown*) • perfect (*had been fought*)

M1-b   **229**

Verb tenses commonly used in the passive voice

For details about verb tenses in the active voice, see pages 227–28.

Simple tenses (passive voice)

Simple present	*am, is, are* + past participle
▪ general facts	Breakfast *is served* daily.
▪ habitual, repetitive actions	The receipts *are counted* every night.

Simple past	*was, were* + past participle
▪ completed past actions	He *was punished* for being late.

Simple future	*will be* + past participle
▪ future actions, promises, or predictions	The decision *will be made* by the committee next week.

Simple progressive forms (passive voice)

Present progressive	*am, is, are* + *being* + past participle
▪ actions in progress at the present time	The new stadium *is being built* with private money.
▪ future actions (with *go, leave, come, move*, etc.)	Jo *is being moved* to a new class next month.

Past progressive	*was, were* + *being* + past participle
▪ actions in progress at a specific time in the past	We thought we *were being followed*.

Perfect tenses (passive voice)

Present perfect	*has, have* + *been* + past participle
▪ actions that began in the past and continue to the present	The flight *has been delayed* because of violent storms over the Prairies.
▪ actions that happened at an unknown or unspecific time in the past	Wars *have been fought* throughout history.

Past perfect	*had* + *been* + past participle
▪ actions that began or occurred before another time in the past	He *had been given* all the hints he needed to complete the puzzle.

NOTE: The future progressive, future perfect, and perfect progressive forms are not used in the passive voice.

NOTE: Only transitive verbs, those that take direct objects, may be used in the passive voice. Intransitive verbs such as *occur*, *happen*, *sleep*, *die*, *become*, and *fall* are not used in the passive. (See B2-b.)

▶ The accident ~~was~~ happened suddenly.

▶ Stock prices *fell* ~~were fallen~~ all week.
                    ^

M1-c Use the base form of the verb after a modal.

The modal verbs are *can*, *could*, *may*, *might*, *must*, *shall*, *should*, *will*, and *would*. (*Ought to* is also considered a modal verb.) The modals are used with the base form of a verb to show certainty, necessity, or possibility.

Modals and the verbs that follow them do not change form to indicate tense. For a summary of modals and their meanings, see the chart on pages 232–33. (See also G2-e.)

▶ The art museum will *launch* ~~launches~~ its fundraising campaign next month.
                        ^

   The modal *will* must be followed by the base form *launch*, not the present tense *launches*.

▶ The translator could *speak* ~~spoke~~ many languages, so the ambassador
                        ^

   hired her for the European tour.

   The modal *could* must be followed by the base form *speak*, not the past tense *spoke*.

TIP: Do not use *to* in front of a main verb that follows a modal.

▶ Gina can ~~to~~ drive us home if we miss the last train.

For the use of modals in conditional sentences, see M1-e.

M1-d To make negative verb forms, add *not* in the appropriate place.

If the verb is the simple present or past tense of *be* (*am*, *is*, *are*, *was*, *were*), add *not* after the verb.

   Mario *is not* a member of the club.

verbs with objects • modals (*can, may*, etc.) • avoiding
double negative (*don't have no*) • *if, when* clauses • conditional

M1-e   231

For simple present-tense verbs other than *be*, use *do* or *does* plus *not* before the base form of the verb. (For the correct forms of *do* and *does*, see the chart in G1-a.)

>   *does not*
> ▶ Mariko ~~no~~ want more dessert.
>   ^

> ▶ Mariko does not want~~s~~ more dessert.

For simple past-tense verbs other than *be*, use *did* plus *not* before the base form of the verb.

>   *plant*
> ▶ They did not ~~planted~~ corn this year.
>   ^

In a verb phrase consisting of one or more helping verbs and a present or past participle (*is watching, were living, has played, could have been driven*), use the word *not* after the first helping verb.

>   *not*
> ▶ Inna should have ~~not~~ gone dancing last night.
>   ^

>   *not*
> ▶ Bonnie is ~~no~~ singing this weekend.
>   ^

NOTE: English allows only one negative in an independent clause to express a negative idea; using more than one is an error known as a *double negative* (see G4-d).

>   *any*
> ▶ We could not find ~~no~~ books about the history of our school in the
>   ^
> public library.

M1-e In a conditional sentence, choose verb tenses according to the type of condition expressed in the sentence.

Conditional sentences contain two clauses: a subordinate clause (usually starting with *if, when,* or *unless*) and an independent clause. The subordinate clause (sometimes called the *if* or *unless* clause) states the condition or cause; the independent clause states the result or effect. In each example in this section, the subordinate clause (*if* clause) is marked SUB, and the independent clause is marked IND. (See B3-e on clauses.)

Modals and their meanings

can

- general ability (present)

  Ants *can survive* anywhere, even in space. Jorge *can run* a marathon faster than his brother.

- informal requests or permission

  Can you *tell* me where the light is? Sandy *can borrow* my calculator.

could

- general ability (past)

  Lea *could read* when she was only three years old.

- polite, informal requests or permission

  Could you *give* me that pen?

may

- formal requests or permission

  May I *see* the report? Students *may park* only in the yellow zone.

- possibility

  I *may try* to finish my homework tonight, or I *may wake up* early and *finish* it tomorrow.

might

- possibility

  Funding for the language lab *might double* by 2017.

NOTE: *Might* usually expresses a stronger possibility than *may*.

must

- necessity (present or future)

  To be effective, weight-loss programs *must provide* access to a nutritionist.

- strong probability

  Amy *must be* sick. [She is probably sick.]

- near certainty (present or past)

  I *must have left* my wallet at home. [I almost certainly left my wallet at home.]

should

- suggestions or advice

  People with diabetes *should drink* plenty of water every day.

- obligations or duties

  The government *should protect* citizens' rights.

- expectations

  The books *should arrive* soon. [We expect the books to arrive soon.]

→

modals • *can, could, may, might, must, should, will, would* • *if* clauses •
when clauses • conditional • expressing facts • predicting

M1-e   233

will	
■ certainty	If you don't leave now, you *will* be late.
■ requests	*Will* you *help* me study for my test?
■ promises and offers	Jonah *will arrange* the carpool.

would	
■ polite requests	*Would* you *help* me carry these books? I *would like* some coffee. [*Would like* is more polite than *want*.]
■ habitual or repeated actions (past)	Whenever Elena needed help with sewing, she *would call* her aunt.

Factual

Factual conditional sentences express relations based on fact. If the relationship is a scientific truth, use the present tense in both clauses.

> ⌈————— SUB —————⌉ ⌈— IND —⌉
> If water *cools* to 0 °C, it *freezes*.

If the sentence describes a condition that is or was habitually true, use the same tense in both clauses.

> ⌈——————— SUB ———————⌉ ⌈——————— IND ———————⌉
> When Sue *jogs* along the canal, her dog *runs* ahead of her.

> ⌈——————— SUB ———————⌉ ⌈—— IND ——⌉
> Whenever the coach *asked* for help, I *volunteered*.

Predictive

Predictive conditional sentences are used to predict the future or to express future plans or possibilities. To form a predictive sentence, use a present-tense verb in the subordinate clause; in the independent clause, use the modal *will, can, may, should,* or *might* plus the base form of the verb.

> ⌈——————— SUB ———————⌉ ⌈——————— IND ———————⌉
> If you *practise* regularly, your tennis game *should improve*.

> ⌈——————— IND ———————⌉ ⌈—— SUB ——⌉
> We *will lose* our remaining wetlands unless we *act* now.

TIP: In all types of conditional sentences (factual, predictive, and speculative), *if* or *unless* clauses do not use the modal verb *will*.

> ▶   *passes*
> ▶ If Jenna ~~will pass~~ her history test, she will graduate this year.
>   ^

Speculative

Speculative conditional sentences express unlikely, contrary-to-fact, or impossible conditions. English uses the past or past perfect tense in the *if* clause, even for conditions in the present or the future.

UNLIKELY POSSIBILITIES   If the condition is possible but unlikely in the present or the future, use the past tense in the subordinate clause; in the independent clause, use *would*, *could*, or *might* plus the base form of the verb.

┌────── SUB ──────┐┌────── IND ──────┐
If I *won* the lottery, I *would travel* to Egypt.

The writer does not expect to win the lottery. Because this is a possible but unlikely present or future situation, the subordinate clause uses the past tense.

CONDITIONS CONTRARY TO FACT   In conditions that are currently unreal or contrary to fact, use the past-tense verb *were* (not *was*) in the *if* clause for all subjects. (See also G2-g, on the subjunctive mood.)

>   *were*
> ▶ If I ~~was~~ prime minister, I would make children's issues a priority.
>   ^

The writer is not prime minister, so *were* is correct in the *if* clause.

EVENTS THAT DID NOT HAPPEN   In a conditional sentence that speculates about an event that did not happen or was impossible in the past, use the past perfect tense in the *if* clause; in the independent clause, use *would have*, *could have*, or *might have* with the past participle. (See also past perfect tense, p. 228.)

┌────── SUB ──────┐┌────── IND ──────┐
If I *had saved* more money, I *would have visited* Laos last year.

The writer did not save more money and did not travel to Laos. This sentence shows a possibility that did not happen.

┌────── SUB ──────┐ ┌── IND ──┐
If Aunt Grace *had been* alive for your graduation, she *would have been* very proud.

Aunt Grace was not alive at the time of the graduation. This sentence shows an impossible situation in the past.

M1-f Become familiar with verbs that may be followed by gerunds or infinitives.

A gerund is a verb form that ends in *-ing* and is used as a noun: *sleeping*, *dreaming*. (See B3-b.) An infinitive is the word *to* plus the base form of the verb: *to sleep*, *to dream*. (The word *to* is an infinitive marker, not a preposition, in this use.)

A few verbs may be followed by either a gerund or an infinitive; others may be followed by a gerund but not by an infinitive; still others may be followed by an infinitive but not by a gerund.

Verb + gerund or infinitive (no change in meaning)

The following commonly used verbs may be followed by a gerund or an infinitive, with little or no difference in meaning:

begin	hate	love
continue	like	start

I love *skiing*. I love *to ski*.

Verb + gerund or infinitive (change in meaning)

With a few verbs, the choice of a gerund or an infinitive changes the meaning dramatically:

forget	remember	stop	try

She stopped *speaking* to Lucia. [She no longer spoke to Lucia.]

She stopped *to speak* to Lucia. [She paused so that she could speak to Lucia.]

Verb + gerund

These verbs may be followed by a gerund but not by an infinitive:

admit	enjoy	postpone	resist
appreciate	escape	practice	risk
avoid	finish	put off	suggest
deny	imagine	quit	tolerate
discuss	miss	recall	

Bill enjoys *playing* [not *to play*] the piano.

Jamie quit *smoking*.

PRACTICE   hackerhandbooks.com/writersref
   > Multilingual/ESL > M1–8 and M1–9

Verb + infinitive

These verbs may be followed by an infinitive but not by a gerund:

agree	expect	need	refuse
ask	help	offer	wait
beg	hope	plan	want
claim	manage	pretend	wish
decide	mean	promise	would like

Jill has offered *to water* [not *watering*] the plants while we are away.

Joe finally managed *to find* a parking space.

The man refused *to join* the rebellion.

A few of these verbs may be followed either by an infinitive directly or by a noun or pronoun plus an infinitive:

ask	help	promise	would like
expect	need	want	

We asked *to speak* to the congregation.

We asked *Rabbi Abrams to speak* to our congregation.

Alex expected *to get* the lead in the play.

Ira expected *Alex to get* the lead in the play.

Verb + noun or pronoun + infinitive

With certain verbs in the active voice, a noun or pronoun must come between the verb and the infinitive that follows it. The noun or pronoun usually names a person who is affected by the action of the verb.

advise	convince	order	tell
allow	encourage	persuade	urge
cause	have ("own")	remind	warn
command	instruct	require	

                    V   N   ⌐ INF ¬
The class encouraged Luis to tell the story of his escape.

The counsellor *advised Haley to take* four courses instead of the usual five.

Professor Howlett *instructed us to write* our names on the left side of the paper.

Verb + noun or pronoun + unmarked infinitive

An unmarked infinitive is an infinitive without *to*. A few verbs (often called *causative verbs*) may be followed by a noun or pronoun and an unmarked infinitive.

have ("cause")	let ("allow")
help	make ("force")

Jorge *had the valet park* his car.

▶ Please let me ~~to~~ pay for the tickets.

▶ Frank made me ~~to~~ carry his book for him.

NOTE: *Help* can be followed by a noun or pronoun and either an unmarked or a marked infinitive:

Emma *helped Brian wash* the dishes.

Emma *helped Brian to wash* the dishes.

M2 Articles

Articles (*a, an, the*) are part of a category of words known as *noun markers* or *determiners*.

M2-a Be familiar with articles and other noun markers.

Standard English uses noun markers to help identify the nouns that follow. In addition to articles (*a, an,* and *the*), noun markers include

- possessive nouns, such as *Elena's* (See P4-a.)
- possessive pronoun/adjectives: *my, your, his, her, its, our, their* (See B1-b.)
- demonstrative pronoun/adjectives: *this, that, these, those* (See B1-b.)
- quantifiers: *all, any, each, either, every, few, many, more, most, much, neither, several, some,* and so on (See M2-d.)
- numbers: *one, twenty-three,* and so on

Types of nouns

Common or proper

Common nouns

- name general persons, places, things, or ideas
- begin with lowercase

Examples

religion   beauty
knowledge   student
rain   country

Proper nouns

- name specific persons, places, things, or ideas
- begin with capital letter

Examples

Hinduism   Prime Minister Harper
Philip   CN Tower
Vietnam   Renaissance

Count or noncount (common nouns only)

Count nouns

- name persons, places, things, or ideas that can be counted
- have plural forms

Examples

girl, girls
city, cities
goose, geese
philosophy, philosophies

Noncount nouns

- name things or abstract ideas that cannot be counted
- cannot be made plural

Examples

dirt   patience
silver   knowledge
furniture   air

NOTE: See the chart on page 243 for commonly used noncount nouns.

Singular or plural (both common and proper)

**Singular nouns
(count and noncount)**

- represent one person, place, thing, or idea

Examples

backpack   rain
country   beauty
woman   Nile River
achievement   Deer Island

**Plural nouns
(count only)**

- represent more than one person, place, thing, or idea
- must be count nouns

Examples

backpacks   Ural Mountains
countries   Falkland Islands
women   achievements

Specific (definite) or general (indefinite) (count and noncount)

Specific nouns	Examples
■ name persons, places, things, or ideas that can be identified within a group of the same type	*The students* in *Professor Martin's class* should study. *The airplane* carrying *the actor* was late. *The furniture* in *the truck* was damaged.

General nouns	Examples
■ name categories of persons, places, things, or ideas (often plural)	*Students* should study. *Books* help *cultures* connect. *The airplane* has made commuting between *cities* easy.

Using articles and other noun markers

Articles and other noun markers always appear before nouns; sometimes other modifiers, such as adjectives, come between a noun marker and a noun.

      ART N
Felix is reading a book about mythology.

      ART   ADJ   N
We took an exciting trip to Alaska last summer.

NOUN
MARKER ADV   ADJ   N
That very delicious meal was expensive.

In most cases, do not use an article with another noun marker.

      My
▶ ~~The my~~ older brother lives in Quebec.
     ^

Expressions like *a few*, *the most*, and *all the* are exceptions: *a few potatoes*, *all the rain*. See also M2-d.

Types of articles and types of nouns

To choose an appropriate article for a noun, you must first determine whether the noun is *common* or *proper*, *count* or *noncount*, *singular* or *plural*, and *specific* or *general*. The chart on pages 238–39 describes the types of nouns.

Articles are classified as *indefinite* and *definite*. The indefinite articles, *a* and *an*, are used with general nouns. The definite article, *the*, is used with specific nouns. (The last section of the chart, on p. 239, explains general and specific nouns.)

A and *an* both mean "one" or "one among many." Use *a* before a consonant sound: *a banana, a tree, a picture, a happy child, a united family.* Use *an* before a vowel sound: *an eggplant, an occasion, an uncle, an honourable person.* (See also *a, an* in W1.)

The shows that a noun is specific; use *the* with one or more than one specific thing: *the newspaper, the soldiers.*

M2-b Use *the* with most specific common nouns.

The definite article, *the*, is used with most nouns—both count and noncount—that the reader can identify specifically. Usually the identity will be clear to the reader for one of the following reasons. (See also the chart on p. 242.)

1. The noun has been previously mentioned.

   > *the*
   > ▶ A truck cut in front of our van. When truck skidded a few seconds
   >   ^
   > later, we almost crashed into it.

   The article *A* is used before *truck* when the noun is first mentioned. When the noun is mentioned again, it needs the article *the* because readers can now identify which truck skidded—the one that cut in front of the van.

2. A phrase or clause following the noun restricts its identity.

   > *the*
   > ▶ Bryce warned me that computer on his desk had just crashed.
   >   ^
   > The phrase *on his desk* identifies the specific computer.

NOTE: Descriptive adjectives do not necessarily make a noun specific. A specific noun is one that readers can identify within a group of nouns of the same type.

> *a*
> ▶ If I win the lottery, I will buy ~~the~~ brand-new bright red sports car.
>   ^
> The reader cannot identify which specific brand-new bright red sports car the writer will buy. Even though *car* has several adjectives in front of it, it is a general noun in this sentence.

3. A superlative adjective such as *best* or *most intelligent* makes the noun's identity specific. (See also G4-c on comparatives and superlatives.)

> *the*
> ▶ Our petite daughter dated ˄tallest boy in her class.

The superlative *tallest* makes the noun *boy* specific. Although there might be several tall boys, only one boy can be the tallest.

4. The noun describes a unique person, place, or thing.

> *the*
> ▶ During an eclipse, one should not look directly at ˄sun.

There is only one sun in our solar system, so its identity is clear.

5. The context or situation makes the noun's identity clear.

> *the*
> ▶ Please don't slam ˄door when you leave.

Both the speaker and the listener know which door is meant.

6. The noun is singular and refers to a scientific class or category of items (most often animals, musical instruments, and inventions).

> *The tin*
> ▶ ~~Tin~~ whistle is common in traditional Irish music.
> ˄

The writer is referring to the tin whistle as a class of musical instruments.

M2-c Use *a* (or *an*) with common singular count nouns that refer to "one" or "any."

If a count noun refers to one unspecific item (not a whole category), use the indefinite article, *a* or *an*. *A* and *an* usually mean "one among many" but can also mean "any one." (See the chart on p. 242.)

> *a*
> ▶ My English professor asked me to bring ˄dictionary to class.

The noun *dictionary* refers to "one unspecific dictionary" or "any dictionary."

> *an*
> ▶ We want to rent ˄apartment close to the lake.

The noun *apartment* refers to "any apartment close to the lake," not a specific apartment.

Choosing articles for common nouns

Use *the*

- if the reader has enough information to identify the noun specifically

COUNT: Please turn on *the lights*. We're going to *the beach* tomorrow.

NONCOUNT: *The food* throughout Italy is excellent.

Use *a* or *an*

- if the noun refers to one item

and

- if the item is singular but not specific

COUNT: Bring *a pencil* to class. Charles wrote *an essay* about his first job.

NOTE: Do not use *a* or *an* with plural or noncount nouns.

Use a quantifier (*enough, many, some,* etc.)

- if the noun represents an unspecified amount of something
- if the amount is more than one but not all items in a category

COUNT (PLURAL): Amir showed us *some photos* of his trip to India. *Many turtles* return to the same nesting site each year.

NONCOUNT: We didn't get *enough rain* this summer.

NOTE: Sometimes no article conveys an unspecified amount: *Amir showed us photos of his trip to India.*

Use no article

- if the noun represents all items in a category
- if the noun represents a category in general

COUNT (PLURAL): *Students* can attend the show for free. *Runners* must report to the officials' table at 7:00 a.m.

NONCOUNT: *Coal* is a natural resource.

NOTE: *The* is occasionally used when a singular count noun refers to all items in a class or a specific category: *The right whale is endangered in Canada.*

Commonly used noncount nouns

Food and drink

beef, bread, butter, candy, cereal, cheese, cream, meat, milk, pasta, rice, salt, sugar, water, wine

Nonfood substances

air, cement, coal, dirt, gasoline, gold, paper, petroleum, plastic, rain, silver, snow, soap, steel, wood, wool

Abstract nouns

advice, anger, beauty, confidence, courage, employment, fun, happiness, health, honesty, information, intelligence, knowledge, love, poverty, satisfaction, wealth

Other

biology (and other areas of study), clothing, equipment, furniture, homework, jewellery, luggage, machinery, mail, money, news, poetry, pollution, research, scenery, traffic, transportation, violence, weather, work

NOTE: A few noncount nouns (such as *love*) can also be used as count nouns: *He had two loves: music and archery.*

M2-d Use a quantifier such as *some* or *more*, not *a* or *an*, with a noncount noun to express an approximate amount.

Do not use *a* or *an* with noncount nouns. Also do not use numbers or words such as *several* or *many* because they must be used with plural nouns, and noncount nouns do not have plural forms. (See the chart on this page for a list of commonly used noncount nouns.)

▶ Dr. Snyder gave us ~~an~~ information about CUSO-VSO.

▶ Do you have ~~many~~ money with you?

You can use quantifiers such as *enough*, *less*, and *some* to suggest approximate amounts or nonspecific quantities of noncount nouns: *any homework, enough wood, less information, much pollution.*

▶ Vincent's mother told him that she had ~~a~~ *some* news that would surprise him.

M2-e Do not use articles with nouns that refer to all of something or something in general.

When a noncount noun refers to all of its type or to a concept in general, it is not marked with an article.

> *Kindness*
> ► ~~The kindness~~ is a virtue.
>   ^
> The noun represents kindness in general; it does not represent a specific type of kindness.

> ► In some parts of the world, ~~the~~ rice is preferred to all other grains.
>
> The noun *rice* represents rice in general, not a specific type or portion of rice.

In most cases, when you use a count noun to represent a general category, make the noun plural. Do not use unmarked singular count nouns to represent whole categories.

> *Fountains are*
> ► ~~Fountain is~~ an expensive element of landscape design.
>   ^
> *Fountains* is a count noun that represents fountains in general.

EXCEPTION: In some cases, *the* can be used with singular count nouns to represent a class or specific category: *The Chinese alligator is smaller than the American alligator*. See also number 6 in M2-b.

M2-f Do not use articles with most singular proper nouns. Use *the* with most plural proper nouns.

Since singular proper nouns are already specific, they typically do not need an article: *Prime Minister Cameron, Jamaica, Lake Huron, Mount Etna*.

There are, however, many exceptions. In most cases, if the proper noun consists of a common noun with modifiers (adjectives or an *of* phrase), use *the* with the proper noun.

> *the*
> ► We visited Great Wall of China last year.
>   ^

> *the*
> ► Rob wants to work for Canadian Security Intelligence Service.
>   ^

The is used with most plural proper nouns: *the McGregors, the Bahamas, the Finger Lakes, the Northwest Territories*.

Using *the* with geographic nouns

When to omit *the*

streets, squares, parks	Ivy Street, Union Square, Glacier National Park
cities, provinces, counties	Toronto, Saskatchewan, Bee County
most countries, continents	Italy, Nigeria, China, South America, Africa
bays, single lakes	Hudson Bay, Lake Geneva
single mountains, islands	Mount Everest, Crete

When to use *the*

country names with *of* phrase	the United States (of America), the People's Republic of China
large regions, deserts	the East Coast, the Sahara
peninsulas	the Baja Peninsula, the Sinai Peninsula
oceans, seas, gulfs	the Pacific Ocean, the Dead Sea, the Persian Gulf
canals and rivers	the Panama Canal, the Amazon
mountain ranges	the Rocky Mountains, the Alps
groups of islands	the Solomon Islands

Geographic names create problems because there are so many exceptions to the rules. When in doubt about whether or not to use an article, consult the chart on this page, check a dictionary, or ask a native speaker.

M3 Sentence structure

Although their structure can vary widely, sentences in English generally flow from subject to verb to object or complement: *Bears eat fish.* This section focuses on the major challenges that multilingual students face when writing sentences in English. For more details on the parts of speech and the elements of sentences, consult sections B1–B4.

M3-a Use a linking verb between a subject and its complement.

Some languages, such as Russian and Turkish, do not use linking verbs (*is*, *are*, *was*, *were*) between subjects and complements (nouns or adjectives that rename or describe the subject). Every English sentence, however, must include a verb. For more on linking verbs, see G2-e.

▶ Jim *is* intelligent.

▶ Many streets in San Francisco *are* very steep.

M3-b Include a subject in every sentence.

Some languages, such as Spanish and Japanese, do not require a subject in every sentence. Every English sentence, however, must have a subject. Commands are an exception: The subject *you* is understood but not present ([*You*] *Give me the book*).

▶ Your aunt is very energetic. ~~Seems~~ *She seems* young for her age.

The word *it* is used as the subject of a sentence describing the weather or temperature, stating the time, indicating distance, or suggesting an environmental fact.

▶ *It is* ~~Is~~ raining in the valley and snowing in the mountains.

▶ *It is* ~~Is~~ 9:15 a.m.

▶ *It is* ~~Is~~ three hundred kilometres to Regina.

In most English sentences, the subject appears before the verb. Some sentences, however, are inverted: The subject comes after the verb. In these sentences, a placeholder called an *expletive* (*there* or *it*) often comes before the verb.

> EXP V ⌐— S —⌐   ⌐— S —⌐ V
> There are many people here today. (Many people are here today.)

▶ *There is* ~~Is~~ an apple in the refrigerator.

▶ As you know, *there are* many religious sects in India.

Notice that the verb agrees with the subject that follows it: *apple is, sects are*. (See G1-g.)

Sometimes an inverted sentence has an infinitive (*to work*) or a noun clause (*that she is intelligent*) as the subject. In such sentences, the placeholder *it* is needed before the verb. (Also see B3-b and B3-e.)

EXP V ┌─ S ─┐ ┌─ S ─┐ V
It is important to study daily. (To study daily is important.)

 it
▶ Because the road is flooded, ^ is necessary to change our route.

The placeholder *it* is required before the verb *is* because the subject *to change our route* follows the verb.

TIP: The words *here* and *there* are not used as subjects. When they mean "in this place" (*here*) or "in that place" (*there*), they are adverbs, not nouns.

 It   *there.*
▶ I just returned from a vacation in Japan. ~~There~~ is very beautiful ^/
       ^   ^

 This school   *that school*
▶ ~~Here~~ offers a master's degree; ~~there~~ has only a bachelor's program.
  ^   ^

M3-c Do not use both a noun and a pronoun to perform the same grammatical function in a sentence.

English does not allow a subject to be repeated in its own clause.

▶ The doctor ~~she~~ advised me to cut down on salt.

The pronoun *she* cannot repeat the subject, *doctor*.

Do not add a pronoun even when a word group comes between the subject and the verb.

▶ The watch that I bought on vacation ~~it~~ was not expensive.

The pronoun *it* cannot repeat the subject, *watch*.

Some languages allow "topic fronting," placing a word or phrase (a "topic") at the beginning of a sentence and following it with an independent clause that explains something about the topic. This form is not allowed in English because the sentence seems to start with one subject but then introduces a new subject in an independent clause.

 ┌─ TOPIC ─┐┌──── IND CLAUSE ────┐
INCORRECT   The seeds I planted them last fall.

The sentence can be corrected by bringing the topic (*seeds*) into the independent clause.

>   *the seeds*
> ▶ ~~The seeds~~ I planted ~~them~~ last fall.
>   ^

M3-d Do not repeat an object or an adverb in an adjective clause.

Adjective clauses begin with relative pronouns (*who, whom, whose, which, that*) or relative adverbs (*when, where*). Relative pronouns usually serve as subjects or objects in the clauses they introduce; another word in the clause cannot serve the same function. Relative adverbs should not be repeated by other adverbs later in the clause.

>   ┌─────── ADJ CLAUSE ───────┐
> The cat ran under the car that was parked on the street.

> ▶ The cat ran under the car that ~~it~~ was parked on the street.

The relative pronoun *that* is the subject of the adjective clause, so the pronoun *it* cannot be added as a subject.

> ▶ Myrna enjoyed the investment seminars that she attended ~~them~~ last week.

The relative pronoun *that* is the object of the verb *attended*. The pronoun *them* cannot also serve as an object.

Sometimes the relative pronoun is understood but not present in the sentence. In such cases, do not add another word with the same function as the understood pronoun.

> ▶ Myrna enjoyed the investment seminars she attended ~~them~~ last week.

The relative pronoun *that* is understood after *seminars* even though it is not present in the sentence.

If the clause begins with a relative adverb, do not use another adverb with the same meaning later in the clause.

> ▶ The office where I work ~~there~~ is one hour from the city.

The adverb *there* cannot repeat the relative adverb *where*.

M3-e Avoid mixed constructions beginning with *although* or *because*.

A word group that begins with *although* cannot be linked to a word group that begins with *but* or *however*. The result is an error called a *mixed construction* (see also S5-a). Similarly, a word group that begins with *because* cannot be linked to a word group that begins with *so* or *therefore*.

If you want to keep *although* or *because*, drop the other linking word.

▶ Although Linda Holeman is best known for her books for

teens, ~~but~~ she has written several books for adults.

▶ Because German and Dutch are related languages, ~~therefore~~

tourists from Berlin can usually read a few signs in Amsterdam.

If you want to keep the other linking word, omit *although* or *because*.

▶ ~~Although~~ Linda Holeman is best known for her books for

teens, but she has written several books for adults.

▶ ~~Because~~ German and Dutch are related languages/;therefore,

tourists from Berlin can usually read a few signs in Amsterdam.

For advice about using commas and semicolons with linking words, see P1-a, P1-b, and P3-a.

M3-f Do not place an adverb between a verb and its direct object.

Adverbs modifying verbs can appear in various positions: at the beginning or end of a sentence, before or after a verb, or between a helping verb and the main verb.

Slowly, we drove along the rain-slick road.

Mia handled the teapot *very carefully*.

Martin *always* wins our tennis matches.

Christina is *rarely* late for our lunch dates.

My daughter has *often* spoken of you.

The election results were being *closely* followed by analysts.

An adverb cannot appear between a verb and its direct object.

carefully
▶ Mother wrapped ~~carefully~~ the gift.
      ^

The adverb *carefully* cannot appear between the verb, *wrapped*, and its direct object, *the gift*.

M4 Using adjectives

M4-a Distinguish between present participles and past participles used as adjectives.

Both present and past participles may be used as adjectives. The present participle always ends in *-ing*. Past participles usually end in *-ed*, *-d*, *-en*, *-n*, or *-t*. (See G2-a.)

PRESENT PARTICIPLES   confusing, speaking, boring

PAST PARTICIPLES   confused, spoken, bored

Like all other adjectives, participles can come before nouns; they also can follow linking verbs, in which case they describe the subject of the sentence. (See B2-b.)

Use a present participle to describe a person or thing *causing or stimulating an experience.*

The printer came with *confusing instructions.* [The instructions caused confusion.]

Use a past participle to describe a person or thing *undergoing an experience.*

Rachel was *confused* by the instructions. [Rachel experienced confusion.]

Participles that describe emotions or mental states often cause the most confusion.

annoying/annoyed   exhausting/exhausted
boring/bored   fascinating/fascinated
confusing/confused   frightening/frightened
depressing/depressed   satisfying/satisfied
exciting/excited   surprising/surprised

>   *exhausting.*
> Our hike was ~~exhausted.~~
>   ^
>
> *Exhausting* suggests that the hike caused exhaustion.

>   *exhausted*
> The ~~exhausting~~ hikers reached the campground just before
>   ^
>
> sunset.
>
> *Exhausted* describes how the hikers felt.

M4-b Place cumulative adjectives in an appropriate order.

Adjectives usually come before the nouns they modify and may also come after linking verbs. (See B1-d and B2-b.)

      ADJ   N   V   ADJ
Janine wore new shoes. Janine's shoes were new.

Cumulative adjectives, which cannot be joined by the word *and* or separated by commas, must come in a particular order. If you use cumulative adjectives before a noun, the chart on page 252 can help you determine their order. The chart is only a guide; don't be surprised if you encounter exceptions. (See also P2-d.)

>   *smelly red plastic*
> My dorm room has only a small desk and a ~~plastic red smelly~~
>   ^
>
> chair.

>   *clear blue*
> Nice weather, ~~blue clear~~ water, and ancient monuments attract
>   ^
>
> many people to Italy.

Order of cumulative adjectives

FIRST   **ARTICLE OR OTHER NOUN MARKER**   a, an, the, her, this, my, Joe's, two, many, some

EVALUATIVE WORD   attractive, dedicated, delicious, ugly, disgusting

SIZE   large, enormous, small, little

LENGTH OR SHAPE   long, short, round, square

AGE   new, old, young, antique

COLOR   yellow, blue, crimson

NATIONALITY   French, Peruvian, Vietnamese

RELIGION   Catholic, Protestant, Jewish, Muslim

MATERIAL   silver, walnut, wool, marble

LAST   **NOUN/ADJECTIVE**   tree (as in *tree* house), kitchen (as in *kitchen* table)

THE NOUN MODIFIED   house, coat, bicycle, bread, woman, coin

My large blue wool coat is in the attic.

Joe's collection includes *two small antique silver* coins.

M5 Prepositions and idiomatic expressions

M5-a Become familiar with prepositions that show time and place.

The most frequently used prepositions in English are *at*, *by*, *for*, *from*, *in*, *of*, *on*, *to*, and *with*. Prepositions can be difficult to master because the differences among them are subtle and idiomatic. The chart on page 253 is limited to three troublesome prepositions that show time and place: *at*, *on*, and *in*.

Not every possible use is listed in the chart, so don't be surprised when you encounter exceptions and idiomatic uses that you must learn one at a time. For example, in English a person rides *in* a car but *on* a bus, plane, train, or subway.

PRACTICE hackerhandbooks.com/writersref
> Multilingual/ESL > M5–2

At, on, and *in* to show time and place

Showing time

AT   *at* a specific time: *at* 7:20, *at* dawn, *at* dinner

ON   *on* a specific day or date: *on* Tuesday, *on* June 4

IN   *in* a part of a 24-hour period: *in* the afternoon, *in* the daytime
[but *at* night]

in a year or month: *in* 1999, *in* July

in a period of time: finished *in* three hours

Showing place

AT   *at* a meeting place or location: *at* home, *at* the club

at the edge of something: sitting *at* the desk

at the corner of something: turning *at* the intersection

at a target: throwing the snowball *at* Lucy

ON   *on* a surface: placed *on* the table, hanging *on* the wall

on a street: the house *on* Spring Street

on an electronic medium: *on* television, *on* the Internet

IN   *in* an enclosed space: *in* the garage, *in* an envelope

in a geographic location: *in* Charlottetown, *in* Newfoundland

in a print medium: *in* a book, *in* a magazine

▶ My first class starts ~~on~~ *at* 8:00 a.m.

▶ The farmers go to market ~~in~~ *on* Wednesday.

▶ I want to work at one of the biggest companies ~~on~~ *in* the world.

M5-b Use nouns (including *-ing* forms) after prepositions.

In a prepositional phrase, use a noun (not a verb) after the preposition. Sometimes the noun will be a gerund, the *-ing* verb form that functions as a noun (see B3-b).

▶ Our student government is good at ~~save~~ *saving* money.

Distinguish between the preposition *to* and the infinitive marker *to*. If *to* is a preposition, it should be followed by a noun or a gerund.

▶ We are dedicated to ~~help~~ the poor.
               helping

If *to* is an infinitive marker, it should be followed by the base form of the verb.

▶ We want to ~~helping~~ the poor.
          help

To test whether *to* is a preposition or an infinitive marker, insert a word that you know is a noun after the word *to*. If the noun makes sense in that position, *to* is a preposition. If the noun does not make sense after *to*, then *to* is an infinitive marker.

Zoe is addicted *to* _____.

They are planning *to* _____.

In the first sentence, a noun (such as *magazines*) makes sense after *to*, so *to* is a preposition and should be followed by a noun or a gerund: Zoe is addicted *to magazines*. Zoe is addicted *to running*.

In the second sentence, a noun (such as *magazines*) does not make sense after *to*, so *to* is an infinitive marker and must be followed by the base form of the verb: They are planning *to build* a new school.

M5-c Become familiar with common adjective + preposition combinations.

Some adjectives appear only with certain prepositions. These expressions are idiomatic and may be different from the combinations used in your first language.

▶ Paula is married ~~with~~ Jon.
                 to

Check an ESL dictionary for combinations that are not listed in the chart on page 255.

M5-d Become familiar with common verb + preposition combinations.

Many verbs and prepositions appear together in idiomatic phrases. Pay special attention to the combinations that are different from the combinations used in your native language.

▶ Your success depends ~~of~~ your effort.
  on
  ^

  Check an ESL dictionary for combinations that are not listed in the chart below.

Adjective + preposition combinations

accustomed to	connected to	guilty of	preferable to
addicted to	covered with	interested in	proud of
afraid of	dedicated to	involved in	responsible for
angry with	devoted to	involved with	satisfied with
ashamed of	different from	known as	scared of
aware of	engaged in	known for	similar to
committed to	engaged to	made of (*or*	tired of
concerned	excited about	made from)	worried about
about	familiar with	married to	
concerned with	full of	opposed to	

Verb + preposition combinations

agree with	compare with	forget about	speak to (*or*
apply to	concentrate on	happen to	speak with)
approve of	consist of	hope for	stare at
arrive at	count on	insist on	succeed at
arrive in	decide on	listen to	succeed in
ask for	depend on	participate in	take advantage of
believe in	differ from	rely on	take care of
belong to	disagree with	reply to	think about
care about	dream about	respond to	think of
care for	dream of	result in	wait for
compare to	feel like	search for	wait on

Punctuation
and Mechanics

P Punctuation and Mechanics

≡ P1 The comma

The comma was invented to help readers. Without it, sentence parts can collide into one another unexpectedly, causing misreadings.

CONFUSING   If you cook Elmer will do the dishes.

CONFUSING   While we were eating a rattlesnake approached our campsite.

Add commas in the logical places (after *cook* and *eating*), and suddenly all is clear. No longer is Elmer being cooked, the rattlesnake being eaten.

Various rules have evolved to prevent such misreadings and to speed readers along through complex grammatical structures. Those rules are detailed in this section. (P2 explains when not to use commas.)

P1-a Use a comma before a coordinating conjunction joining independent clauses.

When a coordinating conjunction connects two or more independent clauses—word groups that could stand alone as separate sentences—a comma must precede the conjunction. There are seven coordinating conjunctions in English: *and, but, or, nor, for, so,* and *yet.*

A comma tells readers that one independent clause has come to a close and that another is about to begin.

▶ The department sponsored a seminar on university survival skills,
   ^

   and it also hosted a barbecue for new students.

EXCEPTION: If the two independent clauses are short and there is no danger of misreading, the comma may be omitted.

   The plane took off and we were on our way.

TIP: As a rule, do *not* use a comma to separate compound elements that are not independent clauses. (See P2-a.)

▶ A good money manager controls expenses/ and invests surplus

   dollars to meet future needs.

   The word group following *and* is not an independent clause; it is the second half of a compound predicate (*controls . . . and invests*).

P1-b Use a comma after an introductory phrase or clause.

The most common introductory word groups are phrases and clauses functioning as adverbs. Such word groups usually tell when, where, how, why, or under what conditions the main action of the sentence occurred. (See B3-a, B3-b, and B3-e.)

A comma tells readers that the introductory phrase or clause has come to a close and that the main part of the sentence is about to begin.

▶ Near a small stream at the bottom of the canyon, the park

rangers discovered an abandoned mine.

> The comma tells readers that the introductory prepositional phrase has come to a close.

▶ When Irwin was ready to iron, his cat tripped on the extension

cord.

> Without the comma, readers may have Irwin ironing his cat. The comma signals that *his cat* is the subject of a new clause, not part of the introductory one.

EXCEPTION: The comma may be omitted after a short adverb clause or phrase if there is no danger of misreading.

> In no time we were at 1500 metres.

Sentences also frequently begin with participial phrases describing the noun or pronoun immediately following them. The comma tells readers that they are about to learn the identity of the person or thing described; therefore, the comma is usually required even when the phrase is short. (See B3-b.)

▶ Thinking his walk to his apartment was routine, Thomas D'Arcy

McGee paid no attention to the man walking behind him.

▶ Buried under layers of younger rocks, the earth's oldest rocks

contain no fossils.

NOTE: Other introductory word groups include transitional expressions and absolute phrases (see P1-f).

P1-c Use a comma between all items in a series.

When three or more items are presented in a series, those items should be separated from one another with commas. Items in a series may be single words, phrases, or clauses.

▶ Bubbles of air, leaves, ferns, bits of wood, and insects are often
   ^
found trapped in amber.

▶ Leonard Cohen has been inducted into the Canadian Music Hall

of Fame, the Canadian Songwriters Hall of Fame, and the American
                                              ^
Rock and Roll Hall of Fame.

Although some writers view the comma between the last two items as optional, most experts advise using the comma because its omission can result in ambiguity or misreading.

▶ David willed his oldest niece all of his property, houses, and
                                                          ^
warehouses.

Did Uncle David will his property *and* houses *and* warehouses — or simply his property, consisting of houses and warehouses? If the former meaning is intended, a comma is necessary to prevent ambiguity.

▶ The activities include touring the Parliament Building, listening

to a carillon concert, watching a video about the Tulip Festival,
                                                                ^
and skating on the Rideau Canal.

Without the comma, the activities might seem to include a lecture about skating, not participating in skating. The comma makes it clear that *skating on the Rideau Canal* is a separate item in the series.

P1-d Use a comma between coordinate adjectives not joined with *and*. Do not use a comma between cumulative adjectives.

When two or more adjectives each modify a noun separately, they are coordinate.

Roberto is a *warm, gentle, affectionate* father.

TEST: If the adjectives can be joined with *and*, the adjectives are coordinate, so you should use commas: *warm* and *gentle* and *affectionate* (*warm, gentle, affectionate*).

Adjectives that do not modify the noun separately are cumulative.

Three large grey shapes moved slowly toward us.

Beginning with the adjective closest to the noun *shapes*, these modifiers lean on one another, piggyback style, with each modifying a larger word group. *Grey* modifies *shapes*, *large* modifies *grey shapes*, and *three* modifies *large grey shapes*. Cumulative adjectives cannot be joined with *and* (not *three* and *large* and *grey shapes*).

COORDINATE ADJECTIVES

▶ Should patients with severe‚ irreversible brain damage
 ^
be put on life support systems?

CUMULATIVE ADJECTIVES

▶ Ira ordered a rich/ chocolate/ layer cake.

P1-e Use commas to set off nonrestrictive elements. Do not use commas to set off restrictive elements.

Certain word groups that modify nouns or pronouns can be restrictive or nonrestrictive—that is, essential or not essential to the meaning of a sentence. These word groups are usually adjective clauses, adjective phrases, or appositives.

Restrictive elements

A restrictive element defines or limits the meaning of the word it modifies; it is therefore essential to the meaning of the sentence and is not set off with commas. If you remove a restrictive modifier from a sentence, the meaning changes significantly, becoming more general than you intended.

RESTRICTIVE (NO COMMAS)

The campers need clothes *that are durable*.

Scientists *who study the earth's structure* are called geologists.

The first sentence does not mean that the campers need clothes in general. The intended meaning is more limited: The campers need durable clothes. The second sentence does not mean that scientists in general are called geologists; only those scientists who specifically study the earth's structure are called geologists. The italicized word groups are essential and are therefore not set off with commas.

Nonrestrictive elements

A nonrestrictive modifier describes a noun or pronoun whose meaning has already been clearly defined or limited. Because the modifier contains nonessential or parenthetical information, it is set off with commas. If you remove a nonrestrictive element from a sentence, the meaning does not change dramatically. Some meaning may be lost, but the defining characteristics of the person or thing described remain the same.

NONRESTRICTIVE (WITH COMMAS)

The campers need sturdy shoes, *which are expensive.*

The scientists, *who represented five different universities*, met to review applications for the Northern Science Award.

In the first sentence, the campers need sturdy shoes, and the shoes happen to be expensive. In the second sentence, the scientists met to review applications for the Northern Science Award; that they represented five different universities is informative but not critical to the meaning of the sentence. The nonessential information in both sentences is set off with commas.

NOTE: Often it is difficult to tell whether a word group is restrictive or nonrestrictive without seeing it in context and considering the writer's meaning. Both of the following sentences are grammatically correct, but their meanings are slightly different.

The dessert made with fresh raspberries was delicious.

The dessert, made with fresh raspberries, was delicious.

In the first example, the phrase *made with fresh raspberries* tells readers which of two or more desserts the writer is referring to. In the example with commas, the phrase merely adds information about the dessert.

Adjective clauses

Adjective clauses are patterned like sentences, containing subjects and verbs, but they function within sentences as modifiers of nouns or pronouns. They always follow the word they modify, usually immediately. Adjective clauses begin with a relative pronoun (*who, whom, whose, which, that*) or with a relative adverb (*where, when*). (See B3-e.)

Nonrestrictive adjective clauses are set off with commas; restrictive adjective clauses are not.

NONRESTRICTIVE CLAUSE (WITH COMMAS)

▶ Ed's house, which is located on five hectares, was completely

furnished with bats in the rafters and mice in the kitchen.

The adjective clause *which is located on five hectares* does not restrict the meaning of *Ed's house*; the information is nonessential and is therefore enclosed in commas.

RESTRICTIVE CLAUSE (NO COMMAS)

▶ The trumpeter swans/ that were born at the Toronto Zoo/ were

released into the wild.

Because the adjective clause *that were born at the Toronto Zoo* identifies one particular group of swans, not all swans, the information is essential and is therefore not enclosed in commas.

NOTE: Use *that* only with restrictive (essential) clauses. Many writers prefer to use *which* only with nonrestrictive (nonessential) clauses, but usage varies.

Adjective phrases

Prepositional or verbal phrases functioning as adjectives may be restrictive or nonrestrictive. (See B3-a and B3-b.) Nonrestrictive phrases are set off with commas; restrictive phrases are not.

NONRESTRICTIVE PHRASE (WITH COMMAS)

▶ The helicopter, with its million-candlepower spotlight

illuminating the area, circled above.

The *with* phrase is nonessential because its purpose is not to specify which of two or more helicopters is being discussed.

RESTRICTIVE PHRASE (NO COMMAS)

▶ One corner of the attic was filled with newspapers/ dating from

the early 1900s.

Dating from the early 1900s restricts the meaning of *newspapers*, so the comma should be omitted.

▶ The bill/ proposed by Minister of State Fletcher/ would limit

a senator's term to eight years.

Proposed by Minister of State Fletcher identifies exactly which bill is meant.

Appositives

An appositive is a noun or noun phrase that renames a nearby noun. Nonrestrictive appositives are set off with commas; restrictive appositives are not.

NONRESTRICTIVE APPOSITIVE (WITH COMMAS)

▶ Darwin's most important book, *On the Origin of Species,* was the
                              ^   ^
result of many years of research.

Most important restricts the meaning to one book, so the appositive *On the Origin of Species* is nonrestrictive and should be set off with commas.

RESTRICTIVE APPOSITIVE (NO COMMAS)

▶ The song/ "Viva la Vida/ " was blasted out of huge amplifiers at the

concert.

Once they've read *song*, readers still don't know precisely which song the writer means. The appositive following *song* restricts its meaning, so the appositive should not be enclosed in commas.

P1-f Use commas to set off transitional and parenthetical expressions, absolute phrases, and word groups expressing contrast.

Transitional expressions

Transitional expressions serve as bridges between sentences or parts of sentences. They include conjunctive adverbs such as *however, therefore,* and *moreover* and transitional phrases such as *for example, as a matter of fact,* and *in other words.* (For complete lists of these expressions, see P3-a.)

When a transitional expression appears between independent clauses in a compound sentence, it is preceded by a semicolon and is usually followed by a comma. (See P3-a.)

▶ Minh did not understand our language; moreover, he was
                                              ^
unfamiliar with our customs.

When a transitional expression appears at the beginning of a sentence or in the middle of an independent clause, it is usually set off with commas.

▶ As a matter of fact, lacrosse is Canada's official summer sport.
                     ^

▶ Natural foods are not always salt free; celery, for example,
                                                 ^   ^
contains more sodium than most people would imagine.

EXCEPTION: If a transitional expression blends smoothly with the rest of the sentence, calling for little or no pause in reading, it does not need to be set off with a comma. Expressions such as *also, at least, certainly, consequently, indeed, of course, moreover, no doubt, perhaps, then,* and *therefore* do not always call for a pause.

Alice's bicycle is broken; *therefore* you will need to borrow Sue's.

Parenthetical expressions

Expressions that are distinctly parenthetical, providing only supplemental information, should be set off with commas.

▶ Evolution, as far as we know, doesn't work this way.
           ^   ^

▶ The bass weighed about five kilograms, give or take a few
                                        ^
hundred grams.

Absolute phrases

An absolute phrase, which modifies the whole sentence, usually consists of a noun followed by a participle or participial phrase. (See B3-d.) Absolute phrases may appear at the beginning or at the end of a sentence. Wherever they appear, they should be set off with commas.

```
┌──────────── ABSOLUTE PHRASE ────────────┐
│    N   PARTICIPLE                        │
```
The sun appearing for the first time in a week, we were at last able to begin the archaeological dig.

▶ Elvis Presley made music industry history in the 1950s, his
^
records having sold more than ten million copies.

NOTE: Do not insert a comma between the noun and the participle in an absolute construction.

▶ The next contestant/being five years old, the emcee adjusted the
height of the microphone.

Word groups expressing contrast

Sharp contrasts beginning with words such as *not*, *never*, and *unlike* are set off with commas.

▶ The Epicurean philosophers sought mental, not bodily, pleasures.
^   ^

▶ Unlike Robert, Celia loved dance contests.
^

P1-g Use commas to set off words and phrases according to convention.

Direct address, yes and no

▶ Forgive me, Angela, for forgetting your birthday.
^   ^

▶ Yes, the loan will probably be approved.
^

Interrogative tags, mild interjections

▶ The film was faithful to the book, wasn't it?
^

▶ Well, cases like these are difficult to decide.
^

Direct quotations

▶ In his book *Shake Hands with the Devil*, Roméo Dallaire
wrote, "We all helped to create the mess that has murdered and
^
displaced millions and destabilized the whole central African
region" (5).

▶ "Happiness in marriage is entirely a matter of chance," says
⌄
Charlotte Lucas in *Pride and Prejudice*, a novel that ends with two

happy marriages (69; ch. 6).

See P5-a on the use of quotation marks and pages 397–98 on citing literary sources in MLA style.

Dates

In dates, the year is set off from the rest of the sentence with a pair of commas.

▶ On October 5, 1813, Tecumseh was killed in the Battle of the
⌄   ⌄
Thames.

EXCEPTIONS: Commas are not necessary if the date is inverted or if only the month and year are given.

The security alert system went into effect on 15 April 2009.

January 2008 was an extremely cold month.

Addresses

In a text sentence, the elements of an address or a place name are separated with commas. A postal code, however, is not preceded by a comma.

▶ John Lennon was born in Liverpool, England, in 1940.
⌄   ⌄

▶ Please send the package to Greg Tarvin at 708 Spring Street,
⌄
Hamilton, ON L8N 2P1.
⌄

Personal titles

If a title follows a name, separate the title from the rest of the sentence with a pair of commas.

▶ Sandra Belinsky, MD, has been appointed to the hospital board.
⌄   ⌄

Numbers

In numbers more than four digits long, use spaces to separate the numbers into groups of three, starting from the right. In numbers four digits long, a space is optional.

3 500 [*or* 3500]

100 000

5 000 000

NOTE: Commas are sometimes used in numbers of four or more digits, especially in US publications or in writing intended for a US audience.

P1-h Use a comma to prevent confusion.

In certain situations, a comma is necessary to prevent confusion. If the writer has intentionally left out a word or phrase, for example, a comma may be needed to signal the omission.

▶ To err is human; to forgive, divine.
               ^

If two words in a row echo each other, a comma may be needed for ease of reading.

▶ All of the catastrophes that we had feared might happen,
                                                         ^

happened.

Sometimes a comma is needed to prevent readers from grouping words in ways that do not match the writer's intention.

▶ Patients who can, walk up and down the halls several times
                ^

a day.

P2 Unnecessary commas

Many common misuses of the comma result from misunderstanding of the major comma rules presented in P1.

P2-a Do not use a comma between compound elements that are not independent clauses.

Though a comma should be used before a coordinating conjunction joining independent clauses (see P1-a), this rule should not be extended to other compound word groups.

PRACTICE hackerhandbooks.com/writersref
  > Punctuation and mechanics > P2–3 and P2–4

▶ Marie Curie discovered radium/ and later applied her work

on radioactivity to medicine.

And links two verbs in a compound predicate: *discovered* and *applied*.

▶ Jake told us that his illness is serious/ but that changes in

his lifestyle can improve his chances for survival.

The coordinating conjunction *but* links two subordinate clauses, each beginning with *that*: *that his illness is serious* and *that changes in his lifestyle*. . . .

P2-b Do not use a comma to separate a verb from its subject or object.

A sentence should flow from subject to verb to object without unnecessary pauses. Commas may appear between these major sentence elements only when a specific rule calls for them.

▶ Zoos large enough to give the animals freedom to roam/ are

becoming more popular.

The comma should not separate the subject, *Zoos*, from the verb, *are becoming*.

Writing with sources

MLA-style citation

▶ Catherine Ford writes/ that the way Canada welcomes immigrants

"contributes most heavily to the mosaic of race, creed, class and

culture" (141).

The comma should not separate the verb, *writes*, from its object, the subordinate clause beginning with *that*. A signal phrase ending in a word like *writes* or *says* is followed by a comma only when a direct quotation immediately follows: *Ford writes, "It is Canada's treatment of newcomers that contributes most heavily to the mosaic of race, creed, class and culture" (141).* (See also P5-e.)

P2-c Do not use a comma before the first or after the last item in a series.

Though commas are required between items in a series (P1-c), do not place them either before or after the whole series.

no comma to separate verb from subject or object • before or after
a series • between adjectives • with essential word groups

P2-e 271

▶ Other causes of asthmatic attacks are/ stress, change in

temperature, and cold air.

▶ Ironically, even novels that focus on horror, evil, and alienation/

often have themes of spiritual renewal and redemption.

P2-d Do not use a comma between cumulative adjectives, between an adjective and a noun, or between an adverb and an adjective.

Commas are required between coordinate adjectives (those that can be joined with *and*), but they do not belong between cumulative adjectives (those that cannot be joined with *and*). (For a full discussion, see P1-d.)

▶ In the corner of the closet, we found an old/ maroon hatbox.

A comma should never be used between an adjective and the noun that follows it.

▶ It was a senseless, dangerous/ mission.

Nor should a comma be used between an adverb and an adjective that follows it.

▶ The Hillside is a good home for severely/ malnourished children.

P2-e Do not use commas to set off restrictive or mildly parenthetical elements.

Restrictive elements are modifiers or appositives that restrict the meaning of the nouns they follow. Because they are essential to the meaning of the sentence, they are not set off with commas. (For a full discussion of restrictive and nonrestrictive elements, see P1-e.)

▶ Drivers/ who think they own the road/ make cycling a dangerous

sport.

The modifier *who think they own the road* restricts the meaning of *Drivers* and is therefore essential to the meaning of the sentence. Putting commas around the *who* clause falsely suggests that all drivers think they own the road.

▶ Margaret Mead's book/ *Coming of Age in Samoa/* stirred up

considerable controversy when it was published in 1928.

Since Mead wrote more than one book, the appositive contains information essential to the meaning of the sentence.

Although commas should be used with distinctly parenthetical expressions (see P1-f), do not use them to set off elements that are only mildly parenthetical.

▶ Texting has/ essentially/ replaced e-mail for casual communication.

P2-f Do not use a comma to set off a concluding adverb clause that is essential to the meaning of the sentence.

When adverb clauses introduce a sentence, they are nearly always followed by a comma (see P1-b). When they conclude a sentence, however, they are not set off by commas if their content is essential to the meaning of the earlier part of the sentence. Adverb clauses beginning with *after*, *as soon as*, *because*, *before*, *if*, *since*, *unless*, *until*, and *when* are usually essential.

▶ Don't visit Paris at the height of the tourist season/ unless you

have booked hotel reservations.

Without the *unless* clause, the meaning of the sentence might at first seem broader than the writer intended.

When a concluding adverb clause is nonessential, it should be preceded by a comma. Clauses beginning with *although*, *even though*, *though*, and *whereas* are usually nonessential.

▶ The lecture seemed to last only a short time, although the clock
                                             ^
said it had gone on for more than an hour.

P2-g Do not use a comma after a phrase that begins an inverted sentence.

Though a comma belongs after most introductory phrases (see P1-b), it does not belong after phrases that begin an inverted sentence. In an inverted sentence, the subject follows the verb, and a phrase that ordinarily would follow the verb is moved to the beginning.

▶ At the bottom of the hill/ sat the stubborn mule.

P2-h Avoid other common misuses of the comma.

Do not use a comma in the following situations.

AFTER A COORDINATING CONJUNCTION (*AND, BUT, OR, NOR, FOR, SO, YET*)

▶ Occasionally TV talk shows are performed live, but/ more often they are taped.

AFTER *SUCH AS* OR *LIKE*

▶ Shade-loving plants such as/ begonias, impatiens, and coleus can add colour to a shady garden.

BEFORE *THAN*

▶ Touring Crete was more thrilling for us/ than visiting the Greek islands frequented by the rich.

AFTER *ALTHOUGH*

▶ Although/ the air was balmy, the water was too cold for swimming.

BEFORE A PARENTHESIS

▶ At InterComm, Sylvia began at the bottom/ (with only three and a half walls and a swivel chair), but within three years she had been promoted to supervisor.

TO SET OFF AN INDIRECT (REPORTED) QUOTATION

▶ Samuel Goldwyn once said/ that a verbal contract isn't worth the paper it's written on.

WITH A QUESTION MARK OR AN EXCLAMATION POINT

▶ "Why don't you try it?/ " she coaxed. "You can't do any worse than the rest of us."

P3 The semicolon and the colon

The semicolon is used to connect major sentence elements of equal grammatical rank (see P3-a and P3-b). The colon is used primarily to call attention to the words that follow it (see P3-d). In addition, the colon has some conventional uses (see P3-e).

P3-a Use a semicolon with independent clauses.

Between independent clauses with no coordinating conjunction

When two independent clauses appear in one sentence, they are usually linked with a comma and a coordinating conjunction (*and*, *but*, *or*, *nor*, *for*, *so*, *yet*). The coordinating conjunction signals the relation between the clauses. If the clauses are closely related and the relation is clear without a conjunction, they may be linked with a semicolon instead.

> In film, a low-angle shot makes the subject look powerful; a high-angle shot does just the opposite.

A semicolon must be used whenever a coordinating conjunction has been omitted between independent clauses. To use merely a comma creates a type of run-on sentence known as a *comma splice*. (See G6.)

▶ In 1534, Jacques Cartier sailed to Canada while trying to find a route to Asia**/;** in 1535, he made a second voyage to Canada.

Between independent clauses with a transitional expression

Transitional expressions include conjunctive adverbs and transitional phrases.

CONJUNCTIVE ADVERBS

accordingly	furthermore	moreover	still
also	hence	nevertheless	subsequently
anyway	however	next	then
besides	incidentally	nonetheless	therefore
certainly	indeed	now	thus
consequently	instead	otherwise	
conversely	likewise	similarly	
finally	meanwhile	specifically	

TRANSITIONAL PHRASES

after all	even so	in fact
as a matter of fact	for example	in other words
as a result	for instance	in the first place
at any rate	in addition	on the contrary
at the same time	in conclusion	on the other hand

When a transitional expression appears between independent clauses, it is preceded by a semicolon and usually followed by a comma.

▶ Many corals grow very gradually/; in fact, the creation of a coral
                                      ^

reef can take centuries.

When a transitional expression appears in the middle or at the end of the second independent clause, the semicolon goes *between the clauses.*

▶ Biologists have observed laughter in primates other than humans/;
                                                   ^

chimpanzees, however, sound more like they are panting than

laughing.

Transitional expressions should not be confused with the coordinating conjunctions *and, but, or, nor, for, so,* and *yet,* which are preceded by a comma when they link independent clauses. (See P1-a.)

P3-b Use a semicolon between items in a series containing internal punctuation.

▶ Classic science fiction sagas include *Star Trek,* with Captain Kirk,

Dr. McCoy, and Mr. Spock/; *Battlestar Galactica,* with its
                                        ^

Cylons/; and *Star Wars,* with Han Solo, Luke Skywalker, and
      ^

Darth Vader.

Without the semicolons, the reader would have to sort out the major groupings, distinguishing between important and less important pauses according to the logic of the sentence. By inserting semicolons at the major breaks, the writer does this work for the reader.

P3-c Avoid common misuses of the semicolon.

Do not use a semicolon in the following situations.

BETWEEN A SUBORDINATE CLAUSE AND THE REST OF THE SENTENCE

▶ Although legislation requiring radio stations to include Canadian content was controversial⁄, it has helped many Canadian artists gain recognition.

BETWEEN AN APPOSITIVE AND THE WORD IT REFERS TO

▶ The scientists were fascinated by the species *Argyroneta aquatica⁄,* a spider that lives underwater.

TO INTRODUCE A LIST

▶ Some of my favourite celebrities have their own blogs⁄: Lindsay Lohan, Rosie O'Donnell, and Zach Braff.

BETWEEN INDEPENDENT CLAUSES JOINED BY *AND, BUT, OR, NOR, FOR, SO,* OR *YET*

▶ Five of the applicants had worked with spreadsheets⁄, but only one was familiar with database management.

P3-d Use a colon after an independent clause to direct attention to a list, an appositive, a quotation, or a summary or an explanation.

A LIST

The daily routine should include at least the following: twenty knee bends, fifty sit-ups, fifteen leg lifts, and five minutes of running in place.

AN APPOSITIVE

My roommate is guilty of two of the seven deadly sins: gluttony and sloth.

A QUOTATION

Consider the words of Pierre Trudeau: "I will not leave Ottawa until the country is and the government are irreversibly bilingual."

PRACTICE **hackerhandbooks.com/writersref**
> Punctuation and mechanics > P3–6

A SUMMARY OR AN EXPLANATION

Faith is like love: It cannot be forced.

The novel is clearly autobiographical: The author even gives his own name to the main character.

NOTE: For other ways of introducing quotations, see "Introducing quoted material" on pages 284–85. When an independent clause follows a colon, it may begin with a capital or a lowercase letter (see P8-e).

P3-e Use a colon according to convention.

SALUTATION IN A LETTER   Dear Sir or Madam:

HOURS AND MINUTES   5:30 p.m.

PROPORTIONS   The ratio of women to men was 2:1.

TITLE AND SUBTITLE   *The Glory of Hera: Greek Mythology and the Greek Family*

BIBLIOGRAPHIC ENTRIES   Toronto: Nelson, 2011

NOTE: In biblical references, a colon is ordinarily used between chapter and verse (Luke 2:14). The Modern Language Association (MLA) recommends a period instead (Luke 2.14).

P3-f Avoid common misuses of the colon.

A colon must be preceded by a full independent clause. Therefore, avoid using it in the following situations.

BETWEEN A VERB AND ITS OBJECT OR COMPLEMENT

▶ Some important vitamins found in vegetables are: vitamin A, thiamine, niacin, and vitamin C.

BETWEEN A PREPOSITION AND ITS OBJECT

▶ The heart's two pumps each consist of: an upper chamber, or atrium, and a lower chamber, or ventricle.

AFTER *SUCH AS*, *INCLUDING*, OR *FOR EXAMPLE*

▶ Canadian Interuniversity Sport regulates university athletic teams, including: basketball, soccer, ice hockey, and football.

P4 The apostrophe

P4-a Use an apostrophe to indicate that a noun or an indefinite pronoun is possessive.

The possessive form of a noun or an indefinite pronoun usually indicates ownership, as in *Tim's hat*, *the lawyer's desk*, or *someone's glove*. Frequently, however, ownership is only loosely implied: *the tree's roots*, *a day's work*. If you are not sure whether a word is possessive, try turning it into an *of* phrase: the roots *of the tree*, the work *of a day*.

When to add -'s to a noun

1. If the noun does not end in *-s*, add *-'s*.

   Luck often propels a rock musician's career.

   The Children's Wish Foundation of Canada fulfills the wishes of children who have life-threatening illnesses.

2. If the noun is singular and ends in *-s* or an *s* sound, add *-'s*.

   Lois's sister spent last year in India.

   Her article presents an overview of Marx's teachings.

NOTE: To avoid potentially awkward pronunciation, some writers use only the apostrophe with a singular noun ending in *-s*: *Sophocles'*.

When to add only an apostrophe to a noun

If the noun is plural and ends in *-s*, add only an apostrophe.

   Both diplomats' briefcases were searched by guards.

Joint possession

To show joint possession, use *-'s* or (*-s'*) with the last noun only; to show individual possession, make all nouns possessive.

   Have you seen Joyce and Greg's new camper?

   John's and Marie's expectations of marriage couldn't have been more different.

Joyce and Greg jointly own one camper. John and Marie individually have different expectations.

PRACTICE hackerhandbooks.com/writersref
> Punctuation and mechanics > P4–3 and P4–4

possessives • using -'s or -s' • compound nouns (*father-in-law's*) • *everyone's, somebody's,* etc. • contractions (*isn't*) • no apostrophe

P4-c   279

Compound nouns

If a noun is compound, use -'s (or -s') with the last element.

> My father-in-law's memoir about his childhood in Sri Lanka was published in October.

Indefinite pronouns

Indefinite pronouns refer to no specific person or thing: *everyone, someone, no one, something.* (See B1-b.)

> Someone's raincoat has been left behind.

P4-b Use an apostrophe to mark omissions in contractions and numbers.

In a contraction, the apostrophe takes the place of one or more missing letters.

> It's a shame that Frank can't go on the tour.

It's stands for *it is, can't* for *cannot.*
    The apostrophe is also used to mark the omission of the first two digits of a year (*the class of '08*) or years (*the '60s generation*).

P4-c Do not use an apostrophe to form the plural of numbers, letters, abbreviations, and words mentioned as words.

An apostrophe typically is not used to pluralize numbers, letters, abbreviations, and words mentioned as words. Note the few exceptions and be consistent throughout your paper.

Plural of numbers

Do not use an apostrophe in the plural of any numbers, including decades.

> Oksana skated nearly perfect figure 8s.

> The 1920s are known as the Jazz Age.

Plural of letters

Italicize the letter and use roman (regular) font style for the -*s* ending. Do not italicize academic grades.

Two large *J*s were painted on the door.

He received two Ds for the first time in his life.

EXCEPTIONS: To avoid misreading, use an apostrophe to form the plural of lowercase letters and the capital letters *A* and *I*: *p*'s, *A*'s.

Beginning readers often confuse *b*'s and *d*'s.

MLA NOTE: The Modern Language Association recommends using an apostrophe for the plural of both capital and lowercase letters: *J*'s, *p*'s.

Plural of abbreviations

Do not use an apostrophe to pluralize an abbreviation.

Harriet has thirty DVDs on her desk.

Marco earned two PhDs before his thirtieth birthday.

Plural of words mentioned as words

Generally, omit the apostrophe to form the plural of words mentioned as words. If the word is italicized, the *-s* ending appears in roman (regular) type.

We've heard enough *maybe*s.

Words mentioned as words may also appear in quotation marks. When you choose this option, use the apostrophe.

We've heard enough "maybe's."

P4-d Avoid common misuses of the apostrophe.

Do not use an apostrophe in the following situations.

WITH NOUNS THAT ARE NOT POSSESSIVE
> ► Some ~~outpatient's~~ have special parking permits.
>   *outpatients*
>   ^

IN THE POSSESSIVE PRONOUNS ITS, WHOSE, HIS, HERS, OURS, YOURS, AND THEIRS
> ► Each area has ~~it's~~ own conference room.
>   *its*
>   ^

It's means "it is." The possessive pronoun *its* contains no apostrophe despite the fact that it is possessive.

▶ The short-story collection *When Women Rule* was written by
        whose
Austin Clarke, ~~who's~~ work focuses on the immigrant community
     ^
in Canada.

Who's means "who is." The possessive pronoun is *whose*.

☰ P5 Quotation marks

Writers use quotation marks primarily to enclose direct quotations of
another person's spoken or written words. You will also find these other
uses and exceptions:

- for quotations within quotations (single quotation marks: P5-b)
- for titles of short works (P5-c)
- for words used as words (P5-d)
- with other marks of punctuation (P5-e)
- with brackets and ellipsis marks (P6-b, P6-c)
- no quotation marks for long quotations (P5-a)
- no quotation marks for indirect quotations, summaries, and
  paraphrases (P5-a, MLA-2c, APA-2c, CMS-2c)

P5-a Use quotation marks to enclose direct quotations.

Direct quotations of a person's words, whether spoken or written, must
be in quotation marks.

> "The contract negotiations are stalled," the airline executive told
> reporters, "but I am prepared to work night and day to bring both
> sides together."

In dialogue, begin a new paragraph to mark a change in speaker.

> "Mom, his name is Willie, not William. A thousand times I've told
> you, it's *Willie*."
> "Willie is a derivative of William, Lester. Surely his birth certifi-
> cate doesn't have Willie on it, and I like calling people by their
> proper names."
> "Yes, it does, ma'am. My mother named me Willie K. Mason."
>   — Gloria Naylor

PRACTICE   hackerhandbooks.com/writersref
> Punctuation and mechanics > P5–3 and P5–4

If a single speaker utters more than one paragraph, introduce each paragraph with a quotation mark, but do not use a closing quotation mark until the end of the speech.

Exception: indirect quotations

Do not use quotation marks around indirect quotations. An indirect quotation reports someone's ideas without using that person's exact words. In academic writing, indirect quotation is called *paraphrase* or *summary*. (See R3-c.)

> The airline executive told reporters that although contract negotiations were at a standstill, she was prepared to work hard with both labour and management to bring about a settlement.

Exception: long quotations

Long quotations of prose or poetry are generally set off from the text by indenting. Quotation marks are not used because the indented format tells readers that the quotation is taken word-for-word from the source.

> After making an exhaustive study of the historical record, James Horan evaluates Billy the Kid like this:
>
> > The portrait that emerges of [the Kid] from the thousands of pages of affidavits, reports, trial transcripts, his letters, and his testimony is neither the mythical Robin Hood nor the stereotyped adenoidal moron and pathological killer. Rather Billy appears as a disturbed, lonely young man, honest, loyal to his friends, dedicated to his beliefs, and betrayed by our institutions and the corrupt, ambitious, and compromising politicians in his time. (158)

The number in parentheses is a citation handled according to MLA style. (See MLA-4a.)

MLA, APA, and CMS (*Chicago*) have specific guidelines for what constitutes a long quotation and how it should be indented (see pp. 381, 485, and 506, respectively).

P5-b Use single quotation marks to enclose a quotation within a quotation.

> Megan Marshall notes that what Elizabeth Peabody "hoped to accomplish in her school was not merely 'teaching' but 'educating children morally and spiritually as well as intellectually from the first'" (107).

P5-c Use quotation marks around the titles of short works.

Short works include newspaper and magazine articles, poems, short stories, songs, episodes of television and radio programs, and chapters or subdivisions of books.

> Roch Carrier's short story "The Hockey Sweater" is based on a true story from the author's childhood.

NOTE: Titles of books, plays, Web sites, television and radio programs, films, magazines, and newspapers are put in italics. (See P10-a.)

P5-d Quotation marks may be used to set off words used as words.

Although words used as words are ordinarily italicized (see P10-b), quotation marks are also acceptable. Be consistent throughout your paper.

> The words "accept" and "except" are frequently confused.

> The words *accept* and *except* are frequently confused.

P5-e Use punctuation with quotation marks according to convention.

This section describes the conventions most Canadian publishers use in placing marks of punctuation inside or outside quotation marks. It also explains how to punctuate when introducing quoted material.

Periods and commas

Place periods and commas inside quotation marks.

> "I'm here as part of my co-op placement," I told the classroom teacher. "I'm hoping to become a reading specialist."

This rule applies to single quotation marks as well as double quotation marks. (See P5-b.) It also applies to all uses of quotation marks: for quoted material, for titles of works, and for words used as words.

EXCEPTION: In the Modern Language Association's style of parenthetical in-text citations (see MLA-4a), the period follows the citation in parentheses. (See the example on p. 284.)

David M. Quiring notes that in 1944 poverty in Saskatchewan "had reached legendary proportions, dashing the hopes of the immigrants who had come to this place once thought to be a Garden of Eden" (3).

Colons and semicolons

Put colons and semicolons outside quotation marks.

Harold wrote, "I regret that I am unable to attend the fundraiser for AIDS research"; his letter, however, came with a substantial contribution.

Question marks and exclamation points

Put question marks and exclamation points inside quotation marks unless they apply to the whole sentence.

Contrary to tradition, bedtime at my house is marked by "Mommy, can I tell you a story now?"

Have you heard the old proverb "Do not climb the hill until you reach it"?

In the first sentence, the question mark applies only to the quoted question. In the second sentence, the question mark applies to the whole sentence.

NOTE: In MLA style for a quotation that ends with a question mark or an exclamation point, the parenthetical citation and a period should follow the entire quotation.

Rosie Thomas asks, "Is nothing in life ever straight and clear, the way children see it?" (77).

Introducing quoted material

After a word group introducing a quotation, choose a colon, a comma, or no punctuation at all, whichever is appropriate in context.

FORMAL INTRODUCTION If a quotation is formally introduced, a colon is appropriate. A formal introduction is a full independent clause, not just an expression such as *he said* or *she remarked.*

Thomas Friedman provides a challenging yet optimistic view of the future: "We need to get back to work on our country and on our planet. The hour is late, the stakes couldn't be higher, the project couldn't be harder, the payoff couldn't be greater" (25).

EXPRESSION SUCH AS *HE SAID*   If a quotation is introduced with an expression such as *he said* or *she remarked*—or if it is followed by such an expression—a comma is needed.

> About Newfoundland's weather, Rex Murphy once declared, "Weather is the currency of every Newfoundland conversation, and it may be a misery, but it's our own misery" (289-90).

> "The written record signed, sealed, and swiftly transmitted was essential to military power and the extension of government," Harold Innis wrote when describing the connection between successful empires and the types of communication they used (30).

BLENDED QUOTATION   When a quotation is blended into the writer's own sentence, either a comma or no punctuation is appropriate, depending on the way in which the quotation fits into the sentence structure.

> The future champion could, as he put it, "float like a butterfly and sting like a bee."

> Virginia Woolf wrote in 1928 that "a woman must have money and a room of her own if she is to write fiction" (4).

BEGINNING OF SENTENCE   If a quotation appears at the beginning of a sentence, use a comma after it unless the quotation ends with a question mark or an exclamation point.

> "I've always thought of myself as a reporter," claimed poet Gwendolyn Brooks (162).

> "What is it?" she asked, bracing herself.

INTERRUPTED QUOTATION   If a quoted sentence is interrupted by explanatory words, use commas to set off the explanatory words.

> "With regard to air travel," Stephen Ambrose notes, "Jefferson was a full century ahead of the curve" (53).

If two successive quoted sentences from the same source are interrupted by explanatory words, use a comma before the explanatory words and a period after them.

> "Everyone agrees journalists must tell the truth," Bill Kovach and Tom Rosenstiel write. "Yet people are befuddled about what 'the truth' means" (37).

P5-f   Avoid common misuses of quotation marks.

Do not use quotation marks to draw attention to familiar slang, to disown trite expressions, or to justify an attempt at humour.

▶ The economist estimated that single-family home prices would decline another 5 percent by the end of the year, emphasizing that this was only a /ballpark figure./

Do not use quotation marks around the title of your own essay.

▦ **P6** Other punctuation marks

P6-a End punctuation

The period

Use a period to end all sentences except direct questions or genuine exclamations. Also use periods in abbreviations according to convention.

TO END SENTENCES   Most sentences should end with a period. Problems sometimes arise when a writer must choose between a period and a question mark or between a period and an exclamation point.

If a sentence reports a question instead of asking it directly, it should end with a period, not a question mark.

▶ The professor asked whether talk therapy was more beneficial

than antidepressants̸.
        ^

If a sentence is not a genuine exclamation, it should end with a period, not an exclamation point. (See also p. 287.)

▶ After years of working her way through school, Geeta finally

graduated with high honours̸.
        ^

IN ABBREVIATIONS   A period is conventionally used in abbreviations of titles and Latin words or phrases, including the time designations for morning and afternoon.

Mr.	i.e.	a.m. (or AM)
Ms.	e.g.	p.m. (or PM)
Dr.	etc.	

NOTE: If a sentence ends with a period marking an abbreviation, do not add a second period.

Do not use a period with postal abbreviations for provinces and territories and US states: AB, NU, TX.

Current usage is to omit the period in abbreviations of organization and country names, academic degrees, and designations for eras.

NATO	UNESCO	UCLA	BS	BC
IRS	AFL-CIO	NIH	PhD	BCE

The question mark

A direct question should be followed by a question mark.

What is the horsepower of a 777 engine?

If a polite request is written in the form of a question, it may be followed by a period.

Would you please send me your catalogue of lilies.

TIP: Do not use a question mark after an indirect question, one that is reported rather than asked directly. Use a period instead.

▶ He asked me who was teaching the mythology course this year?.
^

NOTE: Questions in a series may be followed by question marks even when they are not complete sentences.

We wondered where Calamity had hidden this time. Under the sink? Behind the furnace? On top of the bookcase?

The exclamation point

Use an exclamation point after a word group or sentence to express exceptional feeling or to provide special emphasis. The exclamation point is rarely appropriate in academic writing.

When Gloria entered the room, I switched on the lights, and we all yelled, "Surprise!"

TIP: Do not overuse the exclamation point.

▶ In the fisherman's memory, the fish lives on, increasing in length

and weight with each passing year, until at last it is big enough

to shade a fishing boat!.
^

This sentence doesn't need to be pumped up with an exclamation point. It is emphatic enough without it.

▶ Whenever I see my favourite hitter, Aaron Hill, in the batter's box,

I dream of making it to the big leagues**⁄.** My team would win
          ^
every time!

The first exclamation point should be deleted so that the second one will have more force.

P6-b The dash, parentheses, and brackets

The dash

When typing, use two hyphens to form a dash (--). Do not put spaces before or after the dash. If your word processing program has what is known as an "em-dash" (—), you may use it instead, with no space before or after it.

A dash can be used to set off parenthetical material that deserves emphasis.

> Everything that went wrong—from the peeping Tom at Theodora's window last night to my head-on collision today—we blamed on our move.

A pair of dashes is useful to enclose an appositive that contains commas. An appositive is a noun or noun phrase that renames a nearby noun. Ordinarily appositives are set off with commas (see P1-e), but when the appositive itself contains commas, a pair of dashes helps readers see the relative importance of all the pauses.

> In my hometown, the basic needs of people—food, clothing, and shelter—are less costly than in a big city like Toronto.

A dash is a dramatic, somewhat informal way to introduce a list, a restatement, an amplification, or a striking shift in tone or thought.

> Along the wall are the bulk liquids—sesame seed oil, honey, safflower oil, and that half-liquid "peanuts only" peanut butter.

> In his last semester, Peter tried to pay more attention to his priorities—applying to graduate school, getting financial aid, and finding a roommate.

> Everywhere we looked there were little kids—a box of Cracker Jacks in one hand and Mommy or Daddy's sleeve in the other.

> Kiere took a few steps back, came running full speed, kicked a mighty kick—and missed the ball.

In the first two examples, the writer could also use a colon. (See P3-d.)
The colon is more formal than the dash and not quite as dramatic.

TIP: Unless there is a specific reason for using the dash, avoid it. Unnecessary dashes create a choppy effect.

▶ Insisting that students use computers as instructional

tools ⫻ for information retrieval ⫻ makes good sense. Herding

them ⫻ sheeplike ⫻ into computer technology does not.

Parentheses

Use parentheses to enclose supplemental material, minor digressions,
and afterthoughts.

> Nurses record patients' vital signs (temperature, pulse, and blood
> pressure) several times a day.

Use parentheses to enclose letters or numbers labelling items in
a series.

> Regulations stipulated that only the following equipment could be used
> on the survival mission: (1) a knife, (2) ten metres of parachute line,
> (3) a book of matches, (4) a poncho, (5) an E tool, and (6) a signal flare.

TIP: Do not overuse parentheses. Rough drafts are likely to contain
more afterthoughts than necessary. As writers head into a sentence, they
often think of additional details, occasionally working them in as best
they can with parentheses. Usually such sentences should be revised so
that the additional details no longer seem to be afterthoughts.

▶ Researchers have said that three million ~~(estimates run as~~
  from
  ~~high as~~ four million)Canadians have diabetes.
  to

Brackets

Use brackets to enclose any words or phrases that you have inserted
into an otherwise word-for-word quotation.

> "What made the experience [of seeing great horned owls] even more
> special was that it happened in the middle of Calgary," Bruce Masterman reports (26).

The sentence quoted from the *of seeing great horned owls* article did
not contain the words (since the context of the full article made clear

what experience was meant), so the writer needed to clarify in brackets.

The Latin word "sic" in brackets indicates that an error in a quoted sentence appears in the original source.

> According to the review, Nelly Furtado's performance was brilliant, "exceding [sic] the expectations of even her most loyal fans."

Do not overuse "sic," however, since calling attention to others' mistakes can appear snobbish. The preceding quotation, for example, might have been paraphrased instead: *According to the review, even Nelly Furtado's most loyal fans were surprised by the brilliance of her performance.*

P6-c The ellipsis mark

The ellipsis mark consists of three spaced periods. Use an ellipsis mark to indicate that you have deleted words from an otherwise word-for-word quotation.

> Reuben reports that "when the amount of cholesterol circulating in the blood rises over . . . 300 milligrams per 100, the chances of a heart attack increase dramatically."

If you delete a full sentence or more in the middle of a quoted passage, use a period before the three ellipsis dots.

> "The Kaiapo," writes David Suzuki, "are famous for their ferocity. . . . [W]hen there is a crisis, it doesn't matter how well you have been received; you are not Kaiapo" (186).

For the use of brackets to change a lowercase letter to a capital (and vice versa) in MLA style, see page 381.

TIP: Ordinarily, do not use the ellipsis mark at the beginning or at the end of a quotation. Readers will understand that the quoted material is taken from a longer passage. If you have cut some words from the end of the final quoted sentence, however, MLA requires an ellipsis mark, as in the first example on page 381.

In quoted poetry, use a full line of ellipsis dots to indicate that you have dropped a line or more from the poem, as in this example from "To His Coy Mistress" by Andrew Marvell:

> Had we but world enough, and time,
> This coyness, lady, were no crime.
> . . . .
> But at my back I always hear
> Time's wingèd chariot hurrying near; (1-2, 21-22)

The ellipsis mark may also be used to indicate a hesitation or an interruption in speech or to suggest unfinished thoughts.

> "The apartment building next door . . . it's going up in flames!" yelled Marcia.

> Before falling into a coma, the victim whispered, "It was a man with a tattoo on his . . . "

P6-d The slash

Use the slash to separate two or three lines of poetry that have been run into your text. Add a space both before and after the slash.

> In the opening lines of "Jordan," George Herbert pokes gentle fun at popular poems of his time: "Who says that fictions only and false hair / Become a verse? Is there in truth no beauty?" (1-2).

More than three lines of poetry should be handled as an indented quotation. (See p. 282.)

The slash may occasionally be used to separate paired terms such as *pass/fail* and *producer/director*. Do not use a space before or after the slash. Be sparing in this use of the slash. In particular, avoid the use of *and/or*, *he/she*, and *his/her*. Instead of using *he/she* and *his/her* to solve sexist language problems, you can usually find more graceful alternatives. (See W4-e and G3-a.)

P7 Spelling and hyphenation

You learned to spell from repeated experience with words in both reading and writing, but especially writing. Words have a look, a sound, and even a feel to them as the hand moves across the page. As you proofread, you can probably tell if a word doesn't look quite right. In such cases, the solution is obvious: Look up the word in the dictionary. (See W6-a.)

P7-a Become familiar with the major spelling rules.

i *before* e *except after* c

Use *i* before *e* except after *c* or when sounded like *ay*, as in *neighbour* and *weigh*.

I BEFORE *E*	relieve, believe, sieve, niece, fierce, frieze
E BEFORE *I*	receive, deceive, sleigh, freight, eight
EXCEPTIONS	seize, either, weird, height, foreign, leisure

Suffixes

FINAL SILENT -*E*　Generally, drop a final silent -*e* when adding a suffix that begins with a vowel. Keep the final -*e* if the suffix begins with a consonant.

combine, combination	achieve, achievement
desire, desiring	care, careful
prude, prudish	entire, entirety
remove, removable	gentle, gentleness

Words such as *changeable, acknowledgment, judgment, argument,* and *truly* are exceptions.

FINAL -*Y*　When adding -*s* or -*d* to words ending in -*y*, ordinarily change -*y* to -*ie* when the -*y* is preceded by a consonant but not when it is preceded by a vowel.

comedy, comedies	monkey, monkeys
dry, dried	play, played

With proper names ending in -*y*, however, do not change the -*y* to -*ie* even if it is preceded by a consonant: *the Dougherty family, the Doughertys.*

FINAL CONSONANTS　If a final consonant is preceded by a single vowel *and* the consonant ends a one-syllable word or a stressed syllable, double the consonant when adding a suffix beginning with a vowel.

bet, betting	occur, occurrence
commit, committed	

Plurals

-*S* OR -*ES*　Add -*s* to form the plural of most nouns; add -*es* to singular nouns ending in -*s*, -*sh*, -*ch*, and -*x*.

table, tables	church, churches
paper, papers	dish, dishes

Ordinarily add -*s* to nouns ending in -*o* when the -*o* is preceded by a vowel. Add -*es* when it is preceded by a consonant.

radio, radios	hero, heroes
video, videos	tomato, tomatoes

OTHER PLURALS　To form the plural of a hyphenated compound word, add -*s* to the chief word even if it does not appear at the end.

mother-in-law, mothers-in-law

English words derived from other languages such as Latin, Greek, or French sometimes form the plural as they would in their original language.

medium, media   chateau, chateaux
criterion, criteria

> **ESL**   Spelling varies slightly among English-speaking countries. This can be particularly confusing for multilingual students in Canada, who may have learned British or American English. Following is a list of some common words spelled differently in Canadian, American, and British English. Consult a dictionary for others.
>
> | CANADIAN | AMERICAN | BRITISH |
> |---|---|---|
> | cancelled, travelled | canceled, traveled | cancelled, travelled |
> | colour, humour | color, humor | colour, humour |
> | judgment | judgment | judgement |
> | cheque | check | cheque |
> | realize, apologize | realize, apologize | realise, apologise |
> | defence | defense | defence |
> | anemia, anaesthetic | anemia, anesthetic | anaemia, anaesthetic |
> | theatre, centre | theater, center | theatre, centre |
> | fetus | fetus | foetus |
> | mould, smoulder | mold, smolder | mould, smoulder |
> | civilization | civilization | civilisation |
> | connection, inflection | connection, inflection | connexion, inflexion |
> | licorice | licorice | liquorice |

P7-b Discriminate between words that sound alike but have different meanings.

Words that sound alike or nearly alike but have different meanings and spellings are called *homophones*. The following sets of words are so commonly confused that a good writer will double-check their every use.

affect (verb: to exert an influence)
effect (verb: to accomplish; noun: result)

its (possessive pronoun: of or belonging to it)
it's (contraction for *it is* or *it has*)

loose (adjective: free, not securely attached)
lose (verb: to fail to keep, to be deprived of)

principal (adjective: most important; noun: head of a school)
principle (noun: a fundamental guideline or truth)

their (possessive pronoun: belonging to them)
they're (contraction for *they are*)
there (adverb: that place or position)

who's (contraction for *who is* or *who has*)
whose (possessive form of *who*)

your (possessive pronoun: belonging to you)
you're (contraction for *you are*)

To check for correct use of these and other commonly confused words, consult the glossary of usage (W1).

P7-c Consult the dictionary to determine whether to hyphenate a compound word.

The dictionary will tell you whether to treat a compound word as a hyphenated compound (*water-repellent*), one word (*waterproof*), or two words (*water table*). If the compound word is not in the dictionary, treat it as two words.

► The prosecutor chose not to cross‑examine any witnesses.

► All students are expected to record their data in a small

   note⁀book.

► Alice walked through the looking/glass into a backward world.

P7-d Hyphenate two or more words used together as an adjective before a noun.

► Mrs. Douglas gave Toshiko a seashell and some newspaper‑wrapped

   fish to take home to her mother.

► Richa Gupta is not yet a well‑known candidate.

   Newspaper-wrapped and *well-known* are adjectives used before the nouns *fish* and *candidate*.

   Generally, do not use a hyphen when such compounds follow the noun.

hyphen • compounds (*cross-examine, well-known*) •
numbers (*one-half, forty-two*) • prefixes, suffixes (*ex-boss, mayor-elect*)

P7-g   **295**

▶ After our television campaign, Richa Gupta will be well/known.

Do not use a hyphen to connect *-ly* adverbs to the words they modify.

▶ A slowly/moving truck tied up traffic.

NOTE: When two or more hyphenated adjectives in a row modify the same noun, you can suspend the hyphens.

Do you prefer first-, second-, or third-class tickets?

P7-e Hyphenate fractions and certain numbers when they are spelled out.

For numbers written in words, use a hyphen in all fractions and in compound numbers from twenty-one to ninety-nine.

▶ One-fourth of my income pays for child care, and one-third
   ^   ^
pays the rent.

P7-f Use a hyphen with the prefixes *all-*, *ex-* (meaning "former"), and *self-* and with the suffix *-elect*.

▶ The private foundation is funnelling more money into self-help
                                                            ^
projects.

▶ The Student Senate bylaws require the president-elect to attend
                                                    ^
all senate meetings between the election and the official transfer

of office.

P7-g Use a hyphen in certain words to avoid ambiguity or to separate awkward double or triple letters.

Without the hyphen, there would be no way to distinguish between words such as *re-creation* and *recreation*.

Bicycling in the city is my favourite form of recreation.

The film was praised for its astonishing re-creation of nineteenth-century London.

Hyphens are sometimes used to separate awkward double or triple letters in compound words (*anti-intellectual*, *cross-stitch*). Always check a dictionary for the standard form of the word.

P7-h Check for correct hyphenation at the ends of lines.

Some word processing programs and other computer applications automatically generate word breaks at the ends of lines. When you're writing an academic paper, it's best to set your computer application not to hyphenate automatically. This setting will ensure that only words already containing a hyphen (such as *long-distance*, *pre-Roman*) will be hyphenated at the ends of lines. (See also C6.)

E-mail addresses, URLs, and other electronic addresses need special attention when they occur at the end of a line of text or in bibliographic citations. You can't rely on your computer application to divide these terms correctly, so you must make a decision in each case. Do not insert a hyphen to divide electronic addresses. Instead, break an e-mail address after the @ symbol or before a period. Break a URL after a slash or a double slash or before any other punctuation mark.

> I repeatedly e-mailed Janine at janine.r.rose@dunbaracademy .org before I gave up and called her cell phone.

> To find a postal code quickly, I always use the Canada Post Web site at http://www.canadapost.ca/cpotools/apps/fpc/ personal/findByCity.

For breaks in URLs in MLA, APA, and CMS (*Chicago*) documentation styles, see MLA-5a, APA-5a, and CMS-5a, respectively.

P8 Capitalization

In addition to the rules in this section, a good dictionary can tell you when to use capital letters.

P8-a Capitalize proper nouns and words derived from them; do not capitalize common nouns.

Proper nouns are the names of specific persons, places, and things. All other nouns are common nouns. The following types of words are usually capitalized: names of deities, religions, religious followers, sacred books; words of family relationship used as names; particular places;

nationalities and their languages, races, tribes; educational institutions, departments, degrees, particular courses; government departments, organizations, political parties; historical movements, periods, events, documents; specific electronic sources; and trade names.

PROPER NOUNS	COMMON NOUNS
God (used as a name)	a god
Book of Common Prayer	a sacred book
Uncle Pedro	my uncle
Father (used as a name)	my father
Lake Ontario	a picturesque lake
the Capital Centre	a centre for advanced studies
the Maritimes	a province
Commonwealth Stadium	a football stadium
University of Windsor	a university
Geology 101	geology
Canada Border Services	a federal agency
Phi Kappa Psi	a fraternity
a Liberal	an independent
the Enlightenment	the eighteenth century
the Treaty of Versailles	a treaty
the World Wide Web, the Web	a home page
the Internet, the Net	a computer network
Advil	a painkiller

Months, holidays, and days of the week are treated as proper nouns; the seasons and numbers of the days of the month are not.

> Our academic year begins on a Tuesday in early September, right after Labour Day.

> Graduation is in early summer, on the second of June.

EXCEPTION: Capitalize Fourth of July (or July Fourth) when referring to the US holiday.

Names of school subjects are capitalized only if they are names of languages. Names of particular courses are capitalized.

> This semester Austin is taking math, geography, geology, French, and English.

> Professor Obembe offers Modern American Fiction 501 to graduate students.

CAUTION: Do not capitalize common nouns to make them seem important: *Our company is currently hiring computer programmers* (not *Company, Computer Programmers*).

P8-b Capitalize titles of persons when used as part of a proper name but usually not when used alone.

Professor Margaret Barnes; Dr. Sinyee Sein; John Scott Williams Jr.

Attorney General Marshall was reprimanded for badgering the witness.

The attorney general was appointed last year.

Usage varies when the title of an important public figure is used alone: *The queen* [or *Queen*] *visited Ottawa in April.*

P8-c Capitalize the first, last, and all major words in titles and subtitles of works.

In both titles and subtitles of works (books, articles, songs, artwork, and online documents), major words—nouns, pronouns, verbs, adjectives, and adverbs—should be capitalized. Minor words—articles, prepositions, and coordinating conjunctions—are not capitalized unless they are the first or last word of a title or subtitle.

Capitalize the second part of a hyphenated term in a title if it is a major word but not if it is a minor word. Capitalize chapter titles and the titles of other major divisions of a work following the same guidelines used for titles of complete works.

Seizing the Enigma: The Race to Break the German U-Boat Codes
A River Runs through It
"I Want to Hold Your Hand"
The Canadian Green Page

To learn why some of the titles in the list are italicized and some are put in quotation marks, see P10-a and P5-c.

P8-d Capitalize the first word of a sentence.

The first word of a sentence should be capitalized. When a sentence appears within parentheses, capitalize its first word unless the parentheses appear within another sentence.

Early detection of breast cancer significantly increases survival rates. (See table 2.)

Early detection of breast cancer significantly increases survival rates (see table 2).

titles with names (*Premier Hughes*) • titles and subtitles •
to begin a sentence • after a colon • abbreviations (*CRA, NHL*)

P8-f   299

Capitalize the first word of a quoted sentence but not a quoted phrase.

> Robert Hughes writes, "There are only about sixty Watteau paintings on whose authenticity all experts agree" (102).

> Russell Baker has written that in this country, sports are "the opiate of the masses" (46).

If a quoted sentence is interrupted by explanatory words, do not capitalize the first word after the interruption. (See P5-e.)

> "If you want to go out," he said, "tell me now."

When quoting poetry, copy the poet's capitalization exactly. Many poets capitalize the first word of every line of poetry; a few contemporary poets dismiss capitalization altogether.

> it was the week   that
> i felt the city's narrow breezes rush about
> me   —Don L. Lee

P8-e Capitalize the first word after a colon if it begins an independent clause.

If a word group following a colon could stand on its own as a complete sentence, capitalize the first word.

> Clinical trials called into question the safety profile of the drug: A high percentage of participants reported hypertension and kidney problems.

> Preferences vary among academic disciplines. See MLA-5a, APA-5a, and CMS-5a for MLA, APA, and CMS (*Chicago*) style, respectively.

Always use lowercase for a list or an appositive that follows a colon.

> Students were divided into two groups: residents and commuters.

P8-f Capitalize abbreviations according to convention.

Abbreviations for government agencies, companies, and other organizations as well as call numbers for radio and television stations are capitalized.

> CRA, CSIS, DKNY, IBM, WCRB, KNBC-TV

≣ **P9** Abbreviations and numbers

P9-a Use standard abbreviations for titles immediately before and after proper names.

TITLES BEFORE PROPER NAMES	TITLES AFTER PROPER NAMES
Mr. Rafael Zabala	William Albert Sr.
Ms. Nancy Linehan	Thomas Hines Jr.
Mrs. Edward Horn	Anita Lor, PhD
Dr. Margaret Simmons	Robert Simkowski, MD
Rev. John Stone	Margaret Chin, LLD
Prof. James Russo	Polly Stein, DDS

Abbreviate a title only if it is used with a proper name.

> *professor*
> ► My history ~~prof.~~ is an expert on twentieth-century race relations in
>   ^
> South Africa.

Avoid redundant titles such as *Dr. Amy Day, MD*. Choose one title or the other: *Dr. Amy Day* or *Amy Day, MD*.

P9-b Use abbreviations only when you are sure your readers will understand them.

Familiar abbreviations, written without periods, are acceptable.

CIA	FBI	MD	CUPE
NBA	NHL	PhD	CD-ROM
RSVP	CBC	USA	ESL

Game show host Alex Trebek graduated from the University of Ottawa with a BA in philosophy.

My new computer has eight USB ports.

NOTE: When using an unfamiliar abbreviation (such as CASW for Canadian Association of Social Workers) throughout a paper, write the full name followed by the abbreviation in parentheses at the first mention of the name. Then use just the abbreviation throughout the rest of the paper.

P9-c Use *BC*, *AD*, *a.m.*, *p.m.*, *No.*, and *$* only with specific dates, times, numbers, and amounts.

The abbreviation *BC* ("before Christ") follows a date, and *AD* ("*anno Domini*") precedes a date. Acceptable alternatives are *BCE* ("before the common era") and *CE* ("common era"), both of which follow a date.

40 BC (or 40 BCE)	4:00 a.m. (or AM)	No. 12 (or no. 12)
AD 44 (or 44 CE)	6:00 p.m. (or PM)	$150

Avoid using *a.m.*, *p.m.*, *No.*, or *$* when not accompanied by a specific figure.

▶ The premier argued that the new sales tax would raise
much-needed $ ~~money~~ for the province.
      money
      ^

P9-d Be sparing in your use of Latin abbreviations.

Latin abbreviations are acceptable in footnotes and bibliographies and in informal writing for comments in parentheses.

cf. (Latin *confer*, "compare")

e.g. (Latin *exempli gratia*, "for example")

et al. (Latin *et alia*, "and others")

etc. (Latin *et cetera*, "and so forth")

i.e. (Latin *id est*, "that is")

N.B. (Latin *nota bene*, "note well")

The text for our sociology class is Harold Simms et al., *Introduction to Social Systems*.

Alfred Hitchcock directed many classic thrillers (e.g., *Psycho*, *Rear Window*, and *Vertigo*).

In formal writing, use the appropriate English phrases.

▶ Many obsolete laws remain on the books; ~~e.g.,~~ a law in Fort
                                for example,
                                    ^

Qu'Appelle, Saskatchewan, makes it illegal for teenagers to walk

down Main Street with their shoes untied.

P9-e Avoid inappropriate abbreviations.

In formal writing, abbreviations for the following are not commonly accepted.

PERSONAL NAMES   Charles (not Chas.)

UNITS OF MEASUREMENT   kilograms (not kg)

DAYS OF THE WEEK   Monday (not Mon.)

HOLIDAYS   Christmas (not Xmas)

MONTHS   January, February, March (not Jan., Feb., Mar.)

COURSES OF STUDY   political science (not poli. sci.)

DIVISIONS OF WRITTEN WORKS   chapter, page (not ch., p.)

STATES, PROVINCES, TERRITORIES, COUNTRIES   Alberta (not AB or Alta.)

PARTS OF A BUSINESS NAME   Adams Lighting Company (not Adams Lighting Co.); Kim and Brothers (not Kim and Bros.)

▶ Canadian Blood Services requires that blood donors be at least
       years   *kilograms,*
seventeen ~~yrs.~~ old, weigh at least fifty ~~kg,~~ and not have given blood
      ^   *weeks.*   ^
in the past eight ~~wks.~~
                  ^

EXCEPTION: Abbreviate states, provinces, and territories in complete addresses, and always abbreviate DC when used with Washington.

P9-f Follow the conventions in your discipline for spelling out or using numerals to express numbers.

In the humanities, which generally follow either Modern Language Association (MLA) style or CMS (*Chicago*) style, use numerals only for specific numbers above one hundred: *353*; *1 020*. Spell out numbers one hundred and below and large round numbers: *eleven, thirty-five, sixty, fifteen million.*

The social sciences and sciences, which follow the style guidelines of the American Psychological Association (APA) or the Council of Science Editors (CSE), use numerals for all but the numbers one through nine.

In all fields, treat related numbers in a passage consistently: *The survey found that 89 of 157 respondents had not taken any courses related to alcohol use.*

When one number immediately follows another, spelling out one number and using numerals for the other is usually effective: *three 100-metre events, 25 four-poster beds.*

▶ It's been ~~8~~ *eight* years since I visited Peru.

▶ Enrollment in the charter school in its first year will be limited to ~~three hundred forty~~ *340* students.

If a sentence begins with a number, spell out the number or rewrite the sentence.

▶ ~~150~~ *One hundred fifty* children in our program need expensive dental treatment.

Rewriting the sentence will also correct the error and may be less awkward if the number is long: *In our program, 150 children need expensive dental treatment.*

P9-g Use numerals according to convention in dates, addresses, and so on.

DATES   July 4, 1776; 56 BC

ADDRESSES   77 Latches Lane, 519 West 42nd Street

PERCENTAGES   55 percent (or 55%)

FRACTIONS, DECIMALS   ½, 0.047

SCORES   7 to 3, 21–18

STATISTICS   average age 37, average weight 180

SURVEYS   4 out of 5

EXACT AMOUNTS OF MONEY $105.37, $106,000

DIVISIONS OF BOOKS   volume 3, chapter 4, page 189

DIVISIONS OF PLAYS   act 3, scene 3 (or act III, scene iii)

IDENTIFICATION NUMBERS   serial number 10988675

TIME OF DAY   4:00 p.m., 1:30 a.m.

▶ The foundation raised ~~four hundred thirty thousand dollars~~ *$430,000* for cancer research.

NOTE: When not using *a.m.* or *p.m.*, write out the time in words (*two o'clock in the afternoon, twelve noon, seven in the morning*).

▤ **P10** Italics

This section describes conventional uses for italics. While italics is recommended by all three style guides covered in this book (MLA, APA, and CMS), some instructors may prefer underlining in student papers. If that is the case in your course, simply substitute underlining for italics in the examples in this section.

Some computer and online applications do not allow for italics. To indicate words that should be italicized, you can use underscore marks or asterisks before and after the italic words.

I am planning to write my senior thesis on _Memoirs of a Geisha_.

NOTE: Excessive use of italics to emphasize words or ideas, especially in academic writing, is distracting and should be avoided.

P10-a Italicize the titles of works according to convention.

Titles of the following types of works, including electronic works, should be italicized.

TITLES OF BOOKS	*The Known World, Middlesex, Encarta*
MAGAZINES	*Maclean's, Canadian Geographic, Salon.com*
NEWSPAPERS	the *Toronto Sun*, the *Calgary Herald*
PAMPHLETS	*Common Sense, Facts about Marijuana*
LONG POEMS	*The Waste Land, Beowulf*
PLAYS	*'Night Mother, Wicked*
FILMS	*Casablanca, The Hurt Locker*
TELEVISION PROGRAMS	*Canadian Idol, Frontline*
RADIO PROGRAMS	*All Things Considered*
MUSICAL COMPOSITIONS	*Porgy and Bess*
CHOREOGRAPHIC WORKS	*Brief Fling*
WORKS OF VISUAL ART	*American Gothic*
ELECTRONIC DATABASES	*ProQuest*
WEB SITES	*ZDNet, Google*
ELECTRONIC GAMES	*Everquest, Call of Duty*

The titles of other works, such as short stories, essays, episodes of radio and television programs, songs, and short poems, are enclosed in quotation marks. (See P5-c.)

NOTE: Do not use italics when referring to the Bible, titles of books in the Bible (Genesis, not *Genesis*), or titles of legal documents (the Constitution, not the *Constitution*). Do not italicize the titles of computer software (Keynote, Photoshop). Do not italicize the title of your own paper.

P10-b Italicize other terms according to convention.

SPACECRAFT, SHIPS, AIRCRAFT
Challenger, Queen Mary 2, Spirit of St. Louis

The success of the Soviets' *Sputnik* energized the US space program.

FOREIGN WORDS
Shakespeare's Falstaff is a comic character known for both his excessive drinking and his general *joie de vivre.*

EXCEPTION: Do not italicize foreign words that have become a standard part of the English language—"laissez-faire," "fait accompli," "modus operandi," and "per diem," for example.

WORDS, LETTERS, NUMBERS AS THEMSELVES
Tomás assured us that the chemicals could probably be safely mixed, but his *probably* stuck in our minds.

Some toddlers have trouble pronouncing the letter *s.*

A big *3* was painted on the stage door.

NOTE: Quotation marks may be used instead of italics to set off words mentioned as words. (See P5-d.)

Basic Grammar

B Basic Grammar

nouns • persons, places, things, ideas •
pronouns (*we, their, who, anyone,* etc.)

B1-b

309

B1 Parts of speech

Traditional grammar recognizes eight parts of speech: noun, pronoun, verb, adjective, adverb, preposition, conjunction, and interjection. Many words can function as more than one part of speech. For example, depending on its use in a sentence, the word *paint* can be a noun (*The paint is wet*) or a verb (*Please paint the ceiling next*).

B1-a Nouns

A noun is the name of a person, place, thing, or concept.

> N   N   N
> The *lion* in the *cage* growled at the *zookeeper*.

Nouns sometimes function as adjectives modifying other nouns. Because of their dual roles, nouns used in this manner may be called *noun/adjectives*.

> N/ADJ   N/ADJ
> The *leather* notebook was tucked in the *student's* backpack.

Nouns are classified in a variety of ways. *Proper* nouns are capitalized, but *common* nouns are not (see P8-a). For clarity, writers choose between *concrete* and *abstract* nouns (see W5-b). The distinction between *count* nouns and *noncount* nouns can be especially helpful to multilingual writers (see M2-a). Most nouns have singular and plural forms; *collective* nouns may be either singular or plural, depending on how they are used (see G1-f and G3-a). *Possessive* nouns require an apostrophe (see P4-a).

B1-b Pronouns

A pronoun is a word used in place of a noun. Usually the pronoun substitutes for a specific noun, known as its *antecedent*.

> When the *battery* wears down, we recharge *it*.

Although most pronouns function as substitutes for nouns, some can function as adjectives modifying nouns. Because they have the

PRACTICE hackerhandbooks.com/writersref
> Basic grammar > B1–5 to B1–8

form of a pronoun and the function of an adjective, such pronouns may be called *pronoun/adjectives*.

PN/ADJ
This bird was at the same window yesterday morning.

Pronouns are classified as personal, possessive, intensive and reflexive, relative, interrogative, demonstrative, indefinite, and reciprocal.

PERSONAL PRONOUNS   Personal pronouns refer to specific persons or things. They always function as noun equivalents.

Singular: I, me, you, she, her, he, him, it

Plural: we, us, you, they, them

POSSESSIVE PRONOUNS   Possessive pronouns indicate ownership.

Singular: my, mine, your, yours, her, hers, his, its

Plural: our, ours, your, yours, their, theirs

Some of these possessive pronouns function as adjectives modifying nouns: *my, your, her, his, its, our, their*.

INTENSIVE AND REFLEXIVE PRONOUNS   Intensive pronouns emphasize a noun or another pronoun (The senator *herself* met us at the door). Reflexive pronouns, which have the same form as intensive pronouns, name a receiver of an action identical with the doer of the action (Paula cut *herself*).

Singular: myself, yourself, himself, herself, itself

Plural: ourselves, yourselves, themselves

RELATIVE PRONOUNS   Relative pronouns introduce subordinate clauses functioning as adjectives (The writer *who won the award* refused to accept it). In addition to introducing the clause, the relative pronoun (in this case *who*) points back to a noun or pronoun that the clause modifies (*writer*). (See B3-e.)

who, whom, whose, which, that

INTERROGATIVE PRONOUNS   Interrogative pronouns introduce questions (*Who* is expected to win the election?).

who, whom, whose, which, what

DEMONSTRATIVE PRONOUNS Demonstrative pronouns identify or point to nouns. Frequently they function as adjectives (*This* chair is my favourite), but they may also function as noun equivalents (*This* is my favourite chair).

> this, that, these, those

INDEFINITE PRONOUNS Indefinite pronouns refer to nonspecific persons or things. Most are always singular (*everyone, each*); some are always plural (*both, many*); a few may be singular or plural (see G1-e). Most indefinite pronouns function as noun equivalents (*Something* is burning), but some can also function as adjectives (*All* campers must check in at the lodge).

all	anything	everyone	nobody	several
another	both	everything	none	some
any	each	few	no one	somebody
anybody	either	many	nothing	someone
anyone	everybody	neither	one	something

RECIPROCAL PRONOUNS Reciprocal pronouns refer to individual parts of a plural antecedent (By turns, the penguins fed *one another*).

> each other, one another

NOTE: Using pronouns correctly can be challenging. See pronoun-antecedent agreement (G3-a), pronoun reference (G3-b), distinguishing between pronouns such as *I* and *me* (G3-c), and distinguishing between *who* and *whom* (G3-d).

B1-c Verbs

The verb of a sentence usually expresses action (*jump, think*) or being (*is, become*). It is composed of a main verb possibly preceded by one or more helping verbs.

>   MV
> The horses *exercise* every day.

>   HV   MV
> The task force report *was* not *completed* on schedule.

Notice that words, usually adverbs, can intervene between the helping verb and the main verb (was *not* completed). (See B1-e.)

PRACTICE hackerhandbooks.com/writersref
  > Basic grammar > B1–9 and B1–10

Helping verbs

There are twenty-three helping verbs in English: forms of *have*, *do*, and *be*, which may also function as main verbs; and nine modals, which function only as helping verbs. *Have*, *do*, and *be* change form to indicate tense; the nine modals do not.

FORMS OF *HAVE*, *DO*, AND *BE*

have, has, had

do, does, did

be, am, is, are, was, were, being, been

MODALS

can, could, may, might, must, shall, should, will, would

The verb phrase *ought to* is often classified as a modal as well.

Main verbs

The main verb of a sentence is always the kind of word that would change form if put into these test sentences:

BASE FORM	Usually I (*walk*, *ride*).
PAST TENSE	Yesterday I (*walked*, *rode*).
PAST PARTICIPLE	I have (*walked*, *ridden*) many times before.
PRESENT PARTICIPLE	I am (*walking*, *riding*) right now.
***-S* FORM**	Usually he/she/it (*walks*, *rides*).

If a word doesn't change form when slipped into the test sentences, you can be certain that it is not a main verb. For example, the noun *revolution*, though it may seem to suggest an action, can never function as a main verb. Just try to make it behave like one (*Today I revolution . . . Yesterday I revolutioned . . .*) and you'll see why.

When both the past-tense and the past-participle forms of a verb end in *-ed*, the verb is regular (*walked*, *walked*). Otherwise, the verb is irregular (*rode*, *ridden*). (See G2-a.)

The verb *be* is highly irregular, having eight forms instead of the usual five: the base form *be*; the present-tense forms *am*, *is*, and *are*; the past-tense forms *was* and *were*; the present participle *being*; and the past participle *been*.

Helping verbs combine with the various forms of main verbs to create tenses. For a survey of tenses, see G2-f.

NOTE: Some verbs are followed by words that look like prepositions but are so closely associated with the verb that they are a part of its meaning. These words are known as *particles.* Common verb-particle combinations include *bring up, call off, drop off, give in, look up, run into,* and *take off.*

Sharon *packed up* her broken laptop and *sent* it *off* to the repair shop.

TIP: You can find more information about using verbs in other sections of the handbook: active verbs (W3), subject-verb agreement (G1), standard English verb forms (G2-a to G2-d), verb tense and mood (G2-f and G2-g), and multilingual/ESL challenges with verbs (M1).

B1-d Adjectives

An adjective is a word used to modify, or describe, a noun or pronoun. An adjective usually answers one of these questions: Which one? What kind of? How many?

ADJ
the *frisky* horse [Which horse?]

ADJ   ADJ
cracked old plates [What kind of plates?]

ADJ
nine months [How many months?]

Adjectives usually precede the words they modify. They may also follow linking verbs, in which case they describe the subject. (See B2-b.)

ADJ
The decision was *unpopular.*

The definite article *the* and the indefinite articles *a* and *an* are also classified as adjectives.

ART   ART   ART
A defendant should be judged on *the* evidence provided to *the* jury, not on hearsay.

Some possessive, demonstrative, and indefinite pronouns can function as adjectives: *their, its, this, all,* and so on (see B1-b). And nouns can function as adjectives when they modify other nouns: *apple pie* (the noun *apple* modifies the noun *pie;* see B1-a).

TIP: You can find more details about using adjectives in G4. If you are a multilingual writer, you may also find help with articles and specific uses of adjectives in M2 and M4.

PRACTICE hackerhandbooks.com/writersref
> Basic grammar > B1–11 to B1–14
              > B1–15 and B1–16 (all parts of speech)

B1-e Adverbs

An adverb is a word used to modify, or qualify, a verb (or verbal), an adjective, or another adverb. It usually answers one of these questions: When? Where? How? Why? Under what conditions? To what degree?

Pull *firmly* on the emergency handle. [Pull how?]

Read the text *first* and *then* work the exercises. [Read when? Work when?]

Adverbs modifying adjectives or other adverbs usually intensify or limit the intensity of the word they modify.

ADV   ADV
Be *extremely* kind, and you will *probably* have many friends.

The words *not* and *never* are classified as adverbs.

B1-f Prepositions

A preposition is a word placed before a noun or pronoun to form a phrase modifying another word in the sentence. The prepositional phrase nearly always functions as an adjective or as an adverb.

P   P   P
The road *to* the summit travels *past* craters *from* an extinct volcano.

To the summit functions as an adjective modifying the noun *road*; *past craters* functions as an adverb modifying the verb *travels*; *from an extinct volcano* functions as an adjective modifying the noun *craters*. (For more on prepositional phrases, see B3-a.)

English has a limited number of prepositions. The most common are included in the following list.

about	beside	from	outside	toward
above	besides	in	over	under
across	between	inside	past	underneath
after	beyond	into	plus	unlike
against	but	like	regarding	until
along	by	near	respecting	unto
among	concerning	next	round	up
around	considering	of	since	upon
as	despite	off	than	with
at	down	on	through	within
before	during	onto	throughout	without
behind	except	opposite	till	
below	for	out	to	

adverbs • prepositions (*in, at, from*, etc.) •
conjunctions (*and, but, after, because*, etc.) • *however* etc.

B1-g 315

Some prepositions are more than one word long. *Along with, as well as, in addition to, next to,* and *rather than* are common examples.

TIP: Prepositions are used in idioms such as *capable of* and *dig up* (see W5-d). For a discussion of specific issues for multilingual writers, see M5.

B1-g Conjunctions

Conjunctions join words, phrases, or clauses, and they indicate the relation between the elements they join.

COORDINATING CONJUNCTIONS A coordinating conjunction is used to connect grammatically equal elements. (See S1-b and S6.) The coordinating conjunctions are *and, but, or, nor, for, so,* and *yet.*

CORRELATIVE CONJUNCTIONS Correlative conjunctions come in pairs. Like coordinating conjunctions, they connect grammatically equal elements. (See S1-b.)

either . . . or	whether . . . or
neither . . . nor	both . . . and
not only . . . but also	

SUBORDINATING CONJUNCTIONS A subordinating conjunction introduces a subordinate clause and indicates the relation of the clause to the rest of the sentence. (See B3-e.) The most common subordinating conjunctions are *after, although, as, as if, because, before, if, in order that, once, since, so that, than, that, though, unless, until, when, where, whether,* and *while.* (For a complete list, see p. 325.)

CONJUNCTIVE ADVERBS Conjunctive adverbs connect independent clauses and indicate the relation between the clauses. The most common conjunctive adverbs are *finally, furthermore, however, moreover, nevertheless, similarly, then, therefore,* and *thus.* (See P3-a for a complete list.)

TIP: The ability to distinguish between conjunctive adverbs and coordinating conjunctions will help you avoid run-on sentences and make punctuation decisions (see G6, P1-a, and P1-b). The ability to recognize subordinating conjunctions will help you avoid sentence fragments (see G5).

B1-h Interjections

An interjection is a word used to express surprise or emotion (*Oh! Hey! Wow!*).

B2 Parts of sentences

Most English sentences flow from subject to verb to any objects or complements. The part of the sentence containing the verb plus its objects, complements, and modifiers is called the *predicate*.

B2-a Subjects

The subject of a sentence names who or what the sentence is about. The simple subject is always a noun or a pronoun; the complete subject consists of the simple subject and any words or word groups modifying the simple subject.

The complete subject

To find the complete subject, ask Who? or What?, insert the verb, and finish the question. The answer is the complete subject.

> ┌─────── COMPLETE SUBJECT ───────┐
> The devastating effects of famine can last for many years.

Who or what lasts for many years? *The devastating effects of famine.*

> ┌─────────────── COMPLETE SUBJECT ───────────────┐
> Adventure novels that contain multiple subplots are often made into successful movies.

Who or what are made into movies? *Adventure novels that contain multiple subplots.*

> ┌─ COMPLETE SUBJECT ─┐
> In our program, student teachers work full-time for ten months.

What or who works full-time for ten months? *Student teachers.* Notice that *In our program, student teachers* is not a sensible answer to the question. (It is not safe to assume that the subject must always appear first in a sentence.)

PRACTICE   hackerhandbooks.com/writersref
> Basic grammar > B2–4 and B2–5

The simple subject

To find the simple subject, strip away all modifiers in the complete subject. This includes single-word modifiers such as *the* and *devastating*, phrases such as *of famine*, and subordinate clauses such as *that contain multiple subplots*.

┌ SS ┐
The devastating effects of famine can last for many years.

A sentence may have a compound subject containing two or more simple subjects joined with a coordinating conjunction such as *and*, *but*, or *or*.

┌── SS ──┐   ┌SS┐
Great commitment and a little luck make a successful actor.

Understood subjects

In imperative sentences, which give advice or issue commands, the subject is understood to be *you*.

[*You*] Put your clothes in the hamper.

Subject after the verb

Although the subject ordinarily comes before the verb (*The planes took off*), occasionally it does not. When a sentence begins with *There is* or *There are* (or *There was* or *There were*), the subject follows the verb. In such inverted constructions, the word *There* is an expletive, an empty word serving merely to get the sentence started.

┌ SS ┐
There are *eight planes waiting to take off.*

Occasionally a writer will invert a sentence for effect.

┌ SS ┐
Joyful is *the child whose school closes for snow.*

In questions, the subject frequently appears between the helping verb and the main verb.

HV   ┌── SS ──┐ MV
Do *Kenyan marathoners* train year-round?

TIP: The ability to recognize the subject of a sentence will help you edit for a variety of problems: sentence fragments (G5), subject-verb agreement (G1), choice of pronouns such as *I* and *me* (G3-c), missing subjects (M3-b), and repeated subjects (M3-c).

B2-b Verbs, objects, and complements

Section B1-c explains how to find the verb of a sentence. A sentence's verb is classified as linking, transitive, or intransitive, depending on the kinds of objects or complements the verb can (or cannot) take.

Linking verbs and subject complements

Linking verbs connect the subject to a subject complement, a word or word group that completes the meaning of the subject by renaming or describing it.

If the subject complement renames the subject, it is a noun or noun equivalent (sometimes called a *predicate noun*).

┌──────────────────── S ────────────────────┐ ┌─ V ─┐┌─ SC ─┐
An e-mail requesting personal information may be a scam.

If the subject complement describes the subject, it is an adjective or adjective equivalent (sometimes called a *predicate adjective*).

┌────────── S ──────────┐┌─V─┐ SC
Last month's temperatures were mild.

Whenever they appear as main verbs (rather than helping verbs), the forms of *be*—*be, am, is, are, was, were, being, been*—usually function as linking verbs. In the preceding examples, for instance, the main verbs are *be* and *were*.

Verbs such as *appear, become, feel, grow, look, make, seem, smell, sound,* and *taste* are linking when they are followed by a word group that renames or describes the subject.

┌── S ──┐┌─ V ──┐   SC
As it thickens, the sauce will look unappealing.

Transitive verbs and direct objects

A transitive verb takes a direct object, a word or word group that names a receiver of the action.

┌──── S ────┐ V ┌──── DO ────┐
The hungry cat clawed the bag of dry food.

The simple direct object is always a noun or pronoun, in this case *bag*. To find it, simply strip away all modifiers.

Transitive verbs usually appear in the active voice, with the subject doing the action and a direct object receiving the action. Active-voice sentences can be transformed into the passive voice, with the subject receiving the action instead. (See also W3-a.)

ACTIVE VOICE   Volunteers distributed food and clothing.

PASSIVE VOICE   Food and clothing were distributed by volunteers.

Transitive verbs, indirect objects, and direct objects

The direct object of a transitive verb is sometimes preceded by an indirect object, a noun or pronoun telling to whom or for whom the action of the sentence is done.

    S   V   IO ┌── DO ──┐   S ┌─ V ─┐ IO ┌ DO ┐
You give her some yarn, and she will knit you a scarf.

Transitive verbs, direct objects, and object complements

The direct object of a transitive verb is sometimes followed by an object complement, a word or word group that renames or describes the object.

    S   V   DO ┌──── OC ────┐
People often consider chivalry a thing of the past.

┌─ S ─┐   V   DO ┌──── OC ────┐
The kiln makes clay firm and strong.

When the object complement renames the direct object, it is a noun or pronoun (such as *thing*). When it describes the direct object, it is an adjective (such as *firm* and *strong*).

Intransitive verbs

Intransitive verbs take no objects or complements.

┌──── S ────┐   V
The audience laughed.

┌──── S ────┐   V
The driver accelerated in the straightaway.

Nothing receives the actions of laughing and accelerating in these sentences, so the verbs are intransitive. Notice that such verbs may or may not be followed by adverbial modifiers. In the second sentence, *in the straightaway* is an adverbial prepositional phrase modifying *accelerated*.

NOTE: The dictionary will tell you whether a verb is transitive or intransitive. Some verbs have both transitive and intransitive functions.

TRANSITIVE   Sandra *flew* her small plane over the canyon.

INTRANSITIVE   A flock of geese *flew* overhead.

In the first example, *flew* has a direct object that receives the action: *her small plane*. In the second example, the verb is followed by an adverb (*overhead*), not by a direct object.

B3 Subordinate word groups

Subordinate word groups include phrases and clauses. Phrases are subordinate because they lack a subject and a verb; they are classified as prepositional, verbal, appositive, and absolute (see B3-a to B3-d). Subordinate clauses have a subject and a verb, but they begin with a word (such as *although*, *that*, or *when*) that marks them as subordinate (see B3-e; see also B4-a).

B3-a Prepositional phrases

A prepositional phrase begins with a preposition such as *at, by, for, from, in, of, on, to,* or *with* (see B1-f) and usually ends with a noun or noun equivalent: *on the table, for him, by sleeping late.* The noun or noun equivalent is known as the *object of the preposition*.

Prepositional phrases function either as adjectives or as adverbs. When functioning as an adjective, a prepositional phrase nearly always appears immediately following the noun or pronoun it modifies.

The hut had *walls of mud*.

Adjective phrases usually answer one or both of the questions Which one? and What kind of? If we ask Which walls? or What kind of walls? we get a sensible answer: *walls of mud*.

Adverbial prepositional phrases usually modify the verb, but they can also modify adjectives or other adverbs. When a prepositional phrase modifies the verb, it can appear nearly anywhere in a sentence.

James *walked* his dog *on a leash*.

Sabrina *will in time adjust* to life in Ecuador.

During a mudslide, the terrain *can change* drastically.

Adverbial word groups usually answer one of these questions: When? Where? How? Why? Under what conditions? To what degree?

James walked his dog *how*? *On a leash*.

Sabrina will adjust to life in Ecuador *when*? *In time*.

The terrain can change drastically *under what conditions*? *During a mudslide*.

B3-b Verbal phrases

A verbal is a verb form that does not function as the verb of a clause. Verbals include infinitives (the word *to* plus the base form of the verb), present participles (the *-ing* form of the verb), and past participles (the verb form usually ending in *-d*, *-ed*, *-n*, *-en*, or *-t*). (See G2-a.) Instead of functioning as the verb of a clause, a verbal functions as an adjective, a noun, or an adverb.

ADJECTIVE	*Broken* promises cannot be fixed.
NOUN	Constant *complaining* becomes wearisome.
ADVERB	Can you wait *to celebrate*?

Verbals with objects, complements, or modifiers form verbal phrases. Like verbals, verbal phrases function as adjectives, nouns, or adverbs. Verbal phrases are ordinarily classified as participial, gerund, and infinitive.

Participial phrases

Participial phrases always function as adjectives. Their verbals are either present participles (such as *dreaming*, *asking*) or past participles (such as *stolen*, *reached*).

Participial phrases frequently appear immediately following the noun or pronoun they modify.

Congress shall make no *law abriding the freedom of speech or of the press*.

Unlike other word groups that function as adjectives (prepositional phrases, infinitive phrases, adjective clauses), which must always follow the noun or pronoun they modify, participial phrases are often movable. They can precede the word they modify.

Being a weight-bearing joint, the *knee* is among the most often

injured.

They may also appear at some distance from the word they modify.

Last night we saw a *play* that affected us deeply, *written with*

profound insight into the lives of immigrants.

Gerund phrases

Gerund phrases are built around present participles (verb forms that end in *-ing*), and they always function as nouns: usually as subjects, subject complements, direct objects, or objects of a preposition.

                    DO

Lizards usually enjoy sunning themselves.

Infinitive phrases

Infinitive phrases, usually constructed around *to* plus the base form of the verb (*to call, to drink*), can function as nouns, as adjectives, or as adverbs. When functioning as a noun, an infinitive phrase may appear in almost any noun slot in a sentence, usually as a subject, subject complement, or direct object.

                  S

To give her speech without fainting was her goal.

Infinitive phrases functioning as adjectives usually appear immediately following the noun or pronoun they modify.

You have the *right to be heard.*

Adverbial infinitive phrases usually qualify the meaning of the verb, telling when, where, how, why, under what conditions, or to what degree an action occurred.

phrases • gerund (*eating well*) • *-ing* verb form • infinitive
(*to watch birds*) • appositive • absolute • clauses with *who, that,* etc.

B3-e   323

Volunteers *rolled up* their pants *to wade through the flood waters.*

NOTE: In some constructions, the infinitive is unmarked; in other words, the *to* does not appear. (See also M1-f.)

Graphs and charts can help researchers [*to*] *present complex data.*

B3-c Appositive phrases

Appositive phrases describe nouns or pronouns. Instead of modifying nouns or pronouns, however, appositive phrases rename them. In form they are nouns or noun equivalents.

Bloggers, *conversationalists at heart*, are the online equivalent of radio talk show hosts.

B3-d Absolute phrases

An absolute phrase modifies a whole clause or sentence, not just one word. It consists of a noun or noun equivalent usually followed by a participial phrase.

Her words reverberating in the hushed arena, the party leader urged the crowd to support her former opponent.

B3-e Subordinate clauses

Subordinate clauses are patterned like sentences, having subjects and verbs and sometimes objects or complements. But they function within sentences as adjectives, adverbs, or nouns. They cannot stand alone as complete sentences.

Adjective clauses

Adjective clauses modify nouns or pronouns, usually answering the question Which one? or What kind of ? They begin with a relative pronoun (*who, whom, whose, which,* or *that*) or occasionally with a relative adverb (usually *when, where,* or *why*). (See p. 325.)

The coach chose *players who would benefit from intense drills.*

In addition to introducing the clause, the relative pronoun points back to the noun that the clause modifies.

A *book that goes unread* is a writer's worst nightmare.

Relative pronouns are sometimes "understood."

The things [*that*] *we cherish most* are the things [*that*] *we might lose.*

The parts of an adjective clause are often arranged as in sentences (subject/verb/object or complement).

          S V DO
Sometimes it is our closest friends who disappoint us.

Frequently, however, the object or complement appears first.

         DO S V
They can be the very friends whom we disappoint.

TIP: For punctuation of adjective clauses, see P1-e and P2-e. For advice about avoiding repeated words in adjective clauses, see M3-d.

Adverb clauses

Adverb clauses modify verbs, adjectives, or other adverbs, usually answering one of these questions: When? Where? Why? How? Under what conditions? To what degree? They always begin with a subordinating conjunction (such as *after, although, because, that, though, unless,* or *when*). (For a complete list, see p. 325.)

When the sun went down, the hikers *prepared* their camp.

Kate *would have made* the team *if she hadn't broken her ankle.*

Noun clauses

A noun clause functions just like a single-word noun, usually as a subject, a subject complement, a direct object, or an object of a preposition. It usually begins with one of the following words: *how, if, that, what, whatever, when, where, whether, which, who, whoever, whom, whomever, whose, why.* (For a complete list, see p. 325.)

clauses with *who*, *that*, etc. • clauses with *if*, *when*, etc. •
clauses with *that*, *which*, etc. • sentence types

B4

325

Words that introduce subordinate clauses

Words introducing adverb clauses

Subordinating conjunctions: after, although, as, as if, because, before, even though, if, in order that, since, so that, than, that, though, unless, until, when, where, whether, while

Words introducing adjective clauses

Relative pronouns: that, which, who, whom, whose
Relative adverbs: when, where, why

Words introducing noun clauses

Relative pronouns: that, which, who, whom, whose
Other pronouns: what, whatever, whichever, whoever, whomever
Other subordinating words: how, if, when, whenever, where, wherever, whether, why

———— S ————
Whoever leaves the house last must double-lock the door.

———————— DO ————————
Copernicus argued that the sun is the centre of the universe.

The subordinating word introducing the clause may not play a significant role in the clause. In the preceding example sentences, *Whoever* is the subject of its clause, but *that* does not perform a function in its clause.

As with adjective clauses, the parts of a noun clause may appear in normal order (subject/verb/object or complement) or out of normal order.

    S   V   ┌── DO ──┐
Loyalty is what keeps a friendship strong.

    DO   S   V
Quebec is where we live.

B4 Sentence types

Sentences are classified in two ways: according to their structure (simple, compound, complex, and compound-complex) and according to their purpose (declarative, imperative, interrogative, and exclamatory).

B4-a Sentence structures

Depending on the number and types of clauses they contain, sentences are classified as simple, compound, complex, or compound-complex.

Clauses come in two varieties: independent and subordinate. An independent clause contains a subject and a predicate, and it either stands alone or could stand alone as a sentence. A subordinate clause also contains a subject and a predicate, but it functions within a sentence as an adjective, an adverb, or a noun; it cannot stand alone. (See B3-e.)

Simple sentences

A simple sentence is one independent clause with no subordinate clauses.

┌──────────────── INDEPENDENT CLAUSE ────────────────┐
Without a passport, Eva could not visit her parents in Lima.

A simple sentence may contain compound elements—a compound subject, verb, or object, for example—but it does not contain more than one full sentence pattern. The following sentence is simple because its two verbs (*comes in* and *goes out*) share a subject (*Spring*).

┌──────────── INDEPENDENT CLAUSE ────────────┐
Spring comes in like a lion and goes out like a lamb.

Compound sentences

A compound sentence is composed of two or more independent clauses with no subordinate clauses. The independent clauses are usually joined with a comma and a coordinating conjunction (*and*, *but*, *or*, *nor*, *for*, *so*, *yet*) or with a semicolon. (See P1-a and P3-a.)

INDEPENDENT   INDEPENDENT
┌──── CLAUSE ────┐   ┌──────── CLAUSE ────────┐
The car broke down, but a rescue van arrived within minutes.

┌──── INDEPENDENT CLAUSE ────┐ ┌─ INDEPENDENT CLAUSE ─┐
A shark was spotted near shore; people left immediately.

sentence structures • simple • compound • complex • compound-
complex • independent + subordinate clauses • sentence purpose

B4-b   327

Complex sentences

A complex sentence is composed of one independent clause with one or more subordinate clauses. (See B3-e.)

> SUBORDINATE
> ┌──── CLAUSE ────┐
> If you leave late, take a cab home.

> SUBORDINATE
> ┌───── CLAUSE ──────┐
> What matters most to us is a quick commute.

Compound-complex sentences

A compound-complex sentence contains at least two independent clauses and at least one subordinate clause. The following sentence contains two independent clauses, each of which contains a subordinate clause.

> ┌──── INDEPENDENT CLAUSE ────┐   ┌──── INDEPENDENT CLAUSE ────
> │   ┌── SUB CL ──┐   ┌── SUB CL ──
> Tell the doctor how you feel, and she will decide whether you
>
> ┌─────────────────┐
> └─────────────────┘
> can go home.

B4-b Sentence purposes

Writers use declarative sentences to make statements, imperative sentences to issue requests or commands, interrogative sentences to ask questions, and exclamatory sentences to make exclamations.

DECLARATIVE	The echo sounded in our ears.
IMPERATIVE	Love your neighbour.
INTERROGATIVE	Did the better team win tonight?
EXCLAMATORY	We're here to save you!

R

Researching

R Researching

Academic research assignments ask you to pose a question worth exploring, to read widely in search of possible answers, to interpret what you read, to draw reasoned conclusions, and to support those conclusions with valid and well-documented evidence. The process takes time—for researching and for drafting, revising, and documenting the paper in the style recommended by your instructor (see the tabbed dividers marked MLA and APA/CMS). Before beginning a research project, set a realistic schedule of deadlines.

One student created a calendar to map out her tasks for a paper assigned on October 3 and due October 31, keeping in mind that some tasks might overlap or need to be repeated.

RESEARCH TIP: Think of research as a process. As your topic evolves, you may find new questions arising that require you to create a new

SAMPLE CALENDAR FOR A RESEARCH ASSIGNMENT

2	3	4	5	6	7	8
	Receive and analyze the assignment.	Pose questions you might explore.	→ Talk with a reference librarian; plan a → search strategy.		Settle on a topic; narrow the focus.	Revise research questions. Locate → sources.
9	**10**	**11**	**12**	**13**	**14**	**15**
Read, take notes, and → compile a working bibliography. →				Draft a working thesis and an outline.	Draft the paper. →	
16	**17**	**18**	**19**	**20**	**21**	**22**
→ Draft the paper.→			Visit the writing centre for feedback.	Do additional research → if needed.		
23	**24**	**25**	**26**	**27**	**28**	**29**
Ask peers for feedback. Revise the paper; → if necessary, revise the thesis.				Prepare a list of → works cited.		Proofread the final draft. →
30	**31**					
Proofread the final draft. →	**Submit the final draft.**					

search strategy, find additional sources, and challenge your initial assumptions. Keep an open mind throughout the process, be curious, and enjoy the detective work.

R1 Conducting research

Throughout this tabbed section, you will encounter examples related to three sample research papers:

- A paper on Internet surveillance in the workplace, written by a student in an English composition class (see pp. 436–40). The student, Anna Orlov, uses the MLA (Modern Language Association) style of documentation. (See highlights of Orlov's research process on pp. 432–35.)

- A paper on the limitations of medications to treat childhood obesity, written by a student in a psychology class (see pp. 488–96). The student, Luisa Mirano, uses the APA (American Psychological Association) style of documentation.

- A paper on the extent to which Civil War general Nathan Bedford Forrest can be held responsible for the Fort Pillow massacre, written by a student in a history class (see pp. 532–37). The student, Ned Bishop, uses the CMS (*Chicago Manual of Style*) documentation system.

R1-a Pose questions worth exploring.

Working within the guidelines of your assignment, pose a few questions that seem worth researching—questions that you want to explore, that you feel would interest your audience, and about which there is a substantial debate. Here, for example, are some preliminary questions jotted down by students enrolled in a variety of courses in different disciplines.

- Should the CRTC broaden its definition of indecency to include violence?
- Which geological formations are the safest repositories for nuclear waste?
- What was Marcus Garvey's contribution to the fight for racial equality?
- How can governments and zoos help preserve Asia's endangered snow leopard?

- Why was amateur archaeologist Heinrich Schliemann such a controversial figure in his own time?

Approaching your topic with a series of worthwhile questions can help you focus your research and guide you toward developing an answer. As you think about possible questions, make sure that they are appropriate lines of inquiry for a research paper. Choose questions that are narrow (not too broad), challenging (not too bland), and grounded (not too speculative).

Choosing a narrow question

If your initial question is too broad, given the length of the paper you plan to write, look for ways to restrict your focus. Here, for example, is how two students narrowed their initial questions.

TOO BROAD	NARROWER
What are the hazards of fad diets?	Why are low-carbohydrate diets hazardous?
What are the benefits of stricter auto emissions standards?	How will stricter auto emissions standards create new, more competitive auto industry jobs?

Choosing a challenging question

Your research paper will be more interesting to both you and your audience if you base it on an intellectually challenging line of inquiry. Draft questions that provoke thought or engage readers in a debate.

TOO BLAND	CHALLENGING
What is obsessive-compulsive disorder?	Why is obsessive-compulsive disorder so difficult to treat?
How does DNA testing work?	How reliable is DNA testing?

You may need to address a bland question in the course of answering a more challenging one. For example, if you were writing about promising treatments for obsessive-compulsive disorder, you would no doubt answer the question "What is obsessive-compulsive disorder?" at some point in your paper. It would be a mistake, however, to use the bland question as the focus for the whole paper.

Choosing a grounded question

Finally, you will want to make sure that your research question is grounded, not too speculative. Although speculative questions—such as those that address morality or beliefs—are worth asking and may receive some attention in a research paper, they are inappropriate central questions. For most college and university courses, the central argument of a research paper should be grounded in facts.

TOO SPECULATIVE	GROUNDED
Is it wrong to share pornographic personal photos by cell phone?	What role should the government play in regulating mobile content?
Do medical scientists have the right to experiment on animals?	How have technology breakthroughs made medical experiments on animals increasingly unnecessary?

R1-b Map out a search strategy.

A search strategy is a systematic plan for tracking down sources. To create a search strategy appropriate for your research question, consult a reference librarian and take a look at your library's Web site, which will give you an overview of available resources.

Including the library in your plan

Reference librarians are information specialists who can save you time by steering you toward relevant and reliable sources. With the help of an expert, you can make the best use of electronic databases, Web search engines, the library's catalogue, and other reference tools.

Before you ask a reference librarian for help, be sure you have thought through the following questions:

- What is your assignment?
- In which academic discipline are you writing?
- What is your tentative research question?
- How long will the paper be?
- How much time can you spend on the project?

It's a good idea to bring a copy of the assignment with you.

In addition to speaking with a reference librarian, take some time to explore your library's Web site. You will typically find links to the library's catalogue and to a variety of databases and electronic sources. You may also find resources listed by subject, research guides, information about interlibrary loans, and links to Web sites selected by librarians for their quality. Many libraries also offer online reference assistance to help you locate information and refine your search strategy.

finding sources • search strategy • resources • reference librarians • using the library • finding sources to fit your purpose

R1-b   335

NOTE FOR ONLINE STUDENTS: Even if you are unable to visit the library, as an enrolled student you can still use its resources. Most libraries offer chat reference services and remote access to online databases, though you may have to follow special procedures to use them. Check your library's Web site for information for distance learners.

Starting with your library's databases

You may be tempted to go straight to the Internet and ignore your library's resources, but using them early and often in the research process can save you time in the end. Libraries make a wide range of quality materials readily available, and they weed out questionable sources.

While a general Internet search might seem quick and convenient, it is often more time-consuming and can be less reliable than a search in a library's databases. Initial Internet searches may generate thousands of results. Figuring out which of these are credible, relevant, and worth further investigation can require many additional steps:

- Refining search terms (See the chart on p. 338.)
- Narrowing the domain name to include only .org, .gc.ca, or .edu sites
- Weeding out any advertisements associated with results
- Scanning titles and sometimes content for relevant results
- Combing through sites to determine their currency and relevance as well as the credibility of their authors

Starting with your library's collection of databases can save time and effort. Because you can limit library database searches to only academic databases, you can count on finding reliable sources. Not all of the results will be worth examining in detail, but many library searches automatically sort them into subject categories that allow you to view narrowed results with just one click.

Choosing an appropriate search strategy

No single search strategy works for every topic. For some topics, it may be appropriate to search for information in newspapers, magazines, and Web sites. For others, the best sources might be found in scholarly journals and books and specialized reference works. Still other topics might be enhanced by field research—interviews, surveys, or direct observation.

With the help of a reference librarian, each of the students mentioned on page 332 constructed a search strategy appropriate for his or her research question.

ANNA ORLOV Anna Orlov's topic, Internet surveillance in the workplace, was current and influenced by technological changes, so she relied heavily on recent sources, especially those online. To find information on her topic, Orlov decided to

- search her library's general database for articles in magazines, newspapers, and journals
- check the library's catalogue for recently published books
- use Web search engines, such as *Google*, to locate articles and government publications that might not show up in a database search

LUISA MIRANO Luisa Mirano's topic, the limitations of medications for childhood obesity, is the subject of psychological studies as well as articles in newspapers and magazines aimed at the general public. Thinking that both scholarly and popular works would be appropriate, Mirano decided to

- locate books through the library's online catalogue
- check a specialized encyclopedia, *Encyclopedia of Psychology*
- search a specialized database, *PsycINFO*, for scholarly articles
- search her library's general database for popular articles

NED BISHOP Ned Bishop's topic, Nathan Bedford Forrest's role in the Fort Pillow massacre, has been investigated and debated by professional historians. Given the nature of his historical topic, Ned Bishop decided to

- locate books through the library's online catalogue
- locate scholarly articles by searching a specialized database, *America: History and Life*
- locate newspaper articles from 1864 by searching the historical archive at the *New York Times* Web site
- search the Web for other historical primary sources (See p. 353.)

R1-c To locate articles, search a database or consult a print index.

Libraries subscribe to a variety of electronic databases (sometimes called *periodical* or *article databases*) that give students access to articles and other materials without charge. Because many databases are limited to relatively recent works, you may need to consult a print index as well.

What databases offer

Your library has access to databases that can lead you to articles in periodicals such as newspapers, magazines, and scholarly or technical journals. General databases cover several subject areas; subject-specific databases cover one subject area in depth.

Many databases, especially general databases, include the full text of at least some articles; others list only citations or citations with short summaries called *abstracts* (see also p. 352). When the full text is not available, a citation usually will give you enough information to track down an article. Your library's Web site will help you determine which articles are available in your library, either in print or in electronic form.

Your library might subscribe to some of the following databases.

GENERAL DATABASES

The information in general databases is not restricted to a specific discipline or subject area. You may find searching a general database helpful in the early stages of your research process.

Academic Search Premier. An interdisciplinary database that indexes thousands of popular and scholarly journals on all subjects.

Expanded Academic ASAP. An interdisciplinary database that indexes the contents of magazines, newspapers, and scholarly journals in all subject areas.

JSTOR. A full-text archive of scholarly journals from many disciplines; unlike most databases, it includes articles published decades ago but does not include articles from the most recent issues of publications.

LexisNexis. A database that is particularly strong in coverage of news, business, legal, and political topics.

ProQuest. A database of periodical articles. Through *ProQuest*, your library may subscribe to databases in subjects such as nursing, biology, and psychology.

SUBJECT-SPECIFIC DATABASES

Libraries have access to dozens of specialized databases, each of which covers a specific area of research. To find out what's available, consult your library's Web site or ask your reference librarian. The following are examples of subject-specific databases.

ERIC. A database offering education-related documents and abstracts of articles published in education journals.

Refining keyword searches in databases and search engines

Although command terms and characters vary in electronic databases and Web search engines, some common functions are listed here.

- Use quotation marks around words that are part of a phrase: "gateway drug".
- Use AND to connect words that must appear in a document: hyperactivity AND children. In some search engines—*Google*, for example—AND is assumed, so typing it is unnecessary. Other search engines require a plus sign instead: hyperactivity + children.
- Use NOT in front of words that must not appear in a document: Persian Gulf NOT war. Some search engines require a minus sign (hyphen) instead: Persian Gulf -war.
- Use OR if only one of the terms must appear in a document: "mountain lion" OR cougar.
- Use an asterisk as a substitute for letters that might vary: "marine biolog*" (to find *marine biology* or *marine biologist*, for example).
- Use parentheses to group a search expression and combine it with another: (standard OR student OR test*) AND reform.

NOTE: Many search engines and databases offer an advanced search option for refining your search with filters for exact phrases that must appear, specific words that should not appear, date restrictions, and so on.

MLA International Bibliography. A database of literary criticism, with citations of articles, books, and dissertations.

PsycINFO. A comprehensive database of psychology research, including abstracts of articles in journals and books.

Public Affairs Information Service International (PAIS International). A database of books, journals, government documents, and reports in the social sciences.

PubMed. A database offering millions of abstracts of medical research studies.

How to search a database

To find articles on your topic in a database, start by searching with keywords, terms that describe the information you need. If the first keyword you try results in too few or no matches, experiment with synonyms or ask a librarian for suggestions. For example, if you're searching for sources on a topic related to education, you might also want to try the terms *teaching, learning,* and *curriculum.* If your keyword search results in too many matches, narrow it by using one of the strategies in the chart on page 338.

For her paper on Internet surveillance in the workplace, Anna Orlov conducted a keyword search in a general database. She typed in *"internet use"* and *employee* and *surveillance* (see the database screen on this page).

Making the most of your handbook

Freewriting, listing, and clustering can help you come up with additional search terms.

► Ways to explore your subject: **C1-b**

This search brought up twenty possible articles, some of which looked promising. (See p. 433 for Orlov's annotated list of search results.) Orlov e-mailed several full-text articles to herself and printed citations to other sources so that she could locate them in the library.

When to use a print index

A print index to periodical articles is a useful tool when you are researching a historical topic, especially from the early to mid-twentieth century. *The Readers' Guide to Periodical Literature* and *Poole's Index to Periodical Literature* index magazine articles beginning around

DATABASE SCREEN: KEYWORD SEARCH

1900, many of which are too old to appear in electronic databases. You can usually access the print articles themselves in your library's shelves or on microfilm.

R1-d To locate books, consult the library's catalogue.

The books your library owns are listed along with other resources in its catalogue. You can search the catalogue by author, title, or subject.

If your first search calls up too few results, try different keywords or search for books on broader topics. If your search gives you too many results, use the strategies in the chart on page 338 or try an advanced search tool to combine concepts and limit your results. If those strategies don't work, ask a librarian for suggestions.

When Luisa Mirano, whose topic was childhood obesity, entered the term *obesity* into the library's catalogue, she was faced with an unmanageable number of hits. She narrowed her search by adding two more specific terms to *obesity*: *child** (to include the terms *child*, *children*, and *childhood*) and *treatment*. When she still got too many results, she limited the first two terms to subject searches to find books that had obesity in children as their primary subject (see screen 1). Screen 2 shows the complete record for one of the books she found. The call number, listed beside *Availability*, is the book's address on the shelf. When you're retrieving a book from the shelf, take time to scan other books in the area since they are likely to be on the same topic.

RESEARCH TIP: The catalogue record for a book lists related subject headings. These headings are a good way to locate other books on your

LIBRARY CATALOGUE SCREEN 1: ADVANCED SEARCH

LIBRARY CATALOGUE SCREEN 2: COMPLETE RECORD FOR A BOOK

subject. For example, the record in screen 2 lists *obesity in children* and *obesity in adolescence* as related subject headings. By clicking on these terms, Mirano found more books on her subject. Subject headings can be useful terms for a database search as well.

R1-e To locate other sources, use a variety of online tools.

You can find a variety of reliable sources by using online tools beyond those offered by your library. For example, most governments and agencies post information on their Web sites to communicate with citizens. The sites of many private organizations, such as Médecins sans frontières and the Sierra Club Canada, contain useful information about current issues. Museums and libraries often post digital versions of primary sources, such as photographs, political speeches, and classic literary texts.

Although the Internet at large can be a rich source of information, some of which can't be found anywhere else, it lacks quality control. The material on many sites has not necessarily been reviewed by experts. So when you're not working with your library's tools to locate online sources, carefully evaluate what you find (see R2).

This section describes the following Web resources: search engines, directories, digital archives, government and news sites, blogs, and wikis.

Search engines

When using a search engine, such as *Google* or *Yahoo!*, focus your search as narrowly as possible. You can refine your search by using many of the tips in the chart on page 338 or by using the search engine's advanced search form. For her paper on Internet surveillance in the workplace, Anna Orlov had difficulty restricting the number of hits. When she typed the words *Internet, surveillance, workplace,* and *privacy* into a search engine, she received more than 80 000 matches. After examining the first page of her results and viewing some that looked promising, Orlov grouped her search terms into the phrases *"Internet surveillance"* and *"workplace privacy"* and added the term *employee* to narrow the focus. The result was 422 matches. To refine her search further, Orlov clicked on Advanced Search and restricted her search to sites with URLs ending in .org and to those updated in the last three months. (See the results screen on p. 343.)

Directories

If you want to find good resources on topics too broad for a search engine, try a directory. Unlike search engines, directories are put together by information specialists who choose reputable sites and arrange them by topic: education, health, politics, and so on.

Try the following directories for scholarly research.

Internet Scout Project: http://scout.wisc.edu/Archives

Librarian's Internet Index: http://www.lii.org

Open Directory Project: http://www.dmoz.org

WWW Virtual Library: http://www.vlib.org

Digital archives

Archives are a good place to find primary sources: the texts of poems, books, speeches, and historically significant documents; photographs; and political cartoons. (See p. 353.)

The materials in these sites are usually limited to official documents and older works because of copyright laws.

SEARCH ENGINE SCREEN: RESULTS OF AN ADVANCED SEARCH

Web Results 1 - 5 of about 9 over the past 3 months for "Internet surveillance" employee "workplace privacy"

Web Results 1 - 5 of about 9 over the past 3 months for "Internet surveillance" employee "workplace privacy" site:.org(0.44 seconds)

Tip: Try removing quotes from your search to get more results.

EPIC/PI - Privacy & Human Rights 2000
Now the supervision of **employee**'s performance, behavior and... [89] Information and
Privacy Commissioner/Ontario, **Workplace Privacy**: The Need for a..
www.privacyinternational.org/survey/phr2000/threats.html - 131k Cached - Similar pages

Privacy and Human Rights 2003: Threats to Privacy
Other issues that raise **workplace privacy** concerns are employer requirements that
employees complete medical tests, questionnaires, and polygraph tests..
www.privacyinternational.org/survey/phr2003/threats.htm - 279k Cached - Similar pages
[More results from www.privacyinternational.org]

[PDF] Monitoring **Employee** E-Mail And Internet Usage: Avoiding The..
File Format: PDF/Adobe Acrobat -View as HTML
Internet surveillance by employers in the American workplace. At present, US **employees**
in the private workplace have no constitutional, common law or statu
lsr.nellco.org/cgi/viewcontent.cgi?article=1006&context=suffolk/ip -Similar pages

Previous EPIC Top News
The agencies plan to use RFID to track **employees**' movements and in ID cards... For more
information on **workplace privacy**, see the EPIC **Workplace Privacy** ...
www.epic.org/news/2005.html - 163k Cached - Similar pages

Archives Canada: http://www.archivescanada.ca

CBC Digital Archives: http://archives.cbc.ca

Eurodocs: http://eudocs.lib.byu.edu

Google Books: http://books.google.com

Google Scholar: http://scholar.google.com

Library and Archives Canada: http://www.collectionscanada.gc.ca

The New York Public Library Digital Collections: http://www
.nypl.org/digital

Online Books Page: http://digital.library.upenn.edu/books

Government and news sites

For current topics, both government and news sites can prove useful.
Many government agencies at every level provide online information.
Government-maintained sites include resources such as legal texts,

facts and statistics, government reports, and searchable reference data-bases. Here are just a few government sites:

Census of Canada: http://www12.statcan.ca/english/census /index.cfm

Industry Canada, Programs and Services: http://www.ic.gc.ca /eic/site/ic1.nsf/eng/h_00006.html

Justice Laws: http://laws.justice.gc.ca/en

Statistics Canada: http://www.statcan.gc.ca

United Nations: http://www.un.org

Many news organizations offer up-to-date information on the Web. Some require registration and may charge fees for some articles. (Find out if your library subscribes to news sites so that you can access them at no charge.) The following news sites offer many free resources.

BBC: http://www.bbc.co.uk

Canoe: http://www.canoe.ca

Kidon Media-Link: http://www.kidon.com/media-link

New York Times: http://nytimes.com

Blogs

A blog (short for *Weblog*) is a site that contains text or multimedia entries usually written and maintained by one person, with comments contributed by readers. Though some blogs are personal diaries and others are devoted to partisan politics, many journalists and aca-demics maintain blogs that cover topics of interest to researchers. Some blogs feature short essays that provide useful insights or analysis; others point to new developments in a particular area of interest. The following Web sites can lead you to a wide range of blogs.

Academic Blog Portal: http://academicblogs.org

Google Blog Search: http://blogsearch.google.ca

Science Blogs: http://scienceblogs.com

Technorati: http://technorati.com

Wikis

A wiki is a collaborative Web site with many contributions and with content that may change frequently. *Wikipedia*, the collaborative online encyclopedia, is one of the most frequently consulted wikis.

government sites • news sites • blogs • wikis •
other search tools • references • encyclopedias, atlases, etc.

R1-f   345

In general, *Wikipedia* may be helpful if you're checking for some-thing that is common knowledge (facts available in multiple sources, such as dates and well-known historical events) or looking for current information about a topic in contemporary culture that isn't covered elsewhere. However, many scholars do not consider *Wikipedia* and wikis in general to be appropriate sources for academic research. Authorship is not limited to experts; articles may be written by amateurs who are not well informed. And because the articles can be changed by anyone, controversial texts are often altered to reflect a particular perspective and are susceptible to bias. When possible, locate and cite another, more reliable source for any useful information you find in a wiki.

R1-f Use other search tools.

In addition to articles, books, and online sources, you may want to consult references such as encyclopedias and almanacs. Citations in scholarly works can also lead you to additional sources.

Reference works

The reference section of the library holds both general and specialized encyclopedias, dictionaries, almanacs, atlases, and biographical refer-ences, some available in electronic form through the library's Web site. Such works often provide a good overview of your subject and include references to the most significant works on a topic. Check with a refer-ence librarian to see which works are most appropriate for your project.

GENERAL REFERENCE WORKS   General reference works are good places to check facts and get basic information. Here are a few frequently used general references:

> *The Canadian Encyclopedia*
>
> *Canadian Oxford Dictionary*
>
> *Dictionary of Canadian Biography*
>
> *National Geographic Atlas of the World*
>
> *Statistical Abstract of the United States*

Although general encyclopedias are often a good place to find background for your topic, you should rarely use them in your final paper. Most instructors expect you to rely on more specialized sources.

SPECIALIZED REFERENCE WORKS   Specialized reference works often explore a topic in depth, usually in the form of articles written by leading authorities. They offer a quick way to gain an expert's overview of a complex topic. Many specialized works are available, including these:

Contemporary Authors

Encyclopedia of Bioethics

Encyclopedia of Crime and Justice

Encyclopedia of Psychology

Encyclopedia of World Environmental History

International Encyclopedia of Communication

New Encyclopedia of Africa

Bibliographies and scholarly citations as shortcuts

Scholarly books and articles list the works the author has cited, usually at the end. These lists can be useful shortcuts to additional reliable sources on your topic. For example, most of the scholarly articles Luisa Mirano consulted contained citations to related research studies; through these citations, she quickly located other sources related to her topic, treatments for childhood obesity.

R1-g Conduct field research, if appropriate.

Your own field research can enhance or be the focus of a writing project. For a composition class, for example, you might want to interview a local politician about a current issue, such as the use of alternative energy sources. For a sociology class, you might decide to conduct a survey regarding campus trends in community service. At work, you might need to learn how food industry executives have responded to reports that their products are contributing to health problems.

NOTE: Colleges and universities often require researchers to submit projects to an institutional review board (IRB) if the research involves human subjects outside of a classroom setting. Before administering a survey or conducting other fieldwork, check with your instructor to see if IRB approval is required.

R2 Evaluating sources

You can often locate dozens or even hundreds of potential sources for your topic—far more than you will have time to read. Your challenge will be to determine what kinds of sources you need and to zero in on a

bibliographies • field research • interviews • surveys • how sources
work in a paper • selecting sources • scanning search results

R2-b   347

reasonable number of quality sources, those truly worthy of your time and attention.

Later, once you have decided on some sources worth consulting, your challenge will be to read them with an open mind and a critical eye.

R2-a Think about how sources might contribute to your writing.

How you plan to use sources will affect how you evaluate them. Not every source must directly support your thesis; sources can have other functions in a paper. They can

- provide background information or context for your topic
- explain terms or concepts that your readers might not understand
- provide evidence for your argument
- lend authority to your argument
- offer alternative interpretations and countercvidence to your argument

For examples of how student writers use sources for a variety of purposes, see MLA-1c, APA-1c, and CMS-1c.

R2-b Select sources worth your time and attention.

Sections R1-c through R1-e show how to refine your searches in databases, in the library's catalogue, and in search engines. This section explains how to scan through the results for the most promising sources and how to preview them to see whether they are likely to live up to your expectations and meet your needs.

Scanning search results

As you scan through a list of search results, watch for clues indicating whether a source might be useful for your purposes or is not worth pursuing. (For an annotated list of one student's search results, see p. 433.) You will need to use somewhat different strategies when scanning search results from a database, a library catalogue, and a Web search engine.

**Making the most
of your handbook**

Annotating bibliography entries can help you evaluate sources.

- ▶ Maintain a working bibliography: R3-a
- ▶ Summarize sources: A1-c
- ▶ Analyze sources: A1-d
- ▶ Consider how sources inform your argument: MLA-1c, APA-1c, CMS-1c

DATABASES   Most databases (see p. 337) list at least the following information, which can help you decide if a source is relevant, current, scholarly enough (see the chart on p. 352), and a suitable length for your purposes.

> Title and brief description (How relevant?)
>
> Date (How current?)
>
> Name of periodical (How scholarly?)
>
> Length (How extensive in coverage?)

At the bottom of this page are just a few of the hits Ned Bishop came up with when he consulted a general database for articles on the Fort Pillow massacre, using the search term *Fort Pillow*.

Many databases allow you to sort your list of results by relevance or date; sorting may help you scan the information more efficiently. By scanning the titles in his search results, Bishop saw that only one contained the words *Fort Pillow*. The name of the periodical in which it appeared, *Journal of American History*, suggested that the source was scholarly. The 1989 publication date was not a problem, since currency is not necessarily a criterion for historical sources. The article's length (eight pages) is given in parentheses at the end of the citation. While the article may seem short, the topic—a statistical note—is narrow enough to ensure adequate depth of coverage. Bishop decided that the article was worth consulting. Because the other sources were irrelevant or too broad, he decided not to consult them.

LIBRARY CATALOGUES   A library's catalogue usually lists enough basic information about books, periodicals, DVDs, and other material to give you a first impression. A book's title and date of publication, for example, will often be your first clues as to whether the book is worth consulting. If a title looks interesting, you can click on it for further

EVALUATING SEARCH RESULTS: LIBRARY DATABASE

Popular magazine. Not relevant.	☐ **Black, blue and gray: the other Civil War; African-American soldiers, sailors and spies were the** Mark **unsung heroes.** *Ebony* Feb 1991 v46 n4 p96(6) View <u>text and retrieval choices</u>
Movie review. Not relevant.	☐ **The Civil War.** (movie reviews) Lewis Cole. *The Nation* Dec 3, 1990 v251 n19 p694(5) Mark View <u>text and retrieval choices</u>
Subject too broad.	☐ **The hard fight was getting into the fight at all.** (black soldiers in the Civil War) Jack Fincher. Mark *Smithsonian* Oct 1990 v21 n7 p46(13) View <u>text and retrieval choices</u>
Brief scholarly article. Matches the student's topic. Promising.	☑ **The Fort Pillow massacre: a statistical note.** John Cimprich, Robert C. Mainfort Jr.. *Journal of America* Mark *History* Dec 1989 v76 n3 p830(8) View <u>extended citation and retrieval choices</u>

EVALUATING SEARCH RESULTS: INTERNET SEARCH ENGINE

American **Obesity** Association - **Childhood Obesity**
Childhood Obesity. Obesity in **children** ... Note: The term "**childhood obesity**" may refer
to both **children** and adolescents. In general, we ...
www.**obesity**.org/subs/**childhood**/ - 17k - Jan 8, 2005 - Cached - Similar pages

> Content from a research-based organization. Promising.

Childhood Obesity
KS Logo, **Childhood Obesity**. advertisement. Source. ERIC Clearinghouse on Teaching and
Teacher Education. Contents. ... Back to the Top Causes of **Childhood Obesity**. ...
www.kidsource.com/kidsource/content2/**obesity**.html - 18k - Cached - Similar pages

> Popular rather than scholarly source. Not relevant.

Childhood Obesity, June 2002 Word on Health - National Institutes ...
Childhood Obesity on the Rise, an article in the June 2002 edition of The NIH Word on
Health - Consumer Information Based on Research from the National ...
www.nih.gov/news/WordonHealth/ jun2002/**childhoodobesity**.htm - 22k -
Cached - Similar pages

> Content too general. Not relevant.

MayoClinic.com - **Childhood obesity**: Parenting advice
... **Childhood obesity**: Parenting advice By Mayo Clinic staff. ... Here are some other tips to
help your **obese child** — and yourself: Be a positive role model. ...
www.mayoclinic.com/invoke.cfm?id=FL00058 - 42k - Jan 8, 2005 - Cached - Similar pages

> Popular and too general. Not relevant.

---

information about its subject matter and length. The table of contents also can offer a glimpse of what's inside. (See also p. 341.)

WEB SEARCH ENGINES   Because anyone can publish a Web site, legitimate sources and unreliable sources live side-by-side online. As you scan through search results, look for the following clues about the probable relevance, currency, and reliability of a site—but be aware that the clues are by no means foolproof.

The title, keywords, and lead-in text (How relevant?)

A date (How current?)

An indication of the site's sponsor or purpose (How reliable?)

The URL, especially the domain name extension: for example, .com, .edu, .gc.ca, or .org (How relevant? How reliable?)

At the top of this page are a few of the results that Luisa Mirano retrieved after typing the keywords *childhood obesity* into a search engine; she limited her search to works with those words in the title.

Mirano found the first site, sponsored by a research-based organization, promising enough to explore for her paper. The second and fourth sites held less promise because they seemed to offer popular rather than scholarly information. In addition, the second site was full of distracting commercial advertisements. Mirano rejected the third source not because she doubted its reliability—in fact, research from the National Institutes of Health was what she hoped to find—but because a skim of its contents revealed that the information was too general for her purposes.

COMMON FEATURES OF A SCHOLARLY SOURCE

1   Formal presentation includes abstract and research methods.
2   Includes review of previous research studies.
3   Reports original research.
4   Includes references.
5   Often has multiple authors who are academics.

Cyberbullying: Using Virtual Scenarios to Educate and Raise Awareness

Vivian H. Wright, Joy J. Burnham, Christopher T. Inman, and Heather N. Ogorchock

Abstract

This study examined cyberbullying in three distinct phases to facilitate a multifaceted understanding of cyberbullying. The phases included (a) a quantitative survey, (b) a qualitative focus group, and (c) development of educational scenarios/simulations (within the Second Life virtual environment). Phase III was based on adolescent feedback about cyberbullying from Phases I and II of this study. In all three phases, adolescent reactions to cyberbullying were examined and reported to raise awareness and to educate others about cyberbullying. Results from scenario development indicate that simulations created in a virtual environment are engaging and have the potential to be powerful tools in helping schools address problems such as cyberbullying education and prevention. (Keywords: cyberbullying, virtual worlds, Second Life, teacher education, counselor education)

Introduction

Cyberbullying has gained attention and recognition in recent years (Beale & Hall, 2007; Carney, 2008; Casey-Canon, Hayward, & Gowen, 2001; Kowalski & Limber, 2007; Li, 2007; Shariff, 2005). The increased interest and awareness of cyberbullying relates to such factors as the national media attention after several publicized cyberbullying tragedies (Maag, 2007; Stelter, 2008; Zifcak, 2006), the attenuation of communication boundaries (i.e., cell phones, the Internet, and computer network connections), and the exponential increase in technology use among youth. Nonetheless, with the escalation of technology and the easy access and popularity of technological devices among youth, presently there remains a critical gap in the literature related to cyberbullying and its possible effects on school-aged children and adolescents. Because cyberbullying has the potential to impact youth across systems (i.e., home, school, and the community), we believe that parents, "school professionals" (Li, 2007, p. 1778), and mental health providers must not only be made aware of cyberbullying and its consequences, but must also have access to ways to deal with this growing concern.

Two years ago, cyberbullying was considered to be a "new territory" for exploration (Li, 2007, p. 1778) because there was limited information about bullying through "electronic means" (Li, p. 1780). In contrast, today studies on cyberbullying, including some descriptions of the worst cyberbullying incidences (Maag, 2007; Stelter, 2008; Zifcak, 2006), are becoming more prevalent (Beale & Hall, 2007; Carney, 2008; Kowalski & Limber, 2007; Li, 2007). At this time, there is a need to raise awareness about the effects of cyberbullying and to create educational opportunities to serve multiple audiences (i.e., teachers, teacher educators, school administrators, school counselors, mental health professionals, students, parents) in the quest to identify and hopefully prevent cyberbullying in the future. Consequently, to facilitate a multifaceted understanding of

Volume 26/ Number 1 Fall 2009   Journal of Computing in Teacher Education   35
Copyright © 2009 ISTE (International Society for Technology in Education). 800.336.5191 (U.S. & Canada) or 541.302.3777 (Int'l), iste@iste.org, www.iste.org

---

Abstract

This study examined cyberbullying in three distinct phases to facilitate a multifaceted understanding of cyberbullying. The phases included (a) a quantitative survey, (b) a qualitative focus group, and (c) development of educational scenarios/simulations (within the Second Life virtual environment). Phase III was based on adolescent feedback about cyberbullying from Phases I and II of this study. In all three phases, adolescent reactions to cyberbullying were examined and reported to raise awareness and to

2

Research suggests that cyberbullying has distinct gender and age differences. According to the literature, girls are more likely to be online and to cyberbully (Beale & Hall, 2007; Kowalski & Limber, 2007; Li, 2006, 2007). This finding is "opposite of what happens off-line," where boys are more likely to bully than girls (Beale & Hall, p. 8). Age also appears to be a factor in cyberbullying. Cyberbullying increases in the elementary years, peaks during the middle school years, and declines in the high school years (Beale & Hall). Based on the literature, cyberbullying is a growing concern among middle school-aged children (Beale & Hall; Hinduja & Patchin, 2008; Kowalski & Limber, 2007; Li, 2007; Pellegrini & Bartini, 2000; Smith, Mahdavi, Carvalho, & Tippett, 2006; Williams & Guerra, 2007). Of the middle school grades, 6th grade students are usually the

3 Table 2: Percentage of Students Who Experienced Cyberbullying through Various Methods

	E-mail	Facebook	MySpace	Cell Phone	Online Video	Chat Rooms
Victim	35.3%	11.8%	52.9%	50%	14.7%	11.8%
Bully	17.6%	0%				

4 **References**

Bainbridge, W. S. (2007, July). The scientific research potential of virtual worlds. *Science, 317,* 472–476.

5

Vivian H. Wright is an associate professor of instructional technology at the University of Alabama. In addition to teaching in the graduate program, Dr. Wright works with teacher educators on innovative ways to infuse technology in the curriculum to enhance teaching and learning. She has helped initiate and develop projects such as the Master Technology Teacher and Technology on Wheels. Dr. Wright's scholarship includes publications and presentations in the research areas of K–12 technology integration, emerging technologies, and asynchronous education.

Wright, Vivian H., et al. "Cyberbullying: Using Virtual Scenarios to Educate and Raise Awareness." *Journal of Computing in Teacher Education* 26.1 (2009): 35-42.

COMMON FEATURES OF A POPULAR SOURCE

1   Often has a provocative title.
2   Author is typically a staff reporter, not an expert.
3   The bulk of the article presents anecdotes about the topic.
4   Presents a summary of research but no original research.
5   No consistent citation of sources.

Technology

The cyber-bullies are always with you... ❶

The anonymity of the internet makes it easy for bullies to ruin the lives of their teenage victims

PHIL MCKENNA

RYAN HALLIGAN was taunted for months. Classmates spread rumours via instant messaging that the 13-year-old boy was gay. A popular female classmate pretended to like him and chatted with him online only to copy their personal exchanges and share them with her friends. Unable to cope, Halligan, of Essex Junction, Vermont, killed himself.

The anonymity of the internet makes it easy to ruin the lives of their teenage victims

PHIL MCKENNA ❷

RYAN HALLIGAN was taunted for months. Classmates spread rumours via instant messaging that the 13-year-old boy was gay. ❸ A popular female classmate pretended to like him and chatted with him online only to copy their personal exchanges and share them with her friends. Unable to cope, Halligan, of Essex Junction, Vermont, killed himself.

ONLINE BULLIES ATTACK ADULTS TOO

❹ A study last month by the Pew Internet & American Life Project based in Washington DC found that one-third of US teenage internet users have been targets

"The lack of face-to-face contact might tempt bullies to new levels of cruelty"

communication. "There is a ❺ distancing of the self and immediacy in response that we don't have in any other form of communication," she says. "On the computer, it's like it's not really you."

So what can be done? Led by Ruth Aylett of Heriot-Watt University in Edinburgh, UK,

Meanwhile, some governments have taken legislative action. In January 2006, the US Congress passed a law making it a federal crime to "annoy, abuse, threaten or harass" another person over the internet. Approximately 36 states have enacted similar legislation. And in South Korea, the "internet real-

McKenna, Phil. "The Cyber-Bullies Are Always with You. . . ." *New Scientist* July 2007: 26-27.

Determining if a source is scholarly

For many academic assignments, you will be asked to use scholarly sources. These are written by experts for a knowledgeable audience and usually go into more depth than works written for a general audience. (Scholarly sources are sometimes called *refereed* or *peer-reviewed* because the work is evaluated by experts in the field before publication.) To determine if a source is scholarly, look for the following:

- Formal language and presentation
- Authors with academic or scientific credentials
- Footnotes or a bibliography documenting the works cited by the author in the source
- Original research and interpretation (rather than a summary of other people's work)
- Quotations from and analysis of primary sources (in humanities disciplines such as literature, history, and philosophy)
- A description of research methods or a review of related research (in the sciences and social sciences)

See pages 350–51 for a sample scholarly source and popular source.

NOTE: In some databases, searches can be limited to refereed or peer-reviewed journals.

Selecting appropriate versions of electronic sources

An online source may appear as an abstract, an excerpt, or a full-text article or book. It is important to distinguish among these versions of sources and to use a complete version of a source for your research.

Abstracts and excerpts are shortened versions of complete works. An abstract—a summary of a work's contents—might appear in a database record for a periodical article. An excerpt is the first few sentences or paragraphs of a newspaper or magazine article; it sometimes appears in a list of hits in an online search. Abstracts and excerpts often provide enough information for you to determine whether the complete article would be useful for your paper. Both are brief (usually fewer than five hundred words) and generally do not contain enough information to function alone as sources in a research paper. Reading the complete article is the best way to understand the author's argument before referring to it in your own writing. A full-text work may appear online as a PDF (portable document format) file or as an HTML file (sometimes called a *text file*). If your source is available in both formats, choose the PDF file for your research because it will include page numbers for your citations.

R2-c Read with an open mind and a critical eye.

As you begin reading the sources you have chosen, keep an open mind. Do not let your personal beliefs prevent you from listening to new ideas and opposing viewpoints. Your research question—not a snap judgment about the question—should guide your reading.

When you read critically, you are not necessarily judging an author's work harshly; you are simply examining its assumptions, assessing its evidence, and weighing its conclusions. (For one student's careful reading of a source text, see p. 434.)

Academic English   When you research on the Web, it is easy to ignore views different from your own. Web pages that appeal to you will often link to other pages that support the same viewpoint. If your sources all seem to agree with you—and with one another—seek out opposing views and evaluate them with an open mind.

Distinguishing between primary and secondary sources

As you begin assessing evidence in a source, determine whether you are reading a primary or a secondary source. Primary sources are original documents such as letters, diaries, photographs, legislative bills, laboratory studies, field research reports, and eyewitness accounts. Secondary sources are commentaries on primary sources—another writer's opinions about or interpretation of a primary source. A primary source for Ned Bishop was Nathan Bedford Forrest's official report on the battle at Fort Pillow. Bishop also consulted a number of secondary sources, some of which relied heavily on primary sources such as letters.

Although a primary source is not necessarily more reliable than a secondary source, it has the advantage of being a firsthand account. Naturally, you can better evaluate what a secondary source says if you have first read any primary sources it discusses.

Being alert for signs of bias

Some sources are more objective than others. Even publications that are considered reputable can be editorially biased. For example, *Canadian Business Magazine* and *Financial Post Magazine* are credible sources, but they are also likely to interpret events differently. If you are uncertain about a periodical's special interests, consult *Magazines for Libraries*. To check for bias in a book, see what book reviewers have written about it. A reference librarian can help you locate reviews and assess the credibility of both the book and the reviewers.

Evaluating all sources

Checking for signs of bias

- Does the author or publisher endorse political or religious views that could affect objectivity?
- Is the author or publisher associated with a special-interest group, such as Greenpeace or the National Firearms Association of Canada, that might present only one side of an issue?
- Are alternative views presented and addressed? How fairly does the author treat opposing views? (See A3-c.)
- Does the author's language show signs of bias?

Assessing an argument

- What is the author's central claim or thesis?
- How does the author support this claim—with relevant and sufficient evidence or with just a few anecdotes or emotional examples?
- Are statistics consistent with those you encounter in other sources? Have they been used fairly? (It is possible to "lie" with statistics by using them selectively or by omitting details.) Does the author explain where the statistics come from?
- Are any of the author's assumptions questionable?
- Does the author consider opposing arguments and refute them persuasively? (See A3-c.)
- Does the author fall prey to any logical fallacies? (See A3-a.)

Like publishers, some authors are more objective than others. If you have reason to believe that a writer is particularly biased, you will want to assess his or her arguments with special care. For questions to ask about a source's possible bias, see the chart on this page.

Assessing the author's argument

In nearly all academic writing, there is some element of argument, so don't be surprised to encounter experts who disagree. When you find areas of disagreement, you will want to read each source's arguments with special care, testing them with your own critical intelligence. The questions in the chart on this page can help you weigh the strengths and weaknesses of each author's argument.

Making the most of your handbook

Good academic writers read critically.

▶ Judging whether a source is reasonable: A3-a

▶ Judging whether a source is fair: A3-c

Evaluating Web sources

Authorship

- Does the Web site or document have an author? You may need to do some clicking and scrolling to find the author's name. If you have landed directly on an internal page of a site, for example, you may need to navigate to the home page or find an "about this site" link to learn the name of the author.
- If there is an author, can you tell whether he or she is knowledgeable and credible? When the author's qualifications aren't listed on the site itself, look for links to the author's home page, which may provide evidence of his or her interests and expertise.

Sponsorship

- Who, if anyone, sponsors the site? The sponsor of a site is often named and described on the home page and is sometimes listed alongside the copyright date: © 2009 University of Toronto.
- What does the URL tell you? The domain name extension often indicates the type of group hosting the site: commercial (.com), educational (.edu), nonprofit (.org), governmental (.gc.ca or .gov), military (.mil), or network (.net). URLs may also indicate a country of origin: .ca (Canada) or .jp (Japan), for instance.

Purpose and audience

- Why was the site created: To argue a position? To sell a product? To inform readers?
- Who is the site's intended audience?

Currency

- How current is the site? Check for the date of publication or the latest update, often located at the bottom of the home page or at the beginning or end of an internal page.
- How current are the site's links? If many of the links no longer work, the site may be too dated for your purposes.

R2-d Assess Web sources with special care.

Web sources can provide valuable information, but verifying their credibility may take time. Before using a Web source in your paper, make sure you know who created the material and for what purpose.

Many sophisticated-looking sites contain questionable information. Even a well-designed hate site may at first appear unbiased and

EVALUATING A WEB SITE: CHECKING RELIABILITY

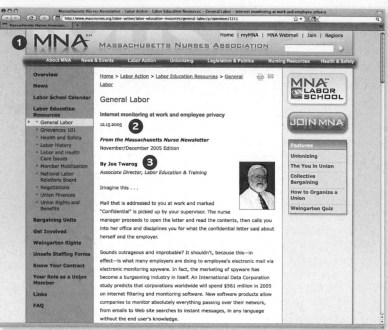

1   This article on Internet monitoring is on a site sponsored by the Massachusetts Nurses Association, a professional health care association and union whose staff and members advocate for nurses in the workplace. The URL ending .org marks this sponsor as a nonprofit organization.

2   Clear dates of publication show currency.

3   The author is a credible expert whose credentials can be verified.

---

informative. Sites with reliable information, however, can stand up to careful scrutiny. For a checklist on evaluating Web sources, see the chart on page 355.

In researching Internet surveillance and workplace privacy, Anna Orlov encountered sites that raised her suspicions. In particular, some sites were authored by surveillance software companies, which have an obvious interest in emphasizing the benefits of such software to company management. When you know something about the creator of a site and have a sense of the site's purpose, you can quickly determine whether a source is reliable, credible, and worth a closer look. Consider, for example, the two sites pictured on this page and on page 357. Anna Orlov decided that the first Web site would be more useful for her project than sites like the second.

EVALUATING A WEB SITE: CHECKING PURPOSE

1   The site is sponsored by a company that specializes in employee monitoring software.

2   Repeated links for trial downloads and purchase suggest the site's intended audience: consumers seeking to purchase software (probably not researchers seeking detailed information about employees' use of the Internet in the workplace).

3   The site appears to provide information and even shows statistics from studies, but ultimately the purpose of the site is to sell a product.

R3 Managing information; avoiding plagiarism

An effective researcher is a good record keeper. Whether you decide to keep records on paper or on your computer—or both—your challenge as a researcher will be to find systematic ways of managing information. More specifically, you will need methods for maintaining a working bibliography, keeping track of source materials, and taking notes without plagiarizing your sources. (For more on avoiding plagiarism, see MLA-2 for MLA style, APA-2 for APA style, and CMS-2 for CMS style.)

R3-a Maintain a working bibliography.

Keep a record of any sources you decide to consult. You will need this record, called a *working bibliography*, when you compile the list of sources that will appear at the end of your paper. The format of this list depends on the documentation style you are using. (For MLA style, see MLA-4b; for APA style, see APA-4b; for CMS style, see CMS-4c.) Using the proper style in your working bibliography will ensure that you have all the information you need to correctly cite any sources you use. Your working bibliography will probably contain more sources than you will actually include in your list of works cited in your final paper.

Most researchers print or save bibliographic information from the library's online catalogue, its periodical databases, and the Web. The information you need to collect is given in the chart on page 360. If you download a visual, you must gather the same information as for a print source.

For Web sources, some bibliographic information may not be available, but spend time looking for it before assuming that it doesn't exist. When information isn't available on the home page, you may have to drill into the site, following links to interior pages. Look especially for the author's name, the date of publication (or latest update), and the name of any sponsoring organization. Do not omit such information unless it is genuinely unavailable.

Once you have created a working bibliography, you can annotate it. Writing several brief sentences summarizing key points of a source will help you identify how it relates to your argument and to your other sources. You should evaluate the source in your own words and use quotations sparingly. Clarifying the source's ideas at this stage will help you separate them from your own and avoid plagiarizing them later.

SAMPLE ANNOTATED BIBLIOGRAPHY ENTRY (MLA STYLE)

Gonsalves, Chris. "Wasting Away on the Web." *eWeek.com*. Ziff Davis Enterprise
Holdings, 8 Aug. 2005. Web. 16 Feb. 2009.

Summarize the source.

Annotations should be three to seven sentences long.

In this editorial, Gonsalves considers the implications of several surveys, including one in which 61% of respondents said that their companies have the right to spy on them. The author agrees with this majority, claiming that it's fine if his company chooses to monitor him as long as the company discloses its monitoring practices. He argues that "the days of Internet freedom at work are

Use quotations sparingly. Put quotation marks around any words from the source.

MODELS   hackerhandbooks.com/writersref
> Model papers > MLA annotated bibliography: Orlov
> APA annotated bibliography: Haddad

keeping records • building a bibliography • annotated bibliography •
keeping copies of sources • taking notes • avoiding plagiarism

R3-c   359

justifiably finished," adding that he would prefer not to

know the extent of the surveillance. Gonsalves writes for

eWeek.com, a publication focused on technology products.

He presents himself as an employee who is comfortable with

being monitored, but his job may be a source of bias. This

editorial contradicts some of my other sources, which claim

that employees want to know and should know all the

details of their company's monitoring procedures.

R3-b Keep track of source materials.

The best way to keep track of source materials is to save a copy of each one. Many database subscription services will allow you to e-mail, save, or print citations or full texts of articles, and you can easily download, copy, or take screen shots of information from the Web.

Working with photocopies, printouts, and electronic files—as opposed to relying on memory or hastily written notes—has several benefits. You can highlight key passages, perhaps even colour-coding them to reflect topics in your outline. You can annotate the source in the margins by hand or with your word processing program's comment feature and get a head start on note taking (for an example, see the annotated article on p. 434). Finally, you reduce the chances of unintentional plagiarism, since you will be able to compare your use of a source in your paper with the actual source, not just with your notes (see R3-c).

NOTE: It's especially important to keep print or electronic copies of Web sources, which may change or even become inaccessible over time. Make sure that your copy includes the site's URL and your date of access.

TIP: Your school may provide citation software, which allows researchers to download references directly from online sources. Similarly, many databases format citations with a mouse click, and Web sites offer fill-in-the-blank forms for generating formatted citations. You must proofread such citations carefully, however, because the programs sometimes provide incorrect results.

R3-c As you take notes, avoid unintentional plagiarism.

When you take notes and jot down ideas, be very careful not to use language from your sources unless you clearly identify borrowed words and phrases as quotations. Even if you half-copy the author's

Information for a working bibliography

For an entire book

- All authors; any editors or translators
- Title and subtitle
- Edition (if not the first)
- Publication information: city, publisher, and date

For a periodical article

- All authors of the article
- Title and subtitle of the article
- Title of the magazine, journal, or newspaper
- Date; volume, issue, and page numbers

For a periodical article retrieved from a database (in addition to preceding information)

- Name of the database and an item number, if available
- Name of the subscription service
- URL of the subscription service (for an online database)
- Accession number or other number assigned by the database
- Digital object identifier (DOI), if there is one
- Date you retrieved the source

NOTE: Use particular care when printing or saving articles in PDF format. These files may not include some of the elements you need to properly cite the source. You may need to record additional information from the database or Web site where you retrieved the file.

For a Web source (including visuals)

- All authors, editors, or creators of the source
- Editor or compiler of the Web site, if there is one
- Title and subtitle of the source
- Title of the site
- Publication information for the source, if available
- Page or paragraph numbers, if any
- Date of online publication (or latest update)
- Sponsor of the site
- Date you accessed the source
- The site's URL

NOTE: For the exact bibliographic format to use in your working bibliography and in the final paper, see MLA-4b, APA-4b, or CMS-4c.

sentences—either by mixing the author's phrases with your own without using quotation marks or by plugging your synonyms into the author's sentence structure—you are committing plagiarism, a serious academic offence. (For examples of this kind of plagiarism, see MLA-2, APA-2, and CMS-2.)

To prevent unintentional borrowing, resist the temptation to look at the source as you take notes—except when you are quoting. Keep the source close by so you can check for accuracy, but don't try to put ideas in your own words with the source's sentences in front of you. When you need to quote the exact words of a source, make sure you copy the words precisely and put quotation marks around them.

TIP: Be especially careful when using copy and paste functions in electronic files. Some researchers have unintentionally plagiarized their sources because they lost track of which words came from sources and which were their own. To prevent unintentional plagiarism, put quotation marks around any exact language you save from your sources.

Academic English Even in the early stages of note taking, it is important to keep in mind that, in Canada, written texts are considered an author's property. (This "property" isn't a physical object, so it is often referred to as *intellectual property*.) The author (or publisher) owns the language as well as any original ideas contained in the writing, whether the source is published in print or electronic form. When you use another author's property in your own writing, you need to follow certain conventions for citing the material; if you don't, you risk committing *plagiarism*.

Summarizing, paraphrasing, and quoting are three ways of taking notes. Be sure to include exact page references for all three types of notes, since you will need the page numbers later if you use the information in your paper.

Summarizing without plagiarizing

A summary condenses information, perhaps reducing a chapter to a short paragraph or a paragraph to a single sentence. A summary should be written in your own words; if you use phrases from the source, put them in quotation marks.

On page 362 is a passage from a source about mountain lions. Following the passage is the student's summary. (The bibliographic information is recorded in MLA style.)

ORIGINAL SOURCE

In some respects, the increasing frequency of mountain lion encounters in California has as much to do with a growing *human* population as it does with rising mountain lion numbers. The scenic solitude of the western ranges is prime cougar habitat, and it is falling swiftly to the developer's spade. Meanwhile, with their ideal habitat already at its carrying capacity, mountain lions are forcing younger cats into less suitable terrain, including residential areas. Add that cougars have generally grown bolder under a lengthy ban on their being hunted, and an unsettling scenario begins to emerge.
— Rychnovsky, Ray. "Clawing into Controversy." *Outdoor Life* Jan. 1995: 38–42. Print. [p. 40]

SUMMARY

Source: Rychnovsky, Ray. "Clawing into Controversy." *Outdoor Life* Jan. 1995: 38–42. Print. [p. 40]

Encounters between mountain lions and humans are on the rise in California because increasing numbers of lions are competing for a shrinking habitat. As the lions' wild habitat shrinks, older lions force younger lions into residential areas. These lions have lost some of their fear of humans because of a ban on hunting (Rychnovsky 40).

Paraphrasing without plagiarizing

Like a summary, a paraphrase is written in your own words; but whereas a summary reports significant information in fewer words than the source, a paraphrase retells the information in roughly the same number of words. If you retain occasional choice phrases from the source, use quotation marks so that later you will know which phrases are not your own.

As you read the following paraphrase of the original source at the top of this page, notice that the language is significantly different from that in the original.

PARAPHRASE

Source: Rychnovsky, Ray. "Clawing into Controversy." *Outdoor Life* Jan. 1995: 38–42. Print. [p. 40]

Californians are encountering mountain lions more frequently because increasing numbers of humans and a rising population of lions are competing for the same territory. Humans have moved into mountainous regions once dominated by the lions, and the wild habitat that is left cannot sustain the current lion population.

Therefore, the older lions are forcing younger lions into residential areas. And because of a ban on hunting, these younger lions have become bolder—less fearful of encounters with humans (Rychnovsky 40).

Using quotation marks to avoid plagiarizing

A quotation consists of the exact words from a source. In your notes, put all quoted material in quotation marks; do not assume that you will remember later which words, phrases, and passages you have quoted and which are your own. When you quote, be sure to copy the words of your source exactly, including punctuation and capitalization.

QUOTATION

Source: Rychnovsky, Ray. "Clawing into Controversy." *Outdoor Life* Jan. 1995: 38–42. Print. [p. 40]

Rychnovsky explains that as humans expand residential areas into mountain ranges, the cougar's natural habitat "is falling swiftly to the developer's spade" (40).

Avoiding Internet plagiarism

UNDERSTAND WHAT PLAGIARISM IS.   When you use another author's intellectual property—language, visuals, or ideas—in your own writing without giving proper credit, you commit a kind of academic theft called *plagiarism*.

TREAT WEB SOURCES IN THE SAME WAY YOU TREAT PRINT SOURCES.   Any language that you find on the Internet must be carefully cited, even if the material is in the public domain or is publicly accessible on free sites. When you use material from Web sites sponsored by governments (.gc.ca or .gov sites) or by nonprofit organizations (.org sites), you must acknowledge that material, too, as intellectual property owned by those agencies.

KEEP TRACK OF WHICH WORDS COME FROM SOURCES AND WHICH ARE YOUR OWN.   To prevent unintentional plagiarism when you copy and paste passages from Web sources to an electronic file, put quotation marks around any text that you have inserted into your own notes or paper. In addition, during note taking and drafting, you might use highlighting or a different colour font to draw attention to text taken from sources—so that material from articles, Web sites, and other sources stands out unmistakably as someone else's words.

Integrating and citing sources to avoid plagiarism

Source text

What I observed at the "French for the Future" conference would have provided fodder for both the supporters and the critics of immersion French. These teenagers were poised, comfortable, and relatively articulate while engaging in a free-flowing discussion about generosity, charity, taxation, and foreign aid—in French. On the other hand, most of them had clearly learned their French from hearing other English-speaking students, and routinely made mistakes that no native French-speakers would ever make. It was a discussion that was sometimes naïve and sometimes shrewd and sophisticated—like many discussions of public policy by teenagers—being carried on by English-Canadian students from across the country talking to each other in French.

—Graham Fraser, *Sorry, I Don't Speak French: Confronting the Canadian Crisis That Won't Go Away*, p. 185

NOTE: The examples in this chart follow MLA style (see MLA-4). For information on APA and CMS (*Chicago*) styles, see APA-4 and CMS-4.

If you are using an exact sentence from a source, with no changes . . .	→	. . . put quotation marks around the sentence. Use a signal phrase and include a page number in parentheses.
		Fraser writes, "These teenagers were poised, comfortable, and relatively articulate" (185).
If you are using a few exact words from the source but not an entire sentence . . .	→	. . . put quotation marks around the exact words that you have used from the source. Use a signal phrase and include a page number in parentheses.
		The teenagers' conversations were, according to Fraser, "sometimes shrewd and sophisticated" (185).
If you are using near-exact words from the source but changing some word forms (*I* to *she*, *walk* to *walked*) or adding words to clarify and make the quotation flow with your own text . . .	→	. . . put quotation marks around the quoted words, and put brackets around your changes. Use a signal phrase and follow the quotation with the page number in parentheses.
		Fraser is impressed that the students can "engag[e] in a free-flowing discussion about generosity, charity, taxation, and foreign aid—in French" (185).

Fraser writes that "most of the teenagers were poised, comfortable, and relatively articulate" (185).

If you are paraphrasing or summarizing the source, using the author's ideas but not any of the author's exact words . . .	→ . . . introduce the ideas with a signal phrase and put the page number at the end of your sentence. Do not use quotation marks. (See MLA-2, APA-2, and CMS-2.)

Fraser notes that English-speaking students do make errors when speaking French but is pleased to hear these students having serious discussions in French (185).

If you have used the source's sentence structure but substituted a few synonyms for the author's words . . .	→ STOP! This is a form of plagiarism even if you use a signal phrase and a page number. Change your sentence by using one of the techniques given in this chart or in MLA-3, APA-3, or CMS-3.

PLAGIARIZED

Fraser claims that the students were confident, at ease, and fairly fluent while having a discussion in French.

INTEGRATED AND CITED CORRECTLY

Fraser claims that the "teenagers were poised, comfortable, and relatively articulate while engaging in a free-flowing discussion . . . in French" (185).

AVOID WEB SITES THAT BILL THEMSELVES AS "RESEARCH SERVICES" AND SELL ESSAYS. When you use Web search engines to research a topic, you will often see links to sites that appear to offer legitimate writing support but that actually sell university and college essays. Of course, submitting a paper that you have purchased is cheating, but even using material from such a paper is considered plagiarism.

For more on avoiding plagiarism while working with sources, see MLA-2, APA-2, or CMS-2.

≣ R4 Choosing a documentation style

The various academic disciplines use their own style for citing sources and for listing the works that are cited in a paper. *A Canadian Writer's Reference* describes three commonly used styles: MLA (Modern Language Association), APA (American Psychological Association), and CMS (*Chicago Manual of Style*). See the appropriate tabbed section for details about each style.

NOTE: For a list of style manuals in a variety of disciplines, visit *Research and Documentation Online* at hackerhandbooks.com/resdoc.

R4-a Select a style appropriate for your discipline.

In researched writing, sources are cited for several reasons. First, it is important to acknowledge the contributions of others. If you fail to credit sources properly, you commit plagiarism, a serious academic offence. Second, by choosing appropriate sources, you will add credibility to your work; in a sense, you are calling on authorities to serve as expert witnesses. The more care you have taken in choosing reliable sources, the stronger your argument will be. Finally—and most importantly—you are engaging in a scholarly conversation: When you cite your sources, you show readers where they can pursue your topic in greater depth.

All of the academic disciplines cite sources for these same reasons. However, the different styles for citing sources are based on the values and intellectual goals of scholars in different disciplines.

MLA and APA in-text citations

MLA style and APA style both use citations in the text of a paper that refer to a list of works at the end of the paper. The systems work somewhat differently, however, because MLA style was created for scholars in English composition and literature and APA style was created for researchers in the social sciences.

MLA IN-TEXT CITATION

Brandon Conran argues that the story is written from "a bifocal point of view" (111).

APA IN-TEXT CITATION

As researchers Yanovski and Yanovski (2002) have explained, obesity was once considered "either a moral failing or evidence of underlying psychopathology" (p. 592).

While MLA and APA styles work in a similar way, some basic disciplinary differences show up in these key elements:

- author's name
- date of publication
- page numbers
- verb tense in signal phrases

MLA style gives the author's full name when it is first mentioned. This approach emphasizes authorship and interpretation. APA style, which uses only the last names of authors, gives a date after the author's name. This approach reflects the social scientist's concern with the currency of research. MLA style places the date in the works cited list but omits it in the text. While currency is important, what someone had to say a century ago may be as significant as the latest contribution to the field.

Both styles include page numbers for quotations. MLA style requires page numbers for summaries and paraphrases as well; with a page number, readers can easily find the original passage that has been summarized or paraphrased. While APA does not require page numbers for summaries and paraphrases, it recommends that writers use a page number if doing so would help readers find the passage in a longer work.

Finally, MLA style uses the present tense (such as *argues*) to introduce cited material, whereas APA style uses the past or present perfect tense (such as *argued* or *have argued*) in signal phrases. The present tense evokes the timelessness of a literary text; the past or present perfect tense emphasizes that research or experimentation occurred in the past.

CMS footnotes or endnotes

Most historians and many scholars in the humanities use the style of footnotes or endnotes recommended by *The Chicago Manual of Style* (CMS). Historians base their work on a wide variety of primary and secondary sources, all of which must be cited. The CMS note system has the virtue of being relatively unobtrusive; even when a paper or an article is thick with citations, readers will not be overwhelmed. In the text of the paper, only a raised number appears. Readers who are interested can consult the accompanying numbered note, which is given either at the foot of the page or at the end of the paper.

TEXT

Historian Albert Castel quotes several eyewitnesses on both the Union and the Confederate sides as saying that Forrest ordered his men to stop firing.[7]

NOTE

7. Albert Castel, "The Fort Pillow Massacre: A Fresh Examination of the Evidence," *Civil War History* 4, no. 1 (1958): 44-45.

The CMS system gives as much information as the MLA or APA system, but less of that information appears in the text of the paper.

MLA

MLA Papers

MLA MLA Papers

MLA | 369 – 440

Directory to MLA in-text citation models

Directory to MLA works cited models

→

Directory to MLA works cited models (continued)

BOOKS (PRINT) (continued)

29. Foreword, introduction, preface, or afterword, 409
30. Book with a title in its title, 411
31. Book in a series, 411
32. Republished book, 411
33. Publisher's imprint, 411

ONLINE SOURCES

34. Entire Web site, 412
35. Short work from a Web site, 413
36. Web site with an author using a pseudonym, 413
37. Article in an online journal, 413
38. Article in an online magazine, 415
39. Article in an online newspaper, 415
40. Work from a database, 415
41. Online book-length work, 417
42. Part of an online book, 417
43. Digital archives, 417
44. Entry in an online reference work, 418
45. Online poem, 418
46. Entire blog (Weblog), 418
47. Entry or comment in a blog (Weblog), 418
48. Academic course or department home page, 418
49. Online video clip, 419
50. Online abstract, 419
51. Online editorial or letter to the editor, 419
52. Online review, 419
53. E-mail message, 419
54. Posting to an online discussion list, 420
55. Entry in a wiki, 420

AUDIO AND VISUAL SOURCES (INCLUDING ONLINE VERSIONS)

56. Digital file, 420
57. Podcast, 421
58. Musical score, 421
59. Sound recording, 421
60. Film, 421
61. DVD, 422
62. Special feature on a DVD, 422
63. CD-ROM, 422
64. Computer software or video game, 422
65. Radio or television program, 422
66. Radio or television interview, 423
67. Live performance, 423
68. Lecture or public address, 423
69. Work of art, 423
70. Cartoon, 424
71. Advertisement, 424
72. Map or chart, 424

OTHER SOURCES (INCLUDING ONLINE VERSIONS)

73. Government document, 424
74. Historical document, 425
75. Legal source, 425
76. Pamphlet or brochure, 426
77. Unpublished dissertation, 426
78. Published dissertation, 426
79. Abstract of a dissertation, 426
80. Published proceedings of a conference, 427
81. Paper in conference proceedings, 427
82. Published interview, 427
83. Personal interview, 427
84. Personal letter, 427
85. Published letter, 428
86. Manuscript, 428

MLA Papers

Most English instructors and some humanities instructors will ask you to document your sources with the Modern Language Association (MLA) system of citations described in MLA-4. When writing an MLA paper that is based on sources, you face three main challenges: (1) supporting a thesis, (2) citing your sources and avoiding plagiarism, and (3) integrating quotations and other source material.

Examples in this tabbed section are drawn from a student's research about online monitoring of employees' computer use. Anna Orlov's research paper, in which she argues that electronic surveillance in the workplace threatens employees' privacy, appears on pages 436–40. (See highlights of Anna Orlov's research process on pp. 432–35.)

MLA-1 Supporting a thesis

Most research assignments ask you to form a thesis, or main idea, and to support that thesis with well-organized evidence.

MLA-1a Form a working thesis.

Once you have read a variety of sources and considered your issue from different perspectives, you are ready to form a working thesis: a one-sentence (or occasionally a two-sentence) statement of your central idea (see also C2-a). Because it is a working, or tentative, thesis, you can remain flexible and revise it as your ideas develop. In a research paper, your thesis will answer the central research question you pose (see R1-a). Here, for example, are Anna Orlov's research question and working thesis.

RESEARCH QUESTION

Should employers monitor their employees' online activities in the workplace?

WORKING THESIS

Employers should not monitor their employees' online activities because electronic surveillance can compromise workers' privacy.

After you have written a rough draft and perhaps done more reading, you may decide to revise your thesis, as Orlov did.

REVISED THESIS

Although companies often have legitimate concerns that lead them to monitor employees' Internet usage—from expensive security breaches to reduced productivity—the benefits of electronic surveillance are outweighed by its costs to employees' privacy and autonomy.

The thesis usually appears at the end of the introductory paragraph. To read Anna Orlov's thesis in the context of her introduction, see page 436.

PRACTICE **hackerhandbooks.com/writersref**
> MLA > MLA 1–1

MLA-1b Organize ideas with a rough outline.

The body of your paper will consist of evidence in support of your thesis. Instead of getting tangled up in a formal outline early in the process, sketch an informal plan that organizes your ideas in bold strokes. Anna Orlov, for example, used this simple plan to outline the structure of her argument:

- Compared with older types of surveillance, electronic surveillance allows employers to monitor workers more efficiently.
- Some experts argue that companies have important financial and legal reasons to monitor employees' Internet usage.
- But monitoring employees' Internet usage may lower worker productivity when the threat to privacy creates distrust.
- Current laws do little to protect employees' privacy rights, so employees and employers have to negotiate the potential risks and benefits of electronic surveillance.

After you have written a rough draft, a more formal outline can be a useful way to shape the complexities of your argument. See C1-d for an example.

> **Making the most of your handbook**
>
> It's helpful to start off with a working thesis and a rough outline— especially when writing from sources.
>
> ▶ Drafting a working thesis: C1-c
>
> ▶ Sketching a plan: C1-d

MLA-1c Use sources to inform and support your argument.

Used thoughtfully, the source materials you have gathered will make your argument more complex and convincing for readers. Sources can play several different roles as you develop your points.

Providing background information or context

You can use facts and statistics to support generalizations or to emphasize the importance of your topic, as student writer Anna Orlov does in her introduction.

As the Internet has become an integral tool of businesses, company policies on Internet usage have become as common as policies regarding vacation days or sexual harassment. A 2005 study by the American Management Association and ePolicy Institute found that 76% of companies monitor employees' use of the Web, and the number of companies that block employees' access to certain Web sites has increased 27% since 2001 (1).

Explaining terms or concepts

If readers are unlikely to be familiar with words or ideas important to your topic, you must explain them. Quoting or paraphrasing a source can help you define terms and concepts in accessible language.

> One popular monitoring method is keystroke logging, which is done by means of an undetectable program on employees' computers. . . . As Lane explains, these programs record every key entered into the computer in hidden directories that can later be accessed or uploaded by supervisors; the programs can even scan for keywords tailored to individual companies (128-29).

Supporting your claims

As you draft your argument, make sure to back up your assertions with facts, examples, and other evidence from your research. (See also A2-e.) Orlov, for example, uses an anecdote from one of her sources to support her claim that limiting computer access causes resentment among a company's staff.

> Monitoring online activities can have the unintended effect of making employees resentful. . . . Kesan warns that "prohibiting personal use can seem extremely arbitrary and can seriously harm morale. . . . Imagine a concerned parent who is prohibited from checking on a sick child by a draconian company policy" (315-16). As this analysis indicates, employees can become disgruntled when Internet usage policies are enforced to their full extent.

Lending authority to your argument

Expert opinion can give weight to your argument. (See also A2-e.) But don't rely on experts to make your argument for you. Construct your argument in your own words and, when appropriate, cite the judgment of an authority in the field to support your position.

> Additionally, many experts disagree with employers' assumption that online monitoring can increase productivity. Employment law attorney Joseph Schmitt argues that, particularly for employees who are paid a salary rather than an hourly wage, "a company shouldn't care whether employees spend one or 10 hours on the Internet as long as they are getting their jobs done—and provided that they are not accessing inappropriate sites" (qtd. in Verespej).

Anticipating and countering objections

Do not ignore sources that seem contrary to your position or that offer arguments different from your own. Instead, use them to give voice to opposing points of view and to state potential objections to your argument before you counter them (see A-2f). Anna Orlov, for example, cites conflicting evidence to acknowledge that some readers may feel that unlimited Internet access in the workplace hinders productivity. In doing so, she creates an opportunity to counter that objection and persuade those readers.

> On the one hand, computers and Internet access give employees powerful tools to carry out their jobs; on the other hand, the same technology offers constant temptations to avoid work. As a 2005 study by *Salary.com* and *America Online* indicates, the Internet ranked as the top choice among employees for ways of wasting time on the job; it beat talking with co-workers—the second most popular method—by a margin of nearly two to one (Frauenheim).

≡ MLA-2 Citing sources; avoiding plagiarism

Your research paper is a collaboration between you and your sources. To be fair and ethical, you must acknowledge your debt to the writers of those sources. If you don't, you commit plagiarism, a serious academic offence.

In general, these three acts are considered plagiarism: (1) failing to cite quotations and borrowed ideas, (2) failing to enclose borrowed language in quotation marks, and (3) failing to put summaries and paraphrases in your own words. Definitions of plagiarism may vary; it's a good idea to find out how your school defines academic dishonesty.

MLA-2a Cite quotations and borrowed ideas.

Sources are cited for two reasons:

1. to tell readers where your information comes from — so that they can assess its reliability and, if interested, find and read the original source

2. to give credit to the writers from whom you have borrowed words and ideas

**Making the most
of your handbook**

When you use exact language from a source, you need to show that it is a quotation.

▶ Quotation marks for direct quotations: **P5-a**

You must cite anything you borrow from a source, including direct quotations; statistics and other specific facts; visuals such as cartoons, graphs, and diagrams; and any ideas you present in a summary or paraphrase.

The only exception is common knowledge—information your readers could easily find in any number of general sources. For example, most encyclopedias will tell readers that Alfred Hitchcock directed *Notorious* in 1946 and that Emily Dickinson published only a handful of her many poems during her lifetime.

As a rule, when you have seen information repeatedly in your reading, you don't need to cite it. However, when information has appeared in only one or two sources, when it is highly specific (as with statistics), or when it is controversial, you should cite the source. If a topic is new to you and you are not sure what is considered common knowledge or what is controversial, ask your instructor or someone else with expertise. When in doubt, cite the source.

The Modern Language Association recommends a system of in-text citations. Here, briefly, is how the MLA citation system usually works:

1. The source is introduced by a signal phrase that names its author.
2. The material being cited is followed by a page number in parentheses.
3. At the end of the paper, a list of works cited (arranged alphabetically by authors' last names) gives complete publication information about the source.

IN-TEXT CITATION

Legal scholar Jay Kesan points out that the law holds employers liable for employees' actions such as violations of copyright laws, the distribution of offensive or graphic sexual material, and illegal disclosure of confidential information (312).

ENTRY IN THE LIST OF WORKS CITED

Kesan, Jay P. "Cyber-Working or Cyber-Shirking? A First Principles Examination of Electronic Privacy in the Workplace." *Florida Law Review* 54.2 (2002): 289-332. Print.

This basic MLA format varies for different types of sources. For a detailed discussion of other models, see MLA-4.

MLA-2b Enclose borrowed language in quotation marks.

To indicate that you are using a source's exact phrases or sentences, you must enclose them in quotation marks unless they have been set off from the text by indenting (see p. 381). To omit the quotation marks is to claim—falsely—that the language is your own. Such an omission is plagiarism even if you have cited the source.

ORIGINAL SOURCE

Without adequate discipline, the World Wide Web can be a tremendous time sink; no other medium comes close to matching the Internet's depth of materials, interactivity, and sheer distractive potential.

— Frederick Lane, *The Naked Employee*, p. 142

PLAGIARISM

Frederick Lane points out that if people do not have adequate discipline, the World Wide Web can be a tremendous time sink; no other medium comes close to matching the Internet's depth of materials, interactivity, and sheer distractive potential (142).

BORROWED LANGUAGE IN QUOTATION MARKS

Frederick Lane points out that for those not exercising self-control, "the World Wide Web can be a tremendous time sink; no other medium comes close to matching the Internet's depth of materials, interactivity, and sheer distractive potential" (142).

MLA-2c Put summaries and paraphrases in your own words.

A summary condenses information from a source; a paraphrase conveys the information by using roughly the same number of words as the original source. When you summarize or paraphrase, it is not enough to name the source; you must restate the source's meaning using your own language. (See also R3-c.) You commit plagiarism if you half-copy the author's sentences—either by mixing the author's phrases with your own without using quotation marks or by plugging your synonyms into the author's sentence structure.

The first paraphrase of the following source is plagiarized—even though the source is cited—because too much of its language is borrowed from the original. The underlined strings of words have been copied exactly (without quotation marks). In addition, the writer has closely echoed the sentence structure of the source, merely substituting some synonyms (*restricted* for *limited*, *modern era* for *computer age*, *monitoring* for *surveillance*, and *inexpensive* for *cheap*).

ORIGINAL SOURCE

In earlier times, surveillance was limited to the information that a supervisor could observe and record firsthand and to primitive counting devices. In the computer age surveillance can be instantaneous, unblinking, cheap, and, maybe most importantly, easy.
> — Carl Botan and Mihaela Vorvoreanu, "What Do Employees Think about Electronic Surveillance at Work?" p. 126

PLAGIARISM: UNACCEPTABLE BORROWING

Scholars Carl Botan and Mihaela Vorvoreanu argue that in earlier times monitoring of employees was restricted to the information that a supervisor could observe and record firsthand. In the modern era, monitoring can be instantaneous, inexpensive, and, most importantly, easy (126).

To avoid plagiarizing an author's language, resist the temptation to look at the source while you are summarizing or paraphrasing. After you have read the original passage, set the source aside. Ask yourself, "What is the author's meaning?" In your own words, state the author's basic point. Return to the source and check that you haven't used the author's language or sentence structure or misrepresented the author's ideas. When you fully understand another writer's meaning, you can more easily and accurately present those ideas in your own words.

ACCEPTABLE PARAPHRASE

Scholars Carl Botan and Mihaela Vorvoreanu claim that the nature of workplace surveillance has changed over time. Before the arrival of computers, managers could collect only small amounts of information about their employees based on what they saw or heard. Now, because computers are standard workplace technology, employers can monitor employees efficiently (126).

MLA-3 Integrating sources

Quotations, summaries, paraphrases, and facts will help you develop your argument, but they cannot speak for you. You can use several strategies to integrate information from research sources into your paper while maintaining your own voice.

MLA-3a Use quotations appropriately.

Limiting your use of quotations

Although it is tempting to insert many quotations in your paper and to use your own words only for connecting passages, do not quote excessively. In your academic writing, keep the emphasis on your ideas; use your own words to summarize and to paraphrase your sources and to explain your points. Sometimes, however, quotations can be the most effective way to integrate a source's ideas.

WHEN TO USE QUOTATIONS

- When language is especially vivid or expressive
- When exact wording is needed for technical accuracy
- When it is important to let the debaters of an issue explain their positions in their own words
- When the words of an authority lend weight to an argument
- When the language of a source is the topic of your discussion (as in an analysis or interpretation)

It is not always necessary to quote full sentences from a source. To reduce your reliance on the words of others, you can often integrate language from a source into your own sentence structure. (For the use of signal phrases in integrating quotations, see MLA-3b.)

> Kizza and Ssanyu observe that technology in the workplace has been accompanied by "an array of problems that needed quick answers" such as electronic monitoring to prevent security breaches (4).

Using the ellipsis mark and brackets

Two useful marks of punctuation, the ellipsis mark and brackets, allow you to keep quoted material to a minimum and to integrate it smoothly into your text.

The ellipsis mark To condense a quoted passage, you can use the ellipsis mark (three periods, with spaces between) to indicate that you have left words out. What remains must be grammatically complete.

> Lane acknowledges the legitimate reasons that many companies have for monitoring their employees' online activities, particularly management's concern about preventing "the theft of information that can be downloaded to a . . . disk, e-mailed to oneself . . . , or even posted to a Web page for the entire world to see" (12).

The writer has omitted from the source the words *floppy or Zip* before *disk* and *or a confederate* after *oneself.*

On the rare occasions when you want to leave out one or more full sentences, use a period before the three ellipsis dots.

> Charles Lewis, director of the Center for Public Integrity, points out that "by 1987, employers were administering nearly 2,000,000 polygraph tests a year to job applicants and employees. . . . Millions of workers were required to produce urine samples under observation for drug testing . . ." (22).

Ordinarily, do not use an ellipsis mark at the beginning or at the end of a quotation. Your readers will understand that the quoted material is taken from a longer passage, so such marks are not necessary. The only exception occurs when you have dropped words at the end of the final quoted sentence. In such cases, put three ellipsis dots before the closing quotation mark and parenthetical reference, as in the previous example.

Make sure omissions and ellipsis marks do not distort the meaning of your source.

Brackets   Brackets allow you to insert your own words into quoted material. You can insert words in brackets to clarify a confusing reference or to keep a sentence grammatical in your context. You also use brackets to indicate that you are changing a letter from capital to lowercase (or vice versa) to fit into your sentence.

> Legal scholar Jay Kesan notes that "[a] decade ago, losses [from employees' computer crimes] were already mounting to five billion dollars annually" (311).

This quotation began *A decade ago . . .* in the source, so the writer indicated the change to lowercase with brackets and inserted words in brackets to clarify the meaning of *losses.*

To indicate an error such as a misspelling in a quotation, insert [sic], including the brackets, right after the error.

> Johnson argues that "while online monitoring is often imagined as harmles [sic], the practice may well threaten employees' rights to privacy" (14).

Setting off long quotations

When you quote more than four typed lines of prose or more than three lines of poetry, set off the quotation by indenting it one inch (2.5 cm) from the left margin.

Long quotations should be introduced by an informative sentence, usually followed by a colon. Quotation marks are unnecessary because the indented format tells readers that the passage is taken word-for-word from the source.

> Botan and Vorvoreanu examine the role of gender in company practices of electronic surveillance:
>
>> There has never been accurate documentation of the extent of gender differences in surveillance, but by the middle 1990s, estimates of the proportion of surveilled employees that were women ranged from 75% to 85%. . . . Ironically, this gender imbalance in workplace surveillance may be evening out today because advances in surveillance technology are making surveillance of traditionally male dominated fields, such as long-distance truck driving, cheap, easy, and frequently unobtrusive. (127)

Notice that at the end of an indented quotation the parenthetical citation goes outside the final mark of punctuation. (When a quotation is run into your text, the opposite is true. See the sample citations on p. 380.)

MLA-3b Use signal phrases to integrate sources.

Whenever you include a paraphrase, summary, or direct quotation of another writer in your paper, prepare your readers for it with a *signal phrase*. A signal phrase usually names the author of the source and often provides some context. It commonly appears before the source material. To vary your sentence structure, you may decide to interrupt source material with a signal phrase or place the signal phrase after your paraphrase, summary, or direct quotation.

When you write a signal phrase, choose a verb that is appropriate for the way you are using the source (see MLA-1c). Are you providing background, explaining a concept, supporting a claim, lending authority, or refuting a belief? See the chart on page 383 for a list of verbs commonly used in signal phrases. Note that MLA style calls for verbs in the present or present perfect tense (*argues* or *has argued*) to introduce source material unless you include a date that specifies the time of the original author's writing.

Marking boundaries

Readers need to move from your words to the words of a source without feeling a jolt. Avoid dropping quotations into the text without warning. Instead, provide clear signal phrases, including at least the author's name, to indicate the boundary between your words and the source's words. (The signal phrase is highlighted in the second example.)

Using signal phrases in MLA papers

To avoid monotony, try to vary both the language and the placement of your signal phrases.

Model signal phrases

In the words of researchers Greenfield and Davis, ". . ."

As legal scholar Jay Kesan has noted, ". . ."

The ePolicy Institute, an organization that advises companies about reducing risks from technology, reports that ". . ."

". . .," writes Daniel Tynan, ". . ."

". . .," attorney Schmitt claims.

Kizza and Ssanyu offer a persuasive counterargument: ". . ."

Verbs in signal phrases

acknowledges	comments	endorses	reasons
adds	compares	grants	refutes
admits	confirms	illustrates	rejects
agrees	contends	implies	reports
argues	declares	insists	responds
asserts	denies	notes	suggests
believes	disputes	observes	thinks
claims	emphasizes	points out	writes

DROPPED QUOTATION

Some experts have argued that a range of legitimate concerns justifies employer monitoring of employee Internet usage. "Employees could accidentally (or deliberately) spill confidential corporate information . . . or allow worms to spread throughout a corporate network" (Tynan).

QUOTATION WITH SIGNAL PHRASE

Some experts have argued that a range of legitimate concerns justifies employer monitoring of employee Internet usage. As *PC World* columnist Daniel Tynan points out, "Employees could accidentally (or deliberately) spill confidential corporate information . . . or allow worms to spread throughout a corporate network."

Establishing authority

Good research writing uses evidence from reliable sources. The first time you mention a source, include in the signal phrase the author's title, credentials, or experience — anything that would help your readers recognize the source's authority. (Signal phrases are highlighted in the next two examples.)

SOURCE WITH NO CREDENTIALS

Jay Kesan points out that the law holds employers liable for employees' actions such as violations of copyright laws, the distribution of offensive or graphic sexual material, and illegal disclosure of confidential information (312).

SOURCE WITH CREDENTIALS

Legal scholar Jay Kesan points out that the law holds employers liable for employees' actions such as violations of copyright laws, the distribution of offensive or graphic sexual material, and illegal disclosure of confidential information (312).

When you establish your source's authority, as with the phrase *Legal scholar* in the previous example, you also signal to readers your own credibility as a responsible researcher who has located trustworthy sources.

Introducing summaries and paraphrases

Introduce most summaries and paraphrases with a signal phrase that names the author and places the material in the context of your argument. Readers will then understand that everything between the signal phrase and the parenthetical citation summarizes or paraphrases the cited source.

Without the signal phrase (highlighted) in the following example, readers might think that only the quotation at the end is being cited, when in fact the whole paragraph is based on the source.

Frederick Lane believes that the personal computer has posed new challenges for employers worried about workplace productivity. Whereas early desktop computers were primitive enough to prevent employees from using them to waste time, the machines have become so sophisticated that they now make non-work-related computer activities easy and inviting. Many employees spend considerable company time customizing features and playing games on their computers. But perhaps most problematic from the employer's point of view, Lane asserts, is giving employees access to the Internet, "roughly the equivalent of installing a gazillion-channel television set for each employee" (15-16).

There are times when a summary or a paraphrase does not require a signal phrase naming the author. When the context makes clear where the cited material begins, you may omit the signal phrase and include the author's last name in parentheses.

Integrating statistics and other facts

When you are citing a statistic or another specific fact, a signal phrase is often not necessary. In most cases, readers will understand that the citation refers to the statistic or fact (not the whole paragraph).

> Roughly 60% of responding companies reported disciplining employees who had used the Internet in ways the companies deemed inappropriate; 30% had fired their employees for those transgressions (Greenfield and Davis 347).

There is nothing wrong, however, with using a signal phrase to introduce a statistic or another fact.

Putting source material in context

Readers should not have to guess why source material appears in your paper. A signal phrase can help you connect your own ideas and those of another writer by clarifying how the source will contribute to your paper (see R2-a).

If you use another writer's words, you must explain how they relate to your point. In other words, you must put the source in context. It's a good idea to embed a quotation between sentences of your own. In addition to introducing it with a signal phrase, follow it with interpretive comments that link the quotation to your paper's argument (see also MLA-3c).

QUOTATION WITH EFFECTIVE CONTEXT

The difference, Lane argues, between old methods of data gathering and electronic surveillance involves quantity:

> Technology makes it possible for employers to gather enormous amounts of data about employees, often far beyond what is necessary to satisfy safety or productivity concerns. And the trends that drive technology—faster, smaller, cheaper—make it possible for larger and larger numbers of employers to gather ever-greater amounts of personal data. (3-4)

In an age when employers can collect data whenever employees use their computers—when they send e-mail, surf the Web, or even arrive at or depart from their workstations—the challenge for both employers and employees is to determine how much is too much.

MLA-3c Synthesize sources.

When you synthesize multiple sources in a research paper, you create a conversation about your research topic. You show readers that your argument is based on your active analysis and integration of ideas, not just a list of quotations and paraphrases. Your synthesis will show how your sources relate to one another; one source may support, extend, or counter the ideas of another. Readers should be able to see how each source functions in your argument (see R2-a).

Considering how sources relate to your argument

Before you integrate sources and show readers how they relate to one another, consider how each one might contribute to your own argument. As student writer Anna Orlov became more informed about Internet surveillance in the workplace, she asked herself these questions: *What do I think about monitoring employees online? Which sources might extend or illustrate the points I want to make? Which sources voice opposing points of view that I need to address?* With these questions in mind, Orlov read and annotated sources, including an argument in favour of workplace surveillance. (See the example on p. 434.)

Placing sources in conversation

When you synthesize sources, you show readers how the ideas of one source relate to those of another by connecting and analyzing the ideas in the context of your argument. Keep the emphasis on your own writing. After all, you've done the research and thought through the issues, so you should control the conversation. The thread of your argument should be easy to identify and to understand, with or without your sources.

SAMPLE SYNTHESIS (DRAFT)

Student writer Anna Orlov begins with a claim that needs support. → Productivity is not easily measured in the wired workplace. As a result, employers find it difficult to determine how much freedom to allow their employees. On the one hand, computers and Internet access give employees powerful tools to carry out their jobs; on the other hand, the same technology offers constant

Signal phrases indicate how sources contribute to Orlov's paper and show that the ideas that follow are not her own. → temptations to avoid work. As a 2005 study by *Salary.com* and *America Online* indicates, the Internet ranked as the top choice among employees for ways of wasting time on the job (Frauenheim). Chris Gonsalves, an editor for

Student writer

Source 1

Source 2

eWeek.com, argues that technology has changed the terms
between employers and employees: "While bosses can
easily detect and interrupt water-cooler chatter," he
writes, "the employee who is shopping at Lands' End or
IMing with fellow fantasy baseball managers may actually
appear to be working." The gap between observable
behaviors and actual online activities has motivated some
employers to invest in surveillance programs.

Student writer

rlov presents a
ounterposition
> extend her
rgument.

Many experts, however, disagree with employers'
assumption that online monitoring can increase productivity.
Employment law attorney Joseph Schmitt argues that, particularly for salaried employees, "a company shouldn't care
whether employees spend one or 10 hours on the Internet
as long as they are getting their jobs done—and provided
that they are not accessing inappropriate sites" (qtd. in
Verespej). Other experts even argue that time spent on
personal Internet browsing can actually be productive
for companies. According to Bill Coleman, an executive at
Salary.com, "Personal Internet use and casual office conversations often turn into new business ideas or suggestions
for gaining operating efficiencies" (qtd. in Frauenheim).
Employers, in other words, may benefit from showing more
faith in their employees' ability to exercise their autonomy.

Source 3

Student writer

Source 4

Student writer

rlov builds her
ase—each
uoted passage
ffers a more
etailed claim
r example in
upport of her
rger claim.

In this draft, Orlov uses her own analyses to shape the conversation among her sources. She does not simply string quotations together
or allow her sources to overwhelm her writing. The final sentence, written in her own voice, gives her an opportunity to explain to readers how
the various sources support her argument.

When synthesizing sources, ask yourself the following questions:

- Which sources inform, support, or extend your argument?
- Have you varied the function of sources—to provide background, to explain concepts, to lend authority, and to anticipate
  counterarguments? Do you use signal phrases to indicate these
  functions?
- Do you explain how your sources support your argument?
- Do you connect and analyze sources in your own voice?
- Is your own argument easy to identify and to understand, with
  or without your sources?

Reviewing an MLA paper: Use of sources

Use of quotations

- Is quoted material enclosed in quotation marks (unless it has been set off from the text)? (See MLA-2b.)
- Is quoted language word-for-word accurate? If not, do brackets or ellipsis marks indicate the changes or omissions? (See pp. 380–81.)
- Does a clear signal phrase (usually naming the author) prepare readers for each quotation and for the purpose the quotation serves? (See MLA-3b.)
- Does a parenthetical citation follow each quotation? (See MLA-4a.)
- Is each quotation put in context? (See MLA-3c.)

Use of summaries and paraphrases

- Are summaries and paraphrases free of plagiarized wording—not copied or half-copied from the source? (See MLA-2c.)
- Are summaries and paraphrases documented with parenthetical citations? (See MLA-4a.)
- Do readers know where the cited material begins? In other words, does a signal phrase mark the boundary between your words and the summary or paraphrase? Or does the context alone make clear exactly what you are citing? (See MLA-3b.)
- Does a signal phrase prepare readers for the purpose the summary or paraphrase has in your argument?

Use of statistics and other facts

- Are statistics and facts (other than common knowledge) documented with parenthetical citations? (See MLA-2a.)
- If there is no signal phrase, will readers understand exactly which facts are being cited? (See MLA-3b.)

≡ MLA-4 Documenting sources

In English and other humanities classes, you may be asked to use the MLA (Modern Language Association) system for documenting sources, which is set forth in the *MLA Handbook for Writers of Research Papers,* 7th ed. (New York: MLA, 2009).

MLA recommends in-text citations that refer readers to a list of works cited. A typical in-text citation names the author of the source, often in a signal phrase, and gives a page number in parentheses. At the end of the paper, a list of works cited provides publication information about the source; the list is alphabetized by authors' last names (or by titles for works without authors). There is a direct connection between the in-text citation and the alphabetized listing. In the following example, that connection is highlighted in orange.

IN-TEXT CITATION

Jay Kesan notes that even though many companies now routinely monitor employees through electronic means, "there may exist less intrusive safeguards for employers" (293).

ENTRY IN THE LIST OF WORKS CITED

Kesan, Jay P. "Cyber-Working or Cyber-Shirking? A First Principles Examination of Electronic Privacy in the Workplace." *Florida Law Review* 54.2 (2002): 289-332. Print.

For a list of works cited that includes this entry, see page 440.

MLA-4a MLA in-text citations

MLA in-text citations are made with a combination of signal phrases and parenthetical references. A signal phrase introduces information taken from a source (a quotation, summary, paraphrase, or fact); usually the signal phrase includes the author's name. The parenthetical reference comes after the cited material, often at the end of the sentence. It includes at least a page number (except for unpaginated sources, such as those found online). In the models in MLA-4a, the elements of the in-text citation are highlighted in orange.

IN-TEXT CITATION

Kwon points out that the Fourth Amendment does not give employees any protections from employers' "unreasonable searches and seizures" (6).

Readers can look up the author's last name in the alphabetized list of works cited, where they will learn the work's title and other publication information. If readers decide to consult the source, the page number will take them straight to the passage that has been cited.

For a directory to the in-text citation models in this section, see page 371, immediately following the tabbed divider.

Basic rules for print and online sources

The MLA system of in-text citations, which depends heavily on authors' names and page numbers, was created with print sources in mind. Although many online sources have unclear authorship and lack page numbers, the basic rules are the same for both print and online sources.

The models in this section (items 1–5) show how the MLA system usually works and explain what to do if your source has no author or page numbers.

1. Author named in a signal phrase Ordinarily, introduce the material being cited with a signal phrase that includes the author's name. In addition to preparing readers for the source, the signal phrase allows you to keep the parenthetical citation brief.

> Frederick Lane reports that employers do not necessarily have to use software to monitor how their employees use the Web: employers can "use a hidden video camera pointed at an employee's monitor" and even position a camera "so that a number of monitors [can] be viewed at the same time" (147).

The signal phrase—*Frederick Lane reports*—names the author; the parenthetical citation gives the page number of the book in which the quoted words may be found.

Notice that the period follows the parenthetical citation. When a quotation ends with a question mark or an exclamation point, leave the end punctuation inside the quotation mark and add a period at the end of your sentence. (See also the note on p. 284.)

> O'Connor asks a critical question: "When does Internet surveillance cross the line between corporate responsibility and invasion of privacy?" (16).

2. Author named in parentheses If a signal phrase does not name the author, put the author's last name in parentheses along with the page number. Use no punctuation between the name and the page number.

> Companies can monitor employees' every keystroke without legal penalty, but they may have to combat low morale as a result (Lane 129).

3. Author unknown Either use the complete title in a signal phrase or use a short form of the title in parentheses. Titles of books are italicized; titles of articles are put in quotation marks.

> A popular keystroke logging program operates invisibly on workers' computers yet provides supervisors with details of the workers' online activities ("Automatically").

TIP: Before assuming that a Web source has no author, do some detective work. Often the author's name is available but is not easy to find. For example, it may appear at the end of the page, in tiny print. Or it may appear on another page of the site, such as the home page.

NOTE: If a source has no author and is sponsored by a corporation or government agency, name the corporation or agency as the author (see items 8 and 17 on pp. 392 and 395, respectively).

4. Page number unknown Do not include the page number if a work lacks page numbers, as is the case with many Web sources. Even if a printout from a Web site shows page numbers, treat the source as unpaginated in the in-text citation because not all printouts give the same page numbers. (When the pages of a Web source are stable, as in PDF files, supply a page number in your in-text citation.)

> As a 2005 study by *Salary.com* and *America Online* indicates, the Internet
> ranked as the top choice among employees for ways of wasting time on the
> job; it beat talking with co-workers—the second most popular method—by
> a margin of nearly two to one (Frauenheim).

If a source has numbered paragraphs or sections, use "par." (or "pars.") or "sec." (or "secs.") in the parentheses: (Smith, par. 4). Notice that a comma follows the author's name.

5. One-page source If the source is one page long, MLA allows (but does not require) you to omit the page number. Even so, it's a good idea to supply the page number because without it readers may not know where your citation ends or, worse, may not realize that you have provided a citation at all.

NO PAGE NUMBER IN CITATION

> Anush Yegyazarian reports that in 2000 the National Labor Relations Board's
> Office of the General Counsel helped win restitution for two workers who had
> been dismissed because their employers were displeased by the employees'
> e-mails about work-related issues. The case points to the ongoing struggle to
> define what constitutes protected speech in the workplace.

PAGE NUMBER IN CITATION

> Anush Yegyazarian reports that in 2000 the National Labor Relations Board's
> Office of the General Counsel helped win restitution for two workers who had
> been dismissed because their employers were displeased by the employees'
> e-mails about work-related issues (62). The case points to the ongoing
> struggle to define what constitutes protected speech in the workplace.

Variations on the basic rules

This section describes the MLA guidelines for handling a variety of situations not covered by the basic rules in items 1–5. These rules for in-text citations are the same for both print and online sources.

6. Two or three authors Name the authors in a signal phrase, as in the following example, or include their last names in the parenthetical reference: (Kizza and Ssanyu 2).

> Kizza and Ssanyu note that "employee monitoring is a dependable, capable, and very affordable process of electronically or otherwise recording all employee activities at work" and elsewhere (2).

When three authors are named in the parentheses, separate the names with commas: (Alton, Davies, and Rice 56).

7. Four or more authors Name all of the authors or include only the first author's name followed by "et al." (Latin for "and others"). The format you use should match the format in your works cited entry (see item 3 on p. 399).

> The study was extended for two years, and only after results were reviewed by an independent panel did the researchers publish their findings (Blaine et al. 35).

8. Organization as author When the author is a corporation or an organization, name that author either in the signal phrase or in the parentheses. (For a government agency as author, see item 17 on p. 395.)

> According to a 2001 survey of human resources managers by the American Management Association, more than three-quarters of the responding companies reported disciplining employees for "misuse or personal use of office telecommunications equipment" (2).

In the list of works cited, the American Management Association is treated as the author and alphabetized under *A*. When you give the organization name in parentheses, abbreviate common words in the name: "Assn.," "Dept.," "Natl.," "Soc.," and so on.

> In a 2001 survey of human resources managers, more than three-quarters of the responding companies reported disciplining employees for "misuse or personal use of office telecommunications equipment" (Amer. Management Assn. 2).

9. Authors with the same last name If your list of works cited includes works by two or more authors with the same last name, include the author's first name in the signal phrase or first initial in the parentheses.

> Estimates of the frequency with which employers monitor employees' use of the
> Internet each day vary widely (A. Jones 15).

10. Two or more works by the same author Mention the title of the work in the signal phrase or include a short version of the title in the parentheses.

> The American Management Association and ePolicy Institute have tracked
> employers' practices in monitoring employees' e-mail use. The groups' 2003
> survey found that one-third of companies had a policy of keeping and reviewing
> employees' e-mail messages ("2003 E-mail" 2); in 2005, more than 55% of
> companies engaged in e-mail monitoring ("2005 Electronic" 1).

Titles of articles and other short works are placed in quotation marks; titles of books are italicized.

In the rare case when both the author's name and a short title must be given in parentheses, separate them with a comma.

> A 2004 survey found that 20% of employers responding had employees' e-mail
> "subpoenaed in the course of a lawsuit or regulatory investigation," up 7%
> from the previous year (Amer. Management Assn. and ePolicy Inst., "2004
> Workplace" 1).

11. Two or more works in one citation To cite more than one source in the parentheses, give the citations in alphabetical order and separate them with a semicolon.

> Several researchers have analyzed the reasons that companies monitor
> employees' use of the Internet at work (Botan and Vorvoreanu 128-29; Kesan
> 317-19; Kizza and Ssanyu 3-7).

Multiple citations can be distracting, so you should not overuse the technique. If you want to point to several sources that discuss a particular topic, consider using an information note instead (see MLA-4c).

12. Repeated citations from the same source When your paper is about a single work of fiction or nonfiction (such as an essay), you do not need to include the author's name each time you quote from or paraphrase the work. After you mention the author's name at the beginning of your paper, you may include just the page numbers in your parenthetical citations.

> In Susan Glaspell's short story "A Jury of Her Peers," two women accompany their husbands and a county attorney to an isolated house where a farmer named John Wright has been choked to death in his bed with a rope. The chief suspect is Wright's wife, Minnie, who is in jail awaiting trial. The sheriff's wife, Mrs. Peters, has come along to gather some personal items for Minnie, and Mrs. Hale has joined her. Early in the story, Mrs. Hale sympathizes with Minnie and objects to the way the male investigators are "snoopin' round and criticizin'" her kitchen (191). In contrast, Mrs. Peters shows respect for the law, saying that the men are doing "no more than their duty" (191).

In a paper with multiple sources, if you are citing a source more than once in a paragraph, you may omit the author's name after the first mention in the paragraph as long as it is clear that you are still referring to the same source.

13. Encyclopedia or dictionary entry Unless an entry in an encyclopedia or a dictionary has an author, the source will be alphabetized in the list of works cited under the word or entry that you consulted (see item 27 on p. 409). Either in your text or in your parenthetical citation, mention the word or entry. No page number is required, since readers can easily look up the word or entry.

> The word *crocodile* has a surprisingly complex etymology ("Crocodile").

14. Multivolume work If your paper cites more than one volume of a multivolume work, indicate in the parentheses the volume you are referring to, followed by a colon and the page number.

> In his studies of gifted children, Terman describes a pattern of accelerated language acquisition (2: 279).

If you cite only one volume of a multivolume work throughout your paper, you will include the volume number in the list of works cited and will not need to include it in the parentheses. (See the second example in item 26, at the top of p. 409.)

15. Entire work Use the author's name in a signal phrase or a parenthetical citation. There is no need to use a page number.

> Lane explores the evolution of surveillance in the workplace.

16. Selection in an anthology   Put the name of the author of the selection (not the editor of the anthology) in the signal phrase or the parentheses.

> In "Love Is a Fallacy," the narrator's logical teachings disintegrate when Polly
> declares that she should date Petey because "[h]e's got a raccoon coat"
> (Shulman 379).

In the list of works cited, the work is alphabetized by the author's last name, not by the name of the editor of the anthology. (See item 24 on pp. 407–08.)

> Shulman, Max. "Love Is a Fallacy." *Current Issues and Enduring Questions*. Ed. Sylvan
> Barnet and Hugo Bedau. 8th ed. Boston: Bedford, 2008. 371-79. Print.

17. Government document   When a government agency is the author, you will alphabetize it in the list of works cited under the name of the government, such as *Canada* or *United States* (see item 73 on p. 424). For this reason, you must name the government as well as the agency in your in-text citation.

> Online monitoring by the United States Department of the Interior over a
> one-week period found that employees' use of "sexually explicit and gambling
> websites . . . accounted for over 24 hours of Internet use" and that "computer
> users spent over 2,004 hours accessing game and auction sites" during the
> same period (3).

18. Historical document   For a historical document, such as the Constitution Act, 1867, or the United States Constitution, provide the document title, neither italicized nor in quotation marks, along with relevant article and section numbers. In parenthetical citations, use common abbreviations such as "art.," "pt.," and "sec." and abbreviations of well-known titles (Can. Const. Act, pt. 2, sec. 6).

> The Charter of Rights and Freedoms guarantees every Canadian "the right to life,
> liberty and security of the person" (sec. 7).

For other historical documents, cite as you would any other work, by the first element in the works cited entry (see item 74 on p. 425).

19. Legal source   For legislative acts (laws) and court cases, name the act or case either in a signal phrase or in parentheses. Italicize the names of cases but not the names of acts.

> The Youth Criminal Justice Act came into force in 2003.

The 1930 ruling in *Edwards v. Canada (Attorney General)*, informally known in Canada as the Persons Case, acknowledged that women have the same political rights as men.

20. Visual such as a photograph, map, or chart To cite a visual that has a figure number in the source, use the abbreviation "fig." and the number in place of a page number in your parenthetical citation: (Manning, fig. 4). Spell out the word "figure" if you refer to it in your text.

To cite a visual that does not have a figure number in a print source, use the visual's title or a general description in your text and cite the author and page number as for any other source.

For a visual that is not contained in a source such as a book or periodical, identify the visual in your text and then cite it using the first element in the works cited entry: the photographer's or artist's name or the title of the work. (See items 69 and 72 on pp. 423 and 424.)

Photographs such as *Firefighting Exercise* (Royal) and *Women Manufacturing Cartridges* (Morant) demonstrate the Canadian government's attempt to document the contributions of women on the home front during World War II.

21. E-mail, letter, or personal interview Cite e-mail messages, personal letters, and personal interviews by the name listed in the works cited entry, as you would for any other source. Identify the type of source in your text if you feel it is necessary. (See item 53 on p. 419 and items 83 and 84 on p. 427.)

22. Web site or other electronic source Your in-text citation for an electronic source should follow the same guidelines as for other sources. If the source lacks page numbers but has numbered paragraphs, sections, or divisions, use those numbers with the appropriate abbreviation in your in-text citation: "par.," "sec.," "ch.," "pt.," and so on. Do not add such numbers if the source itself does not use them; simply give the author or title in your in-text citation.

Julian Hawthorne points out profound differences between his father and Ralph Waldo Emerson but concludes that, in their lives and their writing, "together they met the needs of nearly all that is worthy in human nature" (ch. 4).

23. Indirect source (source quoted in another source) When a writer's or a speaker's quoted words appear in a source written by someone else, begin the parenthetical citation with the abbreviation "qtd. in."

According to Bill Coleman, an executive at *Salary.com,* "Personal Internet use and casual office conversations often turn into new business ideas or suggestions for gaining operating efficiencies" (qtd. in Frauenheim).

Literary works and sacred texts

Literary works and sacred texts are usually available in a variety of editions. Your list of works cited will specify which edition you are using, and your in-text citation will usually consist of a page number from the edition you consulted (see item 24). When possible, give enough information—such as book parts, play divisions, or line numbers—so that readers can locate the cited passage in any edition of the work (see items 25–27).

24. Literary work without parts or line numbers   Many literary works, such as most short stories and many novels and plays, do not have parts or line numbers. In such cases, simply cite the page number.

> At the end of Kate Chopin's "The Story of an Hour," Mrs. Mallard drops dead upon learning that her husband is alive. In the final irony of the story, doctors report that she has died of a "joy that kills" (25).

25. Verse play or poem   For verse plays, give act, scene, and line numbers that can be located in any edition of the work. Use arabic numerals and separate the numbers with periods.

> In Shakespeare's *King Lear,* Gloucester, blinded for suspected treason, learns a profound lesson from his tragic experience: "A man may see how this world goes / with no eyes" (4.2.148-49).

For a poem, cite the part, stanza, and line numbers, if it has them, separated by periods.

> The Green Knight claims to approach King Arthur's court "because the praise of you, prince, is puffed so high, / And your manor and your men are considered so magnificent" (1.12.258-59).

For poems that are not divided into numbered parts or stanzas, use line numbers. For a first reference, use the word "lines": (lines 5-8). Thereafter use just the numbers: (12-13).

26. Novel with numbered divisions   When a novel has numbered divisions, put the page number first, followed by a semicolon and the book, part, or chapter in which the passage may be found. Use abbreviations such as "bk.," "pt.," and "ch."

> One of Kingsolver's narrators, teenager Rachel, pushes her vocabulary beyond its limits. For example, Rachel complains that being forced to live in the Congo with her missionary family is "a sheer tapestry of justice" because her chances of finding a boyfriend are "dull and void" (117; bk. 2, ch. 10).

27. Sacred text When citing a sacred text such as the Bible or the Quran, name the edition you are using in your works cited entry (see item 28 on p. 409). In your parenthetical citation, give the book, chapter, and verse (or their equivalent), separated with periods. Common abbreviations for books of the Bible are acceptable.

> Consider the words of Solomon: "If your enemy is hungry, give him bread to eat; and if he is thirsty, give him water to drink" (*Oxford Annotated Bible,* Prov. 25.21).

The title of a sacred work is italicized when it refers to a specific edition of the work, as in the preceding example. If you refer to the book in a general sense in your text, neither italicize it nor put it in quotation marks. (See also the note in P10-a, p. 305.)

> The Bible and the Quran provide allegories that help readers understand how to lead a moral life.

MLA-4b MLA list of works cited

An alphabetized list of works cited, which appears at the end of your research paper, gives publication information for each of the sources you have cited in the paper. Include only sources that you have quoted, summarized, or paraphrased. (For information about preparing the list, see p. 431; for a sample list of works cited, see p. 440.)

For a directory to the works cited models in this section, see pages 371–72, immediately following the tabbed divider.

General guidelines for works cited in MLA style

In an MLA works cited entry, invert the first author's name (last name first, followed by a comma and the first name); put all other names in normal order. In titles of works, capitalize all words except articles (*a, an, the*), prepositions (*into, between,* and so on), coordinating conjunctions (*and, but, or, nor, for, so, yet*), and the *to* in infinitives—unless they are the first or last word of the title or subtitle. Use quotation marks for titles of articles and other short works, such as brief documents from Web sites; italicize titles of books and other long works, such as entire Web sites.

Give the city of publication without a state name. Shorten publishers' names, usually to the first principal word ("Wiley" for "John Wiley and Sons," for instance); abbreviate "University" and "Press" in the names of university publishers: U of Alberta P. For the date of publication, use the date on the title page or the most recent date on the copyright page.

For all works cited entries, include the medium in which a work was published, produced, or delivered. Usually put the medium at the end of the entry, capitalized but neither italicized nor in quotation marks. Typical designations for the medium are "Print," "Web," "Television," "CD," "Film," "DVD," "Photograph," "Performance," "Lecture," "MP3 file," and "PDF file." (See specific items throughout MLA-4b.)

Listing authors (print and online)

Alphabetize entries in the list of works cited by authors' last names (or by title if a work has no author). The author's name is important because citations in the text of the paper refer to it and readers will look for it at the beginning of an entry in the alphabetized list.

NAME CITED IN TEXT

According to Nancy Flynn, . . .

BEGINNING OF WORKS CITED ENTRY

Flynn, Nancy.

1. Single author

author: last name first | title (book) | city of publication | publisher | date | medium

Mohan, Suruchi. *Divine Music.* Calgary: Bayeux, 2009. Print.

2. Two or three authors

first author: last name first | second author: in normal order | title (book)

Blake, Raymond, and Jeffrey Keshen. *Narrating a Nation: Canadian History Post-*

city of publication | publisher | date | medium

Confederation. Toronto: McGraw, 2010. Print.

first author: last name first | other authors: in normal order | title (newspaper article)

Farmer, John, John Azzarello, and Miles Kara. "Real Heroes, Fake Stories."

newspaper title | date of publication | page(s) | medium

New York Times 14 Sept. 2008: WK10. Print.

3. Four or more authors

first author: last name first | other authors: in normal order

Giltrow, Janet, Richard Gooding, Daniel Burgoyne, and Marlene Sawatsky. *Academic*

title (book) | edition number | city of publication | publisher | date | medium

Writing: An Introduction. 2nd ed. Peterborough: Broadview, 2009. Print.

Name all the authors or name the first author followed by "et al." (Latin for "and others"). In an in-text citation, use the same form for the authors' names as you use in the works cited entry. See item 7 on page 392.

4. Organization as author

author: organization name,
not abbreviated   title (book)

Canadian Education Association. *The Promise and Problem of Literacy for Canada: An*

                          city of   publisher, with
                          publication common abbreviations   date   medium

Agenda for Action. Toronto: Can. Educ. Assn., 2004. Print.

For a publication by a government agency, see item 73. Your in-text citation should also treat the organization as the author (see item 8 on p. 392).

5. Unknown author

Article or other short work

       title   magazine   date of
  (magazine article)   title   publication   page(s) medium

"Global Targets, Local Ingenuity." *Economist* 25 Sept. 2010: 34-35. Print.

      title   title   city of   date of
  (TV episode)   (TV program)   producer   network station broadcast   broadcast

"Something's Fishy." *Marketplace.* Prod. Greg Sadler. CBC. CBLT, Toronto, 2 Apr. 2010.

     medium

Television.

For other examples of an article with no author and of a television program, see items 13 and 65, respectively.

Book, entire Web site, or other long work

                                          city of
              title (book)   publication publisher   date   medium

Oxford Canadian Spelling Bee Dictionary. Toronto: Oxford UP, 2008. Print.

                                       no
title (Web site)   sponsor of site   date medium   access date

Famous Five. Lib. and Archives Can., n.d. Web. 29 Sept. 2010.

Before concluding that the author of an online source is unknown, check carefully (see the tip at the top of p. 391). Also remember

organization, company • no author • two or more works
by one author • article • journal • magazine
MLA-4b **401**

that an organization or a government may be the author (see items 4 and 73).

6. Two or more works by the same author If your list of works cited includes two or more works by the same author, first alphabetize the works by title (ignoring the article *A*, *An*, or *The* at the beginning of a title). Use the author's name for the first entry only; for subsequent entries, use three hyphens followed by a period. The three hyphens must stand for exactly the same name or names as in the first entry.

Shields, Carol. *Jane Austen: A Life*. New York: Penguin, 2005.

---. *The Stone Diaries*. Vintage Can., 1993. Print.

Articles in periodicals (print)

This section shows how to prepare works cited entries for articles in print magazines, journals, and newspapers. See "General guidelines" and "Listing authors" on pages 398 and 399 for how to handle basic parts of the entries. See also "Online sources" beginning on page 412 for articles from Web sites and articles accessed through a library's database.

For articles appearing on consecutive pages, provide the range of pages (see items 7 and 8). When an article does not appear on consecutive pages, give the first page number followed by a plus sign: 32+. For dates requiring a month, abbreviate all but May, June, and July. For an illustrated citation of an article in a periodical, see pages 402–03.

7. Article in a journal (paginated by volume or by issue)

author: last
name first   article title   journal title

Blackburn, Robin. "Economic Democracy: Meaningful, Desirable, Feasible?" *Daedalus*

volume,
issue   year   page(s)   medium

136.3 (2007): 36-45. Print.

8. Article in a monthly magazine

author: last
name first   article title   magazine title

Cowan, James. "Why We'll Never Escape Facebook." *Report on Business Magazine*

date:
month + year   page(s)   medium

July 2010: 28-34. Print.

Citation at a glance: Article in a periodical (MLA)

To cite an article in a print periodical in MLA style, include the following elements:

1   Author of article
2   Title and subtitle of article
3   Title of periodical
4   Volume and issue number (for journal)
5   Date or year of publication
6   Page number(s) of article
7   Medium

TABLE OF CONTENTS

JOURNAL TITLE PAGE

3 ● STUDIES IN CANADIAN LITERATURE

S C L / É L C

STUDIES IN CANADIAN LITERATURE
ÉTUDES EN LITTÉRATURE CANADIENNE

4
VOLUME 34 NUMBER 2
PUBLISHED BY
THE UNIVERSITY OF NEW BRUNSWICK
© 2009 **5**

FIRST PAGE OF ARTICLE

2 [A Desire for the Real: The Power of Film
      in *The Englishman's Boy*

1 ROBERT ZACHARIAS

Let us . . . be on our guard against the hallowed philosophers'
myth of a 'pure, will-less, painless, timeless knower.' . . . All these
concepts presuppose an eye such as no living being can imagine,
an eye required to have no direction, to abrogate its active and
interpretative powers.

— Friedrich Nietzsche (255)

MIDWAY THROUGH GUY VANDERHAEGHE's award-winning
novel *The Englishman's Boy* (1996), Damon Ira Chance, an
infamous and reclusive Hollywood studio head, invites a
hapless young Canadian screenwriter named Harry Vincent to his man-
sion for dinner. The year is 1923, and the filmmaker believes Americans
must steel themselves for conflict; news of Lenin's revolution reverber-
ates around the world, and Mussolini's blackshirts have just marched
on Rome. Speaking of the power of cinema in a hushed voice over an
after-dinner cigar, Chance admires Mussolini's use of film and announces that he intends to harness the new medium to rewrite the story of
the Cypress Hills Massacre of 1873 as a mythic history of the settling
of the American west. The scene closes with the producer announcing
that "the mind's highest struggle is to interpret the world" (110) and
that since, as he claimed earlier, the "the new century [is] going to be
a century governed by images" (106), he plans to interpret the world
through film. He then declares that he's tired, and Harry stumbles out
into the night.

WORKS CITED ENTRY FOR AN ARTICLE IN A PRINT PERIODICAL

```
   ┌──────1──────┐ ┌──────────────────────2──────────────────────┐
```
Zacharias, Robert. "A Desire for the Real: The Power of Film in *The Englishman's Boy*."

```
    ┌──────────3──────────┐ ┌─4─┐ ┌─5─┐  ┌─6─┐ ┌─7─┐
```
Studies in Canadian Literature 34.2 (2009): 245-63. Print.

For more on citing print periodical articles in MLA style, see pages 401–04.

9. Article in a weekly magazine

| author:
last name first | article title | magazine
title | date: day +
month + year | page(s) | medium |

Sorensen, Chris. "Which Way Is Up?" *Maclean's* 4 Oct. 2010: 48. Print.

10. Article in a daily newspaper Give the page range of the article. If the article does not appear on consecutive pages, use a plus sign (+) after the first page number. If the city of publication is not obvious from the title of the newspaper, include the city in brackets after the name of the newspaper.

If sections are identified by letter, include the section letter as part of the page number. If sections are numbered, include the section number between the date and the page number, using the abbreviation "sec."

Page number with section letter

| author: last
name first | article title |

Howlett, Karen. "Criminal Allegations: Public Guardian's Office Has Troubled History."

| newspaper title | date: day +
month + year | name of
edition | page | medium |

Globe and Mail 10 Aug. 2007, Toronto ed.: A6. Print.

Page number with section number

| author: last
name first | article title | newspaper title | city of
publication |

Knox, David Blake. "Lord Archer, Storyteller." *Sunday Independent* [Dublin]

| date: day +
month + year | section | page | medium |

14 Sept. 2008, sec. 2: 9. Print.

11. Abstract of a journal article Include the word "Abstract" after the title of the article.

Walker, Joyce. "Narratives in the Database: Memorializing September 11th Online."

   Abstract. *Computers and Composition* 24.2 (2007): 121. Print.

12. Article with a title in its title   Use single quotation marks around a title of a short work or a quoted term that appears in an article title. Italicize a title or term normally italicized. (See also P5-c.)

Knowles, Ric. "'My Passion, My World': An Interview with Derrick Chua." *Canadian*
   Theatre Review 14.2 (2010): 50-54. Print.

13. Editorial or other unsigned article   Begin with the article title and alphabetize the entry by the title in the list of works cited.

"Farely Frustrated." Editorial. *Metro* [Toronto] 18 Nov. 2009: 1. Print.

14. Letter to the editor

Saffrey, Leslie. "FEMA's 'Eat-Cake' Attitude." Letter. *Globe and Mail* 6 Sept. 2005: A16.
   Print.

15. Review   For a review of a book, a film, or another type of work, begin with the name of the reviewer and the title of the review, if it has one. Add the words "Rev. of" and the title of the work reviewed, followed by the author, director, or other significant contributor. Give the publication information for the periodical in which the review appears. If the review has no author and no title, begin with "Rev. of" and alphabetize the entry by the first principal word in the title of the work reviewed.

Basilières, Michel. "Diderot Derivative." Rev. of *Beatrice and Virgil*, by Yann Martel.
   Literary Review of Canada 18.5 (2010): 19. Print.

Farquharson, Vanessa. "In Praise of Scrunchy-Faced Women." Rev. of *Miss Potter*, dir.
   Chris Noonan. *National Post* 12 Jan. 2007: E4. Print.

Books (print)

Items 16–33 apply to print books. For online books, see items 41 and 42. For an illustrated citation of a print book, see page 406.

16. Basic format for a book

author: last
name first   book title   city of
                                                                                             publication

Hepburn, Allan. *Enchanted Objects: Visual Art in Contemporary Fiction.* Toronto:

   publisher   date   medium

   U of Toronto P, 2010. Print.

Take the information about the book from its title page and copy-right page. Use a short form of the publisher's name; omit terms such as "Press," "Inc.," and "Co." except when naming university presses ("Howard UP," for example). If the copyright page lists more than one date, use the most recent one.

17. Book with an author and an editor

author: last name first	book title	editor(s): in normal order

Barbauld, Anna Letitia. *Selected Poetry and Prose*. Ed. William McCarthy and Elizabeth

city of publication	publisher	date	medium

Kraft. Peterborough: Broadview, 2002. Print.

The abbreviation "Ed." means "Edited by," so it is the same for one or multiple editors.

18. Book with an author and a translator   "Trans." means "Translated by," so it is the same for one or multiple translators.

Leroux, Georges. *Partita for Glenn Gould: An Inquiry into the Nature of Genius*. Trans.

Donald Winkler. Montreal: McGill-Queen's UP, 2010. Print.

19. Book with an editor   Begin with the editor's name. For one editor, use "ed." (for "editor") after the name; for multiple editors, use "eds." (for "editors").

Stott, Jon C., and Raymond E. Jones, eds. *The Harbrace Anthology of Short Fiction*. 5th

ed. Toronto: Nelson, 2010. Print.

20. Graphic narrative or illustrated book   For a book that combines text and illustrations, begin your citation with the person you wish to emphasize (writer, illustrator, artist) and list any other contributors after the title of the book. Use the abbreviation "illus." and other common labels to identify contributors. If the writer and illustrator are the same person, cite the work as you would a book, with no labels.

Gerard, Shannon, illus. *Sword of My Mouth: A Post-Rapture Graphic Novel*. By Jim Munroe.

Toronto: No Media Kings, 2010. Print.

Blackley, Kaja. *Kid K-OS: The Agents of Doom*. Illus. Alex Hawley. Toronto: Art House 7,

2010. Print.

Thompson, Craig. *Blankets*. Marietta: Top Shelf, 2005.

Citation at a glance: Book (MLA)

To cite a print book in MLA style, include the following elements:

1 Author
2 Title and subtitle
3 City of publication
4 Publisher (or imprint-publisher)
5 Date of publication
6 Medium

TITLE PAGE

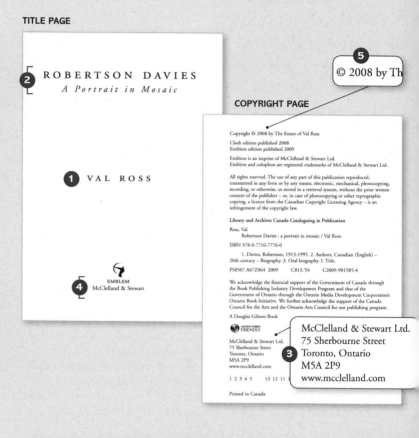

COPYRIGHT PAGE

WORKS CITED ENTRY FOR A PRINT BOOK

Ross, Val. *Robertson Davies: A Portrait in Mosaic.* Toronto: Emblem-McClelland, 2008.

Print.

For more on citing print books in MLA style, see pages 404–11.

21. Book with an author using a pseudonym Give the author's name as it appears on the title page (the pseudonym), and follow it with the author's real name in brackets.

Dinesen, Isak [Karen Blixen]. *Winter's Tales*. 1942. New York: Vintage, 1993. Print.

22. Book in a language other than English If your readers are not familiar with the language of the book, include a translation of the title, italicized and in brackets. Capitalize the title according to the conventions of the book's language, and give the original publication information.

Nemtsov, Boris, and Vladimir Milov. *Putin. Itogi. Nezavisimyi Ekspertnyi Doklad*

  [*Putin. The Results: An Independent Expert Report*]. Moscow: Novaya Gazeta,

  2008. Print.

23. Entire anthology An anthology is a collection of works on a common theme, often with different authors for the selections and usually with an editor for the entire volume. (For an anthology with one editor, use the abbreviation "ed." after the editor's name. For more than one editor, use "eds.")

Erickson, Paul A., and Liam Donat Murphy, eds. *Readings for a History of Anthropological*

  Theory. 3rd ed. Toronto: U of Toronto P, 2010. Print.

24. One or more selections from an anthology

One selection from anthology

author of selection: last name first	title of selection	title of anthology

Gray, Thomas Alan. "One Day Winner." *Frontier: A Collection of New Canadian Short*

	editor(s) of anthology: in normal order	city of publication	publisher	date	page(s) of selection

  Stories. Ed. Rachelle McCallum. Maple Ridge: Polar Expressions, 2008. 36-37.

medium

Print.

The abbreviation "Ed." means "Edited by," so it is the same for one or multiple editors. For an illustrated citation of a selection from an anthology, see pages 410–11.

Two or more selections, with separate anthology entry

If you use two or more works from the same anthology in your paper, provide an entry for the entire anthology (see item 23) and give a shortened entry for each selection. Use the medium only in the entry for the complete anthology. For an illustrated citation of a selection from an anthology, see pages 410–11.

| author of selection | title of selection | editor(s): last name(s) | page(s) of selection |

Gray, Thomas Alan. "One Day Winner." McCallum 36-37.

| editor(s) of anthology | title of anthology |

McCallum, Rachelle, ed. *Frontier: A Collection of New Canadian Short Stories.*

| city of publication | publisher | date | medium |

Maple Ridge: Polar Expressions, 2008. Print.

| author of selection | title of selection | editor(s): last name(s) | page(s) of selection |

Ryder, Wanda. "The Visit." McCallum 13-14.

25. Edition other than the first   Include the number of the edition (2nd, 3rd, and so on). If the book has a translator or an editor in addition to the author, give the name of the translator or editor before the edition number, using the abbreviation "Trans." for "Translated by" (see item 18) or "Ed." for "Edited by" (see item 17).

Grescoe, Paul. *Trip of a Lifetime: The Making of the Rocky Mountaineer.* 3rd ed.

Vancouver: Armstrong, 2010. Print.

26. Multivolume work   Include the total number of volumes before the city and publisher, using the abbreviation "vols." If the volumes were published over several years, give the inclusive dates of publication. The abbreviation "Ed." means "Edited by," so it is the same for one or multiple editors.

| author: last name first | title | editor: in normal order | total volumes | city of publication | publisher | inclusive dates | medium |

Stark, Freya. *Letters.* Ed. Lucy Moorehead. 8 vols. Salisbury: Compton, 1974-82. Print.

If you cite only one of the volumes in your paper, include the volume number before the city and publisher and give the date of publication for that volume. After the date, give the medium of publication followed by the total number of volumes.

author: last name first	title	editor: in normal order	volume cited	city of publication	publisher	date of volume	medium

Stark, Freya. *Letters*. Ed. Lucy Moorehead. Vol. 5. Salisbury: Compton, 1978. Print.

total volumes

8 vols.

27. Encyclopedia or dictionary entry   List the author of the entry (if there is one), the title of the entry, the title of the reference work, the edition number (if any), the date of the edition, and the medium. Volume and page numbers are not necessary because the entries in the source are arranged alphabetically and are therefore easy to locate.

Posner, Rebecca. "Romance Languages." *The Encyclopaedia Britannica: Macropaedia.*

15th ed. 1987. Print.

"Sonata." *Canadian Oxford Dictionary*. 2nd ed. 2004. Print.

28. Sacred text   Give the title of the sacred text (taken from the title page), italicized; the editor's or translator's name (if any); publication information; and the medium. Add the name of the version, if there is one.

The Oxford Annotated Bible with the Apocrypha. Ed. Herbert G. May and Bruce M.

Metzger. New York: Oxford UP, 1965. Print. Rev. Standard Vers.

The Qur'an: Translation. Trans. Abdullah Yusuf Ali. Elmhurst: Tahrike, 2000. Print.

29. Foreword, introduction, preface, or afterword

author of foreword: last name first	book part		book title

Skelton, David. Foreword. *Stay, Breathe with Me: Stories of Courage, Healing, and Love.*

author of book: in normal order	city of publication	publisher	date	page(s) of foreword	medium

By Helen Allison. Burns Lake: Cairndow, 2010. x-xiv. Print.

If the book part has a title, include it in quotation marks immediately after the author's name and before the label for the book part. If the author of the book part is also the author or editor of the complete work, give only the last name of the author the second time it is used.

Ozick, Cynthia. "Portrait of the Essay as a Warm Body." Introduction. *The Best American*

Essays 1998. Ed. Ozick. Boston: Houghton, 1998. xv-xxi. Print.

Citation at a glance: Selection from an anthology (MLA)

To cite a selection from a print anthology in MLA style, include the following elements:

1 Author of selection
2 Title of selection
3 Title and subtitle of anthology
4 Editor(s) of anthology
5 City of publication
6 Publisher
7 Date of publication
8 Page number(s) of selection
9 Medium

TITLE PAGE

FIRST PAGE OF SELECTION

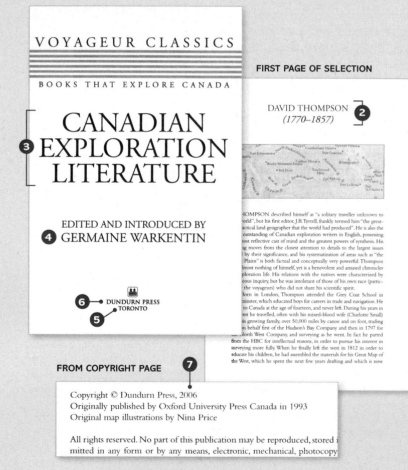

VOYAGEUR CLASSICS

BOOKS THAT EXPLORE CANADA

3 CANADIAN
EXPLORATION
LITERATURE

EDITED AND INTRODUCED BY
4 GERMAINE WARKENTIN

6 DUNDURN PRESS
TORONTO
5

DAVID THOMPSON **2**
(1770–1857)

HOMPSON described himself as "a solitary traveller unknown to orld", but his first editor, J.B. Tyrrell, frankly termed him "the great-actical land geographer that the world had produced". He is also the outstanding of Canadian exploration writers in English, possessing most reflective cast of mind and the greatest powers of synthesis. His ng moves from the closest attention to details to the largest issues by their significance, and his systematization of areas such as "the Plains" is both factual and conceptually very powerful. Thompson almost nothing of himself, yet is a benevolent and amused chronicler ploration life. His relations with the natives were characterized by eous inquiry, but he was intolerant of those of his own race (partic-the voyageurs) who did not share his scientific spirit.
Born in London, Thompson attended the Grey Coat School in minster, which educated boys for careers in trade and navigation. He to Canada at the age of fourteen, and never left. During his years in est he travelled, often with his mixed-blood wife (Charlotte Small) is growing family, over 50,000 miles by canoe and on foot, trading n behalf first of the Hudson's Bay Company and then in 1797 for North West Company, and surveying as he went. In fact he parted from the HBC for intellectual reasons, in order to pursue his interest in surveying more fully. When he finally left the west in 1812 in order to educate his children, he had assembled the materials for his Great Map of the West, which he spent the next few years drafting and which is now

FROM COPYRIGHT PAGE **7**

Copyright © Dundurn Press, 2006
Originally published by Oxford University Press Canada in 1993
Original map illustrations by Nina Price

All rights reserved. No part of this publication may be reproduced, stored i mitted in any form or by any means, electronic, mechanical, photocopy

WORKS CITED ENTRY FOR A SELECTION FROM AN ANTHOLOGY

```
         ┌─────2─────┐ ┌──────3──────┐   ┌────4────┐
"David Thompson (1770-1857)." Canadian Exploration Literature. Ed. Germaine Warkentin.
  ┌─5─┐ ┌──6──┐ ┌─7─┐ ┌──8──┐ ┌─9─┐
  Toronto: Dundurn, 2006. 269-317. Print.
```

For more on citing selections from anthologies in MLA style, see pages 407–08.

30. Book with a title in its title If the book title contains a title normally italicized, neither italicize the internal title nor place it in quotation marks.

Woodson, Jon. *A Study of Joseph Heller's* Catch-22: *Going Around Twice*. New York: Lang,

2001. Print.

If the title within the title is normally put in quotation marks, retain the quotation marks and italicize the entire book title.

Millás, Juan José. *"Personality Disorders" and Other Stories*. Trans. Gregory B. Kaplan.

New York: MLA, 2007. Print. MLA Texts and Trans.

31. Book in a series After the publication information, give the medium of publication and then the series name as it appears on the title page, followed by the series number, if any.

Douglas, Dan. *Assessing Languages for Specific Purposes*. Cambridge: Cambridge UP,

2000. Print. Cambridge Applied Linguistics Ser.

32. Republished book After the title of the book, give the original publication date, followed by the current publication information. If the republished book contains new material, such as an introduction or afterword, include information about the new material after the original date.

Trilling, Lionel. *The Liberal Imagination*. 1950. Introd. Louis Menand. New York: New

York Review of Books, 2008. Print.

33. Publisher's imprint If a book was published by a division (an imprint) of a publishing company, give the name of the imprint, a hyphen, and the name of the publisher.

Echlin, Kim. *The Disappeared*. Toronto: Black Cat-Grove, 2009. Print.

Online sources

MLA guidelines assume that readers can locate most online sources by entering the author, title, or other identifying information in a search engine or a database. Consequently, the *MLA Handbook* does not require a Web address (URL) in citations for online sources. If your instructor requires one, see the note at the end of item 34.

MLA style calls for a sponsor or a publisher in works cited entries for most online sources. If a source has no sponsor or publisher, use the abbreviation "N.p." (for "No publisher") in the sponsor position. If there is no date of publication or update, use "n.d." (for "no date") after the sponsor. For an article in an online journal or an article from a database, give page numbers if they are available; if they are not, use the abbreviation "n. pag." (See item 37.)

34. Entire Web site

sponsor of site

| author: last name first | title of Web site | (personal page) | update medium |

Peterson, Susan Lynn. *The Life of Martin Luther.* Susan Lynn Peterson, 2005. Web.

date of access:
day + month + year

24 Jan. 2009.

Web site with organization (group) as author

organization name: not abbreviated | title of Web site | sponsor: abbreviated update medium

Canadian Library Association. *Canadian Library Association.* CLA, 2010. Web.

date of access:
day + month + year

14 Sept. 2010.

Web site with no author

title of Web site | sponsor of site

The Canadian Country Atlas Digital Project. Rare Books and Special Collections Div., McGill U,

date of access:
update medium day + month + year

June 2003. Web. 6 Aug. 2010.

Web site with editor

See item 19 (p. 405) for listing the name(s) of editor(s).

Halsall, Paul, ed. *Internet Modern History Sourcebook.* Fordham U, 22 Sept. 2001. Web.

19 Jan. 2009.

Web site with no title

Use the label "Home page" or another appropriate description in place of a title.

Aikenhead, Glen. Home page. U of Saskatchewan, n.d. Web. 30 May 2010.

NOTE: If your instructor requires a URL for Web sources, include the URL, enclosed in angle brackets, at the end of the entry. When a URL in a works cited entry must be divided at the end of a line, break it after a slash. Do not insert a hyphen.

Harbeck, James. *How to Explain Grammar*. James Harbeck, 2010. Web. 24 Jan. 2010.

    <http://www.harbeck.ca/James/syntax.html>.

35. Short work from a Web site   Short works include articles, poems, and other documents that are not book length or that appear as internal pages on a Web site. For an illustrated citation of a short work from a Web site, see pages 414–15.

Short work with author

author: last
name first   title of short work   title of
Web site   sponsor   no update
date   medium

Shiva, Vandana. "Bioethics: A Third World Issue." *NativeWeb*. NativeWeb, n.d. Web.

date of access:
day + month + year

22 Jan. 2010.

Short work with no author

title of
short work   title of
Web site   sponsor
of site   update
date   medium   date of access:
day + month + year

"Coming Home." *The Wounded Platoon*. PBS Online, 18 May 2010. Web. 1 June 2010.

36. Web site with an author using a pseudonym   Begin the entry with the pseudonym and add the author's or creator's real name, if known, in brackets. Follow with the information required for a Web site or a short work from a Web site (see item 34 or 35).

Grammar Girl [Mignon Fogarty]. "What Is the Plural of 'Mouse'?" *Grammar Girl: Quick and Dirty Tips for Better Writing*. Holtzbrinck, 16 Sept. 2008. Web. 10 Nov. 2010.

37. Article in an online journal

author: last name first   article title

Mason, John Edwin. "'Mannenberg': Notes on the Making of an Icon and Anthem."

journal title   volume,
issue   year   not
paginated   medium   date of access:
day + month + year

African Studies Quarterly 9.4 (2007): n. pag. Web. 23 Feb. 2010.

Citation at a glance: Short work from a Web site (MLA)

To cite a short work from a Web site in MLA style, include the following elements:

1   Author of short work (if any)
2   Title of short work
3   Title of Web site
4   Sponsor of Web site ("N.p." if none)
5   Update date ("n.d." if none)
6   Medium
7   Date you accessed the source

INTERNAL PAGE OF WEB SITE

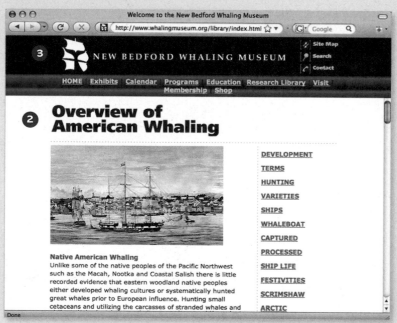

FOOTER ON HOME PAGE

the local area. It houses the most extensive collection of art, artifacts, and manuscripts pertaining to American whaling in the age of sail - late eighteenth century to the early twentieth, when sailing ships dominated merchant trade and whaling.

18 Johnny Cake Hill | New Bedford, MA | 02740-6398 | Tel. (508) 997-0046
Fax: (508) 997-0018 | Library Fax: (508) 207-1064

©Copyright 2009 Old Dartmouth Historical Society / New Bedford Whaling Museum

WORKS CITED ENTRY FOR A SHORT WORK FROM A WEB SITE

┌────────2────────┐ ┌────────3────────┐ ┌────4────┐
"Overview of American Whaling." *New Bedford Whaling Museum.* Old Dartmouth Hist.

┌──────────────────────┐ ┌─5─┐ ┌─6─┐ ┌────7────┐
Soc./New Bedford Whaling Museum, 2009. Web. 27 Oct. 2009.

For more on citing sources from Web sites in MLA style, see pages 412–13.

38. Article in an online magazine Give the author; the title of the article, in quotation marks; the title of the magazine, italicized; the sponsor or publisher of the site (use "N.p." if there is none); the date of publication; the medium; and your date of access.

Pettifor, Eric. "Copyright Bill Gives Big Media Control." *backofthebook.ca.* Single Lane
    Media, 2 June 2010. Web. 30 Nov. 2010.

39. Article in an online newspaper Give the author; the title of the article, in quotation marks; the title of the newspaper, italicized; the sponsor or publisher of the site (use "N.p." if there is none); the date of publication; the medium; and your date of access.

Golombek, Jamie. "Sometimes, You Just Get Lucky with Deadlines." *financialpost.com.*
    National Post, 28 Aug. 2010. Web. 3 Sept. 2010.

40. Work from a database For a source retrieved from a library's subscription database, first list the publication information for the source (see items 7–15) and then provide information about the database. For an illustrated citation of an article from a database, see page 416.

author(s) of source   title of article   journal title
┌──────────────┐ ┌──┐   ┌──────────────────────┐
Goodare, Julian. "The Scottish Presbyterian Movement in 1596." *Canadian Journal of History*

volume,   database   date of access:
issue   year   page(s)   name   medium   day + month + year
┌──┐ ┌────┐ ┌──────┐ ┌──────────┐ ┌──┐ ┌────────────────┐
45.1 (2010): 21-48. *General OneFile.* Web. 24 Nov. 2010.

Barrera, Rebeca María. "A Case for Bilingual Education." *Scholastic Parent and Child*
    Nov.-Dec. 2004: 72-73. *Academic Search Premier.* Web. 1 Feb. 2009.

Williams, Jeffrey J. "Why Today's Publishing World Is Reprising the Past." *Chronicle
    of Higher Education* 13 June 2008: n. pag. *LexisNexis Academic.* Web.
    29 Sept. 2009.

Citation at a glance: Article from a database (MLA)

To cite an article from a database in MLA style, include the following elements:

1 Author of article
2 Title of article
3 Title of periodical
4 Volume and issue numbers (for journal)
5 Date or year of publication
6 Page number(s) of article ("n. pag." if none)
7 Name of database
8 Medium
9 Date you accessed the source

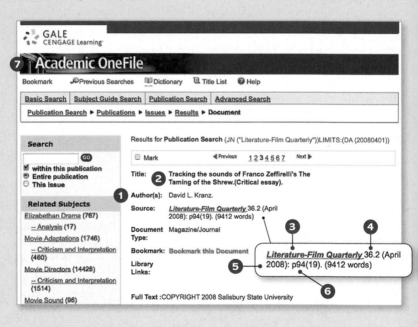

WORKS CITED ENTRY FOR AN ARTICLE FROM A DATABASE

┌─── 1 ───┐ ┌──────────────── 2 ────────────────┐
Kranz, David L. "Tracking the Sounds of Franco Zeffirelli's *The Taming of the Shrew*."

┌────── 3 ──────┐ ┌4┐ ┌─5─┐ ┌─6─┐ ┌──── 7 ────┐ ┌8┐
Literature-Film Quarterly 36.2 (2008): 94-112. *Academic OneFile*. Web.

┌── 9 ──┐
28 Oct. 2009.

For more on citing articles from a database in MLA style, see item 40.

41. Online book-length work   Cite an online book or an online book-length work, such as a play or a long poem, as you would a short work from a Web site (see item 35), but italicize the title of the work.

editors · · · · · · · · · · · · · · title of work

Anderson, Terry, and Fathi Elloumi, eds. *Theory and Practice of Online Learning*. *Centre for*

title of Web site · · sponsor of site · update · medium · date of access: day + month + year

Distance Education. Athabasca U, 2004. Web. 14 Dec. 2010.

Give the print publication information for the work, if available (see items 16–33), followed by the title of the Web site, the medium, and your date of access.

author: last name first · · · · · · book title · · · · · · editor of original book

Jacobs, Harriet A. *Incidents in the Life of a Slave Girl: Written by Herself*. Ed. L. Maria Child.

city of publication · year · · title of Web site · · medium · date of access: day + month + year

Boston, 1861. *Documenting the American South*. Web. 3 Feb. 2010.

42. Part of an online book   Begin as for a part of a print book (see item 29 on p. 409). If the online book part has no page numbers, use "N. pag." following the publication information. End with the Web site on which the work is found, the medium, and your date of access.

O'Donnell, Darren. "White Mice." *Inoculations*. Toronto: Coach House, 2001. N. pag. *Coach House Books: Online Editions*. Web. 3 June 2010.

43. Digital archives   Digital archives are online collections of documents or records—books, letters, photographs, data—that have been converted to digital form. Cite publication information for the original document, if it is available, using the models throughout section MLA-4b. Then give the location of the document, if any, neither italicized nor in quotation marks; the name of the archive, italicized; the medium ("Web"); and your date of access.

Fiore, Mark. *Shockwaves*. 18 Oct. 2001. *September 11 Digital Archive*. Web. 3 Apr. 2009.

Cartwright, George. *Captain Cartwright Visiting His Fox-Traps*. 1792. Lib. and Archives Can. *Early Images of Canada: Illustrations from Rare Books*. Web. 3 Dec. 2010.

Austin-Smith, Peter. Letter to the Friends of the Blomidon Naturalists Society. 24 Apr. 1990. Acadia U. *Esther Clark Wright Archives*. Web. 31 Mar. 2010.

44. Entry in an online reference work Give the author of the entry, if there is one. Otherwise begin with the title of the entry, in quotation marks. Then give the title of the site; the sponsor and the update date (use "n.d." if there is none); the medium; and your date of access.

Latouche, Daniel. "Lévesque, René." *The Canadian Encyclopedia*. Historica-Dominion,

2010. Web. 31 Aug. 2010.

45. Online poem Cite as you would a short work from a Web site (item 35) or part of an online book (item 42).

Bell, Acton [Anne Brontë]. "Mementos." *Poems by Currer, Ellis, and Acton Bell*.

London, 1846. N. pag. *A Celebration of Women Writers*. Web. 18 Sept. 2009.

46. Entire blog (Weblog) Cite a blog as you would an entire Web site (see item 34).

Akin, David. *David Akin's On the Hill*. N.p., 7 Dec. 2010. Web. 22 Dec. 2010.

47. Entry or comment in a blog (Weblog) Cite an entry or a comment (a response to an entry) in a blog as you would a short work from a Web site (see item 35). If the comment or entry has no title, use the label "Weblog entry" or "Weblog comment." Follow with the remaining information as for an entire blog in item 46.

Paikin, Steve. "A Brilliant Debate." *The Agenda*. TVOntario, 29 Nov. 2010. Web.

15 Dec. 2010.

Johan. "Welcome to the Modern World." *The Agenda*. TVOntario, 8 Dec. 2010. Web.

15 Dec. 2010.

48. Academic course or department home page Cite as a short work from a Web site (see item 35). For a course home page, begin with the name of the instructor and the title of the course or title of the page (use "Course home page" if there is no other title). For a department home page, begin with the name of the department and the label "Dept. home page."

McIntosh, D. F. "CHM223: Physical Chemistry for Pharmacy." *University of Toronto*. Dept.

of Chemistry, U of Toronto, 2010. Web. 4 Sept. 2010.

Faculty of Community Services. Dept. home page. *Ryerson University*. Ryerson U, 2010.

Web. 24 Sept. 2010.

online sources • dictionary, encyclopedia • poem • blog • course
home page • video clip • abstract • editorial • review • e-mail

MLA-4b **419**

49. Online video clip Cite as you would a short work from a Web site (see item 35).

author: last
name first   video title   title of
Web site   sponsor   update   medium

Murphy, Beth. "Tips for a Good Profile Piece." *YouTube*. YouTube, 7 Sept. 2008. Web.

     date of access:
day + month + year

19 Apr. 2010.

50. Online abstract Cite as you would an abstract of a journal article (see item 11), giving whatever print information is available, followed by the medium and your date of access. If you found the abstract in an online periodical database, include the name of the database after the print publication information (see item 40).

Turner, Fred. "Romantic Automatism: Art, Technology, and Collaborative Labor in

     Cold War America." Abstract. *Journal of Visual Culture* 7.1 (2008): 5. Web.

     25 Oct. 2009.

51. Online editorial or letter to the editor Cite as you would an editorial or a letter to the editor in a print publication (see item 13 or 14), followed by information for a short work from a Web site (see item 35).

McGowan, Stuart. "City Needs Clear Sponsorship Guidelines." Letter. *Fort Saskatchewan*

     Record. Sun Media, 10 Aug. 2010. Web. 3 Sept. 2010.

52. Online review Begin the entry as you would for a review in a magazine or newspaper (see item 15). If the review is published in print as well as online, first give publication information as for an article in a periodical (see items 7–10). Then add the Web site on which the review appears, the medium ("Web"), and your date of access. If the review is published only on the Web, give the information required for a short work from a Web site (see item 35). If you found the review in a database, cite as in item 40.

Lamey, Andy. "The Thinking Man's Marxist." Rev. of *Why Not Socialism?* by G. A. Cohen.

     Literary Review of Canada. Lit. Rev. of Can., June 2010. Web. 16 June 2010.

53. E-mail message Begin with the writer's name and the subject line. Then write "Message to" followed by the name of the recipient. End with the date of the message and the medium ("E-mail").

Lowe, Walter. "Review Questions." Message to the author. 15 Mar. 2010. E-mail.

54. Posting to an online discussion list   When possible, cite archived versions of postings. If you cannot locate an archived version, keep a copy of the posting for your records. Begin with the author's name, followed by the title or subject line, in quotation marks (use the label "Online posting" if the posting has no title). Then proceed as for a short work from a Web site (see item 35).

Fainton, Peter. "Re: Backlash against New Labour." *Media Lens Message Board*. Media

Lens, 7 May 2008. Web. 2 June 2008.

55. Entry in a wiki   A wiki is an online reference that is openly edited by its users. Treat an entry in a wiki as you would a short work from a Web site (see item 35). Because wiki content is, by definition, collectively edited and can be updated frequently, do not include an author. Give the title of the entry; the name of the wiki, italicized; the sponsor or publisher of the wiki (use "N.p." if there is none); the date of the last update; the medium; and your date of access.

"Hip Hop Music." *Wikipedia*. Wikimedia Foundation, 2 Mar. 2010. Web. 18 Mar. 2010.

"Negation in Languages." *UniLang Wiki*. UniLang, 12 Jan. 2009. Web. 9 Mar. 2010.

Audio and visual sources (including online versions)

56. Digital file   A digital file is any document or image that exists in digital form, independent of a Web site. To cite a digital file, begin with information required for the source (such as a photograph, a report, a sound recording, or a radio program), following the guidelines throughout MLA-4b. Then for the medium, indicate the type of file: "JPEG file," "PDF file," "MP3 file," and so on.

photographer   photograph title

Gilroy, G. Barry. *Canadian Infantrymen Surrounded by Dutch Civilians Celebrating the*

date of
composition   location of photograph   medium:
file type

Liberation of the Netherlands. 9 May 1945. Lib. and Archives Can. JPEG file.

"The Fiddle Tree at the Celtic Colours International Festival." *Concerts on Demand*. CBC

Radio, 12 Oct. 2009. MP3 file.

Canadian Mental Health Association, Ontario. *The Windows of Opportunity for Mental

Health Reform in Ontario*. Toronto: CMHA ON, 2010. PDF file.

57. Podcast   If you view or listen to a podcast online, cite it as you
would a short work from a Web site (see item 35). If you download the
podcast and view or listen to it on a computer or portable player, cite
it as a digital file (see item 56).

Podcast online

"Canada's Foreign Policy." Narr. Brian Bow. *Connect2Canada*. Govt. of Can., 5 June 2010.

Web. 31 Aug. 2010.

Podcast downloaded as digital file

"Canada's Foreign Policy." Narr. Brian Bow. *Connect2Canada*. Govt. of Can., 5 June 2010.

MP3 file.

58. Musical score   For print and online, begin with the composer's
name; the title of the work, italicized (unless it is named by form,
number, and key); and the date of composition. For a print source, give
the place, publisher, date of publication, and medium. For an online
source, give the title of the Web site; the publisher or sponsor; the
date of Web publication; the medium; and your date of access.

Handel, G. F. *Messiah: An Oratorio*. N.d. *CCARH Publications: Scores and Parts*. Center for

Computer Assisted Research in the Humanities, 2003. Web. 5 Jan. 2009.

59. Sound recording   Begin with the name of the person you want to
emphasize: the composer, conductor ("Cond."), or performer ("Perf.").
For a long work, give the title, italicized (unless it is named by form,
number, and key); the names of pertinent artists (such as performers,
readers, or musicians); and the orchestra and conductor, if relevant.
End with the manufacturer, the date, and the medium.

Bizet, Georges. *Carmen*. Perf. Jennifer Laramore, Thomas Moser, Angela Gheorghiu,

and Samuel Ramey. Bavarian State Orch. and Chorus. Cond. Giuseppe Sinopoli.

Warner, 1996. CD.

For a song, put the title in quotation marks. If you include the
name of the album or CD, italicize it.

Voisine, Roch. "Avant de partir." *Best of Roch*. RCA, 2007. CD.

60. Film   Typically, begin with the title, italicized, followed by the
director and lead actors ("Perf.") or narrator ("Narr."); the distributor;
the year of the film's release; and the medium ("Film," "Videocassette").

If your paper emphasizes a person involved with the film, you may begin with that person, as in the first example in item 61.

movie title   director   major performers

Frozen River. Dir. Courtney Hunt. Perf. Melissa Leo, Charlie McDermott, and Misty Upham.

                release
      distributor   date   medium

       Sony, 2008. Film.

61. DVD   For a film on DVD, cite as you would a film, giving "DVD" as the medium. If you are citing the film as a whole, use the model in item 60. If your paper emphasizes a particular person, begin with that person's name and title, as shown here.

Reitman, Jason, dir. *Up in the Air*. Perf. George Clooney, Vera Farmiga, and Anna

     Kendrick. Paramount, 2009. DVD.

For any other work on DVD, such as an educational work or a game, cite as you would a film, giving whatever information is available about the author, director, distributor, and so on.

Across the Drafts: Students and Teachers Talk about Feedback. Harvard Expository

     Writing Program, 2005. DVD.

62. Special feature on a DVD   Begin with the title of the feature, in quotation marks, and the names of any important contributors, as for films or DVDs (item 60 or 61). End with information about the DVD, as in item 61, including the disc number, if any.

"Sweeney's London." Prod. Eric Young. *Sweeney Todd: The Demon Barber of Fleet Street*.

     Dir. Tim Burton. DreamWorks, 2007. DVD. Disc 2.

63. CD-ROM   After publication information, add the medium ("CD-ROM").

"Pimpernel." *The Canadian Oxford Dictionary*. Toronto: Oxford UP, 2002. CD-ROM.

64. Computer software or video game   List the developer or author of the software (if any); the title, italicized; the distributor and date of publication; and the platform or medium.

Désilets, Patrice, creative dir. *Assassin's Creed II*. Ubisoft, 2009. Xbox 360.

65. Radio or television program   Begin with the title of the radio segment or television episode (if there is one), in quotation marks. Then give the title of the program or series, italicized; relevant information about the program, such as the writer ("By"), director ("Dir."), performers

("Perf."), or narrator ("Narr."); the network; the local station (if any) and location; the date of broadcast; and the medium ("Television," "Radio"). For a program you accessed online, after the information about the program give the network, the original broadcast date, the title of the Web site, the medium ("Web"), and your date of access.

"Machines of the Gods." *Ancient Discoveries*. History Channel. 14 Oct. 2008. Television.

"Who's Minding the Store?" *Marketplace*. Narr. Erica Johnson. Prod. Catherine Clark. CBC,
12 Mar. 2010. *CBC.ca*. Web. 31 Aug. 2010.

66. Radio or television interview Begin with the name of the person who was interviewed, followed by the word "Interview" and the interviewer's name, if relevant. End with information about the program as in item 65.

Harrington, Rex. Interview by Paula Todd. *Person 2 Person*. TVOntario. CICA, Toronto,
5 May 2007. Television.

67. Live performance For a live performance of a concert, a play, a ballet, or an opera, begin with the title of the work performed, italicized. Then give the author or composer of the work ("By"); relevant information such as the director ("Dir."), the choreographer ("Chor."), the conductor ("Cond."), or the major performers ("Perf."); the orchestra or the theater, ballet, or opera company, if any; the theater and location; the date of the performance; and the label "Performance."

The Brothers Size. By Tarell Alvin McCraney. Dir. Bijan Sheibani. Young Vic Theatre,
London. 15 Oct. 2008. Performance.

Piano Concerto No. 1. By Frédéric Chopin. Cond. Michael Newnham. Perf. Jan Lisiecki and
Symphony New Brunswick. Capitol Theatre, Moncton. 18 Oct. 2010. Performance.

68. Lecture or public address Begin with the speaker's name, followed by the title of the lecture (if any), in quotation marks; the organization sponsoring the lecture; the location; the date; and a label such as "Lecture" or "Address."

Tallamy, Douglas. "Bringing Nature Home." Edwards Charitable Foundation. Toronto
Botanical Garden. 27 Oct. 2010. Lecture.

69. Work of art Cite the artist's name; the title of the artwork, italicized; the date of composition; the medium of composition (for instance, "Lithograph on paper," "Photograph," "Charcoal on paper"); and the institution and city in which the artwork is located. For artworks found online, omit the medium of composition and include the title of the Web site, the medium ("Web"), and your date of access.

Constable, John. *Dedham Vale*. 1802. Oil on canvas. Victoria and Albert Museum, London.

Grauerholz, Angela. *Jewish Cemetery*. 2004. Natl. Gallery of Can., Ottawa. *National Gallery of Canada*. Web. 1 Sept. 2010.

70. Cartoon   Give the cartoonist's name; the title of the cartoon, if it has one, in quotation marks; the label "Cartoon" or "Comic strip"; publication information; and the medium. To cite an online cartoon, instead of publication information give the title of the Web site, the sponsor or publisher, the medium, and your date of access.

Aislin, Terry. "Iggy's Big Red Tent." Cartoon. *Montrealgazette.com*. Postmedia Network, 1 Sept. 2010. Web. 1 Sept. 2010.

71. Advertisement   Name the product or company being advertised, followed by the word "Advertisement." Give publication information for the source in which the advertisement appears.

Pringles Multigrain. Advertisement. *Reader's Digest*. Sept. 2010: 121. Print.

Kia. Advertisement. *Globe and Mail*. Globe and Mail, n.d. Web. 4 Dec. 2010.

72. Map or chart   Cite a map or a chart as you would a book or a short work within a longer work. Use the word "Map" or "Chart" following the title. Add the medium and, for an online source, the sponsor or publisher and the date of access.

Gates, Guilbert. "Examining Victorian Literature, Title by Title." Chart. *New York Times* 4 Dec. 2010, New York ed.: C1. Print.

"Serbia." Map. *Syrena Maps*. Syrena, 2 Feb. 2001. Web. 17 Mar. 2009.

Other sources (including online versions)

This section includes a variety of sources not covered elsewhere. For online sources, consult the appropriate model in this section and also see items 34–55.

73. Government document   Treat the government agency as the author, giving the name of the government followed by the name of the department and the agency, if any. For print sources, add the medium at the end of the entry. For online sources, follow the model for an entire Web site (item 34) or a short work from a Web site (item 35).

government   department   agency

Canada. Indian and Northern Affairs Canada. Can. Northern Economic Development

document title

Agency. "Northern Project Management Office (NPMO) Summary." *Canadian*

Web site title   publisher/sponsor

Northern Economic Development Agency. Indian and Northern Affairs Can.,

publication date   date of access: medium day + month + year

18 May 2010. Web. 1 July 2010.

Canada. Minister of Indian Affairs and Northern Dev. *Gathering Strength: Canada's*
Aboriginal Action Plan. Ottawa: Minister of Public Works and Govt. Services Can.,
2000. Print.

74. Historical document   To cite a historical document, such as the Constitution Act, 1867, or the US Constitution, begin with the document author, if it has one, and then give the document title, neither italicized nor in quotation marks, and the document date. For a print version, continue as for a selection in an anthology (see item 24) or for a book (with the title not italicized). For an online version, cite as a short work from a Web site (see item 35).

Macdonald, John A. A Federal Union. 1865. *Great Canadian Speeches: From John A.*
Macdonald to Adrienne Clarkson. Ed. Dennis Gruending. Markham: Fitzhenry, 2004.
31-35. Print.

The Royal Charter for Incorporating the Hudson's Bay Company. 1670. *Canadian*
Constitutional Documents: A Legal History. William F. Maton, 2001. Web. 23 Oct.
2010.

75. Legal source

Legislative act (law)

Begin with the name of the act, neither italicized nor in quotation marks. Then provide the act's *Statutes of Canada* volume and chapter numbers; its date of enactment; and the medium of publication.

Personal Information Protection and Electronic Documents Act. SC 2000, ch. 5. 13 Apr.
2000. Print.

Court case

Name the first plaintiff and the first defendant. Then give the year of publication (in parentheses for continuous volume numbering, in brackets for numbering by calendar year); the volume, name, and page numbers of the law report; the neutral citation, if applicable (the year of the decision, the court name, and the case number); and publication information. Do not italicize the name of the case. (In the text of the paper, the name of the case is italicized; see item 19 on p. 395.)

Arsenault-Cameron v. Prince Edward Island, [2000] 1 SCR 3, 2000 SCC 1. *Judgments of the Supreme Court of Canada*. Lexum, Faculty of Law, U of Montreal, n.d. Web. 17 Feb. 2009.

76. Pamphlet or brochure   Cite as you would a book (see items 16–33).

Canadian Coalition for Immunization Awareness and Promotion. *Immunize Your Kids!* Ottawa: Can. Public Health Assn., 2009. Print.

77. Unpublished dissertation   Begin with the author's name, followed by the dissertation title in quotation marks; the abbreviation "Diss."; the name of the institution; the year the dissertation was accepted; and the medium of the dissertation.

Gregory, T. R. "The C-Value Enigma." Diss. U of Guelph, 2002. Print.

78. Published dissertation   After the title (italicized) and before the book's publication information, give the abbreviation "Diss.," the name of the institution, and the year the dissertation was accepted. Add the medium of publication at the end.

Estrada, Mariko. *Effects of Anxiety on Children's Working Memory*. Diss. U of Toronto, 2009. Toronto: U of Toronto Press, 2010. Print.

79. Abstract of a dissertation   Cite an abstract as you would an unpublished dissertation. After the dissertation date, give the abbreviation *DA* or *DAI* (for *Dissertation Abstracts* or *Dissertation Abstracts International*), followed by the volume and issue numbers; the year of publication; inclusive page numbers or, if the abstract is not numbered, the item number; and the medium of publication. For an abstract accessed in an online database, give the item number in place of the page number, followed by the name of the database, the medium, and your date of access.

Zyla, Benjamin. "A Bridge Not Too Far? Canada and European Security, 1989-2001." Diss. Royal Military Coll. of Can., 2008. *DAI* 69.10 (2009): AATNR42149. *ProQuest Dissertations and Theses*. Web. 1 Sept. 2010.

80. Published proceedings of a conference Cite as you would a book, adding the name, date, and location of the conference after the title and before the publication information.

Bose, Prosenjit, ed. *Proceedings*. Proc. of the 19th Annual Can. Conf. on Computational

Geometry, 20-22 Aug. 2007, Carleton U. Montreal: McGill-Queen's UP, 2008. Print.

81. Paper in conference proceedings Cite as you would a selection in an anthology (see item 24), giving information about the conference after the title and editors of the proceedings (see item 80).

Bitner, Steven, and Ovidiu Daescu. "Finding Segments and Triangles Spanned by

Points in R3." *Proceedings*. Ed. Prosenjit Bose. Proc. of the 19th Annual Can.

Conf. on Computational Geometry, 20-22 Aug. 2007, Carleton U. Montreal:

McGill-Queen's UP, 2008. 17-20. Print.

82. Published interview Name the person interviewed, followed by the title of the interview (if there is one). If the interview does not have a title, include the word "Interview" after the interviewee's name. Give publication information for the work in which the interview was published.

Egoyan, Atom. "Interview with Canadian-Armenian Filmmaker Atom Egoyan."

Ethnomusicology Forum 18.1 (2009): 73-82. Print.

If you wish to include the name of the interviewer, put it after the title of the interview (or after the name of the interviewee if there is no title).

Riley, Michael. "A Master of Disguise." Interview by Anne Brodie. *M&C*. WotR, 29 June

2010. Web. 2 Sept. 2010.

83. Personal interview To cite an interview that you conducted, begin with the name of the person interviewed. Then write "Personal interview" or "Telephone interview," followed by the date of the interview.

Akufo, Dautey. Personal interview. 11 Apr. 2010.

84. Personal letter To cite a letter that you received, begin with the writer's name and add the phrase "Letter to the author," followed by the date. Add the medium ("MS" for "manuscript," or a handwritten letter; "TS" for "typescript," or a typed letter).

Primak, Shoshana. Letter to the author. 6 May 2010. TS.

85. Published letter Begin with the writer of the letter, the words "Letter to" and the recipient, and the date of the letter (use "N.d." if the letter is undated). Then add the title of the collection and proceed as for a selection in an anthology (see item 24).

Grey Owl. Letter to William Deacon. 10 May 1935. *Canada: A Portrait in Letters,*
    1800-2000. Ed. Charlotte Gray. Toronto: Anchor-Random, 2004. 362-66. Print.

86. Manuscript Give the author, a title or a description of the manuscript, and the date of composition, followed by the abbreviation "MS" for "manuscript" (handwritten) or "TS" for "typescript." Add the name and location of the institution housing the material. For a manuscript found online, give the preceding information but omit "MS" or "TS." Then list the title of the Web site, the medium ("Web"), and your date of access.

Arendt, Hannah. *Between Past and Present*. N.d. 1st draft. Hannah Arendt Papers.
    MS Div., Lib. of Cong. *Manuscript Division, Library of Congress*. Web. 24 Apr. 2009.

MLA-4c MLA information notes (optional)

Researchers who use the MLA system of parenthetical documentation may also use information notes for one of two purposes:

1. to provide additional material that is important but might interrupt the flow of the paper
2. to refer to several sources that support a single point or to provide comments on sources

Information notes may be either footnotes or endnotes. Footnotes appear at the foot of the page; endnotes appear on a separate page at the end of the paper, just before the list of works cited. For either style, the notes are numbered consecutively throughout the paper. The text of the paper contains a raised arabic numeral that corresponds to the number of the note.

TEXT

In the past several years, employees have filed a number of lawsuits against employers because of online monitoring practices.[1]

NOTE

1. For a discussion of federal law applicable to electronic surveillance in the workplace, see Kesan 293.

MLA-5 MLA manuscript format; student research process and sample paper

The following guidelines are consistent with advice given in the *MLA Handbook for Writers of Research Papers*, 7th ed. (New York: MLA, 2009), and with typical requirements for student papers. For a sample MLA paper, see pages 436–40.

MLA-5a MLA manuscript format

Formatting the paper

Papers written in MLA style should be formatted as follows.

Materials and font   Use good-quality 8½″ × 11″ (216 mm × 279 mm) white paper. If your instructor does not require a specific font, choose one that is standard and easy to read (such as Times New Roman).

Title and identification   MLA does not require a title page. On the first page of your paper, place your name, your instructor's name, the course title, and the date on separate lines against the left margin. Then centre your title. (See p. 436 for a sample first page.)

    If your instructor requires a title page, ask for formatting guidelines. A format similar to the one on page 532 may be acceptable.

Pagination   Put the page number preceded by your last name in the upper right corner of each page, one-half inch (1.5 cm) below the top edge. Use arabic numerals (1, 2, 3, and so on).

Margins, line spacing, and paragraph indents   Leave margins of one inch (2.5 cm) on all sides of the page. Left-align the text.

    Double-space throughout the paper. Do not add extra space above or below the title of the paper or between paragraphs.

    Indent the first line of each paragraph one-half inch (1.5 cm) from the left margin.

Capitalization and italics   In titles of works, capitalize all words except articles (*a, an, the*), prepositions (*to, from, between,* and so on), coordinating conjunctions (*and, but, or, nor, for, so, yet*), and the *to* in infinitives—unless they are the first or last word of the title or subtitle. Follow these guidelines in your paper even if the title appears in all capital or all lowercase letters in the source.

In the text of an MLA paper, when a complete sentence follows a colon, lowercase the first word following the colon unless the sentence is a direct quotation or a well-known expression or principle. (See the examples in item 1 on p. 390.)

Italicize the titles of books, periodicals, and other long works, such as Web sites. Use quotation marks around the titles of periodical articles, short stories, poems, and other short works. (If your instructor prefers underlining, use it consistently in place of italics.)

Long quotations   When a quotation is longer than four typed lines of prose or three lines of verse, set it off from the text by indenting the entire quotation one inch (2.5 cm) from the left margin. Double-space the indented quotation, and do not add extra space above or below it.

Quotation marks are not needed when a quotation has been set off from the text by indenting. See page 436 for an example.

URLs (Web addresses)   When you need to break a URL at the end of a line in the text of your paper, break it only after a slash and do not insert a hyphen. For MLA rules on dividing URLs in your list of works cited, see page 431.

Headings   MLA neither encourages nor discourages the use of headings and provides no guidelines for their use. If you would like to insert headings in a long essay or research paper, check first with your instructor.

Visuals   MLA classifies visuals as tables and figures (figures include graphs, charts, maps, photographs, and drawings). Label each table with an arabic numeral ("Table 1," "Table 2," and so on) and provide a clear caption that identifies the subject. Capitalize the caption as you would a title (see P8-c); do not italicize the label and caption or place them in quotation marks. The label and caption should appear on separate lines above the table, flush with the left margin.

For a table that you have borrowed or adapted, give the source below the table in a note like the following:

Source: David N. Greenfield and Richard A. Davis; "Lost in Cyberspace: The Web @ Work"; *CyberPsychology and Behavior* 5.4 (2002): 349; print.

For each figure, place the figure number (using the abbreviation "Fig.") and a caption below the figure, flush left. Capitalize the caption as you would a sentence; include source information following the caption. (When referring to the figure in your paper, use the abbreviation "fig." in parenthetical citations; otherwise spell out the word.) See page 439 for an example of a figure in a paper.

Place visuals in the text, as close as possible to the sentences that relate to them, unless your instructor prefers that visuals appear in an appendix.

Preparing the list of works cited

Begin the list of works cited on a new page at the end of the paper. Centre the title "Works Cited" about one inch (2.5 cm) from the top of the page. Double-space throughout. See page 440 for a sample list of works cited.

Alphabetizing the list   Alphabetize the list by the last names of the authors (or editors); if a work has no author or editor, alphabetize by the first word of the title other than *A, An,* or *The.*

If your list includes two or more works by the same author, use the author's name for the first entry only. For subsequent entries, use three hyphens followed by a period. List the titles in alphabetical order. (See item 6 on p. 401.)

Indenting   Do not indent the first line of each works cited entry, but indent any additional lines one-half inch (1.5 cm). This technique highlights the beginning of each entry, making it easy for readers to scan the alphabetized list. See page 440.

URLs (Web addresses)   If you need to include a URL in a works cited entry and it must be divided across lines, break the URL only after a slash. Do not insert a hyphen at the end of the line. Insert angle brackets around the URL. (See the note following item 34 on p. 413.) If your word processing program automatically turns URLs into links (by underlining them and changing the color), turn off this feature.

MLA-5b Highlights of one student's research process

The following pages describe key steps in student writer Anna Orlov's research process, from selecting a research question to documenting sources. At each step, cross-references in the margins point to more discussion and examples elsewhere in the handbook. Samples from Orlov's process illustrate strategies and skills she used to create an accurate and effective essay. See pages 436–40 for Orlov's final paper.

Making the most of your handbook
Highlights of one student's research process (MLA style)

Anna Orlov, a student in a composition class, was assigned a research essay related to technology and the workplace. The assignment called for her to use a variety of print and electronic sources and to follow MLA style. She developed some questions and strategies to guide her research and writing.

"How do I begin a research paper?"

Before getting started, Orlov worked with a writing tutor to break her research plan into several stages. (Section numbers in blue refer to relevant discussions throughout the book.)

- Ask worthwhile questions about my topic.   C1-b, R1-a
- Talk with a reference librarian about useful types of sources and where to find them.   R1-b
- Consider how each source can contribute to my paper.   R2-a
- Decide which search results are worth a closer look.   R2-b
- Evaluate the sources.   R2-c, R2-d
- Take notes and keep track of the sources.   R3
- Write a working thesis.   C1-c, MLA-1a
- Write a draft and integrate sources.   C2, MLA-3, MLA-4a
- Document sources.   MLA-4

R1-a: Posing questions for a research paper

Orlov began by jotting down her research question: *Is Internet surveillance in the workplace fair or unfair to employees?* She thought the practice might be unfair but wanted to consider all sides of the issue. Orlov knew she would have to be open-minded and flexible and revisit her main ideas as she examined the information and arguments in her sources.

"What sources do I need, and where should I look for them?"

R2-a: Roles sources can play in a paper

Orlov worked with a reference librarian to develop a search strategy. She looked for sources that would provide that background, evidence, and counterevidence.

R1-b: Working with reference librarians

Library databases Because her topic was current, Orlov turned to her library's subscription databases for trustworthy, scholarly, up-to-date articles with concrete examples of workplace Internet surveillance.

R1-c to R1-e: Searching databases, library catalogues, and the Web

Library catalogues Orlov looked for recently published books that could offer in-depth context, including the history of online monitoring and the laws governing workplace surveillance. One book on the topic had the subject heading "electronic monitoring in the workplace." Using that heading as a search term, Orlov found a more focused list of books.

getting started • forming a research plan • posing questions •
finding sources • search terms • search results
MLA-5b 433

The Web Using a general search engine, Orlov found Web sites, articles, and government publications that would explain the software used by employers and various opinions held by those who use the Internet and e-mail in the workplace.

"What search terms should I use?"

Orlov asked a librarian to help her conduct a narrower search with her library's general periodical database. She could count on the database for fewer, more reliable results than an Internet search could provide.

Orlov's search terms	Date restrictions
employee	Past five years
internet use	**Number of results**
surveillance	20

R1-c and p. 338: Refining key-word searches, selecting search terms

"How do I select sources from my search results?"

Orlov used several criteria to decide which results from her general periodical database search were worth a closer look. Would a source

- be relevant to her topic?
- provide authoritative support?
- provide background information?
- offer a range of views or evidence that Orlov could address when forming her argument?

R2: Evaluating sources

DATABASE SCREEN: SEARCH RESULTS

This article's focus on surveillance cameras was not relevant.

"A New Look at Big Brother"
Business Week Online, December 20, 2007, Technology, 959 words, Peter Burrows

Orlov would want to respond to this survey if she argued that Internet surveillance is unfair.

"Wasting Away on the Web; More Employers Taking Workers' Web Use Seriously"
eWeek, August 8, 2005, 692 words, Chris Gonsalves

The *Wall Street Journal* is widely respected and might offer background for Orlov's topic.

"Snooping E-Mail by Software Is Now a Workplace Norm"
The Wall Street Journal Online, March 9, 2005, Pui-Wing Tam et al.

Orlov wondered if the *Progressive* had a political slant. She made a note to check for bias.

"Snooping Bosses; Electronic Surveillance Program"
The Progressive, February 1, 2006: 14, Barbara Ehrenreich

Reviewed by legal experts, a law review article could provide legal context and lend credibility.

"Cyber-Working or Cyber-Shirking? A First Principles Examination of Electronic Privacy in the Workplace"
Florida Law Review 54.2 (2002): 289-332, Jay P. Kesan

"How do I evaluate my sources?"

R2-b to R2-d:
Assessing
print and
online sources

R3: Managing
your
information

After Orlov had conducted several searches and narrowed her list of results, she downloaded her sources and began evaluating them. She wanted to see what evidence and claims she would need to address to strengthen her argument.

She looked carefully at an article in *eWeek*, an online business computing magazine. To keep track of her thoughts about the author's text, she made notes in the margins as she read. Taking good notes would help her to begin forming her own lines of argument and avoid plagiarism.

ORLOV'S NOTES ON AN ARTICLE

Wasting Away on the Web

Opinion: More employers are taking workers' Web use seriously.

Writer is sympathetic to employers?

By Chris Gonsalves
2005-08-08

SECTION: OPINION; Pg. 26

Consider statistics. Is spending work time on personal Internet use so bad?

The issue of IT surveillance was driven home last month when Salary.com and America Online released a survey of 10,000 American workers, many of whom admitted that goofing off on the Internet was their primary method of frittering away the workday. In a sign of the times, it beat out socializing with co-workers, 45 percent to 23 percent.

Strong case for surveillance, but I'm not convinced. Counter with useful workplace Web surfing?

While bosses can easily detect and interrupt water-cooler chatter, the employee who is shopping at Lands' End or IMing with fellow fantasy baseball managers may actually appear to be working. Thwarting the activity is a technology challenge, and it's one that more and more enterprises are taking seriously, despite resistance from privacy advocates and some employees themselves.

Common examples— readers can relate.

Does the AMA side with employers? Survey results— good for background and counter-argument.

According to the American Management Association, 78 percent of large U.S. employers are regularly checking workers' e-mail messages, Internet use, computer files and phone calls. Nearly half of such employers store employee e-mail messages for review. The AMA also found that 65 percent of enterprises had disciplined employees for misuse of e-mail or the Internet at work, and 27 percent had actually fired someone over such offenses.

According to a recent poll of workers in technology-related fields published by the executive recruiting company FPC, 61 percent said they felt their bosses had the right to cyber-spy on them, but only with consent. Just 28 percent felt IT had the right to monitor their activity without consent, and only 1 percent said an employer never has the right to monitor Internet use.

Employees want employers to be up front about monitoring.

"It's not surprising that companies want to assure that their employees' time is predominantly spent on work-related computer usage," said FPC President Ron Herzog. "The majority of employees ... would like to be informed, so it is always in the company's best interest to have an Internet usage policy clearly outlining the company's expectations, which all employees sign upon hiring."

When is workplace surveillance unfair and when not?

As the stakes grow beyond a few wasted man-hours and some misappropriated bandwidth, it grows increasingly important for IT to let everyone in the company know they might be watched.

Executive Editor/News Chris Gonsalves can be contacted at chris_gonsalves@ziffdavis.com.
LOAD-DATE: August 8, 2005
LANGUAGE: English

Copyright 2005 Ziff Davis Media Inc. All Rights Reserved

"How do I integrate sources into my paper?"

C1-c and
MLA-1a: Writing
a working thesis

After reading and evaluating a number of sources, Orlov wrote her working thesis: *Though companies may have legitimate reasons to monitor employees' Internet usage, electronic surveillance is more unfair than beneficial to employees since it threatens their privacy.* She then sketched an informal plan to organize her ideas and began writing a rough draft. As she wrote and revised, she integrated sources from her research.

C1–C2: Planning
and drafting

R3-c and
MLA-2: Quoting,
summarizing, and
paraphrasing

For example, Orlov had selected a book on electronic surveillance in the workplace, written by Frederick Lane III. She looked through the table of contents and selected a few chapters that seemed relevant to her working thesis. She read the chapters for ideas and information that she could paraphrase, summarize, or quote to provide background, support her argument, and help her counter the kind of pro-surveillance position that Chris Gonsalves takes in his *eWeek* article.

"How do I keep track of and document my sources?"

R3-b: Keeping
track of source
materials

Because Orlov took careful notes about publication information and page numbers for source material throughout her research process, she didn't need to hunt down information as she cited her sources.

MLA-4:
Documenting
sources

She followed the MLA (Modern Language Association) system to document her sources.

ENTRY IN WORKS CITED LIST

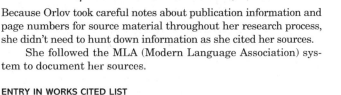

author   title and subtitle

Lane, Frederick S., III. *The Naked Employee: How Technology Is*

                                        city of
                                        publication   publisher

Compromising Workplace Privacy. New York: Amer. Management Assn.,

publication
date   medium

2003. Print.

MLA-5c Sample research paper: MLA style

On the following pages is a research paper on the topic of electronic surveillance in the workplace, written by Anna Orlov, a student in a composition class. Orlov's paper is documented with in-text citations and a list of works cited in MLA style. Annotations in the margins of the paper draw your attention to Orlov's use of MLA style and her effective writing.

MODELS   hackerhandbooks.com/writersref
   > Model papers   > MLA research papers: Orlov; Daly; Levi
            > MLA annotated bibliography: Orlov

Orlov 1

Anna Orlov

Professor Willis

English 101

17 March 2009

Title is centred.

Online Monitoring:

A Threat to Employee Privacy in the Wired Workplace

Opening sentences provide background for the thesis.

As the Internet has become an integral tool of businesses, company policies on Internet usage have become as common as policies regarding vacation days or sexual harassment. A 2005 study by the American Management Association and ePolicy Institute found that 76% of companies monitor employees' use of the Web, and the number of companies that block employees' access to certain Web sites has increased 27% since 2001 (1). Unlike other company rules, however, Internet usage policies often include language authorizing companies to secretly monitor their employees, a practice that raises questions about rights in the

Thesis asserts Orlov's main point.

workplace. Although companies often have legitimate concerns that lead them to monitor employees' Internet usage—from expensive security breaches to reduced productivity—the benefits of electronic surveillance are outweighed by its costs to employees' privacy and autonomy.

While surveillance of employees is not a new phenomenon, electronic surveillance allows employers to monitor workers with unprecedented

Summary and long quotation are each introduced with a signal phrase naming the author.

efficiency. In his book *The Naked Employee*, Frederick Lane describes offline ways in which employers have been permitted to intrude on employees' privacy for decades, such as drug testing, background checks, psychological exams, lie detector tests, and in-store video surveillance. The difference, Lane argues, between these old methods of data gathering and electronic surveillance involves quantity:

Long quotation is set off from the text; quotation marks are omitted.

> Technology makes it possible for employers to gather enormous amounts of data about employees, often far beyond what is necessary to satisfy safety or productivity concerns. And the trends that drive technology—faster, smaller, cheaper—make it possible for larger and larger numbers of employers to gather

Page number is given in parentheses after the final period.

> ever-greater amounts of personal data. (3-4)

In an age when employers can collect data whenever employees use their

---

Marginal annotations indicate MLA-style formatting and effective writing.

Orlov 2

computers—when they send e-mail, surf the Web, or even arrive at or depart from their workstations—the challenge for both employers and employees is to determine how much is too much.

Another key difference between traditional surveillance and electronic surveillance is that employers can monitor workers' computer use secretly. One popular monitoring method is keystroke logging, which is done by means of an undetectable program on employees' computers. The Web site of a vendor for Spector Pro, a popular keystroke logging program, explains that the software can be installed to operate in "Stealth" mode so that it "does not show up as an icon, does not appear in the Windows system tray, . . . [and] cannot be uninstalled without the Spector Pro password which YOU specify" ("Automatically"). As Lane explains, these programs record every key entered into the computer in hidden directories that can later be accessed or uploaded by supervisors; the programs can even scan for keywords tailored to individual companies (128-29).

Some experts have argued that a range of legitimate concerns justifies employer monitoring of employee Internet usage. As PC World columnist Daniel Tynan points out, companies that don't monitor network traffic can be penalized for their ignorance: "Employees could accidentally (or deliberately) spill confidential information . . . or allow worms to spread throughout a corporate network." The ePolicy Institute, an organization that advises companies about reducing risks from technology, reported that breaches in computer security cost institutions $100 million in 1999 alone (Flynn). Companies also are held legally accountable for many of the transactions conducted on their networks and with their technology. Legal scholar Jay Kesan points out that the law holds employers liable for employees' actions such as violations of copyright laws, the distribution of offensive or graphic sexual material, and illegal disclosure of confidential information (312).

These kinds of concerns should give employers, in certain instances, the right to monitor employee behavior. But employers rushing to adopt surveillance programs might not be adequately weighing the effect such programs can have on employee morale. Employers must consider the possibility that employees will perceive surveillance as a breach of trust that can make them feel like disobedient children, not responsible

Clear topic sentences, like this one, are used throughout the paper.

Source with an unknown author is cited by a shortened title.

Orlov anticipates objections and provides sources for opposing views.

Transition helps readers move from one paragraph to the next.

Orlov 3

adults who wish to perform their jobs professionally and autonomously.

Orlov treats both sides fairly; she provides a transition to her own argument.

Yet determining how much autonomy workers should be given is complicated by the ambiguous nature of productivity in the wired workplace. On the one hand, computers and Internet access give employees powerful tools to carry out their jobs; on the other hand, the same technology offers constant temptations to avoid work. As a 2005 study by *Salary.com* and *America Online* indicates, the Internet ranked as the top choice among employees for ways of wasting time on the job; it beat talking with co-workers—the second most popular method—by a margin of nearly two to one (Frauenheim). Chris Gonsalves, an editor for *eWeek.com*, argues that the technology has changed the terms between employers and employees: "While bosses can easily detect and interrupt water-cooler chatter," he writes, "the employee who is shopping at Lands' End or IMing with fellow fantasy baseball managers may actually appear to

No page number is available for this Web source.

be working." The gap between behaviors that are observable to managers and the employee's actual activities when sitting behind a computer has created additional motivations for employers to invest in surveillance programs. "Dilbert," a popular cartoon that spoofs office culture, aptly captures how rampant recreational Internet use has become in the workplace (see fig. 1).

Orlov counters opposing views and provides support for her argument.

But monitoring online activities can have the unintended effect of making employees resentful. As many workers would be quick to point out, Web surfing and other personal uses of the Internet can provide needed outlets in the stressful work environment; many scholars have argued that limiting and policing these outlets can exacerbate tensions between

Orlov uses a brief signal phrase to move from her argument to the words of a source.

employees and managers. Kesan warns that "prohibiting personal use can seem extremely arbitrary and can seriously harm morale. . . . Imagine a concerned parent who is prohibited from checking on a sick child by a draconian company policy" (315-16). As this analysis indicates, employees can become disgruntled when Internet usage policies are enforced to their full extent.

Additionally, many experts disagree with employers' assumption that online monitoring can increase productivity. Employment law attorney Joseph Schmitt argues that, particularly for employees who are paid a salary rather than an hourly wage, "a company shouldn't care whether employees spend one or 10 hours on the Internet as long as they are

Orlov 4

Fig. 1. This "Dilbert" comic strip suggests that personal Internet usage is widespread in the workplace (Adams 106).

Illustration has figure number, caption, and source information.

getting their jobs done—and provided that they are not accessing inappropriate sites" (qtd. in Verespej). Other experts even argue that time spent on personal Internet browsing can actually be productive for companies. According to Bill Coleman, an executive at *Salary.com*, "Personal Internet use and casual office conversations often turn into new business ideas or suggestions for gaining operating efficiencies" (qtd. in Frauenheim). Employers, in other words, may benefit from showing more faith in their employees' ability to exercise their autonomy.

Orlov cites an indirect source: words quoted in another source.

Employees' right to privacy and autonomy in the workplace, however, remains a murky area of the law. Although evaluating where to draw the line between employee rights and employer powers is often a duty that falls to the judicial system, the courts have shown little willingness to intrude on employers' exercise of control over their computer networks. Federal law provides few guidelines related to online monitoring of employees, and only Connecticut and Delaware require companies to disclose this type of surveillance to employees (Tam et al.). "It is unlikely that we will see a legally guaranteed zone of privacy in the American workplace," predicts Kesan (293). This reality leaves employees and employers to sort the potential risks and benefits of technology in contract agreements and terms of employment. With continuing advances in technology, protecting both employers and employees will require greater awareness of these programs, better disclosure to employees, and a more public discussion about what types of protections are necessary to guard individual freedoms in the wired workplace.

Orlov sums up her argument and suggests a course of action.

Orlov 5

Heading is centred.

Works Cited

Adams, Scott. *Dilbert and the Way of the Weasel*. New York: Harper, 2002.
Print.

American Management Association and ePolicy Institute. "2005 Electronic
Monitoring and Surveillance Survey." *American Management
Association*. Amer. Management Assn., 2005. Web. 15 Feb. 2009.

"Automatically Record Everything They Do Online! Spector Pro 5.0
FAQ's." *Netbus.org*. Netbus.Org, n.d. Web. 17 Feb. 2009.

Flynn, Nancy. "Internet Policies." *ePolicy Institute*. ePolicy Inst., n.d.
Web. 15 Feb. 2009.

Frauenheim, Ed. "Stop Reading This Headline and Get Back to Work."
CNET News.com. CNET Networks, 11 July 2005. Web. 17 Feb.
2009.

Gonsalves, Chris. "Wasting Away on the Web." *eWeek.com*. Ziff Davis
Enterprise Holdings, 8 Aug. 2005. Web. 16 Feb. 2009.

Kesan, Jay P. "Cyber-Working or Cyber-Shirking? A First Principles
Examination of Electronic Privacy in the Workplace." *Florida
Law Review* 54.2 (2002): 289-332. Print.

Lane, Frederick S., III. *The Naked Employee: How Technology Is
Compromising Workplace Privacy*. New York: Amer. Management
Assn., 2003. Print.

Tam, Pui-Wing, et al. "Snooping E-Mail by Software Is Now a Workplace
Norm." *Wall Street Journal* 9 Mar. 2005: B1+. Print.

Tynan, Daniel. "Your Boss Is Watching." *PC World*. PC World
Communications, 6 Oct. 2004. Web. 17 Sept. 2009.

Verespej, Michael A. "Inappropriate Internet Surfing." *Industry Week*.
Penton Media, 7 Feb. 2000. Web. 16 Feb. 2009.

List is alphabetized by authors' last names (or by title when a work has no author).

Abbreviation "n.d." indicates that the online source has no update date.

First line of each entry is at the left margin; extra lines are indented ¹/₂" (1.5 cm).

Double-spacing is used throughout.

A work with four authors is listed by the first author's name and the abbreviation "et al." (for "and others").

APA
CMS

APA and CMS
Papers

APA/CMS APA and CMS Papers

Directory to APA in-text citation models

Directory to APA reference list models

→

*Directory to **CMS-style note and bibliography models** is on page 498.*

This tabbed section shows how to document sources in APA style for the social sciences and fields like nursing and business, and in CMS (*Chicago*) style for history and some humanities classes. It also includes discipline-specific advice on three important topics: supporting a thesis, citing sources and avoiding plagiarism, and integrating sources.

NOTE: For advice on finding and evaluating sources and on managing information in courses across the disciplines, see the tabbed section R, Researching.

APA Papers

Many writing assignments in the social sciences are either reports of original research or reviews of the literature (previously published research) on a particular topic. Often an original research report contains a "review of the literature" section that places the writer's project in the context of previous research.

Most social science instructors will ask you to document your sources with the American Psychological Association (APA) system of in-text citations and references described in APA-4. You face three main challenges when writing a social science paper that draws on sources: (1) supporting a thesis, (2) citing your sources and avoiding plagiarism, and (3) integrating quotations and other source material.

Examples in this section appear in APA style and are drawn from one student's research for a review of the literature on treatments for childhood obesity. Luisa Mirano's complete paper appears on pages 488–96.

≣ APA-1 Supporting a thesis

Most assignments ask you to form a thesis, or main idea, and to support that thesis with well-organized evidence. In a paper reviewing the literature on a topic, this thesis analyzes the often competing conclusions drawn by a variety of researchers.

APA-1a Form a working thesis.

Once you have read a variety of sources and considered your issue from different perspectives, you are ready to form a working thesis: a one-sentence (or occasionally a two-sentence) statement of your central idea. (See also C1-c.) Because it is a working, or tentative, thesis, you can remain flexible and revise it as your ideas develop. Ultimately, your thesis will express not just your opinion but your informed, reasoned answer to your research question (see R1-a). Here, for example, is a research question posed by Luisa Mirano, a student in a psychology class, followed by her thesis in answer to that question.

RESEARCH QUESTION

Is medication the right treatment for the escalating problem of childhood obesity?

WORKING THESIS

Treating cases of childhood obesity with medication alone is too narrow an approach for this growing problem.

Notice that the thesis expresses a view on a debatable issue—an issue about which intelligent, well-meaning people might disagree. The writer's job is to persuade such readers that this view is worth taking seriously.

PRACTICE hackerhandbooks.com/writersref
> APA > APA 1–1 and APA 1–2

APA-1b Organize your ideas.

The American Psychological Association encourages the use of headings to help readers follow the organization of a paper. For an original research report, the major headings often follow a standard model: Method, Results, Discussion. The introduction is not given a heading; it consists of the material between the title of the paper and the first heading.

For a literature review, headings will vary. The student who wrote about treatments for childhood obesity used four questions to focus her research; the questions then became headings in her paper (see pp. 488–96).

> **Making the most of your handbook**
>
> A working thesis and rough outline can help writers get started.
>
> ▶ Drafting a working thesis: C1-c
>
> ▶ Sketching a plan: C1-d

APA-1c Use sources to inform and support your argument.

Used thoughtfully, your source materials will make your argument more complex and convincing for readers. Sources can play several different roles as you develop your points.

Providing background information or context

You can use facts and statistics to support generalizations or to establish the importance of your topic, as student writer Luisa Mirano does in her introduction.

> In March 2004, U.S. Surgeon General Richard Carmona called attention to a health problem in the United States that, until recently, has been overlooked: childhood obesity. Carmona said that the "astounding" 15% child obesity rate constitutes an "epidemic." Since the early 1980s, that rate has "doubled in children and tripled in adolescents." Now more than 9 million children are classified as obese.

Explaining terms or concepts

If readers are unlikely to be familiar with a word, a phrase, or an idea important to your topic, you must explain it for them. Quoting or paraphrasing a source can help you define terms and concepts in accessible

language. Luisa Mirano uses a scholarly source to explain how one of
the major obesity drugs functions.

> Sibutramine suppresses appetite by blocking the reuptake of the
> neurotransmitters serotonin and norepinephrine in the brain (Yanovski &
> Yanovski, 2002, p. 594).

Supporting your claims

As you draft your argument, make sure to back up your assertions
with facts, examples, and other evidence from your research (see also
A2-e). Luisa Mirano, for example, uses one source's findings to support
her central idea that the medical treatment of childhood obesity has
limitations.

> As journalist Greg Critser (2003) noted in his book *Fat Land*, use of weight-loss
> drugs is unlikely to have an effect without the proper "support system"—one that
> includes doctors, facilities, time, and money (p. 3).

Lending authority to your argument

Expert opinion can add credibility to your argument (see also A2-e). But
don't rely on experts to make your argument for you. Construct your
argument in your own words and, when appropriate, cite the judgment
of an authority in the field for support.

> Both medical experts and policymakers recognize that solutions might come not
> only from a laboratory but also from policy, education, and advocacy. A handbook
> designed to educate doctors on obesity called for "major changes in some aspects
> of western culture" (Hoppin & Taveras, 2004, Conclusion section, para. 1).

Anticipating and countering alternative interpretations

Do not ignore sources that seem contrary to your position or that offer
interpretations different from your own. Instead, use them to give
voice to opposing points of view and alternative interpretations before
you counter them (see A2-f). Readers often have objections in mind
already, whether or not they agree with you. Mirano uses a source to
acknowledge value in her opponents' position that medication alone
can successfully treat childhood obesity.

> As researchers Yanovski and Yanovski (2002) have explained, obesity was once
> considered "either a moral failing or evidence of underlying psychopathology"
> (p. 592). But this view has shifted: Many medical professionals now consider
> obesity a biomedical rather than a moral condition, influenced by both genetic

and environmental factors. Yanovski and Yanovski have further noted that the development of weight-loss medications in the early 1990s showed that "obesity should be treated in the same manner as any other chronic disease . . . through the long-term use of medication" (p. 592).

≡ APA-2 Citing sources; avoiding plagiarism

Your research paper is a collaboration between you and your sources. To be fair and ethical, you must acknowledge your debt to the writers of those sources. Failure to do so is a form of academic dishonesty known as *plagiarism*.

Three different acts are considered plagiarism: (1) failing to cite quotations and borrowed ideas, (2) failing to enclose borrowed language in quotation marks, and (3) failing to put summaries and paraphrases in your own words. It's a good idea to find out how your school defines and addresses academic dishonesty. (See also R3-c.)

APA-2a Cite quotations and borrowed ideas.

Sources are cited for two reasons:

- to tell readers where your information comes from—so that they can assess its reliability and, if interested, find and read the original source
- to give credit to the writers from whom you have borrowed words and ideas

You must cite anything you borrow from a source, including direct quotations; statistics and other specific facts; visuals such as tables, graphs, and diagrams; and any ideas you present in a summary or paraphrase.

The only exception is common knowledge—information that your readers may know or could easily locate in any number of reference sources. For example, most general encyclopedias will tell readers that Sigmund Freud wrote *The Interpretation of Dreams* and that chimpanzees can learn American Sign Language.

As a rule, when you have seen certain information repeatedly in your reading, you don't need to cite it. However, when information has appeared in only a few sources, when it is highly specific (as with statistics), or when it is controversial, you should cite the source.

The American Psychological Association recommends an author-date system of citations. The following is a brief description of how the author-date system often works.

1. The source is introduced by a signal phrase that includes the last name of the author followed by the date of publication in parentheses.
2. The material being cited is followed by a page number in parentheses.
3. At the end of the paper, an alphabetized list of references gives complete publication information for the source.

IN-TEXT CITATION

As researchers Yanovski and Yanovski (2002) have explained, obesity was once considered "either a moral failing or evidence of underlying psychopathology" (p. 592).

ENTRY IN THE LIST OF REFERENCES

Yanovski, S. Z., & Yanovski, J. A. (2002). Drug therapy: Obesity. *The New England Journal of Medicine, 346,* 591-602.

This basic APA format varies for different types of sources. For a detailed discussion and other models, see APA-4.

APA-2b Enclose borrowed language in quotation marks.

To indicate that you are using a source's exact phrases or sentences, you must enclose them in quotation marks unless they have been set off from the text by indenting (see p. 453). To omit the quotation marks is to claim—falsely—that the language is your own. Such an omission is plagiarism even if you have cited the source.

ORIGINAL SOURCE

In an effort to seek the causes of this disturbing trend, experts have pointed to a range of important potential contributors to the rise in childhood obesity that are unrelated to media: a reduction in physical education classes and after-school athletic programs, an increase in the availability of sodas and snacks in public schools, the growth in the number of fast-food outlets across the country, the trend toward "super-sizing" food portions in restaurants, and the increasing number of highly processed high-calorie and high-fat grocery products.

—Henry J. Kaiser Family Foundation, "The Role of Media in Childhood Obesity" (2004), p. 1

PLAGIARISM

According to the Henry J. Kaiser Family Foundation (2004), experts have pointed to a range of important potential contributors to the rise in childhood obesity that are unrelated to media (p. 1).

BORROWED LANGUAGE IN QUOTATION MARKS

According to the Henry J. Kaiser Family Foundation (2004), "experts have pointed to a range of important potential contributors to the rise in childhood obesity that are unrelated to media" (p. 1).

NOTE: When quoted sentences are set off from the text by indenting, quotation marks are not needed (see p. 453).

APA-2c Put summaries and paraphrases in your own words.

Summaries and paraphrases are written in your own words. A summary condenses information; a paraphrase conveys the information using roughly the same number of words as in the original source. When you summarize or paraphrase, it is not enough to name the source; you must restate the source's meaning using your own language. (See also R3-c.) You commit plagiarism if you half-copy the author's sentences—either by mixing the author's phrases with your own without using quotation marks or by plugging your own synonyms into the author's sentence structure. The following paraphrases are plagiarized—even though the source is cited—because their language and sentence structure are too close to those of the source.

ORIGINAL SOURCE

In an effort to seek the causes of this disturbing trend, experts have pointed to a range of important potential contributors to the rise in childhood obesity that are unrelated to media.

—Henry J. Kaiser Family Foundation, "The Role of Media in Childhood Obesity" (2004), p. 1

UNACCEPTABLE BORROWING OF PHRASES

According to the Henry J. Kaiser Family Foundation (2004), experts have indicated a range of significant potential contributors to the rise in childhood obesity that are not linked to media (p. 1).

UNACCEPTABLE BORROWING OF STRUCTURE

According to the Henry J. Kaiser Family Foundation (2004), experts have identified a variety of key factors causing a rise in childhood obesity, factors that are not tied to media (p. 1).

To avoid plagiarizing an author's language, resist the temptation to look at the source while you are summarizing or paraphrasing. After you have read the passage you want to paraphrase, set the source aside. Ask yourself, "What is the author's meaning?" In your own words, state your understanding of the author's basic point. Return to the source and check that you haven't used the author's language or sentence structure or misrepresented the author's ideas. When you fully understand another writer's meaning, you can more easily and accurately present those ideas in your own words.

ACCEPTABLE PARAPHRASE

A report by the Henry J. Kaiser Family Foundation (2004) described causes other than media for the childhood obesity crisis (p. 1).

☰ APA-3 Integrating sources

Quotations, summaries, paraphrases, and facts will help you develop your argument, but they cannot speak for you. You can use several strategies to integrate information from sources into your paper while maintaining your own voice.

APA-3a Use quotations appropriately.

In your academic writing, keep the emphasis on your ideas; use your own words to summarize and to paraphrase your sources and to explain your points. Sometimes, however, quotations can be the most effective way to integrate a source.

WHEN TO USE QUOTATIONS

- When language is especially vivid or expressive
- When exact wording is needed for technical accuracy
- When it is important to let the debaters of an issue explain their positions in their own words
- When the words of an authority lend weight to an argument
- When the language of a source is the topic of your discussion

Limiting your use of quotations Although it is tempting to insert many quotations in your paper and to use your own words only for connecting passages, do not quote excessively. It is almost impossible to integrate numerous long quotations smoothly into your own text. It is not always necessary to quote full sentences from a source. To reduce your reliance on the words of others, you can often integrate language from a source into your own sentence structure.

> Carmona (2004) advised the subcommittee that the situation constitutes an "epidemic" and that the skyrocketing statistics are "astounding."

> As researchers continue to face a number of unknowns about obesity, it may be helpful to envision treating the disorder, as Yanovski and Yanovski (2002) suggested, "in the same manner as any other chronic disease" (p. 592).

Using the ellipsis mark To condense a quoted passage, you can use the ellipsis mark (three periods, with spaces between) to indicate that you have omitted words. What remains must be grammatically complete.

> Roman (2003) reported that "social factors are nearly as significant as individual metabolism in the formation of . . . dietary habits of adolescents" (p. 345).

The writer has omitted the words *both healthy and unhealthy* from the source.

When you want to leave out one or more full sentences, use a period before the three ellipsis dots.

> According to Sothern and Gordon (2003), "Environmental factors may contribute as much as 80% to the causes of childhood obesity. . . . Research suggests that obese children demonstrate decreased levels of physical activity and increased psychosocial problems" (p. 104).

Ordinarily, do not use an ellipsis mark at the beginning or at the end of a quotation. Readers will understand that you have taken the quoted material from a longer passage, so such marks are not necessary. The only exception occurs when you have dropped words at the end of the final quoted sentence. In such cases, put three ellipsis dots before the closing quotation mark. Make sure that omissions and ellipsis marks do not distort the meaning of your source.

Using brackets Brackets allow you to insert your own words into quoted material. You can insert words in brackets to clarify a confusing reference or to keep a sentence grammatical in your context.

> The cost of treating obesity currently totals $117 billion per year—a price, according to the surgeon general, "second only to the cost of [treating] tobacco use" (Carmona, 2004).

To indicate an error such as a misspelling in a quotation, insert [*sic*], italicized and with brackets around it, right after the error. (See P6-b.)

Setting off long quotations   When you quote forty or more words from a source, set off the quotation by indenting it one-half inch (1.5 cm) from the left margin. Use the normal right margin and do not single-space the quotation.

Long quotations should be introduced by an informative sentence, usually followed by a colon. Quotation marks are unnecessary because the indented format tells readers that the passage is taken word-for-word from the source.

> Yanovski and Yanovski (2002) have described earlier treatments of obesity that
> focused on behavior modification:
>
>> With the advent of behavioral treatments for obesity in the 1960s, hope
>> arose that modification of maladaptive eating and exercise habits would
>> lead to sustained weight loss, and that time-limited programs would
>> produce permanent changes in weight. Medications for the treatment
>> of obesity were proposed as short-term adjuncts for patients, who
>> would presumably then acquire the skills necessary to continue to lose
>> weight, reach "ideal body weight," and maintain a reduced weight
>> indefinitely. (p. 592)

Notice that at the end of an indented quotation the parenthetical citation goes outside the final mark of punctuation. (When a quotation is run into your text, the opposite is true. See the sample citations on p. 452.)

APA-3b Use signal phrases to integrate sources.

Whenever you include a paraphrase, summary, or direct quotation of another writer's work in your paper, prepare your readers for it with a signal phrase. A signal phrase usually names the author of the source, gives the publication year in parentheses, and often provides some context. It commonly appears before the source material. To vary your sentence structure, you may decide to interrupt source material with a signal phrase or place the signal phrase after your paraphrase, summary, or direct quotation. It is generally acceptable in the social sciences to call authors by their last name only, even on a first mention. If your paper refers to two authors with same last name, use initials as well.

Using signal phrases in APA papers

To avoid monotony, try to vary both the language and the placement of
your signal phrases.

Model signal phrases

In the words of Carmona (2004), "..."

As Yanovski and Yanovski (2002) have noted, "..."

Hoppin and Taveras (2004), medical researchers, pointed out that "..."

"...," claimed Critser (2003).

"...," wrote Duenwald (2004), "..."

Researchers McDuffie et al. (2003) have offered a compelling argument
for this view: "..."

Hilts (2002) answered objections with the following analysis: "..."

Verbs in signal phrases

admitted	contended	reasoned
agreed	declared	refuted
argued	denied	rejected
asserted	emphasized	reported
believed	insisted	responded
claimed	noted	suggested
compared	observed	thought
confirmed	pointed out	wrote

When you write a signal phrase, choose a verb that is appropriate
for the way you are using the source (see APA-1c). Are you providing
background, explaining a concept, supporting a claim, lending authority, or refuting an argument? See the chart on this page for a list of
verbs commonly used in signal phrases. Note that APA requires using
verbs in the past tense or present perfect tense (*explained* or *has
explained*) to introduce source material. Use the present tense only for
discussing the results of an experiment (*the results show*) or knowledge that has been clearly established (*researchers agree*).

Marking boundaries

Readers need to move from your words to the words of a source
without feeling a jolt. Avoid dropping direct quotations into your
text without warning. Instead, provide clear signal phrases, including at least the author's name and the year of publication. Signal
phrases mark the boundaries between source material and your

own words; they can also tell readers why a source is worth quoting.
(The signal phrase is highlighted in the second example.)

DROPPED QUOTATION

Obesity was once considered in a very different light. "For many years, obesity
was approached as it if were either a moral failing or evidence of underlying
psychopathology" (Yanovski & Yanovski, 2002, p. 592).

QUOTATION WITH SIGNAL PHRASE

Obesity was once considered in a very different light. As researchers Yanovski and
Yanovski (2002) have explained, obesity was widely thought of as "either a moral
failing or evidence of underlying psychopathology" (p. 592).

Using signal phrases with summaries and paraphrases

As with quotations, you should introduce most summaries and paraphrases with a signal phrase that mentions the author and the year
and places the material in the context of your argument. Readers will
then understand where the summary or paraphrase begins.

Without the signal phrase (highlighted) in the following example,
readers might think that only the last sentence is being cited, when
in fact the whole paragraph is based on the source.

Carmona (2004) advised a Senate subcommittee that the problem of childhood
obesity is dire and that the skyrocketing statistics—which put the child
obesity rate at 15%—are cause for alarm. More than 9 million children,
double the number in the early 1980s, are classified as obese. Carmona
warned that obesity can cause myriad physical problems that only worsen
as children grow older.

There are times, however, when a summary or a paraphrase does
not require a signal phrase naming the author. When the context makes
clear where the cited material begins, you may omit the signal phrase
and include the author's name and the year in parentheses. Unless the
work is short, also include the page number in the parentheses.

Integrating statistics and other facts

When you are citing a statistic or another specific fact, a signal phrase
is often not necessary. In most cases, readers will understand that the
citation refers to the statistic or fact (not the whole paragraph).

In purely financial terms, the drugs cost more than $3 a day on average
(Duenwald, 2004).

There is nothing wrong, however, with using a signal phrase to introduce a statistic or another fact.

Duenwald (2004) reported that the drugs cost more than $3 a day on average.

Putting source material in context

Readers should not have to guess why source material appears in your paper. If you use another writer's words, you must explain how they relate to your point. In other words, you must put the source in context. It's a good idea to embed a quotation between sentences of your own, introducing it with a signal phrase and following it up with interpretive comments that link the quotation to your paper's argument. (See also APA-3c.)

QUOTATION WITH EFFECTIVE CONTEXT

A report by the Henry J. Kaiser Family Foundation (2004) outlined trends that may have contributed to the childhood obesity crisis, including food advertising for children as well as

> a reduction in physical education classes . . . , an increase in the availability of sodas and snacks in public schools, the growth in the number of fast-food outlets . . . , and the increasing number of highly processed high-calorie and high-fat grocery products. (p. 1)

Addressing each of these areas requires more than a doctor armed with a prescription pad; it requires a broad mobilization not just of doctors and concerned parents but of educators, food industry executives, advertisers, and media representatives.

APA-3c Synthesize sources.

When you synthesize multiple sources in a research paper, you create a conversation about your research topic. You show readers that your argument is based on your active analysis and integration of ideas, not just a list of quotations and paraphrases. Your synthesis will show how your sources relate to one another; one source may support, extend, or counter the ideas of another. Readers should be able to see how each one functions in your argument (see R2-a).

Considering how sources relate to your argument

Before you integrate sources and show readers how they relate to one another, consider how each one might contribute to your own argument. As student writer Luisa Mirano became more informed through

her research about treatments for childhood obesity, she asked herself
these questions: *What do I think about the various treatments for
childhood obesity? Which sources might support my ideas? Which
sources might help extend or illustrate the points I want to make?
What common counterarguments do I need to address to strengthen
my position?* Mirano kept these questions in mind as she read and
annotated sources.

Placing sources in conversation

When you synthesize sources, you show readers how the ideas of one
source relate to those of another by connecting and analyzing the ideas
in the context of your argument. Keep the emphasis on your own writing.
After all, you've done the research and thought through the issues, so
you should control the conversation. The thread of your argument should
be easy to identify and to understand, with or without your sources.

SAMPLE SYNTHESIS (DRAFT)

tudent writer
uisa Mirano
egins with
claim that
eeds support.

ignal phrases
dicate how
ources
ontribute to
Mirano's paper
nd show that
e ideas that
llow are not
er own.

Mirano interprets
nd connects
urces. Each
aragraph ends
ith her own
oughts.

Medical treatments have clear costs for individual
patients, including unpleasant side effects, little information
about long-term use, and uncertainty that they will yield
significant weight loss. The financial burden is heavy as well;
the drugs cost more than $3 a day on average (Duenwald,
2004). In each of the clinical trials, use of medication was
accompanied by expensive behavioral therapies, including
counseling, nutrition education, fitness advising, and
monitoring. As Critser (2003) noted in his book *Fat Land,*
use of weight-loss drugs is unlikely to have an effect without
the proper "support system"—one that includes doctors,
facilities, time, and money (p. 3). For many families, this
level of care is prohibitively expensive.

Both medical experts and policymakers recognize
that solutions might come not only from a laboratory but
also from policy, education, and advocacy. A handbook
designed to educate doctors on obesity called for "major
changes in some aspects of western culture" (Hoppin &
Taveras, 2004, Conclusion section, para. 1). Solving the
childhood obesity problem will require broad mobilization of
doctors and concerned parents and also of educators, food
industry executives, advertisers, and media representatives.

Student writer

Source 1

Student writer

Source 2

Student writer

Source 3

Student writer

In this draft, Mirano uses her own analyses to shape the conversation among her sources. She does not simply string quotations and statistics together or allow her sources to overwhelm her writing. The final sentence, written in her own voice, gives her an opportunity to explain to readers how her sources support and extend her argument. When synthesizing sources, ask yourself these questions:

- Which sources inform, support, or extend your argument?
- Have you varied the functions of sources—to provide background, explain concepts, lend authority, and anticipate counterarguments? Do your signal phrases indicate these functions?
- Do you explain how your sources support your argument?
- Do you connect and analyze sources in your own voice?
- Is your own argument easy to identify and to understand, with or without your sources?

APA-4 Documenting sources

In most social science classes, you will be asked to use the APA system for documenting sources, which is set forth in the *Publication Manual of the American Psychological Association,* 6th ed. (Washington: APA, 2010). APA recommends in-text citations that refer readers to a list of references.

An in-text citation usually gives the author of the source (often in a signal phrase), the year of publication, and at times a page number in parentheses. At the end of the paper, a list of references provides publication information about the source (see p. 496 for a sample list). The direct link between the in-text citation and the entry in the reference list is highlighted in green in the following example.

IN-TEXT CITATION

Yanovski and Yanovski (2002) reported that "the current state of the treatment for obesity is similar to the state of the treatment of hypertension several decades ago" (p. 600).

ENTRY IN THE LIST OF REFERENCES

Yanovski, S. Z., & Yanovski, J. A. (2002). Drug therapy: Obesity. *The New England Journal of Medicine, 346,* 591-602.

For a reference list that includes this entry, see page 496.

APA-4a APA in-text citations

APA's in-text citations provide at least the author's last name and the year of publication. For direct quotations and some paraphrases, a page number is given as well.

For a directory to the in-text citation models in this section, see page 443, immediately following the tabbed divider.

NOTE: APA style requires the use of the past tense or the present perfect tense in signal phrases introducing cited material: *Smith (2005) reported . . . , Smith (2005) has argued. . . .*

1. Basic format for a quotation Ordinarily, introduce the quotation with a signal phrase that includes the author's last name followed by the year of publication in parentheses. Put the page number preceded by "p." (or "pp." for more than one page) in parentheses after the quotation.

> Critser (2003) noted that despite growing numbers of overweight Americans, many health care providers still "remain either in ignorance or outright denial about the health danger to the poor and the young" (p. 5).

If the author is not named in the signal phrase, place the author's name, the year, and the page number in parentheses after the quotation: (Critser, 2003, p. 5).

NOTE: APA style requires the year of publication in an in-text citation. Do not include a month, even if the entry in the reference list includes the month.

2. Basic format for a summary or a paraphrase Include the author's last name and the year either in a signal phrase introducing the material or in parentheses following it. Give a page number to help readers find the passage. (For the use of paragraph numbers and headings in online sources, see "No page numbers" on pp. 462–63.)

> Yanovski and Yanovski (2002) explained that sibutramine suppresses appetite by blocking the reuptake of the neurotransmitters serotonin and norepinephrine in the brain (p. 594).

> Sibutramine suppresses appetite by blocking the reuptake of the neurotransmitters serotonin and norepinephrine in the brain (Yanovski & Yanovski, 2002, p. 594).

3. Work with two authors Give the names of both authors in the signal phrase or the parentheses each time you cite the work. In the parentheses, use "&" between the authors' names; in the signal phrase, use "and."

According to Sothern and Gordon (2003), "Environmental factors may contribute as much as 80% to the causes of childhood obesity" (p. 104).

Obese children often engage in limited physical activity (Sothern & Gordon, 2003, p. 104).

4. Work with three to five authors Identify all authors in the signal phrase or the parentheses the first time you cite the source.

In 2003, Berkowitz, Wadden, Tershakovec, and Cronquist concluded, "Sibutramine . . . must be carefully monitored in adolescents, as in adults, to control increases in [blood pressure] and pulse rate" (p. 1811).

In subsequent citations, use the first author's name followed by "et al." in either the signal phrase or the parentheses.

As Berkowitz et al. (2003) advised, "Until more extensive safety and efficacy data are available, . . . weight-loss medications should be used only on an experimental basis for adolescents" (p. 1811).

5. Work with six or more authors Use the first author's name followed by "et al." in the signal phrase or the parentheses.

McDuffie et al. (2002) tested 20 adolescents, aged 12-16, over a three-month period and found that orlistat, combined with behavioral therapy, produced an average weight loss of 4.4 kg, or 9.7 pounds (p. 646).

6. Work with unknown author If the author is unknown, mention the work's title in the signal phrase or give the first word or two of the title in the parenthetical citation. Titles of short works such as articles and chapters are put in quotation marks; titles of long works such as books and reports are italicized. (For online sources with no author, see item 12 on p. 462.)

Children struggling to control their weight must also struggle with the pressures of television advertising that, on the one hand, encourages the consumption of junk food and, on the other, celebrates thin celebrities ("Television," 2002).

NOTE: In the rare case when "Anonymous" is specified as the author, treat it as if it were a real name: (Anonymous, 2001). In the list of references, also use the name Anonymous as the author.

7. **Organization as author** If the author is a government agency or another organization, name the organization in the signal phrase or in the parenthetical citation the first time you cite the source.

Obesity puts children at risk for a number of medical complications, including
Type 2 diabetes, hypertension, sleep apnea, and orthopedic problems (Henry J.
Kaiser Family Foundation, 2004, p. 1).

If the organization has a familiar abbreviation, you may include it in brackets the first time you cite the source and use the abbreviation alone in later citations.

FIRST CITATION   (Canadian Institute for Health Information [CIHI], 2009)

LATER CITATIONS   (CIHI, 2009)

8. **Authors with the same last name** To avoid confusion, use initials with the last names if your reference list includes two or more authors with the same last name.

Research by E. Smith (1989) revealed that. . . .

9. **Two or more works by the same author in the same year** When your list of references includes more than one work by the same author in the same year, use lowercase letters ("a," "b," and so on) with the year to order the entries in the reference list. (See item 6 on p. 465.) Use those same letters with the year in the in-text citation.

Research by Durgin (2003b) has yielded new findings about the role of
counselling in treating childhood obesity.

10. **Two or more works in the same parentheses** When your parenthetical citation names two or more works, put them in the same order that they appear in the reference list, separated with semicolons.

Researchers have indicated that studies of pharmacological treatments for
childhood obesity are inconclusive (Berkowitz et al., 2003; McDuffie et al.,
2002).

11. Personal communication Personal interviews, memos, letters, e-mail, and similar unpublished communications should be cited in the text only, not in the reference list. (Use the first initial with the last name in parentheses.)

> One of Atkinson's colleagues, who has studied the effect of the media on children's eating habits, has contended that advertisers for snack foods will need to design ads responsibly for their younger viewers (F. Johnson, personal communication, October 20, 2009).

12. Electronic source When possible, cite electronic sources, including online sources, as you would any other source, giving the author and the year.

> Atkinson (2001) found that children who spent at least four hours a day watching TV were less likely to engage in adequate physical activity during the week.

Electronic sources sometimes lack authors' names, dates, or page numbers.

Unknown author

If no author is named in the source, mention the title of the source in the signal phrase or give the first word or two of the title in the parentheses (see also item 6). (If an organization serves as the author, see item 7.)

> The body's basal metabolic rate, or BMR, is a measure of its at-rest energy requirement ("Exercise," 2003).

Unknown date

When the date is unknown, use the abbreviation "n.d." (for "no date").

> Attempts to establish a definitive link between television programming and children's eating habits have been problematic (Magnus, n.d.).

No page numbers

APA requires page numbers for quotations, summaries, and paraphrases. When an electronic source lacks stable numbered pages, include paragraph numbers or headings, if the source has them, to help readers locate the particular passage you are citing.

If the source has numbered paragraphs, use the paragraph number preceded by the abbreviation "para.": (Hall, 2008, para. 5). If the source contains headings, cite the appropriate heading in parentheses; you may also indicate the paragraph under the heading that you are referring to, even if the paragraphs are not numbered.

Hoppin and Taveras (2004) pointed out that several other medications were classified by the Drug Enforcement Administration as having the "potential for abuse" (Weight-Loss Drugs section, para. 6).

NOTE: Electronic files in portable document format (PDF) often have stable page numbers. For such sources, give the page number in the parenthetical citation.

13. Indirect source If you use a source that was cited in another source (a secondary source), name the original source in your signal phrase. List the secondary source in your reference list and include it in your parenthetical citation, preceded by the words "as cited in." In the following example, Satcher is the original source, and Critser is the secondary source, given in the reference list.

Former surgeon general Dr. David Satcher described "a nation of young people seriously at risk of starting out obese and dooming themselves to the difficult task of overcoming a tough illness" (as cited in Critser, 2003, p. 4).

14. Sacred or classical text Identify the text, the version or edition you used, and the relevant part (chapter, verse, line). It is not necessary to include the source in the reference list.

Peace activists have long cited the biblical prophet's vision of a world without war: "And they shall beat their swords into plowshares, and their spears into pruning hooks; nation shall not lift up sword against nation, neither shall they learn war any more" (Isaiah 2:4, Revised Standard Version).

APA-4b APA list of references

In APA style, the alphabetical list of works cited, which appears at the end of the paper, is titled "References." For advice on preparing the list, see pages 486–87. For a sample reference list, see page 496.

For a directory to the reference list models in this section, see pages 443–44, immediately following the tabbed divider.

Alphabetize entries in the reference list by authors' last names; if a work has no author, alphabetize it by its title. Place the date of publication immediately after the first element of the citation.

In APA style, titles of books are italicized; titles of articles are neither italicized nor put in quotation marks. (For rules on capitalization of titles, see p. 485.)

Some sources include a unique, permanent number called a digital object identifier (DOI). Use the DOI at the end of a reference list entry for a print or an online source that has one. (See also p. 472.)

General guidelines for listing authors (print and online)

In APA style, all authors' names are inverted (the last name comes first), and initials are used for all first and middle names.

NAME AND DATE CITED IN TEXT

Duncan (2008) has reported that. . . .

BEGINNING OF ENTRY IN THE LIST OF REFERENCES

Duncan, B. (2008).

1. Single author

author: last name
+ initial(s)   year   title (book)

Egeland, J. (2008). *A billion lives: An eyewitness report from the frontlines of humanity.*

place of
publication   publisher

New York, NY: Simon & Schuster.

2. Multiple authors
List up to seven authors by last names followed by initials. Use an ampersand (&) before the name of the last author. If there are more than seven authors, list the first six followed by three ellipsis dots and the last author's name. (See pp. 460–61 for citing works with multiple authors in the text of your paper.)

Two to seven authors

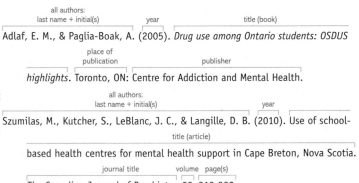

all authors:
last name + initial(s)   year   title (book)

Adlaf, E. M., & Paglia-Boak, A. (2005). *Drug use among Ontario students: OSDUS*

place of
publication   publisher

highlights. Toronto, ON: Centre for Addiction and Mental Health.

all authors:
last name + initial(s)   year

Szumilas, M., Kutcher, S., LeBlanc, J. C., & Langille, D. B. (2010). Use of school-

title (article)

based health centres for mental health support in Cape Breton, Nova Scotia.

journal title   volume page(s)

The Canadian Journal of Psychiatry, 55, 319-328.

Eight or more authors

Mulvaney, S. A., Mudasiru, E., Schlundt, D. G., Baughman, C. L., Fleming, M., VanderWoude, A., . . . Rothman, R. (2008). Self-management in Type 2 diabetes: The adolescent perspective. *The Diabetes Educator, 34,* 118-127.

3. Organization as author

author:
organization name — year — title (book)

Canadian Psychological Association. (2000). *Canadian code of ethics for psychologists*

edition number — place of publication — organization as author and publisher

(3rd ed.). Ottawa, ON: Author.

If the publisher is not the same as the author, give the publisher's name at the end as you would for any other source.

4. Unknown author Begin the entry with the work's title.

title (book) — year — place of publication — publisher

Canadian Oxford Dictionary. (2004). Don Mills, ON: Oxford University Press.

title (article) — year + month + day (for weekly publication) — journal title — volume, issue — page(s)

Order in the jungle. (2008, March 15). *The Economist, 386*(8571), 83-85.

5. Two or more works by the same author Use the author's name for all entries. List the entries by year, the earliest first.

Klein, R. (1999). The Hebb legacy. *Canadian Journal of Experimental Psychology, 53*, 1-3.

Klein, R. (2009). On the control of attention. *Canadian Journal of Experimental Psychology, 63*, 240-252.

6. Two or more works by the same author in the same year List the works alphabetically by title. In the parentheses, following the year add "a," "b," and so on. Use these same letters when giving the year in the in-text citation. (See also p. 486.)

Elkind, D. (2008a, Spring). Can we play? *Greater Good, 4*(4), 14-17.

Elkind, D. (2008b, June 27). The price of hurrying children [Web log post]. Retrieved from http://blogs.psychologytoday.com/blog/digital-children

Articles in periodicals (print)

For a journal or a magazine, give only the volume number if the publication is paginated continuously throughout each volume; give the volume and issue numbers if each issue begins on page 1. Italicize the volume number and put the issue number, not italicized, in parentheses.

For all periodicals, when an article appears on consecutive pages, provide the range of pages. When an article does not appear on consecutive pages, give all page numbers: A1, A17. (See also "Online sources" beginning on p. 472.) For an illustrated citation of an article in a print journal or magazine, see page 467.

7. Article in a journal

                  all authors:
                  last name + initial(s)   year   article title

Pagani, L. S., Derevensky, J. L., & Japel, C. (2010). Does early emotional distress predict

                                              journal title   volume

later child involvement in gambling? *The Canadian Journal of Psychiatry, 55,*

page(s)

507-513.

8. Article in a magazine
Cite as you would a journal article, but give the year and the month for monthly magazines; add the day for weekly magazines.

McKibben, B. (2007, October). Carbon's new math. *National Geographic, 212*(4), 32-37.

9. Article in a newspaper

author: last name
+ initial(s)   year + month + day   article title

DeParle, J. (2010, November 12). Defying trend, Canada lures more migrants. *The New*

newspaper title   page(s)

York Times, p. A1.

Give the year, month, and day for daily and weekly newspapers. Use "p." or "pp." before page numbers.

10. Article with three to seven authors

Ungar, M., Brown, M., Liebenberg, L., Othman, R., Kwong, W. M., Armstrong, M., & Gilgun, J. (2007). Unique pathways to resilience across cultures. *Adolescence, 42,* 287-310.

11. Article with eight or more authors
List the first six authors followed by three ellipsis dots and the last author.

Krippner, G., Granovetter, M., Block, F., Biggart, N., Beamish, T., Hsing, Y., . . . O'Riain, S. (2004). Polanyi Symposium: A conversation on embeddedness. *Socio-Economic Review, 2,* 109-135.

12. Abstract of a journal article

Lahm, K. (2008). Inmate-on-inmate assault: A multilevel examination of prison violence [Abstract]. *Criminal Justice and Behavior, 35*(1), 120-137.

Citation at a glance: Article in a journal or magazine (APA)

To cite an article in a print journal or magazine in APA style, include the following elements:

1 Author
2 Year of publication for journal; complete date for magazine
3 Title of article
4 Name of journal or magazine
5 Volume number; issue number, if required (see p. 466)
6 Page number(s) of article

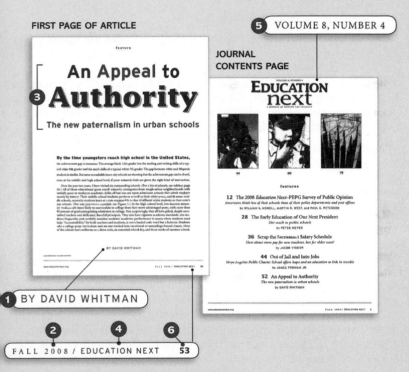

FIRST PAGE OF ARTICLE

5 VOLUME 8, NUMBER 4

3 An Appeal to **Authority**
The new paternalism in urban schools

By the time youngsters reach high school in the United States,

BY DAVID WHITMAN

FALL 2008 / EDUCATION NEXT 53

JOURNAL CONTENTS PAGE

EDUCATION next

features

12 The 2008 *Education Next*–PEPG Survey of Public Opinion
Americans think less of their schools than of their police departments and post offices
by WILLIAM G. HOWELL, MARTIN R. WEST, and PAUL E. PETERSON

28 The Early Education of Our Next President
Not much in public schools
by PETER MEYER

36 Scrap the Sacrosanct Salary Schedule
How about more pay for new teachers, less for older ones?
by JACOB VIGDOR

44 Out of Jail and Into Jobs
Maya Angelou Public Charter School offers hope and an education to kids in trouble
by JAMES FORMAN JR.

52 An Appeal to Authority
The new paternalism in urban schools
by DAVID WHITMAN

1 BY DAVID WHITMAN

2 **4** **6**
FALL 2008 / EDUCATION NEXT 53

REFERENCE LIST ENTRY FOR AN ARTICLE IN A PRINT JOURNAL OR MAGAZINE

—1— —2— ———————————3———————————
Whitman, D. (2008). An appeal to authority: The new paternalism in urban schools.

———4——— —5— —6—
Education Next, 8(4), 53-58.

For variations on citing articles in print journals or magazines in APA style, see pages 466–68.

13. Letter to the editor Follow the appropriate model for a journal, magazine, or newspaper (see items 7–9) and insert the words "Letter to the editor" in brackets after the title of the letter. If the letter has no title, use the bracketed words as the title.

Park, T. (2008, August). Defining the line [Letter to the editor]. *Scientific American, 299*(2), 10.

14. Editorial or other unsigned article

The global justice movement [Editorial]. (2005). *Multinational Monitor, 26*(7/8), 6.

15. Newsletter article

Setting the stage for remembering. (2006, September). *Mind, Mood, and Memory, 2*(9), 4-5.

16. Review Give the author and title of the review (if any) and, in brackets, the type of work, the title, and the author for a book or the year for a motion picture. If the review has no author or title, use the material in brackets as the title.

Applebaum, A. (2008, February 14). A movie that matters [Review of the motion picture *Katyn*, 2007]. *The New York Review of Books, 55*(2), 13-15.

Agents of change. (2008, February 2). [Review of the book *The power of unreasonable people: How social entrepreneurs create markets that change the world,* by J. Elkington & P. Hartigan]. *The Economist, 386*(8565), 94.

Books (print)

Items 17–29 apply to print books. For online books, see items 36 and 37. For an illustrated citation of a print book, see page 470.

Take the information about a book from its title page and copyright page. Give the city and province or territory for Canadian cities; the city and state for US cities; and the city and country for all other cities. Use postal abbreviations for provinces, territories, and states; don't abbreviate country names. Do not give a province, territory, or state if the publisher's name includes it (a university press, for example).

17. Basic format for a book

author: last name + initial(s)   year of publication   book title

McKenzie, F. R. (2008). *Theory and practice with adolescents: An applied approach.*

place of publication   publisher

Chicago, IL: Lyceum Books.

18. Book with an editor

all editors:
last name + initial(s)
year of
publication
book title

Cohen, D. J., & Volkmar, F. R. (Eds.). (1997). *Handbook of autism and pervasive*

edition
place of
publication
publisher

developmental disorders (2nd ed.). Toronto, ON: Wiley.

The abbreviation "Eds." is for multiple editors. If the book has one editor, use "Ed."

19. Book with an author and an editor

author: last name
+ initial(s)
year of
publication
book title
name(s) of editor(s):
in normal order

McLuhan, M. (2003). *Understanding me: Lectures and interviews* (S. McLuhan & D. Staine,

place of publication
(city, province or state)
publisher

Eds.). Toronto, ON: McClelland & Stewart.

The abbreviation "Eds." is for multiple editors. If the book has one editor, use "Ed."

20. Book with an author and a translator
After the title, name the translator, followed by "Trans.," in parentheses. Add the original date of publication at the end of the entry.

Dickner, N. (2009). *Nikolski* (L. Lederhendler, Trans.). Toronto, ON: Vintage Canada.

(Original work published 2005)

21. Edition other than the first

Barlow, D. H., Durand, V. M., & Stewart, S. H. (2009). *Abnormal psychology: An*

integrative approach (2nd ed.). Toronto, ON: Nelson.

If the entry also requires volume numbers (see item 23), put the volume numbers after the edition number: (3rd ed., Vols. 1-3).

22. Article or chapter in an edited book or an anthology

author of chapter:
last name + initial(s)
year of
publication
title of chapter

Denton, N. A. (2006). Segregation and discrimination in housing. In R. G. Bratt,

book editor(s):
in normal order
book title

M. E. Stone, & C. Hartman (Eds.), *A right to housing: Foundation of a new*

page(s)
for chapter
place of
publication
publisher

social agenda (pp. 61-81). Philadelphia, PA: Temple University Press.

Citation at a glance: Book (APA)

To cite a print book in APA style, include the following elements:

1 Author
2 Year of publication
3 Title and subtitle
4 Place of publication
5 Publisher

TITLE PAGE

COPYRIGHT PAGE

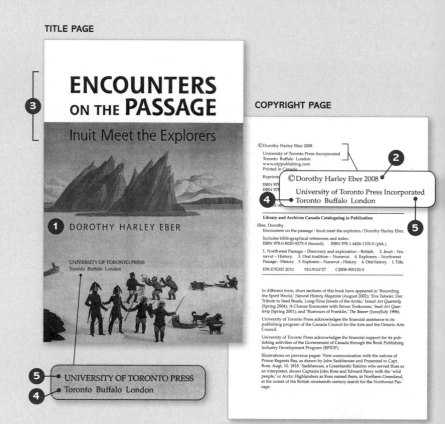

REFERENCE LIST ENTRY FOR A PRINT BOOK

Eber, D. H. (2008). *Encounters on the passage: Inuit meet the explorers.* Toronto, ON:
University of Toronto Press.

For more on citing print books in APA style, see pages 468–71.

The abbreviation "Eds." is for multiple editors. If the book has one editor, use "Ed."

23. Multivolume work   Give the number of volumes after the title.

Pao, R. V., & Christy, K. (Eds.). (1968). *Synthesis of passive networks* (Vols. 1-2). Toronto, ON: University of Toronto Press.

If the work is published in an edition other than the first (see item 21), put the edition number before the volume numbers: (3rd ed., Vols. 1-3).

24. Introduction, preface, foreword, or afterword

Wilson, W. B. (2009). Foreword. In S. Paschall, *Birth of a boom: Lives and legacies of Saskatchewan entrepreneurs*. Saskatoon, SK: Prairie Policy Centre.

25. Dictionary or other reference work

Podesto, M. (Ed.). (2010). *The ultimate medical encyclopedia: Visualize, heal, prevent*. Richmond Hill, ON: Firefly Books.

26. Article in a reference work

Wylde, B. (2008). Homeopathy. In S. Torkos, *The Canadian encyclopedia of natural medicine* (pp. 73-85). Toronto, ON: Wiley.

27. Republished book

Williams, R. (2001). *The long revolution*. Peterborough, ON: Broadview Press. (Original work published 1961)

28. Book with a title in its title   If the book title contains another book title or an article title, neither italicize the internal title nor place it in quotation marks.

Marcus, L. (Ed.). (1999). *Sigmund Freud's* The interpretation of dreams*: New interdisciplinary essays*. Manchester, England: Manchester University Press.

29. Sacred or classical text   It is not necessary to list sacred works such as the Bible or the Quran or classical Greek and Roman works in your reference list. See item 14 on page 463 for how to cite these sources in the text of your paper.

Online sources

When citing an online article, include publication information as for a print periodical (see items 7–16) and add information about the online version (see items 30–35).

Use a retrieval date for an online source only if the content is likely to change. Most of the examples in this section do not show a retrieval date because the content of the sources is stable; if you are unsure about whether to use a retrieval date, consult your instructor.

If the source includes a DOI (digital object identifier), use the DOI in place of a URL at the end of the entry. (See p. 487 for guidelines about breaking a DOI or a URL at the end of a line.)

30. Article in an online journal

author: last   year of
name + initial(s) publication   article title

Harris, G. E. (2010). Educational psychologists' perspectives on their professional

                                                journal title

    practice in Newfoundland and Labrador. *Canadian Journal of School Psychology,*

    volume page(s)   DOI

    25, 205-220. doi:10.1177/0829573510366726

If there is no DOI, include the URL for the journal's home page.

Lee, E. K., & Douglass, A. B. (2010). Sleep in psychiatric disorders: Where are we

    now? *The Canadian Journal of Psychiatry, 55,* 403-412. Retrieved from http://

    publications.cpa-apc.org/browse/sections/0

31. Article in an online magazine
Give the author, date, article title, and magazine title. Follow with the volume, issue, and page numbers, if they are available. End with the URL for the magazine's home page.

Lundy, D. (2010, July/August). Stanstead: A town on the border. *Canadian Geographic,*

    130(4). Retrieved from http://www.canadiangeographic.ca/magazine/

Rupley, S. (2010, February 26). The myth of the benign monopoly. *Salon.* Retrieved from

    http://www.salon.com/

32. Article in an online newspaper
Give the author, date, article title, and newspaper title. Follow with the page numbers, if they are available. End with the URL for the newspaper's home page.

Murphy, R. (2010, September 11). Nine years later, tragedy replaced by farce. *National*

    Post. Retrieved from http://www.nationalpost.com/

33. Supplemental material published only online If a journal, magazine, or newspaper contains extra material (an article or a chart, for example) only in its online version, give whatever publication information is available in the source and add the description "Supplemental material" in brackets after the title.

Molotkow, A. (2010, September). And the brat came back [Supplemental material]. *The Walrus*. Retrieved from http://www.walrusmagazine.com/

34. Article from a database Start with the publication information for the source (see items 7–16). If the database entry includes a DOI for the article, use the DOI number at the end. For an illustrated citation of a work from a database, see page 474.

all authors:
last name + initial(s)   year   article title

Eskritt, M., & McLeod, K. (2008). Children's note taking as a mnemonic tool.

          journal title   volume page(s)   DOI

Journal of Experimental Child Psychology, 101, 52-74. doi:10.1016

/jecp.2008.05.007

If there is no DOI, include the URL for the home page of the journal. If the URL is not included in the database entry, you can search for it on the Web.

Howard, K. R. (2007). Childhood overweight: Parental perceptions and readiness for
    change. *The Journal of School Nursing, 23,* 73-79. Retrieved from http://jsn
    .sagepub.com/

35. Abstract for an online article

Brockerhoff, E. G., Jactel, H., Parrotta, J. A., Quine, C. P., & Sayer, J. (2008). Plantation
    forests and biodiversity: Oxymoron or opportunity? [Abstract]. *Biodiversity and
    Conservation, 17,* 925-951. doi:10.1007/s10531-008-9380-x

36. Online book

Adams, B. (2004). *The theory of social revolutions.* Retrieved from http://www
    .gutenberg.org/catalog/world/readfile?fk_files=44092 (Original work
    published 1913)

37. Chapter in an online book

Clinton, S. J. (1999). What can be done to prevent childhood obesity? In *Understanding
    childhood obesity* (pp. 81-98). Retrieved from http://www.questia.com/

Citation at a glance: Article from a database (APA)

To cite an article from a database in APA style, include the following elements:

1 Author(s)
2 Date of publication
3 Title of article
4 Name of periodical
5 Volume number; issue number, if required (see p. 465)

6 Page number(s)
7 DOI (digital object identifier)
8 URL for journal's home page (if there is no DOI)

ON-SCREEN VIEW OF DATABASE RECORD

New Search	Publications	Company Profiles	Thesaurus	More ▾
		Sign In to My EBSCOhost	📁 Folder	New Features!	Help

Searching: **Business Source Premier**   Choose Databases »

☐ Suggest Subject Terms

AN 27711104   in Select a Field (optional) ▾
and ▾   in Select a Field (optional) ▾
and ▾   in Select a Field (optional) ▾

[Search] [Clear] ❓

Basic Search | Advanced Search | Visual Search | Search History/Alerts | Preferences »

◀ 1 of 1 ▶   Result List | Refine Search

🗋 Citation   Cited References (38)   🖨 ✉ 💾 📄 📤 📁

Times Cited in this Database (3)

Title: ❸ International Human Rights and Consumer Quality of Life: An Ethical Perspective.

Authors: Hill, Ronald Paul[1]
Felice, William F.[2] ❶
Ainscough, Thomas[3]   ❷   ❺   ❻

Source: ❹ Journal of Macromarketing; Dec2007, Vol. 27 Issue 4, p370-379, 10p, 2 charts

Document Type: Article

Subject Terms: *PRIMARY commodities
*MACROMARKETING

END OF DATABASE RECORD

ISSN: 0276-1467

DOI: 10.1177/027614670307128 ❼

REFERENCE LIST ENTRY FOR AN ARTICLE FROM A DATABASE

Hill, R. P., Felice, W. F., & Ainscough, T. (2007). International human rights and
consumer quality of life: An ethical perspective. *Journal of Macromarketing,*
27, 370-379. doi:10.1177/027614670307128

For more on citing articles from a database in APA style, see item 34.

38. Online reference work

Swain, C. M. (2004). Sociology of affirmative action. In N. J. Smelser & P. B. Baltes

(Eds.), *International encyclopedia of the social and behavioral sciences.* Retrieved

from http://www.sciencedirect.com/science/referenceworks/9780080430768

Include a retrieval date only if the content of the work is likely to
change.

39. Report or long document from a Web site
List the author's name,
publication date (or "n.d." if there is no date), document title (in italics),
and URL for the document. Give a retrieval date only if the content of
the source is likely to change. If a source has no author, begin with the
title and follow it with the date in parentheses (see item 4 on p. 465).

Source with date

all authors:
last name + initial(s)   online publication date   document title

Cain, A., & Burris, M. (1999, April). *Investigation of the use of mobile phones while driving.*

URL

Retrieved from http://www3.cutr.usf.edu/pdf/mobile_phone.PDF

Source with no date

Archer, D. (n.d.). *Exploring nonverbal communication.* Retrieved from http://nonverbal
.ucsc.edu

40. Section in a Web document

author (organization)   year   title of section

National Institute on Media and the Family. (2009). Mobile networking. In

title of Web document

Guide to social networking: Risks. Retrieved from http://www.mediafamily.org

URL

/network_pdf/MediaWise_Guide_to_Social_Networking_Risks_09.pdf

For an illustrated citation of a section in a Web document, see page 478.

41. Short work from a Web site

NATO statement endangers patients in Afghanistan. (2010, March 11). *Médecins*

sans frontières/Doctors without borders. Retrieved from http://www

.doctorswithoutborders.org/

42. Document from a university or government agency Web site

Abbott, A. H. (1900). *Experimental psychology and the laboratory in Toronto.* Retrieved

from York University, Toronto, Classics in the History of Psychology website:

http://psychclassics.yorku.ca/Abbott/

43. Article in an online newsletter   Cite as an online article (see items
30–32), giving the title of the newsletter and whatever other information is available, including volume and issue numbers.

Sugonyaev, E. S. (2000). Feature species: The chalcid wasp *Encyrtus infidus. Arctic*

Insect News, 11, 3-4. Retrieved from http://www.biology.ualberta.ca/bsc/english

/newsletters.htm#arctic

44. Podcast

organization as producer   date of posting

National Academies (Producer). (2007, June 6). Progress in preventing childhood

podcast title   descriptive label   series title

obesity: How do we measure up? [Audio podcast]. *The sounds of science podcast.*

URL

Retrieved from http://media.nap.edu/podcasts/

writer/
presenter   date of posting   podcast title

Hoehn, K. (2008, October). Research opportunities: Anatomy and physiology

descriptive label   Web site hosting podcast

[Audio podcast]. Retrieved from Mount Royal University website:

URL

http://research.mtroyal.ca/content.php?page=presentations

45. Blog (Weblog) post   Give the writer's name, the date of the post, and the subject. In brackets following the subject, add the label "Web log post." Give the URL at the end. For a response to a post, use the label "Web log comment."

writer date of posting   comment title   descriptive label

Baxter, D. (2010, September 8). Mood 24/7 beta test and survey [Web log post].

URL

  Retrieved from http://blog.psychlinks.ca/mood-247-beta-test-and-survey/

46. Online audio or video file   Give the medium or a description of the source file in brackets following the title.

writer/ no   descriptive
presenter date title   label   URL

Chomsky, N. (n.d.). The new imperialism [Audio file]. Retrieved from http://www

  .rhapsody.com/noamchomsky

Hamilton, R. (Narrator). (2010, August 2). Five years after Garang [Slide show].

  Retrieved from http://pulitzercenter.org/slideshows/five-years-after-garang

47. Entry in a wiki   Begin with the title of the entry and the date of posting, if there is one (use "n.d." for "no date" if there is not). Then add your retrieval date and the URL for the wiki entry. Include the date of retrieval because the content of a wiki can change frequently. If an author or an editor is identified, include that name at the beginning of the entry.

Ethnomethodology. (n.d.). Retrieved June 18, 2010, from http://stswiki.org/index

  .php?title/Ethnomethodology

48. Data set or graphic representation   Give information about the type of source in brackets following the title. If there is no title, give a brief description of the content of the source in brackets in place of the title.

Statistics Canada. (2010). *Live births, by age and marital status of mother, Canada,*

  annual (140 series) [CANSIM data]. Retrieved from http://cansim2.statcan.gc.ca/

Gallup. (2008, October 23). *No increase in proportion of first-time voters* [Graphs].

  Retrieved from http://www.gallup.com/poll/111331/No-Increase-Proportion

  -First-Time-Voters.aspx

49. Conference hearing

Freiman, M. J. (2009, December 7). Testimony before the Canadian Parliamentary
    Coalition to Combat Antisemitism. Retrieved from http://www.cpcca.ca
    /09.12.07transcript-E.pdf

50. E-mail E-mail messages, letters, and other personal communications are not included in the list of references. (See item 11 on p. 462
for citing these sources in the text of your paper.)

51. Online posting If an online posting is not archived, cite it as a
personal communication in the text of your paper and do not include
it in the list of references. If the posting is archived, give the URL and
the name of the discussion list if it is not part of the URL.

Paul, S. (2010, August 18). Spouse sponsorship in Canada [Electronic mailing list
    message]. Retrieved from http://groups.yahoo.com/group/canadian_immigration
    /message/67303

Other sources (including online versions)

52. Dissertation from a database

Marshall, B. L. (2009). *Silent grief: Narratives of bereaved adult siblings* (Doctoral
    dissertation). Available from Theses Canada database. (AMICUS No. 37949299)

53. Unpublished dissertation

Conrad, D. (2004). *"Life in the sticks": Youth experiences, risk, and popular
    theatre process* (Unpublished doctoral dissertation). University of Alberta,
    Edmonton.

54. Government document

Statistics Canada. (2010). *Canada year book 2010.* Ottawa, ON: Minister of Industry.

Statistics Canada, Census Operations Division. (2010, January). *2006 census dictionary*
    (Catalogue No. 92-566-X). Retrieved from http://www12.statcan.gc.ca
    /census-recensement/2006/ref/dict/pdf/92-566-eng.pdf

55. Report from a private organization If the publisher is also the
author, begin with the publisher's name in the author position. For a
print source, use "Author" in the publisher position at the end of the

entry (see item 3 on p. 465); for an online source, give the URL. If the report has a number, put the number in parentheses following the title.

Canadian Alliance on Mental Illness and Mental Health. (2006, February). *Framework for action on mental illness and mental health*. Retrieved from http://www.cmha.ca /data/1/rec_docs/601_CAMIMH English Lowres.pdf

56. Legal source

Vancouver (City) v. Ward, 2010 SCC 27 (2010). Retrieved from Canadian Legal Information Institute website: http://www.canlii.org/en/ca/scc/doc/2010 /2010scc27/2010scc27.html

57. Conference proceedings

Ménard, E., Nesset, V., & Mas, S. (2010). *Proceedings of CAIS conference 2010: Information science: Synergy through diversity*. Montreal, QC: Concordia University.

58. Paper presented at a meeting or symposium (unpublished)

Panayotidis, E. L., & Stortz, P. (2010, October). *Visual myth-making and the university campus: University of Toronto's pictorial maps, 1932, 1937*. Paper presented at the 16th biennial conference of the Canadian History of Education Association, Toronto, ON.

59. Poster session at a conference

Wager, V. (2010, June). *Toward an electronic health record in a community health facility*. Poster session presented at the annual conference of ARMA Canada, London, ON.

60. Map or chart

Manitoba Keewatinowi Okimakanak Territory and First Nations [Map]. Retrieved from http://www.mkonorth.com/mkocommunities.html

61. Advertisement

Rosetta Stone [Advertisement]. (2010, September). *Scientific American, 303*(3), 31.

62. Published interview

Hadfield, C. (2009, July 20). Canada and the moon: Past and future missions [Interview]. Retrieved from http://www.cbc.ca

63. Lecture, speech, or address

King, R. (2010, March 5). *From Manitoba to Matisse.* Lecture at the Winnipeg Art Gallery, Winnipeg, MB.

64. Work of art or photograph

Hardy, P. (1997). *A tribute to Canadian wildlife* [Outdoor mural]. Ottawa, ON.

Brueghel, P. (n.d.). *The peasants' wedding.* Art Gallery of Ontario, Toronto, ON.

65. Brochure, pamphlet, or fact sheet

Ryerson University. (n.d.). *BScN* [Brochure]. http://www.ryerson.ca/nursing/pdf /BScN_brochure.pdf

World Health Organization. (2007, October). *Health of indigenous peoples* (No. 326) [Fact sheet]. Retrieved from http://www.who.int/mediacentre/factsheets/fs326 /en/index.html

66. Presentation slides

Boeninger, C. F. (2008, August). *Web 2.0 tools for reference and instructional services* [Presentation slides]. Retrieved from http://libraryvoice.com/archives/2008 /08/04/opal-20-conference-presentation-slides/

67. Film or video (motion picture) Give the director, producer, and other relevant contributors, followed by the year of the film's release, the title, the description "Motion picture" in brackets, the country where the film was made, and the studio. If you viewed the film on videocassette or DVD, indicate that medium in brackets in place of "Motion picture." If the original release date and the date of the DVD or videocassette are different, add "Original release" and that date in parentheses at the end of the entry. If the motion picture would be difficult for your readers to find, include the name and address of its distributor instead of the country and studio.

Swerhone, E. (Director), Engel, C., Jensen-Carr, M., Swerhone, E., & von Helmolt, V. (Producers). (2009). *Ballet high* [DVD]. Canada: Merit Motion Pictures.

interview • lecture • artwork • brochure • slides • film • video •
TV program • recording • software • video game • formatting a paper

APA-5   **483**

Spurlock, M. (Director). (2004). *Super size me* [Motion picture]. Available from IDP
Films, 1133 Broadway, Suite 926, New York, NY 10010

68. Television program   List the producer and the date of the program. Give the title, followed by "Television broadcast" in brackets, the city, and the television network or service.

Underwood, C. (Series producer). (2010, September 11). *The nature of things* [Television
broadcast]. Toronto, ON: CBC-TV.

For a television series, use the year in which the series was produced, and follow the title with "Television series" in brackets. For an episode in a series, list the writer and director and the year. After the episode title, put "Television series episode" in brackets. Follow with information about the series.

Hawkins, N. (Producer). (2010). *Allen Gregg in conversation* [Television series]. Toronto,
ON: TVO.

Gregg, A. (Writer). (2010). Annie Leonard [Television series episode]. In N. Hawkins
(Producer), *Allen Gregg in conversation*. Toronto, ON: TVO.

69. Sound recording

Fielding, R. (2004). Off to school no more. On *Acoustic workshop* [CD]. Toronto, ON:
Borealis Records.

70. Computer software or video game   Add the words "Computer software" in brackets after the title of the program.

Robin's Quest [Computer software]. (2010). Moncton, NB: Gogii Games.

≣ **APA-5** Manuscript format;
sample paper

The American Psychological Association makes a number of recommendations for formatting a paper and preparing a list of references. The following guidelines are consistent with advice given in the *Publication Manual of the American Psychological Association*, 6th ed. (Washington: APA, 2010).

APA-5a Manuscript format

The APA manual provides guidelines for papers prepared for publication in a scholarly journal; it does not provide separate guidelines for papers prepared for undergraduate classes. The formatting guidelines in this section and the sample paper on pages 488–96 can be used for either type of paper. (See p. 497 for alternative formatting.) If you are in doubt about the specific format preferred or required in your course, ask your instructor.

Formatting the paper

Many instructors in the social sciences require students to follow APA guidelines for formatting a paper.

Materials and font Use good-quality 8½″ × 11″ (216 mm × 279 mm) white paper. If your instructor does not require a specific font, choose one that is standard and easy to read (such as Times New Roman).

Title page Begin at the top left with the words "Running head," followed by a colon and the title of your paper (shortened to no more than fifty characters) in all capital letters. Put the page number 1 flush with the right margin.

About halfway down the page, centre the full title of your paper (capitalizing all words of four letters or more), your name, and your school's name. At the bottom of the page, you may add the heading "Author Note," centred, followed by a brief paragraph that lists specific information about the course or department or provides acknowledgments or contact information. See page 488 for a sample title page.

Some instructors may instead require a title page like the one on page 497. If in doubt about the requirements in your course, check with your instructor.

Page numbers and running head Number all pages with arabic numerals (1, 2, and so on) in the upper right corner about one-half inch (2.5 cm) from the top of the page. The title page should be numbered 1.

On every page, in the upper left corner on the same line as the page number, place a running head. The running head consists of the title of the paper (shortened to no more than fifty characters) in all capital letters. (On the title page only, include the words "Running head" followed by a colon before the shortened title.) See pages 488–96. (See an alternative running head on p. 497.)

Margins, line spacing, and paragraph indents   Use margins of one inch (2.5 cm) on all sides of the page. Left-align the text.

Double-space throughout the paper. Indent the first line of each paragraph one-half inch (1.5 cm).

Capitalization, italics, and quotation marks   Capitalize all words of four letters or more in titles of works and in headings that appear in the text of the paper. Capitalize the first word after a colon if the word begins a complete sentence.

Italicize the titles of books, periodicals, and other long works, such as Web sites. Use quotation marks around the titles of periodical articles, short stories, poems, and other short works.

NOTE: APA has different requirements for titles in the reference list. See page 487.

Long quotations and footnotes   When a quotation is longer than forty words, set it off from the text by indenting it one-half inch (1.5 cm) from the left margin. Double-space the quotation. Do not use quotation marks around it. See page 495 for an example.

If you insert a footnote number in the text of your paper, place the note at the bottom of the page on which the number appears. Insert an extra double-spaced line between the last line of text on the page and the footnote. Double-space the footnote and indent the first line one-half inch (1.5 cm). Begin the note with the superscript arabic numeral that corresponds to the number in the text. See page 490 for an example.

Abstract   If your instructor requires an abstract, include it immediately after the title page. Centre the word "Abstract" one inch (2.5 cm) from the top of the page; double-space the abstract.

An abstract is a 100-to-150-word paragraph that provides readers with a quick overview of your essay. It should express your main idea and your key points; it might also briefly suggest any implications or applications of the research you discuss in the paper. See page 489 for an example.

Headings   Although headings are not always necessary, their use is encouraged in the social sciences. For most undergraduate papers, one level of heading will usually be sufficient.

In APA style, major headings are centred and boldface. Capitalize the first word of the heading along with all words except articles, short prepositions, and coordinating conjunctions. See the sample paper on pages 488–96 for the use of headings.

Visuals APA classifies visuals as tables and figures (figures include graphs, charts, drawings, and photographs). Keep visuals as simple as possible.

Label each table with an arabic numeral (Table 1, Table 2, and so on) and provide a clear title. The label and title should appear on separate lines above the table, flush left and double-spaced.

Below the table, give its source in a note. If any data in the table require an explanatory footnote, use a superscript lowercase letter in the body of the table and in a footnote following the source note. Double-space source notes and footnotes and do not indent the first line of each note. See page 493 for an example of a table in a student paper.

For each figure, place a label and a caption below the figure, flush left and double-spaced. The label and caption need not appear on separate lines.

In the text of your paper, discuss significant features of each visual. Place the visual as close as possible to the sentences that relate to it unless your instructor prefers that visuals appear in an appendix.

Preparing the list of references

Begin your list of references on a new page at the end of the paper. Centre the title "References" one inch (2.5 cm) from the top of the page, and double-space throughout. For a sample reference list, see page 496.

Indenting entries Use a hanging indent in the reference list: Type the first line of each entry flush left and indent any additional lines one-half inch (1.5 cm), as shown on page 496.

Alphabetizing the list Alphabetize the reference list by the last names of the authors (or editors); when a work has no author (or editor), alphabetize by the first word of the title other than *A*, *An*, or *The*.

If your list includes two or more works by the same author, arrange the entries by year, the earliest first. If your list includes two or more works by the same author in the same year, arrange the works alphabetically by title. Add the letters "a," "b," and so on within the parentheses after the year. Use only the year and the letter for articles in journals: (2002a). Use the full date and the letter for articles in magazines and newspapers in the reference list: (2005a, July 7). Use only the year and the letter in the in-text citation.

Authors' names Invert all authors' names and use initials instead of first names. Separate the names with commas. With two to seven authors, use an ampersand (&) before the last author's name. If there are eight or more authors, give the first six authors, three ellipsis dots, and the last author (see p. 464).

Titles of books and articles   Italicize the titles and subtitles of books. Do not italicize or use quotation marks around the titles of articles. Capitalize only the first word of the title and subtitle (and all proper nouns) of books and articles. Capitalize names of periodicals as you would capitalize them normally (see P8-c).

Abbreviations for page numbers   Abbreviations for "page" and "pages" ("p." and "pp.") are used before page numbers of newspaper articles and articles in edited books (see item 9 on p. 466 and item 22 on p. 469) but not before page numbers of articles in magazines and scholarly journals (see items 7 and 8 on p. 466).

Breaking a URL or DOI   When a URL or a DOI (digital object identifier) must be divided, break it after a double slash or before any other mark of punctuation. Do not insert a hyphen, and do not add a period at the end.

For information about the exact format of each entry in your list, consult the models on pages 464–83.

APA-5b Sample research paper: APA style

On pages 488–96 is a research paper on the effectiveness of treatments for childhood obesity, written by Luisa Mirano, a student in a psychology class. Mirano's assignment was to write a review of the literature and document it with APA-style citations and references. (See p. 497 for a sample of alternative formatting.)

MODELS   hackerhandbooks.com/writersref
> Model papers > APA papers: Mirano; Charat; Gibson; Riss
> APA annotated bibliography: Haddad

A running head, which will be used in the printed journal article, consists of a title (shortened to no more than fifty characters) in all capital letters. On the title page, it is preceded by the label "Running head." Page numbers appear in the upper right corner.

Running head: CAN MEDICATION CURE OBESITY IN CHILDREN?   1

Full title, writer's name, and school name are centred halfway down the page.

Can Medication Cure Obesity in Children?

A Review of the Literature

Luisa Mirano

Northwest-Shoals Community College

An author's note lists specific information about the course or department and can provide acknowledgments and contact information.

Author Note

This paper was prepared for Psychology 108, Section B, taught by Professor Kang.

Marginal annotations indicate APA-style formatting and effective writing.

Abstract

In recent years, policymakers and medical experts have expressed alarm
about the growing problem of childhood obesity in the United States.
While most agree that the issue deserves attention, consensus dissolves
around how to respond to the problem. This literature review examines one
approach to treating childhood obesity: medication. The paper compares
the effectiveness for adolescents of the only two drugs approved by the
Food and Drug Administration (FDA) for long-term treatment of obesity,
sibutramine and orlistat. This examination of pharmacological treatments
for obesity points out the limitations of medication and suggests the need
for a comprehensive solution that combines medical, social, behavioral,
and political approaches to this complex problem.

Abstract appears on
a separate page.

CAN MEDICATION CURE OBESITY IN CHILDREN?   3

Can Medication Cure Obesity in Children?

A Review of the Literature

In March 2004, U.S. Surgeon General Richard Carmona called attention to a health problem in the United States that, until recently, has been overlooked: childhood obesity. Carmona said that the "astounding" 15% child obesity rate constitutes an "epidemic." Since the early 1980s, that rate has "doubled in children and tripled in adolescents." Now more than 9 million children are classified as obese.[1] While the traditional response to a medical epidemic is to hunt for a vaccine or a cure-all pill, childhood obesity is more elusive. The lack of success of recent initiatives suggests that medication might not be the answer for the escalating problem. This literature review considers whether the use of medication is a promising approach for solving the childhood obesity problem by responding to the following questions:

1. What are the implications of childhood obesity?

2. Is medication effective at treating childhood obesity?

3. Is medication safe for children?

4. Is medication the best solution?

Understanding the limitations of medical treatments for children highlights the complexity of the childhood obesity problem in the United States and underscores the need for physicians, advocacy groups, and policymakers to search for other solutions.

What Are the Implications of Childhood Obesity?

Obesity can be a devastating problem from both an individual and a societal perspective. Obesity puts children at risk for a number of medical complications, including Type 2 diabetes, hypertension, sleep apnea, and orthopedic problems (Henry J. Kaiser Family Foundation, 2004, p. 1). Researchers Hoppin and Taveras (2004) have noted that obesity is often associated with psychological issues such as depression, anxiety, and binge eating (Table 4).

Obesity also poses serious problems for a society struggling to cope with rising health care costs. The cost of treating obesity currently totals

---

[1]Obesity is measured in terms of body-mass index (BMI): weight in kilograms divided by square of height in meters. A child or an adolescent with a BMI in the 95th percentile for his or her age and gender is considered obese.

Marginal annotations:

Full title, centred.

Mirano sets up her organization by posing four questions.

Mirano states her thesis.

Headings, centred, help readers follow the organization.

In a signal phrase, the word "and" links the names of two authors; the date is given in parentheses.

Mirano uses a footnote to define an essential term that would be cumbersome to define within the text.

CAN MEDICATION CURE OBESITY IN CHILDREN?   4

$117 billion per year—a price, according to the surgeon general, "second
only to the cost of [treating] tobacco use" (Carmona, 2004). And as the
number of children who suffer from obesity grows, long-term costs will
only increase.

Is Medication Effective at Treating Childhood Obesity?

The widening scope of the obesity problem has prompted medical
professionals to rethink old conceptions of the disorder and its causes.
As researchers Yanovski and Yanovski (2002) have explained, obesity was
once considered "either a moral failing or evidence of underlying
psychopathology" (p. 592). But this view has shifted: Many medical
professionals now consider obesity a biomedical rather than a moral
condition, influenced by both genetic and environmental factors. Yanovski
and Yanovski have further noted that the development of weight-loss
medications in the early 1990s showed that "obesity should be treated in
the same manner as any other chronic disease . . . through the long-term
use of medication" (p. 592).

The search for the right long-term medication has been complicated.
Many of the drugs authorized by the Food and Drug Administration (FDA) in
the early 1990s proved to be a disappointment. Two of the medications—
fenfluramine and dexfenfluramine—were withdrawn from the market because
of severe side effects (Yanovski & Yanovski, 2002, p. 592), and several others
were classified by the Drug Enforcement Administration as having the
"potential for abuse" (Hoppin & Taveras, 2004, Weight-Loss Drugs section,
para. 6). Currently only two medications have been approved by the FDA for
long-term treatment of obesity: sibutramine (marketed as Meridia) and
orlistat (marketed as Xenical). This section compares studies on the
effectiveness of each.

Sibutramine suppresses appetite by blocking the reuptake of the
neurotransmitters serotonin and norepinephrine in the brain (Yanovski
& Yanovski, 2002, p. 594). Though the drug won FDA approval in 1998,
experiments to test its effectiveness for younger patients came
considerably later. In 2003, University of Pennsylvania researchers
Berkowitz, Wadden, Tershakovec, and Cronquist released the first
double-blind placebo study testing the effect of sibutramine on
adolescents, aged 13-17, over a 12-month period. Their findings are
summarized in Table 1.

After 6 months, the group receiving medication had lost 4.6 kg

Because the author
(Carmona) is not
named in the signal
phrase, his name
and the date appear
in parentheses.

Ellipsis mark
indicates omitted
words.

In a parenthetical
citation, an
ampersand links the
names of two authors.

Mirano draws
attention to an
important article.

CAN MEDICATION CURE OBESITY IN CHILDREN? 5

(about 10 pounds) more than the control group. But during the second half of the study, when both groups received sibutramine, the results were more ambiguous. In months 6-12, the group that continued to take sibutramine gained an average of 0.8 kg, or roughly 2 pounds; the control group, which switched from placebo to sibutramine, lost 1.3 kg, or roughly 3 pounds (p. 1808). Both groups received behavioral therapy covering diet, exercise, and mental health.

These results paint a murky picture of the effectiveness of the medication: While initial data seemed promising, the results after one year raised questions about whether medication-induced weight loss could be sustained over time. As Berkowitz et al. (2003) advised, "Until more extensive safety and efficacy data are available, . . . weight-loss medications should be used only on an experimental basis for adolescents" (p. 1811).

A study testing the effectiveness of orlistat in adolescents showed similarly ambiguous results. The FDA approved orlistat in 1999 but did not authorize it for adolescents until December 2003. Roche Laboratories (2003), maker of orlistat, released results of a one-year study testing the drug on 539 obese adolescents, aged 12-16. The drug, which promotes weight loss by blocking fat absorption in the large intestine, showed some effectiveness in adolescents: an average loss of 1.3 kg, or roughly 3 pounds, for subjects taking orlistat for one year, as opposed to an average gain of 0.67 kg, or 1.5 pounds, for the control group (pp. 8-9). See Table 1.

Short-term studies of orlistat have shown slightly more dramatic results. Researchers at the National Institute of Child Health and Human Development tested 20 adolescents, aged 12-16, over a three-month period and found that orlistat, combined with behavioral therapy, produced an average weight loss of 4.4 kg, or 9.7 pounds (McDuffie et al., 2002, p. 646). The study was not controlled against a placebo group; therefore, the relative effectiveness of orlistat in this case remains unclear.

Is Medication Safe for Children?

While modest weight loss has been documented for both medications, each carries risks of certain side effects. Sibutramine has been observed to increase blood pressure and pulse rate. In 2002, a

For a source with six or more authors, the first author's surname followed by "et al." is used for the first and subsequent references.

Table 1

Effectiveness of Sibutramine and Orlistat in Adolescents

Medication	Subjects	Treatment[a]	Side effects	Average weight loss/gain
Sibutramine	Control	0-6 mos.: placebo 6-12 mos.: sibutramine	Mos. 6-12: increased blood pressure; increased pulse rate	After 6 mos.: loss of 3.2 kg (7 lb) After 12 mos.: loss of 4.5 kg (9.9 lb)
	Medicated	0-12 mos.: sibutramine	Increased blood pressure; increased pulse rate	After 6 mos.: loss of 7.8 kg (17.2 lb) After 12 mos.: loss of 7.0 kg (15.4 lb)
Orlistat	Control	0-12 mos.: placebo	None	Gain of 0.67 kg (1.5 lb)
	Medicated	0-12 mos.: orlistat	Oily spotting; flatulence; abdominal discomfort	Loss of 1.3 kg (2.9 lb)

Note. The data on sibutramine are adapted from "Behavior Therapy and Sibutramine for the Treatment of Adolescent Obesity," by R. I. Berkowitz, T. A. Wadden, A. M. Tershakovec, & J. L. Cronquist, 2003, *Journal of the American Medical Association, 289*, pp. 1807-1809. The data on orlistat are adapted from *Xenical (Orlistat) Capsules: Complete Product Information*, by Roche Laboratories, December 2003, retrieved from http://www.rocheusa.com/products/xenical/pi.pdf

[a]The medication and/or placebo were combined with behavioral therapy in all groups over all time periods.

Mirano uses a table to summarize the findings presented in two sources.

A note gives the source of the data.

A content note explains data common to all subjects.

CAN MEDICATION CURE OBESITY IN CHILDREN? 7

consumer group claimed that the medication was related to the deaths of 19 people and filed a petition with the Department of Health and Human Services to ban the medication (Hilts, 2002). The sibutramine study by Berkowitz et al. (2003) noted elevated blood pressure as a side effect, and dosages had to be reduced or the medication discontinued in 19 of the 43 subjects in the first six months (p. 1809).

The main side effects associated with orlistat were abdominal discomfort, oily spotting, fecal incontinence, and nausea (Roche Laboratories, 2003, p. 13). More serious for long-term health is the concern that orlistat, being a fat-blocker, would affect absorption of fat-soluble vitamins, such as vitamin D. However, the study found that this side effect can be minimized or eliminated if patients take vitamin supplements two hours before or after administration of orlistat (p. 10). With close monitoring of patients taking the medication, many of the risks can be reduced.

Is Medication the Best Solution?

The data on the safety and efficacy of pharmacological treatments of childhood obesity raise the question of whether medication is the best solution for the problem. The treatments have clear costs for individual patients, including unpleasant side effects, little information about long-term use, and uncertainty that they will yield significant weight loss.

In purely financial terms, the drugs cost more than $3 a day on average (Duenwald, 2004). In each of the clinical trials, use of medication was accompanied by an expensive regime of behavioral therapies, including counseling, nutritional education, fitness advising, and monitoring. As journalist Greg Critser (2003) noted in his book *Fat Land,* use of weight-loss drugs is unlikely to have an effect without the proper "support system"—one that includes doctors, facilities, time, and money (p. 3). For some, this level of care is prohibitively expensive.

A third complication is that the studies focused on adolescents aged 12-16, but obesity can begin at a much younger age. Few data exist to establish the safety or efficacy of medication for treating very young children.

While the scientific data on the concrete effects of these medications in children remain somewhat unclear, medication is not the only avenue for addressing the crisis. Both medical experts and

---

When this article was first cited, all four authors were named. In subsequent citations of a work with three to five authors, "et al." is used after the first author's name.

Mirano develops the paper's thesis.

CAN MEDICATION CURE OBESITY IN CHILDREN? 8

policymakers recognize that solutions might come not only from a laboratory but also from policy, education, and advocacy. A handbook designed to educate doctors on obesity called for "major changes in some aspects of western culture" (Hoppin & Taveras, 2004, Conclusion section, para. 1). Cultural change may not be the typical realm of medical professionals, but the handbook urged doctors to be proactive and "focus [their] energy on public policies and interventions" (Conclusion section, para. 1).

Brackets indicate a word not in the original source.

The solutions proposed by a number of advocacy groups underscore this interest in political and cultural change. A report by the Henry J. Kaiser Family Foundation (2004) outlined trends that may have contributed to the childhood obesity crisis, including food advertising for children as well as

> a reduction in physical education classes and after-school athletic programs, an increase in the availability of sodas and snacks in public schools, the growth in the number of fast-food outlets . . . , and the increasing number of highly processed high-calorie and high-fat grocery products. (p. 1)

A quotation longer than forty words is indented without quotation marks.

Addressing each of these areas requires more than a doctor armed with a prescription pad; it requires a broad mobilization not just of doctors and concerned parents but of educators, food industry executives, advertisers, and media representatives.

Mirano interprets the evidence; she doesn't just report it.

The barrage of possible approaches to combating childhood obesity—from scientific research to political lobbying—indicates both the severity and the complexity of the problem. While none of the medications currently available is a miracle drug for curing the nation's 9 million obese children, research has illuminated some of the underlying factors that affect obesity and has shown the need for a comprehensive approach to the problem that includes behavioral, medical, social, and political change.

The tone of the conclusion is objective.

List of references begins on a new page. Heading is centred.

List is alphabetized by authors' last names. All authors' names are inverted.

The first line of an entry is at the left margin; subsequent lines indent ½" (1.5 cm).

Double-spacing is used throughout.

References

Berkowitz, R. I., Wadden, T. A., Tershakovec, A. M., & Cronquist, J. L. (2003). Behavior therapy and sibutramine for the treatment of adolescent obesity. *Journal of the American Medical Association, 289,* 1805-1812.

Carmona, R. H. (2004, March 2). *The growing epidemic of childhood obesity.* Testimony before the Subcommittee on Competition, Foreign Commerce, and Infrastructure of the U.S. Senate Committee on Commerce, Science, and Transportation. Retrieved from http://www.hhs.gov/asl/testify/t040302.html

Critser, G. (2003). *Fat land.* Boston, MA: Houghton Mifflin.

Duenwald, M. (2004, January 6). Slim pickings: Looking beyond ephedra. *The New York Times,* p. F1. Retrieved from http://nytimes.com/

Henry J. Kaiser Family Foundation. (2004, February). *The role of media in childhood obesity.* Retrieved from http://www.kff.org /entmedia/7030.cfm

Hilts, P. J. (2002, March 20). Petition asks for removal of diet drug from market. *The New York Times,* p. A26. Retrieved from http:// nytimes.com/

Hoppin, A. G., & Taveras, E. M. (2004, June 25). Assessment and management of childhood and adolescent obesity. *Clinical Update.* Retrieved from http://www.medscape.com/viewarticle/481633

McDuffie, J. R., Calis, K. A., Uwaifo, G. I., Sebring, N. G., Fallon, E. M., Hubbard, V. S., & Yanovski, J. A. (2002). Three-month tolerability of orlistat in adolescents with obesity-related comorbid conditions. *Obesity Research, 10,* 642-650.

Roche Laboratories. (2003, December). *Xenical (orlistat) capsules: Complete product information.* Retrieved from http://www.rocheusa .com/products/xenical/pi.pdf

Yanovski, S. Z., & Yanovski, J. A. (2002). Drug therapy: Obesity. *The New England Journal of Medicine, 346,* 591-602.

ALTERNATIVE APA TITLE PAGE

Obesity in Children 1

Short title and page
number in the upper
right corner on all
pages.

Can Medication Cure Obesity in Children?

A Review of the Literature

Full title, centred.

Luisa Mirano

Psychology 108, Sector B

Professor Kang

October 31, 2004

Writer's name,
course, instructor's
name, and date, all
centred at the
bottom of the page.

ALTERNATIVE APA RUNNING HEAD

Obesity in Children 5

were classified by the Drug Enforcement Administration as having the

"potential for abuse" (Hoppin & Taveras, 2004, Weight-Loss Drugs

section, para. 6). Currently only two medications have been approved

by the FDA for long-term treatment of obesity: sibutramine (marketed

Marginal annotations indicate APA-style formatting.

Directory to CMS-style note and bibliography models

CMS (*Chicago*) Papers

Most assignments in history and other humanities classes are based to some extent on reading. At times you will be asked to respond to one or two readings, such as essays or historical documents. At other times you may be asked to write a research paper that draws on a wide variety of sources.

Many history instructors and some humanities instructors require you to document sources with footnotes or endnotes based on *The Chicago Manual of Style*, 16th ed. (Chicago: U of Chicago P, 2010). (See CMS-4.) When you write a paper using sources, you face three main challenges: (1) supporting a thesis, (2) citing your sources and avoiding plagiarism, and (3) integrating quotations and other source material.

Examples in this section appear in CMS style and are drawn from one student's research on the Fort Pillow massacre. Sample pages from Ned Bishop's paper appear on pages 532–37.

CMS-1 Supporting a thesis

Most research assignments ask you to form a thesis, or main idea, and to support that thesis with well-organized evidence.

CMS-1a Form a working thesis.

Once you have read a variety of sources and considered your issue from different perspectives, you are ready to form a working thesis: a one-sentence (or occasionally a two-sentence) statement of your central idea. (See also C1-c.) In a research paper, your thesis will answer the central research question that you pose. Here, for example, are student writer Ned Bishop's research question and working thesis statement.

RESEARCH QUESTION

To what extent was Confederate Major General Nathan Bedford Forrest responsible for the massacre of Union troops at Fort Pillow?

WORKING THESIS

By encouraging racism among his troops, Nathan Bedford Forrest was directly responsible for the massacre of Union troops at Fort Pillow.

Notice that the thesis expresses a view on a debatable issue—an issue about which intelligent, well-meaning people might disagree. The writer's job is to persuade such readers that this view is worth taking seriously. To read Ned Bishop's thesis in the context of his introduction, see page 533.

CMS-1b Organize your ideas.

The body of your paper will consist of evidence in support of your thesis. Instead of getting tangled up in a formal outline early in the process, sketch an informal plan that organizes your ideas in bold strokes. Ned Bishop, for example, used a simple outline to structure his ideas. In the paper itself, these points became headings that help readers follow his line of argument.

> What happened at Fort Pillow?
>
> Did Forrest order the massacre?
>
> Can Forrest be held responsible for the massacre?

CMS-1c Use sources to inform and support your argument.

Used thoughtfully, your source materials will make your argument more complex and convincing for readers. Sources can play several different roles as you develop your points.

Providing background information or context

You can use facts and statistics to support generalizations or to establish the importance of your topic, as student writer Ned Bishop does early in his paper.

> Fort Pillow, Tennessee, which sat on a bluff overlooking the Mississippi River, had been held by the Union for two years. It was garrisoned by 580 men, 292 of them from United States Colored Heavy and Light Artillery regiments, 285 from the white Thirteenth Tennessee Cavalry. Nathan Bedford Forrest commanded about 1,500 troops.[1]

Explaining terms or concepts

If readers are unlikely to be familiar with a word, a phrase, or an idea important to your topic, you must explain it for them. Quoting or paraphrasing a source can help you define terms and concepts clearly and concisely.

> The Civil War practice of giving no quarter to an enemy—in other words, "denying [an enemy] the right of survival"—defied Lincoln's mandate for humane and merciful treatment of prisoners.[9]

Supporting your claims

As you draft your argument, make sure to back up your assertions with facts, examples, and other evidence from your research (see also A2-e). Ned Bishop, for example, uses an eyewitness report of the racially motivated violence perpetrated by Nathan Bedford Forrest's troops.

> The slaughter at Fort Pillow was no doubt driven in large part by racial hatred. . . .
> A Southern reporter traveling with Forrest makes clear that the discrimination was deliberate: "Our troops maddened by the excitement, shot down the ret[r]eating Yankees, and not until they had attained t[h]e water's edge and turned to beg for mercy, did any prisoners fall in [t]o our hands—Thus the whites received quarter, but the negroes were shown no mercy."[19]

Lending authority to your argument

Expert opinion can give weight to your argument (see also A2-e). But don't rely on experts to make your argument for you. Construct your argument in your own words and, when appropriate, cite the judgment of an authority in the field for support.

> Fort Pillow is not the only instance of a massacre or threatened massacre of black soldiers by troops under Forrest's command. Biographer Brian Steel Wills points out that at Brice's Cross Roads in June 1864, "black soldiers suffered inordinately" as Forrest looked the other way and Confederate soldiers deliberately sought out those they termed "the damned negroes."[21]

Anticipating and countering alternative interpretations

Do not ignore sources that seem contrary to your position or that offer interpretations different from your own. Instead, use them to give voice to opposing points of view and alternative interpretations before you counter them (see A2-f). Readers often have objections in mind already, whether or not they agree with you. Ned Bishop, for example, presents conflicting evidence to acknowledge that some readers may credit Nathan Bedford Forrest with stopping the massacre. In doing so, Bishop creates an opportunity to counter that objection and persuade those readers that Forrest can be held accountable.

> Hurst suggests that the temperamental Forrest "may have ragingly ordered a massacre and even intended to carry it out—until he rode inside the fort and viewed the horrifying result" and ordered it stopped.[15] While this is an intriguing interpretation of events, even Hurst would probably admit that it is merely speculation.

CMS-2 Citing sources; avoiding plagiarism

Your research paper is a collaboration between you and your sources. To be fair and ethical, you must acknowledge your debt to the writers of those sources. Failure to do so is a form of academic dishonesty known as *plagiarism.*

Three different acts are generally considered plagiarism: (1) failing to cite quotations and borrowed ideas, (2) failing to enclose borrowed language in quotation marks, and (3) failing to put summaries and paraphrases in your own words. Definitions of plagiarism may vary; it's a good idea to find out how your school defines and addresses academic dishonesty. (See also R3-c.)

CMS-2a Cite quotations and borrowed ideas.

You must cite anything you borrow from a source, including direct quotations; statistics and other facts; visuals such as tables, maps, and photographs; and any ideas you present in a summary or paraphrase.

The only exception is common knowledge—information your readers could easily find in any number of general sources. For example, most encyclopedias will tell readers that the Korean War ended in 1953 and that Frederick Banting was the first Canadian to receive a Nobel Prize. As a rule, when you have seen certain information repeatedly in your reading, you don't need to cite it. However, when information has appeared in only a few sources, when it is highly specific (as with statistics), or when it is controversial, you should cite the source.

CMS citations consist of superscript numbers in the text of the paper that refer readers to notes with corresponding numbers either at the foot of the page (footnotes) or at the end of the paper (endnotes).

TEXT

Governor John Andrew was not allowed to recruit black soldiers from out of state. "Ostensibly," writes Peter Burchard, "no recruiting was done outside Massachusetts but it was an open secret that Andrew's agents were working far and wide."[1]

NOTE

1. Peter Burchard, *One Gallant Rush: Robert Gould Shaw and His Brave Black Regiment* (New York: St. Martin's, 1965), 85.

PRACTICE hackerhandbooks.com/writersref
> CMS (*Chicago*) > CMS 2–1 to CMS 2–5

This basic CMS format varies for different types of sources. For a detailed discussion and other models, see CMS-4. When you use footnotes or endnotes, you will usually need to provide a bibliography as well (see CMS-4b).

CMS-2b Enclose borrowed language in quotation marks.

To indicate that you are using a source's exact phrases or sentences, you must enclose them in quotation marks unless they have been set off from the text by indenting (see p. 506). To omit the quotation marks is to claim—falsely—that the language is your own. Such an omission is plagiarism even if you have cited the source.

ORIGINAL SOURCE

For many Southerners it was psychologically impossible to see a black man bearing arms as anything but an incipient slave uprising complete with arson, murder, pillage, and rapine.

—Dudley Taylor Cornish, *The Sable Arm*, p. 158

PLAGIARISM

According to Civil War historian Dudley Taylor Cornish, for many Southerners it was psychologically impossible to see a black man bearing arms as anything but an incipient slave uprising complete with arson, murder, pillage, and rapine.[2]

BORROWED LANGUAGE IN QUOTATION MARKS

According to Civil War historian Dudley Taylor Cornish, "For many Southerners it was psychologically impossible to see a black man bearing arms as anything but an incipient slave uprising complete with arson, murder, pillage, and rapine."[2]

NOTE: When quoted sentences are set off from the text by indenting, quotation marks are not needed (see p. 506).

CMS-2c Put summaries and paraphrases in your own words.

Summaries and paraphrases are written in your own words. A summary condenses information; a paraphrase conveys the information using roughly the same number of words as in the original source. When you summarize or paraphrase, it is not enough to name the source; you must restate the source's meaning using your own language. (See also R3-c.) You commit plagiarism if you half-copy the author's sentences— either by mixing the author's phrases with your own without using quotation marks or by plugging your own synonyms into the author's sentence structure.

The first paraphrase of the following source is plagiarized—even though the source is cited—because too much of its language is borrowed from the original. The underlined strings of words have been copied exactly (without quotation marks). In addition, the writer has closely followed the sentence structure of the original source, merely making a few substitutions (such as *Fifty percent* for *Half* and *angered and perhaps frightened* for *enraged and perhaps terrified*).

ORIGINAL SOURCE

Half of the force holding Fort Pillow were Negroes, former slaves now enrolled in the Union Army. Toward them Forrest's troops had the fierce, bitter animosity of men who had been educated to regard the colored race as inferior and who for the first time had encountered that race armed and fighting against white men. The sight enraged and perhaps terrified many of the Confederates and aroused in them the ugly spirit of a lynching mob.

—Albert Castel, "The Fort Pillow Massacre," pp. 46–47

PLAGIARISM: UNACCEPTABLE BORROWING

Albert Castel suggests that much of the brutality at Fort Pillow can be traced to racial attitudes. Fifty percent of the troops holding Fort Pillow were Negroes, former slaves who had joined the Union Army. Toward them Forrest's soldiers displayed the savage hatred of men who had been taught the inferiority of blacks and who for the first time had confronted them armed and fighting against white men. The vision angered and perhaps frightened the Confederates and aroused in them the ugly spirit of a lynching mob.[3]

To avoid plagiarizing an author's language, resist the temptation to look at the source while you are summarizing or paraphrasing. After you have read the passage you want to paraphrase, set the source aside. Ask yourself, "What is the author's meaning?" In your own words, state your understanding of the author's basic point. Return to the source and check that you haven't used the author's language or sentence structure or misrepresented the author's ideas. When you fully understand another writer's meaning, you can more easily and accurately present those ideas in your own words.

ACCEPTABLE PARAPHRASE

Albert Castel suggests that much of the brutality at Fort Pillow can be traced to racial attitudes. Nearly half of the Union troops were blacks, men whom the Confederates had been raised to consider their inferiors. The shock and perhaps fear of facing armed ex-slaves in battle for the first time may well have unleashed the fury that led to the massacre.[3]

CMS-3 Integrating sources

Quotations, summaries, paraphrases, and facts will help you develop your argument, but they cannot speak for you. You can use several strategies to integrate information from sources into your paper while maintaining your own voice.

CMS-3a Use quotations appropriately.

In your academic writing, keep the emphasis on your ideas; use your own words to summarize and to paraphrase your sources and to explain your points. Sometimes, however, quotations can be the most effective way to integrate a source.

WHEN TO USE QUOTATIONS

• When language is especially vivid or expressive
• When exact wording is needed for technical accuracy
• When it is important to let the debaters of an issue explain their positions in their own words
• When the words of an authority lend weight to an argument
• When the language of a source is the topic of your discussion

Limiting your use of quotations   Although it is tempting to insert many quotations in your paper and to use your own words only for connecting passages, do not quote excessively. It is almost impossible to integrate numerous long quotations smoothly into your own text.

It is not always necessary to quote full sentences from a source. To reduce your reliance on the words of others, you can often integrate language from a source into your own sentence structure.

> As Hurst has pointed out, until "an outcry erupted in the Northern press," even the Confederates did not deny that there had been a massacre at Fort Pillow.[4]

> Union surgeon Dr. Charles Fitch testified that after he was in custody, he "saw" Confederate soldiers "kill every negro that made his appearance dressed in Federal uniform."[20]

Two useful marks of punctuation, the ellipsis mark and brackets, allow you to keep quoted material to a minimum and to integrate it smoothly into your text.

PRACTICE   hackerhandbooks.com/writersref
> CMS (*Chicago*) > CMS 3–1 to CMS 3–4

Using the ellipsis mark To condense a quoted passage, you can use the ellipsis mark (three periods, with spaces between) to indicate that you have omitted words. What remains must be grammatically complete.

> Union surgeon Fitch's testimony that all women and children had been evacuated from Fort Pillow before the attack conflicts with Forrest's report: "We captured . . . about 40 negro women and children."[6]

The writer has omitted several words not relevant to the issue at hand: *164 Federals, 75 negro troops, and.*

When you want to leave out one or more full sentences, use a period before the three ellipsis dots. For an example, see the long quotation on page 507.

Ordinarily, do not use an ellipsis mark at the beginning or at the end of a quotation. Readers will understand that you have taken the quoted material from a longer passage, so such marks are not necessary. The only exception occurs when you have dropped words at the end of the final quoted sentence. In such cases, put three ellipsis dots before the closing quotation mark.

Using brackets Brackets allow you to insert your own words into quoted material, perhaps to explain a confusing reference or to keep a sentence grammatical in your context.

> According to Albert Castel, "It can be reasonably argued that he [Forrest] was justified in believing that the approaching steamships intended to aid the garrison [at Fort Pillow]."[7]

NOTE: To indicate an error such as a misspelling in a quotation, insert the word [*sic*], italicized and with brackets around it, right after the error. (See the example on p. 507 and in P6-b for more information.)

Setting off long quotations CMS style allows you some flexibility in deciding whether to set off a long quotation or run it into your text. For emphasis, you may want to set off a quotation of more than four or five typed lines of text; almost certainly you should set off quotations of ten or more lines. To set off a quotation, indent it one-half inch (1.5 cm) from the left margin and use the normal right margin. Double-space the indented quotation.

Long quotations should be introduced by an informative sentence, often followed by a colon. Quotation marks are unnecessary because the indented format tells readers that the passage is taken word-for-word from the source.

In a letter home, Confederate officer Achilles V. Clark recounted what happened at
Fort Pillow:

> Words cannot describe the scene. The poor deluded negroes would run up to
> our men fall upon their knees and with uplifted hands scream for mercy but
> they were ordered to their feet and then shot down. The whitte [*sic*] men
> fared but little better. . . . I with several others tried to stop the butchery
> and at one time had partially succeeded, but Gen. Forrest ordered them shot
> down like dogs, and the carnage continued.[8]

CMS-3b Use signal phrases to integrate sources.

Whenever you include a paraphrase, summary, or direct quotation of
another writer's work in your paper, prepare your readers for it with a
signal phrase. A signal phrase usually names the author of the source
and often provides some context. It commonly appears before the source
material. To vary your sentence structure, you may decide to interrupt
source material with a signal phrase or place the signal phrase after
your paraphrase, summary, or direct quotation.

When the signal phrase includes a verb, choose one that is appropriate for the way you are using the source (see CMS-1c). Are you providing background, explaining a concept, supporting a claim, lending
authority, or refuting an argument? See the chart on page 508 for a list
of verbs commonly used in signal phrases.

Note that CMS style calls for verbs in the present tense or present
perfect tense (*points out* or *has pointed out*) to introduce source material unless you include a date that specifies the time of the original
author's writing.

The first time you mention an author, use the full name: *Shelby
Foote argues. . . .* When you refer to the author again, you may use
the last name only: *Foote raises an important question.*

Marking boundaries

Readers need to move from your words to the words of a source without feeling a jolt. Avoid dropping quotations into your text without
warning. Instead, provide clear signal phrases, usually including
the author's name, to indicate the boundary between your words and
the source's words. (The signal phrase is highlighted in the second
example.)

Using signal phrases in CMS papers

To avoid monotony, try to vary both the language and the placement of your signal phrases.

Model signal phrases

In the words of historian James M. McPherson, ". . ."[1]

As Dudley Taylor Cornish has argued, ". . ."[2]

In a letter to his wife, a Confederate soldier who witnessed the massacre wrote that ". . ."[3]

". . .," claims Benjamin Quarles.[4]

". . .," writes Albert Castel, ". . ."[5]

Shelby Foote offers an intriguing interpretation: ". . ."[6]

Verbs in signal phrases

admits	compares	insists	rejects
agrees	confirms	notes	reports
argues	contends	observes	responds
asserts	declares	points out	suggests
believes	denies	reasons	thinks
claims	emphasizes	refutes	writes

DROPPED QUOTATION

Not surprisingly, those testifying on the Union and Confederate sides recalled events at Fort Pillow quite differently. Unionists claimed that their troops had abandoned their arms and were in full retreat. "The Confederates, however, all agreed that the Union troops retreated to the river with arms in their hands."[9]

QUOTATION WITH SIGNAL PHRASE

Not surprisingly, those testifying on the Union and Confederate sides recalled events at Fort Pillow quite differently. Unionists claimed that their troops had abandoned their arms and were in full retreat. "The Confederates, however," writes historian Albert Castel, "all agreed that the Union troops retreated to the river with arms in their hands."[9]

Using signal phrases with summaries and paraphrases

As with quotations, you should introduce most summaries and paraphrases with a signal phrase that mentions the author and places the

material in the context of your argument. Readers will then understand where the summary or paraphrase begins.

Without the signal phrase (highlighted) in the following example,
readers might think that only the last sentence is being cited, when
in fact the whole paragraph is based on the source.

> According to Jack Hurst, official Confederate policy was that black soldiers were to
> be treated as runaway slaves; in addition, the Confederate Congress decreed that
> white Union officers commanding black troops be killed. Confederate Lieutenant
> General Kirby Smith went one step further, declaring that he would kill all captured
> black troops. Smith's policy never met with strong opposition from the Richmond
> government.[10]

Integrating statistics and other facts

When you are citing a statistic or another specific fact, a signal phrase
is often not necessary. In most cases, readers will understand that
the citation refers to the statistic or another fact (not the whole
paragraph).

> Of 295 white troops garrisoned at Fort Pillow, 168 were taken prisoner. Black
> troops fared worse, with only 58 of 262 captured and most of the rest presumably
> killed or wounded.[12]

There is nothing wrong, however, with using a signal phrase to introduce a statistic or fact.

> Shelby Foote notes that of 295 white troops garrisoned at Fort Pillow, 168 were
> taken prisoner but that black troops fared worse, with only 58 of 262 captured and
> most of the rest presumably killed or wounded.[12]

Putting source material in context

Readers should not have to guess why source material appears in your
paper. If you use another writer's words, you must explain how they
relate to your point. In other words, you must put the source in context.
It's a good idea to embed a quotation between sentences of your own,
introducing it with a signal phrase and following it up with interpretive
comments that link the quotation to your paper's argument.

QUOTATION WITH EFFECTIVE CONTEXT

> In a respected biography of Nathan Bedford Forrest, Hurst suggests that the
> temperamental Forrest "may have ragingly ordered a massacre and even intended

to carry it out—until he rode inside the fort and viewed the horrifying result" and ordered it stopped.[11] While this is an intriguing interpretation of events, even Hurst would probably admit that it is merely speculation.

NOTE: When you bring other sources into a conversation about your research topic, you are synthesizing. For more on synthesis, see MLA-3c.

☰ CMS-4 Documenting sources

In history and some humanities courses, you may be asked to use the documentation system set forth in *The Chicago Manual of Style*, 16th ed. (Chicago: U of Chicago P, 2010). In *Chicago* (CMS) style, superscript numbers in the text of the paper refer readers to notes with corresponding numbers either at the foot of the page (footnotes) or at the end of the paper (endnotes). A bibliography is often required as well; it appears at the end of the paper and gives publication information for all the works cited in the notes.

TEXT

A Union soldier, Jacob Thompson, claimed to have seen Forrest order the killing, but when asked to describe the six-foot-two general, he called him "a little bit of a man."[12]

FOOTNOTE OR ENDNOTE

12. Brian Steel Wills, *A Battle from the Start: The Life of Nathan Bedford Forrest* (New York: HarperCollins, 1992), 187.

BIBLIOGRAPHY ENTRY

Wills, Brian Steel. *A Battle from the Start: The Life of Nathan Bedford Forrest.* New York: HarperCollins, 1992.

CMS-4a First and subsequent notes for a source

The first time you cite a source, the note should include publication information for that work as well as the page number on which the passage being cited may be found.

1. Peter Burchard, *One Gallant Rush: Robert Gould Shaw and His Brave Black Regiment* (New York: St. Martin's, 1965), 85.

For subsequent references to a source you have already cited, you may simply give the author's last name, a short form of the title, and the page or pages cited. A short form of the title of a book is italicized; a short form of the title of an article is put in quotation marks.

4. Burchard, *One Gallant Rush,* 31.

When you have two consecutive notes from the same source, you may use "Ibid." (meaning "in the same place") and the page number for the second note. Use "Ibid." alone if the page number is the same.

5. Jack Hurst, *Nathan Bedford Forrest: A Biography* (New York: Knopf, 1993), 8.

6. Ibid., 174.

CMS-4b CMS-style bibliography

A bibliography, which appears at the end of your paper, lists every work you have cited in your notes; in addition, it may include works that you consulted but did not cite. For advice on constructing the list, see page 531. A sample bibliography appears on page 537.

NOTE: If you include a bibliography, *The Chicago Manual of Style* suggests that you shorten all notes, including the first reference to a source, as described at the top of this page. Check with your instructor, however, to see whether using an abbreviated note for a first reference to a source is acceptable.

CMS-4c Model notes and bibliography entries

The following models are consistent with guidelines in *The Chicago Manual of Style*, 16th ed. For each type of source, a model note appears first, followed by a model bibliography entry. The note shows the format you should use when citing a source for the first time. For subsequent citations of a source, use shortened notes (see CMS-4a). For a directory to models in this section, see page 498.

Some online sources, typically periodical articles, use a permanent locator called a digital object identifier (DOI). Use the DOI, when it is available, in place of a URL in your citations of online sources.

When a URL (Web address) or a DOI must break across lines, do not insert a hyphen or break at a hyphen if the URL or DOI contains one. Instead, break after a colon or a double slash or before any other mark of punctuation.

Books (print and online)

1. Basic format for a print book

1. Richard Gwyn, *John A.: The Man Who Made Us* (Toronto: Random House Canada, 2007), 242.

Gwyn, Richard. *John A.: The Man Who Made Us*. Toronto: Random House Canada, 2007.

For an illustrated citation of a print book, see pages 514–15.

2. Basic format for an online book

2. John Dewey, *Democracy and Education* (1916; ILT Digital Classics, 1994), chap. 4, http://www.ilt.columbia.edu/publications/dewey.html.

Dewey, John. *Democracy and Education*. 1916. ILT Digital Classics, 1994. http://www.ilt.columbia.edu/publications/dewey.html.

3. Basic format for an e-book (electronic book)

3. Stieg Larsson, *The Girl with the Dragon Tattoo* (Toronto: Penguin Canada, 2010), Kindle edition, chap. 3.

Larsson, Stieg. *The Girl with the Dragon Tattoo*. Toronto: Penguin Canada, 2010. Kindle edition.

4. Two or more authors

For a work with two or three authors, give all authors' names in both the note and the bibliography entry. For a work with four or more authors, in the note give the first author's name followed by "et al." (for "and others"); in the bibliography entry, list all authors' names.

4. Chris Stringer and Peter Andrews, *The Complete World of Human Evolution* (London: Thames and Hudson, 2005), 45.

Stringer, Chris, and Peter Andrews. *The Complete World of Human Evolution*. London: Thames and Hudson, 2005.

4. Lynn Hunt et al., *The Making of the West: Peoples and Cultures,* 3rd ed. (Boston: Bedford/St. Martin's, 2009), 541.

Hunt, Lynn, Thomas R. Martin, Barbara H. Rosenwein, R. Po-chia Hsia, and Bonnie G. Smith. *The Making of the West: Peoples and Cultures*. 3rd ed. Boston: Bedford/St. Martin's, 2009.

5. Organization as author

5. Guelph Historical Society, *Guelph: Perspectives on a Century of Change, 1900-2000* (Guelph, ON: Guelph Historical Society), 24.

Guelph Historical Society. *Guelph: Perspectives on a Century of Change, 1900-2000.* Guelph, ON: Guelph Historical Society.

6. Unknown author

6. *The Men's League Handbook on Women's Suffrage* (London, 1912), 23.

The Men's League Handbook on Women's Suffrage. London, 1912.

7. Multiple works by the same author

In the bibliography, use six hyphens in place of the author's name in the second and subsequent entries. Arrange the entries alphabetically by title.

Granatstein, Jack. *History and War*. Toronto: University of Toronto Press, 2006.

------. *Whose War Is It?* Toronto: Phyllis Bruce Books, 2008.

8. Edited work without an author

8. Ramsay Cook, ed., *Confederation* (Toronto: University of Toronto Press, 1967), 127.

Cook, Ramsay, ed. *Confederation*. Toronto: University of Toronto Press, 1967.

9. Edited work with an author

9. Ted Poston, *A First Draft of History,* ed. Kathleen A. Hauke (Athens: University of Georgia Press, 2000), 46.

Poston, Ted. *A First Draft of History*. Edited by Kathleen A. Hauke. Athens: University of Georgia Press, 2000.

10. Translated work

10. Tonino Guerra, *Abandoned Places,* trans. Adria Bernardi (Barcelona: Guernica, 1999), 71.

Guerra, Tonino. *Abandoned Places*. Translated by Adria Bernardi. Barcelona: Guernica, 1999.

11. Edition other than the first

11. Arthur Silver, *The French Canadian Idea of Confederation, 1864-1900*, 2nd ed. (Toronto: University of Toronto Press, 1997), 34.

Silver, Arthur. *The French Canadian Idea of Confederation, 1864-1900*. 2nd ed. Toronto: University of Toronto Press, 1997.

16. Work with a title in its title Use quotation marks around any title within an italicized title.

16. J. Brooks Bouson, ed., *Margaret Atwood: "The Robber Bride," "The Blind Assassin," "Oryx and Crake"* (London: Continuum, 2010), 36.

Bouson, J. Brooks, ed. *Margaret Atwood: "The Robber Bride," "The Blind Assassin," "Oryx and Crake."* London: Continuum, 2010.

17. Letter in a published collection If the letter writer's name is part of the book title, begin the note with only the writer's last name but begin the bibliography entry with the full name. (Also see p. 519.)

17. Langton to William Langton, 27 June 1837, in *A Gentlewoman in Upper Canada: The Journals, Letters, and Art of Anne Langton*, ed. Barbara Williams (Toronto: University of Toronto Press, 2008), 127.

Langton, Anne. *A Gentlewoman in Upper Canada: The Journals, Letters, and Art of Anne Langton*. Edited by Barbara Williams. Toronto: University of Toronto Press, 2008.

For an illustrated citation of a letter in a published collection, see pages 518–19.

18. Work in a series

18. R. Keith Schoppa, *The Columbia Guide to Modern Chinese History,* Columbia Guides to Asian History (New York: Columbia University Press, 2000), 256-58.

Schoppa, R. Keith. *The Columbia Guide to Modern Chinese History*. Columbia Guides to Asian History. New York: Columbia University Press, 2000.

19. Encyclopedia or dictionary entry

19. *Encyclopaedia Britannica,* 15th ed., s.v. "Red River Rebellion."

19. Margery Fee and Janice McAlpine, *Oxford Guide to Canadian English Usage*, 2nd ed. (Toronto: Oxford University Press, 2007), s.v. "Sasquatch."

Fee, Margery, and Janice McAlpine. *Oxford Guide to Canadian English Usage*. 2nd ed. Toronto: Oxford University Press, 2007.

The abbreviation "s.v." is for the Latin *sub verbo* ("under the word").
Well-known reference works such as encyclopedias do not require publication information and are usually not included in the bibliography.

20. Sacred text

20. Matt. 20:4-9 (Revised Standard Version).

20. Quran 18:1-3.

Sacred texts are usually not included in the bibliography.

21. Source quoted in another source

21. Ron Grossman and Charles Leroux, "A Local Outpost of Democracy," *Chicago Tribune*, March 5, 1996, quoted in William Julius Wilson and Richard P. Taub, *There Goes the Neighborhood: Racial, Ethnic, and Class Tensions in Four Chicago Neighborhoods and Their Meaning for America* (New York: Knopf, 2006), 18.

Grossman, Ron, and Charles Leroux. "A Local Outpost of Democracy." *Chicago Tribune*, March 5, 1996. Quoted in William Julius Wilson and Richard P. Taub, *There Goes the Neighborhood: Racial, Ethnic, and Class Tensions in Four Chicago Neighborhoods and Their Meaning for America* (New York: Knopf, 2006), 18.

Articles in periodicals (print and online)

22. Article in a print journal Include the volume and issue numbers and the date; end the bibliography entry with the page range of the article.

For an illustrated citation of an article in a journal, see pages 520–21.

22. Barbara A. Spellman and Simone Schnall, "Embodied Rationality," *Queen's Law Journal* 35, no. 1 (2009): 119.

Spellman, Barbara A., and Simone Schnall. "Embodied Rationality." *Queen's Law Journal* 35, no. 1 (2009): 117-64.

23. Article in an online journal Give the DOI if the article has one; if there is no DOI, give the URL for the article. For an unpaginated online article, in your note you may include locators, such as numbered paragraphs (if the article has them), or headings from the article.

23. Brian Lennon, "New Media Critical Homologies," *Postmodern Culture* 19, no. 2 (2009), http://pmc.iath.virginia.edu/text-only/issue.109/19.2lennon.txt.

Lennon, Brian. "New Media Critical Homologies." *Postmodern Culture* 19, no. 2 (2009). http://pmc.iath.virginia.edu/text-only/issue.109/19.2lennon.txt.

24. Journal article from a database Give whatever identifying information is available in the database listing: a DOI for the article; the name of the database and the number assigned by the database; or a "stable" or "persistent" URL for the article.

For an illustrated citation of an article from a database, see pages 522–23.

24. Constant Leung, "Language and Content in Bilingual Education," *Linguistics and Education* 16, no. 2 (2005): 239, doi:10.1016/j.linged.2006.01.004.

Leung, Constant. "Language and Content in Bilingual Education." *Linguistics and Education* 16, no. 2 (2005): 238-52. doi:10.1016/j.linged.2006.01.004.

Citation at a glance: Article in a scholarly journal (CMS)

To cite a print article in a scholarly journal in CMS (*Chicago*) style, include the following elements:

1 Author
2 Title of article
3 Title of journal
4 Volume and issue numbers

5 Year of publication
6 Page number(s) cited (for notes); page range of article (for bibliography)

TITLE PAGE OF JOURNAL

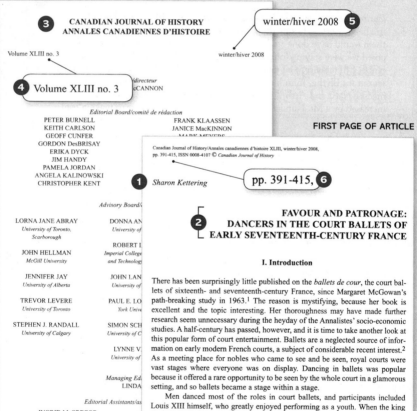

③ CANADIAN JOURNAL OF HISTORY
ANNALES CANADIENNES D'HISTOIRE

winter/hiver 2008 **⑤**

Volume XLIII no. 3

winter/hiver 2008

/directeur
cCANNON

④ Volume XLIII no. 3

Editorial Board/comité de rédaction

PETER BURNELL
KEITH CARLSON
GEOFF CUNFER
GORDON DesBRISAY
ERIKA DYCK
JIM HANDY
PAMELA JORDAN
ANGELA KALINOWSKI
CHRISTOPHER KENT

FRANK KLAASSEN
JANICE MacKINNON
MARK MEYERS

FIRST PAGE OF ARTICLE

Canadian Journal of History/Annales canadiennes d'histoire XLIII, winter/hiver 2008,
pp. 391-415, ISSN 0008-4107 © *Canadian Journal of History*

① *Sharon Kettering*

pp. 391-415, **⑥**

Advisory Board/

LORNA JANE ABRAY
University of Toronto,
Scarborough

JOHN HELLMAN
McGill University

JENNIFER JAY
University of Alberta

TREVOR LEVERE
University of Toronto

STEPHEN J. RANDALL
University of Calgary

DONNA AN
University of

ROBERT I
Imperial College
and Technolog

JOHN LAN
University of

PAUL E. LO
York Unive

SIMON SCH
University of C

LYNNE V.
University of

Managing Ed
LINDA

Editorial Assistants/as
INGRID McGREGOR

Translator/
DENYSE SAINT-C

FAVOUR AND PATRONAGE:
② DANCERS IN THE COURT BALLETS OF
EARLY SEVENTEENTH-CENTURY FRANCE

I. Introduction

There has been surprisingly little published on the *ballets de cour*, the court ballets of sixteenth- and seventeenth-century France, since Margaret McGowan's path-breaking study in 1963.[1] The reason is mystifying, because her book is excellent and the topic interesting. Her thoroughness may have made further research seem unnecessary during the heyday of the Annalistes' socio-economic studies. A half-century has passed, however, and it is time to take another look at this popular form of court entertainment. Ballets are a neglected source of information on early modern French courts, a subject of considerable recent interest.[2] As a meeting place for nobles who came to see and be seen, royal courts were vast stages where everyone was on display. Dancing in ballets was popular because it offered a rare opportunity to be seen by the whole court in a glamorous setting, and so ballets became a stage within a stage.

Men danced most of the roles in court ballets, and participants included Louis XIII himself, who greatly enjoyed performing as a youth. When the king danced, the dances were known as *grands ballets du Roy* or royal ballets. Louis's brother, Gaston d'Orléans, and his cousin, the prince de Condé, also danced in

[1] Margaret McGowan, *L'art du ballet de cour en France, 1581-1643* (Paris, 1963) with a list of archival sources, pp. 251-309 ; idem, *The Court Ballets of Louis XIII. A Collection of Working Designs for Costumes 1615-33* (London, 1989); idem, *Dance in the Renaissance: European Fashion, French Obsession* (New Haven, 2008). Marie-Françoise Christout has written extensively on court ballets, see below and especially, *Le ballet de cour de Louis XIV (1643-1672)* (Paris, 1967). Also see

NOTE

1. Sharon Kettering, "Favour and Patronage: Dancers in the Court Ballets of Early Seventeenth-Century France," *Canadian Journal of History* 43, no. 3 (2008): 393.

BIBLIOGRAPHY

Kettering, Sharon. "Favour and Patronage: Dancers in the Court Ballets of Early Seventeenth-Century France." *Canadian Journal of History* 43, no. 3 (2008): 391-415.

For more on citing articles from scholarly journals in CMS (*Chicago*) style, see page 517.

25. Article in a print magazine

25. Jason Kirby, "Read like a Billionaire," *Maclean's*, July 5, 2010, 60.

Kirby, Jason. "Read like a Billionaire." *Maclean's*, July 5, 2010, 60.

26. Article in an online magazine Include the URL for the article.

26. Katharine Mieszkowski, "A Deluge Waiting to Happen," *Salon*, July 3, 2008, http://www.salon.com/news/feature/2008/07/03/floods/index.html.

Mieszkowski, Katharine. "A Deluge Waiting to Happen." *Salon*, July 3, 2008. http://www.salon.com/news/feature/2008/07/03/floods/index.html.

27. Magazine article from a database Give whatever identifying information is available in the database listing: a DOI for the article; the name of the database and the number assigned by the database; or a "stable" or "persistent" URL for the article.

27. "Facing Facts in Afghanistan," *National Review*, November 2, 2009, 14, Expanded Academic ASAP (A209905060).

"Facing Facts in Afghanistan." *National Review*, November 2, 2009, 14. Expanded Academic ASAP (A209905060).

28. Article in a print newspaper Page numbers are not necessary; a section letter or number, if available, is sufficient.

28. Brian MacLeod, "Media Must Explain Why Truth Matters," *Niagara Falls Review*, November 24, 2010, sec. A.

MacLeod, Brian. "Media Must Explain Why Truth Matters." *Niagara Falls Review*, November 24, 2010, sec. A.

32. Book review

32. Benjamin Wittes, "Remember the Titan," review of *Louis D. Brandeis: A Life*, by Melvin T. Urofsky, *Wilson Quarterly* 33, no. 4 (2009): 100.

Wittes, Benjamin. "Remember the Titan." Review of *Louis D. Brandeis: A Life*, by Melvin T. Urofsky. *Wilson Quarterly* 33, no. 4 (2009): 100-101.

33. Letter to the editor Do not use the letter's title, even if the publication gives one.

33. Andrew Petter, letter to the editor, *Literary Review of Canada*, April 2010.

Petter, Andrew. Letter to the editor. *Literary Review of Canada*, April 2010.

Online sources

For most Web sites, include an author if a site has one, the title of the site, the sponsor, the date of publication or modified date (date of most recent update), and the site's URL. Do not italicize a Web site title unless the site is an online book or periodical. Use quotation marks for the titles of sections or pages in a Web site. If a site does not have a date of publication or modified date, give the date you accessed the site ("accessed on January 3, 2010").

34. Web site

34. Aulavik National Park of Canada, Parks Canada, last modified August 7, 2010, http://www.pc.gc.ca/eng/pn-np/nt/aulavik/index.aspx.

Aulavik National Park of Canada. Parks Canada. Last modified August 7, 2010. http://www.pc.gc.ca/eng/pn-np/nt/aulavik/index.aspx.

35. Short work from a Web site Place the title of the short work in quotation marks.

For an illustrated citation of a primary source from a Web site, see pages 526–27.

35. George P. Landow, "Victorian and Victorianism," Victorian Web, last modified August 2, 2009, http://victorianweb.org/vn/victor4.html.

Landow, George P. "Victorian and Victorianism." Victorian Web. Last modified August 2, 2009. http://victorianweb.org/vn/victor4.html.

36. Online posting or e-mail If an online posting has been archived, include a URL. E-mails that are not part of an online discussion are treated as personal communications (see item 42). Online postings and e-mails are not included in the bibliography.

36. Susanna J. Sturgis to Copyediting-L discussion list, July 17, 2010, http://listserv.indiana.edu/archives/copyediting-l.html.

book review • letter to the editor • online sources • Web site •
e-mail • blog • podcast • audio or video • government document

CMS-4c   **525**

37. Blog (Weblog) post   Treat as a short document from a Web site (see item 35). Put the title of the posting in quotation marks, and italicize the name of the blog. Insert "blog" in parentheses after the name if the word "blog" is not part of the name.

> 37. Miland Brown, "The Flawed Montevideo Convention of 1933," *World History Blog*, May 31, 2008, http://www.worldhistoryblog.com/2008/05/flawed-montevideo -convention-of-1933.html.

> Brown, Miland. "The Flawed Montevideo Convention of 1933." *World History Blog*. May 31, 2008. http://www.worldhistoryblog.com/2008/05/flawed-montevideo-convention -of-1933.html.

38. Podcast   Treat as a short work from a Web site (see item 35), including the following, if available: the author's (or speaker's) name; the title of the podcast, in quotation marks; an identifying number, if any; the title of the site on which the podcast appears; the sponsor of the site; and the URL. Before the URL, identify the type of podcast or file format and the date of posting or your date of access.

> 38. Paul Tiyambe Zeleza, "Africa's Global Past," Episode 40, Africa Past and Present, African Online Digital Library, podcast audio, April 29, 2010, http://afripod .aodl.org/.

> Zeleza, Paul Tiyambe. "Africa's Global Past." Episode 40. Africa Past and Present. African Online Digital Library. Podcast audio. April 29, 2010. http://afripod.aodl.org/.

39. Online audio or video   Cite as a short work from a Web site (see item 35). If the source is a downloadable file, identify the file format or medium before the URL.

> 39. Fredric Jameson, "Future of Culture, Future of Utopia," Jackman Humanities Institute, University of Toronto, December 5, 2007, http://www.youtube.com /watch?v=yxtUgTLqMAk.

> Jameson, Fredric. "Future of Culture, Future of Utopia." Jackman Humanities Institute, University of Toronto. December 5, 2007. http://www.youtube.com/watch?v =yxtUgTLqMAk.

Other sources (including online versions)

40. Government document

> 40. Statistics Canada, *Foreign and Domestic Investment in Canada* (Ottawa: Minister of Industry, 2005), 10.

> Statistics Canada. *Foreign and Domestic Investment in Canada*. Ottawa: Minister of Industry, 2005.

45. Video or DVD

45. *The Secret of Roan Inish,* directed by John Sayles (1993; Culver City, CA: Columbia TriStar Home Video, 2000), DVD.

The Secret of Roan Inish. Directed by John Sayles. 1993; Culver City, CA: Columbia TriStar Home Video, 2000. DVD.

46. Sound recording

46. Gustav Holst, *The Planets,* Royal Philharmonic Orchestra, conducted by André Previn, Telarc 80133, compact disc.

Holst, Gustav. *The Planets.* Royal Philharmonic Orchestra. Conducted by André Previn. Telarc 80133, compact disc.

47. Musical score or composition

47. Antonio Vivaldi, *L'Estro armonico,* op. 3, ed. Eleanor Selfridge-Field (Mineola, NY: Dover, 1999).

Vivaldi, Antonio. *L'Estro armonico,* op. 3. Edited by Eleanor Selfridge-Field. Mineola, NY: Dover, 1999.

48. Work of art

48. Robert Davidson, *Eagles,* gouache and watercolour on paper, 1991, Vancouver Art Gallery, Vancouver, BC.

Davidson, Robert. *Eagles.* Gouache and watercolour on paper, 1991. Vancouver Art Gallery, Vancouver, BC.

49. Performance

49. Athol Fugard, *The Road to Mecca,* directed by Morris Ertman, Rosebud Theatre, Rosebud, AB, October 23, 2010.

Fugard, Athol. *The Road to Mecca.* Directed by Morris Ertman. Rosebud Theatre, Rosebud, AB, October 23, 2010.

CMS-5 Manuscript format; sample pages

The following guidelines for formatting a CMS-style paper and preparing its endnotes and bibliography are based on *The Chicago Manual of Style,* 16th ed. (Chicago: U of Chicago P, 2010). For pages from a sample paper, see CMS-5b.

CMS-5a Manuscript format

Formatting the paper

CMS manuscript guidelines are fairly generic because they were not created with a specific type of writing in mind.

Materials and font Use good-quality 8½″ × 11″ (216 mm × 279 mm) white paper. If your instructor does not require a specific font, choose one that is standard and easy to read (such as Times New Roman).

Title page Include the full title of your paper, your name, the course title, the instructor's name, and the date. See page 532 for a sample title page.

Pagination Using arabic numerals, number the pages in the upper right corner. Do not number the title page but count it in the numbering; that is, the first page of the text will be numbered 2. Depending on your instructor's preference, you may also use a short title or your last name before the page numbers to help identify pages.

Margins and line spacing Leave margins of at least one inch (2.5 cm) at the top, bottom, and sides of the page. Double-space the body of the paper, including long quotations that have been set off from the text. (For line spacing in notes and the bibliography, see p. 531.) Left-align the text.

Long quotations You can choose to set off a long quotation of five to ten typed lines by indenting the entire quotation one-half inch (1.5 cm) from the left margin. (You should always set off quotations of ten or more lines.) Double-space the quotation; do not use quotation marks. (See p. 533 for a long quotation in the text of a paper; see also pp. 506–07.)

Capitalization and italics In titles of works, capitalize all words except articles (*a, an, the*), prepositions (*at, from, between*, and so on), coordinating conjunctions (*and, but, or, nor, for, so, yet*), and *to* and *as*—unless one of these words is first or last in the title or subtitle. Follow these guidelines in your paper even if the title is styled differently in the source.

Lowercase the first word following a colon even if the word begins a complete sentence. When the colon introduces a series of sentences or questions, capitalize all sentences in the series, including the first.

Italicize the titles of books, periodicals, and other long works. Use quotation marks around the titles of periodical articles, short stories, poems, and other short works.

Visuals CMS classifies visuals as tables and illustrations (illustrations, or figures, include drawings, photographs, maps, and charts). Keep visuals as simple as possible.

Label each table with an arabic numeral ("Table 1," "Table 2," and so on) and provide a clear title that identifies the table's subject. The label and the title should appear on separate lines above the table, flush left. Below the table, give its source in a note like this one:

> Source: Norman Hilmer and J. L. Granatstein, *Empire to Umpire: Canada and the World into the 21st Century* (Toronto: Nelson, 2008), 145.

For each figure, place a label and a caption below the figure, flush left. The label and caption need not appear on separate lines. The word "Figure" may be abbreviated "Fig."

In the text of your paper, discuss significant features of each visual. Place visuals as close as possible to the sentences that relate to them unless your instructor prefers that visuals appear in an appendix.

URLs (Web addresses) When a URL must break across lines, do not insert a hyphen or break at a hyphen if the URL contains one. Instead, break the URL after a colon or a double slash or before any other mark of punctuation. If your word processing program automatically turns URLs into links (by underlining them and changing the colour), turn off this feature.

Headings CMS does not provide guidelines for the use of headings in student papers. If you would like to insert headings in a long essay or research paper, check first with your instructor. See the sample pages of a CMS-style paper on pages 532–37 for typical placement and formatting of headings.

Preparing the endnotes

Begin the endnotes on a new page at the end of the paper. Centre the title "Notes" about one inch (2.5 cm) from the top of the page, and number the pages consecutively with the rest of the manuscript. See page 536 for an example.

Indenting and numbering Indent the first line of each note one-half inch (1.5 cm) from the left margin; do not indent additional lines in the note. Begin the note with the arabic numeral that corresponds to the number in the text. Put a period after the number.

Line spacing Single-space each note and double-space between notes (unless your instructor prefers double-spacing throughout).

Preparing the bibliography

Typically, the notes in CMS-style papers are followed by a bibliography, an alphabetically arranged list of all the works cited or consulted. Centre the title "Bibliography" about one inch (2.5 cm) from the top of the page. Number bibliography pages consecutively with the rest of the paper. See page 537 for a sample bibliography.

Alphabetizing the list   Alphabetize the bibliography by the last names of the authors (or editors); when a work has no author or editor, alphabetize it by the first word of the title other than *A, An,* or *The.*

If your list includes two or more works by the same author, use six hyphens instead of the author's name in all entries after the first. Arrange the entries alphabetically by title.

Indenting and line spacing   Begin each entry at the left margin, and indent any additional lines one-half inch (1.5 cm). Single-space each entry and double-space between entries (unless your instructor prefers double-spacing throughout).

CMS-5b Sample pages from a research paper: CMS style

Following are pages from a research paper by Ned Bishop, a student in a history class. The assignment required CMS-style endnotes and bibliography. Bishop followed CMS guidelines in preparing his manuscript as well.

MODELS   hackerhandbooks.com/writersref
   > Model papers > CMS (*Chicago*) papers: Bishop; Benjamin

Title of paper.

The Massacre at Fort Pillow:

Holding Nathan Bedford Forrest Accountable

Writer's name.

Ned Bishop

Title of course,
instructor's name,
and date.

History 214

Professor Citro

March 22, 2008

Marginal annotations indicate CMS-style formatting and effective writing.

Bishop 2

Although Northern newspapers of the time no doubt exaggerated
some of the Confederate atrocities at Fort Pillow, most modern sources
agree that a massacre of Union troops took place there on April 12,
1864. It seems clear that Union soldiers, particularly black soldiers,
were killed after they had stopped fighting or had surrendered or were
being held prisoner. Less clear is the role played by Major General Nathan
Bedford Forrest in leading his troops. Although we will never know whether
Forrest directly ordered the massacre, evidence suggests that he was
responsible for it.

What happened at Fort Pillow?

Fort Pillow, Tennessee, which sat on a bluff overlooking the
Mississippi River, had been held by the Union for two years. It was
garrisoned by 580 men, 292 of them from United States Colored Heavy
and Light Artillery regiments, 285 from the white Thirteenth Tennessee
Cavalry. Nathan Bedford Forrest commanded about 1,500 troops.[1]

The Confederates attacked Fort Pillow on April 12, 1864, and had
virtually surrounded the fort by the time Forrest arrived on the battlefield.
At 3:30 p.m., Forrest demanded the surrender of the Union forces, sending
in a message of the sort he had used before: "The conduct of the officers
and men garrisoning Fort Pillow has been such as to entitle them to being
treated as prisoners of war. . . . Should my demand be refused, I cannot be
responsible for the fate of your command."[2] Union Major William Bradford,
who had replaced Major Booth, killed earlier by sharpshooters, asked for an
hour to consider the demand. Forrest, worried that vessels in the river were
bringing in more troops, "shortened the time to twenty minutes."[3] Bradford
refused to surrender, and Forrest quickly ordered the attack.

The Confederates charged to the fort, scaled the parapet, and fired
on the forces within. Victory came quickly, with the Union forces running
toward the river or surrendering. Shelby Foote describes the scene like this:

> Some kept going, right on into the river, where a number drowned
> and the swimmers became targets for marksmen on the bluff. Others,
> dropping their guns in terror, ran back toward the Confederates with
> their hands up, and of these some were spared as prisoners, while
> others were shot down in the act of surrender.[4]

In his own official report, Forrest makes no mention of the massacre.
He does make much of the fact that the Union flag was not lowered by the

*Thesis asserts
Bishop's main point.*

*Headings, centred,
help readers follow
the organization.*

*Statistics are cited
with an endnote.*

*Ellipsis mark
indicates that words
have been omitted.*

*Quotation is cited
with an endnote.*

*Long quotation is
set off from text by
indenting. Quotation
marks are omitted.*

*Bishop uses a
primary source as
well as secondary
sources.*

Union forces, saying that if his own men had not taken down the flag, "few, if any, would have survived unhurt another volley."[5] However, as Jack Hurst points out and Forrest must have known, in this twenty-minute battle, "Federals running for their lives had little time to concern themselves with a flag."[6]

> Quotation is introduced with a signal phrase.

The federal congressional report on Fort Pillow, which charged the Confederates with appalling atrocities, was strongly criticized by Southerners. Respected writer Shelby Foote, while agreeing that the report was "largely" fabrication, points out that the "casualty figures . . . indicated strongly that unnecessary killing had occurred."[7] In an important article, John Cimprich and Robert C. Mainfort Jr. argue that the most trustworthy evidence is that written within about ten days of the battle, before word of the congressional hearings circulated and Southerners realized the extent of Northern outrage. The article reprints a group of letters and newspaper sources written before April 22 and thus "untainted by the political overtones the controversy later assumed."[8] Cimprich and Mainfort conclude that these sources "support the case for the occurrence of a massacre" but that Forrest's role remains "clouded" because of inconsistencies in testimony.[9]

> Bishop draws attention to an article that reprints primary sources.

Did Forrest order the massacre?

> Topic sentence states the main idea for this section.

We will never really know whether Forrest directly ordered the massacre, but it seems unlikely. True, Confederate soldier Achilles Clark, who had no reason to lie, wrote to his sisters that "I with several others tried to stop the butchery . . . but Gen. Forrest ordered them [Negro and white Union troops] shot down like dogs, and the carnage continued."[10] But it is not clear whether Clark heard Forrest giving the orders or was just reporting hearsay. Many Confederates had been shouting "No quarter! No quarter!" and, as Shelby Foote points out, these shouts were "thought by some to be at Forrest's command."[11] A Union soldier, Jacob Thompson, claimed to have seen Forrest order the killing, but when asked to describe the six-foot-two general, he called him "a little bit of a man."[12]

> Bishop presents a balanced view of the evidence.

Perhaps the most convincing evidence that Forrest did not order the massacre is that he tried to stop it once it had begun. Historian Albert Castel quotes several eyewitnesses on both the Union and Confederate sides as saying that Forrest ordered his men to stop firing.[13] In a letter to his wife three days after the battle, Confederate soldier Samuel Caldwell

Bishop 4

wrote that "if General Forrest had not run between our men & the Yanks with his pistol and sabre drawn not a man would have been spared."[14]

In a respected biography of Nathan Bedford Forrest, Hurst suggests that the temperamental Forrest "may have ragingly ordered a massacre and even intended to carry it out—until he rode inside the fort and viewed the horrifying result" and ordered it stopped.[15] While this is an intriguing interpretation of events, even Hurst would probably admit that it is merely speculation.

Can Forrest be held responsible for the massacre?

Even assuming that Forrest did not order the massacre, he can still be held accountable for it. That is because he created an atmosphere ripe for the possibility of atrocities and did nothing to ensure that it wouldn't happen. Throughout his career Forrest repeatedly threatened "no quarter," particularly with respect to black soldiers, so Confederate troops had good reason to think that in massacring the enemy they were carrying out his orders. As Hurst writes, "About all he had to do to produce a massacre was issue no order against one."[16] Dudley Taylor Cornish agrees:

> It has been asserted again and again that Forrest did not order a massacre. He did not need to. He had sought to terrify the Fort Pillow garrison by a threat of no quarter, as he had done at Union City and at Paducah in the days just before he turned on Pillow. If his men did enter the fort shouting "Give them no quarter; kill them; kill them; it is General Forrest's orders," he should not have been surprised.[17]

The slaughter at Fort Pillow was no doubt driven in large part by racial hatred. Numbers alone suggest this: of 295 white troops, 168 were taken prisoner, but of 262 black troops, only 58 were taken into custody, with the rest either dead or too badly wounded to walk.[18] A Southern reporter traveling with Forrest makes clear that the discrimination was deliberate: "Our troops maddened by the excitement, shot down the ret[r]eating Yankees, and not until they had attained t[h]e water's edge and turned to beg for mercy, did any prisoners fall in [t]o our hands—Thus the whites received quarter, but the negroes were shown no mercy."[19] Union surgeon Dr. Charles Fitch, who was taken prisoner by Forrest, testified that after he was in custody he "saw" Confederate soldiers "kill every negro that made his appearance dressed in Federal uniform."[20]

Topic sentence for this section reinforces the thesis.

Notes begin on a
new page.

First line of each
note is indented
½˝ (1.5 cm).

Note number is
not raised and is
followed by a period.

Authors' names are
not inverted.

Last name and title
refer to an earlier
note by the same
author.

Notes are single-
spaced, with double-
spacing between
notes. (Some
instructors may
prefer double-
spacing throughout.)

Notes

1. John Cimprich and Robert C. Mainfort Jr., eds., "Fort Pillow
Revisited: New Evidence about an Old Controversy," *Civil War History* 28,
no. 4 (1982): 293-94.

2. Quoted in Brian Steel Wills, *A Battle from the Start: The Life of
Nathan Bedford Forrest* (New York: HarperCollins, 1992), 182.

3. Ibid., 183.

4. Shelby Foote, *The Civil War, a Narrative: Red River to Appomattox*
(New York: Vintage, 1986), 110.

5. Nathan Bedford Forrest, "Report of Maj. Gen. Nathan B. Forrest,
C. S. Army, Commanding Cavalry, of the Capture of Fort Pillow," *Shotgun's
Home of the American Civil War*, accessed March 6, 2008, http://www
.civilwarhome.com/forrest.htm.

6. Jack Hurst, *Nathan Bedford Forrest: A Biography* (New York: Knopf,
1993), 174.

7. Foote, *Civil War*, 111.

8. Cimprich and Mainfort, "Fort Pillow," 305.

9. Ibid., 305.

10. Ibid., 299.

11. Foote, *Civil War*, 110.

12. Quoted in Wills, *Battle from the Start*, 187.

13. Albert Castel, "The Fort Pillow Massacre: A Fresh Examination of
the Evidence," *Civil War History* 4, no. 1 (1958): 44-45.

14. Cimprich and Mainfort, "Fort Pillow," 300.

15. Hurst, *Nathan Bedford Forrest*, 177.

16. Ibid.

17. Dudley Taylor Cornish, *The Sable Arm: Black Troops in the Union
Army, 1861-1865* (Lawrence: University Press of Kansas, 1987), 175.

18. Foote, *Civil War*, 111.

19. Cimprich and Mainfort, "Fort Pillow," 304.

20. Quoted in Wills, *Battle from the Start*, 189.

21. Ibid., 215.

22. Quoted in Hurst, *Nathan Bedford Forrest*, 177.

23. Quoted in James M. McPherson, *Battle Cry of Freedom: The Civil
War Era* (New York: Oxford University Press, 1988), 402.

Bishop 8

Bibliography

Castel, Albert. "The Fort Pillow Massacre: A Fresh Examination of the Evidence." *Civil War History* 4, no. 1 (1958): 37-50.

Cimprich, John, and Robert C. Mainfort Jr., eds. "Fort Pillow Revisited: New Evidence about an Old Controversy." *Civil War History* 28, no. 4 (1982): 293-306.

Cornish, Dudley Taylor. *The Sable Arm: Black Troops in the Union Army, 1861-1865.* Lawrence: University Press of Kansas, 1987.

Foote, Shelby. *The Civil War, a Narrative: Red River to Appomattox.* New York: Vintage, 1986.

Forrest, Nathan Bedford. "Report of Maj. Gen. Nathan B. Forrest, C. S. Army, Commanding Cavalry, of the Capture of Fort Pillow." Shotgun's Home of the American Civil War. Accessed March 6, 2008. http://www .civilwarhome.com/forrest.htm.

Hurst, Jack. *Nathan Bedford Forrest: A Biography.* New York: Knopf, 1993.

McPherson, James M. *Battle Cry of Freedom: The Civil War Era.* New York: Oxford University Press, 1988.

Wills, Brian Steel. *A Battle from the Start: The Life of Nathan Bedford Forrest.* New York: HarperCollins, 1992.

L

Writing about
Literature

All good writing about literature attempts to answer a question, spoken or unspoken, about the text:

- Why does Hamlet hesitate for so long before killing his uncle, King Claudius?
- How does street language function in Gwendolyn Brooks's "We Real Cool"?
- What does Orwell's "Shooting an Elephant" imply about the role the British played in imperial India?
- What does the relationship between Hana and Kip in Michael Ondaatje's novel *The English Patient* suggest about love and nationality?
- What is the connection between Latin and Gaelic in Brian Friel's play *Translations*?
- Why does Margaret Atwood make so many biblical allusions in *The Handmaid's Tale*?
- In what ways does Louise Erdrich's *Love Medicine* draw on oral narrative traditions?
- Why does it matter that Robert Hayden's poem "Those Winter Sundays" is about winter Sundays (as opposed to, say, winter Tuesdays)?

The goal of a literature paper should be to address such questions with a meaningful interpretation, presented both forcefully and persuasively.

L1 Reading to form an interpretation

L1-a Get involved in the work; be an active reader.

Read the work through once, closely and carefully. Think of it as speaking to you: What is it telling you? Asking you? Trying to make you feel? Then go back and read it a second time. If the work provides an introduction and footnotes, read them attentively. They may be a source of important information. Use the dictionary to look up words that are unfamiliar to you or words with subtle nuances that may affect the work's meaning.

Rereading is a central part of the process of developing your interpretation. You should read short works several times, first to get an overall impression and then again to focus on meaningful details. With longer works, such as novels or plays, read the most important chapters or scenes more than once while keeping in mind the work as a whole.

As you read and reread, interact with the work by posing questions and looking for possible answers. The chart that begins on page 546 suggests some questions about literature that may help you become a more active reader.

Annotating the work

Annotating the work is a way to focus your reading. If you own a copy of the work, you should feel free to make notes on it. If you do not, make a photocopy. The first time you read the work through, you may want to pencil a check mark next to passages you find especially significant. On a more careful rereading, pay particular attention to these passages and jot down your ideas and reactions in the margins of the page.

Here is one student's annotation of a poem by Shakespeare.

Rhyming pattern of sonnet

Shall I compare *thee* to a summer's day?

Thou art more lovely and more *temperate:*

Rough winds do shake the darling buds of May,

And summer's lease hath all too short a date.

Who? (Must be a loved one.)

Pleasant-natured (like pleasant weather)?

Sometime *too hot* the eye of heaven shines,

And often is his gold complexion dimmed;

And every (fair) from (fair) sometimes declines,

By chance, or nature's changing course, untrimmed.

Fair = beauty, or more than beauty?

Summer is fleeting and not always perfect. (But lover is perfect?)

But thy eternal summer shall not fade,

Nor lose possession of that fair thou ow'st

Nor shall death brag thou wand'rest in his shade,

When in eternal lines to time thou grow'st.

What are "eternal lines to time"? Ask in class?

Death would be proud to claim the lover but can't?

So long as men can breathe or eyes can see,

So long lives *this,* and this gives life to thee.

Final couplet seems to signal a shift in thought.

This = the poem? (Art, like the writer's love, is eternal.)

NOTE TAKING ON A LITERARY WORK

```
Notes on Chrysanthemums.doc - Microsoft Word
File  Edit  View  Insert  Format  Tools  Table  Window  Help
Times New Roman  ▼ 14  ▼  B  I  U  ▐▀ ▀▀ ▀▀ ▀▀ ▀▀ ▼  ▀▀  ✎ ▼ A ▼                    »  F
 L   ·  · · 1 · · · 1 · · · 1 · · · 2 · · · 1 · · · 3 · · · 1 · · · 4 · · · 1 · · · 5 · · ·
```

Notes on "Chrysanthemums"

Eliza's gardening clothes—"clodhopper" shoes and a dress "covered by a big corduroy apron"—not very feminine.

The words "strong," "strength," "power," and "powerful" pop up in connection with Eliza and her gardening. Why?

Conversation with pots-and-pans repairman about growing chrysanthemums is sexually charged—"Her breast swelled passionately."

Is she attracted to the travelling repairman or just his way of life? She envies his freedom to sleep outdoors in his wagon: "I wish women could do such things."

Bathtub scene after repairman leaves—awakened sexuality, romance.

What do chrysanthemums symbolize? Beauty? Femininity? Source of pride? Strength? All of these?

Eliza sees chrysanthemums tossed into a ditch. Disillusion.

Taking notes

Note taking is also an important part of rereading a work of literature. In your notes you can try out ideas and develop your perspective on the work. At the top of this page are some notes one student took on a short story, "Chrysanthemums," by John Steinbeck. Notice that some of these notes pose questions for further thought.

Discussing the work

As you may have discovered, class discussions can lead to interesting insights about a literary work, perhaps by calling attention to details that you failed to notice on a first reading. Discussions don't always need to occur face-to-face. In many classes, they happen online in discussion forums, chat rooms, blogs, or wikis. On page 544, for example, is a set of blog postings about a character in Joyce Carol Oates's short story "Where Are You Going, Where Have You Been?"

CONVERSATION ABOUT A SUBJECT

Dr. Connolly's Blog | ENG 101, Section 4

❶ Who is Arnold Friend?
Posted by **Professor Barbara Connolly**, Thu Mar 4, 2010 4:36 PM

At one point during the story Arnold Friend demands, "Don't you know who I am?" Who do you think he is? Does the reader or Connie ever really know?

View comments | Add a comment

---

4 comments on
"Who is Arnold Friend?" Original post

❷ Posted by **Zoe Marshall**, Thu Mar 4, 2010 7:23 PM
I think we're not supposed to know who Arnold Friend is. When he first arrives at Connie's house she asks him, "Who the hell do you think you are?" but Arnold ignores her question by changing the subject. He never tells her who he really is, only that he's her friend and her lover.

Posted by **Mirabel Chavez**, Thu Mar 4, 2010 7:47 PM
Connie is always pretending to be something else to her friends, her boyfriends, and her family. Oates describes her as having two sides: one for home and one for when she's away from home. Pretending is something Connie and Arnold have in common.

Posted by **Jon Fietze**, Thu Mar 4, 2010 8:04 PM
I found a lot of parallels between Arnold and the wolf in "Little Red Riding Hood." For example, Connie notices Arnold's hair, his teeth, and his grin. It reminded me of that part in "Little Red Riding Hood" when Little Red says, "Oh, Grandmother, what big teeth you have!"

Posted by **Yuko Yoshikawa**, Thu Mar 4, 2010 11:11 PM
I was thinking the same thing. Plus, Arnold seems like he's dressing up to hide who he is. Connie thinks that his hair is like a wig, and later that his face is a mask. It reminded me of when the wolf puts on the grandmother's clothing to trick Little Red Riding Hood, just like Arnold is trying to trick Connie.

---

1 Instructor's prompt.
2 A series of student responses to the prompt.

L1-b Form an interpretation.

After rereading, jotting notes, and perhaps discussing the work, you are ready to start forming an interpretation. At this stage, try to focus on a single aspect of the work. Look through your notes and annotations for recurring questions and insights related to the aspect you have chosen.

Focusing on a central issue

In forming an interpretation, you should try to focus on a central issue. Your job is not to say everything about the work that can possibly be said. It is to develop a sustained, in-depth interpretation that illuminates the work in some specific way. You may think, for example, that *Huckleberry Finn* is an interesting book because it not only contains humour and brilliant descriptions of scenery but also tells a serious story of one boy's coming of age. But to develop this general response into an interpretation, you will have to find a focus. For example, you might address the ways in which the runaway slave Jim uses humour to preserve his dignity. Or you might examine the ironic contradictions between what Huck says and what his heart tells him.

Asking questions that lead to an interpretation

Good interpretations generally arise from good questions. What is it about the work that puzzles, intrigues, or unsettles you? What do you want to know more about? What are you uncertain about? By asking yourself such questions, you will push yourself to move beyond your first impressions to deeper insights and better ideas.

Some interpretations answer questions about literary techniques, such as the writer's handling of plot, setting, and character. Others respond to questions about social context as well—what a work reveals about the time and culture in which it was written. Both kinds of questions are included in the chart that begins on page 546.

Often you will find yourself writing about both technique and social context. For example, Margaret Peel, a student who wrote about Langston Hughes's poem "Ballad of the Landlord" (see p. 564), addressed the following question, which touches on both language and race:

> How does the poem's language—through its four voices—dramatize the experience of a black man in a society dominated by whites?

Questions to ask about literature

Questions about technique

Plot. What central conflicts drive the plot? Are they internal (within a character) or external (between characters or between a character and a force)? How are conflicts resolved? Why are events revealed in a particular order?

Setting. Does the setting (time and place) create an atmosphere, give an insight into a character, suggest symbolic meanings, or hint at the theme of the work?

Character. What seems to motivate the central characters? Do any characters change significantly? If so, what—if anything—have they learned from their experiences? Do sharp contrasts between characters highlight important themes?

Point of view. Does the point of view—the perspective from which the story is narrated or the poem is spoken—influence our understanding of events? Does the narration reveal the character of the speaker, or does the speaker merely observe others? Is the narrator perhaps innocent, naive, or deceitful?

Theme. Does the work have an overall theme (a central insight about people or a truth about life, for example)? If so, how do details in the work serve to illuminate this theme?

Language. Does language—such as formal or informal, standard or dialect, prosaic or poetic, cool or passionate—reveal the character of speakers? How do metaphors, similes, and sensory images contribute to the work? How do recurring images enrich the work and hint at its meaning? To what extent do sentence rhythms and sounds underscore the writer's meaning?

Questions about social context

Historical context. What does the work reveal about—or how was it shaped by—the time and place in which it was written? Does the work appear to promote or undermine a philosophy that was popular in its time, such as social Darwinism in the late nineteenth century or the women's movement in the mid-twentieth century?

Class. How does social class shape or influence characters' choices and actions? How does class affect the way characters view—or are viewed by—others? What economic struggles or power relationships does the work reflect or depict?

Race and culture. Are any characters portrayed as being caught between cultures: between the culture of home and the culture of work or school, for example, or between a traditional and an emerging culture? Are any characters engaged in a conflict with society because of their race or ethnic background? To what extent does the work celebrate a specific culture and its traditions?

Gender. Are any characters' choices restricted because of gender? What are the power relationships between the sexes, and do these change during the course of the work? Do any characters resist the gender roles society has assigned to them? Do other characters choose to conform to those roles?

Archetypes (or universal types). Does a character, an image, or a plot fit a pattern—or type—that has been repeated in stories throughout history and across cultures? (For example, nearly every culture has stories about heroes, quests, redemption, and revenge.) How does an archetypal character, image, or plot line correspond to or differ from others like it?

In the introduction of your paper, you will usually announce your interpretation in a one- or two-sentence thesis. The thesis answers the central question that you posed. Here, for example, is Margaret Peel's two-sentence thesis:

> Langston Hughes's "Ballad of the Landlord" is narrated through four voices, each with its own perspective on the poem's action. These opposing voices—of a tenant, a landlord, the police, and the press—dramatize a black man's experience in a society dominated by whites.

L2 Planning the paper

L2-a Draft a thesis.

When planning your paper, it is good to have a working or preliminary thesis in mind. This preliminary thesis will reflect the current state of your thinking about the work and will likely change and evolve as you plan and draft. (See also C1-c and C2-a on thesis statements.)

In its final form, your thesis will address the central question you asked about the work. It will likely appear at the end of your introduction and will announce your essay's main point. When drafting your thesis, aim for a strong, assertive summary of your interpretation. On page 548, for example, are two successful thesis statements taken from student essays, together with the central question each student had posed.

QUESTION

In his poem "All the Spikes but the Last," is F. R. Scott justified in his criticism of E. J. Pratt for his poem "Towards the Last Spike"?

THESIS

In his poem "All the Spikes but the Last," F. R. Scott is incorrect in his assertion that E. J. Pratt does not acknowledge the Chinese workers in Pratt's poem "Towards the Last Spike."

QUESTION

What is the significance of the explorer Robert Walton in Mary Shelley's novel *Frankenstein*?

THESIS

Through the character of Walton, Shelley suggests that the most profound sort of knowledge is not a knowledge of nature's secrets but a knowledge of the limits of knowledge itself.

As in other writing, the thesis of a literature paper should not be too factual, too broad, or too vague (see also C2-a). For an essay on Douglas Coupland's *Microserfs*, for example, the following would all make poor thesis statements.

TOO FACTUAL

Microserfs is a series of journal entries by its main character, Daniel.

TOO BROAD

In *Microserfs*, Douglas Coupland examines the effect of technology on society.

TOO VAGUE

Microserfs is Coupland's most innovative novel.

The following thesis statement is sharply focused and presents a central idea that requires discussion and support. It connects a general point (that Coupland sees technology and big business as alienating) to those specific aspects of the novel the paper will address (the characters' isolation, the characters' search to find meaning in their lives).

ACCEPTABLE THESIS

In Coupland's *Microserfs*, the characters' social isolation and loneliness, products of a technology-driven world, are replaced with meaning only when the characters leave the big corporation to start their own company.

L2-b Sketch an outline.

Your thesis may strongly suggest a method of organization, in which case you will have little difficulty jotting down your essay's key points. Consider, for example, the following informal outline, based on a thesis that leads naturally to a three-part organization.

Thesis: In Zora Neale Hurston's novel *Their Eyes Were Watching God*, Janie grows into independence through a series of marriages: first to Logan Killicks, who treats her as a source of farm labour; next to Jody Starks, who sees her as a symbol of his own power; and then to Tea Cake, with whom she shares a passionate and satisfying love that leads her to self-discovery.

—Marriage to Logan Killicks: arranged by grandmother, Janie as labour, runs away
—Marriage to Jody Starks: Eatonville, Jody as mayor, violence, Jody's death
—Marriage to Tea Cake: younger man, love, shooting, return to Eatonville

If your thesis does not by itself suggest a method of organization, turn to your notes and begin putting them into categories that relate to the thesis. For example, one student who was writing about Euripides's play *Medea* constructed the following formal outline from her notes.

Thesis: Although Medea professes great love for her children, Euripides gives us reason to doubt her sincerity: Medea does not hesitate to use the children as weapons in her bloody battle with Jason, and from the outset she displays little real concern for their fate.

I. From the beginning of the play, Medea is a less than ideal mother.
   A. Her first words about the children are hostile.
   B. Her first actions suggest indifference.
II. In three scenes Medea appears to be a loving mother, but in each of these scenes we have reason to doubt her sincerity.
III. Throughout the play, as Medea plots her revenge, her overriding concern is not her children but her reputation.
   A. Fearing ridicule, she is proud of her reputation as one who can "help her friends and hurt her enemies."
   B. Her obsession with reputation may stem from the Greek view of reputation as a means of immortality.
IV. After she kills her children, Medea reveals her real concern.
   A. She shows no remorse.
   B. She revels in Jason's agony over their death.

Whether to use a formal or an informal outline is to some extent a matter of personal preference. For most purposes, you will probably find that an informal outline is sufficient, perhaps even preferable. (See also C1-d.)

≡ **L3** Writing the paper

L3-a Draft an introduction that announces your interpretation.

The introduction to a literature paper is usually one paragraph long. In most cases, you will want to begin the paragraph with a few sentences that provide context for your thesis and to end it with a thesis that sums up your interpretation. You may also want to note the question or issue that motivated your interpretation. In this way, you will help your reader understand not only what your idea or thesis *is* but also why it *matters*.

The following is an introductory paragraph announcing a student's interpretation of one aspect of the novel *Frankenstein*; the thesis is highlighted.

> In Mary Shelley's novel *Frankenstein*, Walton's ambition as an explorer, to find a passage to the North Pole, mirrors Frankenstein's ambition as a scientist, to discover and master the secret of life. But where Frankenstein is ultimately destroyed by his quest for knowledge, Walton turns back from his quest when he learns of Frankenstein's fate. Walton's story might seem unimportant, but paired with Frankenstein's, it keeps us from missing one of the novel's most important themes. Through Walton, Shelley suggests that the most profound and useful sort of knowledge is not a knowledge of nature's secrets but a knowledge of the limits of knowledge itself.

L3-b Support your interpretation with evidence from the work; avoid simple plot summary.

Your thesis and preliminary outline will point you toward details in the work relevant to your interpretation. As you begin drafting the body of your paper, make good use of those details.

Supporting your interpretation

As a rule, each paragraph in the body of your paper should focus on some aspect of your overall interpretation and should include a topic sentence that states the main idea of the paragraph. (See also C4-a.)

The rest of the paragraph should present details and perhaps quotations from the work that back up your interpretation. In the following paragraph, which develops part of the outline sketched on page 549, the topic sentence comes first. It sums up the significance of Janie's marriage to Logan Killicks in Zora Neale Hurston's novel *Their Eyes Were Watching God.*

> Janie finds her marriage to Logan Killicks unsatisfying because she did not choose him and cannot love him. The marriage is arranged by Janie's grandmother and caretaker, Nanny, so that Janie will have a secure home after Nanny dies. When Janie objects to the marriage, Nanny tells her, "'Tain't Logan Killicks Ah wants you to have, baby, it's protection" (15). Janie marries Logan even though she does not love him. She "wait[s] for love to begin" (22), but love never comes. At first, Logan dotes on Janie, but as time passes, he demands more and more work from her. Although she works hard in the kitchen, he wants her to perform traditionally masculine tasks such as chopping wood, plowing fields, and shovelling manure. When Janie suggests that they each have their roles—"Youse in yo' place and Ah'm in mine"—Logan asserts his authority over her and doesn't seem to relate to her as family: "You ain't got no particular place. It's wherever Ah need yuh" (31). As husband and wife, Janie and Logan are estranged from each other. Janie tells him, "You ain't done me no favor by marryin' me" (31). To escape this loveless and demeaning marriage, Janie runs away with Joe Starks.

Notice that the writer has quoted dialogue from the novel to lend both flavour and substance to her interpretation (quotations are cited with page numbers). Notice too that the writer is *interpreting* the work: She is not merely summarizing the plot.

Avoiding simple plot summary

In a literature paper, it is tempting to rely heavily on plot summary and avoid interpretation. You can resist this temptation by paying special attention to your topic sentences. The following rough-draft topic sentence, for instance, led to a plot summary rather than an interpretation.

> As they drift down the river on a raft, Huck and the runaway slave Jim have many philosophical discussions.

The student's revised topic sentence, which announces an interpretation, is much better.

> The theme of dawning moral awareness is reinforced by the many philosophical discussions between Huck and Jim, the runaway slave, as they drift down the river on a raft.

Usually a little thought and preparation can make the difference between a plot summary that cannot be developed and a focused, forceful interpretation. As with all writing, revision is key. To avoid simple plot summary, keep the following strategies in mind as you write.

- When you write for an academic audience, you can assume that readers have read the work. You may need to include some summary as background, but the emphasis should be on your ideas about the work.

- Pose questions that lead to an interpretation or judgment of the work rather than to a summary. The questions in the chart that begins on page 546 can help steer you away from summary and toward interpretation.

- Read your essay out loud. If you hear yourself listing events from the work, stop and revise.

- Rather than organizing your paper according to the work's sequence of events, organize it in a way that brings out the relationships among your ideas.

L4 Observing the conventions of literature papers

The academic discipline of English literature has certain conventions, or standard practices, that scholars in the field use when writing about literature. These conventions help scholars communicate their ideas clearly and efficiently. If you adhere to these conventions, you will enhance your credibility and enable your readers to focus more easily on your ideas.

L4-a Refer to authors, titles, and characters according to convention.

The first time you refer to an author of a literary work or a secondary source, such as a critical essay, use the author's full name: *Virginia Woolf is known for her experimental novels.* In subsequent references, you may use the last name only: *Woolf's early work was largely overlooked.* As a rule, do not use personal titles such as *Mr.* or *Ms.* or *Dr.* when referring to authors.

When you mention the title of a short story, an essay, or a short or medium-length poem, put the title in quotation marks.

"The Progress of Love," by Alice Munro

"Coming Home Again," by Chang-Rae Lee

"Promises like Pie-Crust," by Christina Rossetti

Italicize the titles of novels, nonfiction books, plays, and long poems.

The Poisonwood Bible, by Barbara Kingsolver

I Know Why the Caged Bird Sings, by Maya Angelou

M. Butterfly, by David Henry Hwang

Howl, by Allen Ginsberg

Refer to each character by the name most often used for him or her in the work. If, for instance, a character's name is Lambert Strether and he is always referred to as "Strether," do not call him "Lambert" or "Mr. Strether." Similarly, write "Lady Macbeth," not "Mrs. Macbeth."

L4-b Use the present tense to describe fictional events.

Perhaps because fictional events have not actually occurred in the past, the literary convention is to describe them in the present tense. Until you become used to this convention, you may find yourself shifting between present and past tense. As you revise your draft, make sure that you have used the present tense consistently.

INCONSISTENT USE OF TENSES

Octavia demands blind obedience from James and from all of her children. When James and Ty caught two redbirds in their trap, they wanted to play with them; Octavia, however, had other plans for the birds (89-90).

CONSISTENT USE OF THE PRESENT TENSE

Octavia demands blind obedience from James and from all of her children. When James and Ty catch two redbirds in their trap, they want to play with them; Octavia, however, has other plans for the birds (89-90).

NOTE: When integrating quotations from the work into your own text, you will need to be alert to the problem of shifting tenses. See L5-c.

L4-c Use MLA style to format passages quoted from the work.

Unless your instructor suggests otherwise, use MLA (Modern Language Association) style for formatting passages quoted from literary works.

MLA style usually requires that you name the author of the work quoted and give a page number for the exact location of the passage in the work. When writing about nonfiction articles and books, introduce a quotation with a signal phrase naming the author (*John Smith points out that* "...") or place the author's name and page number in parentheses at the end of the quoted passage: "..." *for all time (Smith 22).*

When writing about a single work of fiction, however, you do not need to include the author's name each time you quote from the work. You will mention the author's name in the introduction to your paper. Then, when you are quoting from the work, you may include just the page number in parentheses following the quotation (see p. 558). You may, of course, use the author's name in a signal phrase to highlight the author's role or technique (see p. 557), but you are not required to do so. (See also L5-a.)

See L5 for additional MLA guidelines for handling citations in the text of your paper. (See also MLA-3.)

L5 Integrating quotations from the work

Integrating quotations from a literary work can lend vivid support to your argument, but keep most quotations fairly short. You can use long quotations to present extended passages you will discuss at length, but use them sparingly. Excessive use of long quotations may interrupt the flow of your interpretation, making your paper more difficult to read and understand.

Integrating quotations smoothly into your own text can present a challenge. Because of the complexities of literature, do not be surprised to find yourself puzzling over the most graceful way to tuck in a short phrase or the clearest way to introduce a more extended passage from the work.

L5-a Do not confuse the work's author with a narrator, speaker, or character.

When introducing quotations from a literary work, make sure that you don't confuse the author with the narrator of a story, the speaker of a poem, or a character in a story or play. Instead of naming the author, you can refer to the narrator or speaker—or to the work itself.

INAPPROPRIATE

Poet Andrew Marvell describes his fear of death like this: "But at my back I always hear / Time's wingèd chariot hurrying near" (21-22).

APPROPRIATE

Addressing his beloved in an attempt to win her sexual favours, the speaker of the poem argues that death gives them no time to waste: "But at my back I always hear / Time's wingèd chariot hurrying near" (21-22).

APPROPRIATE

The poem "To His Coy Mistress" says as much about fleeting time and death as it does about sexual passion. Its most powerful lines are "But at my back I always hear / Time's wingèd chariot hurrying near" (21-22).

In the last example, you could mention the author as well: *Marvell's poem "To His Coy Mistress" says as much.* . . . Although the author is mentioned, readers will not confuse him with the speaker of the poem.

L5-b Provide context for quotations.

When you quote the words of a narrator, speaker, or character in a literary work, you should name who is speaking and provide a context for the quoted words. In the following examples, the quoted dialogue is from Tennessee Williams's play *The Glass Menagerie* and Alistair MacLeod's short story "In the Fall."

Laura is so completely under Amanda's spell that when urged to make a wish on the moon, she asks, "What shall I wish for, Mother?" (1.5.140).

When the narrator's mother wants to sell the family horse, his father responds, "He doesn't eat much now since all of his teeth has gone bad" (9).

L5-c As you integrate quotations, avoid shifts in tense.

Because it is conventional to write about literature in the present tense (see L4-b) and because literary works often use other tenses, you will need to exercise some care when weaving quotations into your own writing. One student's first draft of a paper on Nadine Gordimer's short story "Friday's Footprint" included the following awkward sentence, in which the present-tense main verb *sees* is followed by the past-tense verb *blushed* in the quotation.

TENSE SHIFT

When Rita sees Johnny's relaxed attitude, "she blushed, like a wave of illness" (159).

When revising, the writer considered two ways to avoid the distracting shift from present to past tense: to paraphrase the reference to Rita's blushing and reduce the length of the quotation or to change the verb in the quotation to the present tense, using brackets to indicate the change.

REVISION 1

When Rita sees Johnny's relaxed attitude, she is overcome with embarrassment, "like a wave of illness" (159).

REVISION 2

When Rita sees Johnny's relaxed attitude, "she blushe[s], like a wave of illness" (159).

Using brackets around just one letter of a word can seem fussy, so the writer chose the first revision. (See also L5-d.)

L5-d To indicate changes in a quotation, use brackets and the ellipsis mark.

Two marks of punctuation, square brackets and the ellipsis mark (three spaced periods), show readers that you have modified a quoted passage in some way.

Brackets are used for additions, as in the following example from a paper on Khaled Hosseini's novel *A Thousand Splendid Suns*.

Laila, fearful, confides in Tariq: "It's the whistling, the damn whistling [of the rockets], I hate more than anything" (156).

Because some readers might not understand the meaning of *whistling* out of context, the writer has supplied a clarification in brackets. Brackets are also used to change words or letters to keep a quoted sentence grammatical in your context, as in the last example in L5-c, or to change a capital letter to lowercase or vice versa, as on page 561.

The ellipsis mark is used to indicate omissions. In the following example from a paper on Tim O'Brien's "How to Tell a True War Story," the writer has omitted some words from the original in order to keep the quoted passage brief.

> O'Brien warns his readers bluntly that they should not seek noble themes in war stories: "If at the end of a war story you feel uplifted, . . . then you have been made the victim of a very old and terrible lie" (347).

If you want to omit one or more full sentences from a quotation, use a period before the three ellipsis dots.

> O'Brien regards war as fundamentally immoral: "A true war story is never moral. . . . If a story seems moral, do not believe it" (347).

Usually you do not need an ellipsis mark at the beginning or at the end of a quotation. But if you have dropped words at the end of the final quoted sentence, put three ellipsis dots before the closing quotation mark and parenthetical reference, as in the example on page 561.

Remember to use brackets and ellipsis marks sparingly. The purpose of quoting is to show your readers the actual language of the work. Excessive alterations can undermine a quotation's effectiveness as evidence.

L5-e Enclose embedded quotations in single quotation marks.

In writing about literature, you may sometimes want to use a quotation with another quotation embedded in it—when you are quoting dialogue in a novel, for example. In such cases, set off the main quotation with double quotation marks, as you usually would, and set off the embedded quotation with single quotation marks. The following example from a student paper quotes lines from Amy Tan's novel *The Hundred Secret Senses*.

> Early in the novel the narrator's half-sister Kwan sees—or thinks she sees—ghosts: "'Libby-ah,' she'll say to me. 'Guess who I see yesterday, you guess.' And I don't have to guess that she's talking about someone dead" (3).

L5-f Use MLA style to cite passages from the work.

MLA guidelines for citing quotations differ somewhat for short stories or novels, poems, and plays.

Short stories or novels

To cite a passage from a short story or a novel, use a page number in parentheses after the quoted words.

> The narrator of Madeleine Thien's "Simple Recipes" remembers a conversation with her mother in which the mother described guilt as something one could "shrink" and "compress." After a time, according to the mother, "you can blow it off your body like a speck of dirt" (12).

If a novel has numbered divisions, give the page number and a semicolon; then indicate the book, part, or chapter in which the passage is found. Use abbreviations such as "bk." and "ch."

> White relies on past authors to help retell the legend of King Arthur. The narrator does not provide specifics about Lancelot's tournament at Corbin, instead telling readers, "If you want to read about the Corbin tournament, Malory has it" (489; bk. 3, ch. 39).

When a quotation from a work of fiction takes up four or fewer typed lines, put it in quotation marks and run it into the text of your essay, as in the two previous examples. When a quotation is five lines or longer, set it off from the text by indenting one inch (2.5 cm) from the left margin; when you set a quotation off from the text, do not use quotation marks. Put the parenthetical citation after the final mark of punctuation.

> Sister's tale begins with "I," and she makes every event revolve around herself, even her sister's marriage:
>
> > I was getting along fine with Mama, Papa-Daddy and Uncle Rondo until my sister Stella-Rondo just separated from her husband and came back home again. Mr. Whitaker! Of course I went with Mr. Whitaker first, when he first appeared here in China Grove, taking "Pose Yourself" photos, and Stella-Rondo broke us up. (88)

Poems

To cite lines from a poem, use line numbers in parentheses at the end of the quotation. For the first reference, use the word "lines": (lines 1-2). Thereafter, use just the numbers: (12-13).

> The opening lines of Frost's "Fire and Ice" strike a conversational tone: "Some say the world will end in fire, / Some say in ice" (1-2).

Enclose quotations of three or fewer lines of poetry in quotation marks within your text, and indicate line breaks with a slash, as in the example just given.

When you quote four or more lines of poetry, set the quotation off from the text by indenting one inch (2.5 cm), and omit the quotation marks. Put the line numbers in parentheses after the final mark of punctuation.

In "Rivers of Canada," Bliss Carman describes the irresistible allure of Canada's rivers:

> I hear the brawling rapid, the thunder of the fall,
> And when I think upon them I cannot stay at all.
> At the far end of the carry, where the wilderness begins,
> Set me down with my canoe-load—and forgiveness of
>   my sins.
> O all the mighty rivers beneath the Polar Star,
> They call me and call me to follow them afar. (5-10)

NOTE: If any line of the poem takes up more than one line of your paper, carry the extra words to the next line of the paper and indent them an additional one-quarter inch (0.5 cm), as in the previous example. Alternatively, you may indent the entire poem a little less than one inch (2.5 cm) to fit the long line.

Plays

To cite lines from a play, include the act number, scene number, and line numbers (as many of these as are available) in parentheses at the end of the quotation. Separate the numbers with periods, and use arabic numerals unless your instructor prefers roman numerals.

Two attendants silently watch as the sleepwalking Lady Macbeth struggles with her conscience: "Here's the smell of the blood still. All the perfumes of Arabia will not sweeten this little hand" (5.1.50-51).

If no act, scene, or line numbers are available, use a page number.

When a quotation from a play takes up four or fewer typed lines in your paper and is spoken by only one character, put quotation marks around it and run it into the text of your essay, as in the previous example. If the quotation consists of two or three lines from a verse play, use a slash for line breaks, as for poetry (see p. 558). When a quotation by a single character in a play is five typed lines or longer (or more than three lines in a verse play), indent it one inch (2.5 cm) from the left margin and omit quotation marks. Include the citation in parentheses after the final mark of punctuation.

Speaking to Electra, Clytemnestra complains about the sexual double standard that has allowed her husband to justify sacrificing her other daughter, Iphigenia, to the gods. She asks what would have happened if Menelaus, and not his wife Helen, had been seized by the Trojans:

> If Menelaus had been raped from home on the sly, should I have
> had to kill Orestes so my sister's husband could be rescued? You
> think your father would have borne it? He would have killed me.
> Then why was it fair for him to kill what belonged to me and not
> be killed? (1041-45)

When quoting dialogue between two or more characters in a play, no matter how many lines you use, set the quotation off from the text. Type each character's name in all capital letters at a one-inch (2.5-cm) indent from the left margin. Indent subsequent lines under the character's name an additional one-quarter inch (0.5 cm).

In the opening act of *Translations*, Friel pointedly contrasts the monolingual Captain Lancey with the multilingual Irish:

> HUGH. . . . [Lancey] then explained that he does not speak Irish.
> Latin? I asked. None. Greek? Not a syllable. He speaks—on his
> own admission—only English; and to his credit he seemed suitably
> verecund—James?
> JIMMY. *Verecundus*—humble.
> HUGH. Indeed—he voiced some surprise that we did not speak his
> language. (act 1)

L6 Using secondary sources

Many literature papers rely wholly on primary sources—the literary work or works under discussion. You document such papers with MLA in-text citations as explained in L5-f. If a list of works cited is required, it will consist of the literary work or works (see L6-a).

In addition to relying on primary sources, some literature papers draw on secondary sources: articles or books of literary criticism, biographies of the author, the author's own essays or autobiography, or histories of the era in which the work was written. When you use secondary sources, you must document them with MLA in-text citations and a list of works cited as explained in L6-a. (For an example of a paper that uses secondary sources, see pp. 568–73.)

Keep in mind that even when you use secondary sources, your main goal should be to develop and communicate your own understanding and interpretation of the literary work.

L6-a Use MLA style to document secondary sources.

Most literature papers use the documentation system recommended by the Modern Language Association (MLA), as set forth in the *MLA Handbook for Writers of Research Papers*, 7th ed. (New York: MLA, 2009). (For complete details, see MLA-4.)

MLA recommends in-text citations that refer readers to a list of works cited. An in-text citation names the author of the source, often in a signal phrase, and gives the page number in parentheses. At the end of the paper, a list of works cited provides publication information about the sources used in the paper.

MLA IN-TEXT CITATION

Finding Butler's science fiction novel *Xenogenesis* more hopeful than *Frankenstein*, Theodora Goss and John Paul Riquelme note that "[h]uman and creature never bridge their differences in Shelley's narrative, but in Butler's they do . . ." (437).

The signal phrase names the authors of the secondary source; the number in parentheses is the page on which the quoted words appear.

The in-text citation is used in combination with a list of works cited at the end of the paper. Anyone interested in knowing additional information about the secondary source can consult the list of works cited. Here, for example, is the works cited entry for the work referred to in the sample in-text citation.

ENTRY IN THE LIST OF WORKS CITED

Goss, Theodora, and John Paul Riquelme. "From Superhuman to Posthuman: The Gothic Technological Imaginary in Mary Shelley's *Frankenstein* and Octavia Butler's *Xenogenesis*." *Modern Fiction Studies* 53.3 (2007): 434-59. Print.

As you document secondary sources with in-text citations and a list of works cited, you can consult the models and explanations in MLA-4.

L6-b Avoid plagiarism.

The rules about plagiarism are the same for literature papers as for other research writing. To be fair and ethical, you must acknowledge your debt to the writers of any sources you use. If you don't, you commit plagiarism, a serious academic offence.

In general, three different acts are considered plagiarism: (1) failing to cite quotations and borrowed ideas, (2) failing to enclose borrowed language in quotation marks, and (3) failing to put summaries and paraphrases in your own words. You may want to check out your school's plagiarism policy if you are unfamiliar with it.

If an interpretation was suggested to you by a critic's work or if an obscure point was clarified by someone else's research, it is your responsibility to cite the source (as explained in L6-a). In addition to citing the source, you must place any borrowed language in quotation marks. In the following example, the plagiarized words are underlined.

ORIGINAL SOURCE

Here again Glaspell's story reflects a larger truth about the lives of rural women. Their isolation induced madness in many. The rate of insanity in rural areas, especially for women, was a much-discussed subject in the second half of the nineteenth century.
— Elaine Hedges, "Small Things Reconsidered: 'A Jury of Her Peers,'" p. 59

PLAGIARISM

Glaspell may or may not want us to believe that Minnie Wright's murder of her husband is an insane act, but Minnie's loneliness and isolation certainly could have driven her mad. As Elaine Hedges notes, the rate of insanity in rural areas, especially for women, was a much-discussed subject in the second half of the nineteenth century (59).

BORROWED LANGUAGE IN QUOTATION MARKS

Glaspell may or may not want us to believe that Minnie Wright's murder of her husband is an insane act, but Minnie's loneliness and isolation certainly could have driven her mad. As Elaine Hedges notes, "The rate of insanity in rural areas, especially for women, was a much-discussed subject in the second half of the nineteenth century" (59).

Sometimes writers plagiarize unintentionally because they have difficulty paraphrasing a source's ideas. In the first paraphrase of the following source, the writer has copied the underlined words (without quotation marks) and followed the sentence structure of the source too closely, merely plugging in synonyms (*prowess* for *skill*, *respect* for *esteem*, and so on).

ORIGINAL SOURCE

Mothers [in the late nineteenth century] were advised to teach their daughters to make small, exact stitches, not only for durability but as a way of instilling habits of patience, neatness, and diligence. But such stitches also became a badge of one's needlework skill, a source of self-esteem and of status, through the recognition and admiration of other women.

—Elaine Hedges, "Small Things Reconsidered: 'A Jury of Her Peers,'" p. 62

PLAGIARISM: UNACCEPTABLE BORROWING

One of the final clues in the story, the irregular stitching in Minnie's quilt patches, connects immediately with Mrs. Hale and Mrs. Peters. In the late nineteenth century, explains Elaine Hedges, small, exact stitches were valued not only for their durability. They became a badge of one's prowess with the needle, a source of self-respect and of prestige, through the recognition and approval of other women (62).

ACCEPTABLE PARAPHRASE

One of the final clues in the story, the irregular stitching in Minnie's quilt patches, connects immediately with Mrs. Hale and Mrs. Peters. In the late nineteenth century, explains Elaine Hedges, precise needlework was valued for more than its strength. It was a source of pride to women, a way of gaining status in the community of other women (62).

Although the acceptable version uses a few words found in the original source, it does not borrow entire phrases without quotation marks or closely mimic the structure of the original. To write an acceptable paraphrase, resist the temptation to look at the source while you write; instead, write from memory. When you write from memory, you will be more likely to use your own words. Ask yourself, "What is the author's meaning?" and then in your own words, state your understanding of the author's basic point.

L7 Sample papers

Following are two sample essays. The first, by Margaret Peel, has no secondary sources. (Langston Hughes's "Ballad of the Landlord," the poem on which the essay is based, appears on p. 567.) The second essay, by Dan Larson, uses secondary sources. (The short story on which the paper is based begins on p. 574.)

Peel 1

Margaret Peel

Professor Lin

English 102

20 April 2010

Opposing Voices in "Ballad of the Landlord"

Langston Hughes's "Ballad of the Landlord" is narrated through four voices, each with its own perspective on the poem's action. These opposing voices—of a tenant, a landlord, the police, and the press— dramatize a black man's experience in a society dominated by whites.

The main voice in the poem is that of the tenant, who, as the last line tells us, is black. The tenant is characterized by his informal, nonstandard speech. He uses slang ("Ten Bucks"), contracted words (*'member, more'n*), and nonstandard grammar ("These steps is broken down"). This colloquial English suggests the tenant's separation from the world of convention, represented by the formal voices of the police and the press, which appear later in the poem.

Although the tenant uses nonstandard English, his argument is organized and logical. He begins with a reasonable complaint and a gentle reminder that the complaint is already a week old: "My roof has sprung a leak. / Don't you 'member I told you about it / Way last week?" (lines 2-4). In the second stanza, he appeals diplomatically to the landlord's self-interest: "These steps is broken down. / When you come up yourself / It's a wonder you don't fall down" (6-8). In the third stanza, when the landlord has responded to his complaints with a demand for rent money, the tenant becomes more forceful, but his voice is still reasonable: "Ten Bucks you say is due? / Well, that's Ten Bucks more'n I'll pay you / Till you fix this house up new" (10-12).

The fourth stanza marks a shift in the tone of the argument. At this point the tenant responds more emotionally, in reaction to the landlord's threats to evict him. By the fifth stanza, the tenant has unleashed his anger: "Um-huh! You talking high and mighty" (17). Hughes uses an exclamation point for the first time; the tenant is raising his voice at last. As the argument gets more heated, the tenant finally resorts to the language of violence: "You ain't gonna be able to say a word / If I land my fist on you" (19-20).

Thesis states Peel's main idea.

Details from the poem illustrate Peel's point.

The first citation for lines of the poem includes the word "lines." Subsequent citations from the poem are cited with line numbers alone.

Topic sentence focuses on an interpretation.

Marginal annotations indicate MLA-style formatting and effective writing.

Peel 2

These are the last words the tenant speaks in the poem. Perhaps Hughes wants to show how black people who threaten violence are silenced. When a new voice is introduced—the landlord's—the poem shifts to a frantic tone:

> *Police! Police!*
> *Come and get this man!*
> *He's trying to ruin the government*
> *And overturn the land!* (21-24)

This response is clearly an overreaction to a small threat. Instead of dealing with the tenant directly, the landlord shouts for the police. His hysterical voice—marked by repetitions and punctuated with exclamation points—reveals his disproportionate fear and outrage. And his conclusions are equally excessive: this black man, he claims, is out to "ruin the government" and "overturn the land." Although the landlord's overreaction is humorous, it is sinister as well, because the landlord knows that, no matter how excessive his claims are, he has the police and the law on his side.

In line 25, the regular meter and rhyme of the poem break down, perhaps showing how an arrest disrupts everyday life. The "voice" in lines 25-29 has two parts: the clanging sound of the police ("Copper's whistle! / Patrol bell!") and, in sharp contrast, the unemotional, factual tone of a police report ("Arrest. / Precinct Station. / Iron cell.").

The last voice in the poem is the voice of the press, represented in newspaper headlines: "MAN THREATENS LANDLORD / TENANT HELD NO BAIL / JUDGE GIVES NEGRO 90 DAYS IN COUNTY JAIL" (31-33). Meter and rhyme return here, as if to show that once the tenant is arrested, life can go on as usual. The language of the press, like that of the police, is cold and distant, and it gives the tenant less and less status. In line 31, he is a "man"; in line 32, he has been demoted to a "tenant"; and in line 33, he has become a "Negro," or just another statistic.

By using four opposing voices in "Ballad of the Landlord," Hughes effectively dramatizes different views of minority assertiveness. To the tenant, assertiveness is informal and natural, as his language shows; to the landlord, it is a dangerous threat, as his hysterical response suggests. The police response is, like the language that describes it, short and sharp. Finally, the press's view of events, represented by the headlines, is

[margin notes]

Transition prepares readers for the next topic.

Peel interprets the landlord's response.

Peel shows how meter and rhyme support the poem's meaning.

Peel sums up her interpretation.

Peel 3

distant and unsympathetic.

Peel concludes with an analysis of the poem's political significance.

      By the end of the poem, we understand the predicament of the black man. Exploited by the landlord, politically oppressed by those who think he's out "to ruin the government," physically restrained by the police and the judicial system, and denied his individuality by the press, he is saved only by his own sense of humor. The very title of the poem suggests his— and Hughes's—sense of humor. The tenant is singing a *ballad* to his oppressors, but this ballad is no love song. It portrays the oppressors, through their own voices, in an unflattering light: the landlord as cowardly and ridiculous, the police and press as dull and soulless. The tenant may lack political power, but he speaks with vitality, and no one can say he lacks dignity or the spirit to survive.

Peel 4

Work Cited

Hughes, Langston. "Ballad of the Landlord." *Poetry: An Introduction*.
    Ed. Michael Meyer. 6th ed. Boston: Bedford, 2010. 417-18. Print.

Ballad of the Landlord

LANGSTON HUGHES

Landlord, landlord,
My roof has sprung a leak.
Don't you 'member I told you about it
Way last week?

Landlord, landlord,
These steps is broken down.
When you come up yourself
It's a wonder you don't fall down.

Ten Bucks you say I owe you?
Ten Bucks you say is due?
Well, that's Ten Bucks more'n I'll pay you
Till you fix this house up new.

What? You gonna get eviction orders?
You gonna cut off my heat?
You gonna take my furniture and
Throw it in the street?

Um-huh! You talking high and mighty.
Talk on—till you get through.
You ain't gonna be able to say a word
If I land my fist on you.

Police! Police!
Come and get this man!
He's trying to ruin the government
And overturn the land!

Copper's whistle!
Patrol bell!
Arrest.

Precinct Station.
Iron cell.
Headlines in press:

MAN THREATENS LANDLORD
TENANT HELD NO BAIL
JUDGE GIVES NEGRO 90 DAYS IN COUNTY JAIL

Larson 1

Dan Larson

Professor Duncan

English 102

19 April 2010

The Transformation of Mrs. Peters:

An Analysis of "A Jury of Her Peers"

In Susan Glaspell's 1917 short story "A Jury of Her Peers," two
women accompany their husbands and a county attorney to an isolated
house where a farmer named John Wright has been choked to death in
his bed with a rope. The chief suspect is Wright's wife, Minnie, who is in
jail awaiting trial. The sheriff's wife, Mrs. Peters, has come along to gather
some personal items for Minnie, and Mrs. Hale has joined her. Early in the
story, Mrs. Hale sympathizes with Minnie and objects to the way the male
investigators are "snoopin' round and criticizin'" her kitchen (191). In
contrast, Mrs. Peters shows respect for the law, saying that the men are
doing "no more than their duty" (191). By the end of the story, however,
Mrs. Peters has joined Mrs. Hale in a conspiracy of silence, lied to the men,
and committed a crime—hiding key evidence. What causes this dramatic
change?

One critic, Leonard Mustazza, argues that Mrs. Hale recruits
Mrs. Peters "as a fellow 'juror' in the case, moving the sheriff's wife away
from her sympathy for her husband's position and towards identification
with the accused wom[a]n" (494). While this is true, Mrs. Peters also
reaches insights on her own. Her observations in the kitchen lead her to
understand Minnie's grim and lonely plight as the wife of an abusive farmer,
and her identification with both Minnie and Mrs. Hale is strengthened as the
men conducting the investigation trivialize the lives of women.

The first evidence that Mrs. Peters reaches understanding on her own
surfaces in the following passage:

> The sheriff's wife had looked from the stove to the sink—
> to the pail of water which had been carried in from
> outside. . . . That look of seeing into things, of seeing
> through a thing to something else, was in the eyes of the
> sheriff's wife now. (194)

Something about the stove, the sink, and the pail of water connects with

---

Marginal annotations:

The opening lines name the story and establish context.

Present tense is used to describe details from the story.

Quotations from the story are cited with page numbers in parentheses.

The opening paragraph ends with Larson's research question.

The thesis asserts Larson's main point.

A long quotation is set off by indenting; no quotation marks are needed; ellipsis dots indicate a sentence omitted from the source.

Marginal annotations indicate MLA-style formatting and effective writing.

Larson 2

her own experience, giving Mrs. Peters a glimpse into the life of Minnie Wright. The details resonate with meaning.

Social historian Elaine Hedges argues that such details, which evoke the drudgery of a farm woman's work, would not have been lost upon Glaspell's readers in 1917. Hedges tells us what the pail and the stove, along with another detail from the story—a dirty towel on a roller—would have meant to women of the time. Laundry was a dreaded all-day affair. Water had to be pumped, hauled, and boiled; then the wash was rubbed, rinsed, wrung through a wringer, carried outside, and hung on a line to dry. "What the women see, beyond the pail and the stove," writes Hedges, "are the hours of work it took Minnie to produce that one clean towel" (56).

On her own, Mrs. Peters discovers clues about the motive for the murder. Her curiosity leads her to pick up a sewing basket filled with quilt pieces and then to notice something strange: a sudden row of badly sewn stitches. "What do you suppose she was so—nervous about?" asks Mrs. Peters (195). A short time later, Mrs. Peters spots another clue, an empty birdcage. Again she observes details on her own, in this case a broken door and hinge, suggesting that the cage has been roughly handled.

In addition to noticing details, both women draw conclusions from them and speculate on their significance. When Mrs. Hale finds the dead canary beneath a quilt patch, for example, the women conclude that its neck has been wrung and understand who must have wrung it.

As the women speculate on the significance of the dead canary, each connects the bird with her own experience. Mrs. Hale knows that Minnie once sang in the church choir, an activity that Mr. Wright put a stop to, just as he put a stop to the bird's singing. Also, as a farmer's wife, Mrs. Hale understands the desolation and loneliness of life on the prairie. She sees that the bird was both a thing of beauty and a companion. "If there had been years and years of—nothing, then a bird to sing to you," says Mrs. Hale, "it would be awful—still—after the bird was still" (198). To Mrs. Peters, the stillness of the canary evokes memories of the time when she and her husband homesteaded in the northern plains. "I know what stillness is," she says, as she recalls the death of her first child, with no one around to console her (198).

Larson summarizes ideas from a secondary source and then quotes from that source; he names the author in a signal phrase and gives a page number in parentheses.

Topic sentences present Larson's interpretation.

Details from the story provide evidence for the interpretation.

Larson 3

Elaine Hedges has written movingly of the isolation that women experienced on late-nineteenth- and early-twentieth-century farms of the West and Midwest:

> Women themselves reported that it was not unusual to spend five months in a log cabin without seeing another woman . . . or to spend one and a half years after arriving before being able to take a trip to town. . . . (54)

To combat loneliness and monotony, says Hedges, many women bought canaries and hung the cages outside their sod huts. The canaries provided music and color, a "spot of beauty" that "might spell the difference between sanity and madness" (60).

Mrs. Peters and Mrs. Hale understand—and Glaspell's readers in 1917 would have understood—what the killing of the bird means to Minnie. For Mrs. Peters, in fact, the act has a special significance. When she was a child, a boy axed her kitten to death and, as she says, "If they hadn't held me back I would have . . . hurt him" (198). She has little difficulty comprehending Minnie's murderous rage, for she has felt it herself.

Although Mrs. Peters's growing empathy for Minnie stems largely from her observations, it is also prompted by her negative reaction to the patronizing comments of the male investigators. At several points in the story, her body language reveals her feelings. For example, when Mr. Hale remarks that "women are used to worrying over trifles," both women move closer together and remain silent. When the county attorney asks, "for all their worries, what would we do without the ladies?" the women do not speak, nor do they "unbend" (190). The fact that the women respond in exactly the same way reveals the extent to which they are bonding.

Both women are annoyed at the way in which the men criticize and trivialize the world of women. The men question the difficulty of women's work. For example, when the county attorney points to the dirty towel on the rack as evidence that Minnie wasn't much of a housekeeper, Mrs. Hale replies, "There's a great deal of work to be done on a farm" (190). Even the importance of women's work is questioned. The men kid the women for trying to decide if Minnie was going to quilt or knot patches together for a quilt and laugh about such trivial concerns. Those very

---

Ellipsis dots indicate omitted words within the sentence and at the end of the sentence.

Transition serves as a bridge from one section of the paper to the next.

quilts, of course, kept the men warm at night and cost them nothing beyond the price of thread.

The men also question the women's wisdom and intelligence. For example, when the county attorney tells the women to keep their eyes out for clues, Mr. Hale replies, "But would the women know a clue if they did come upon it?" (191). The women's response is to stand motionless and silent. The irony is that the men don't see the household clues that are right in front of them.

By the end of the story, Mrs. Peters has been so transformed that she risks lying to the men. When the county attorney walks into the kitchen and notices the birdcage the women have found, he asks about the whereabouts of the bird. Mrs. Hale replies, "We think the cat got it" (197), even though she knows from Mrs. Peters that Minnie was afraid of cats and would not have owned one. Instead of correcting the lie, Mrs. Peters elaborates on it, saying of cats, "They're superstitious, you know; they leave" (198). Clearly Mrs. Hale is willing to risk lying because she is confident that Mrs. Peters won't contradict her.

> Larson gives evidence that Mrs. Peters has been transformed.

The Mrs. Peters character may have been based on a real sheriff's wife. Seventeen years before writing "A Jury of Her Peers," Susan Glaspell covered a murder case for the *Des Moines Daily News*. A farmer's wife, Margaret Hossack, was accused of murdering her sleeping husband with two axe blows to the head. In one of her newspaper reports, Glaspell wrote that the sheriff's wife sat next to Mrs. Hossack and "frequently applied her handkerchief to her eyes" (qtd. in Ben-Zvi 30).

> Larson draws on a secondary source that gives background on Glaspell's life.

We do not know from the short story the ultimate fate of Minnie Wright, but Margaret Hossack, whose case inspired the story, was found guilty, though the case was later thrown out by the Iowa Supreme Court. However, as Linda Ben-Zvi points out, the women's guilt or innocence is not the issue:

> Whether Margaret Hossack or Minnie Wright committed
> murder is moot; what is incontrovertible is the brutality
> of their lives, the lack of options they had to redress
> grievances or to escape abusive husbands, and the
> complete disregard of their plight by the courts and by
> society. (38)

These are the issues that Susan Glaspell wished to stress in "A Jury of Her Peers."

Larson's conclusion echoes his main point without dully repeating it.

These are also the issues that Mrs. Peters comes to understand as the story unfolds, with her understanding deepening as she identifies with Minnie and Mrs. Hale and is repulsed by male attitudes. Her transformation becomes complete when the men joke that she is "married to the law" and she responds by violating the law: hiding key evidence, the dead canary.

Larson 6

Works Cited

Ben-Zvi, Linda. "'Murder, She Wrote': The Genesis of Susan Glaspell's
    Trifles." *Theatre Journal* 44.2 (1992): 141–62. Rpt. in *Susan
    Glaspell: Essays on Her Theater and Fiction*. Ed. Linda Ben-Zvi.
    Ann Arbor: U of Michigan P, 1995. 19-48. Print.

Glaspell, Susan. "A Jury of Her Peers." *Literature and Its Writers: A
    Compact Introduction to Fiction, Poetry, and Drama*. Ed. Ann
    Charters and Samuel Charters. 5th ed. Boston: Bedford, 2010.
    185-201. Print.

Hedges, Elaine. "Small Things Reconsidered: 'A Jury of Her Peers.'"
    Women's Studies 12.1 (1986): 89-110. Rpt. in *Susan Glaspell:
    Essays on Her Theater and Fiction*. Ed. Linda Ben-Zvi. Ann
    Arbor: U of Michigan P, 1995. 49-69. Print.

Mustazza, Leonard. "Generic Translation and Thematic Shift in Susan
    Glaspell's *Trifles* and 'A Jury of Her Peers.'" *Studies in Short
    Fiction* 26.4 (1989): 489-96. Print.

The works cited
page lists the
primary source
(Glaspell's story) and
secondary sources.

A Jury of Her Peers
SUSAN GLASPELL

When Martha Hale opened the storm-door and got a cut of the north wind, she ran back for her big woolen scarf. As she hurriedly wound that round her head her eye made a scandalized sweep of her kitchen. It was no ordinary thing that called her away—it was probably further from ordinary than anything that had ever happened in Dickson County. But what her eye took in was that her kitchen was in no shape for leaving: her bread all ready for mixing, half the flour sifted and half unsifted.

She hated to see things half done; but she had been at that when the team from town stopped to get Mr. Hale, and then the sheriff came running in to say his wife wished Mrs. Hale would come too—adding, with a grin, that he guessed she was getting scary and wanted another woman along. So she had dropped everything right where it was.

"Martha!" now came her husband's impatient voice. "Don't keep folks waiting out here in the cold."

She again opened the storm-door, and this time joined the three men and the one woman waiting for her in the big two-seated buggy.

After she had the robes tucked around her she took another look at the woman who sat beside her on the back seat. She had met Mrs. Peters the year before at the county fair, and the thing she remembered about her was that she didn't seem like a sheriff's wife. She was small and thin and didn't have a strong voice. Mrs. Gorman, sheriff's wife before Gorman went out and Peters came in, had a voice that somehow seemed to be backing up the law with every word. But if Mrs. Peters didn't look like a sheriff's wife, Peters made it up in looking like a sheriff. He was to a dot the kind of man who could get himself elected sheriff—a heavy man with a big voice, who was particularly genial with the law-abiding, as if to make it plain that he knew the difference between criminals and non-criminals. And right there it came into Mrs. Hale's mind, with a stab, that this man who was so pleasant and lively with all of them was going to the Wrights' now as a sheriff.

"The country's not very pleasant this time of year," Mrs. Peters at last ventured, as if she felt they ought to be talking as well as the men.

Mrs. Hale scarcely finished her reply, for they had gone up a little hill and could see the Wright place now, and seeing it did not make her feel like talking. It looked very lonesome this cold March morning. It had always been a lonesome-looking place. It was down in a hollow, and the poplar trees around it were lonesome-looking trees. The men were looking at it and talking about what had happened. The county attorney was bending to one side of the buggy, and kept looking steadily at the place as they drew up to it.

"I'm glad you came with me," Mrs. Peters said nervously, as the two women were about to follow the men in through the kitchen door.

Even after she had her foot on the door-step, her hand on the knob, Martha Hale had a moment of feeling she could not cross that threshold. And the reason it seemed she couldn't cross it now was simply because she hadn't crossed it before. Time and time again it had been in her mind, "I ought to go over and see Minnie Foster"—she still thought of her as Minnie Foster, though for twenty years she had been Mrs. Wright. And then there was always something to do and Minnie Foster would go from her mind. But *now* she could come.

The men went over to the stove. The women stood close together by the door. Young Henderson, the county attorney, turned around and said, "Come up to the fire, ladies."

Mrs. Peters took a step forward, then stopped. "I'm not—cold," she said.

And so the two women stood by the door, at first not even so much as looking around the kitchen.

The men talked for a minute about what a good thing it was the sheriff had sent his deputy out that morning to make a fire for them, and then Sheriff Peters stepped back from the stove, unbuttoned his outer coat, and leaned his hands on the kitchen table in a way that seemed to mark the beginning of official business. "Now, Mr. Hale," he said in a sort of semi-official voice, "before we move things about, you tell Mr. Henderson just what it was you saw when you came here yesterday morning."

The county attorney was looking around the kitchen.

"By the way," he said, "has anything been moved?" He turned to the sheriff. "Are things just as you left them yesterday?"

Peters looked from cupboard to sink; from that to a small worn rocker a little to one side of the kitchen table.

"It's just the same."

"Somebody should have been left here yesterday," said the county attorney.

"Oh—yesterday," returned the sheriff, with a little gesture as of yesterday having been more than he could bear to think of. "When I had to send Frank to Morris Center for that man who went crazy—let me tell you. I had my hands full *yesterday*. I knew you could get back from Omaha by today, George, and as long as I went over everything here myself —"

"Well, Mr. Hale," said the county attorney, in a way of letting what was past and gone go, "tell just what happened when you came here yesterday morning."

Mrs. Hale, still leaning against the door, had that sinking feeling of the mother whose child is about to speak a piece. Lewis often wandered along and got things mixed up in a story. She hoped he would tell this straight and plain, and not say unnecessary things that would just make things harder for Minnie Foster. He didn't begin at once, and she noticed that he looked queer—as if standing in that kitchen and having to tell what he had seen there yesterday morning made him almost sick.

"Yes, Mr. Hale?" the county attorney reminded.

"Harry and I had started to town with a load of potatoes," Mrs. Hale's husband began.

Harry was Mrs. Hale's oldest boy. He wasn't with them now, for the very good reason that those potatoes never got to town yesterday and he was taking them this morning, so he hadn't been home when the sheriff stopped to say he wanted Mr. Hale to come over to the Wright place and tell the county attorney his story there, where he could point it all out. With all Mrs. Hale's other emotions came the fear now that maybe Harry wasn't dressed warm enough—they hadn't any of them realized how that north wind did bite.

"We come along this road," Hale was going on, with a motion of his hand to the road over which they had just come, "and as we got in sight of the house I says to Harry, 'I'm goin' to see if I can't get John Wright to take a telephone.' You see," he explained to Henderson, "unless I can get somebody to go in with me they won't come out this branch road except for a price *I* can't pay. I'd spoke to Wright about it once before; but he put me off, saying folks talked too much anyway, and all he asked was peace and quiet—guess you know about how much he talked himself. But I thought maybe if I went to the house and talked about it before his wife, and said all the women-folks liked the telephones, and that in this lonesome stretch of road it would be a good thing—well, I said to Harry that that was what I was going to say—though I said at the same time that I didn't know as what his wife wanted made much difference to John —"

Now there he was!—saying things he didn't need to say. Mrs. Hale tried to catch her husband's eye, but fortunately the county attorney interrupted with:

"Let's talk about that a little later, Mr. Hale. I do want to talk about that, but I'm anxious now to get along to just what happened when you got here."

When he began this time, it was very deliberately and carefully: "I didn't see or hear anything. I knocked at the door. And still it was all quiet inside. I knew they must be up—it was past eight o'clock. So I knocked again, louder, and I thought I heard somebody say, 'Come in.' I wasn't sure—I'm not sure yet. But I opened the door—this door," jerking a hand toward the door by which the two women stood, "and there, in that rocker"—pointing to it—"sat Mrs. Wright."

Everyone in the kitchen looked at the rocker. It came into Mrs. Hale's mind that that rocker didn't look in the least like Minnie Foster—the Minnie Foster of twenty years before. It was a dingy red, with wooden rungs up the back, and the middle rung was gone, and the chair sagged to one side.

"How did she—look?" the county attorney was inquiring.

"Well," said Hale, "she looked—queer."

"How do you mean—queer?"

As he asked it he took out a note-book and pencil. Mrs. Hale did not like the sight of that pencil. She kept her eye fixed on her husband, as if to keep him from saying unnecessary things that would go into that note-book and make trouble.

Hale did speak guardedly, as if the pencil had affected him too.

"Well, as if she didn't know what she was going to do next. And kind of—done up."

"How did she seem to feel about your coming?"

"Why, I don't think she minded—one way or other. She didn't pay much attention. I said, 'Ho' do, Mrs. Wright? It's cold, ain't it?' And she said, 'Is it?'—and went on pleatin' at her apron.

"Well, I was surprised. She didn't ask me to come up to the stove, or to sit down, but just set there, not even lookin' at me. And so I said: 'I want to see John.'

"And then she—laughed. I guess you would call it a laugh.

"I thought of Harry and the team outside, so I said, a little sharp, 'Can I see John?' 'No,' says she—kind of dull like. 'Ain't he home?' says I. Then she looked at me. 'Yes,' says she, 'he's home.' 'Then why can't I see him?' I asked her, out of patience with her now. ''Cause he's dead' says she, just as quiet and dull—and fell to pleatin' her apron. 'Dead?' says I, like you do when you can't take in what you've heard.

"She just nodded her head, not getting a bit excited, but rockin' back and forth.

"'Why—where is he?' says I, not knowing what to say.

"She just pointed upstairs—like this"—pointing to the room above.

"I got up, with the idea of going up there myself. By this time I—didn't know what to do. I walked from there to here; then I says: 'Why, what did he die of?'

"'He died of a rope around his neck,' says she; and just went on pleatin' at her apron."

Hale stopped speaking, and stood staring at the rocker, as if he were still seeing the woman who had sat there the morning before. Nobody spoke; it was as if every one were seeing the woman who had sat there the morning before.

"And what did you do then?" the county attorney at last broke the silence.

"I went out and called Harry. I thought I might—need help. I got Harry in, and we went upstairs." His voice fell almost to a whisper. "There he was—lying over the —"

"I think I'd rather have you go into that upstairs," the county attorney interrupted, "where you can point it all out. Just go on now with the rest of the story."

"Well, my first thought was to get that rope off. It looked —"

He stopped, his face twitching.

"But Harry, he went up to him, and he said, 'No, he's dead all right, and we'd better not touch anything.' So we went downstairs.

"She was still sitting that same way. 'Has anybody been notified?' I asked. 'No,' says she, unconcerned.

"'Who did this, Mrs. Wright?' said Harry. He said it businesslike, and she stopped pleatin' at her apron. 'I don't know,' she says. 'You don't *know*?' says Harry. 'Weren't you sleepin' in the bed with him?' 'Yes,' says she, 'but I was on the inside.' 'Somebody slipped a rope round his neck and strangled him, and you didn't wake up?' says Harry. 'I didn't wake up,' she said after him.

"We may have looked as if we didn't see how that could be, for after a minute she said, 'I sleep sound.'

"Harry was going to ask her more questions, but I said maybe that weren't our business; maybe we ought to let her tell her story first to the coroner or the sheriff. So Harry went fast as he could over to High Road—the Rivers' place, where there's a telephone."

"And what did she do when she knew you had gone for the coroner?" The attorney got his pencil in his hand all ready for writing.

"She moved from that chair to this one over here"—Hale pointed to a small chair in the corner—"and just sat there with her hands held together and looking down. I got a feeling that I ought to make some conversation, so I said I had come in to see if John wanted to put in a telephone; and at that she started to laugh, and then she stopped and looked at me—scared."

At the sound of a moving pencil the man who was telling the story looked up.

"I dunno—maybe it wasn't scared," he hastened: "I wouldn't like to say it was. Soon Harry got back, and then Dr. Lloyd came, and you, Mr. Peters, and so I guess that's all I know that you don't."

He said that last with relief, and moved a little, as if relaxing. Everyone moved a little. The county attorney walked toward the stair door.

"I guess we'll go upstairs first—then out to the barn and around there."

He paused and looked around the kitchen.

"You're convinced there was nothing important here?" he asked the sheriff. "Nothing that would—point to any motive?"

The sheriff too looked all around, as if to re-convince himself.

"Nothing here but kitchen things," he said, with a little laugh for the insignificance of kitchen things.

The county attorney was looking at the cupboard—a peculiar, ungainly structure, half closet and half cupboard, the upper part of it being built in the wall, and the lower part just the old-fashioned kitchen cupboard. As if its queerness attracted him, he got a chair and opened the upper part and looked in. After a moment he drew his hand away sticky.

"Here's a nice mess," he said resentfully.

The two women had drawn nearer, and now the sheriff's wife spoke.

"Oh—her fruit," she said, looking to Mrs. Hale for sympathetic understanding. She turned back to the county attorney and explained: "She worried about that when it turned so cold last night. She said the fire would go out and her jars might burst."

Mrs. Peters' husband broke into a laugh.

"Well, can you beat the woman! Held for murder, and worrying about her preserves!"

The young attorney set his lips.

"I guess before we're through with her she may have something more serious than preserves to worry about."

"Oh, well," said Mrs. Hale's husband, with good-natured superiority, "women are used to worrying over trifles."

The two women moved a little closer together. Neither of them spoke. The county attorney seemed suddenly to remember his manners—and think of his future.

"And yet," said he, with the gallantry of a young politician, "for all their worries, what would we do without the ladies?"

The women did not speak, did not unbend. He went to the sink and began washing his hands. He turned to wipe them on the roller towel—whirled it for a cleaner place.

"Dirty towels! Not much of a housekeeper, would you say, ladies?"

He kicked his foot against some dirty pans under the sink.

"There's a great deal of work to be done on a farm," said Mrs. Hale stiffly.

"To be sure. And yet" —with a little bow to her— "I know there are some Dickson County farm-houses that do not have such roller towels." He gave it a pull to expose its full length again.

"Those towels get dirty awful quick. Men's hands aren't always as clean as they might be."

"Ah, loyal to your sex, I see," he laughed. He stopped and gave her a keen look. "But you and Mrs. Wright were neighbors. I suppose you were friends, too."

Martha Hale shook her head.

"I've seen little enough of her of late years. I've not been in this house—it's more than a year."

"And why was that? You didn't like her?"

"I liked her well enough," she replied with spirit. "Farmers' wives have their hands full, Mr. Henderson. And then —" She looked around the kitchen.

"Yes?" he encouraged.

"It never seemed a very cheerful place," said she, more to herself than to him.

"No," he agreed; "I don't think anyone would call it cheerful. I shouldn't say she had the home-making instinct."

"Well, I don't know as Wright had, either," she muttered.

"You mean they didn't get on very well?" he was quick to ask.

"No; I don't mean anything," she answered, with decision. As she turned a little away from him, she added: "But I don't think a place would be any the cheerfuller for John Wright's bein' in it."

"I'd like to talk to you about that a little later, Mrs. Hale," he said. "I'm anxious to get the lay of things upstairs now."

He moved toward the stair door, followed by the two men.

"I suppose anything Mrs. Peters does'll be all right?" the sheriff inquired. "She was to take in some clothes for her, you know—and a few little things. We left in such a hurry yesterday."

The county attorney looked at the two women whom they were leaving alone there among the kitchen things.

"Yes—Mrs. Peters," he said, his glance resting on the woman who was not Mrs. Peters, the big farmer woman who stood behind the sheriff's wife. "Of course Mrs. Peters is one of us," he said, in a manner of entrusting responsibility. "And keep your eye out, Mrs. Peters, for anything that might be of use. No telling; you women might come upon a clue to the motive—and that's the thing we need."

Mr. Hale rubbed his face after the fashion of a showman getting ready for a pleasantry.

"But would the women know a clue if they did come upon it?" he said; and, having delivered himself of this, he followed the others through the stair door.

The women stood motionless and silent, listening to the footsteps, first upon the stairs, then in the room above them.

Then, as if releasing herself from something strange, Mrs. Hale began to arrange the dirty pans under the sink, which the county attorney's disdainful push of the foot had deranged.

"I'd hate to have men comin' into my kitchen," she said testily—"snoopin' round and criticizin'."

"Of course it's no more than their duty," said the sheriff's wife, in her manner of timid acquiescence.

"Duty's all right," replied Mrs. Hale bluffly; "but I guess that deputy sheriff that come out to make the fire might have got a little of this on." She gave the roller towel a pull. "Wish I'd thought of that sooner! Seems mean to talk about her for not having things slicked up, when she had to come away in such a hurry."

She looked around the kitchen. Certainly it was not "slicked up." Her eye was held by a bucket of sugar on a low shelf. The cover was off the wooden bucket, and beside it was a paper bag—half full.

Mrs. Hale moved toward it.

"She was putting this in there," she said to herself—slowly.

She thought of the flour in her kitchen at home—half sifted, half not sifted. She had been interrupted, and had left things half done. What had interrupted Minnie Foster? Why had that work been left half done? She made a move as if to finish it,—unfinished things always bothered her,—and then she glanced around and saw that Mrs. Peters was watching her—and she didn't want Mrs. Peters to get that feeling she had got of work begun and then—for some reason—not finished.

"It's a shame about her fruit," she said, and walked toward the cupboard that the county attorney had opened, and got on the chair, murmuring: "I wonder if it's all gone."

It was a sorry enough looking sight, but "Here's one that's all right," she said at last. She held it toward the light. "This is cherries, too." She looked again. "I declare I believe that's the only one."

With a sigh, she got down from the chair, went to the sink, and wiped off the bottle.

"She'll feel awful bad, after all her hard work in the hot weather. I remember the afternoon I put up my cherries last summer."

She set the bottle on the table, and, with another sigh, started to sit down in the rocker. But she did not sit down. Something kept her from sitting down in that chair. She straightened—stepped back, and, half turned away, stood looking at it, seeing the woman who had sat there "pleatin' at her apron."

The thin voice of the sheriff's wife broke in upon her: "I must be getting those things from the front-room closet." She opened the door into the other room, started in, stepped back. "You coming with me, Mrs. Hale?" she asked nervously. "You—you could help me get them."

They were soon back—the stark coldness of that shut-up room was not a thing to linger in.

"My!" said Mrs. Peters, dropping the things on the table and hurrying to the stove.

Mrs. Hale stood examining the clothes the woman who was being detained in town had said she wanted.

"Wright was close!" she exclaimed, holding up a shabby black skirt that bore the marks of much making over. "I think maybe that's why she kept so much to herself. I s'pose she felt she couldn't do her part; and then, you don't enjoy things when you feel shabby. She used to wear pretty clothes and be lively—when she was Minnie Foster, one of the town girls, singing in the choir. But that—oh, that was twenty years ago."

With a carefulness in which there was something tender, she folded the shabby clothes and piled them at one corner of the table. She looked up at Mrs. Peters, and there was something in the other woman's look that irritated her.

"She don't care," she said to herself. "Much difference it makes to her whether Minnie Foster had pretty clothes when she was a girl."

Then she looked again, and she wasn't so sure; in fact, she hadn't at any time been perfectly sure about Mrs. Peters. She had that shrinking manner, and yet her eyes looked as if they could see a long way into things.

"This all you was to take in?" asked Mrs. Hale.

"No," said the sheriff's wife; "she said she wanted an apron. Funny thing to want," she ventured in her nervous little way, "for there's not much to get you dirty in jail, goodness knows. But I suppose just to make her feel more natural. If you're used to wearing an apron—. She said they were in the bottom drawer of this cupboard. Yes—here they are. And then her little shawl that always hung on the stair door."

She took the small gray shawl from behind the door leading upstairs, and stood a minute looking at it.

Suddenly Mrs. Hale took a quick step toward the other woman.

"Mrs. Peters!"

"Yes, Mrs. Hale?"

"Do you think she—did it?"

A frightened look blurred the other thing in Mrs. Peters' eyes.

"Oh, I don't know," she said, in a voice that seemed to shrink away from the subject.

"Well, I don't think she did," affirmed Mrs. Hale stoutly. "Asking for an apron, and her little shawl. Worryin' about her fruit."

"Mr. Peters says—." Footsteps were heard in the room above; she stopped, looked up, then went on in a lowered voice: "Mr. Peters says—it looks bad for her. Mr. Henderson is awful sarcastic in a speech, and he's going to make fun of her saying she didn't—wake up."

For a moment Mrs. Hale had no answer. Then, "Well, I guess John Wright didn't wake up—when they was slippin' that rope under his neck," she muttered.

"No, it's *strange*," breathed Mrs. Peters. "They think it was such a—funny way to kill a man."

She began to laugh; at the sound of the laugh, abruptly stopped.

"That's just what Mr. Hale said," said Mrs. Hale, in a resolutely natural voice. "There was a gun in the house. He says that's what he can't understand."

"Mr. Henderson said, coming out, that what was needed for the case was a motive. Something to show anger—or sudden feeling."

"Well, I don't see any signs of anger around here," said Mrs. Hale, "I don't —" She stopped. It was as if her mind tripped on something. Her eye was caught by a dishtowel in the middle of the kitchen table. Slowly she moved toward the table. One half of it was wiped clean, the other half messy. Her eyes made a slow, almost unwilling turn to the bucket of sugar and the half empty bag beside it. Things begun—and not finished.

After a moment she stepped back, and said, in that manner of releasing herself:

"Wonder how they're finding things upstairs? I hope she had it a little more redd up up there. You know,"—she paused, and feeling gathered,—"it seems kind of *sneaking*: locking her up in town and coming out here to get her own house to turn against her!"

"But, Mrs. Hale," said the sheriff's wife, "the law is the law."

"I s'pose 'tis," answered Mrs. Hale shortly.

She turned to the stove, saying something about that fire not being much to brag of. She worked with it a minute, and when she straightened up she said aggressively:

"The law is the law—and a bad stove is a bad stove. How'd you like to cook on this?"—pointing with the poker to the broken lining. She opened the oven door and started to express her opinion of the oven; but she was swept into her own thoughts, thinking of what it would mean, year after year, to have that stove to wrestle with. The thought of Minnie Foster trying to bake in that oven—and the thought of her never going over to see Minnie Foster—.

She was startled by hearing Mrs. Peters say: "A person gets discouraged—and loses heart."

The sheriff's wife had looked from the stove to the sink—to the pail of water which had been carried in from outside. The two women stood there silent, above them the footsteps of the men who were looking for evidence against the woman who had worked in that kitchen. That look of seeing into things, of seeing through a thing to something else, was in the eyes of the sheriff's wife now. When Mrs. Hale next spoke to her, it was gently:

"Better loosen up your things, Mrs. Peters. We'll not feel them when we go out."

Mrs. Peters went to the back of the room to hang up the fur tippet she was wearing. A moment later she exclaimed, "Why, she was piecing a quilt," and held up a large sewing basket piled high with quilt pieces.

Mrs. Hale spread some of the blocks on the table.

"It's log-cabin pattern," she said, putting several of them together. "Pretty, isn't it?"

They were so engaged with the quilt that they did not hear the footsteps on the stairs. Just as the stair door opened Mrs. Hale was saying:

"Do you suppose she was going to quilt it or just knot it?"

The sheriff threw up his hands.

"They wonder whether she was going to quilt it or just knot it!"

There was a laugh for the ways of women, a warming of hands over the stove, and then the county attorney said briskly:

"Well, let's go right out to the barn and get that cleared up."

"I don't see as there's anything so strange," Mrs. Hale said resentfully, after the outside door had closed on the three men—"our taking up our time with little things while we're waiting for them to get the evidence. I don't see as it's anything to laugh about."

"Of course they've got awful important things on their minds," said the sheriff's wife apologetically.

They returned to an inspection of the block for the quilt. Mrs. Hale was looking at the fine, even sewing, and preoccupied with thoughts of the woman who had done that sewing, when she heard the sheriff's wife say, in a queer tone:

"Why, look at this one."

She turned to take the block held out to her.

"The sewing," said Mrs. Peters, in a troubled way. "All the rest of them have been so nice and even—but—this one. Why, it looks as if she didn't know what she was about!"

Their eyes met—something flashed to life, passed between them; then, as if with an effort, they seemed to pull away from each other. A moment Mrs. Hale sat there, her hands folded over that sewing which was so unlike all the rest of the sewing. Then she had pulled a knot and drawn the threads.

"Oh, what are you doing, Mrs. Hale?" asked the sheriff's wife, startled.

"Just pulling out a stitch or two that's not sewed very good," said Mrs. Hale mildly.

"I don't think we ought to touch things," Mrs. Peters said, a little helplessly.

"I'll just finish up this end," answered Mrs. Hale, still in that mild, matter-of-fact fashion.

She threaded a needle and started to replace bad sewing with good. For a little while she sewed in silence. Then, in that thin, timid voice, she heard:

"Mrs. Hale!"

"Yes, Mrs. Peters?"

"What do you suppose she was so—nervous about?"

"Oh, *I* don't know," said Mrs. Hale, as if dismissing a thing not important enough to spend much time on. "I don't know as she was—nervous. I sew awful queer sometimes when I'm just tired."

She cut a thread, and out of the corner of her eye looked up at Mrs. Peters. The small, lean face of the sheriff's wife seemed to have tightened up. Her eyes had that look of peering into something. But next moment she moved, and said in her thin, indecisive way:

"Well, I must get those clothes wrapped. They may be through sooner than we think. I wonder where I could find a piece of paper—and string."

"In that cupboard, maybe," suggested Mrs. Hale, after a glance around.

One piece of the crazy sewing remained unripped. Mrs. Peters' back turned, Martha Hale now scrutinized that piece, compared it with the dainty, accurate sewing of the other blocks. The difference was startling. Holding this block made her feel queer, as if the distracted thoughts of the woman who had perhaps turned to it to try and quiet herself were communicating themselves to her.

Mrs. Peters' voice roused her.

"Here's a bird-cage," she said. "Did she have a bird, Mrs. Hale?"

"Why, I don't know whether she did or not." She turned to look at the cage Mrs. Peters was holding up. "I've not been here in so long." She sighed. "There was a man round last year selling canaries cheap—but I don't know as she took one. Maybe she did. She used to sing real pretty herself."

Mrs. Peters looked around the kitchen.

"Seems kind of funny to think of a bird here." She half laughed—an attempt to put up a barrier. "But she must have had one—or why would she have a cage? I wonder what happened to it."

"I suppose maybe the cat got it," suggested Mrs. Hale, resuming her sewing.

"No; she didn't have a cat. She's got that feeling some people have about cats—being afraid of them. When they brought her to our house yesterday, my cat got in the room, and she was real upset and asked me to take it out."

"My sister Bessie was like that," laughed Mrs. Hale.

The sheriff's wife did not reply. The silence made Mrs. Hale turn round. Mrs. Peters was examining the bird-cage.

"Look at this door," she said slowly. "It's broke. One hinge has been pulled apart."

Mrs. Hale came nearer.

"Looks as if someone must have been—rough with it."

Again their eyes met—startled, questioning, apprehensive. For a moment neither spoke nor stirred. Then Mrs. Hale, turning away, said brusquely:

"If they're going to find any evidence, I wish they'd be about it. I don't like this place."

"But I'm awful glad you came with me, Mrs. Hale." Mrs. Peters put the bird-cage on the table and sat down. "It would be lonesome for me—sitting here alone."

"Yes, it would, wouldn't it?" agreed Mrs. Hale, a certain determined naturalness in her voice. She had picked up the sewing, but now it dropped in her lap, and she murmured in a different voice: "But I tell you what I *do* wish, Mrs. Peters. I wish I had come over sometimes when she was here. I wish—I had."

"But of course you were awful busy, Mrs. Hale. Your house—and your children."

"I could've come," retorted Mrs. Hale shortly. "I stayed away because it weren't cheerful—and that's why I ought to have come. I"—she looked around—"I've never liked this place. Maybe because it's down in a hollow and you don't see the road. I don't know what it is, but it's a lonesome place, and always was. I wish I had come over to see Minnie Foster sometimes. I can see now —" She did not put it into words.

"Well, you mustn't reproach yourself," counseled Mrs. Peters. "Somehow, we just don't see how it is with other folks till—something comes up."

"Not having children makes less work," mused Mrs. Hale, after a silence, "but it makes a quiet house—and Wright out to work all day—and no company when he did come in. Did you know John Wright, Mrs. Peters?"

"Not to know him. I've seen him in town. They say he was a good man."

"Yes—good," conceded John Wright's neighbor grimly. "He didn't drink, and kept his word as well as most, I guess, and paid his debts. But he was a hard man, Mrs. Peters. Just to pass the time of day with him—." She stopped, shivered a little. "Like a raw wind that gets to the bone." Her eye fell upon the cage on the table before her, and she added, almost bitterly: "I should think she would've wanted a bird!"

Suddenly she leaned forward, looking intently at the cage. "But what do you s'pose went wrong with it?"

"I don't know," returned Mrs. Peters; "unless it got sick and died."

But after she said it she reached over and swung the broken door. Both women watched it as if somehow held by it.

"You didn't know—her?" Mrs. Hale asked, a gentler note in her voice.

"Not till they brought her yesterday," said the sheriff's wife.

"She—come to think of it, she was kind of like a bird herself. Real sweet and pretty, but kind of timid and—fluttery. How—she—did—change."

That held her for a long time. Finally, as if struck with a happy thought and relieved to get back to everyday things, she exclaimed:

"Tell you what, Mrs. Peters, why don't you take the quilt in with you? It might take up her mind."

"Why, I think that's a real nice idea, Mrs. Hale," agreed the sheriff's wife, as if she too were glad to come into the atmosphere of a simple kindness. "There couldn't possibly be any objection to that, could there? Now, just what will I take? I wonder if her patches are in here—and her things?"

They turned to the sewing basket.

"Here's some red," said Mrs. Hale, bringing out a roll of cloth. Underneath that was a box. "Here, maybe her scissors are in here—and her things." She held it up. "What a pretty box! I'll warrant that was something she had a long time ago—when she was a girl."

She held it in her hand a moment; then, with a little sigh, opened it.

Instantly her hand went to her nose.

"Why—!"

Mrs. Peters drew nearer—then turned away.

"There's something wrapped up in this piece of silk," faltered Mrs. Hale.

"This isn't her scissors," said Mrs. Peters, in a shrinking voice.

Her hand not steady, Mrs. Hale raised the piece of silk. "Oh, Mrs. Peters!" she cried. "It's —"

Mrs. Peters bent closer.

"It's the bird," she whispered.

"But, Mrs. Peters!" cried Mrs. Hale. "*Look* at it! Its *neck*—look at its neck! It's all—other side *to.*"

She held the box away from her.

The sheriff's wife again bent closer.

"Somebody wrung its neck," said she, in a voice that was slow and deep.

And then again the eyes of the two women met—this time clung together in a look of dawning comprehension, of growing horror. Mrs. Peters looked from the dead bird to the broken door of the cage. Again their eyes met. And just then there was a sound at the outside door.

Mrs. Hale slipped the box under the quilt pieces in the basket, and sank into the chair before it. Mrs. Peters stood holding to the table. The county attorney and the sheriff came in from outside.

"Well, ladies," said the county attorney, as one turning from serious things to little pleasantries, "have you decided whether she was going to quilt it or knot it?"

"We think," began the sheriff's wife in a flurried voice, "that she was going to—knot it."

He was too preoccupied to notice the change that came in her voice on that last.

"Well, that's very interesting, I'm sure," he said tolerantly. He caught sight of the bird-cage. "Has the bird flown?"

"We think the cat got it," said Mrs. Hale in a voice curiously even.

He was walking up and down, as if thinking something out.

"Is there a cat?" he asked absently.

Mrs. Hale shot a look up at the sheriff's wife.

"Well, not *now*," said Mrs. Peters. "They're superstitious, you know; they leave."

She sank into her chair.

The county attorney did not heed her. "No sign at all of anyone having come in from the outside," he said to Peters, in the manner of continuing an interrupted conversation. "Their own rope. Now let's go upstairs again and go over it, piece by piece. It would have to have been someone who knew just the —"

The stair door closed behind them and their voices were lost.

The two women sat motionless, not looking at each other, but as if peering into something and at the same time holding back. When they spoke now it was as if they were afraid of what they were saying, but as if they could not help saying it.

"She liked the bird," said Martha Hale, low and slowly. "She was going to bury it."

"When I was a girl," said Mrs. Peters, under her breath, "my kitten—there was a boy took a hatchet, and before my eyes—before I could get there—" She covered her face an instant. "If they hadn't held me back I would have"—she caught herself, looked upstairs where footsteps were heard, and finished weakly—"hurt him."

Then they sat without speaking or moving.

"I wonder how it would seem," Mrs. Hale at last began, as if feeling her way over strange ground—"never to have had any children around?" Her eyes made a slow sweep of the kitchen, as if seeing what that kitchen had meant through all the years. "No, Wright wouldn't like the bird," she said after that—"a thing that sang. She used to sing. He killed that too." Her voice tightened.

Mrs. Peters moved uneasily.

"Of course we don't know who killed the bird."

"I knew John Wright," was Mrs. Hale's answer.

"It was an awful thing was done in this house that night, Mrs. Hale," said the sheriff's wife. "Killing a man while he slept—slipping a thing round his neck that choked the life out of him."

Mrs. Hale's hand went out to the bird-cage.

"His neck. Choked the life out of him."

"We don't *know* who killed him," whispered Mrs. Peters wildly. "We don't *know*."

Mrs. Hale had not moved. "If there had been years and years of—nothing, then a bird to sing to you, it would be awful—still—after the bird was still."

It was as if something within her not herself had spoken, and it found in Mrs. Peters something she did not know as herself.

"I know what stillness is," she said, in a queer, monotonous voice. "When we homesteaded in Dakota, and my first baby died—after he was two years old—and me with no other then—"

Mrs. Hale stirred.

"How soon do you suppose they'll be through looking for the evidence?"

"I know what stillness is," repeated Mrs. Peters, in just the same way. Then she too pulled back. "The law has got to punish crime, Mrs. Hale," she said in her tight little way.

"I wish you'd seen Minnie Foster," was the answer, "when she wore a white dress with blue ribbons, and stood up there in the choir and sang."

The picture of that girl, the fact that she had lived neighbor to that girl for twenty years, and had let her die for lack of life, was suddenly more than she could bear.

"Oh, I *wish* I'd come over here once in a while!" she cried. "That was a crime! Who's going to punish that?"

"We mustn't take on," said Mrs. Peters, with a frightened look toward the stairs.

"I might 'a' known she needed help! I tell you, it's *queer*, Mrs. Peters. We live close together, and we live far apart. We all go through the same things—it's all just a different kind of the same thing! If it weren't—why do you and I *understand*? Why do we *know*—what we know this minute?"

She dashed her hand across her eyes. Then, seeing the jar of fruit on the table, she reached for it and choked out:

"If I was you I wouldn't *tell* her her fruit was gone! Tell her it *ain't*. Tell her it's all right—all of it. Here—take this in to prove it to her! She—she may never know whether it was broke or not."

She turned away.

Mrs. Peters reached out for the bottle of fruit as if she were glad to take it—as if touching a familiar thing, having something to do, could keep her from something else. She got up, looked about for something to wrap the fruit in, took a petticoat from the pile of clothes she had brought from the front room, and nervously started winding that round the bottle.

"My!" she began, in a high, false voice, "it's a good thing the men couldn't hear us! Getting all stirred up over a little thing like a—dead canary." She hurried over that. "As if that could have anything to do with—with—My, wouldn't they *laugh*?"

Footsteps were heard on the stairs.

"Maybe they would," muttered Mrs. Hale—"maybe they wouldn't."

"No, Peters," said the county attorney incisively; "it's all perfectly clear, except the reason for doing it. But you know juries when it comes to women. If there was some definite thing—something to show. Something to make a story about. A thing that would connect up with this clumsy way of doing it."

In a covert way Mrs. Hale looked at Mrs. Peters. Mrs. Peters was looking at her. Quickly they looked away from each other. The outer door opened and Mr. Hale came in.

"I've got the team round now," he said. "Pretty cold out there."

"I'm going to stay here awhile by myself," the county attorney suddenly announced. "You can send Frank out for me, can't you?" he asked the sheriff. "I want to go over everything. I'm not satisfied we can't do better."

Again, for one brief moment, the two women's eyes found one another.

The sheriff came up to the table.

"Did you want to see what Mrs. Peters was going to take in?"

The county attorney picked up the apron. He laughed.

"Oh, I guess they're not very dangerous things the ladies have picked out."

Mrs. Hale's hand was on the sewing basket in which the box was concealed. She felt that she ought to take her hand off the basket. She did not seem able to. He picked up one of the quilt blocks which she had piled on to cover the box. Her eyes felt like fire. She had a feeling that if he took up the basket she would snatch it from him.

But he did not take it up. With another little laugh, he turned away, saying:

"No; Mrs. Peters doesn't need supervising. For that matter, a sheriff's wife is married to the law. Ever think of it that way, Mrs. Peters?"

Mrs. Peters was standing beside the table. Mrs. Hale shot a look up at her; but she could not see her face. Mrs. Peters had turned away. When she spoke, her voice was muffled.

"Not—just that way," she said.

"Married to the law!" chuckled Mrs. Peters' husband. He moved toward the door into the front room, and said to the county attorney:

"I just want you to come in here a minute, George. We ought to take a look at these windows."

"Oh—windows," said the county attorney scoffingly.

"We'll be right out, Mr. Hale," said the sheriff to the farmer, who was still waiting by the door.

Hale went to look after the horses. The sheriff followed the county attorney into the other room. Again—for one final moment—the two women were alone in that kitchen.

Martha Hale sprang up, her hands tight together, looking at that other woman, with whom it rested. At first she could not see her eyes, for the sheriff's wife had not turned back since she turned away at that suggestion of being married to the law. But now Mrs. Hale made her turn back. Her eyes made her turn back. Slowly, unwillingly, Mrs. Peters turned her head until her eyes met the eyes of the other woman. There was a moment when they held each other in a steady, burning look in which there was no evasion nor flinching. Then Martha Hale's eyes pointed the way to the basket in which was hidden the thing that would make certain the conviction of the other woman—that woman who was not there and yet who had been there with them all through that hour.

For a moment Mrs. Peters did not move. And then she did it. With a rush forward, she threw back the quilt pieces, got the box, tried to put it in her handbag. It was too big. Desperately she opened it, started to take the bird out. But there she broke—she could not touch the bird. She stood there helpless, foolish.

There was the sound of a knob turning in the inner door. Martha Hale snatched the box from the sheriff's wife, and got it in the pocket of her big coat just as the sheriff and the county attorney came back into the kitchen.

"Well, Henry," said the county attorney facetiously, "at least we found out that she was not going to quilt it. She was going to—what is it you call it, ladies?"

Mrs. Hale's hand was against the pocket of her coat.

"We call it—knot it, Mr. Henderson."

Acknowledgments

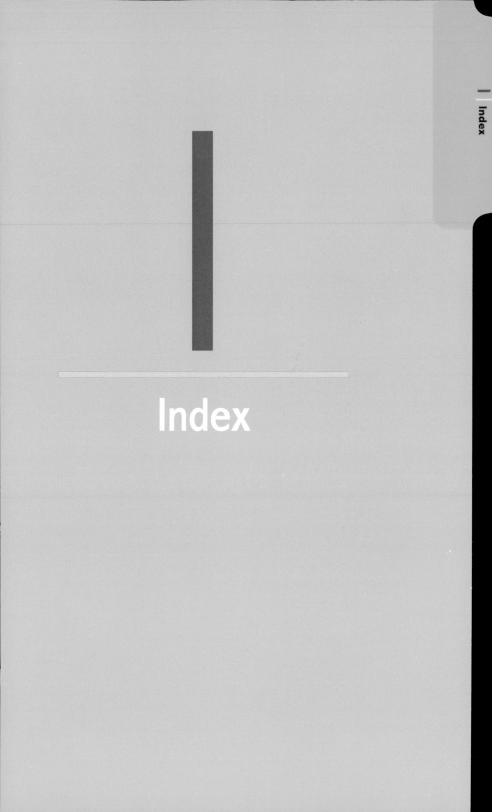

Index

Index

In addition to giving you page numbers, this index shows you which tabbed section to flip to. For example, the entry "*a* vs. *an*" directs you to section **W** (Word Choice), page 139, and to section **M** (Multilingual Writers and ESL Challenges), pages 239–40. Just flip to the appropriate tabbed section and then track down the exact pages you need.

Visiting the writing center

Gather your materials.

- Gather any materials your instructor has provided: the assignment, sample papers, your syllabus.
- Gather your own materials: a printout of your draft; copies of sources you have cited; previous papers with comments and grades.

Organize your materials and prepare questions.

- Read over the assignment carefully. Ask your instructor to clarify anything you don't understand.
- Look at previous papers with instructor comments. Can any of those comments help you revise your current paper?
- Create a list of questions about your draft, noting a few issues to focus your time with the tutor—places where you aren't sure of a phrase or a verb or where you need help thinking through an idea.

Check the writing centre's Web site.

- Find out where the writing center is located and when it's open.
- Make an appointment, if one is required.
- Find out if there is a limit to the number of appointments you can make or the number of drafts you can review with a tutor.
- If English is not your first language, check for tutors who are specially trained to assist multilingual students.

Visit the writing centre.

- Participate actively by asking questions and taking notes.
- Understand the limitations of your visit. In most cases, you should expect to cover one or two major issues, not the entire paper.
- Understand the tutor's role. Most tutors will give you suggestions, but they will not write or edit your paper.

Reflect on your visit.

- As soon as possible after your visit, write down anything you didn't have time to write during the session and clarify any notes you took so that you understand them when you revise your paper.
- Use your notes to review your entire paper for the problems you and the tutor discussed.
- Do not feel obligated to follow advice that you disagree with or are not comfortable following. Tutors provide feedback and suggestions, but you must decide which changes will help you accurately express your meaning.
- As you clarify your notes and revise, keep track of other questions or goals for the next writing centre visit.

A List of Charts

Directory to model papers and other sample documents

Visit **hackerhandbooks.com/writersref** for more than thirty model documents in five citation styles.

Multilingual/ESL Menu

A complete section for multilingual writers:

ESL and Academic English notes in other sections:

A List of Grammatical Terms

Boldface codes refer to sections of this book.

Revision Symbols

Letter-number codes refer to sections of this book.

abbr	faulty abbreviation **P9**	p	error in punctuation
adj	misuse of adjective **G4**	⌃,	comma **P1**
add	add needed word **S2**	no ,	no comma **P2**
adv	misuse of adverb **G4**	;	semicolon **P3**
agr	faulty agreement **G1, G3-a**	:	colon **P3**
appr	inappropriate language **W4**	⌄'	apostrophe **P4**
art	article **M2**	" "	quotation marks **P5**
awk	awkward	. ?	period, question mark,
cap	capital letter **P8**	!	exclamation point,
case	error in case **G3-c, G3-d**	— ( )	dash, parentheses,
cliché	cliché **W5-e**	[ ] ...	brackets, ellipsis mark,
coh	coherence **C4-d**	/	slash **P6**
coord	faulty coordination **S6-c**	pass	ineffective passive **W3**
cs	comma splice **G6**	pn agr	pronoun agreement **G3-a**
dev	inadequate development **C4-b**	proof	proofreading problem **C3-d**
dm	dangling modifier **S3-e**	ref	error in pronoun reference **G3-b**
-ed	error in -ed ending **G2-d**		
emph	emphasis **S6**	run-on	run-on sentence **G6**
ESL	ESL grammar **M1, M2, M3, M4, M5**	-s	error in -s ending **G2-c**
		sexist	sexist language **W4-e**
exact	inexact language **W5**	shift	distracting shift **S4**
frag	sentence fragment **G5**	sl	slang **W4-c**
fs	fused sentence **G6**	sp	misspelled word **P7**
gl/us	see glossary of usage **W1**	sub	faulty subordination **S6-d**
hyph	error in use of hyphen **P7**	sv agr	subject-verb agreement **G1, G2-c**
idiom	idiom **W5-d**		
inc	incomplete construction **S2**	t	error in verb tense **G2-f**
irreg	error in irregular verb **G2-a**	trans	transition needed **C4-d**
		usage	see glossary of usage **W1**
ital	italics **P10**	v	voice **W3**
jarg	jargon **W4-a**	var	sentence variety **S6-b, S6-c, S7**
lc	lowercase letter **P8**		
mix	mixed construction **S5**	vb	verb error **G2**
mm	misplaced modifier **S3-b**	w	wordy **W2**
mood	error in mood **G2-g**	//	faulty parallelism **S1**
nonst	nonstandard usage **W4-c**	⌃	insert
num	error in use of number **P9**	x	obvious error
om	omitted word **S2**	#	insert space
¶	new paragraph **C4**	‿	close up space

Detailed Menu